Social, Managerial, and Organizational Dimensions of Enterprise Information Systems

Maria Manuela Cruz–Cunha
Polytechnic Institute of Cavado and Ave, Portugal

BUSINESS SCIENCE REFERENCE

Hershey · New York

Director of Editorial Content:	Kristin Klinger
Senior Managing Editor:	Jamie Snavely
Assistant Managing Editor:	Michael Brehm
Publishing Assistant:	Sean Woznicki
Typesetter:	Michael Brehm
Cover Design:	Lisa Tosheff
Printed at:	Yurchak Printing Inc.

Published in the United States of America by
Business Science Reference (an imprint of IGI Global)
701 E. Chocolate Avenue
Hershey PA 17033
Tel: 717-533-8845
Fax: 717-533-8661
E-mail: cust@igi-global.com
Web site: http://www.igi-global.com/reference

Library of Congress Cataloging-in-Publication Data

Social, managerial and organizational dimensions of enterprise information
systems / Maria Manuela Cruz-Cunha, editor.
      p. cm.
  Includes bibliographical references and index.
  Summary: "This book is a compilation of contributions on the main issues, challenges, opportunities and developments related with enterprise information systems as tools for competitiveness in SMEs, from the social, managerial and organizational perspectives"--Provided by publisher.
  ISBN 978-1-60566-856-7 (hbk.) -- ISBN 978-1-60566-857-4 (ebook) 1. Management information systems. 2. Information technology--Management. 3. Small business--Management. I. Cruz-Cunha, Maria Manuela, 1964- II. Title.

  HD30.213.S63 2010
  658.4'038011--dc22

                              2009012048

British Cataloguing in Publication Data
A Cataloguing in Publication record for this book is available from the British Library.

Valentina Janev, *The Mihajlo Pupin Institute, Serbia*
Vasiliki Moumtzi, *Research Programmes Division, ALTEC S.A, Greece*
Vladanka Acimovic-Raspopovic, *University of Belgrade, Serbia*
Vladimír Modrák, *Technical University of Kosice, Slovakia*
Wai M. Cheung, *University of Bath, UK*
William Lawless, *Paine College, USA*
Z. J. Pei, *Kansas State University, USA*

Table of Contents

Section 4
Critical Success Factors and Case Studies

Detailed Table of Contents

Section 1
Models, Applications and Solutions

The first section presents the main frameworks, approaches, methodologies and models that support enterprise information systems.

In Chapter 1, "Enterprise Systems Approach," Targowski defines The enterprise system approach by its evolution and major milestones of architectural planning. The ES architectures are multi-faceted solutions; hence it is defined in the scope of the Enterprise Organization Architecture (EOA), Enterprise Functional Architecture (EFA), Enterprise Processive Architecture (EPA), Enterprise Information Architecture (EIA), Enterprise Software Architecture (ESA), Enterprise Network Architecture (ENA), Enterprise Service Architecture (ESA), Business Component Architecture (BCA), Enterprise Information Infrastructure (EII), and Enterprise Configurations. A composite ES architecture is presented as a transitional architecture, which is currently practiced by most enterprises. The near future of the ES approach will be rather limited to the ways of delivering ES applications within a framework of Service-Oriented Architecture (SOA) and the cloud computing, which satisfies effective large-scale operations. The progressive process of organization/business virtualization and the urgent need for more sustainable enterprise development should lead to new development of enterprise systems.

In the Chapter 2, "Modeling Software Development Processes", Chroust, Kuhrmann and Schoitsch discuss the WHY and WHAT of modelling a software development process as they investigate the components of a software process and propose a 5-dimensional grid of attributes of existing models: strategy and path, levels, main subprocesses, components and aura. Specific process models, currently used or historically important, are described. This is followed by an extensive discussion of methods and problems of modelling a software process, followed by a shorter discussion on the enactment of process models via Software Engineering Environments. The chapter closes with a discussion of the human factors of introducing and enacting a process model.

Giorgio Bruno, in Chapter 3, "People-oriented Enterprise Information Systems," states that current notations and languages do not emphasize the participation of users in business processes and consider them essentially as service providers. Moreover, they follow a centralized approach as all the interactions originate from or end in a business process; direct interactions between users cannot be represented. What is missing from this approach is that human work is cooperative and cooperation takes place through structured interactions called conversations; the notion of conversation is at the center of the language/ action perspective. However, the problem of effectively integrating conversations and business processes is still open and this chapter proposes a notation called POBPN (People-Oriented Business Process Notation) and a perspective, referred to as conversation-oriented perspective, for its solution.

In "Doing business on the globalised networked economy: Technology and business challenges for accounting information systems," Chapter 4, Koumpis and Protogeros present a set of challenges that are to be faced by Accounting Information Systems. More specifically, these include the support of interoperable accounting processes, for virtual and networked enterprises and for open-book accounting as well as the creation of novel interface metaphors that will automate and increase the usability of accounting information systems, and last but not least the provision of integrated e-accounting platforms.

Chapter 5, "Recent Developments in Supplier Selection and Order Allocation Process," by Aktar and Ustun, states that the purchasing department can play a key role in cost reduction, and hence supplier selection and order allocation are the most important functions of purchasing management. In view of its complexity, the chapter is focused especially on the final selection stage that consists of determining the best mixture of suppliers and allocating orders among them so as to satisfy different purchasing requirements. In recent years, many researchers used new integrated models for supplier selection and order allocation. They combine multi-criteria approaches such as AHP/ANP and linear programming (LP), mixed integer programming (MIP), non-linear programming (NLP), mixed integer non-linear programming (MINLP) and goal programming (GP) with different achievement scalarizing functions. In this chapter, after the stages of supplier selection process are explained, these new integrated models are introduced and their constraints, variables, and goals/objectives of these models are explained in detail. Then the solution methods of these integrated models are given. Finally, different integrated models are compared by considering their advantages and disadvantages.

In Chapter 6, "Complex Information Technology-Intensive Firms: A New Paradigmatic Firm-Theoretical Imperative! (Or a Pragmatically Impractical Interpretation of the Nature of the Virtualized Firm?)," Jelen and Kolakovic show how profoundly the design elements of firms have been affected by the current version of IT and propose elements of a framework that resiliently accommodates such effects. This framework can guide the practitioner designer for further refinements in the conception of CITI firms. The discoveries and framework elements are the result of our grounded theory methodology study in which executives, professionals, practitioners, entrepreneurs, and high-level decision-makers from a variety of firms participated.

In Chapter 7, "A Methodology for the Auditing of Technological Knowledge Management," Aris and Ayuso present a methodology for auditing technological knowledge management that allows the proposed solution to be aligned with the competitive strategy of organisations, as well as with their processes, key competences, and the associated knowledge resources. That enables the solution to be technologically oriented and to be applied to different types of business, from SOHO and SME to large companies. Firstly, the authors present their view regarding knowledge management, which is a technological perspective; specify the context of application and objectives. Secondly, they analyse the characteristics of knowledge as the object to be managed and we will identify, analyse and criticise the most relevant knowledge management approaches, models and methodologies related to their objectives, then outlining the requirements that technological knowledge management must meet. Thirdly, they present the components of the model on which the methodology is based, and describe its stages and tasks. Then they analyse the advantages of the model and methodology regarding other proposals.

In Chapter 8, "E-CRM and CMS Systems: Potential for More Dynamic Businesses," according to Fernandes, any change in customer's behaviour affects the customer's value. In addition, profitability and economic viability also change. Most companies still do not know entirely their customer base characteristics. They find difficult to define criteria that segment their customer base to find high-value customers. They need to focus on target selections to carry on with marketing campaigns which involve high investments. Given the potential of e-CRM and CMS as powerful tools to guide customer-oriented understanding and analysis, greater attention is required. Several companies, operating within the same business and having access to the same information and technology, differ in e-CRM performance. Without sufficient evidence, managers are prone to making investment decisions that are neither efficient nor effective. So it is imperative to base the decision of e-CRM and CMS adoption, on not only their analytical power, but also on economic viability criteria for sustainable business dynamics.

According to Lima in Chapter 9, "Integrating Production Planning and Control Business Processes," organizations have production planning and control (PPC) processes supported by systems that execute mainly repetitive calculations. Based on these calculation results, decisions are taken by production managers. These decision processes make the connection between different levels of aggregation of information and could benefit from the increment of the level of automation. An increased level of application of business process modelling languages is proposed in order to contribute to increment the level of process automation and the detail of business analysis. Thus, concepts of integration of production management processes, specifically of production planning and control processes are presented. These concepts, the application of Business Process Modelling Language (BPML) and some solutions of PPC integration compose the core content of this work. Additionally, criteria for evaluation of these processes of integration are identified and discussed. Finally, it is presented an industrial case supported by BPML model.

Finally, in Chapter 10, "Environments for Virtual Enterprise Integration," Cunha, Putnik and Ávila introduce the virtual enterprise model as an emerging approach to answer to the new requirements of the business environment, relying on dynamically reconfigurable partnerships, with extremely high performances, strongly time-oriented while highly focused on cost and quality, in permanent alignment with the market, and strongly supported by information and communication technology, dictating a paradigm shift face to the traditional organizational models. Networking and reconfiguration dynamics are main characteristic of this model, which claim for enabling and supporting environments, at bearable costs. To the authors, some existing technologies and Internet-based environments can partially support this organizational model, but the reconfiguration dynamics can only by assured by environments able to managing, controlling and enabling networking and dynamics in virtual enterprise creation/ reconfiguration. Several environments are introduced in the chapter, and particular focus is given to the market of resources, an environment coping with the requirements of the virtual enterprise model.

Section 2
Supporting Technologies and Tools

Section 2 introduces some relevant tools associated to the development of enterprise information systems.

In Chapter 11, "Tool-Support for Software Development Processes," Kuhrmann, Kalus and Chroust present software development projects as complex. The more complex a project is, the higher are the requirements related to the software development process. The implementation of a process is a great challenge. This, in part, has to do with human factors (acceptance, etc.) as the benefits of a formal development process might not be obvious immediately and it may take a while until the process becomes the lifeblood of a team. A crucial step towards implementing, enacting and enforcing a process is to provide tool support for the many activities the process asks for. Tool support is necessary to guarantee efficiency in the project, to do the housekeeping and to minimize the "overhead" of the process. This chapter describes challenges and options for supporting process models by tools. Furthermore it describes concrete samples and shows how tool chains can be created with commercial tools as well as with open source tools.

Chapter 12, "Enterprise Tomography: An Efficient Approach for Semi-Automatic Localization of Integration Concepts in VLBAs", by Aalmink and Gómez, addresses Enterprise Tomography as an interdisciplinary approach for an efficient application lifecycle management of enterprise platforms and very large business applications (VLBA). Enterprise tomography semi-automatically identifies and localizes semantic integration concepts and visualizes integration ontologies in semantic genres. Especially delta determination of integration concepts is performed in dimension space and time. Enterprise tomography supports software and data comprehension. SMEs, large scaled development organizations and maintenance organizations can benefit from this new approach. This methodology is useful for tracking database changes of business processes or coding changes within a specific domain. In this way root cause analysis is supported.

Chapter 13, "Workflow as a Tool in the Development of Information Systems," by Leiva, Caro and Guevara, proposes a cooperative methodology for Information System (IS) development, focusing on the end user's collaboration in the process, providing the training and tools required to obtain the characteristics of the processes in which he/she is involved and actively integrating the user in the IS development team. Each of the steps involved in IS development is coordinated by a Meta-CASE tool based on a Workflow Management System (WfMS). An important characteristic of the methodology is the utilization of tools that allow to realize functions of reengineering to adapt existing systems allowing to add new functionalities or modifying the already existing ones. This methodology provides a high degree of reliability in the development of the system, creating competitive advantages for the organization by reducing times and costs in the generation of the information system (IS).

In Chapter 14, "Designing Open-Source OMIS Environment for Virtual Teams to Support Inter-Enterprise Collaboration," Kam Hou Vat discusses that today companies large and small have taken to open source as a way to increase collaboration, reduce development costs, provide a friendly platform for their products and services. In the specific context of establishing enterprise information systems (EIS) to enable organizations (especially small and medium enterprises) to integrate and coordinate their business processes, the stakes can be high in light of maintaining a company's competitive advantages. Whether open source will work at any company depends on both the capabilities of the company and the maturity of the open source processes and hence the software to support them. This chapter investigates the context of knowledge networks among virtual teams of professionals as the case-in-point discussion on a specific type of open source knowledge environment based on the Wiki technology, called organizational memory information system (OMIS) to support people working within and across organizational boundaries with technology. The issues of trust and shared understanding among organizations using the relevant OMIS environment is also deliberated in the discussion alongside the technology alignment and process adaptation for managing the OMIS-based collaboration among members of the knowledge networks.

Chapter 15

Finally in the last chapter of this section, "Information Systems Planning in Web 2.0 Era: A New Model Approach", José Sousa, argues that since the early development in the 90s, organizations had been growing in a rapid way, becoming each more difficult to manage. Organization business cycle changed from seven years in 1970-1980 to 12-18 months in the 90s, and is even shorter in our time. This addressed the organizations world to a new and complex reality. To be able to deal with this reality, organizations set a big pressure in information access and information turn out to be the most valuable organization asset. Nevertheless, this asset, the information object, has some main characteristics like, exists in large quantities, has many different forms, is very volatile and it also must have confidentially, integrity and availability and all this together can be very hard to manage. It is clear that the management of this information reality is only possible with the adoption of information technologies and planning that adoption and implementation is a central need in order to get the correct solution for the organization ecosystem.

Section 3
Managerial and Organizational Issues

This section discusses challenges, opportunities and concerns related to the managerial, social and organizational aspects of enterprise information systems adoption and exploitation.

Chapter 16

Chapter 16, "From User Participation to Stakeholder Management in Enterprise Information System Projects," by Boonstra, focuses on how managers and sponsors of enterprise information system (EIS) projects can identify and manage stakeholders engaged in the project. This chapter argues that this activity should go beyond the traditional ideas about user participation and management involvement. Also suppliers, customers, government agencies, business partners and the general public can have a clear interest in the ways that the system will be designed and implemented. This chapter proposes to apply identification, analysis and intervention techniques from organization and management disciplines in the IS field to enhance the changes for the successfulness of enterprise information system implementations. Some of these techniques are combined in a coherent method that may help implementers of complex IS projects to identify and categorize stakeholders and to consider appropriate ways of involvement during the various stages of the project.

In "Industrialism: Reduction Either Complexity Patterns," Michelini and Razzolli discuss the wealth generation mechanisms of the industrialism from its intrinsic cultural start, associated with the western-world stile. The prospected remarks single out several characterising features, in opposition to the east-Asia habits and cultural marks. Among other points, noteworthy remarks lead to prise complexity , instead of exploiting the reductionism. This is recognised as the robot age sign, opposed to the industry age patterns. The discussion does not provide full solutions, rather it suggests looking at the industrialism founding motivations (up to the cultural backing), in view to devise worthy alternatives.

As in Chapter 18, "Enterprise Modelling in support of Organisation Design and Change" by Ajaefobi, Rahimifard and Weston, enterprises are increasingly operating under uncertain conditions arising from: governments that introduce new regulations; a marketplace which is shaped by ongoing change in customer requirements; change in capital markets that orient overall market directions; an advancing base of technology; and increasing competition which can arise from a growing number of sources (Monfared, 2000). Consequently, organisations are expected to change rapidly in response to emerging requirements. Classical theories and more recently "method-based" organisation (re)design and change approaches have been proposed and tried with varying degrees of successes. This chapter contribution discusses the role of enterprise and simulation modelling in support of organisation (re)design and change. The capabilities and constraints of some widely acknowledged public domain enterprise modelling frameworks and methods are reviewed. A modelling approach which integrates the use of enterprise modelling, causal loop modelling, and simulation modeling is described. The approach enables the generation of coherent and semantically rich models of organisations. The integrated modelling approach has been applied and tested in a number of Manufacturing Enterprises and one case study application is described.

Chapter 19, "Communication in the Manufacturing Industry: An Empirical Study of the Management of
Engineering Drawing in a Shipyard," by Aslesen and Moen, is based on a case study of one shipyard's
effort to make the flow of engineering drawings feeding into its production process more reliable. To
construct a ship, detailed drawings of every part of the product is an essential input. For these drawings
to be reliable, they must include all relevant information, they have to follow each other in a proper line
of order, and they should be released according to production milestones. In the shipyard in study, an
analysis was initiated to explore the management of engineering drawing. Main findings show that the
usability of ICT is limited for this purpose, and that to really make an effort in order for engineering
drawings to be reliable a more basic understanding of the interpersonal communication at work in a
one-off project environment is fundamental.

According to Chapter 20, "Preconditions for Requisite Holism of Information Bases for the Invention-
Innovation Process Management," by Mulej, Potočan and Ženko, innovation belongs to main open issues
of the modern business. Information for the invention-innovation process is an even more open issue,
because informed guessing about the future needs of future potential customers is a best case scenario.
This is especially true in SMEs with their limited human resources, but the market provides no allowances for them anyway. SMEs are 99% of all organizations in EU or Slovenia. They provide +50% of
jobs and +70% of new jobs. But they can hardly survive with no or poor innovation capacity, including
a requisitely holistic consideration of the entire invention-innovation-diffusion process. The information
system must be adapted to this fact in order to support business quality in line with the demands of the
modern rather global than local market. But the usual enterprise information systems cover better the
daily routine and past performance than future and innovation issues.

In the last chapter of Section 3, "Exploring Enterprise Information Systems," Tabatabaie, Paige and Kimble address the concept of an Enterprise Information System (EIS), that has arisen from the need to deal with the increasingly volatile requirements of modern large-scale organisations. An EIS is a platform capable of supporting and integrating a wide range of activities across an organisation. In principle, the concept is useful and applicable to any large and SMEs, international or national business organisation. However, the range of applications for EIS is growing and they are now being used to support e-government, health care, and non-profit / non-governmental organisations. This chapter reviews research and development efforts related to EIS, and as a result attempts to precisely define the boundaries for the concept of EIS, (i.e., identifying what is and what is not an EIS). Based on this domain analysis, a proposal for using goal-oriented modelling techniques for building EIS is constructed; the proposal is made more concrete through illustration via an example.

Section 4
Critical Succes Factors and Case Studies

Section 4 describes and discusses motivations, trends, cases studies, successful cases of enterprise information systems implementation and exploitation.

Chapter 22

Hui-Lien Tung, Paine College, USA
Tina Marshall-Bradley, Paine College, USA
Joseph Wood, US Army, USA
Donald A. Sofge, Naval Research Laboratory, USA
James Grayson, Augusta State University, USA
Margo Bergman, Michael E. DeBakey VA Medical Center, USA
W.F. Lawless, Paine College, USA

In Chapter 22, "Enterprise Information Systems: Two Case Studies," Tung, Marshall-Bradley, Wood et al, start at the point that Enterprise Information Systems provide a platform that enables small organizations and distant collections of organizations to better integrate and coordinate their operations. The authors provide a theory of organizations and review two case studies beginning to use EIS-type architectures that form common information infrastructures to be more responsive, flexible and agile first for a system of medical organizations and second for a small college. The system of organizations is a distributed collection of military medical department research centers (MDRC) whose mission is to train physicians how to conduct and publish research and the small college is providing a liberal arts education (Future College). Both MDRC and Future College (pseudonyms) are reorganizing their operations. The authors also review theory for the approach, the two case studies, field evidence, computational models, and future prospects.

Chapter 23

In Chapter 23, "Modern ICT technologies in business administration: The case of the DERN project for a Digital Enterprise Research Network," Koumpis and Moumtzi present the DERN project and discuss a set of complementary methodologies that have been used to promote intra-enterprise training in the area of modern business administration technologies and corporate capacity building. The major end product of the research they introduced is a Learning Assets Management system (LAM) interoperable with best breed of the following: (a) human resources management systems and Employee Performance & Talent Management Suite (b) ERP systems and accounting engines and (c) learning management systems.

Chapter 24

As discussed in Chapter 24, "Motivations and Trends for IT/IS Adoption: Insights From Portuguese Companies," by Varajão, Trigo and Barroso, over the last few decades, information systems and technologies have taken on a wide variety of roles within organizations, ranging from operational support to the strategic support of the company. There have therefore been significant changes in the motives for their adoption that are vital to understand in order to guarantee that investment is properly managed. With the purpose of identifying and characterizing the motivations currently behind the adoption of information technologies in large Portuguese companies, which systems the companies have been implementing, in which systems they intend to invest in short-term and what is the current role of information technology within the organization, we carried out a study with the participation of several chief information officers. The findings of this study reveal that the reasons for adoption and the role that information systems and technologies play is evolving in Portuguese companies and that the adoption of certain types of systems such as Enterprise Resource Planning systems is now consolidated, while the adoption of other systems like Business Intelligence systems should increase significantly in the near future.

Chapter 25

In Chapter 25, "Semantic Web Based Integration of Knowledge Resources for Expertise Finding," Janev, Duduković and Vraneš discuss the challenges of expertise data integration and expert finding in modern organizations using an illustrative case study of a concrete research-intensive establishment, the

Mihajlo Pupin Institute (MPI). The chapter presents how the latest semantic technologies (Ontologies, Web services, Semantic Wiki) could be used on the top of the commercial ERP (Enterprise Resource Planning) software (SAP®) and the open-source ECM (Enterprise Content Management) software (Alfresco) in order to ensure meaningful search and retrieval of expertise for in-house users as well as the integration into the Semantic Web community space. This chapter points out the necessary adjustments in enterprise knowledge management infrastructure in the light of uprising initiatives for standardization of the Semantic Web data.

Preface

ABOUT THE SUBJECT

"An enterprise system has the Herculean task of seamlessly supporting and integrating a full range of business processes by uniting functional islands and making their data visible across the organization in real time." (Strong & Volkoff, 2004, p. 22).

For the last decades, it is being recognized that that enterprise computer-based solutions no longer consist of isolated or dispersedly developed and implemented MRP solutions, electronic commerce solutions, ERP solutions, transposing the functional islands to the so-called 'islands of information'. Solutions must be integrated, built on a single system, and supported by a common information infrastructure central to the organization, ensuring that information can be shared across all functional levels and management, so that it lets users instantly see data entered anywhere in the system and, simultaneously, seamlessly allows the integration and coordination of the enterprise business processes.

The topic of Enterprise Information Systems (EIS) is gaining an increasingly relevant strategic impact on global business and the world economy, and organizations are undergoing hard investments (in cost and effort) in search of the rewarding benefits of efficiency and effectiveness that this range of solutions promise. But as we all know this is not an easy task! It is not only a matter of financial investment! It is much more, as the book will show. EIS are responsibly by tremendous gains and even result in tremendous losses.

Responsiveness, flexibility, agility and business alignment are requirements of competitiveness that enterprises search for. And we hope that the models, solutions, tools and case studies presented and discussed in this book can contribute to highlight new ways to identify opportunities and overtake trends and challenges of EIS selection, adoption and exploitation.

ORGANIZATION OF THE BOOK

This book is a compilation of 25 contributions to the discussion of the main issues, challenges, opportunities and developments related with Enterprise Information Systems from the social, managerial and organizational perspectives, in a very comprehensive way, and to the dissemination of current achievements and practical solutions and applications.

These 25 chapters are written by a group of 54 authors that includes many internationally renowned and experienced authors in the EIS field and a set of younger authors, showing a promising potential for research and development. Contributions came from the USA, Latin America, several countries of Eastern and Western Europe and Asia. At the same time, the book integrates contributions from academe, research institutions and industry, representing a good and comprehensive representation of the state-of-the-art approaches and developments that address the several dimensions of this fast evolutionary thematic.

"Social, Managerial and Organizational Dimensions of Enterprise Information Systems" is organized in four sections:

- **Section 1: Models, Applications and Solutions** presents the main frameworks, approaches, methodologies and models that support Enterprise Systems.
- **Section 2: Supporting Technologies and Tools** introduces some tools associated to the development of EIS
- **Section 3: Managerial and Organizational Issues** discusses challenges, opportunities and concerns related to the managerial, social and organizational aspects of EIS adoption and exploitation.
- **Section 4: Critical Success Factors and Case Studies** describes and discusses motivations, trends, cases studies, successful cases of EIS implementation and exploitation.

The first section, "Models, Applications and Solutions" includes ten chapters summarized below.

In chapter one, "Enterprise Systems Approach," Targowski defines the enterprise system approach by its evolution and major milestones of architectural planning. The ES architectures are multi-faceted solutions; hence it is defined in the scope of the Enterprise Organization Architecture (EOA), Enterprise Functional Architecture (EFA), Enterprise Processive Architecture (EPA), Enterprise Information Architecture (EIA), Enterprise Software Architecture (ESA), Enterprise Network Architecture (ENA), Enterprise Service Architecture (ESA), Business Component Architecture (BCA), Enterprise Information Infrastructure (EII), and Enterprise Configurations. A composite ES architecture is presented as a transitional architecture, which is currently practiced by most enterprises. The near future of the ES approach will be rather limited to the ways of delivering ES applications within a framework of Service-Oriented Architecture (SOA) and cloud computing, which satisfies effective large-scale operations. The progressive process of organization/business virtualization and the urgent need for more sustainable enterprise development should lead to new development of enterprise systems.

In the second chapter, "Modeling Software Development Processes," Chroust, Kuhrmann and Schoitsch discuss the WHY and WHAT of modelling a software development process, as they investigate the components of a software process and propose a 5-dimensional grid of attributes of existing models: strategy and path, levels, main subprocesses, components and aura. Specific process models, currently used or historically important, are described. This is followed by an extensive discussion of methods and problems of modelling a software process, followed by a shorter discussion on the enactment of process models via software engineering environments. The chapter closes with a discussion of the human factors of introducing and enacting a process model.

Giorgio Bruno, in chapter three, "People-Oriented Enterprise Information Systems," states that current notations and languages do not emphasize the participation of users in business processes and consider them essentially as service providers. Moreover, they follow a centralized approach as all the interactions originate from or end in a business process; direct interactions between users cannot be represented. What is missing from this approach is that human work is cooperative and cooperation takes place through structured interactions called conversations; the notion of conversation is at the center of the language/action perspective. However, the problem of effectively integrating conversations and business processes is still open and this chapter proposes a notation called POBPN (People-Oriented Business Process Notation) and a perspective, referred to as conversation-oriented perspective, for its solution.

In "Doing Business on the Globalised Networked Economy: Technology and Business Challenges for Accounting Information Systems," the fourth chapter, Koumpis and Protogeros present a set of challenges that are to be faced by accounting information systems. More specifically, these include the support of interoperable accounting processes, for virtual and networked enterprises and for open-book accounting as well as the creation of novel interface metaphors that will automate and increase the usability of accounting information systems, and last but not least the provision of integrated e-accounting platforms.

Chapter five, "Recent Developments in Supplier Selection and Order Allocation Process," by Aktar and Ustun, states that the purchasing department can play a key role in cost reduction, and hence supplier selection and order allocation are the most important functions of purchasing management. In view of its complexity, the chapter is focused especially on the final selection stage that consists of determining the best mixture of suppliers and allocating orders among them so as to satisfy different purchasing requirements. In recent years, many researchers used new integrated models for supplier selection and order allocation. They combine multi-criteria approaches such as AHP/ANP and linear programming (LP), mixed integer programming (MIP), non-linear programming (NLP), mixed integer non-linear programming (MINLP) and goal programming (GP) with different achievement scalarizing functions. In this chapter, after the stages of supplier selection process are explained, these new integrated models are introduced and their constraints, variables, and goals/objectives of these models are explained in detail. Then, the solution methods of these integrated models are given. Finally, different integrated models are compared by considering their advantages and disadvantages.

In chapter six, "Complex Information Technology-Intensive Firms: A New Paradigmatic Firm-Theoretical Imperative! (Or a Pragmatically Impractical Interpretation of the Nature of the Virtualized Firm?)," Jelen and Kolakovic show how profoundly the design elements of firms have been affected by the current version of IT and propose elements of a framework that resiliently accommodates such effects. This framework can guide the practitioner designer for further refinements in the conception of CITI firms. The discoveries and framework elements are the result of our grounded theory methodology study in which executives, professionals, practitioners, entrepreneurs, and high-level decision-makers from a variety of firms participated.

In chapter seven, "A Methodology for the Auditing of Technological Knowledge Management," Aris and Ayuso present a methodology for auditing technological knowledge management that allows the proposed solution to be aligned with the competitive strategy of organisations, as well as with their processes, key competences, and the associated knowledge resources. That enables the solution to be technologically oriented and to be applied to different types of business, from SOHO and SME to large companies. Firstly, the authors present their view regarding knowledge management, which is a technological perspective; specify the context of application and objectives. Secondly, they analyse the characteristics of knowledge as the object to be managed and we will identify, analyse and criticise the most relevant knowledge management approaches, models and methodologies related to their objectives, then outlining the requirements that technological knowledge management must meet. Thirdly, they present the components of the model on which the methodology is based, and describe its stages and tasks. Then, they analyse the advantages of the model and methodology regarding other proposals.

In chapter eight, "E-CRM and CMS Systems: Potential for more Dynamic Businesses," according to Fernandes, any change in customer's behaviour affects the customer's value. In addition, profitability and economic viability also change. Most companies still do not know entirely their customer base characteristics. They find difficult to define criteria that segment their customer base to find high-value customers. They need to focus on target selections to carry on with marketing campaigns which involve high investments. Given the potential of e-CRM and CMS as powerful tools to guide customer-oriented understanding and analysis, greater attention is required. Several companies, operating within the same business and having access to the same information and technology, differ in e-CRM performance. Without sufficient evidence, managers are prone to making investment decisions that are neither efficient nor effective. So it is imperative to base the decision of e-CRM and CMS adoption, on not only their analytical power, but also on economic viability criteria for sustainable business dynamics.

According to Lima in chapter nine, "Integrating Production Planning and Control Business Processes," organizations have production planning and control (PPC) processes supported by systems that execute mainly repetitive calculations. Based on these calculation results, decisions are taken by production managers. These decision processes make the connection between different levels of aggregation of information and could benefit from the increment of the level of automation. An increased level of application of business process modelling languages is proposed in order to contribute to increment the level of process automation and the detail of business analysis. Thus, concepts of integration of production management processes, specifically of production planning and control processes are presented. These concepts, the application of Business Process Modelling Language (BPML) and some solutions of PPC integration compose the core content of this work. Additionally, criteria for evaluation of these processes of integration are identified and discussed. Finally, it is presented an industrial case supported by BPML model.

Finally, in chapter ten, "Environments for Virtual Enterprise Integration," Cunha and Putnik, introduce the virtual enterprise model as an emerging approach to answer to the new requirements of the business environment, relying on dynamically reconfigurable partnerships, with extremely high performances, strongly time-oriented while highly focused on cost and quality, in permanent alignment with the market, and strongly supported by information and communication technology, dictating a paradigm shift face to the traditional organizational models. Networking and reconfiguration dynamics are main characteristic of this model, which claim for enabling and supporting environments, at bearable costs. To the authors, some existing technologies and Internet-based environments can partially support this organizational model, but the reconfiguration dynamics can only by assured by environments able to managing, controlling and enabling networking and dynamics in virtual enterprise creation/ reconfiguration. Several environments are introduced in the chapter, and particular focus is given to the market of resources, an environment coping with the requirements of the virtual enterprise model.

The second section "Supporting Technologies and Tools" contains five chapters.

In chapter 11, "Tool-Support for Software Development Processes," Kuhrmann, Kalus and Chroust present software development projects as complex. The more complex a project is, the higher are the requirements related to the software development process. The implementation of a process is a great challenge. This, in part, has to do with human factors (acceptance, etc.) as the benefits of a formal development process might not be obvious immediately and it may take a while until the process becomes the lifeblood of a team. A crucial step towards implementing, enacting and enforcing a process is to provide tool support for the many activities the process asks for. Tool support is necessary to guarantee efficiency in the project, to do the housekeeping and to minimize the "overhead" of the process. This chapter describes challenges and options for supporting process models by tools. Furthermore it describes concrete samples and shows how tool chains can be created with commercial tools as well as with open source tools.

Chapter 12, "Enterprise Tomography: An Efficient Approach for Semi-Automatic Localization of Integration Concepts in VLBAs" by Aalmink and Gómez, addresses enterprise tomography as an interdisciplinary approach for an efficient application lifecycle management of enterprise platforms and very large business applications (VLBA). Enterprise tomography semi-automatically identifies and localizes semantic integration concepts and visualizes integration ontologies in semantic genres. Especially delta determination of integration concepts is performed in dimension space and time. Enterprise tomography supports software and data comprehension. SMEs, large scaled development organizations and maintenance organizations can benefit from this new approach. This methodology is useful for tracking database changes of business processes or coding changes within a specific domain. In this way, root cause analysis is supported.

Chapter 13, "Workflow as a Tool in the Development of Information Systems," by Leiva, Caro and Guevara, proposes a cooperative methodology for Information System (IS) development, focusing on the end user's collaboration in the process, providing the training and tools required to obtain the characteristics of the processes in which he/she is involved and actively integrating the user in the IS development team. Each of the steps involved in IS development is coordinated by a Meta-CASE tool based on a Workflow Management System (WfMS). An important characteristic of the methodology is the utilization of tools that allow to realize functions of reengineering to adapt existing systems allowing to add new functionalities or modifying the already existing ones. This methodology provides a high degree of reliability in the development of the system, creating competitive advantages for the organization by reducing times and costs in the generation of the information system (IS).

In chapter 14, "Designing Open-Source OMIS Environment for Virtual Teams to Support Inter-Enterprise Collaboration," Kam Hou Vat discusses that today companies large and small have taken to open source as a way to increase collaboration, reduce development costs, provide a friendly platform for their products and services. In the specific context of establishing enterprise information systems (EIS) to enable organizations (especially small and medium enterprises) to integrate and coordinate their business processes, the stakes can be high in light of maintaining a company's competitive advantages. Whether open source will work at any company depends on both the capabilities of the company and the maturity of the open source processes and hence the software to support them. This chapter investigates the context of knowledge networks among virtual teams of professionals as the case-in-point discussion on a specific type of open source knowledge environment based on the Wiki technology, called organizational memory information system (OMIS) to support people working within and across organizational boundaries with technology. The issues of trust and shared understanding among organizations using the relevant OMIS environment is also deliberated in the discussion alongside the technology alignment and process adaptation for managing the OMIS-based collaboration among members of the knowledge networks.

Finally in the last chapter of this section, "Information Systems Planning in Web 2.0 Era: A New Model Approach," José Sousa argues that since the early development in the 90s, organizations had been growing in a rapid way, becoming each more difficult to manage. Organization business cycle changed from seven years in 1970-1980 to 12-18 months in the 90s, and is even shorter in our time. This addressed the organizations world to a new and complex reality. To be able to deal with this reality, organizations set a big pressure in information access and information turn out to be the most valuable organization asset. Nevertheless, this asset, the information object, has some main characteristics like, exists in large quantities, has many different forms, is very volatile and it also must have confidentially, integrity and availability and all this together can be very hard to manage. It is clear that the management of this information reality is only possible with the adoption of information technologies and planning that adoption and implementation is a central need in order to get the correct solution for the organization ecosystem.

And now, concerning the six chapters included in the third section "Managerial and organizational issues."

Chapter 16, "Identifying and Managing Stakeholders in Enterprise Information System Projects", by Boonstra focuses on how managers and sponsors of enterprise information system (EIS) projects can identify and manage stakeholders engaged in the project. This chapter argues that this activity should go beyond the traditional ideas about user participation and management involvement. Also suppliers, customers, government agencies, business partners and the general public can have a clear interest in the ways that the system will be designed and implemented. This chapter proposes to apply identification, analysis and intervention techniques from organization and management disciplines in the IS field to enhance the changes for the successfulness of enterprise information system implementations. Some of these techniques are combined in a coherent method that may help implementers of complex IS projects to identify and categorize stakeholders and to consider appropriate ways of involvement during the various stages of the project.

In "Industrialism: Reduction Either Complexity Patterns," Michelini and Razzolli discuss the wealth generation mechanisms of the industrialism from its intrinsic cultural start, associated with the western-world stile. The prospected remarks single out several characterising features, in opposition to the east-Asia habits and cultural marks. Among other points, noteworthy remarks lead to prise «complexity», instead of exploiting the reductionism. This is recognised as the «robot age» sign, opposed to the «industry age» patterns. The discussion does not provide full solutions, rather it suggests looking at the industrialism founding motivations (up to the cultural backing), in view to devise worthy alternatives.

As in chapter 18, "Enterprise Modelling in sSpport of Organisation Design and Change" by Ajaefobi, Rahimifard and Weston, enterprises are increasingly operating under uncertain conditions arising from: governments that introduce new regulations; a marketplace which is shaped by ongoing change in customer requirements; change in capital markets that orient overall market directions; an advancing base of technology; and increasing competition which can arise from a growing number of sources (Monfared, 2000). Consequently, organisations are expected to change rapidly in response to emerging requirements. Classical theories and more recently "method-based" organisation (re)design and change approaches have been proposed and tried with varying degrees of successes. This chapter contribution discusses the role of enterprise and simulation modelling in support of organisation (re)design and change. The capabilities and constraints of some widely acknowledged public domain enterprise modelling frameworks and methods are reviewed. A modelling approach which integrates the use of enterprise modelling, causal loop modelling, and simulation modeling is described. The approach enables the generation of coherent and semantically rich models of organisations. The integrated modelling approach has been applied and tested in a number of Manufacturing Enterprises and one case study application is described.

Chapter 19, "Communication in the Manufacturing Industry: An Empirical Study of the Management of Engineering Drawing in a Shipyard," by Aslesen and Moen, is based on a case study of one shipyard's effort to make the flow of engineering drawings feeding into its production process more reliable. To construct a ship, detailed drawings of every part of the product is an essential input. For these drawings to be reliable, they must include all relevant information, they have to follow each other in a proper line of order, and they should be released according to production milestones. In the shipyard in study, an analysis was initiated to explore the management of engineering drawing. Main findings show that the usability of ICT is limited for this purpose, and that to really make an effort in order for engineering drawings to be reliable a more basic understanding of the interpersonal communication at work in a one-off project environment is fundamental.

According to chapter 20, "Preconditions for Requisite Holism of Information Bases for the Invention-Innovation Process Management," by Mulej, Potočan and Ženko, innovation belongs to main open issues of the modern business. Information for the invention-innovation process is an even more open issue, because informed guessing about the future needs of future potential customers is a best case scenario. This is especially true in SMEs with their limited human resources, but the market provides no allowances for them anyway. SMEs are 99% of all organizations in EU or Slovenia. They provide +50% of jobs and +70% of new jobs. But they can hardly survive with no or poor innovation capacity, including a requisitely holistic consideration of the entire invention-innovation-diffusion process. The information system must be adapted to this fact in order to support business quality in line with the demands of the modern rather global than local market. But the usual enterprise information systems cover better the daily routine and past performance than future and innovation issues.

In the last chapter of section three, "Exploring Enterprise Information Systems," Tabatabaie, Paige and Kimble address the concept of an Enterprise Information System (EIS), that has arisen from the need to deal with the increasingly volatile requirements of modern large-scale organisations. An EIS is a platform capable of supporting and integrating a wide range of activities across an organisation. In principle, the concept is useful and applicable to any large and SMEs, international or national business organisation. However, the range of applications for EIS is growing and they are now being used to support e-government, health care, and non-profit / non-governmental organisations. This chapter reviews research and development efforts related to EIS, and as a result attempts to precisely define the boundaries for the concept of EIS (i.e., identifying what is and what is not an EIS). Based on this domain analysis, a proposal for using *goal-oriented modelling* techniques for building EIS is constructed; the proposal is made more concrete through illustration via an example.

Section four, "Critical Success Factors and Case Studies," includes four chapters.

In chapter 22, "Enterprise Information Systems: Two Case Studies," Tung, Marshall-Bradley, Wood et al., start at the point that enterprise information systems provide a platform that enables small organizations and distant collections of organizations to better integrate and coordinate their operations. The authors provide a theory of organizations and review two case studies beginning to use EIS-type architectures that form common information infrastructures to be more responsive, flexible and agile first for a system of medical organizations and second for a small college. The system of organizations is a distributed collection of military medical department research centers (MDRC) whose mission is to train physicians how to conduct and publish research and the small college is providing a liberal arts education (Future College). Both MDRC and Future College (pseudonyms) are reorganizing their operations. The authors also review theory for the approach, the two case studies, field evidence, computational models, and future prospects.

In chapter 23, "Modern ICT Technologies in Business Administration: The Case of the DERN Project for a Digital Enterprise Research Network," Koumpis and Moumtzi present the DERN project and discuss a set of complementary methodologies that have been used to promote intra-enterprise training in the area of modern business administration technologies and corporate capacity building. The major end product of the research they introduced is a Learning Assets Management system (LAM) interoperable with best breed of the following: (a) human resources management systems and Employee Performance & Talent Management Suite (b) ERP systems and accounting engines and (c) learning management systems.

As discussed in chapter 24, "Motivations and Trends for IT/IS Adoption: Insights From Portuguese Companies," by Varajão, Trigo and Barroso, over the last few decades, information systems and technologies have taken on a wide variety of roles within organizations, ranging from operational support to the strategic support of the company. There have therefore been significant changes in the motives for their adoption that are vital to understand in order to guarantee that investment is properly managed. With the purpose of identifying and characterizing the motivations currently behind the adoption of information technologies in large Portuguese companies, which systems the companies have been implementing, in which systems they intend to invest in short-term and what is the current role of information technology within the organization, we carried out a study with the participation of several chief information officers. The findings of this study reveal that the reasons for adoption and the role that information systems and technologies play is evolving in Portuguese companies and that the adoption of certain types of systems such as enterprise resource planning systems is now consolidated, while the adoption of other systems like business intelligence systems should increase significantly in the near future.

In chapter 25, "Semantic Web Based Integration of Knowledge Resources for Expertise Finding," Janev, Duduković and Vraneš discuss the challenges of expertise data integration and expert finding in modern organizations using an illustrative case study of a concrete research-intensive establishment, the Mihajlo Pupin Institute (MPI). The chapter presents how the latest semantic technologies (Ontologies, Web services, Semantic Wiki) could be used on the top of the commercial ERP (Enterprise Resource Planning) software (SAP®) and the open-source ECM (Enterprise Content Management) software (Alfresco) in order to ensure meaningful search and retrieval of expertise for in-house users as well as the integration into the Semantic Web community space. This chapter points out the necessary adjustments in enterprise knowledge management infrastructure in the light of uprising initiatives for standardization of the Semantic Web data.

EXPECTATIONS

The book provides researchers, scholars, professionals with some of the most advanced research, solutions and discussions of Enterprise Information Systems under the social, managerial and organizational dimensions.

This book is expected to be read by academics (teachers, researchers and students of several graduate and postgraduate courses) and by professionals of Information Technology, IT managers, Information Resources managers, Enterprise managers (including top level managers), and also technology solutions developers.

I strongly hope it meets your expectations!

Maria Manuela Cruz-Cunha
Barcelos, February 2009

REFERENCES

Strong, D. M., & Volkoff, O. (2004). A Roadmap for Enterprise System Implementation. *Computer-Aided Design & Applications, 37*(6), 22-29.

Acknowledgment

Editing a book is a quite hard but compensating and enriching task, as it involves an set of different activities like contacts with authors and reviewers, discussion and exchange of ideas and experiences, process management, organization and integration of contents, and many other, with the permanent objective of creating a book that meets the public expectations. And this task cannot be accomplished without a great help and support from many sources. As editor I would like to acknowledge the help, support and believe of all who made possible this creation.

First of all, the edition of this book would not have been possible without the ongoing professional support of the team of professionals of IGI Global. I am grateful to Dr. Mehdi Khosrow-Pour, Senior Acquisitions Editor, and to Jan Travers, Managing Director, for the opportunity. A very very special mention of gratitude is due to Julia Mosemann, Assistant Development Editor, for her professional support and friendly words of advisory, encouragement and prompt guidance.

Special thanks go also to all the staff at IGI Global, whose contributions throughout the process of production and making this book available all over the world was invaluable.

We are grateful to all the authors, for their insights and excellent contributions to this book. Also we are grateful to most of the authors who simultaneously served as referees for chapters written by other authors, for their insights, valuable contributions, prompt collaboration and constructive comments. Thank you all, authors and reviewers, you made this book! The communication and exchange of views within this truly global group of recognized individualities from the scientific domain and from industry was an enriching and exciting experience!

I am also grateful to all who accede to contribute to this book, some of them with high quality chapter proposals, but unfortunately, due to several constraints could not have seen their work published.

A special thanks to my institution, the Polytechnic Institute of Cávado and Ave, for providing the material resources and all the necessary logistics.

Thank you.

Maria Manuela Cruz-Cunha
Barcelos, Febrary 2009

Section 1
Models, Applications and Solutions

Chapter 1
The Enterprise Systems Approach

Andrew Targowski
Western Michigan University, USA

ABSTRACT

The enterprise system approach is defined by its evolution and major milestones of architectural planning. The ES architectures are multi-faceted solutions, hence it is defined in the scope of the enterprise organization architecture (EOA), enterprise functional architecture (EFA), enterprise processive architecture (EPA), enterprise information architecture (EIA), enterprise software architecture (ESA), enterprise network architecture (ENA), enterprise service architecture (ESA), business component architecture (BCA), enterprise information infrastructure (EII), and enterprise configurations. A composite ES architecture is presented as a transitional architecture, which is currently practiced by most enterprises. The near future of the ES approach will be rather limited to the ways of delivering ES' applications within a framework of service-oriented architecture (SOA) and the cloud computing, which satisfies effective large-scale operations. The progressive process of organization/business virtualization and the urgent need for more sustainable enterprise development should lead to new development of enterprise systems.

INTRODUCTION

The purpose of this study is to define the Enterprise Systems approach, its evolution, and major milestones of its architectural planning. The former is done mostly in a graphic manner and based on graphic models, which should be self-explanatory. The ES architectures are multi-faceted solutions,

hence they will defined in the scope of the Enterprise Organization Architecture (EOA), Enterprise Functional Architecture (EFA), Enterprise Processive Architecture (EPA), Enterprise Information Architecture (EIA), Enterprise Software Architecture (ESA), Enterprise Network Architecture (ENA), Enterprise Service Architecture (ESA), Business Component Architecture (BCA), Enterprise Information Infrastructure (EII), and Enterprise Configurations. Such enterprise architectures concerning

DOI: 10.4018/978-1-60566-856-7.ch001

hardware and data have been left undefined due to the limits of this chapter.

The ES approach became necessary in the 1990s when the complexity of enterprise systems became the major issue in systems development and was integrated into thousands of IT solutions. It was necessary to provide a general, well-modeled map of IT systems and services that could help in understanding the rising enterprise complexity, which had to be contained and explored for the sake of enterprise operations.

Trends of Enterprise Systems Development

The process of IT-driven enterprise formation will take sharp turns in the 21st century while more technologies and standards will be developed and further challenge business and IT executives. The single major question for application acquisition in the past was "make or buy?" It was assumed that whether an application was "made" or "bought," it would almost inevitably be run inside the enterprise firewall. But in the 21st century the IT industry is entering a period of massive innovation and growth in alternative delivery models, ranging from

- EAI through to full-blown BPI, SaaS, and SOA. So now, the costs, risks, benefits, and sustainability associated with each one must be carefully evaluated. A 21st-century enterprise systems portfolio will contain an eclectic mix of delivery models as the economics of delivery change and technology progresses. It is extremely important that any enterprise application strategy is fully informed about current capabilities of different delivery models and is aware of how these may develop over time.

Before Ford revolutionized carmaking, automobiles were assembled by teams of skilled craftsmen in custom-built workshops. Similarly,

most corporate data centers today house armies of "systems administrators" who are the craftsmen of the Information Age. There are an estimated 7,000 such data centers in America alone. It is not surprising that that they are inefficient. On average, only 6% of server capacity is used and nearly the 30% that are no longer in use at all, no one has bothered to remove. Many data centers will be consolidated and given a big reengineering. For example, Hewlett-Packard (HP) used to have 85 data centers with 19,000 IT workers worldwide. One can expect that it will be cut down to six facilities in America with just 8,000 employees by the end of 2008 and the budget cut from 4% to 2% of revenue (*The Economist*, October 28, 2008, p. 6).

- As a result of such operations integrations, data centers are becoming factories for computing services on an industrial scale. Software is increasingly being delivered as an online service and wireless networks are connecting to more and more devices.. All these allow computing to be disaggregated into components or "services," in IT terminology. This trend leads to the development of *cloud computing*, in which information is permanently stored in servers on the Internet and cached temporarily on clients that include desktops, entertainment centers, table computers, notebooks, wall computers, handhelds, sensors, monitors, etc. Cloud computing is a general concept that incorporates software as a service (SaaS), Web 2.0, and other technology concepts in which the common theme is reliance on the Internet for satisfying the computing needs of the users. For example, Google Apps provides common business applications online that are accessed from a user's web browser, while the software and data are stored on the Google's servers farms. Since *cloud computing* applies the Internet for data transportation, it will be a questionable path for distributing corporate data, which, up until now, were transmitted through private networks.

The enormous applications of the Internet and its cost and time cutting practices in delivering services lead to the development of *virtual enterprises*, which are organizations without walls but with a cyberspace. The virtualization of business and the society takes very convincing forms in the beginning of the 21st century. Hence, one can predict that the following trend in the development of ES will take place:

- To support the development and operations of *virtual enterprise (VE)*, which is a temporary alliance of enterprises that come together to share skills or core competencies and resources in order to better respond to business opportunities, and whose cooperation is supported by computer networks. It is a manifestation of Collaborative Networks and a particular case of *Virtual Organization* (VO). VO defies the conventional rule for operating an organization. It does so by accomplishing tasks traditionally meant for an organization much bigger, better resourced, and financially stable. A company having the technical capability with the right human skill set and another with the solution may come together to create a VO. The VE (a kind of VO) does not exist in the physical sense but on an electronic network representing a partnership of businesses existing as a nebulous form of business organization that only exists to meet a market opportunity. Today, there are numerous virtual enterprises on the Internet. Virtual Music Enterprises is one example of a virtual enterprise Virtual Enterprise California lists several other examples. Another example of a Virtual Enterprise would be an educational class operating worldwide and in which students

in many locations come together in a "virtual classroom" to form a virtual business. They do not conduct real transactions, nor do they sell real merchandise. The purpose of the class is simply to learn how to start and run a business. The business is usually replaced at the end of the year for the next group of students. The students do business with many companies, and even hold trade fairs and grand openings. One of examples of new emerging ES are: e-commerce, collaborative communication (MS SharePoint), and so forth. A more new ES' development and implementations one can expect in the near future (Targowski 2009a).

The financial crisis which touched the world in October 2008 should change the development of ES. Since the failure of banks and financial institutions has something to do with the enormous complexity of created enterprises, which get out of control? For example Lehman Brothers and Wachovia Bank were not economically vital and sustainable firms in 2008 because their business practices did not adequately consider the long-term consequences of their actions. The collapse of Enron in the 2000s showed the importance of internal policies such as maintaining adequate controls and good corporate governance practices on a firm's sustainability. Environmental stewardship requires consideration of how to use natural resources in a productive, efficient, and profitable manner. Concern for how goods and services are produced, packaged, transported, used, and recycled calls for examining supply chain policies as well as energy and environmental impacts. Social responsibility starts, but does not end, with the employee and a firm's hiring, opportunity and training practices. The needs of other stakeholders (suppliers, customers, investors) and their cultural concerns, as well as the community at large and even the future generations are increasingly important. Hence, the expected trend in the development of ES should lead towards the development of:

- *Sustainable enterprise* and supporting an appropriate information infrastructure. Sustainability has been defined as "meeting the needs of the present without compromising the ability of future generations to meet their needs." This definition calls for business organizations to operate in a manner that values the well-being of stakeholders (customers, suppliers, employees and investors) in sustaining economic prosperity while also taking care of their employees and the environment. The core concept of sustainability seeks to encourage the adoption and implementation of practices that aim at the "*triple bottom line:*"
  i.   Economic vitality,
  ii. Environmental stewardship, and
  iii. Social responsibility.

While initially, sustainability was viewed as primarily focusing on preserving the earth's resources, its broader meaning today encompasses the achievement of economic prosperity while caring not only for the planet's resources, but also for the well-being of employees, society, and culture and future generations. Each of the three segments of the triple-bottom line will require businesses to examine and refocus their current policies and practices, as well as supporting the information infrastructure.

Companies have long engaged in head-to-head competition in search of sustained, profitable growth. They have fought for competitive advantage, battled over market shares, and struggled for differentiation. Yet in today's overcrowded industries, competing head-on results in nothing but a bloody "Red Ocean" of rivals fighting over a shrinking profit pool. Kim and Mauborgne (2005) developed a strategy of Blue Ocean for uncontested market space, ripping for growth. Such strategic moves, termed "value innovation," create

powerful leaps in value for both the firm and its buyers, rendering rivals obsolete and unleashing new demand. It leads to:

- Development of *value-creation enterprise*. Examples of such enterprises include: Barnes & Noble Bookstores, Cirque du Soleil, and Dell Computers which created new market space (with a new value for customers) that outperformed other books stores, cirques, and PC makers. This new emerging kind of enterprise will need a new set of key enterprise systems.

Table 1 illustrates a typology of emerging new kinds of enterprises, which determine appropriate support of enterprise systems.

The ES are not only being implemented in industrial practice. They also are taught at the university level where courses on enterprise projects are not only undertaken, but also are supported by computer laboratories that introduce students to hands-on use of enterprise software such as SAP and MS Dynamics. One of the leaders in this kind of education is the Western Michigan University and its Business Information Systems Department (Targowski & Tarn 2006).

The presented solutions define the current state of the art and provide generic rather than specific solutions. Perhaps such an approach will make the presented solutions more permanent. The presented future trends of enterprise systems lead to more complex implementations of ES operations. However, more new enterprise systems one must expect, particularly such ones, which will be supporting *virtual enterprise/organization, sustainable enterprise,* and *value-creation enterprise.* Solutions as SOA and *cloud computing* at first glance seem to be more effective. However, whether will they be more reliable it is a big question which will be answered in coming practice of successful and failing users.

This chapter first defines a concept of the enterprise systems approach, its evolution, and then

Table 1. A typology of emerging new kinds of enterprises

CUSTOMER VISION	KINDS OF ENTERPRISES					
Survival (*wisdom*)						**Sustainable Enterprise**
New Value (*satisfaction*)					**Value-Creation Enterprise**	
Fast and Effective Transaction (usefulness and convenience)				**Virtual Enterprise**		
Low Cost (*usefulness*)			**Electronic Enterprise**			
Activities (*convenience*)		**Service Enterprise**				
Product (*productivity*)	**Industrial Enterprise**					
CORE COMPETENCE	Production	Relations	Networking		Innovations	Sustainability
STRATEGY	*Red Ocean Strategy*				*Blue Ocean Strategy*	*Green Ocean Strategy*

reviews major theoretical and industrial solutions being practiced by this approach. It concludes with the assumption that this approach's success will depend on more defined and applied standards which should smooth the flaws of information, communications, and other processes within an enterprise and among enterprises.

THE EMERGENCE OF THE ENTERPRISE SYSTEMS APPROACH

The enterprise systems approach has roots in the General System Theory, defined by Ludwig von Bertalanffy in 1951 and in Cybernetics defined by Norbert Wiener in 1948. Based upon these two theories, the system analysis has been emerging for military large-scale systems, practiced at the RAND Corporation (Hitch 1955). Its applications in military systems were intensified during the first stage of the Cold War and early defined as system engineering (Schlager 1956, Goode & Robert Machol 1957, Chestnut 1967). The

system analysis applications in civil applications led to the development of the system approach for computer applications design (McDonough 1963, Kanter 1966) and system-oriented approach to the conceptualization of social dynamics in sociology (Buckley 1967). Eventually, the system engineering approach was applied as a method of designing "hard" complex products. Its generalization led to the conceptualization of the system approach for "soft" products (Van Gigch (1974).

In the 1970s and 1980s the supply of comprehensive families of mainframe computers (ex. IBM 360 and 370) facilitated the strong development of computer information systems in business and civic/governmental organizations. It was the beginning stage of this kind of applications, which eventually led to the development of the "information archipelago" (McFarlan, McKenny 1983) of disintegrated applications, currently called "legacy systems." In response to this growing crisis, McFarlan offered a concept of the "applications portfolio" (1981), a set of a few key applications which should be controlled carefully by IT managers, currently called Chief Information Officers (CIO). This strategy was widely accepted by computer executive since they had no challenge of more advanced applications.

Eventually, the Application Portfolio led to the long stagnation of the system approach and its vigorous application in the computer information systems development in practice. Targowski contrasted this approach with his ideas of the enterprise systems approach in his book, *Architecture and Planning of Enterprise-wide Information Management Systems* (1990). His hypothesis was that if the enterprise systems are properly planned and designed, they will limit the "information archipelago" and provide the tools for the logical integration of systems within the enterprise. A few years later, as a result of American enterprise dynamics stagnation, Hammer and Champy called for *Reengineering the Corporation* (1993), which must lead to radical redesign of a company's processes, organization, and culture to achieve a quantum leap in performance. Ever since, the system approach was aimed toward the whole enterprise.

Targowski's scholar message (1990) was weak in the industrial circles, but Hammer and Champy's bestseller showed the right direction on how to invigorate ES, at least for IT professionals. Its first step led towards the development of Enterprise Resources Planning (ERP), which integrated MRP I (Material Requirements Planning) with MRP II (Manufacturing Resources Planning). Hence, such software systems, such as SAP, gained world-wide popularity. However, only IBM meant to apply the enterprise systems approach holistically when it offered Computer Integrated Manufacturing (CIM), which contained CAD, CAM, MIS and Office Automation Systems. Unfortunately, IBM quit this kind of systems delivery and switched to the promotion of SAP, which is based on early IBM PICS and COPICS systems (without CAD/CAM). Nowadays, the Enterprise Systems expand ERP toward SCM (Supply Chain Management) and CRM (Customer

Relationships Management). Today, due to off-shore outsourcing of manufacturing, the impetus towards the further development of CAD/CAM within ES is less energetic than used to be in the past in the U.S and in Western Europe.

At the beginning 21st century, the enterprise systems approach is popular and has many scholars, practitioners, and writers occupied which improving this approach, mostly in the scope of enterprise architecture (Rechting & Maier 1997, Carbone 2004). IBM promotes the so -called the Zachman Framework as a classification structure often used in Information Technology departments by the teams responsible for developing and documenting an *Enterprise Architecture*. The Framework is used for organizing architectural "artifacts" in a way that takes into account both who the artifact targets (for example, business owner, and builder) and what particular issue is being addressed (for example, data and functionality). These artifacts may include design documents, specifications, and models. The Zachman Framework is one of the earliest Enterprise Architecture frameworks (Zachman 1987).

Scott Bernard defines enterprise architecture as:

The analysis and documentation of an enterprise in its current and future states from an integrated strategy, business, and technology perspective (2005:31).

Its components are limited to: goals and initiatives; products and services; data and information; systems and applications; and networks and infrastructure as an Enterprise Architecture Cube.

Enterprise architecture as a business strategy was recognized by Ross, Weill, and Robertson (2006) who researched more than 200 companies. They found that the successful companies were those which operated through the enterprise architecture concept. The authors noticed that,

Figure 1. The J. Schekkerman model of enterprise architecture

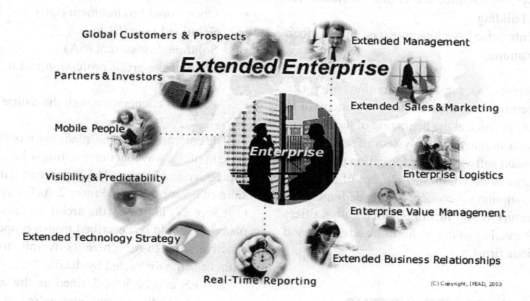

A high-level enterprise architecture creates shared understanding of how a company will operate, but the convergence of people, process, and technology necessary to implement that architecture demands shared understanding of process and data at a more detailed level (2005:49).

Schekkerman (1995) is one of leading specialists who not only recognized the importance of enterprise architecture but in order to pursue its farther right development, founded the independent Institute for Enterprise Architecture Developments (IFEAD) in the Netherlands. IFEAD publishes professional recommendations and provides solutions based on its definition –

'Enterprise Architecture is about understanding all of the different elements that go to make up the enterprise and how those elements interrelate." In that sense, examples of elements are: strategies, business drivers, principles, stakeholders, units, locations, budgets, domains, functions, activities, processes, services, products, information, communications, applications, systems, infrastructure, etc.

The Schekkerman Model of Enterprise Architecture is shown in Figure 1. It is a model of extended enterprise, which goes far beyond the information enterprise architecture.

For example, a very strong user of enterprise architecture concept is the U.S. Department of Defense (DOD), which applies a concept of Enterprise Architecture Framework (DODAF) in order to (Mosto 2004):

- Define a common approach for describing, presenting, and comparing DoD enterprise architectures
- Facilitate the use of common principles, assumptions and terminology

The principal objective of DODAF is:

To ensure that architecture descriptions can be compared and related across organizational boundaries, including Joint and multi-national boundaries

The DoD recognizes a difference between an architecture and systems in the following manner:

- System Architecture is like blueprints for a building
- Enterprise Architecture is like urban planning

However, as far as information enterprise architecture is concerned, the main attention in business practice at the beginning of the 21st century is turning towards a system of servicing of application software and information processing on a large scale within the concept of SOA and cloud computing. A concept of extended enterprise architecture is still in *status nascendi* but offers very promising solutions for more advanced and ambitious firms.

THE ENTERPRISE SYSTEMS APPROACH DEFINED

The enterprise systems (ES) approach has roots in the system approach, which was initiated at the RAND Think Tank of the Air Force in the 1950, by such pioneers as Charles Hitch (1955) and others, who applied this approach in developing complex military systems. In the 1990s, when information systems strategic planning became popular in business enterprises it was evident that the enterprise systems' big-picture can be best defined under the form of the enterprise systems architecture.

The enterprise systems approach is based on the philosophy of the system approach (Klir 1985) and management cybernetics (Beer 1981), graphic-architectural modeling, and was first defined by Targowski (1990) as a comprehensive and cohesive solution to the problem of system development, thus eliminating the fuzziness of the "Applications Portfolio" and the "Information Archipelago" (McFarlan 1981).

The enterprise systems architectural approach involves thought and graphic visualization in the following dimensions:

- Users' groups and their system needs
- Operational Environment (OE)
- Solution Logic (SL)
- Solution Assessment (SA)
- State-of-the-art of profession and technology (SA)
- Peaceful cooperation with the nature (N)

The enterprise systems' planning/modeling is done in such a way that the resulting solutions are expressive and correct. The architectural dimensions of ES are shown in Figure 2. As George Klir (1985, p. 27) indicates, the architectural system planning should be described from a proper perspective so as to recognize its overall structure without being distracted by details.

The ES approach is defined as the art and science of solutions planning applied to fulfill the practical and the synergetic requirements of information technology (IT) advanced enterprise environments, including users and customers. The characteristics that distinguish the work of an system architect from other man-made structures are:

- The suitability of the solutions for use by all stakeholders
- The stability and relative permanence of solution construction for 15 to 25 years
- The communication of solutions' ideas and assessment through the open-ended configuration.

The modeling of the ES architecture begins, when the business and IT strategies are defined and is based on the following principles:

1. *Cybernetization.* A good ES architecture is viable and capable of growing, and adapting to complex, dynamic enterprise operations. This architecture should be self-organizing, with a feedback, and requisite variety.
2. *Systematization.* A good ES architecture is modeled as a set of components and

Figure 2. The dimensions of the enterprise systems approach

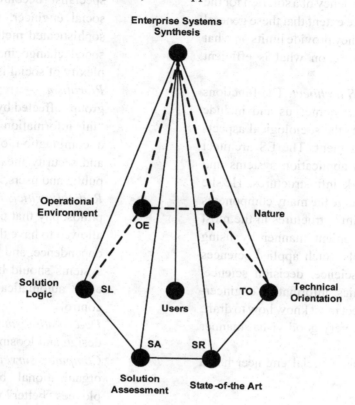

interrelationships in order to accomplish a given goal and produce results outside of ES, despite of the external obstacles.

3. *Cohesiveness.* A good ES architecture makes all components of ES sticking together and it supports the enterprise functions and processes in a harmonious manner.

4. *Categorization.* A good ES architecture requires that ES components are self-contained, independent of each other, and planned without repetition in different forms.

5. *Primitiveness.* A good ES architecture is based on generic elements and relationships. Further extensions of the ES's functionality should have roots in the primitive, generic model of a given element.

6. *Completeness.* A good ES architecture is perceives all major and possible components

of solution logic (SL) and technical orientation (TO).

7. *Value Engineering.* A good ES architecture does not contain unnecessary components but only these ones that are proper for a given solution.

8. *Sustainability.* A good ES architecture supports the reliable development and operations of an enterprise in a long-term perspective, taking into account; economic vitality, environmental stewardship, and social responsibility.

9. *Open*-ended structures. A good ES architecture is open for future improvements and for the insertion of components that are perceivable though not yet available.

The application of these principles in the modeling of ES architecture determines the reliability, quality, and efficiency of a solution for the whole enterprise. To the extent that these general principles are known, they provide limits on what is possible and guidance on what is efficient (Clemson 1984).

Functions of the ES architect. The functions of the ES architect are numerous and include the technical as well as the sociological aspects of information management. The ES architect must be an expert in application systems and their hardware/network infrastructures. He/she must know how to arrange the many components of these applications/infrastructures in the most economical and convenient manner by using graphic modeling tools. Such applied sciences are used as system science, decision science, management, economics, information engineering, etc. The ES architect must know how to draft, render and finish in a very good visual manner the expected solution.

The ES architect as a social engineer has a choice of using:

- *Tools* of information technology, such as system analysis and design, programming high level languages, databases, knowledge bases, utility software for rapid prototyping solutions,
- *Stimulations* defined in information policies on security, privacy, trade, computer crime, intellectual property, ethics, and so forth,
- *Positions* that will influence ES modeling (Mowshowitz 1980):
  - *Technicism* – using IT as an instrument of progress, where success or failure depends on the system design and implementation; social and political consequences are ignore,
  - *Progressive individualism* – humanizing the system with computers as helpers to achieve desirable change,
  - *Elitism* – informing and rescuing society as the mission of the computer

specialist becomes a mission of a social engineer, which is the most sophisticated method of steering the social change in the growing complexity of social issues,
  - *Pluralism* – representing interest groups affected by computer use with "fair information practices" and with a combination of legal, regulatory, and security measures to protect the public and users,
  - *Radical criticism* – protesting the philosophy that computers should be allowed to have their own logic of independence, and that mega computer systems should be developed to operate automatically without human control,
  - *De-evolutionism* – gaining power of design and loosing control over use,
  - *Computer surveillance* – producing organizational benefits, since employees "better" work.

Because these *choices* of ES factors, the architect should have of social awareness about what is he/she is going to develop. Social awareness can be composed of social biases, beliefs, and expectations. Social biases are influenced by the choice of IT tools. For example, a technical bias advocates that technology can solve a social problem, while a non-technical bias supports the view that such a problem can be solved through managerial action such as leadership or an improved market strategy.

The choice of stimulations can influence social beliefs. For example, computers can be seen as strength of the economy or as a threat to an individual privacy and autonomy. Social expectations are the result of a position taken by the ES architect and are determined by the information culture in the scope of values (human and civil rights versus totalitarian slavery, creativity, and electronic friendship versus alienation), symbols (credits cards equate to a cashless society, computer screens equate to a paperless society), competence standards (a lack of computer competence equates to illiteracy), knowledge centers (data, knowledge, wisdom bases), know-how (individual computer skills, social skills that control the information transformations), and futurology ("Star Wars"). The Figure 3 illustrates the ES architect's social awareness about modeled solutions.

THE EVOLUTION OF THE ENTERPRISE SYSTEMS APPROACH

In the early period (the early 1960s) of computer information systems (CIS) development, the paradigm of design was application programming. As shown in Figure 4, the IS concept came as a result of preparing an operational environment for the application of the IBM 1400 and IBM 360 tape/disk computers. The operational environment was organized as a bureaucracy specialized in routines; consequently, this was the logic orientation (SL) of design. The routines were programmed in COBOL, the state of the art (SR) language and processed in batches as a technical orientation (TO). The system assessment (SA) was based on the cost-benefits analysis, which was aiming at the replacement of office clerks by computerized routines. The leading specialist in this time was a programmer, a master handler of computers, who applied the MIND III (practical) (Skolimowski 1984).

In the 1970s with the development of database technology, the system design switched from sequential processing on magnetic tape storage to on-line processing transactions on magnetic disks storage. The operational environment (OE) was slowly transforming into a technocracy which was emphasizing project management.

Solution logic (SL) was oriented towards subsystems using databases; among the most popular were such ones as customer orders, master schedules, inventory control, and bill of material

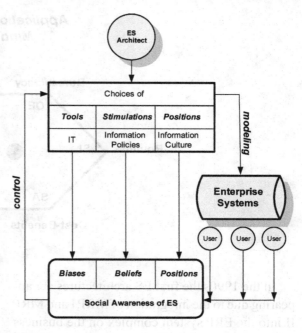

Figure 3. The ES architect as a social engineer

processing (BOMP), cost control, and other. The dominant professional was a system designer. The technical orientation (TO) was on-line processing via remote terminals accessing databases in real time. The state of the art (SR) was database technology and systems assessment was still a cost-benefit analysis. Figure 5 shows a set of key factors defining systems development in the 1970s. A system designer applied the MIND III (practical).

In the 1980s the creeping revolution of personal computers (TO) involved in the Computer Age all workers of an enterprise, particularly business professionals, who soon learned spreadsheets and word editors (OE). Solution logic (SL) put emphasis on sure applications, which were organized in a application portfolio. The complexity of applications grown and required that more attention should be paid on the system life cycle development and end-user involvement in applications implementation ("Joint Application Development"). Hence, a system developer became a key specialist in this process (Figure 6).

Figure 4. Pre-architecture stage of is development in the 1960s

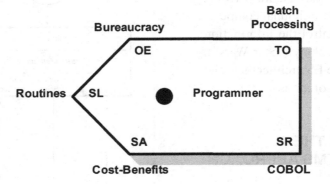

Application Programming
Mind III – 1960s

In the 1990s the first ES architectures are appearing due to the integration of MRP I and MRP II into the ERP system complex on the business side of an enterprise. On the technical side of the enterprise, CAD and CAM evolved into a CIM solution (SL). The operational environment (OE) embraced the whole enterprise and strategic role of IT become a very important factor in a search for business competitive advantage (SA) by Chief Information Officers (CIO). The wide proliferation of enterprise systems required good GUIs to make systems easier to operate by the end-users (SR).

Furthermore, stand-alone PCs were organized into LANs, and building networks were connected into MANs and eventually in WANs and GANs, creating dynamic private computer network grids (TO). Every 18 months personal computers have been doubled their computing speed, so millions of them had to be recycled as they were replaced by faster units (N). Figure 7 reflects the situation in ES in the 1990s. The MIND I (theoretical) and MIND II (creative) as well as MIND III (practical) are engaged in the process of developing the ES architectures.

Figure 5. Pre-architecture stage of IS development in the 1970s

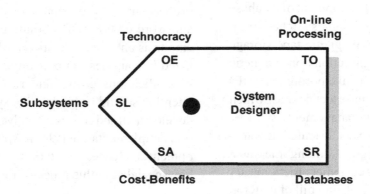

System Design
Mind III – 1970s

Figure 6. Pre-architecture stage of IS development in the 1980s

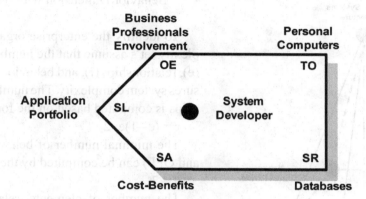

In the 2000s the trend in developing ES takes a sharp turn. The public Internet's web technology passes to enterprise networks, creating Intranets and Extranets (TO).

This leads to the fast emergence of efficient Global Economy, where "the distance is dead." A closed enterprise transforms into an extended enterprise due to such system as SCM and CIM, supported by the Extranet within an emerging Enterprise Information Infrastructure (EII) (SL). The same enterprise is even more expanding, since the Internet allows for instant communication and manufacturing and IT projects are outsourced to offshore subcontractors, mostly in Asia (OP). Since computer programming is done in India, the local IT professionals transform into business process management (BPM) specialists, who conceptualize how to speed up the flow of info-materials and money through the dispersed, electronic enterprise (SR). The offshore outsourcing trend is led by business executives who look for cost minimization and fat bonuses given to them by stockholders, taking full advantage of electronized globalization. Figure 8 explains the challenges for IT architects in the 2000s.

The further evolution of the ES architecture probably will put emphasis on how to operate a

Figure 7. The architecture of enterprise systems in the 1990s

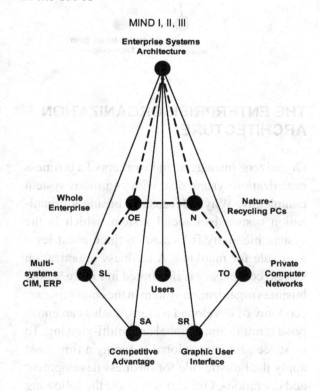

very complex Enterprise Information Infrastructure in the global environment in a reliable and secure manner.

Figure 8. The architecture of enterprise systems in the 2000s

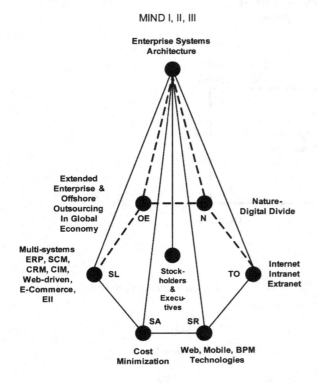

MIND I, II, III

Enterprise Systems Architecture

Extended Enterprise & Offshore Outsourcing In Global Economy

OE

N

Nature-Digital Divide

Multi-systems ERP, SCM, CRM, CIM, Web-driven, E-Commerce, EII

SL

Stock-holders & Execu-tives

TO

Internet Intranet Extranet

SA

SR

Cost Minimization

Web, Mobile, BPM Technologies

THE ENTERPRISE ORGANIZATION ARCHITECTURE

Organizers, managers, and workers of a business organization system deal with enormous system complexity. Why? Because, a business organization system is a social system, which in the system hierarchy is located on the highest level available for mankind. A business organization system complexity is illustrated in Figure 9. Any business organization system in the contemporary economy of developed nations, such as an enterprise is multi-dimensional and multi-viewing. To be successful in the global economy a firm must apply the holistic rule for business development and operations. One can recognize the following dimensions and views of an enterprise:

- World Dimension with 4 views (provided in Figure 9)
- Business Dimension with 13 views
- Behavior Dimension with 6 views

To identify the enterprise organization complexity let's assume that the number of elements (e), relationships (r), and behavior states (s) measures system complexity. The number of relationships is computed based on the formula:

$$r = (e - 1)e : 2$$

The minimal number of behavior states (On and OFF) can be computed by the formula:

$$s = 2^e$$

The number of elements, relationships and states characterizes systems shown in Figure 10.

Let's apply measures of system complexity to a model of an enterprise system shown in Figure 8. There are two possible approaches to this issue. In the Three-Tier approach, called "complete," system complexity is provided in Table 2. In the Two-Tier approach, called "holistic," system complexity is provided in Table 3. It was assumed that a view is composed of e=7, r=21, s=128 for all 23 views.

In "complete" management of a business enterprise, executives, responsible for the so called "big-picture" decisions, must take into account: 27 entities (23 views, 3 dimensions, 1 inter-dimension), 187 elements, 585 relationships, and 11,224 system states in a three-tier hierarchy. This is a huge number of "things" to care for. Therefore, "big-picture" is divided into a series of "small pictures" that are associated with senior, middle, and lower levels of management. In addition, automation of information systems takes care of the majority of well-structured relationships and elements' states. In such a manner system complexity is decomposed and "processable" by individual managers.

In "holistic" management of a business enterprise system, which has emerged as a new mode

Figure 9. A model of enterprise dimensions (D) and views (V)

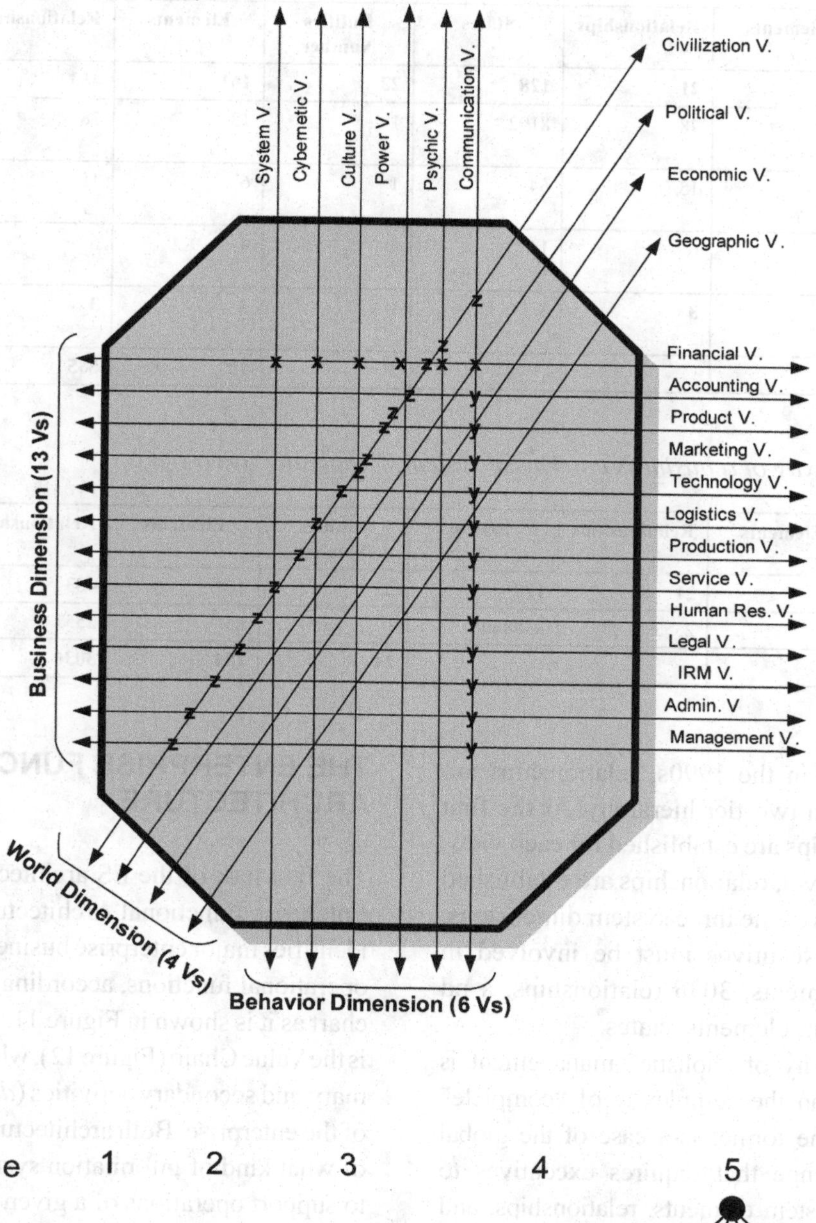

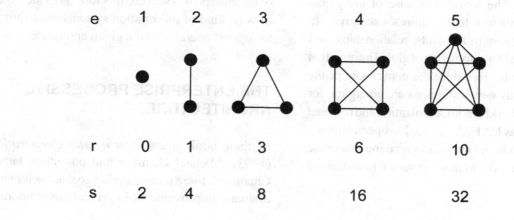

Figure 10.

Table 2. Complexity of a business enterprise system – "complete" (three-tier)

System Level	Elements	Relationships	States	Entities Number	Elements	Relationships	States
Intra-view	7	21	128	23	161	483	2944
Business Dimension	13	78	8192	1	13	78	8192
Behavior Dimension	6	15	64	1	6	15	64
World Dimension	4	6	16	1	4	6	16
Inter-Dimensional	3	3	8	1	3	3	8
Total				27	187	585	11224

Table 3. Complexity of a business enterprise system – "holistic" (two-tier)

System Level	Elements	Relationships	States	Entities Number	Elements	Relationships	States
Intra-view	7	21	128	23	161	483	2944
Inter-view	23	2553	8388608	1	23	2553	8388608
Total				24	184	3036	8391552

of management in the 1990s, relationships are taking place in a two-tier hierarchy. At the first level, relationships are established for each view. At the second level, relationships are established among all views of the three system dimensions. "Big-picture" executives must be involved in 184 system elements, 3036 relationships, a nd 8,391,552 system elements' states.

The complexity of "holistic" management is much bigger than the complexity of "complete" management. The former is a case of the global economy challenge that requires executives to include more system elements, relationships, and states. The need for automation of global information systems is acute. To reduce the complexity of the global economy new institutions are emerging, for example the World Trade Organization and regional treaties such as NAFTA and the European Union.

The ES architect must minimize the enterprise complexity in order to manage such a multifaceted enterprise.

THE ENTERPRISE FUNCTIONAL ARCHITECTURE

The first task of the ES architect is to define the Enterprise Functional Architecture (EFA), which identifies major enterprise business, technical, and operational functions, according the management chart as it is shown in Figure 11. Similar approach is the Value Chain (Figure 12), which identifies primary and secondary activities (*de facto* functions) of the enterprise. Both architectures provide a clue of what kind of information systems are required to support operations of a given enterprise.

THE ENTERPRISE PROCESSIVE ARCHITECTURE

In their book *Reengineering the Corporation* (1993), Michael Hammer and co-author James Champy define a reengineering goal as "achieving dramatic improvements in critical contemporary

Figure 11. The enterprise functional architecture

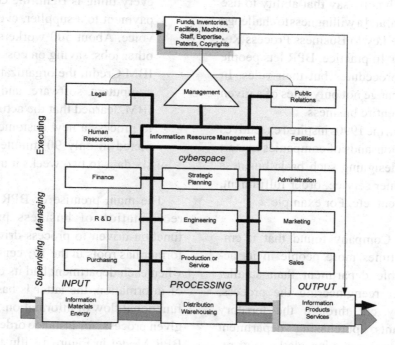

measures of performance such as cost, quality, service and speed." The basic steps of reengineering are:

1. Define business objectives – reassess your business purpose and reposition for greater market penetration;

2. Analyze existing processes – reconfigurate your work for smoother workflow;

3. Invent new ways to work – reconstruct your jobs to match reality;

4. Implement new processes – for ongoing competitiveness.

Figure 12. The Value Chain – The Enterprise Activities Architecture

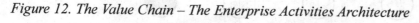
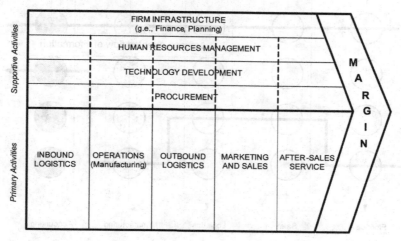

Hammer and Champy say that ability to use insight, imagination, and a willingness to challenge all assumptions are key to Business Process Reengineering (BPR). In practice, BPR lets people change not only procedures but their rules. In effect, they may change not only rules of a given process but of the entire business.

Reengineering in the 1990s inspired executives and managers in thousands of companies to start rethinking and redesigning such basic business practices as customer service, order fulfillment, product development, etc. For example:

- Ford Motor Company found that it employed 100 times more people in its accounts payable department than smaller Mazda. After reengineering the process, the company cut through the territory of accountants, purchasing department staff, warehouse receiving clerks, and reordered them. Now, a receiving clerk at Ford checks the database for the order and delivery compatibility and quality and if

every thing is right, the computer sends a payment to a supplier, even without its invoice. About 500 workers were moved to other jobs, saving on cost.

- IBM Credit, the organization that finances computers, software, and service sold by IBM, learned that the actual work required to process a new customer could be completed in only 90 minutes, instead of the six days to two weeks it used to take.

The main premise of BPR is based on the reorientation of business procedures from function-driven to process-driven. Whereas the former has roots in the 19th century bureaucracy, when each department had its own internal flow of information, the latter is based on the cross-functional flow of information, which supports a given process, for instance order fulfillment. The BPR Model in Figure 13 illustrates this change in business practice.

Reengineering approaches defined by Currid (1995) are:

Figure 13. Functions versus Processes

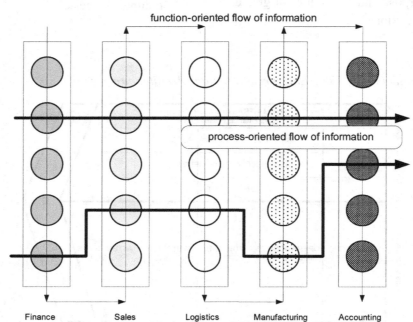

- Streamlining business processes;
- Integrating business processes;
- Transforming business processes.

The seven reengineering business principles defined by Currid (1995) are:

1. Organize work around results, not tasks;
2. Capture data only one time-when it is first created;
3. Allow decision points where work is performed;
4. Incorporate control into information processing;
5. Make people who use a process do the work;
6. Work in parallel instead of sequentially;
7. Treat geographically dispersed resources as one.

The BPR projects lead to Business Process Integration (BPI) via Enterprise Application Integration (EAI). However, EAI typically involves the exchange of information between two applications without regard for business process. BPI, on the other hand, takes into account the overall work flow and the multiple applications required to complete a business process. EIA ensures software compatibility, while BPI applies business rules to operate integrated applications in order to run a business more efficiently. The BPI by Oracle Enterprise Software is shown in Figure 14.

THE ENTERPRISE INFORMATION ARCHITECTURE

Once the Enterprise Functional Architecture is modeled, the next step is the modeling of the Enterprise Information Architecture (EIA) shown in Figure 15. It should contain the main, already developed, information systems and their relationships, and also those, which should be develop in the future.

Among the Business Information Systems (BIS) one can recognize: systems for marketing & sales (CRM), finance, accounting, legal, management and other business functions. Product information Systems (PIS) contain such ones as CADD (Computer-aided Drafting and Design), CAPP (Computer-aide Process Planning), and other ones supporting engineering. Among Operation Information Systems one can include; CAM (Computer-aided Manufacturing), CAP (Computer-aided Publishing), and other. The Inter-organization Systems may be identified by such ones as; SCM (Supply Chain Management) and e-Commerce (B2B, B2C).

Based on the EIA the next task will be to select the right enterprise software and develop the Enterprise Software Architecture.

THE ENTERPRISE SOFTWARE ARCHITECTURE

The Enterprise Software Architecture (ESA) is well described in Figure 16, where the SAP software collaborates with no-SAP software.

The more detailed SAP Software Architecture

Figure 14. The Oracle Enterprise Suite Addressing the Task of BPI by Extracting Business Processes from Applications

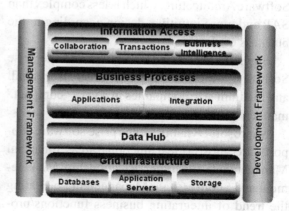

Figure 15. The enterprise information architecture

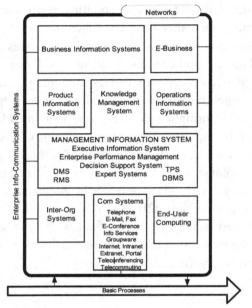

(TPS-Transaction Processing Systems, DBMS-Database Management Systems, DMS-Documents Management Systems, RMS-Records Management System)

is shown in Figure 17, where 22 modules/systems are presented. Needless to say that this software has 500,000 lines of code and 80,000 database tables, for 22+ application modules and 800 business processes, becoming one of the most complex software in the market, more complex than MS Windows.

Figure 18 describes the Oracle Enterprise Suite Software Architecture, which is less complex than SAP and more intuitive, design according to the business cycle.

Figure 19 depicts the MS Dynamics Enterprise Software, which is designed mostly for small and medium size companies in a very "compact" manner.

Microsoft Dynamics enterprise software supports three most critical functional areas: Financial Management; Customer Relationship Management and Supply Chain Management, indicating the trend of integrating business functions/processes into self-contained system federations. The

generic and vendor-independent ESA is defined in Figure 20, where shadow areas identify web-technology driven most popular applications in 2006 (Targowski 2003).

THE ENTERPRISE NETWORK ARCHITECTURE

The Enterprise Network Architecture (ENA) can be composed of two kinds of interconnected networks:

- Private computer grid of networks (Figure 21)
- Public computer set of networks based on web technology, where Intranets are private networks (Figure 22)

THE ENTERPRISE SERVICE-ORIENTED ARCHITECTURE (SOA)

Integration has always been high on the list of concerns for IT professionals, and over the years there have been a number of models and technologies (e.g., DCOM, ORB, COBRA) that tried to address these concerns. The introduction of the Service-oriented Architecture (SOA) in Figure 23, along with associated technologies such as the emergence of the Enterprise Service Bus (ESB) and Business Process Management (BPM) solutions has helped to create more open information infrastructures, which can be penetrated by different service-oriented software modules, particularly web-driven ones. In the past, the integration efforts represented data and information, now they add processes.

In order to apply the SOA, applications need to be "deconstructed" into their component services – each of which performs a specific business function, such as address lookup, customer credit check, and so on (Figure 23). Within the SOA such services can be assembled and delivered

Figure 16. The general enterprise SAP R/3 software architecture (the Targowski model)

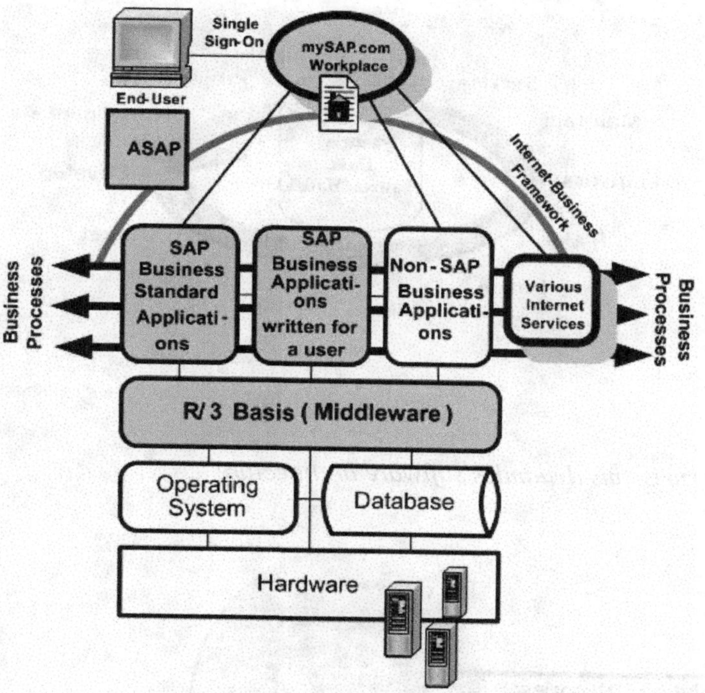

Figure 17. The enterprise SAP R/3 software modules architecture

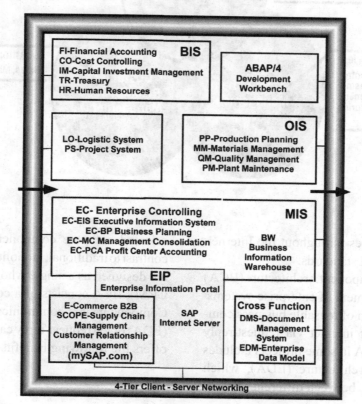

Figure 18. The main applications of the Oracle Enterprise suite

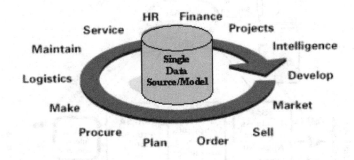

Figure 19. The enterprise ms dynamics software architecture

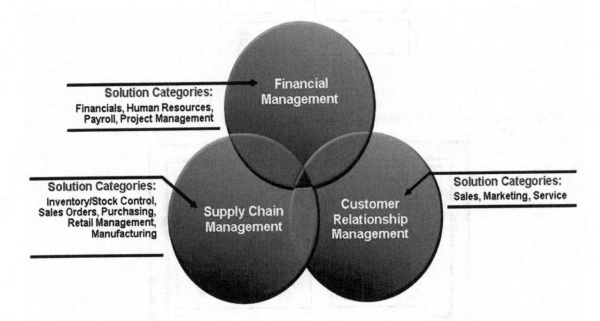

by specialized services throughout the Internet, according to required standards.

The Business Component Architecture (BCA) refers to the development of enterprise systems' service as a collection of reusable business components/services that interact via request/reply (SOA) only. The BCA in some projects includes the Event-driven Architecture (EDA), which continue to exchange between different service-

oriented software components (Figure 24). In contrast to traditional, monolithic applications that are designed as a single whole (e.g., SCM, ERP, CRM), BCA consists of a coalition of Business Components that communicate either via events (EDA) or via request/reply calls (SOA). The BCA offers the following benefits:

Figure 20. The enterprise popular software architecture - 2006

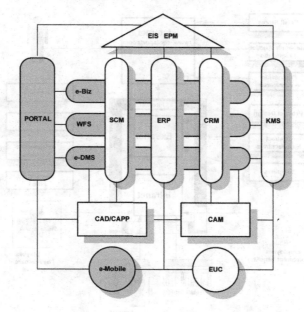

1) BC are easier to develop since are smaller and less complex than whole applications,
2) BC are reusable,
3) BC are easily deployable and modifiable,
   4). BC contributes to easier software configuration management.

The way of using the web-driven services is described in Figure 25. In this mode, it is necessary to apply the Web Service Description Language (WSDL). The following steps are involved in providing and consuming a service:

1. A service provider describes its service using WSDL, which is inserted into the Service Directory, which is accessible through the UDDI (Universal Description, Discovery, and Integration) registry for the retrieval of services provided by various vendors.

Figure 21. The enterprise grip of private computer networks

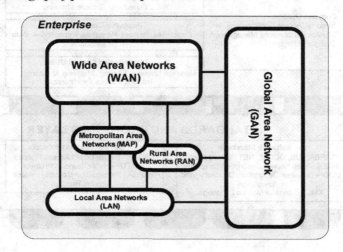

Figure 22. The enterprise public computer networks

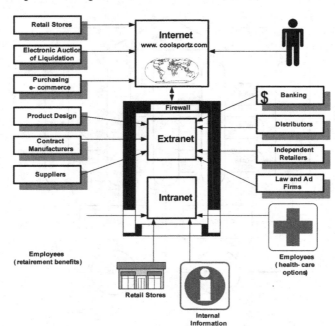

Figure 23. The enterprise services-oriented architecture (SOA)

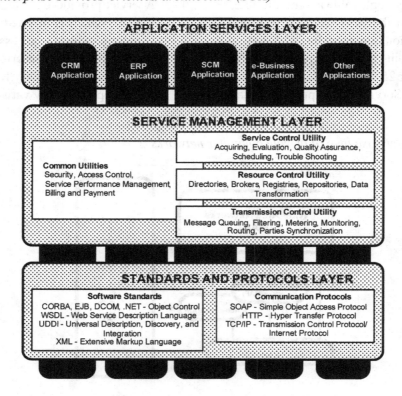

Figure 24. The business component architecture (BCA)

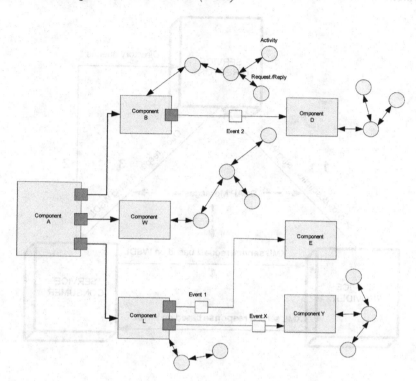

2. A service consumer queries the Service Directory to locate a service provider and find out how to communicate with that service.

3. Part of the WSDL provided by the service provider is passed to the service consumer, informing about a system of request and responses applied by the vendor.

4. The service consumer uses the WSDL to send a request to the service provider.

5. The service provider provides the expected response to service consumer.

Several companies developed Enterprise Application Integration (EAI) solutions during the mid 1990s, but these solutions called middleware were proprietary. Most of these solutions were developed in C/C++ and other proprietary languages. Since 1998, the Java Message Service (JMS) has emerged as the dominant industry standard for enterprise communication, implemented by thousands of companies. Many other communication standards have been developed and the Enterprise Service Bus (ESB) emerged as a channel for communicating all standardized messages (Figure 26).

The ESB supports development in multiple programming languages, becoming a multi-platform enterprise backbone, perhaps the Enterprise Nervous System (ENS) facilitating; communications, connectivity, transformation, portability and security.

THE ENTERPRISE INFORMATION INFRASTRUCTURE

The information management discipline is very young; it is at most 50 years old. However, its professional development has been very strong especially in the last two decades of the 20th

Figure 25. The system of using Web-available services (SOAP – SOA Protocol)

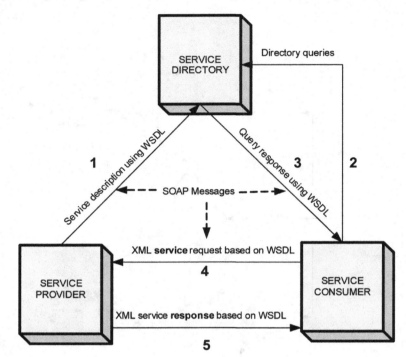

Figure 26. The Enterprise Service Bus (ESB) Architecture

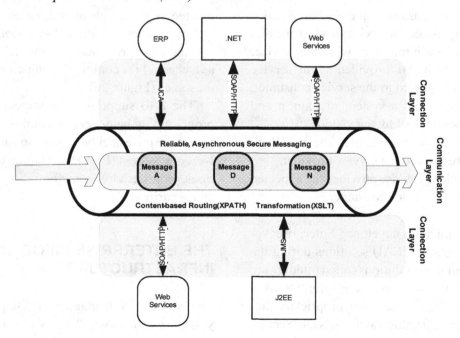

century. Since the beginning, IS have been developed as islands of automation that have been a consequence of an autonomous and eclectic (non-architectural) approach. In the 1980s personal computers triggered a creeping, quiet revolution, known as the Computer Age. In the 1990s, the Internet launched the Communication Age and the phenomena of telecommunication networking and video services. We no longer deal with IS only; we now have to include into an information architecture other forms of information-communication systems and services.

These new systems and services require a new approach towards IT applications in the enterprise. A set of these systems and services is what can be called the Enterprise Information Infrastructure (EII) as it is depicted in Figure 27 (Targowski 2004).

The EII can be considered as an info-communication construction of an enterprise, whose bricks, floors, and walls are made of electronic elements. For many, these elements are invisible even wireless, but their cost is in millions of dollars.

THE ENTERPRISE CONFIGURATIONS

According to the IT criterion, one can distinguish the following configurations of enterprise (Targowski 2003):

- Off-line enterprise, which data processing operates in a batch mode, not on-line and not in real-time,
- On-line enterprise, which processes information on-line through computer networks,
- Integrated enterprise, which applies a common,w enterprise database for the majority of applications,
- Agile enterprise,
- Informed enterprise, which applies knowledge management systems in decision-making,

Figure 27. The Enterprise Information Infrastructure Architecture

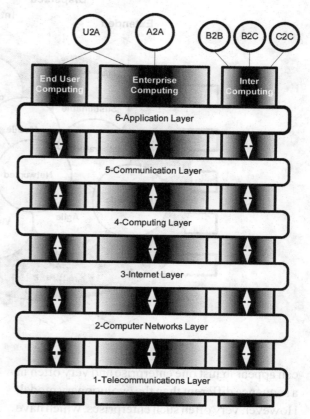

(U2A-User-To-Application, A2A-Application-To-Application
B2B-Business-To-Business, B2C-Business-To-Consumer,
C2C-Consumer-To-Consumer)

- Communicated enterprise,
- Mobile enterprise,
- Electronic entreprise,
- Virtual enterprise, which applies communication technology in connecting different worker locations, when the workers very often operate from their own home, a hotel, a car, or a customer's location[1].
- Sustainable enterprise, which is economically vital, environmentally friendly and socially responsible.

The above sequence of the enterprise evolution is a simplified model, as is each model. In practice, some components of these enterprises

Figure 28. The multi-dimensional, composite enterprise architecture in the 2000s

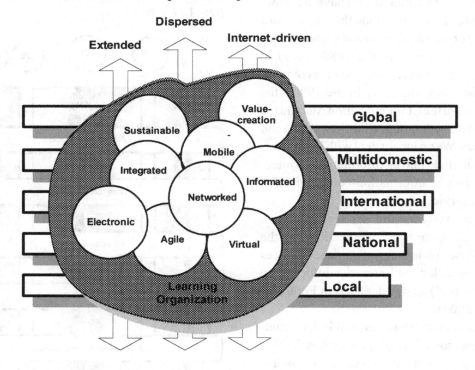

can appear in just one enterprise and very often in a sequence different than the evolutionary model. However, very often such enterprises, which have only a piece of each configuration are considered unfinished solutions with questionable benefits of information technology. The purpose of the enterprise evolution is to know its requirements for each configuration's architecture, budget, developmental skills, and the timeline.

So far the development of IT-driven enterprise has been incremental, leading to a mixture of all the presented enterprise configurations with over the budget projects, overwhelming IT workers, who could not cope with such increasing complexities. As a result of it, CEOs disconnected with CIOs and triggered the outsourcing the IT projects, first inshore and later offshore (looking for cost advantage). Eventually, due to the latter, the quality of IT solutions could be in question and the reliability of solution may be lower.

The nowadays IT-driven enterprise can look as it is shown in Figure 28.

CONCLUSION

The future of the enterprise systems approach will be more complex as IT is still considered as the main factor in achieving competitive advantage in the Global Economy (Targowski 2009b). Only in the U.S. are expenditures for information management 15% of GNP, in the range of $ 2 billion (2006). This enormous amount of financial means will support the development of IT-driven enterprises. Their success will depend on more defined and applied standards, which should smooth the flows of information, communications, and other processes.

REFERENCES

Ackoff, R. L. (1999). *Re-creating the corporation*. New York: Oxford University Press.

Barbour, I. (1993). *Ethics in age of technology*. San Francisco: Harper.

Beer, S. (1981). *The brain of firm*. Chichester, UK: John Wiley & Sons.

Bernard, S. A. (2005). *An introduction to enterprise architecture*. Bloomington, IN: AuthorHouse.

Bernus, P. (2003). *Handbook on enterprise architecture*. New York: Springer.

Bertalanfyy, L. v. (1951). General system theory - a new approach to unity of science (Symposium). *Human Biology, 23*, 303–361.

Buckley, W. (1967). *Sociology and modern systems theory*. Englewood Cliffs, NJ: Prentice Hall.

Carbone, J. A. (2004). *IT architecture toolkit*. Upper Saddle River: Prentice Hall PTR.

Chestnut, H. (1967). *Systems engineering methods*. New York: Wiley.

Clemson, B. (1984). *Cybernetics: A new management tool*. Tumbridge Wells, UK: Abacus Howe.

Currid, Ch. (1995). *Strategies for reengineering your organization*. Roseville, CA: Prima Lifestyles.

Erl, Th. (2004). *Service-oriented architecture*. Upper Saddle River, NJ: Pearson Professional Edition.

Fowler, M. (2002). *Patterns of enterprise application architecture*. Boston: Addison-Wesley Professional.

Goode, H. H., & Machol, R. E. (1957). *System engineering: An introduction to the design of large-scale systems*. New York: McGraw-Hill.

Hammer, M., & Champy, J. (1993). *Reengineering the corporation*. New York: HarperBusiness.

Hitch, Ch. (1955). An application of system analysis. In St. L. Opter (Ed.), *System analysis*. Middlesex, England.

Kanter, J. (1966). Integrated management and control systems. In *The computer and executive* (pp. 45-56). Englewood Cliffs, NJ: Prentice Hall.

Kim, W. Ch., & Mauborgne, R. (2005). *Blue ocean strategy*. Boston: Harvard Business School Press.

Klir, G. J. (1985). *Architect of problem solving*. New York: Plenum Press.

Krafzig, D., et al. (2004). *Enterprise SOA*. Upper Saddle River, NJ: Prentice Hall.

Laszlo, E. (1972). *Introduction to systems philosophy*. New York: Harper Torchbooks.

Marin, J. (1997). *Systems engineering guidebook*. Boca Raton, FL: CRC Press LLC.

McDonough, A. M. (1963). Information management. In *Information economics and management systems*. New York: McGraw-Hill.

McFarlan, F. W. (1981). Portfolio approach to information systems. *Harvard Business Review, 59*, 142–150.

McFarlan, F. W., & McKenney, J. L. (1983). The information archipelago governing the new world. *Harvard Business Review, 61*, 145–156.

McGovern, J. (2003). *The practical guide to enterprise architecture planning*. Hoboken, NJ: Wiley.

Microsoft. (2002). *Application architecture for .NET*.

Mosto, A. (2004). *DoD architecture framework overview*. Retrieved November 2, 2008, from http://www.enterprise-architecture.info/Images/Defence%20C4ISR/DODAF.ppt

Mowshowitz, A. (1980). On an approach to the study of social issues in computing. *Communications of the ACM, 24*(3), 146. doi:10.1145/358568.358592

Mowshowitz, A. (1980). *Human choice and computers, 2.* Amsterdam: North-Holland.

Nadler, D. A., et al. (1992). *Organizational architecture.* San Francisco: Jossey-Bass.

Perks, C., & Beveridge, T. (2002). *Guide to IT architecture.* New York: Springer.

Porter, M. (1990). *The competitive advantage of actions.* New York: Free Press.

Rechtin, E., & Maier, M. (1997). *The art of system architecting.* Boca Raton, FL: CRC Press LLC.

Ross, J. W., Weill, P., & Robertson, D. (2006). *Enterprise architecture as strategy: Creating a foundation for business execution.* Boston: Harvard Business Press.

Schekkerman, J. (2008). *Enterprise architecture good practices guide.* Victoria, Canada: Trafford Publishing.

Schlager, J. (1956). Systems engineering: Key to modern development. *IRE Transactions, EM-3,* 64–66. doi:10.1109/IRET-EM.1956.5007383

Shnaidt, P. (1992). *Enterprise-wide networking.* Carmel, IN: SAMS.

Skolimowski, H. (1981). *Eco-philosophy. designing new tactics for living.* Salem, NH: Marion Boyers.

Skolimowski, H. (1984). *The theater of mind.* Wheaton, IL: The Theosophical Publishing House.

Spewak, St. H. (1993). *Enterprise architecture planning.* Hoboken, NJ: Wiley.

Targowski, A. (1990). *The architecture and planning of enterprise-wide information management systems.* Hershey, PA: Idea Group Publishing.

Targowski, A. (1996). *Global information infrastructure.* Hershey PA: Idea Group Publishing.

Targowski, A. (2003). *Electronic enterprise: Strategy and architecture.* Hershey, PA: IRM Press.

Targowski, A. (2009a). The evolution from data to wisdom in decision-making at the level of real and virtual networks. In C. Camison *et al.* (Eds.), *Connectivity and knowledge management in virtual organizations.* Hershey, PA: Information Science Reference.

Targowski, A. (2009b). *Information technology and societal development.* Hershey, PA: Information Science Reference.

Targowski, A., & Rienzo, T. (2004). *Enterprise information infrastructure.* Kalamazoo, MI: Paradox Associates.

Targowski, A., & Tarn, M. (2006). *Enterprise systems education in the 21st century.* Hershey, PA: IGI Global.

Van Gigch, J. P. (1974). *Applied general systems theory.* New York: Harper & Row.

Wiener, N. (1948). *Cybernetics: Or the control and communication in the animal and the machine.* Cambridge, MA: MIT Press.

Zachman, J. A. (1987). A framework for information systems architecture. *IBM Systems Journal, 26*(3).

ENDNOTE

[1] A virtual enterprise emerged historically before an electronic enterprise, however, the former performs better if is electronic.

Chapter 2
Modeling Software Development Processes

Gerhard Chroust
Kepler University Linz, Austria

Marco Kuhrmann
Technische University München, Germany

Erwin Schoitsch
Austrian Research Centers – ARC, Austria

ABSTRACT

In this chapter the authors discuss the WHY and WHAT of modeling software development processes: defining the components of a software process and proposing 5-dimensional grid of attributes of existing models: strategy and path, levels, main subprocesses, components and aura. Specific process models, currently used or historically important, are described. This is followed by an extensive discussion of methods for and problems of modeling a software process, followed by a shorter discussion on the en-actment of process models via software engineering environments. The chapter closes with a discussion of the human aspects concerning introduction and enactment of a process model.

INTRODUCTION

The Need for a Defined Software Process

Information and Communication Technology (ICT) has become the no. 1 business driver of economy and the key to practically all human activities. The ongoing reduction of the size and the cost of computers together with increased speed and performance allows the implementation of functionalities completely unimaginable even a decade ago. This creates a demand for more software with higher sophistication and with higher quality. Additional requirements are shorter time-to-market together with flexibility and adaptability fo software with respect to answering user needs.

Since approximately 1970 (Royce, 1970) it is understood that the development of a software system is a multi-phase process. Each phase is concerned with contributing a different view and focus of the software artifact to be produced. In order to guarantee an orderly, systematic process this stepwise process should be defined and described

DOI: 10.4018/978-1-60566-856-7.ch002

by a so-called process model. Based on strong statistical evidence this has been supported by Watts Humphrey from the Software Engineering Institute (Humphrey, 1989) introducing the Capability Maturity Model (CMM). It claimed that a defined process model and its appropriate enactment was one of the key steps in order to reach a development capability beyond a certain basic level. Initially only big companies produced 'industrial' software. Due to the multitude of procedures and rules existing in these companies (they often also produced hardware using an appropriate 'development process'), the introduction of a 'software development process' was a somewhat natural innovation (Wang & King, 2000). The trend was intensified by the US Department of Defense's requirement for software contractors to show (and prove) the appropriate level of capability in order to be awarded a contract.

The reduction of the size and the cost of computers (down to PDAs and sophisticated mobile phones) together with an equally dramatic increase in performance and storage has not only provided computers for everybody, but has also created business opportunities for numerous small and very small companies (SMEs), often consisting of one or a few persons, often start-up companies based on a single innovative idea. They profit from the low initial investment, the ability to offer and sell their product world wide via Internet without intermediator or sales organizations. Due to their small size they are able to provide high flexibility and customer-orientation.

Closer investigation of these small and medium companies shows (SPIRE Project Team, 1998) that they often have a highly chaotic, invention-driven production process and a disregard of the associated quality and management processes. As a consequence they cannot guarantee sustainable, verifiable quality, and business return on investment.

In this chapter we present the state-of-the-art of software development process models with respect to the various types, their components,

the strategies they incorporate, giving examples of existing models. We discuss aspects of creating a process model and various human aspects, including issues of introduction of process models. It must be stressed that a software process model in itself is only useful if enacted properly. Therefore we discuss enactment of process models which leads to a short discussion of Software Engineering Environments (for details see Kuhrmann et al. (2010) in this book).

Prominent Process Models are listed in "Selected Process Models - Overview" with their references, therefore in the rest of the text no references to them are given.

BACKGROUND

Software Quality and Software Processes

Quality is the key to successful, sustainable software development. Low quality increases the cost for error correction during development and for maintenance after the delivery of a product. Obviously low quality also reduces market acceptance and hampers later evolution of a product.

In the various disciplines of engineering many different approaches exist to guarantee, to assist or at least to check ex-post the quality, especially the correctness of an industrial product in relation to defined and implicit requirements. The correctness of a product can be established beyond doubt if it is constructed following a proven algorithm or if it has exhaustively been tested. Other methods can only establish correctness to a certain degree (e.g. parallel or inverse construction). Some methods carry over to software engineering, e.g. foolproofing (Nakajo, 1985), inspections (Gilb & Graham, 1993), formal development methods, prototyping, following a well-established process, documentation of work, etc.

For software development (which basically is an engineering discipline!) many of the approaches are not effective, efficient and feasible given the current state-of-the-art of software development (SPIRE Project Team, 1998). It has also to be kept in mind that correctness is only one of the key quality attributes, see ISO/IEC 9126 (ISO/IEC, 2001).

Industrial experience (Humphrey, 1989) shows that following a well-defined and proven software development process is one of the keys to successful software products. It should be remembered, however, that even the best process does not *guarantee* technical quality or usability: nevertheless product quality can be improved by improving process quality. Especially since the seminal work by Watts Humphrey (Humphrey, 1989) the software industry strived for a formal definition of the software development process, supported by several other methods as the basis of high-quality software development. Process assessment methods like CMM (Paulk et al., 1995), CMMI (Chrissis et al., 2006), BOOTSTRAP (Haase et al., 1994), and ISO 15504 (SPICE) (ISO/IEC, 2004) establish the fact that the establishment of a well-defined process is the key to an orderly, "industrial strength" software development.

The complexity of the process also makes it necessary to formally integrate both human actors, stakeholders, and relevant tools into the process definition in order to arrive at a completely formalized, repeatable and auditable process.

The primary purpose of a process model is communication and coordination of all stakeholders and actors of a software development project. The strong involvement of humans also means that human factors (soft factors) play a key role in software development. Some modern developments (e.g. agile methods) put the human factor at the center of their attention.

Software Processes and SMEs

Initially only large companies were interested in documented process models, understanding that these were an important step towards software processes improvement ("SPI") in order to achieve higher maturity in their capabilities of producing high quality software (Humphrey, 1989; Herbsleb, 1996). In contrast to larger firms SMEs lag behind in this initiative due to specific obstacles which prevent them from successfully applying defined and documented process models and SPI (SPIRE Project Team, 1998; Ward et al., 2001):

- Despite evidence to the contrary they frequently hold the view that SPI is too expensive (considering management attention and staff time) and too difficult (lack of expertise) to be cost effective.
- Day-to-day operational crises, financial constraints and changing priorities are likely to drive their improvement plans off course.
- Due to the engineering aspect's domination of their work they are also often caught in the traps of "not invented here", "we are different", and the fear of becoming over- powered by formalism, bureaucracy ("book-keeping") and loss of creativity, see Chroust (2006).

SOFTWARE PROCESS MODELS — BASIC CONCEPTS

Model and Instances

Models in the sense of this chapter are an *abstraction* of some artifacts existing in the real world or being envisioned. In both cases the model is an abstraction, i.e. it contains only certain relevant attributes of the system. Artifacts derived from a model are *instances* of the model (fig. 1).

One danger is that the user mistakes a model for the real artifact. This misunderstanding does not exist in other engineering disciplines. A model is not a miniature version of the final product. It has to be understood

Figure 1. Instantiation of a process model

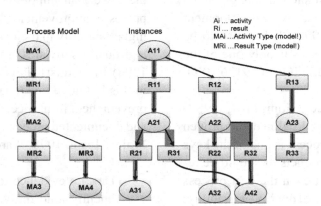

- which attributes of the model correspond to reality (size, material, proportions, views, relation of components, ...) and to what extent,
- how much detail the model shows (granularity, level of abstraction),
- to what extent reality is distorted in the model (properties, materials),
- which properties are represented correctly, and which ones only in an approximate way or not at all.

In order to be useful a model has to have some representational means (textual, graphical, etc.) so as to express the contents of the model. The following properties are of essential importance with respect to representation (exemplar questions are in italics):

Influence on view and thinking: In what direction is the user of the model (or the model itself) biased? *Is the user encouraged to think in terms of transforming documents or enacting activities?*

Expressiveness: What can/cannot be expressed by the model or the representation? What restrictions are imposed? *Can the required skills of developers be indicated in the model?*

Unambiguity: Are all model components unambiguous, can some concepts be expressed in different ways? Are there homonyms, synonyms?

Are there different ways of expressing that a work product depends on some other work product?

Understandability: How easy is it to understand the concepts of the model? *Are for example constraints expressed in a complicated formal mathematical notation?*

Modularity/orthogonality: How far can parts of the model be manipulated independently and how far can model components be combined independently? *Can the development model and the quality assurance model be analyzed independently?*

Effectiveness: To what extent can one express special requirement or constraints? *Can one express that only one design document exists?*

Construction cost, interpretation cost: How difficult and how costly is it to create the model and to interpret its meaning? *How difficult is it to find out in what sequence some development actions have to be performed - by human inspections, and by computer support?*

Tractability: How easy/complex is to the perform operations on the model (additions, deletions)? *Can one quality assurance process be easily replaced by another one?*

Liberality: How strict are the rules for expressing one's concepts in the model? It should be noted here that this question blurs the division between the model concepts and the (probably) associated model building/guidance tool! *Can an* *activity partially be defined and its inputs and outputs defined much later?*

Software Process Models and Representation

In software development the models are used both to (gradually) describe a project's organization and the final software product, which - strictly speaking - again is a model of the process the target computer should execute (e.g. perform a payroll computation).

- Process models are intended to serve as a model for *many* individual software projects and their development processes.
- They have in common that they describe a *sequence of individual activities* in some way.
- In most cases they will give indications in what temporal sequence the activities should be executed ("navigation") and define constraints on the sequencing of the activities.
- For many of the components of the model there will be several instances, e.g. there will be several instances of 'coding a module'.
- They usually describe the intermediate and final work products to a certain level of detail.
- They are intended to support humans in enacting these processes and preferably also support the interpretation by a computer (a "Process Engine").

Several methods for describing a process model exist. The four basic forms for representing a process model are:

Verbal: Originally textual descriptions, e.g. books, were common. The descriptions were written in a more or less structured form, i.e. pure text in the form of a report with chapters and subchapters, etc. or tables.

Graphical: The wish for better visualization created models based on flow charts ('data flow diagrams'), similar to data flow charts of programming and dependency diagrams.

Mathematical/logical: The need for more precision, for more possibilities of analysis and the wish (and need!) to provide computer support so as to assist developers in their work of software development has caused the use of formalized models, either via metamodels, (adapted) programming languages or in mathematic/logical notations.

Metamodel: Metamodel-based processes (OMG, 2005; Friedrich et al., 2008; ISO/IEC, 2007b) have became more important, often also called formal process models. Meta- models in the context of process models answer two essential questions:

- Process Models usually contain several different process components (see "Components of a Process Model"). What are acceptable process components (e.g. activity, role, etc.) and their relationships that can be expressed?
- What are admissible descriptive formats for these process components and their relationships? Again several variants are available.

The advantage of a metamodel-based process is its precision with respect to describing the process components, their relationships and operations for integration into more complex processes. Meta-models provide a language is provided in which process contents has to be described. Formal languages rely on provisions of formal meta-models, similar to the metamodel hierarchies provided for UML (OMG, 2007a,b), using e.g. SPEM (OMG, 2005), a so-called UML-profile. Metamodels ease the definition of tool-support. Metamodels are also well suited to be introduced on the organizational level, as they provide a language able to describe organization-specific contents. This is an impor-

Figure 2. Dimensions of a process model

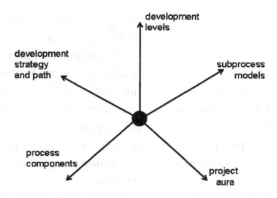

tant feature for process engineers, who have to describe an organization's processes.

Today nearly all commercial process models use a combination of verbal, graphical and formal representations (e.g. RUP, EPF (Haumer, 2006a,b; Foundation, 2007) or V-Model XT). The recent surge of agile methods, e.g. Scrum or XP has again favored the use of verbal and graphical representations, similar to the classic approaches (e.g. ADPS, ESA (ESA, 1991), SSADM (Downs et al., 1988)).

DIMENSIONS OF PROCESS MODELS

Classifying process models means looking for similar structures and philosophies. Depending on the intentions and objectives of a process model we can distinguish five main dimensions which span existing process models, see fig. 2.

These five dimensions are neither fully independent nor orthogonal; not all combinations of values make sense or are feasible. The five dimensions are discussed below:

- Development strategy and path
- Development levels
- Subprocess models
- Process components
- Project aura

Development Strategy and Path

This dimension describes the basic development strategies underlying the development sub-model. Only a few variants exist (fig. 3). They cover all variants: from the initial waterfall model (Royce, 1970) to agile processes (Beck et al., 2002) and special models for embedded systems (Schoitsch, 2008). It should, however, be noted that the classes below are not exclusive. Often iterative and incremental philosophies are combined in a single process model; there is also a large affinity between incremental and agile processes.

Common to all models is that each activity must start with some 'reasonable' input work products (e.g. requirements) to produce some 'reasonably finished' output work products (e.g. a specification). Experience shows that completeness and full correctness of the output work products cannot be achieved in one step (favouring an 'iterative strategy').

The list below also shows that the still continuing discussions (and fights!) for the 'best method' are essentially concerned with the strategy for sequencing the activities (the 'navigation').

Another not yet resolved problem comes from the fact that a model strictly speaking only identifies types of activities and work products but not their instances. As a consequence relationships

Figure 3. Development strategies

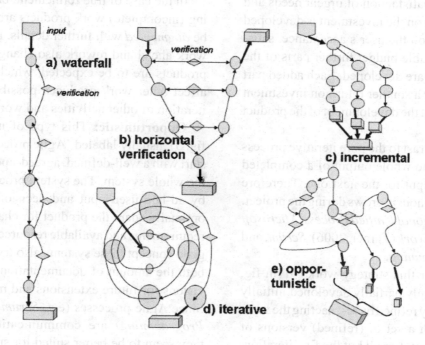

between instances are difficult to describe. This has to be taken into account during enactment, see section "Process Enactment".

Waterfall-type ('sequential'): For this strategy an activity is only considered ready for enactment when all its input work products are in a completed state (Royce, 1970; Boehm, 1976). Based on these input work items further work items are created. An activity is only considered completed when all output work items are completed ('a' in fig. 3).

As a consequence there is a strict alignment of discrete phases, e.g. requirements elicitation, development, test, etc. and it is assumed that with the end of a phase all produced work products are complete and correct. Verification is performed only at the transition from one phase to the next. Practical experience shows that only for a new project, in which all requirements and all technical questions are known, this type of process would be adequate. In reality changes, errors, and modification will always occur and cause rework (Phillips, 1989).

Some widely used models of this category became de-facto standards in some countries or industry segments. Examples are: *ADPS* from IBM, *Hermes* (), *MAESTROII* (Merbeth, 1992; Yourdon, 1990), or *SSADM* (Downs et al., 1988).

Horizontal verification ('v-shaped', 'Vee-model'): *V-shaped* Process Models ('b' in fig. 3) have quality assurance measures assigned to each development phase with respect to a previous phase of the same abstraction level, e.g. the final product versus system requirement, low level design versus technical specifications, etc. The basic structure of the process is otherwise similar to the waterfall-type process models. The difference is the specific quality assurance on the same abstraction layer. Samples are: *V-Modell 97*, *V-Modell XT* (with some limitations) and the *PMOD-Model*.

Incremental: An incremental process model ('c' in fig. 3) has the strategy of decomposing a complex software system into smaller subsystems of decreasing usefulness. A kernel of the product which promises satisfaction of urgent needs and the highest return on the investment is developed first. Depending on the user's acceptance, satisfaction and available budget further parts of the software product are developed. Each added part will usually offer a smaller return on investment until at some point the development of the product is terminated.

This is in contrast to the pure iterative process models, where the whole output of a completed iteration is the input for the next one. Therefore the system continuously grows during the project. Samples are: *Rational Unified Process, Microsoft Solutions Framework* (Turner, 2006), *Scrum,* and *eXtreme Programming.*

Iterative: For this strategy work ('d' in fig. 3) products are only partially developed initially and consecutively refined by re-enacting the *same activity*, but with a set of (refined) versions of input work product. For all but the first iteration, the output work items must also be considered as additional input. Many methods propose this approach (e.g. Prototyping approaches, Spiral Model (Boehm, 1986), Evolutionary development). Samples are: *Rational Unified Process (RUP), V-Modell XT* etc. After several iterations all components are completed. This means the process model has been was repeated as many times. Three variants can be observed:

Refinement: In earlier iterations some details have been left out to be added/inserted in later iterations, but no changes to existing work products are expected.

Work-ahead: Should not all input work products be in final completed stage, but believed to be in a 'good enough', then the next activity in sequence can proceed (Phillips, 1989). Obviously at some later stage the produced work products have to be verified again.

Rework: Both during development and later during maintenance some work products have to be corrected/amended/modified. This means that essentially an iterative process is started (Phillips, 1989).

In the case of true refinement, *only* the existing (incomplete) work products are expected to be *augmented* with further details. In the case of work-ahead and rework also changes to a work products are to be expected, which might even affect other work products, possibly triggering iteration of other activities and work products.

Opportunistic: This type of model ('e' in fig. 3), usually labeled 'Agile process', does not start with a well-defined, agreed-upon concept of the whole system. The system process is guided by ad-hoc user-input and decisions. It tries to optimally adapt the product for changing needs, requirements and available resources. As a synergetic concept these systems also try to minimize both the amount of documentation and the provisions for future extensions and modifications. Since Agile processes (e.g. *Scrum* and *eXtreme Programming)* are communication-intensive, they seem to be better suited for small development teams, in contrast to more formal processes which provide richer support for managing and coordinating large teams.

The various strategies discussed above indicate on the model level in what sequence the various activities should be enacted. It must be born in mind, however, that in reality the sequencing has to be carried out on the instance level. Since to every Activity Type many instances usually exist, the model alone does not exactly specify a sequence between them. The model or the individual project may suggest or even prescribe further sequencing constraints which can be defined in an instance-independent way. These decisions depend on both the intent and the objectives of a project and to some degree on the management style and development philosophy of the enterprise. Choices are:

New work versus rework: Is it more important to start developing a *new work* product or to fix errors in existing work products?

Risk-avoidance versus risk-acceptance: Should risk-prone activities (e.g. based on incomplete information) be carried out early in the development process (yielding more time for experimental later fix-up) or late, hoping by then having more complete information, see Spiral Model (Boehm, 1986)?

Early operability: Is it useful to produce some running subsystem early? This question is related to the incremental development strategy.

Breadth first versus depth first: Should completing of a development level (waterfall type) be preferably chosen instead of the earlier implementation another subsystem providing the chance to show (partial) operability of the system?

Urgency of a subfunction: Are there certain subfunctions of the system which should be produced urgently due to the wish for market entry (cf. incremental or opportunistic strategies)?

Personnel dependent choices: Do some system components have to be worked on within in a certain time window due to personnel/resource availability?

Development Levels

When proceeding in a software development project we can identify several 'levels' of attention: each level focuses on a different aspect of the intended product. There is a strong analogy to building a house (cf. fig. 4). Looking back in history we notice that the development levels only evolved gradually (Chroust, 1992) from the central objective: implementing (coding) the software product.

The different development levels are the result of dissatisfaction with and the inadequacies of the initial attempts to produce software of increasing complexity. In front of the (initially single) phase of "Implementation" several phases were inserted, which were intended to ensure the adequacy of the resulting software product. The desire (and need!) to imbed the software adequately into complete systems has also induced adding two phases following implementation (coding).

Figure 4. House-building und software engineering

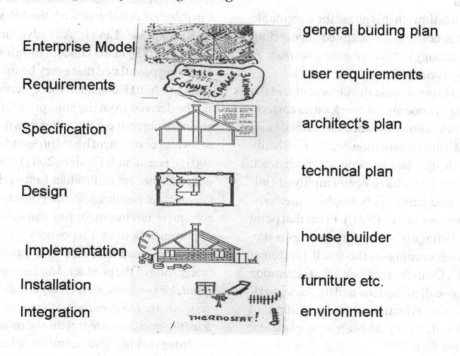

Enterprise Model		general buiding plan
Requirements		user requirements
Specification		architect's plan
Design		technical plan
Implementation		house builder
Installation		furniture etc.
Integration		environment

Development levels can be seen

- as steps of model transformations: All work products developed at the different levels are *models* of some aspect of an intermediate or final product. Thus the transition from one level to the next is a transformation of one set of models into another set of models supporting different views.
- as abstracted view of the final work product: Here the emphasis is put on the different aspects/views by the work products of that level, each answering a specific question of management.

Currently we can distinguish the phases described below. Probably no further predecessor phases are to be expected. At the end of the process, however, further phases can be imagined which are concerned with securing the results of the development. The list of development levels below roughly reflects the historical emergence of these phases (with an analogy to house building, fig. 4) and the relevant management question for each level.

Implementation: In this phase the executable code is written/collected/assembled (depending on the methodology). *Management question: Is the system operational?*

Design: In order to ease development and the understanding of code and to check on its correctness the technical solution has been described independently of all implementation details. Gradually the level of design has became more abstract, higher level notations have been employed (initially pseudocode, later mainly graphical methods, e.g. data flow diagrams or UML). From that point onward one distinguishes 'programming-in-the-large' and 'programming-in-the-small' (deRemer & Kron, 1976). On the human side a first separation between the so-called 'coders' and the 'designers' has emerged, also effecting some 'deskilling' of the coders (Kraft, 1977). *Management question: Can the system be built?*

Specification (Analysis, Architecture): Design and Implementation consider primarily the computer-view of the product. Specification is mainly considered with the user-visible properties and behavior of the system, commonly called 'architecture'. *"The term architecture is used here to describe the attributes of a system as seen by the programmer, i.e. the conceptional structure and functional behavior, as distinct from the organization of the data flow and control, the logical design, and the physical implementation."* (Amdahl & Brooks, 1964, p.21). Similar definitions appear in Blaauw (1972) and Zemanek (1986). *Management question: Is the system acceptable to the user/customer?*

Requirements: The growing complexity of software systems has made it necessary to consider first what was basically expected of the system from *all stakeholders* before committing the system to specification (Boehm et al., 2001; Grünbacher et al., 2001). This has given raise to a new discipline: Requirements Engineering. *Management question: What do the customers/ users and project management expect form the system? Are the demands and wishes compatible, feasible and consistent with the intended use?*

Enterprise Level: Already James Martin (Martin, 1989) in his concept of Information Engineering postulated that every business software product should consider the enterprise context and be derived from the enterprise's fundamental business objectives. With the growth of re-use in software (component based programming (Allen, 2001; Cheesman & Daniels, 2001)) and even more with the concept of Product Lines (Hoyer, 2007; Clements & Northrop, 2002; Pohl et al., 2005) the enterprise environment has gained considerable importance both as a repository for assets (reusable work products) and as a yardstick for the integration of the product. *Management question: What does organisation/enterprise expect from the system? Are the demands and wishes compatible, feasible and consistent with the intended use?*

Integration: The seamless integration with

the environment has also gained importance, especially in view of existing infrastructure (middleware), outsourcing of software development and the growing market of commercially available systems (components). *Management question: Does the system fit into the environment?*

Installation: The installation of a complex software product and the subsequent tuning of interfaces needs a growing amount of attention. *Management question: Is the system adapted to the user's operational environment?*

The levels shown above are 'logically' different. Existing process models often aggregates several of them into one level, e.g. RUP collapses Specification and Design into one level 'Analysis and Design'. ISO/IEC 15288 splits the Requirement Level into two aspects: Stakeholder Requirements and Requirement Analysis, etc. The Enterprise Level is often not explicitly present and included in the Requirements level.

Major Subprocess Models of a Process Model

Software development is to be regarded as an *engineering discipline* and not as a mathematical/logical discipline, see (Naur & Randell, 1969). Numerous activities, besides Design and Implementation of the software product itself have to be performed to successfully execute a project (RUP speaks of 'disciplines'). These other activities have to be performed in a cooperative, parallel manner in order to guarantee the final product's desired quality, marketability etc. Following ISO/IEC 12207 (ISO/IEC, 2007a) other essential activities are Documentation, Quality Management, Project Management, Configuration Management, Product Management and Human Resource Management. They can be formulated somewhat modular and independently. In fact all process models available on the market contain several of these subprocesses.

While some of them are closely linked to the software product (e.g. documentation and quality assurance) others are more concerned with the management of the project. We observe:

- The allocation of activities to different submodels is somewhat arbitrary.
- All submodels should be using the *same* representational mechanism.
- All other submodels are subsidiary to the development process and must to some extent reflect its structure. Typically quality assurance must *be informed about* all work products. Chroust (1994) argues that the *structure* of the quality model should largely be a clone of the structure of the development model.
- Processes of the various submodels have to be *adapted* with respect to their interfaces to one another and especially to the development model.
- The activities of the various submodels have to exchange information via work products.
- Different strategies can be chosen for each subprocess. Typically the way quality assurance is to be performed is dependent on many parameters like requirements of the customer, culture of the organization, risk of the project etc. Similarly project management, too, can be performed in various ways of stringency and intensity.

Development Submodel: The development submodel is usually a member of every process model. The development submodel defines all necessary types of work product, roles, and activities directly related to the contents of the final software product. Sophisticated process models provide complete template architectures for systems to be developed (e.g. RUP, V-Modell XT, SSADM)

Documentation Submodel: For various reasons sufficient documentation is required. Some methods are very document-heavy. Lightweight processes like eXtreme Programming or Scrum try to avoid most of the documentation in favor of 'well-documented' code. Key documentation work products have many objectives and forms: user manuals, operator instructions, on-line help texts, system messages (errors, warning, help). As early as possible during development the transfer of a software product into other languages has to be considered (Chroust, 2007, 2008a; Collins, 2002).

Quality Submodel: This submodel usually contains process components describing (strategic) questions for preparing and executing quality assurance. The audience for this submodel depends on the focus of the process model: If the focus is an organization as a whole, quality is related to the organization's processes. In this case also "software process improvement" (SPI) is considered. Quality submodels are aimed at ensuring the (constructive/analytic) quality of an outcome.

Management Submodel: Every project needs a certain amount of management. The management submodel usually describes artifacts but also concrete methods for the support managers in a project. Concrete examples can be found in Scrum (Schwaber, 2004), which contains management practices related to self-organizing teams. Classic management support can be found e.g. in the V-Modell XT in which extensive reporting, including all artifacts and responsibilities, is defined.

Configuration Submodel: The configuration submodel addresses the administrative management of (all) project work products. Especially product configurations (baselines) have to be managed. This includes tracking of whole releases as well as versioning of particular work products. The configuration submodel also includes methods for the management of changes and the tracking of issue, changes etc. This ensures that at any time the state of the project is known, e.g. for providing information for system hand-over and for management control. Detailed information is made available for the transition of the system into further stages of the life cycle, e.g. from de-

velopment to operation (see (BMVg (ed.), 1997; Dröschel & Wiemers, 1999)).

Role Submodel: The submodel for roles usually describes the organizational setting for projects. Roles can be assigned to work products (responsibility) or to tasks (concrete work). Depending on the concrete embodiment of the role model, the organization can define what person has to carry out which tasks and who is responsible for the tasks have been performed.

Enterprise Submodel: In ISO/IEC 15288 this submodel covers activities which are related to environment, investment, portfolio, etc. It thus explicitly caters for the Enterprise Level.

Maintenance Submodel: The maintenance of a software product was initially (Boehm, 1976; Royce, 1970) considered as the last phase of a software production process. Seen from a product life cycle this is correct, maintenance follows development. If, however, the phases are considered as a *logical* separation into different views on the product, then in reality maintenance is a limited, selective re-iteration of the original product development (Zvegintzov, 1982). *Management question: Have the problems/deficiencies of the system been removed?*

Components of a Process Model

Formally we can describe a process model PM (Chroust, 2000) as:

$$PM = < W, S_W, D, A, S_A, F, I, O, E_R, E_T, ... >$$

The components have the following meaning:

Work Product Types W: Work Products represent the information used by the various activities. They are the basis for understanding, analyzing and creating a given software product.

To a large extent they depend on the chosen development method. Work Products describe essentially the *'WHAT' (the software product is supposed to do)*. Typical work product types are: design documents, storage allocation maps, interface descriptions, requirements statements etc. It can be distinguished between

- work products delivered to the user (e.g. code)
- auxiliary and intermediate work products needed for the development (e.g. test code)
- support data, containing information created/used for managing the process (e.g. quality assurance reports)

Work Product Dependency D: It describes 'logical' dependencies between work products, e.g. "is a submodule of". These relationships partially imply the sequence of creation and also establish a *compatibility requirement* which should be verifiable (e.g. "design conforms to requirements"). In the V-Modell XT, dependencies are modeled in detail for the whole model (called *Work Product Dependencies*). Several classes exist that are used for structural aspects (e.g. part-of relationship), creational aspects (this work product has to be created, because certain other work product need to be created; e.g. System Specification creates Software Specification) and finally content-related aspects, mainly used for quality assurance.

Work Product Structure S_W: This expresses a hierarchical ordering of work product types, useful for understanding, evaluating and storing partial work products.

Activity Types A : Activity types describe the *transformational aspect* of the development process, i.e. *HOW* work products are produced out of other work products. The choice of activities is strongly related to the underlying Result Dependency D, but still leaves considerable freedom in choosing the scope of Activity Types (see also "Modeling a Software Process").

Input Relationship I: The definition of Activity Types also implies which work product types are used as input. Those kinds of relationships can mainly be found in so-called activity-based process models, e.g. RUP. They are, combined with output relationships, the basis for specifying the activity flow and showing the work product flow. We should notice that some process models (e.g. ISO/IEC 12207 and ISO/IEC 15288) do not use the Input Relationship explicitly.

Output Relationship O: This relationship indicates which work product types are produced by an activity type.

Activity Structure S_A: The Activity Structure arranges Activity Types in higher-order structures, usually correlated with development levels. This is supportive of understanding the process. It also structures the development process into "phases" with common objectives or views (e.g. user point of view versus the data processing point of view), typically for better management planning and control.

Activity Flow F : The Activity Types can be considered as the individual steps in the development process. The Activity Flow defines the *'development strategy'*, the desired sequence of Activity Types, which is to some extent already pre-defined by Input Relationship I, Output Relationship O, and the Work Product Dependency D, but there is still considerable freedom which gives raise to different development methods (see section "Navigation in Process Models").

Activity Flow provides important information to project management because it allows control of project progress. Sequencing decisions may also have to take into account non-technical influences like availability of resources, strategic placement of milestones, etc.

Enacting Role E_R: Many models (e.g. V-Model XT, Hermes) provide a description of the individual classes of project members to perform the various actions. The V-Model XT defines approximately 30 roles, Hermes defines 22.

Enacting Tool E_T: Tools are the actual workhorse of development and are essential for providing productivity and quality. For the consistency of development it is often useful to specify which specific *tools* should be used for performing a given activity (e.g. a specific version of a compiler or a design tool). Often these tools can be enabled to be called automatically to perform specific tasks.

The list of components, as shown in fig. 5 and discussed above, comprises the most commonly used descriptive components but more can be added. It has to be noted that essentially *all* process components have to be involved in the process of developing software, but not all components have to be formally defined in the model. This depends, amongst other influences, on the maturity of the software development organization (see section "Evaluation of Software Processes"). Only a few models define the enacting roles E_R, e.g. V-Modell XT or Hermes. And only a few models define enactment tools (E_T), e.g. ADPS, V-Modell XT. Process Models to be used in the assessment following ISO/IEC 15504 only need to contain the Activity Type A, the Work Product Type R, and the Output Relationship O, but not the Input Relationship I. As a consequence these models do not describe a network or an activity flow.

Project Aura

Initially a software product was the result of a single, individual development effort. The next product was again developed independently of all previous (and future) systems. The strife to reduce cost, improve quality and service orientation, however, can only be satisfied by *reuse* of software components, by producing reusable components for later projects (Allen, 2001; Cheesman & Daniels, 2001; Crnkovic et al., 2002), by acquiring externally available product parts (ISO/IEC, 2006), by adopting a Product Line strategy (Hoyer, 2007; Pohl et al., 2005), and by planning for outsourcing ((Kobayashi-Hillary, 2005)). This means that a project has to consider the 'outside' environment beyond its immediate focus. ISO/IEC 15288 therefore has a submodel 'Enterprise Processes'. Product Line Models explicitly cover activities which provide assets from/to the environment (=other projects).

Figure 5. A process meta-model

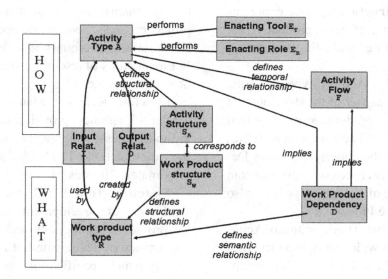

SELECTED PROCESS MODELS – OVERVIEW

Multitudes of process models exist, many on the commercial market, even more in the academic field. In this section some widely accepted, usually commercial process models, are listed. We describe only models which have introduced some degree of innovation; however, it must be taken into account that many of the ideas had often been published and experimentally used in academic projects earlier on, sometimes appearing somewhat hidden in predecessor models. Most of the models are still in use today, but some of them are only of historical importance along the road leading to modern process models. One can also notice that some later models forgo earlier innovations. Historical overviews can be found in Balzert (1989), Garg & Jazayeri (1996), Hausen (1982), and McDermid (1985). For ease of reference the models are arranged alphabetically, irrespective of their date of appearance.

ADPS (Application Development Process Support): IBM's ADPS is a complete Software Engineering Environment which has been based on several predecessor models since 1978 (IBM Corp., 1978), featuring three separate, but connected submodels for Development, Quality Assurance and Project Management. It is supported by a Process Engine to guide and support the users. A repository for storing work products, work product relationships, and an integrated tool model were available.

Innovation: Separate but interconnected submodels for Development, Quality Assurance, Project Management; tool definition and attachment, extensive on-line help texts.

Reference: (Chroust et al., 1988; Mercurio et al., 1990)

Catalysis: Catalysis is a method used to model and develop component-based software systems. It is based on OO-concepts, using and extending the UML for definition, providing a coherent set of abstraction techniques yielding several models of the final system (static, behavioral, interaction). It is useful for implementing Product Lines.

The concept of Product Lines (Hoyer, 2007; Clements & Northrop, 2002; Pohl et al., 2005), such as in the car industry, has introduced a new paradigm: A product is built and marketed as a member of a product. family, sharing many features (called 'assets') with its sibling products.

The assets of the product line have to be generated and maintained independently of the individual projects, resulting in a Product Development Model for building an individual product, an Asset Development Model for performing the provision of new components ("assets") and a Product Line Management model for maintaining/adapting a Product Line over time.

Innovation: Expanding the Project Aura to using/providing software components from outside, especially for Product Lines.

Reference: (D'Souza, 1998; Hoyer, 2007),

HERMES: The HERMES method, prescribed by the Swiss government, supports the management, development and execution of ICT projects in public administration as well as in enterprises. It is similar to the V-Model-97. The associated tool HermesPowerUser is the Process Engine for Hermes, available free of charge.

Innovation: nationwide standard for public administration, detailed Role Model, extensive educational material, multilingual (German, French)

Reference: (Bundesamt f. Informatik, 1995; Swiss Fed. Strategy Unit for Inf. Tech.,2004)

ISO/IEC 12207: "This International Standard establishes a common framework for software life cycle processes, with well-defined terminology, that can be referenced by the software industry. It applies to the acquisition of systems and software products and services, to the supply, development, operation, maintenance, and disposal of software products and the software portion of a system, whether performed internally or externally to an organization" (ISO/IEC, 2007a, p. iii). With respect to process components each process is described by the Activity Type, given by "title", "general goals" and "a list of actions", the Results Type and Output Relation, "observable results expected".

Innovation: international standard, compliant with requirements for process assessment via ISO 15504

Reference: (ISO/IEC, 2007a)

ISO/IEC 15288: "This International Standard provides a common process framework covering the life cycle of man-made systems. This life cycle spans the conception of ideas through to the retirement of a system. It provides the processes for acquiring and supplying systems. In addition, this framework provides for the assessment and improvement of the life cycle processes. ... The processes in this International Standard form a comprehensive set from which an organization can construct system life cycle models appropriate to its products and services. An organization, depending on its purpose, can select and apply an appropriate subset to fulfill that purpose."

Innovation: hardware and software design, Enterprise Model, Acquisition Model, and Aura beyond a single project.

Reference: (ISO/IEC, 2006)

ISO 26262 CD: Road vehicles - functional safety: ISO 26262, consisting of 9 parts, provides a safety lifecycle (management, development, production, operation, service, decommissioning) for the automotive industry, supports tailoring the necessary activities during these lifecycle phases, following an automotive specific risk-based approach for determining risk classes (Automotive Safety Integrity Levels).

It combines the IEC 61508 approach with the V-model, both for hardware and software, and other product and process standards. It takes a reasonable holistic view, taking into account the typical vehicle life time as well as the human driver. "Controllability" of a situation is an important concern, typical for the legal responsibility shared between the driver and the vehicle manufacturer in the automotive context.

Innovation: specific for the automotive industry, explicit risk-based approach, covering the whole system (hardware and software), explicit inclusion of driver responsibility.

Reference: (ISO (ed.), 2008)

ISO 61508 Functional Safety of Electric/ Electronic/Programmable Electronic Systems: For a risk based approach to safety of a *complete system* a holistic safety life cycle models has been developed. Hazard and Risk Analysis phases have been inserted between the establishment of the System Concept and the Requirements Phase. This is necessary because requirements must be based on the System Concept and the Hazard and Risk Analysis. Its focus is based on a safety analysis and the allocation of safety functions besides maintaining the intended and accepted level of safety throughout the complete life cycle of the system. This satisfies the requirement of certifiability of the system and products in context of the overall system which is embedded into the environment involving human interaction (Schoitsch et al., 2008; Schoitsch, 2008). In the realization phase the process model is similar to classical development process models. It can be tailored and thus made domain and application specific.

Innovation: Expanding the aura by using/ providing software components from outside, risk based

Reference: (EC, 1998)

PMOD: This is an evolution of the European Space Agency's standard ESA-PSS-05-0 (1991) and defines the system process for space systems. It provides the main interface to the underlying software processes, relevant to the development of on-board software. It consists of a written set of documents describing the development process in textual form. The model provides tailoring variants for Human-Computer-Interface, Critical, Real Time and Simulation Software.

Innovation: horizontal (v-shaped) verification, tailoring for specific space systems.

Reference: (ESA, 1991; Stragapede, 1999)

PRINCE2: Prince2 (Projects in Controlled Environments) is an extensive project management method addressing organization-level and individual projects. Originally founded in 1989 by Britain Central Computer and Telecommunications Agency (CCTA) it is meanwhile the official standard for IT-projects in Great Britain. Prince2 is in its influence comparable to the Swiss Hermes and the German V-Modell XT. It is accepted and applied in approximately 50 countries.

Innovation: process-oriented, separating the project phases from the relevant processes.

Reference: (Great Britain Office of Government Commerce, 2007)

Rational Unified Process (RUP): The Rational Unified Process (RUP) was originally created by Rational and is now supported by IBM. RUP is an activity-based, phase- organized, SPEM-based (OMG, 2005) process model according to the principles of incremental/iterative approaches. RUP is focused on software development but is not limited to this domain. SPEM (OMG, 2005) is the basis on which to provide sophisticated tool support. Parts of RUP are delivered as open source, named "Open/Basic Unified Process". The corresponding process framework "Eclipse Process Framework" (EPF (Haumer, 2006a,b)) is very popular. It provides a concrete implementation based on SPEM and is additionally available under an open source license. Tools based on the metamodel are the basis for the commercial as well as for the Open Source frame works.

Innovation: overlapping phases and enactment of submodels (called 'disciplines'), iterative development, metamodel

Reference: (Kruchten, 1998; Jacobson et al., 1999; Kroll & Kruchten, 2003; Robillard et al., 2002)

Scrum: Scrum is a management and development method for agile development. It focuses on self-organizing teams. It defines only a small number of entities and concepts. The basic concepts are the *product, sprint backlogs,* and *sprints.* The roles are *team, Scrum master,* and *product owner*. One of the basic concepts of Scrum is time-boxing, defining short deadlines for small chunks of work. They are selected by the team using prioritized lists (sprint backlogs) based on the requirements of the product to be developed (product backlog). The process itself is organized as iterative/incremental with low efforts in management.

Innovation: team development, strict timing of development ('sprints'), time-boxing, short iteration cycles, role model, iterative/incremental approach

Reference: (Koppensteiner, 2008; Schwaber, 2004)

V-Modell 97: Officially "Das V-Modell - Entwicklungsstandard für IT-Systeme des Bundes" regulates the system development process and the maintenance and modification of systems. It defines 4 subprocess models: Development, Quality Assurance, Configuration management, and technical Project Management. The model provides horizontal verification (v-shaped) and considers hardware and software acquisition. It has graphic/tabular descriptions of the activities (including input and output relationships). Extensive tailoring features dependent on the project type are provided.

Innovation: Development, Quality, Management and Configuration Submodel, formalized tailoring process dependent on project characteristics, consideration of hardware and software development

Reference: (BMVg (ed.), 1997; Dröschel & Wiemers, 1999)

V-Modell XT: The V-Modell XT is the standard development process for IT-projects provided by the German government. It is based on the classic V-Modell 97 and was completely re-designed in 2005. The V-Modell XT is an artifact-centered process model with a detailed description of the work products. A formal metamodel is the basis for the process description. It is available as XML-schema and defines all entities and dependency structures, allowing a convenient support by tools.

It provides a sophisticated tailoring model, addressing both the organizational and the project-level. The tailoring guarantees consistency of the model at any time and is widely tool-supported. It is v-shaped, incremental/iterative, and contains iterations as a fundamental concept. It is not focused to software development. It has a wide user community and supports system development as a whole as well as procurement.

Innovation: Completely metamodel-based (via XML-schema) process, change- affinitive, process description and several templates are generated during an automated tailoring, formal metamodel.

Reference: (Friedrich et al., 2008; KBst - Koord. - und Beratungsstelle d. B-Reg. f. Informationstechnik, 2006)

XP - eXtreme Programming: Extreme programming (XP) is a development-centered approach focussing on the software to be developed. XP is focused on change during the development process, not expecting requirements to be fixed or final. XP contains several principles (collected in the "Agile Manifesto" (Beck et al., 2002)) and defines 12 essential practices (Continuous Integration, pair programming, on-site customer, ...). A basic concept of XP is the on intensive and continuing communication both within the development team and with the customers. This approach works well for small teams, but becomes inefficient in large, long-running projects.

Innovation: Human aspects, 12 key principles, reduced documentation, no fixed process model, pair programming, on-site customer

Reference: (Beck et al., 2002; Beck, 2003; Paulk, 2001)

MODELING A SOFTWARE PROCESS

Basic Considerations

Numerous considerations flow into the design of a Process Model. Some of the more salient ones are discussed below.

Problem size: What is the size of the problems and their development time? How much change (requirements etc.) is to be expected during the project? This impacts granularity of work products and configuration models.

Problem complexity: Gradually it has been recognized that we continuously try to solve problems of growing complexity (Lehman, 1980) going from simple, easily specifiable problems to so-called wicked problems (Kopetz, 1997). For the latter it is knows that no initial concept can be implemented without dramatic changes and later adaptation. Depending on the complexity of the problem a more or less flexible, iterative approach may be needed.

Developers' experience and skills: The more experience developers have the less details have to be incorporated in the process model. This includes questions concerning established methods, tools, and approaches.

Optimal granularity: The granularity of REsult Types and Activity Types should be consistent (Chroust, 1992) and should reflect a manageable portion of work to be done by developers without loosing the overview or being annoyed by too much fragmentation of activities and work products.

Development team structure: A certain equivalence between the structure of the development team and the basic structure of the software products (modularization!) is desirable.

Priorities of project objectives: What are the basic constraints of the projects with respect to time to delivery, conformity to specification, quality, maintenance, usability etc.?

Verification/validation needs: They should allow verification of the developed results and their interdependency.

Defining Process Models

Defining a process model is a very difficult, creative, interactive, non-straightforward process. Basically model definition is based on four (partially contradicting) sources: the informal process (including methods and tools) as being currently enacted, the officially prescribed process (mostly ignored, cynically called 'shelfware'), the intended new process (including new ideas, paradigms, etc.) and the experience resulting from pilot projects, if any (Kuhrmann, 2008). Usually it is an iterative learning process.

- Even without a process model the essential work product types to be produced are usually known (a through k in Fig. 6) and can be defined together with (at least some of) the interdependencies (arrows in Fig. 6). The work products and their necessary granularity strongly depends on the typical types of

projects (procurement, development, integration etc.) to be performed. Only essential work product types (e.g. a compiled object code) are considered, not auxiliary minor work product types (like e.g. the compiler listing or the linkage list).

- The Work Product Structure, not shown in Fig. 6, is guided by concerns for practicality and ease of handling larger aggregates of work products.
- The next step usually is to choose an adequate set of Activity Types. Fig. 6 sketches the step from Work Products Types and Work Product Dependencies to the definition of the Activity Types (A through I in Fig. 6). This again requires numerous subtle design decisions. The Activity Types are interpreted as a set of transformations taking care of the dependencies. It can be seen that there is often more than one choice with respect to both the type and the

Figure 6. Result dependency and activity types, see also (Chroust, 2000)

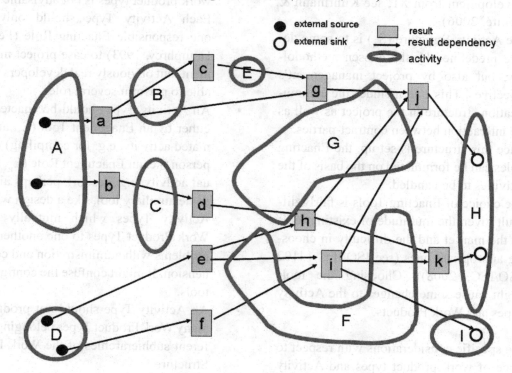

granularity of the activities. Typical and useful sets of Activity Types can be found in commonly available process models like the ISO/IEC 12207. These activities correspond approximately to what ISO/IEC 15504 (ISO/IEC, 2004) calls 'Base Practices'. Depending on the breadth of the model (including subprocess models) a model has some 100 to 250 Activity Types. Activity Types have to be consistent with the underlying Work Product Dependency in order to ensure proper consideration of the implied semantics and dependencies in the development process.

- Choosing the Activity Flow is somewhat easier since this is considerably predetermined by the Work Product Dependency. It should be born in mind that defining the Activity Flow also means defining methods to be used to reach project goals. When an Activity Flow is defined it is advisable also to consider suitable existing methods (e.g. Test Driven Development from XP, see Kuhrmann & Ternité, 2006).
- The Activity Structure (S_A) is to some degree predefined by the chosen methodology, but also by project management's objectives. This also includes the communication structure in the project as well as the interaction between contract-parties.
- Once this structure is set up, the Enacting Roles can be formulated on the basis of the activities to be handled.
- The choice of Enacting Tools is fairly difficult given the multitude of existing tools on the market and the difficulty in choosing appropriate ones (see ISO/IEC 14102 (ISO/IEC, 2008)). Choosing the tools might cause some changes to the Activity Types and Work Products.

Some specific considerations with respect to the choice of work product types and Activity Types are:

- The totality of Activity Types has to 'cover' all work product types by describing the production of *all* Work Product Types.
- It is necessary to choose an appropriate granularity for the Activity Types. Choosing too 'small' an Activity Type means ignoring the available professional software know-how and constrains. At least it hampers the developers. Defining too large an Activity Type makes the assignment of an individual work unit and management control difficult.
- It is of advantage to have each major Work Product to be produced by only one Activity Type. Avoiding producing the same major Work Product Types by different Activity Types make the the assignment of responsibilities for Work Products easier and also eases error detection.
- Defining several Activity Types which all need a similar (or the same) set of input work product types is not advisable.
- Each Activity Type should only have one responsible Enacting Role (Feiler & Humphrey, 1993) to ease project management, but obviously real developers will be able to perform several roles.
- An Activity Type should be enacted fully either by an Enactment Tool (E_T, an automated activity, e.g. for compiling) or by a person, i.e. an Enactment Role (E_R, a manual activity, e.g. design), perhaps aided by some auxiliary tool, like a design wizard.
- Activity Types which mutually supply Work Product Types to one another create problems with administration and comprehension. It might confuse the configuration tools.
- An Activity Type should not produce too many Work Product Types belonging to different subhierarchies of the Work Product Structure.

Verification and Validation

Process Models, to be useful and especially to be amenable to computer interpretation (see section "Process Enactment") have to obey certain syntactical and semantic constraints ("well-formedness rules"): They have to be checked for when defining or customizing a process model. Some of the more stringent rules are:

completeness of work product types: Every Work Product Type has to be produced by an Activity Type and consumed by at least one other. Exceptions might be work products informally coming from outside, e.g. an initial project assignment or some customer intervention.

connectivity of Activity Types: Each Activity Type should have at least one input and output. Exceptions could be 'start activities' which receive the information only informally (e.g. an initial project assignment) or 'end activities' which describe the delivery to a customer.

directedness of the model: All Activity Types should be connected in the sense of a directed graph.

cycle-freeness: Cycles in the Activity Flow F should be avoided or held to a minimum. They cannot be avoided in iterative process models.

Figure 7. Creating and modifying a process model

Even if cycles cannot be avoided on the model level, there is still a chance to avoid them on the instance level.

In this area metamodel-based process models are of advantage since they ensure some of those constraints by the defined process modeling language.

Customizing: Tailoring and Expanding Process Models

In practical life Software Process Models have to be adapted (customized) depending on the projects characteristics. Customizable process models enable organizations to create and introduce a specific process, which is based on a standard process model. Standard process models are often (by necessity) too generic, because they want to address a wide user audience. In most cases standard process models already contain a large amount of prefabricated contents, e.g. descriptions for reference activities and artifacts, knowledge and best practices which might not be needed in a specific case. On the other hand specific project situations might require activities which are not foreseen in the original process models.

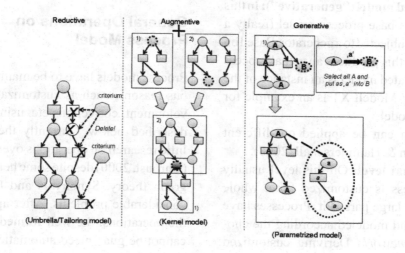

Three approaches can thus be chosen (fig. 7):

Umbrella model - Tailoring ("reductive"): The standard model is supposed to contain all necessary components. Customizing consists of eliminating unnecessary parts – also called *Tailoring*. Components of the given process have to be consistently removed and changed (removal of components might imply changes to other components!). V-Modell XT, and RUP contain elaborate algorithms (Friedrich et al., 2008) for performing tailoring. Tailoring can be supported by tools. So for example RUP (or SPEM-based processes) in general provide sophisticated support for process authors based on e.g. *Eclipse Process Framework* (including a method composer) (Haumer, 2006a,b). For tailoring on the organizational level comparable features are provided by the V-Modell XT. It also covers tailoring on the project-type level. A project assistant guides a project manager through the project set-up in order to determine what kind of work product the project should produce. He is assisted in trimming the given process model according to his needs.

Kernel model ("augmentive"): The standard process model consists of a relatively small basic kernel onto which, depending on need, additional submodels are 'attached', or Activity Types expanded into a larger partial model. RUP is an example for a model of this kind.

Parameterized model ("generative"): In this case the complete base process model (really a 'meta-model') is subjected to a generator. Based on given parameters this produces an actual process model. The generated model is an instance of the original model. V-Modell XT is an example for such a process model.

Customization can be applied on different levels (Kuhrmann & Hammerschall, 2008):

Organizational level: On this level usually a standard process is customized for a whole organization or a large part of it. Processes have to be analyzed and modeled according the chosen *process framework*. Deriving customized processes aiming at a global model for different types of projects across the whole organization is of special interest.

Project-type level: On this level an organization-specific process is customized according to the requirements of a particular project, creating an individual process model for a particular project. This kind of tailoring takes place *before* or *during* the project initialization, cf. V-Modell XT and ADPS.

Project level: On this level, the individual project is already under way. Changes in the process model have to be performed if basic conditions have changed, e.g. tasks or artifacts have to be replaced or redesigned. In unusual cases a project's structure itself has to be reorganized.

Typical project characteristics on which customizing will be based are:

- size of final product
- product platform (e.g. with or without data base, network, ...)
- type of product usage (safety critical, imbedded, ...)
- type of development organization (SME, large enterprises, ...)
- development paradigm (waterfall type, spiral model, ...)
- type of development (forward development, maintenance, reengineering, ...).

General Operations on Process Model

Process models have to be manipulated for various reasons, such as customization, further development, corrections etc. using the operations described below. Currently there seems to be little research on operations over process models (Chroust, 2000) despite some helpful results from graph theory. Synonyms and homonyms pose considerable problems. After applying some of the operations, the well-formedness of a model cannot be guaranteed automatically. Looking at

SPEM and V-Modell XT we can find a (sub-) set of those operations already defined in the underlying metamodels. A set of needed operations could be:

Rename changes consistently the name of some model components.

Union combines two process models. This is useful for e.g. adding a further cooperating subprocess model.

Substitution allows for the replacement of one activity or a small set of subprocess models by some larger submodel. This is useful if more details are desired for an activity. Typical applications are kernel models.

Difference identifies differences between two process models. Especially useful for analysis of different methodologies and for modification.

Intersection identifies process components which are common to two models. Useful for identifying conformity of a process model to some standard model.

Equality tests whether two models are the same. Useful for demonstrating full conformance to a standard model.

PROCESS ENACTMENT / SOFTWARE ENGINEERING ENVIRONMENTS

Initial attempts to support process models by a specific process interpreter ("Process Engine") go back to 1980 (Huenke, 1980). Nowadays the machine supported enactment often makes it difficult to separate issues between model and Process Engine. More details can be found in (Kuhrmann et al., 2010) in this book.

Enacting a Software Process

The complexity of a software process results in a fairly voluminous documentation, if described in the necessary detail. The danger is that the documentation will not be consulted during develop-

ment (cynically called "shelfware"). A solution for the guaranteed (and if necessary enforced) adherence to the process model is the use of a formalized and machine readable process model which is on-line and can be interpreted ("enacted") by a computer program usually, called "Process Engine" or "Model Interpreter" (Kuhrmann et al., 2010). Support of this kind will also perform numerous further services including trivial clerical activities such as recording the status of work products and more advanced features like semantically checking correct relationship between different work products.

An environment providing a Process Engine, a Process Model, the necessary user interfaces, data bases ("Repository") and the required tools is usually referred to as an (Integrated) Software Engineering Environment (SEE) but many other names exist, too (Balzert, 1982; Hausen, 1982; Huenke, 1980; McDermid, 1985; Schäfer, 1995).

From a user perspective a SEE provides a structure as shown in fig 8. Several tasks can be identified:

Interpreting the process model by (gradually) instantiating the process components and then controlling the enactment (Kuhrmann & Kalus, 2008)

Guiding the user (navigation) via the process model through the various activities in the development process (Chroust, 1992, 2000).

Activating automatically the (enactment) tools defined in the process model. The Process Engine can call the tools on behalf of the user. This could be simple auxiliary tools (e.g. an editor) or sophisticated CASE-tools (Kuhrmann et al., 2008).

Administering work products by storing and retrieving them, taking care of versioning etc.

The user performs three basic tasks:

navigation: deciding what to do next, based on the process model, on the status of work products and other activities. The system can give some advice and help by providing priorities etc.

development work: performing the creative

Figure 8. Interfaces in a software engineering environment

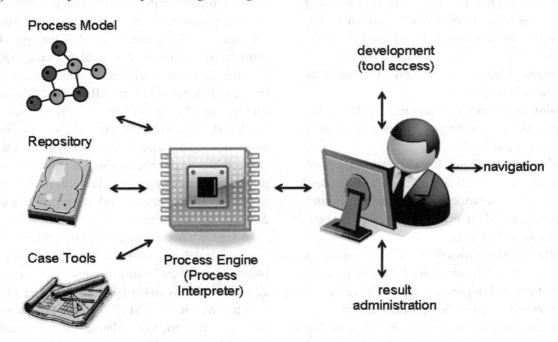

part of software engineering, utilizing the attached CASE tools for creating/modifying work products

administration: As far as this is not automated, the user administers the work products.

Navigation in Process Models

Real processes are instances of the given process model. It is very difficult to define *on the model level* rules for navigation on the *instance level*. To a certain extent a process model defines how to proceed in the course of the software development, but the user must choose the appropriate sequence himself, guided by the process model and the process engine. Some of the strategic considerations discussed in "Development Strategy and Path" however can at least informally be communicated to the developers as a strategic guideline. The software developer will have a certain amount of freedom in choosing the sequence. The Process Engine, however, has to record and support those navigation decisions. *We see an analogy*

to a captain navigating the ship on an individual course based on a general route assignment, on details of ocean maps, and on numerous data like sonar, radar, etc.

A basic hypothesis is that in socio-technical processes like software engineering the navigation has to be largely decided upon by a human being, but the enaction mechanism should provide adequate support for navigation decisions.

Evaluation of Software Processes

It is strongly assumed that the quality of a software process, more precisely *'of the process defined and enacted according to the Process Model'*, plays a key role in software product quality. Since the late 90's the concept of the definition and assessment of software processes has been discussed, especially since W. Humphrey's seminal book (Humphrey, 1989) which defined a 5-level scale for the maturity of a company, the so called Capability Maturity Model (CMM) based on a very large sampling and analysis of industrial software providers (Paulk et al., 1995). In a nutshell the approach is: An enactment of the actual software development (based on recorded data) is compared to a given process reference model. The performance for each individual subprocess ('best practice') is judged on a 4-level scale (not performed, partially fulfilled, largely fulfilled, fully fulfilled). CMM translates this into one single maturity value on the 5-level scale (1: Ad hoc (Chaotic), 2: Repeatable, 3: Defined, 4: Managed, 5: Optimizing). Sometimes (e.g. CMMI) a level 0 'incomplete' is added. The higher the maturity level the higher are the chances for a successful high-quality product and a successful project performance.

In the meantime several similar but competitive approaches have been proposed, e.g. BOOTSTRAP (Haase et al., 1994; Koch, 1993), ISO/IEC 15504 (ISO/IEC, 2004), and CMMI (Kneuper, 2006). BOOTSTRAP and ISO/IEC 15504 return a vector of values for all relevant processes. CMM, CMMI and BOOTSTRAP use their own proprietary model as reference, while ISO/IEC 15504 accepts the user's model (which has to obey certain syntactic constraints) as a reference model.

Many factors contribute to the assessment of maturity levels in a complex way:

- One key is an adequate *quality of the process model* which defines the necessary methods and best practices and is adequately customized for the project at hand.
- The *quality of the Process Engine* plays a further important part since the instantiation, the sequencing ('navigation'), and the activation of tools is largely dependent on the process engine.
- The *quality of the attached tools* is largely responsible for the correctness etc. of work products, but sometimes this influence is over-estimated.
- Last not least the *quality of the human developers* plays the major role. While all tools usually do not provide more than a

30% improvement, the human factor can account for a factor of 300% (Glass, 2001). The human skills are mostly required in two situations: creative design of the various work products and to a lesser extent choosing an optimal navigation strategy.

HUMAN ASPECTS: INTRODUCING AND ENACTING PROCESS MODELS

Importance of Human Factors

Software development is a largely human, personnel-intensive activity, based on human intelligence and engineering ability, by necessity usually performed in teams. Software systems do not exist in isolation, but are imbedded in social and organizational contexts. People and culture determine the use of a system (Chroust, 2006). People are also the main cause of software failures, both with respect to the development process and the use of a software product.

The Individual Developer

With respect to the individual developer several issues have to be considered when introducing a process model. Key issues are:

self-preservation: In case of change people first of all tend to ask: Can it harm me? Is it useful for me? Will it help me (now, in the future)? Is it pleasant to work with?

self-respect related: This includes need for learning and additional qualification, fear of added complexity, loss of knowledge advantage, de-skilling (Kraft, 1977), loss of flexibility, loss of creativity, emphasis on book-keeping and not on productive work, feeling of powerlessness.

self-fulfillment: People need identification with work, pride in work, and workmanship.

loss of flexibility: Many developers fear the loss of work flexibility. Agile processes try to avoid this. On the other hand, too much flexibility can also lead to uncontrolled, chaotic development processes.

creativity: Software developer fear a loss of their creativity (Chroust, 2008a,b; Kraft, 1977). The issue of creativity is multi-faceted and linked to the question as to where and how much creativity is helpful in the development process. It can be stated that in the early stages of the development process creativity is of great significance. The further this process advances, the less creativity is of importance as a more uniform, transparent process has to be enacted. Creativity should be concentrated on the *contents* and not on formal aspects (e.g. naming of modules).

group related problems (peers): Loss of status due to obsolescence of some previously highly appreciated know-how (e.g. process knowledge now incorporated in the model), visibility, and observability by peers, re-organization of work due to computer support, change of group dynamic processes due to computer interfaces, information overload due to enhanced communication, intercultural problems in mixed, geographically and culturally heterogeneous groups (Chroust, 2007).

problems with method, paradigm, and tools: Mismatch of know-how and description, discontinuity of methods and approaches, new terminology, disbelief in the new approach, perseverance in old paradigms, superficial use and double work.

management related problems: They are related to the ability to control information, performance and quality, based on the aggregation of data, their automatic evaluation and comparison ('Big Brother').

organizational problems: They concern reorganization, shifting of work load, change/destruction of informal channels, visibility of external control, changes in the organization.

The Project Manager

Project managers have similar concerns in their functions being subordinates of higher managers (status, self-fulfillment ...). They also experience additional problems in their function as managers: The process models and the SEE make most of the project management information accessible to the software engineers, resulting in the project managers' losing some of the information monopole and causing some emancipation of subordinates. The system will often create the need to show more individual competence.

The Introduction Process

The introduction of a process model (especially if there has been none before) is a very difficult and emotionally laden undertaking, since (as can be seen from above) an introduction of this kind will change, even revert numerous habits, established routines, and traditions (Chroust, 2008b). All stake-holders (especially the software engineers) must be involved, allowing for open discussion and critique, consideration of existing practices and focus on emotional human aspects. (Bouldin, 1989).

FUTURE TRENDS

Software Development Process Models reflect the state of the art and the state-of-the-practice of the software industry. Several trends can be identified: depending on the type of product (high-risk versus fast time-to-market) process models will diversify, either becoming more stringent or becoming more agile. We will find more hybrid-style models, taking the best of both worlds, e.g. stringent process with agile practices.

We also expect increased computer support, both in interpreting and enacting process models, adapting them to individual and project needs. The importance and the use of process models will be re-enforced by the globalization of software development, the systematic reuse of assets together with the growing demands on dependability of software and attempts at establishing certification for software products and software engineers. This will lead to a more holistic point of view taking into account the whole system life cycle from concept to decommissioning (disposal) in which the software processes are only a part of. The evolvement of resilient systems will provoke a further challenge to process models, i.e. will require new dynamic ones for adaptive, self-learning, reasoning autonomous systems cooperating with humans and environment.

CONCLUSION

Process Models (and their computer assisted enactment) are one of the keys to successful, sustainable and high-quality software products. The choice of the process model has to carefully balance the intended types of projects, the existing 'software culture' (practices and methods), the technical and motivational qualification of the personnel, and the state-of-the-art of software engineering. Process models ease the way to a quality capability assessment of companies and promise a high return on investment. This will move software development nearer to becoming a true engineering discipline, able to face new requirements and challenges due to new type of systems.

REFERENCES

Allen, P. (2001). *Realizing e-business with components*. Reading, MA: Addison-Wesley.

Amdahl, G. M., Blaauw, G., & Brooks, F. (1964). Architecture of the IBM system/360. *IBM Journal of Research and Development, 8*(2), 21–36.

Balzert, H. (1982). *Die entwicklung von software systemen*. Reihe Informatik/34, BI Wis- senschaftsverlag.

Balzert, H. (1989). *CASE - systeme und werkzeuge*. B-I Wissenschaftsverlag.

Beck, K. (2003). *Extreme programming*. Reading, MA: Addison-Wesley Longman.

Beck, K., et al. (2002). *Manifesto for agile software development*. Retrieved from http://agilemanifesto.org/

Blaauw, G. (1972). Computer architecture. *El. Rechenanl, 14*(4), 154.

BMVg (Ed.). (1997). *V-Modell - entwicklungsstandard für IT-systeme des bundes (EStddIT) Stand Oct. 1997* (Tech. Rep.). Germany: BMVg.

Boehm, B. (1976). Software engineering. *IEEE Transactions on Computers, C-25*(12), 1226–1241. doi:10.1109/TC.1976.1674590

Boehm, B. (1986). A spiral model of software development and enhancement. *ACM SIGS- OFT - Software Engineering Notes, 11*(4), 22–42.

Boehm, B., Grünbacher, P., & Briggs, B. (2001). Developing groupware for requirements negotiation: Lessons learned. *IEEE Software, 18*(3), 46–55. doi:10.1109/52.922725

Bouldin, B. (1989). *Agents of change - managing the introduction of automated tools*. Your- don Press.

Bundesamt f. Informatik. (1995). *Hermes - führung und abwicklung von informatikprojek- ten* (Tech. Rep.). Bern, Switzerland: Bundesamt f. Informatik, Schweizerische Bundesverwaltung.

Cheesman, J., & Daniels, J. (2001). *UML components*. Reading, MA: Addison Wesley.

Chrissis, M. B., Konrad, M., & Shrum, S. (2006). *CMMI: Guidelines for process integration and product improvement*. Amsterdam: Addison-Wesley Longman.

Chroust, G. (1992). *Modelle der software-ent-wicklung - aufbau und interpretation von vorge-hensmodellen.* Oldenbourg Verlag. 31

Chroust, G. (1994). Partial process models. In M. M. Tanik, W. Rossak, & D. E. Cooke (Eds.), *Software Systems in Engineering, The American Soc. of Mechanical Engineers Engineers,* New Orleans, LA (pp. 197-202).

Chroust, G. (2000). Software process models: Structure and challenges. In Y. Feng, D. Notkin, & M. C. Gaudel (Eds.), *Software: Theory and Practice - Proceedings, IFIP Congress 2000,* Beijing, China (pp. 279-286). Amsterdam: Kluwer.

Chroust, G. (2006). Motivation in component-based software development. In C. Ghaoui (Ed.), *Encyclopedia of human computer interaction* (pp. 414-421). Hershey, PA: Idea Group Reference.

Chroust, G. (2007). Software like a courteous butler - issues of localization under cultural diversity. In *Proceedings of the ISSS 2007. The 51th Annual meeting and Conference for the System Sciences.* Tokyo, Japan: Curran Associates, Inc.

Chroust, G. (2008a). Localization, culture and global communication. In G. D. Putnik & M. M. Cunha (Eds.), *Encyclopedia of networked and virtual organizations* (pp. 829-832). Hershey, PA: Information Science Reference.

Chroust, G. (2008b). Psychologische widerstände bei der einführung computer-gestützter vorgehens-modelle. In R. Höhn, R. Petrasch, & O. Linssen (Eds.), *Proceedings of the Vorgehensmodelle und der product life-cycle - projekt und betrieb von IT-lösungen (15. Workshop der FG WI-VM der GI* (pp. 258-259). Aachen, Germany: Shaker Verlag.

Chroust, G., Gschwandtner, O., & Mutschmann-Sanchez, D. (1988). Das entwicklungssy- stem ADPS der IBM. In T. Gutzwiller & H. Österle (Eds.), *Anleitung zu einer praxisorientier- ten Software-Entwicklungsumgebung, Band 2 AIT Verlag München* (pp. 123-148).

Clements, P., & Northrop, L. (2002). *Software product lines - practices and patterns.* Reading, MA: Addison Wesley.

Collins, R. W. (2002). Software localization for Internet software: Issues and methods. *IEEE Software, 19*(2), 74–80. doi:10.1109/52.991367

IBM Corp. (1978). DV-Verfahrenstechnik - eine methodische vorgehensweise zur entwick- lung von DV-anwendungen. *Schriftenreihe Management- und Methoden-Institut, IBM Deutschland, Form No. SR12-1657-0.*

Crnkovic, I., Larsson, S., & Stafford, J. (2002). Component-based software engineering: Building systems from components. *Software Engineering Notes, 27*(3), 47–50. doi:10.1145/638574.638587

D'Souza, D. (1998). Interface specification, refinement, and design with uml/catalysis. *Jour- nal of Object-Oriented Programming, 11,* 12-18.

deRemer, F., & Kron, H. (1976). Programming-in-the-large versus programming-in-the- small. *IEEE Transactions on Software Engineering, 2*(2), 80–86. doi:10.1109/TSE.1976.233534

Downs, E., Clare, P., & Coe, I. (1988). Structured systems analysis and design method. *Prentice Hall, Englewood Cliffs.*

Dröschel, W., & Wiemers, M. (1999). *Das V-Modell 97.* Oldenburg.

Eclipse Foundation. (2007). *Das eclipse process framework (EPF) online portal.* Retrieved

ESA. (1991). *ESA software engineering standards* (ESA- PSS-05-0 issue 2). Paris: European Space Agency.

Fed, S. Strategy Unit for Inf. Tech. (2004). *Hermes - management and execution of projects in information and communication technolo- gies (ICT) - foundations* (Doc. No. 609.204.e). Retrieved from http://www.hermes.admin.ch/ict_project_management/manuals-utilities

Feiler, P., & Humphrey, W. (1993). Software process development and enactment: Concepts and definitions. In *Proceedings of the 2nd Int'l Conf. on Software Process,* CA (pp. 28-40). Retrieved from http://www.eclipse.org/epf/

Friedrich, J., Hammerschall, U., Kuhrmann, M., & Sihling, M. (2008). *Das V-Modell XT*. Berlin, Germany: Springer.

Garg, P., & Jazayeri, M. (Eds.). (1996). *Process-centered software engineering environ- ments*. Washington, DC: IEEE Computer Soc Press.

Gilb, T., & Graham, D. (1993). *Software inspection*. Reading, MA: Addison-Wesley.

Glass, R. (2001). Frequently forgotten fundamental facts about software engineering. *IEEE Software, 18*(3), 112–110. doi:10.1109/MS.2001.922739

Great Britain Office of Government Commerce. (2007). *Think PRINCE2 (managing suc- cessful projects)* (Tech. Rep.). Great Britain Office of Government Commerce, Sta- tionery Office Books.

Grünbacher, P., Egyed, A., & Medvidovic, N. (2001). Reconciling software requirements and architectures: The CBSP approach. In *Proceedings of the 5th IEEE International Symposium on Requirements Engineering (RE01),* Toronto, Canada.

Haase, V. (1994). Bootstrap: Fine-tuning process assessment. *IEEE Software, 11*(4), 25–35. doi:10.1109/52.300080

Haumer, P. (2006a). *Eclipse process framework composer – part 1: Key concepts*. Retrieved from http://www.eclipse.org/epf/general/EPFComposerOverviewPart1.pdf

Haumer, P. (2006b). *Eclipse process framework composer – part 2: Authoring method con- tent and processes*. Retrieved from http://www.eclipse.org/epf/general/EPFComposerOverviewPart2.pdf

Hausen, H. M. M. (1982). Software engineering environments: State of the art, problems and perspectives. In . *Proceedings of the Compsac, 82,* 326–335.

Herbsleb, J. D., & Goldenson, D. (1996). A systematic survey of CMM experience and results. In *Proceedings of the 18th Int. Conf on Software Engineering* (pp. 323-330).

Hoyer, C. (2007). *ProLiSA - an approach to the specification of product line software architectures*. Unpublished doctoral dissertation, J. Kepler University Linz.

Huenke, H. (Ed.). (1980). *Software engineering environments, Proceedings,* Lahnstein, BRD, North Holland.

Humphrey, W. (1989). *Managing the software process*. Reading, MA: Addison-Wesley.

IEC. (1998). *IEC 61508: Functional safety of electric/electronic/programmable electronic systems, part 1 - 9* (Tech. Rep.). IEC, International Electronic Commission.

ISO (Ed.). (2008). *ISO 26262: Road vehicles - functional safety* (Tech Rep.). International Organization for Standardization.

ISO/IEC. (2001). *ISO/IEC 9126-1:2001 software engineering - product quality - part 1: Quality model* (Tech. Rep.). Internat. Org. for Standardization.

ISO/IEC. (2004). *ISO/IEC 15504-1:2004 information technology - process assessment - part 1: Concepts and vocabulary* (Tech. Rep. ISO/IEC JTC 1/SC 7/WG 10).

ISO/IEC. (2006). *ISO/IEC 15288:2006: Systems engineering - system life cycle processes* (Tech. Rep. ISO/IEC JTC 1/SC 7/WG 7). Internat. Org. for Standarization.

ISO/IEC. (2007a). *ISO/IEC 12207:2007 systems and software engineering - software life cycle processes* (Tech. Rep.). Geneva: Internat. Org. for Standarization, ISO.

ISO/IEC. (2007b). *ISO/IEC 24744: Software engineering – metamodel for development methodologies* (Tech. Rep.). International Organization for Standardization.

ISO/IEC. (2008). *ISO/IEC 14102 - information technology - guideline for the evaluation and selection of case tools* (Tech. Rep.). Geneva: Internat. Org. for Standarization, ISO.

Jacobson, I., Booch, G., & Rumbaugh, J. (1999). The unified process. *IEEE Software, 16*(3), 96–102.

July 9, 2007, from http://www.eclipse.org/epf

KBst - Koord. - und Beratungsstelle d. B-Reg. f. Informationstechnik. (2006). *Das neue V-Modell(R) XT - der Entwicklungsstandard für IT-Systeme des Bundes*. Retrieved from http://www.v-modell-xt.de/

Kneuper, R. (2006). *CMMI - Verbesserung von softwareprozessen mit capability maturity model integration*. Auflage, dpunkt.verlag.

Kobayashi-Hillary, M. (2005). *Outsourcing to India. The offshore advantage*. Berlin, Germany: Springer.

Koch, G. (1993). Process assessment: The bootstrap approach. *Information and Software Technology, 35*(6/7), 387–402. doi:10.1016/0950-5849(93)90010-Z

Kopetz, H. (1997). *Real-time systems - design principles for distributed embedded appli-catins*. Dordrecht, The Netherlands: Kluwer Academic Publishers.

Koppensteiner, S. (2008). *Process mapping and simulation for software projects*. VDM Verlag Dr. Müller.

Kraft, P. (1977). *Programmers and managers*. Heidelberg, Germany: Springer.

Kroll, P., & Kruchten, P. (2003). *The rational unified process made easy – a practicioner's guide to RUP*. Reading, MA: Addison-Wesley.

Kruchten, P. (1998). *The 'rational unified process' - an introduction*. Reading, MA: Addison Wesley.

Kuhrmann, M. (2008). *Konstruktion modularer vorgehensmodelle*. Unpublished doctoral dissertation, Technische Universität München.

Kuhrmann, M., & Hammerschall, U. (2008). *Anpassung des V-Modell XT - Leitfaden zur organisationsspezifischen Anpassung des V-Modell XT*. Projektbericht, Technische Uni-versität München.

Kuhrmann, M., & Kalus, G. (2008). Providing integrated development processes for distri-buted development environments. In *Proceedings of the Workshop on Supporting Distributed Team Work at Computer Supported Cooperative Work (CSCW 2008)*, San Diego, CA.

Kuhrmann, M., Kalus, G., & Chroust, G. (2010). Tool-support for software development pro-cesses. In M. M. Cruz-Cunha (Ed.), *Social, Managerial and Organizational Dimensions of Enterprise Information Systems*. Hershey, PA: Business Science Reference.

Kuhrmann, M., Kalus, G., & Diernhofer, N. (2008). Generating tool-based process- environments from formal process model descriptions – concepts, experiences and samples. In C. Pahl (Ed.), *Proceedings of the IASTED International Conference on Soft- ware Engineering (SE 2008) as part of the 26th IASTED International Multi-Conference on Applied Informatics*. ACTA Press.

Kuhrmann, M., & Ternité, T. (2006). Implementing the Microsoft Solutions framework for agile sw-development as concrete development-method in the V-Modell XT. *In- ternational Transactions on Systems Science and Applications, 1*, 119-126.

Lehman, M. (1980). Programs, life cycles, and laws of software evolution. In M. M. Lehman & L. A. Belady (Eds.), *Program evolution - processes of software change* (pp. 393-450). Academic Press.

Martin, J. (1989). *Information engineering, book I: Introduction*. Englewood Cliffs, NJ: Prentice Hall.

McDermid, J. (Ed.). (1985). *Integrated project support environments*. London: P. Peregrinus Ltd.

Merbeth, G. (1992). MAESTRO-II - das integrierte CASE-System von Softlab. In H. Balzert (Ed.), *CASE - Systeme und Werkzeuge 4. Auflage, B-I Wissenschaftsverlag* (pp. 215-232).

Mercurio, V., Meyers, B., Nisbet, A., & Radin, G. (1990). AD/Cycle strategy and architec- ture. *IBM Systems Journal, 29*(2), 170–188.

Nakajo, T. K. H. (1985). The principles of fool-proofing and their application in manufactu- ring. *Reports of Statistical Application Research JUSE, 32*(2), 10–29.

Naur, P., & Randell, B. (Eds.). (1969). *Software Engineering, Proceedings of the NATO Working Conference Garmisch-Partenkirchen*. Brussels, Belgium: Scientific Affairs Division, NATO.

OMG. (2005). *Software process engineering metamodel specification* (Tech. Rep.). Retrieved from http://www.uml.org/

OMG. (2007a). *Unified modeling language (UML): Infrastructure – version 2.1.1* (Tech, Rep.). Retrieved from http://www.uml.org/

OMG. (2007b). *Unified modeling language (UML): Superstructure – version 2.1.1* (Tech. Rep.). Retrieved from http://www.uml.org/

Paulk, M. (2001). Extreme programming from a CMM perspective. *IEEE Software, 18*(6), 9–26. doi:10.1109/52.965798

Paulk, M., Weber, C., Curtis, B., & Chrissis, M. (Eds.). (1995). *The capability maturity model: Guidelines for improving the software process*. Reading, MA: Addison-Wesley.

Phillips, R. (1989). State change architecture pro-tocols for process models. In *IEEE Pro- ceedings of the Hawaii International Conference on System Sciences (HICSS-22)*, Kona, Hawaii.

Pohl, K., Böckle, G., & van der Linden, F. (2005). *Software product line engineering*. Berlin, Germany: Springer.

Robillard, P., Kruchten, P., & d'Astous, P. (2002). *Software engineering process: With the UPEDU - unified process for education*. Reading, MA: Addison Wesley.

Royce, W. (1970). Managing the development of large software systems. In *Proc. of the IEEE WES- CON* (pp. 1-9).

Schäfer, W. (Ed.). (1995). *Proceedings of the Software Process Technology - 4th European Workshop EWSPT'95 Noordwijkerhout*.

Schoitsch, E. (2008). A holistic view at depend-able embedded software-intensive systems. In G. Chroust, P. Doucek, & J. Klas (Eds.), *Proceedings of the 16th Interdisciplinary Information Management Talks "Managing the Unmanageable"* (pp. 321-344). Schriftenreihe Informatik Nr. 25, Trauner Verlag Linz.

Schoitsch, E., Althammer, E., Sonneck, G., Eriksson, H., & Vinter, J. (2008). Modular cer- tification support - the DECOS concept of generic safety cases. In *Proceedings of IEEE INDIN 2008, 6th International Conference on Industrial Informat-ics*, Daejeon, Korea. IEEE: CFP08INI-CDR.

Schwaber, K. (2004). *Agile project management with scrum*. Redmond, WA: Microsoft Press.

SPIRE Project Team. (1998). *The SPIRE handbook - better, faster, cheaper - software development in small organisations*. Dublin, Ireland: Centre of Software Engineering Ltd.

Stragapede, A. (1999). *ECSS software process model* (Tech. Rep.). Turin, Italy: Alenia Aerospazio - Space Division.

Turner, M. (2006). *Microsoft solutions framework essentials*. Redmond, WA: Microsoft Press.

Wang, Y., & King, G. (2000). *Software engineering processes*. Boca Raton, FL: CRC Press.

Ward, R. P., Fayad, M. E., & Laitinen, M. (2001). Thinking objectively: Software process improvement in the small. *Communications of the ACM, 44*(4), 105–107. doi:10.1145/367211.367291

Yourdon, E. (1990). Softlab's MAESTRO. *American Programmer, 3*(3).

Zemanek, H. (1986). Gedanken zum systementwurf. In H. Maier-Leibniz (Ed.), *Zeugen des wissens* (Vol. XX). Hase and Köhler Verlag Mainz.

Zvegintzov, N. (1982). What life? What cycle? In AFIPS (Ed.), *Proceedings of the National Computer Conference,* Houston, TX (pp. 562-567).

Chapter 3
People–Oriented Enterprise Information Systems

Giorgio Bruno
Politecnico di Torino, Italy

ABSTRACT

Current notations and languages do not emphasize the participation of users in business processes and consider them essentially as service providers. Moreover, they follow a centralized approach as all the interactions originate from or end in a business process; direct interactions between users cannot be represented. What is missing from this approach is that human work is cooperative and cooperation takes place through structured interactions called conversations; the notion of conversation is at the center of the language/action perspective. However, the problem of effectively integrating conversations and business processes is still open and this chapter proposes a notation called POBPN (People-Oriented Business Process Notation) and a perspective, referred to as conversation-oriented perspective, for its solution.

INTRODUCTION

Enterprise Information Systems (EISs) were first conceived as systems providing a repository for business entities and enabling users (subdivided into appropriate roles) to handle such entities. Then the process-oriented approach (Dumas, van der Aalst, & ter Hofstede, 2005) has pointed out that business purposes are achieved through coordinated work to be carried out by means of two kinds of activities: user tasks and automatic procedures. User tasks are units of work that users carry out with the help of a graphical interface in order to achieve a particular purpose. Placing a purchase requisition or filling in the review form for a conference paper are examples of user tasks. Automatic procedures, instead, accomplish their function without requiring any human intervention.

However, as the activities are developed separately from the processes, current notations and languages, such as BPMN (Object Management Group, 2008), XPDL (Workflow Management Coalition, 2007), and BPEL (OASIS, 2007), consider business processes essentially as orchestrators of work, which accomplish this function by means of interactions with external services; it makes little difference if the interaction is directed to a user task or an automatic procedure. This approach, referred to as orchestration-oriented perspective, makes the representation more homogeneous but at the expense of handling human activities as a special case of automatic procedures. If people are involved, they are considered as service providers. Moreover, each interaction that logically takes place between two users, say, A and B, such as A asking B for the approval of a certain request, is mediated by the process and therefore it results in two sequential actual interactions, the first between A and the process and the second between the process and B.

What is missing from the orchestration-oriented perspective is that, in most cases, human work is cooperative and therefore human activities are not performed in isolation but in structured frameworks referred to as conversations (Winograd & Flores, 1986). Conversations are the basis of the language/action perspective (Weigand, 2006), or LAP, which was proposed for the design of information systems and business processes. According to LAP, EISs are mainly tools for coordination.

An example of conversation is the one governing the approval of a purchase requisition (PR). It takes place between two users, denoted as requester and approver: the former is the initiator and the latter is the follower of the conversation. The requester starts the conversation by sending a PR to the approver, who evaluates the PR and sends it back to the requester with three alternative outcomes, that is, "accepted," "rejected," or "to be revised." In the first two cases, the conversation ends, in the third one the conversation continues and the requester may withdraw the PR or submit a revised version. In the latter case, the approver is expected to re-evaluate the revised version and to provide the final outcome ("accepted" or "rejected").

If user tasks are abstracted away, a conversation consists of a number of interactions organized in a control flow specifying their sequence. Interactions are defined in terms of three major attributes: name (embodying the interaction meaning, for example "request," "acceptance," or "rejection"), direction (i.e., initiator-follower or follower-initiator) and the business entity conveyed by the interaction (such as a PR). If the business entities are left unspecified, what remains is the flow that characterizes a particular kind of conversation. This flow, referred to as conversation protocol, is a template that can be specialized by providing the actual types of the business entities exchanged.

Several modeling approaches based on LAP have been proposed (a short survey is given in the next section); however, they mainly focus on the nature of the underlying interactions and do not provide an adequate solution to the integration of conversations and business processes. This integration is a major purpose of this chapter, which proposes a notation called POBPN (People-Oriented Business Process Notation) and a perspective referred to as conversation-oriented perspective.

In POBPN, the top-level representation of a business process clearly separates the contribution of the users involved (in terms of their roles) from that of the automatic activities. The roles participating in the process appear as building blocks and their refinement (in second-level models) is given as a combination of the conversations they are involved in. Such conversations are actualizations of standard conversation protocols obtained by providing the actual types of the business entities exchanged during the interactions. These types come from an information model that complements the process model: this way the behavioral aspects embodied in a business process are integrated with the informational aspects provided by the companion information model. The automatic activities are meant to support the conversations for which the process itself plays the initiator role or the follower one; in the top-level representation of a business process, they are represented by a specific building block, called System.

The RAD approach (Ould, 2005) is based on interacting roles as well, but these roles encompass tasks and control flow activities, while, in POBPN, roles are based on conversations. An extension of RAD towards LAP has been proposed (Beeson & Green, 2003): the basic suggestion is to introduce a middle-level construct in roles, with the purpose of grouping the tasks that are logically involved in a conversation.

This chapter is organized as follows. Section 2 discusses the major limitations of the orchestration-oriented perspective and reports on current research on conversations. Section 3 introduces conversation protocols, whereas sections 4 and 5 illustrate the proposed notation, POBPN, with the help of an example. Section 6 focuses on the differences between the conversation-oriented perspective and the orchestration-oriented one. Section 7 presents the conclusion and the future work.

BACKGROUND

Business processes can be addressed with different orchestration-oriented notations, such as BPMN (Object Management Group, 2008) and UML activity diagrams (Object Management Group, 2007); however, they all have a number of features in common, as follows. They place great emphasis on the control flow of business processes, under the pressure of research on workflow patterns (van der Aalst, ter Hofstede, Kiepuszewski, & Barros, 2003); in contrast, they overlook the information flow (although information items can be included for documentation purposes) and tend to incorporate user tasks as execution steps in the process structures.

In particular, BPMN provides building blocks to represent the actual user tasks. Such building blocks can be placed in swim lanes associated with the roles needed; from an operational point of view, they enable the process to activate a user task, by sending it input information along with the indication of the actual performer(s) required, and then to wait for output information, which notifies the completion of the user task.

This approach, being an attempt at incorporating user tasks in the process structure, does not cope with all the situations taking place in practical applications. It only covers one interaction pattern between a process and a user task, that is, the one in which the user task receives one input message (on its activation) and delivers one output message (on its completion); this pattern is referred to as (1, 1). There are three more task interaction patterns, as follows.

Pattern (1, *) indicates that the task sends a number of intermediate output messages before the completion one. These additional output messages signify that the task has produced information items requiring immediate attention. For example, task "reviewPapers" is started on the arrival of a folder of papers to be reviewed and allows the reviewer to release the reviews one by one.

Pattern (*, 1) indicates that the task may receive additional input messages, after its activation. For example, task "assignPapers" is activated with an initial group of papers and then it may receive additional papers, before its completion.

The fourth pattern (*, *) denotes both a flow of input messages and a flow of output ones. For example, task "evaluatePapers" receives a flow of reviews and provides a flow of papers evaluated, each of which will trigger an immediate notification to its author.

To overcome the above-mentioned limitations, the process, instead of incorporating the user tasks in its control flow, should emphasize the underlying interactions taking place with them.

The notion of interaction is important because it leads to a clear separation between processes and user tasks; however, interactions are part of larger structures encompassing all those exchanged between two parties for a common purpose. At this point, the notion of conversation comes into play.

Winograd and Flores (1986) introduced the term "conversation for action" to indicate the kind of conversation aimed at producing an effect on the real world through the cooperation of two parties. Taking advantage of the theory of speech acts (Austin, 1976), which studies how people act through language, they proposed a novel perspective, referred to as language/action perspective (LAP), for the design of information systems and business processes. According to LAP (Weigand, 2006), information systems are mainly tools for coordination. Conversations may be carried out for different purposes: Winograd (1987) mentions conversations for clarification, for possibilities and for orientation in addition to conversations for action.

Several modeling approaches based on LAP have been proposed, among which stand out Action Workflow, DEMO, and BAT.

In the Action Workflow approach (Medina-Mora, Winograd, Flores, & Flores, 1992), a typical conversation takes place between a requester and a performer and is made up of four major phases, that is, request, commitment, performance, and evaluation, forming the so-called workflow loop. The first two phases establish a commitment between the parties and the last two phases bring the parties to an agreement on the result. The actual workflow might be complicated because negotiations can be made in each phase.

In the DEMO approach (Dietz, 2006), workflow loops are subdivided in three phases, that is, order, execution, and result, and are encapsulated in transactions. Business processes are compositions of roles and transactions, where transactions connect two transactional roles. Transactional roles are compound entities including transactional tasks (i.e., the tasks being part of the transactions the role is involved in) and the

control-flow logic handling their ordering. In the hierarchical structure provided by DEMO, tasks are compared to atoms, transactions to molecules, and business processes to fibers (Dietz, 2003). Transactional roles might not have a one-to-one mapping to organizational roles, because the tasks included in a transactional role might be assigned to different organizational roles: this is needed to support delegation (i.e., the situation in which the actor who receives the order is not the one who delivers the result) but could make the model more difficult to understand.

BAT (Goldkuhl & Lind, 2004) draws upon the ideas of Action Workflow and DEMO and addresses business interactions in an inter-organizational framework. In particular, it analyzes the relationships between a supplier and a customer in a number of situations including single business transactions and frame contracting (with embedded transactions).

Although the above-mentioned LAP approaches yield a deeper understanding of the nature of interactions, they do not provide an operational solution to the integration between business processes and user tasks through conversations. This integration is pursued by the conversation-oriented perspective illustrated in the next sections along with the related notation, POBPN.

CONVERSATION PROTOCOLS

This section illustrates the notion of conversation protocol and shows the notation adopted in POBPN, with the help of a number of examples to be reused in the next sections.

A conversation implies a flow of interactions between the parties, an interaction being the communication of one party's intention to the other party. Intentions can be categorized and identified by specific symbols, as illustrated later on in this section. Examples of intentions are making a request, accepting a request, and providing a reply. An interaction conveys the business entity

Figure 1. Examples of conversation protocols

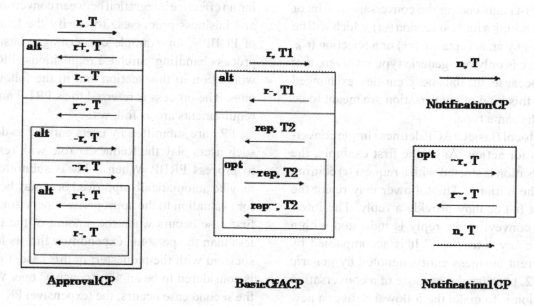

that is the object of the intention. This business entity is referred to as the business content of the interaction.

Conversations can be categorized on the basis of their purpose: for example, there are conversations for approval and conversations for action. If the details of the business content are ignored, all the conversations with the same purpose turn out to have the same interaction flow, and the structure of this flow, called conversation protocol, is the major concern of this section.

A conversation protocol is an abstraction as it is defined independently of the types of the business entities exchanged by the parties; it is a template in which such types are given generic names. When a protocol is actualized, generic types will be replaced with actual types: as will be shown in the next section, an actualized protocol relies on an information model providing the definition of the types of the business entities involved.

State models are often used (Winograd, 1987) to define conversation protocols graphically; POBPN, instead, adopts UML sequence diagrams (Object Management Group, 2007), because they

focus on the essential elements, that is, the interactions, while providing a simple hierarchical structuring mechanism based on fragments. Four examples of protocols are shown in Figure 1.

As a general rule, the lifelines of the two actors involved in the conversation are not shown; however, the initiator is meant to be located on the left side of the diagram and the follower on the right side. The first interaction of a conversation is called initial interaction and the business entity that it conveys is referred to as initial business entity. Timing constraints are not considered so as to keep the examples reasonably simple.

The first protocol in Figure 1 addresses conversations for approval and is called "Approval conversation protocol" (ApprovalCP in short). These conversations start with a request, indicated by symbol "r"; the business content, that is, the entity for which the approval is asked, is denoted by a generic type, such as "T." The follower can accept the request (r+), reject it (r-), or ask for some improvement (r~). The three alternatives are enclosed in a fragment marked with keyword "alt." In the first two cases, the conversation is ended; in the third one, the initiator can then withdraw the request (-r) thus ending the conversation or he or she can submit a revised version (~r), which will be followed by an acceptance (r+) or a rejection (r-).

There is only one generic type involved, that is T, because the business entities exchanged during this kind of conversation are meant to be all of the same type.

Protocol BasicCfACP defines simple conversations for action. As in the first example, the conversation is started with a request (r) coming from the initiator. The follower may reject the request (r-) or may provide a reply. The interaction conveying the reply is indicated with a specific keyword, "rep." It is accompanied by a different business entity, denoted by generic type T2, because the purpose of a conversation for action is to make the follower deliver a new entity as the result of the action caused by the initiator's request. Upon receiving the reply, the initiator may then ask for a clarification (~rep) to be followed by a clarification (rep~) after which the conversation is ended. The sequence of interactions ~rep and rep~ is optional and, therefore, it is enclosed in a fragment marked with keyword "opt".

The protocol of conversations for action can become more complicated (Winograd, 1987), if counter-offers are included.

Protocol NotificationCP consists of one interaction (n), interpreted as a notification (i.e., a simple communication requiring no reply).

Protocol NotificationCP1 ends with a notification, which may be preceded by an optional sequence consisting of a request for clarification (~r) followed by a clarification (r~).

PEOPLE-ORIENTED BUSINESS PROCESSES

As mentioned in the introduction, the conversation-oriented perspective places great emphasis on the participation of users in business processes,

and the notation proposed, POBPN, aims at providing an effective integration between conversations and business processes. To clarify the features of POBPN, an example concerning a business process handling purchase requisitions (PRs) is worked on in this section and in the following ones. The process is referred to as PRBP and its requirements are as follows.

PRs are submitted by users entitled to do so; such users play the Requester role with respect to process PRBP. When a PR is submitted, it may be automatically approved or it may be sent for evaluation to the appropriate supervisor. The first case occurs when the amount of the PR is less than the personal expenditure threshold associated with the requester; in this case, the PR is considered to be an "inexpensive" one. When the second case occurs, the (expensive) PR is directed to the requester's boss (who becomes the supervisor involved). The requester is informed of the result (acceptance or rejection). The supervisor may also ask for some improvement and the requester may provide a revised version of the PR or may withdraw it.

The PRs approved are sent to the purchasing department where they are handled by a number of equivalent buyers. Buyers are assumed to pick pending PRs from a common queue and to include them in purchase orders. In case a buyer has some doubts, he or she can ask the PR requester to make the necessary clarification; when a buyer has included the PR in a purchase order, he or she sends a confirmation to the PR requester.

Sometimes supervisors may ask one or more reviewers to provide third-party reviews of PRs considered to be critical. How this is done can be subjected to different rules: in this case study, the conversation related to a single review is expected to conform to conversation protocol BasicCfACP shown in Figure 1. In addition, if a supervisor has started a review conversation for a certain PR, he or she must wait for its conclusion before starting a new review conversation or taking the final decision, for the same PR.

The analysis of the requirements above leads to the discovery that five roles are involved. Four of them are user roles: Requester, Supervisor, Reviewer, and Buyer. The fifth role involved, the System role, is responsible for all the activities to be performed automatically (such as the approval of inexpensive PRs). These roles take part in several conversations, as follows. For the approval of a PR, its requester interacts with either his/her supervisor or the System; to get support for a critical PR, a supervisor may interact with a number of reviewers; when processing a PR, a buyer interacts with the PR requester (at least to notify him/her that the PR has been included in a purchase order). In addition, since approved PRs need to be processed by the purchasing department, notifications are sent by the System to the buyers.

The above-mentioned four conversations fit the patterns presented in the previous section; however, it is necessary to indicate which business entities are involved. An information model

is then needed, which defines the business entity types along with their most relevant attributes and relationships. This information model is the companion of the process model for two major reasons: firstly, the actualization of conversation protocols into actual conversation types is carried out by replacing the generic types used in the protocols with the actual types provided in the information model. Secondly, in the process model there are a number of data-driven aspects, such as the selection of a conversation follower (to be illustrated later on in this section), and they can be adequately expressed only if an information model is provided.

The companion information model for process PRBP is shown in Figure 2 as a UML class model (Object Management Group, 2007). Only the major items are considered, for the sake of simplicity.

Users are represented by classes marked with stereotype <<role>>. Such classes are not meant to be the actual ones, because the decision on

Figure 2. The companion information model of process PRBP

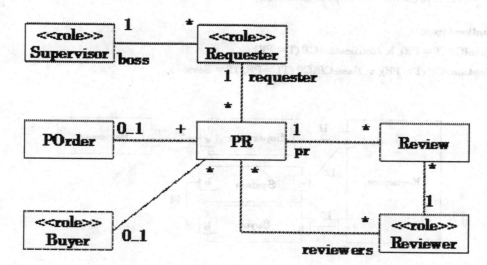

Attributes

PR: float amount. Requester: float threshold.

how to represent users in the information system is postponed to the software development phase; they can be considered as interfaces to the actual classes.

The relationship between role Requester and role Supervisor is a consequence of the requirement that an expensive PR has to be approved by the requester's boss who acts as the supervisor for the PR. Associative attribute "boss" enables the navigation from a requester entity to the corresponding supervisor entity.

A PR is related to one requester entity (which can be reached through associative attribute requester) and possibly to one buyer entity (only in case the PR has been approved). A PR may also be linked to one purchase order (in case it has been approved), to a number of reviewers, as well as to a number of reviews. Purchase Orders are represented by class POrder.

A review is linked to the reviewer entity representing the reviewer who has provided it. Associative attribute "pr" provides the PR associated with a given review.

Relationships PR-Review and PR-Reviewer are both needed in that a reviewer could refuse to provide the review he or she has been asked for. Associative attribute "reviewers" provides the list of Reviewer entities associated with a given PR.

Two relevant attributes are also shown in Figure 2, because they are mentioned in the requirements of PRPB: they are the amount attribute in PR entities and the threshold (for expenditure) attribute in Requester entities.

On the basis of the analysis made so far, the model of process PRBP can be worked out. Its top-level portion is presented in Figure 3 and consists of three parts: the process diagram, the section defining conversation types and the one (Links) showing how the followers of the conversations will be determined.

The approach adopted in POBPN is to represent participating roles as the top-level building blocks (referred to as role participations or simply participations) of the process diagram and to show the conversations involved as ports, depicted as

Figure 3. The top-level representation of process PRBP

Conversation types:

a: ApprovalCP (T = PR); b: NotificationCP (T = PR);

c: Notification1CP (T = PR); v: BasicCfACP (T1 = PR, T2 = Review);

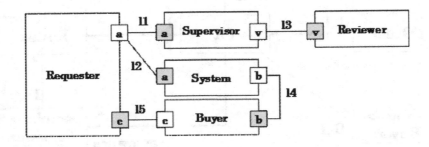

Links:

l1 (PR pr): [pr.amount > pr.requester.threshold] pr.requester.boss.

l2 (PR pr): [pr.amount <= pr.requester.threshold].

l3 (PR pr): pr.reviewers.last(). l5: (PR pr): pr.requester.

small squares on the participation icons. Each conversation gives rise to two ports, one in the initiator role (referred to as initiator port) and the other in the follower role (follower port). Such ports are given identical names but different colors; initiator ports are white, while follower ones are grey. Ports are connected through labeled links, whose details are shown in the Links section. The port names are names of conversation types.

Section "Conversation types" declares conversation type "a" to be based on conversation protocol ApprovalCP with generic type T replaced with entity type PR, while conversation types "b," "c," and "v" are actualizations of protocols NotificationCP, Notification1CP and BasicCfACP, respectively.

Section "Links" contains a number of link definitions, whose purpose is to show how the followers of the corresponding conversations are determined.

A link definition consists of four elements: name, formal parameter, guard (included between square brackets), and follower clause. The formal parameter refers to the initial business entity, that is, the entity conveyed by the initial interaction. In all the definitions shown, the initial business entity is a purchase requisition (whose type is PR) and the formal parameter introduces the name, that is, pr, used (in the guard and in the follower clause of the link definitions) to refer to this entity.

A conversation of type "a" is initiated by a requester and may be followed by a supervisor or by the System. There are two links in competition, l1 and l2, because they have the initiator port in common: the choice is made on the basis of their guards.

The guard of l1, "pr.amount > pr.requester. threshold," consist of two terms, "pr.amount" and "pr.requester.threshold." The evaluation of the first term returns the amount of the current PR, and the evaluation of the second one gives the personal expenditure threshold of the PR

requester: if the guard is true, the follower will be the requester's boss.

In most cases, the follower of a conversation is represented by a business entity related, through a certain path of associations, to the initial business entity: then, the follower clause is needed and it consists of a navigational expression indicating how to reach the follower business entity from the initial one. Two associative attributes are involved in the follower clause of l1, that is, requester and boss: in the information model shown in Figure 2, they determine a path from a PR to a Supervisor entity.

In the definition of link l2, the follower clause is missing, because the follower role is System: when the guard of l2 is true, the conversation is followed by automatic activities and no supervisor is involved.

The definition of link l4 is missing because both the guard and the follower clause are not needed. In general, when the follower clause is missing and the follower role is a user role, such as Buyer in link l4, the assignment of a particular follower will take place at run-time; it is up to the members of the role to decide which of them will follow a new conversation, as it happens with buyers who autonomously pick pending PRs from a common pool. In general, the selection of the performer is a critical issue and several patterns have been proposed (Russell, van der Aalst, ter Hofstede, & Edmond, 2005).

The follower clause in link l3 specifies that the reviewer to be involved is the last added to the collection of reviewers associated with the PR that started the conversation. Link l5 indicates that the follower is the requester of the current PR.

Process diagrams are mainly architectural models, as they show the roles participating in the process and the conversations that may take place between them. Participation building blocks can be refined into second-level models, called participation models, and the next section is dedicated to their illustration.

PARTICIPATION MODELS

Participation models define the involvement of the users (identified by their roles) or the contribution of the System, in the business process being considered. Those related to users are called user participation models and fulfill two major aims: firstly, by looking at them, users get an insight into the overall sequence of interactions they will be involved in; secondly, they are the basis of the implementation of the actual user tasks.

The System participation model (there is at most one in a business process) is mainly meant to handle the automatic activities.

Both types of models are described in this section and the examples given refer to process PRBP: its user participation models are shown in Figure 4.

Basically, user participation models are combinations of conversations. For this reason, their structure is like the one of conversation protocols with interactions replaced by references to conversation types. Such references are placed in constructs similar to the "InteractionUse" items available in UML sequence diagrams (Object Management Group, 2007); however, in POBPN they are called "ConversationUse" items, since their meaning is different. In these items, the conversation type name appears in a small rectangle at the upper left corner: the rectangle is white or grey depending on whether

the current role is the initiator or the follower, respectively.

The Reviewer participation model is based only on conversation "v," and reviewers are followers of such conversations.

The Buyer participation model is a simple sequence of conversations "b" and "c"; buyers are followers of conversations "b" and initiators of conversations "c."

The Requester participation model is based on conversation "a," which, if it ends successfully (i.e., if it ends with r+), is followed by conversation "c." In the optional fragment, operator opt is followed by an informal expression describing when conversation "c" is carried out.

An important feature of user participation models is the ability of structuring conversations hierarchically, as shown in the Supervisor participation model. According to the PRBP requirements presented in the previous section, a supervisor, during conversation "a," and precisely after receiving a new PR or a revised one, may carry out a number of sequential conversations "v." What is needed is the possibility of including a number of conversations "v" into a conversation "a." The original conversations are not modified, but they are combined so as to define the overall behavior of the role. POBPN supports the nesting of ConversationUse items, as follows. ConversationUse items are not black boxes, but they can

Figure 4. The user participation models in process PRBP

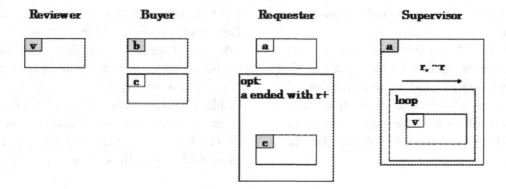

Figure 5. The System participation model in process PRBP

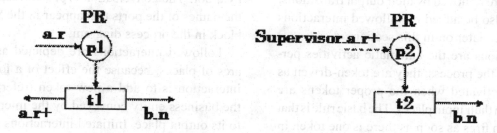

include one or more extensions. An extension is a partition made up of two parts: the first part shows the interaction(s) preceding the extension (referred to as extension points), and the second part contains the conversations (represented by their ConversationUse items) to be carried out before resuming the enclosing conversation. If the enclosed conversations are subjected to constraints, they are placed in appropriate fragments. The Supervisor participation model extends conversation "a": the extension points are interactions "r" or "~r" (referring to the receipt of a new PR or of a revised one, respectively), which are followed by a loop fragment including conversation "v." The loop operator introduces a sequence (possibly empty) of conversations "v."

The System participation model addresses those conversations for which the process itself plays the initiator role or the follower one. In PRBP there are two such conversations: the process is the follower of conversations "a" for inexpensive PRs and the initiator of conversations "b." The related interactions must be dealt with by means of automatic activities and, moreover, control-flow logic is needed to enforce ordering constraints between the activities.

The notation used in System participation models is different from the one adopted in user participation models and follows an orchestration-oriented perspective.

The orchestration-oriented notation used in POBPN is an extension of colored Petri nets (Kristensen, Christensen, & Jensen, 1998) and

is called "interaction nets" to emphasize that its major purpose is to handle interactions, on which orchestrations are based.

This article does not provide a formal definition of interaction nets; instead, it provides two examples, the first of which, shown in Figure 5, defines the System participation model in process PRBP. The second example is given in the next section.

Interaction nets are made up of places, transitions, arcs and interaction symbols.

Places are containers of tokens, which refer to business entities, such as PRs or reviews. They have a name and a label (or place type): the former is written in the circle representing the place and the latter outside the circle and close to it. The label is the name of the type of the business entities that are referred to by the tokens contained in the place. The business entity types are those defined in the companion information model of the process being considered; the one related to process PRBP is shown in Figure 2. This solution eliminates the need for complex data patterns (Russell, ter Hofstede, Edmond, & van der Aalst, 2005) as all the data needed are associated with the tokens: the information flow is integrated with the control flow.

Places may have input arcs and output ones: the input arcs of a place come from its input transitions and the output ones are directed to its output transitions. Transitions have input arcs and output ones, as well: the input arcs of a transition come from its input places and the output ones are directed to its output places.

Tokens are added to places by their input transitions and are removed by their output transitions; they can also be added by followed interactions as described later on in this section.

Transitions are the automatic activities performed by the process; they are token-driven as they are activated when the proper tokens are available in their input places. The basic rule is that a transition fires as soon as there is one token in each of its input places. When it fires, a transition takes the input tokens (i.e., it removes the activating tokens from the corresponding input places), performs an action (which can operate on the business entities referred to by the input tokens), and delivers the appropriate (output) tokens to its output places. When there is a correspondence between the types of the input places and those of the output places, tokens are simply moved from the input places to the output ones: this behavior is referred to as automatic propagation rule. In the other cases, the output tokens must be generated in the action.

The behavior of transitions can be complemented by a textual description that is made up of two sections, that is, the selection rule (introduced by keyword "s") and the action (introduced by keyword "a"). These sections may include operational code, but the examples shown only include informal descriptions, for the sake of simplicity.

If a transition is provided with a suitable selection rule, it can take a variable number of tokens from its input places and the selection can be based on the contents of the business entities linked to the tokens. If the selection rule is omitted, the basic rule is applied.

Interaction symbols are depicted as labeled arcs, which may be either input arcs of places or output arcs of transitions. They represent ordinary interactions or monitored ones.

Ordinary interactions are those in which the process is directly involved and may be divided into followed interactions and initiated ones. Their labels, such as "a.r," consist of the name of a con-

versation type and an interaction name separated by a dot. The conversation types correspond to the names of the ports that appear in the System block in the process diagram.

Followed interactions are depicted as input arcs of places, because the effect of a followed interaction is to add a new token (referring to the business entity conveyed by the interaction) to its output place. Initiated interactions are depicted as output arcs of transitions: when a token flows along such an arc (this occurs by virtue of the automatic propagation rule or by an explicit command issued in the input transition) the corresponding interaction is started and the follower is determined on the basis of the links defined in the top-level process model.

Ordinary interactions appear in the left part of Figure 5. When an inexpensive PR is submitted by a requester, interaction "a.r" is performed and its effect is to add a token (referring to the PR) to place p1 whose type, PR, coincides with the type of the incoming business entity. Transition t1 is then triggered and its action consists in performing two interactions, "a.r+" and "b.n." On the basis of the automatic propagation rule, the business entity taken from place p1 is sent through output interactions "a.r+" and "b.n," without the need of writing any code in the action of t1. The recipient of interaction "a.r+" is the one that started conversation "a," whereas the recipient of interaction "b.n" is determined by link l4 shown in Figure 3, because this interaction is the initial one of a conversation "b."

Monitored interactions are those interactions the process has to be aware of so as to take appropriate actions, although it is not their follower. They are shown dashed and their labels include the initiator role before the conversation type name and the interaction name. One such interaction appears in the right part of Figure 5: its purpose is to enable the activation of conversation "b" when conversation "a" for an expensive PR ends successfully. Conversations "a" for expensive PRs are handled by supervisors, but they are not

Figure 6. The conversation-oriented interaction flow for the scenario proposed

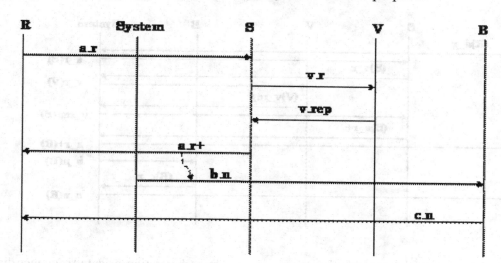

supposed to decide what has to be done after the successful approvals of PRs. It is up to the process to trigger the subsequent processing of approved PRs; therefore, it must be informed of the successful conclusion of a conversation "a" so as to start a conversation "b" with the buyers—these two conversations operate on the same PR.

Monitored interactions can only provide tokens to the process in that they are used to trigger complementary behavior.

COMPARISON OF NOTATIONS

The aim of this section is to provide a comparison between the notations used in the conversation-oriented perspective and in the orchestration-oriented one.

In the former approach, the emphasis is placed on the conversations between users and on how they are organized in participations: the explicit contribution of the process is restricted to the definition of the automatic activities, as shown in Figure 5 for process PRBP.

In the orchestration-oriented perspective, processes are thought of as explicit orchestrators of all the activities, both the automatic ones and

the user tasks. Conversations are not a first-class notion of the approach; therefore, the process has to make up for the lack of conversation-oriented constructs by directly handling the corresponding flow of interactions.

Conversation-oriented notations provide a higher-level representation than orchestration-oriented ones and the difference between them can be easily recognized on the basis of a simple scenario, as follows. The scenario refers to a particular occurrence of process PRBP involving four users: requester R, his/her supervisor S, reviewer V and buyer B. Requester R submits an expensive PR, which is sent to S for evaluation. S asks the support of V and then approves the PR. Buyer B receives the PR from the process and then notifies R of its inclusion in a purchase order.

On the basis of the scenario proposed, process PRBP shown in Figure 3 gives rise to a number of interactions that are graphically represented in the sequence diagram presented in Figure 6. The interaction flow develops as follows. When requester R submits an expensive PR, the process starts a conversation between R and S in conformity to link 11, and the initial interaction takes place. Its label, "a.r," is the name of a conversational interaction, as the interaction name is

Figure 7. The orchestration-oriented interaction flow for the scenario proposed

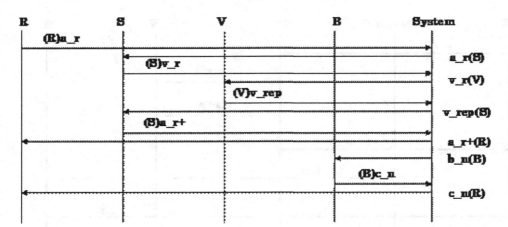

preceded by the name of the conversation type the interaction belongs to.

In the participation model of the supervisor shown in Figure 4, interaction "a.r" is an extension point that can be followed by a number of conversations "v" with reviewers. In the scenario above, supervisor S asks reviewer V to provide a review of the PR and this leads to the pairs of interactions "v.r" and "v.rep" shown in the sequence diagram. Then the PR is approved by supervisor S resulting in interaction "a.r+." This interaction is a monitored one as indicated in the System participation model shown in Figure 5, and therefore it triggers interaction "b.n" between the System and buyer B. The dashed arc connecting interaction "a.r+" and interaction "b.n" emphasizes that "a.r+" is a monitored interaction and "b.n" is a consequence. Buyer B is supposed not to need any additional clarification from the requester and therefore the scenario ends in notification "c.n" sent by B to requester R.

With an interaction-oriented notation, the sequence diagram for the same scenario becomes more complicated, because interactions between users (from an initiator to a follower) are mapped to pairs of sequential interactions involving the process: the first interaction takes place between the initiator and the process, the second one between the process and the follower.

The orchestration-oriented sequence diagram related to the scenario proposed is shown in Figure 7.

For example, interaction "a.r" from requester R to supervisor S is mapped to interaction "(R) a_r" from R to the process, and to interaction "a_r (S)" from the process to S. The name of the interaction is obtained from that of the corresponding conversational interaction by replacing the dot operator with character "_". In addition, in a user-process interaction, the initiator is indicated between parentheses before the interaction name, whereas, in a process-user interaction, the follower is indicated between parentheses after the interaction name. The labels of the process-user interactions are shown on the right of the System lifeline, while those of the user-process interactions are shown above the corresponding lines.

The notion of monitored interaction is not needed, as the process is an explicit orchestrator of all the interactions.

A business process defined with an interaction-oriented notation corresponds to a POBPN process that only includes the System participation model, as all the interactions between users are mapped to pairs of interactions involving the process. As an example, the orchestration-oriented version of process PRBP is shown in Figure 8. It is the second example based on the

Figure 8. The orchestration-oriented model of process PRBP

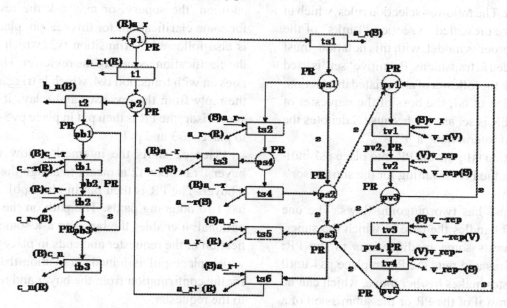

ts1: s: p1.amount > p1.requester.threshold; a: set p1.requester.boss as S.

t1: s: p1.amount <= p1.requester.threshold; a: set p1.requester as R.

tv1: a: set pv1.reviewers.last() as V.

tv2: a: set pv2.requester.boss as S.

interaction nets introduced in the previous section, and includes the description of a number of transitions.

To reduce the complexity of the model, a number of notational simplifications have been introduced, as follows.

If there are two transitions in series (Murata, 1989), the intermediate place (together with its input arc and its output one) can be replaced with a link that directly connects the two transitions and is labeled with the name and type of the place eliminated. Examples of such links are the one connecting transitions tb1 and tb2 and the one connecting tv1 and tv2.

If a place receives tokens only from a followed interaction and it is connected only to one transition, then it can be eliminated and the followed interaction can be directly connected to the transition: this simplification is carried out with several transitions, for example, tb1 and tb2.

The third kind of simplification makes use of ε-arcs: an ε-arc links two places of the same type and its effect is that the tokens included in the source place also belong to the destination place and can trigger its output transitions (the vice versa does not hold); if two places, say p1 and p2, are the source and the destination, respectively, of an ε-arc, p1 is said to be joined to p2.

The interaction labels shown in Figure 8 follow the same convention adopted in Figure 7.

The meaning of the model shown in Figure 8 is as follows. Submitted PRs enter place p1 and then trigger either transition ts1 or transition t1 depending on which selection rule is satisfied. The incoming PR is associated with the input token taken from place p1 and the selection rules and the actions of transitions ts1 and t1 use the place name (i.e., p1) to refer to this PR.

Transition ts1 fires in case of an expensive PR, as shown in its selection rule: its action consists in initiating interaction "a_r (S)" with the proper supervisor. The follower-selection rules, which in POBPN are presented in section "Links" of the top-level process model, with this notation, must be embedded in transitions. Primitive "set" is used to establish the follower of an initiated interaction. In the action of ts1, the boss of the requester of the input PR is set as "S", because S denotes the follower of interaction "a_r".

Transition ts1 puts the PR into place ps1 indicating that the PR is waiting for the supervisor's move.

Place ps1 has two outgoing flows. The one on the left handles the case in which the supervisor requests some modifications to the PR: then ts2 fires and puts the PR in place ps4 until the requester makes his/her move, which can be the withdrawal of the PR or the submission of a revised version: these moves cause ts3 or ts4 to fire, respectively. The firing of ts4 puts the PR in place ps2, where the left path ends. The left path is optional, because ps1 is joined to ps2 and ps2 is joined to both ps3 and pv1. Therefore the supervisor may immediately approve or reject the PR (from place ps3) or ask for external support (from place pv1). If the supervisor accepts or rejects the PR, ts6 or ts5 will fire, respectively; the firing of ts6 puts the PR in place p2 where the interaction flow involving the buyer starts.

The path starting at place pv1 handles the interactions with the reviewers. Transition tv1 fires if the supervisor requests a reviewer's support and initiates interaction "v_r" with the reviewer; the reviewer is the one represented by the last reviewer entity added to the PR, as shown in the action of tv1. The PR is then put in the intermediate place included in the link between transition tv1 and transition tv2 (connected in series) and waits for the arrival of the corresponding review. When this happens, tv2 fires: it relays the review to the supervisor (i.e., the boss of the PR requester, as indicated in the action) and puts the PR in place pv3. Place pv3 is joined to place ps3 and place pv1, as the supervisor, at this point, may issue

the final decision or ask for another review. In addition, the supervisor may ask the reviewer for some clarification: for this reason, place pv3 is also followed by transition tv3, which relays the clarification request to the reviewer. The path goes on with transition tv4, which is triggered by the reply from the reviewer and relays it to the supervisor; the PR is then put in place pv5 joined to places ps3 and pv1.

Place p2 starts the interaction flow with a buyer. Transition t2 is meant to assign the PR to a buyer. The PR is then put in place pb1, which has two outgoing paths. The path on the left is optional: it enables the buyer to ask some clarification of the requester and ends in place pb3 to which place pb1 is joined. Transition tb3 waits for the confirmation from the buyer and relays it to the requester.

CONCLUSION

This article has proposed a notation, POBPN, and a conversation-oriented perspective to effectively integrate conversations and business processes in an intra-organizational context. The involvement of users in business processes is clearly shown by means of participation building blocks appearing in the top-level representation of a business process. Such participation items can be refined into second-level models which are basically combinations of conversation models.

An example has been presented in order to stress the differences between the orchestration-oriented perspective (followed by most of current notations and languages) and the conversation-oriented one. The former is a centralized approach in which all the interactions are explicitly mediated by the process. If a user looks at a process description, he or she cannot immediately identify the interactions he or she will be involved in, as all user activities are intermingled. In the approach proposed, instead, conversation models come first (from the actualization of standard conversation protocols) and the process model is built upon them. The explicit contribution of the process is restricted to those conversations for which the process itself plays the initiator role or the follower one.

Current work is going on in two directions. One line of research is concerned with the inclusion of inter-organizational conversations. For this reason, the similarities between conversation protocols and B2B collaborations or choreographies need to be thoroughly analyzed.

The other line of research is more pragmatic and addresses the automatic mapping of POBPN models to orchestration-oriented ones; the purpose is to take advantage of current technology while preserving the conceptual strength of the conversation-oriented perspective.

REFERENCES

Austin, J. L. (1976). *How to do things with words.* Oxford, UK: Oxford University Press.

Beeson, I., & Green, S. (2003, April 9-11). *Using a language action framework to extend organizational process modelling.* Paper presented at the UK Academy for Information Systems Conference, University of Warwick.

Dietz, J. L. G. (2003). The atoms, molecules and fibers of organizations. *Data & Knowledge Engineering, 47*(3), 301–325. doi:10.1016/S0169-023X(03)00062-4

Dietz, J. L. G. (2006). The deep structure of business processes. *Communications of the ACM, 49*(5), 59–64. doi:10.1145/1125944.1125976

Dumas, M., van der Aalst, W. M. P., & ter Hofstede, A. H. M. (2005). *Process-aware information systems: Bridging people and software through process technology.* New York: John Wiley & Sons.

Goldkuhl, G., & Lind, M. (2004). The generics of business interaction - emphasizing dynamic features through the BAT model. In M. Aakhus & M. Lind (Eds.), *Proceedings of the 9th Conference on the Language-Action Perspective on Communication Modelling (LAP 2004)* (pp. 1-26). New Brunswick, NJ: Rutgers University.

Kristensen, L. M., Christensen, S., & Jensen, K. (1998). The practitioner's guide to coloured Petri nets. *International Journal on Software Tools for Technology Transfer, 2,* 98–132. doi:10.1007/s100090050021

Medina-Mora, R., Winograd, T., Flores, R., & Flores, F. (1992, November 1-4). The action workflow approach to workflow management technology. In J. Turner & R. Kraut (Eds.), *Proceedings of the 1992 ACM Conference on Computer Supported Cooperative Work* (pp. 281-288). Toronto, Canada: ACM Publishing.

Murata, T. (1989). Petri nets: Properties, analysis and applications. *Proceedings of the IEEE, 77*(4), 514–580. doi:10.1109/5.24143

OASIS. (2007). *Web services business process execution language, V.2.0.* Retrieved September 29, 2008, from http://docs.oasis-open.org/wsbpel/2.0/OS/wsbpel-v2.0-OS.html

Object Management Group. (2007). *Unified modeling language: Superstructure, V.2.1.1.* Retrieved September 29, 2008, from http://www.omg.org/docs/formal/07-02-03.pdf

Object Management Group. (2008). *Business process modeling notation, V.1.1.* Retrieved September 29, 2008, from http://www.bpmn.org

Ould, M. (2005). *Business process management: A rigorous approach.* Swindon, UK: The British Computer Society.

Russell, N., ter Hofstede, A. H. M., Edmond, D., & van der Aalst, W. M. P. (2005). Workflow data patterns: Identification, representation and tool support. In L. Delcambre (Ed.), Lecture Notes in Computer Science, 3716 (pp. 353-368). Berlin, Germany: Springer.

Russell, N., van der Aalst, W. M. P., ter Hofstede, A. H. M., & Edmond, D. (2005). Workflow resource patterns: Identification, representation and tool support. In O. Pastor & J. Falcão e Cunha (Eds.), Lecture Notes in Computer Science, 3520 (pp. 216-232). Berlin, Germany: Springer.

van der Aalst, W. M. P., ter Hofstede, A. H. M., Kiepuszewski, B., & Barros, A. P. (2003). Workflow patterns. Distributed and Parallel Databases, 14, 5–51. doi:10.1023/A:1022883727209

Weigand, H. (2006). Two decades of the language-action perspective: Introduction. Communications of the ACM, 49(5), 44–46. doi:10.1145/1125944.1125973

Winograd, T. (1987). A language/action perspective on the design of cooperative work. Human-Computer Interaction, 3, 3–30. doi:10.1207/s15327051hci0301_2

Winograd, T., & Flores, F. (1986). Understanding computers and cognition. Norwood, NJ: Ablex Publishing Corporation.

Workflow Management Coalition. (2007). XML process definition language, V.2.1. Retrieved September 29, 2008, from http://www.wfmc.org

This work was previously published in The International Journal of Enterprise Information Systems 5(4), edited by A. Gunasekaran, copyright 2009 by IGI Publishing (an imprint of IGI Global).

Chapter 4
Doing Business on the Globalised Networked Economy:
Technology and Business Challenges for Accounting Information Systems

Adamantios Koumpis
ALTEC S.A., Greece

Nikos Protogeros
University of Macedonia, Greece

ABSTRACT

In this chapter the authors present a set of challenges that are to be faced by accounting information systems. More specifically, these include the support of interoperable accounting processes, for virtual and networked enterprises and for open-book accounting as well as the creation of novel interface metaphors that will automate and increase the usability of accounting information systems, and last but not least the provision of integrated e-accounting platforms.

INTRODUCTION

As the modern economy depends more and more on information and communication technologies (ICTs), interest in the economic impacts of these technologies is growing. The combination of economic fundamentals triggered a lively public debate on the underlying causes and consequences. The introduction of the World Wide Web and browsers fuelled the growth of the Internet – reaching millions of users worldwide. Paralleling the growth in the number of users was a growth in the number of enterprises wishing to serve this new "online"

population. New ideas and new business models were introduced and investors were happy to pour money into them irrespective of actual profit figures. Many of the new firms went public and prices in the high tech segments of the stock markets soared. Moreover, companies related to Internet infrastructure, computers and software became all the more important.

According to (Coman and Diaconu, 2006) and (Diaconu, 2008) globalization is a historical process, which has been created as a need of improving the resource allocation and to develop bigger markets for the global economy. Ideas about going global can be found in Adam Smith's and David Ricardo's

DOI: 10.4018/978-1-60566-856-7.ch004

works, going through Marx vision about the phenomena until our ages. We can consider it as one of the biggest social processes which the humanity has facing since ever. That's why its impact in the global economy is huge and the accounting sector which is playing a vital role in the information process of the society is very important. That is why one of the main international accounting processes on the actual period is the harmonization of the national accounting systems. The harmonization process is influenced by several factors like culture, politics, economy and also sociological behaviors.

Furthermore, in an increasingly competitive, knowledge-based economy, intangible assets, such as brand awareness, innovation, and employee productivity, have become the key determinants of corporate success. And given that the investments companies make to build those intangible assets - such things as advertising, employee training, and R&D - are flushed through the income statement, balance sheets are increasingly a poor reflection of the value of companies' businesses. And in contrast to the traditional accounting system that is focused on isolated transactions and historical costs, to determine the future value of a company, one should not only look at past history, but need to employ new measures to project forward. In our paper we present some ideas that aim to leverage research efforts in the area of Accounting Information Systems. We position our ideas with respect to ongoing developments in the research fields of accounting, business and computing. The increase of the corporate knowledge capital and the sustainable support of the agility potential of companies is not only a matter of how much intelligence a company shall exhibit in organizing its business related activities but also in the way it shall exploit its accounting infrastructure to respond to existing challenges of the globalised and networked economy.

THE MARKET FOR ACCOUNTING SOFTWARE

An accounting information system (AIS) is the system of records a business keeps to maintain its accounting system. This includes the purchase, sales, and other financial processes of the business. The purpose of an AIS, as it has been historically defined through various commercial system implementations, is to accumulate data and provide decision makers (investors, creditors, and managers) with information to make decision. While this was previously a paper-based process, most modern businesses now use accounting software.

In an Electronic Financial Accounting system, the steps in the accounting cycle are dependent upon the system itself, which in turn are developed by programmers. For example, some systems allow direct journal posting to the various ledgers and others do not. Accounting Information Systems provide efficient delivery of information needed to perform necessary accounting work and to assist in delivery of accurate and informative data to users, especially those who are not familiar with the accounting and financial reporting areas itself. Furthermore, accounting software is typically composed of various modules, different sections dealing with particular areas of accounting. Among the most common are:

Core Modules

- **Accounts receivable:** where the company enters money received
- **Accounts payable:** where the company enters its bills and pays money it owes
- **General ledger:** the company's "books"
- **Billing:** where the company produces invoices to clients/customers
- **Stock/Inventory:** where the company keeps control of its inventory
- **Purchase Order:** where the company orders inventory

- **Sales Order:** where the company records customer orders for the supply of inventory

Non Core Modules

- **Debt Collection:** where the company tracks attempts to collect overdue bills (sometimes part of accounts receivable)
- **Electronic payment processing**
- **Expense:** where employee business-related expenses are entered
- **Inquiries:** where the company looks up information on screen without any edits or additions
- **Payroll:** where the company tracks salary, wages, and related taxes
- **Reports:** where the company prints out data
- **Timesheet:** where professionals (such as attorneys and consultants) record time worked so that it can be billed to clients
- **Purchase Requisition:** where requests for purchase orders are made, approved and tracked

Of course, different vendors use different names for these modules but it all comes around the same modules as mentioned above. Most midmarket and larger applications are sold exclusively through resellers, developers and consultants. Those organizations generally pass on a license fee to the software vendor and then charge the client for installation, customization and support services. Clients can normally count on paying roughly 50-200% of the price of the software in implementation and consulting fees. Other organizations sell to, consult with and support clients directly, eliminating the reseller.

The most complex and expensive business accounting software is frequently part of an extensive suite of software often known as Enterprise resource planning or ERP software. These applications typically have a very long implementation period, often greater than six months. In many cases, these applications are simply a set of functions which require significant integration, configuration and customisation to even begin to resemble an accounting system.

The advantage of a high-end solution is that these systems are designed to support individual company specific processes, as they are highly customisable and can be tailored to exact business requirements. This usually comes at a significant cost in terms of money and implementation time.

As technology improves, software vendors have been able to offer increasingly advanced software at lower prices. This software is suitable for companies at multiple stages of growth. Many of the features of mid market and high-end software (including advanced customization and extremely scalable databases) are required even by small businesses as they open multiple locations or grow in size.

Additionally, with more and more companies expanding overseas or allowing workers to home office, many smaller clients have a need to connect multiple locations. Their options are to employ software-as-a-service or another application that offers them similar accessibility from multiple locations over the internet.

With the increasing dominance of having financial accounts prepared with Accounting Software, as well as some suppliers' claims that anyone can prepare their own books, accounting software can be considered at risk of not providing appropriate information as non-accountants prepare accounting information. As recording and interpretation is left to software and expert systems, the necessity to have a systems accountant overseeing the accountancy system becomes ever more important. The set up of the processes and the end result must be vigorously checked and maintained on a regular basis in order to develop and maintain the integrity of the data and the processes that manage these data.

CHALLENGES

Interoperability of Accounting Processes

Interoperability is today a key issue because of the need of meaningfully connecting several types of autonomous entities i.e. systems, people, software applications, enterprises. Establishing interoperability between pre-defined or dynamically occurring requires infrastructures and theories. Infrastructures can be based on open services facilitating the realisation of interoperability.

Today, however, such services focus on the syntactical and message passing levels of interoperability, paying too little attention to establishing and maintaining shared meaning. Theories are required to guarantee interoperability on the base of consistent relations among the various entities. The aim of a new type of an AIS is to put in practice the most advanced accounting research visions and earlier software engineering and computer science results concerning both these services and these theories.

Specifically, such an AIS will demonstrate the powerfulness of upper ontology (used to breaking down the barriers between distinct domains) to realise universal accounting services for establishing business process interoperability swithin a globalised and networked economy.

The result will be a set of prototype web services that enable interoperability between other (regular) web services by mapping various enterprise accounting models, concepts, queries etc. between distinct semantic domains, aided by emerging technologies for modelling language and ontology integration. Such a prototype could be used to demonstrate the integrated usage of upper ontology and domain ontology.

For example, while accounts are usually distinguished in five different types, namely assets, liabilities, equity, revenues and expenses, this categorisation can be used to drive the separation of functional units within an AIS but can in no case form the basis for a meaningful and sense-making conceptual organisation.

Such web services may form the basis not only for enterprise-wide accounting but also for cross-enterprise accounting operations taking the form of virtual enterprise accounting. We elaborate on this in the next section.

Accounting for the Virtual and Networked Enterprise

A virtual enterprise is defined as a temporary alliance where different companies that are positioned complementary or supplementary along the business activities related value chain are combining their strengths to provide a specific service traditionally provided by a single enterprise. They come together to share competencies and resources in order to better respond to business opportunities, whose cooperation is supported by computer networks and adequate IT tools and protocols (Putnik et al, 2005) and (Protogeros, 2007).

The life-cycle of a virtual enterprise is generally considered to be a four-stage process: creation, operation, evolution and dissolution. Among them, the first step (virtual enterprise creation) involves dynamically generated partnerships and dynamically composed service workflow in order for the successful operation of a virtual enterprise.

We consider a virtual enterprise is dynamically created following a process of order generation, partner search and selection, bid negotiation and contract awarding. Workflow is used to define the business process logics that are shared by the participants of a formed virtual enterprise. If we consider the workflow definition as a "class" in programming, a virtual enterprise can be considered as a running instance of such a class which is triggered by customer requirements, created by its lifecycle, controlled by workflow management, executed by workflow engine and dismantled once its goal is fulfilled (Wang 2006).

The most important requirements for a virtual enterprise have been identified in (Protogeros,

2005) and are related with the field of accounting practices as follows:

- **Global visibility across the virtual enterprise.** Similar to the business field, where there is a need to have an overall visibility on the entire life cycle of the products and/or services produced, starting from its development to its launch into the market, there is an equal need for following the entire path of an accounting operation, as well as its constituent transactions. Such a visibility may be permitted to all the companies' personnel involved in the virtual enterprise operation from all the participating companies.

- **Uniform and consistent business model.** Several researchers define a business process of a virtual enterprise as a set of linked activities that are distributed at member enterprises of the virtual enterprise and collectively realize its common business goal. A uniform business model is very important for the viability of the virtual enterprise. It should support the evolution of the product, process and organisation according to the increasing detail of the attributes representing the same concept (such as the status of an order, the categorization of the order, the customer contact information, the customer account representation, etc.) in a consistent manner.

- **Variable / polymorphic accounting model.** In contrast to the abovementioned business model that needs to be characterised by uniformity, the underlying accounting model of a virtual enterprise does not need such a property. Quite in contrast, the fundamental strength of an accounting model to support the needs of a virtual enterprise relates with the ability to support polymorphic and variable accounting practices. Participating members of a transaction do not need to share a common regulatory

convention or reporting standard as requested by e.g. the various national authorities involved in the process. This is the case of a hypothetical chemical company that operates in Greece and instead of buying some chemical supplies from Germany, where a very strictly operating chemical supplies market exists with not competitive at all prices and complicated procedures for reporting the transfer of chemical goods to the customer, it decides to buy the same quantity from a supplier in a Latin America country, where no complicated reporting procedures need to take place. In both cases the accounting model from the Greek side is the same but there is an obvious change in the use of the accounting model from the side of the supplier.

- **Consistent process and data model.** The data model of the companies can capture various behavioural semantics of the business entities. Thus it is not sufficient to have just a consistent conceptual business model of the business entities for smooth operation (Setrag, 2002). Data semantics and operational behaviour must also be represented and applied consistently.

Assets on the Net: The Case of Open Book Accounting

Almost all users of the Internet and the World Wide Web are familiar with the term of open source software. Though it began as a marketing campaign for free software, open source software is the most prominent example of open source development and often compared to user generated content. Furthermore, OSS allows users to use, change, and improve the software, and to redistribute it in modified or unmodified form and is very often developed in a public, collaborative manner.

Similar to this well-known term, there is a – (yet) less-known – movement for open-book accounting. This is regarded as an extension of the principles of open-book management to include all stakeholders in an organisation, not merely its employees, and specifically its shareholders (including those whose shareholding is managed indirectly, for example through a mutual fund. This effectively means all members of the public. Since almost all accounting records are now kept in electronic form, and since the computers on which they are held are universally-connected, it should be possible for accounting records to be world-readable.

This is an aspiration: at present, organisations run their accounts on systems secured behind firewalls and the release of financial information by publicly-quoted companies is carefully choreographed to ensure that it reaches all participants in the market equally. Nevertheless, price movements before publication of market-sensitive information strongly indicate that insider trading, which is unlawful in most major jurisdictions, had taken place.

Advocates of open-book accounting argue that full transparency in accounting will lead to greater accountability and will help rebuild the trust in financial capitalism that has been so badly damaged by recent events such as the collapse of Lehman Brothers, the federal rescues of AIG, Fannie Mae and Freddie Mac, and the fire-sale of Merrill Lynch to Bank of America(Lowenstein; Bebchuk; Claessens et al; Mads; Bardhan; Jenkinson – all in 2008), not to mention earlier scandals such as the collapse of Enron and Worldcom.

According to (Walker, 2005), the phrase "open book accounting" does not have a specific meaning. It is rather an expression of intent. That intent is to demonstrate the commitment and confidence of partners in a contractual relationship to share information on income and expenditure.

The commitment between commissioners and providers to enter into this way of working needs to be made early in the relationship. This will enable them to describe the type and depth of information to be made available for discussion. The arrangements will depend largely on the nature of the service and length of contract.

Arrangement to access accounts should be clear as vagueness could lead to misinterpretation or confusion. For instance the process may be annual and use independently audited accounts or be more frequent using working figures to identify changes to assumptions in order that joint considerations can be given to these. An exception clause could leave the possibility of more frequent dialogue where circumstances can be described (such as legislative changes) that require this from one side or the other.

It is a very common finding that virtual organisations can always succeed if both providers and commissioners find their way to a win-win situation. Open book accounting can help provide that. Furthermore, open book accounting also helps develop clarity with commissioners about the differences between independent providers, especially the differences between public authorities and private businesses.

The Interface Is the Message

The metaphors and the various conceptual schemes and mental representations that people use for carrying out most types of work tasks and job assignments, spanning from what we call 'simple' and 'everyday' to those we tend to regard as more abstract or sophisticated, and which work and the learning process in general are part of, have a great significance to the way tasks are carried out and work practices are developed for carrying out these tasks. By the use of such a nonmaterial or intangible culture (Lakoff and Johnson, 1980), which is inherent to any specific job assignment, being able to 'serve' it and to sufficiently express its characteristics, it is often possible to improve substantially the way a task is executed, no matter how abstract, complex, detailed or sophisticated may this be. That same nonmaterial or intangible culture also consists of all ideas, values, norms, interaction styles, beliefs and practices that are used by the members of a Community of Practice (CoP) that relates to a specific domain or field of operation.

Figure 1. How should Ronnie the accountant look like? What type of tasks should he be able to accomplish on his own or under the company accountants' guidance and supervision?

Currently, accounting suites exploited the proliferation of graphical user interfaces and desktop computing metaphors but did not innovate in terms of creating their own themes or metaphors. This is an area where major improvements and efficiencies can be gained by the selection of an appropriate metaphor. This does not need to take the form of a personification of the corporate accountant in the same way that Microsoft back in 1995 chose Bob. Bob was a Microsoft software product, released in March 1995, which provided a - then - new, nontechnical interface to desktop computing operations. Despite its ambitious nature, Bob failed to meet the market though he lfet a rich legacy in several other Microsoft products till today. Microsoft Bob was designed for Windows 3.1x and Windows 95 and intended to be a user-friendly interface for Microsoft Windows, supplanting the Program Manager.

Bob included various office suite programs such as a finance application and a word processor. The user interface was designed to be helpful to novice computer users, but many saw its methods of assistance as too cute and involved. Each action, such as creating a new text document, featured the step-by-step tutorials no matter how many times the user had been through the process; some users considered this to be condescending. Users were assisted by cartoon characters whose appearance was usually vaguely related to the task.

In our case, a similar direction would be to choose a cartoon character something like 'Ronnie the Accountant', who could be assigned responsibilities for administering accounting operations that will have been preselected by the design time of the particular AIS within a company. This step might be regarded as adding nothing new in comparison to the customisation process of an accounting software suite but this is not the case: by the time that users interact with a – virtual, though - character, the process of disassociation of certain tasks from the human user to the virtual – computer – character who gets delegated to perform these tasks has started. This is an obviously important transition in the model of operation of the application and, for sure, an irreversible change in the perception and the mental models of the users (just imagine how difficult it is to go back to the command prompt type of interfaces).

Ronnie may be a standard character offered to the users for taking control of routine tasks that the user prefers to delegate to an artificial persona than keep as a set of batch processes to carry out on a – say – weekly basis. A further development might include the provision of a set of cartoon characters that might be assigned responsibilities within the corporate accounting department, taking the form of a mixed reality setting where real human personalities interact and collaborate with artificial characters for certain tasks. Since Microsoft's Bob introduction more than 13 years have passed and the history of interactive computing has seriously been changed since the introduction in 2003 of Second Life, the Internet-based 3D virtual world developed by Linden Research, Inc. Second Life provides a platform for human interaction with a high degree of naturalness. A free downloadable client program called the Second Life Viewer enables its users, called "Residents", to interact with each other through motional avatars, providing an advanced level of a social network service combined with general aspects of a metaverse. Residents can explore, meet other residents, socialize, participate in individual and group activities, and create and trade items (virtual property) and services with one another.

According to our opinion, it is only a matter of time to happen the use of Second Life-like dramaturgical and dramatical elements to supply the AIS with new interaction patterns and styles.

IMPLEMENTATION OF AN E-ACCOUNTING PLATFORM

The lack of a theory specific to the new forms of computing facilitated by pervasive environments may significantly compromise the pace of the developments in the field, since design and evaluation are not based on a solid basis. Similarly, the *e*(lectronic), *m*(obile) and *p*(ervasive)-commerce field, especially in ubiquitous computing environments may require new theories of accounting

to speed up developments. M-accounting is not simply about supporting companies and ventures through mobile devices, but facilitates a new concept and a novel positioning for the accounting profession in a mobile world. In this context, specific emphasis should be given to further investigate both regulatory and socio-cultural issues related to the acceptability of different accounting application and service concepts.

The run-time environment for such a mobile accounting platform needs to have a layered architecture with well defined components, as shown in Figure 2 above. In this architecture, each layer utilizes the services provided by the below layer as well as a layer abstracts the complexities of one service from the above layers. Furthermore, another advantage of the layered architecture is that it facilitates the development of the platform. In the architecture, basically, there are the following components, which of course may vary depending on the specifics of the particular implementation:

Peer Controller, for connecting with P2P Infrastructures, which is divided to the following components:

- **Semantic Registry component:** This component is responsible for the UDDI management by semantically registering accounting or other types of financial services that are provided by the particular corporate peer or are provided by collaborating providers (3rd parties or specialized accountants or auditors). The component uses the UDDI server that is a part of the ERP legacy information system of the Provider. Semantic registry component creates a semantically enhanced UDDI registry where the services of the provider node are published. The registry may uses profiles to create semantic descriptions for the services. The utilization of the component also facilitates the annotation of semantic context for web services utilization.

Figure 2. Run-time environment for a mobile accounting application and service architecture

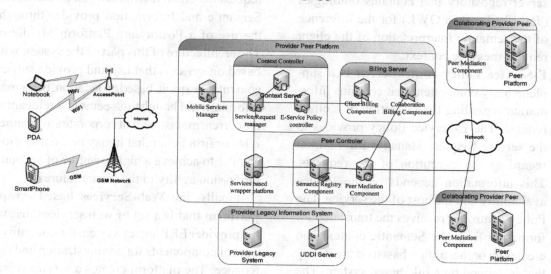

- **Peer Mediation component:** The Peer mediation component act as communication manager between the various accounting service providers. It sends and receives requests for services to other peers. Two peers can communicate by sending request to Peer Mediation components. The Peer Mediator request is encapsulated into standard messages. The definition of the message is based on a common message ontology that will be used from all the provider nodes of the network.

Context Controller consists of the following components:

- **Service Request manager:** Includes the **Computational Model.** The Service request manager is responsible for the completion of a client request. It consolidates all necessary accounting information about the client request and the request execution and undertakes the process of execution. The workflow of the execution may be defined into a BPEL or equivalent semantics language file that is executed from

the content manager. However in order to support dynamic orchestration the Service Request manager uses process templates (semi-structured BPEL files) that are completed and execute with the information retain from the context translation that takes place in the Semantic Context Server and the Policy Controller. It is easy to recognize that a global accounting office with operations all over the world shall need a more powerful context controller, relying on a robust computational model than a small or micro-accounting office that has few clients from the local environment.

- **Semantic context Server** is a server that stores and manipulates information regarding the execution of an accounting service request. It will navigate accounting transaction collections with the use of ontologies and will allow the user to combine information for its particular purpose of use (context). The semantic context server is responsible for the translation of the client request message to set of concepts that define the nodes in the execution process. The translation is also based to context server repository that contains ontologies (described e.g. in OWL) for the inference of the semantic interpretation of the client request message context.

- **E-Service Policy controller:** It is a supplementary component that contains information regarding the execution of a client request. The E-Service Policy provides to the service Request Manager Information regarding the execution of the requests. This information depends on the service availability and the cost of the service. The Policy controller receives the translated information from the Semantic context and creates an orchestration based on the Policy that is defined by a rule based system. The component retains the optimum orchestration based on rule regarding the cost and the time of the process execution.

Billing Server is responsible for the billing of the accounting services that are executed to the provider registered client or to collaborating providers. The billing server also provides information to the existing billing system of the provider. The billing system is manipulated by two sub-system that are the following:

- **Client Billing sub-system** contains all the information regarding the transaction of the provider client when they use the accounting platform.
- **Collaboration Billing sub-system** is responsible for the billing of the collaborating peers billing. This makes increased sense for the case of collaborating networks of accountants that are (usually ad hoc) created for the supply of services to end customers.

Mobile Services Manager handles the client requests. The Mobile Services Manager enables location retrieval mechanisms in order to provide the necessary information to the accounting service

request manager. It will focus on Location Based Semantic and Information provider throughout the use of a Positioning Platform Middleware. The architecture of this part of the system will be based on systems that use and provide sufficient contents to exploit, based on location, the semantic information. Though this seems less relevant with the current mainstream of corporate environments, it is our firm belief that it may be used as a major enabler to achieve a higher degree of accounting profession agility in the (near) future.

Finally, the **Web-Services based wrapper platform** that is a set of web services that wrap the provider ERP legacy system functionality and a set of components for administration and maintenance. The platform creates a service oriented infrastructure that is used for the integration of a particular peer to the particular ERP legacy system of the provider. The creation of the web-service is based to a platform independent Framework that wraps the legacy system of the provider based on semantic conceptualizations. The framework is consisted of software components that develop .NET web services from system conceptualizations. The conceptualization definition is facilitated from a graphical environment. The platform also supports the mechanism for the discovery and invocation of the produced web services.

CONCLUSIONS

Accounting services shall definitely constitute the future of our global economies – as they always did and do in all levels all the years but now the difference will be that this dominance of accounting services shall be evident and apparent in all levels of the society and the economy. This means that the emergence of the accounting service science as an independent branch of the accounting discipline that will be taught, studied, researched and examined shall take place. For sure, this is not a novelty: management and (traditional) accounting as well as computers experienced at some point of their lifetime their transformation from a profession towards a science. And of course there is still a part of the people that don't accept them as such – at the end it is not a matter of taste but a matter of fact what defines something as a science.

The problem that we foresee with accounting services is the basis upon which the formation of the scientific foundations will base: accountants have all the good reason to prefer an accounting background on accounting services; same good is the reason for economists and business and / or management science professionals. Finally computer scientists and sociologists can exhibit some grounded reasons for supplying the basis for this 'new old' science.

Our opinion is sharp-cut: there should be a totally new basis that shall reflect concerns and considerations of all the aforementioned disciplines. Even more: at a great extend, we see the need for introducing an extensive degree of spirituality and transcendal elements in the accounting service science – though the obvious remark is that this comprises an unscientific practice. The reason for this comes from observation of phenomena that dominate our daily personal and working lives: management does not refer to Taylorism but – more and more – relates to leadership, where the latter term connotes terms like an enlighted leader who – more or less – executes his or her powers in a fashion that is totally unscientific and irrational. Additionally, dramatic elements in the organisation and conduct of business processes are not an innovation at all; the same holds for the ritual aspects that can be found in numerous occasions within the modern corporate and business world. The answer to this is simple: there is a need from the people to satisfy several levels of their lives both as individuals as well as members of an organised – professional or non-professional – community and to do so there is a need to introduce transcendal elements that can address parts of the encountered situations in a satisfactory though totally unscientific way.

To know how to do this is an extremely serious and scientific aspect that shall more and more be given increased importance by service scientists and service professionals. We should not forget that religion in all its more or less sense-making realisations constitutes an extremely good case for examining service science in an extremely well-defined application area namely this of intangible spirituality. At least, when you pay for an insurance service or a financial service, there are ways to measure the success or the satisfaction of the supplied (intangible) service in terms of some types of (tangible) results. Religion, on the other hand, does constitute an area where the success of the supplied service does not have a tangible equivalent to use as a benchmark.

What one should be able to see here is all the dangers that can relate with what we expect to happen in terms of a violent and forceful attack of this new type of (should we call them holistic?) accounting services which shall promise to fulfil expectations that are not lying at the area of the traditional accounting service as such. Similarly, one can foresee the need for supplying accounting services for *literally virtual* entities like Second-Life avatars.

Speaking about the future of accounting services one may expect forecasts like global accounting infrastructures (that by the way already and since years exist for e.g. the case of accounting firms operating globally).

The reader may understand the above terms in many different ways. History can teach us a lot – the difficult part is to show willingness for learning from its many lessons. In a similar fashion, one can view phenomena like the open source and free source software communities as some form of service activisms. The underlying cult for both of them may take extremely powerful forms and drive the software and Net economies in unpredictable directions.

The French philosopher Luis Althusser defined a practice as any process of transformation of a determinate product, affected by a determinate human labour, using determinate means (of production). Nowadays that we talk a lot about practices on the Net, in services or e-services, it is tragically timely how much we lack on intellectuals that will be able to transform and process service or technology problems into societal or political ones and vice versa.

REFERENCES

Andenas, M. (2008). Who is going to supervise Europe's financial markets. In M. Adenas & Y. Avgerinos (Eds.), *Financial markets in Europe: Towards a single regulator*. London: Kluwer Law International.

Bardhan, A. (2008). *Of subprimes and subsidies: The political economy of the financial crisis*. Retrieved October 20, 2008, from http://ssrn.com/abstract=1270196

Bebchuk, L. A. (2008). *A plan for addressing the financial crisis* (Harvard Law and Economics Discussion Paper No. 620).

Claessens, S., Kose, M. A., & Terrones, M. (2008). *What happens during recessions, crunches and busts?* IMF Working Paper.

Coman, N., & Diaconu, P. (2006). The impact of globalization on accounting research. In *Proceedings of the International Conference on Business Excellence, ICBE – 2006*, Brasov, Romania.

Diaconu, P., Sr. (2007). *Impact of globalization on international accounting harmonization*. Retrieved October 17, 2008, from http://papers.ssrn.com/sol3/papers.cfm?abstract_id=958478

Jenkinson, N., Penalver, A., & Vause, N. (2008). Financial innovation: What have we learnt? *Bank of England Quarterly Bulletin, 2008*, Q3.

Lakoff, G., & Johnson, M. (1980). *Metaphors we live by*. Chicago: Univ. of Chicago Press.

Lowenstein, R. (2008, April 27). Triple-a failure. *New York Times*.

Protogeros, N. (2005). *Virtual learning enterprise integration technological and organizational perspectives*. Hershey, PA: Idea Group Publishing.

Protogeros, N. (2007). *Agent and Web service technologies in virtual enterprises*. Hershey, PA: Information Science Reference.

Putnik, G. D., Cunha, M. M., Sousa, R., & Ávila, P. (2005). Virtual enterprise integration: challenges of a new paradigm. In G. D. Putnik & M. M. Cunha (Eds.), *Virtual enterprise integration: Technological and organisational perspective*. Hershey, PA: Idea Group Publishing.

Setrag, K. (2002). *Web services and virtual learning enterprises*. Chicago: Tect.

Walker, N. (2005). *Open book accounting – a best value tool*. Good practice guides – Commissioning, Change Agent Team.

Wang, S., Shen, W., & Hao, Q. (2006). An agent-based Web service workflow model for inter-enterprise collaboration. In *Expert systems with applications*. Amsterdam: Elsevier.

Chapter 5
Recent Developments in Supplier Selection and Order Allocation Process

Ezgi Aktar Demirtas
Eskisehir Osmangazi University, Turkey

Ozden Ustun
Dumlupınar University, Turkey

ABSTRACT

Because the purchasing department can play a key role in cost reduction, supplier selection and order allocation are the most important functions of purchasing management. In view of its complexity, it will be focused especially on the final selection stage that consists of determining the best mixture of suppliers and allocating orders among them so as to satisfy different purchasing requirements. In recent years, many researchers used new integrated models for supplier selection and order allocation. They combine multi-criteria approaches such as AHP/ANP and linear programming (LP), mixed integer programming (MIP), non-linear programming (NLP), mixed integer non-linear programming (MINLP) and goal programming (GP) with different achievement scalarizing functions. In this chapter, after the stages of supplier selection process are explained, these new integrated models are introduced and their constraints, variables, and goals/objectives of these models are explained in detail. Then the solution methods of these integrated models are given. Finally, different integrated models are compared by considering their advantages and disadvantages.

INTRODUCTION

With globalization and the emergence of the extended enterprise of interdependent organizations, there has been a steady increase in the outsourcing of parts and services. This has led firms to give more importance to the purchasing function and

its associated decisions. One of those decisions which impact all firms' areas is the supplier selection. Companies need to work with different suppliers to continue their activities. In manufacturing industries the raw materials and component parts can equal up to 70% of the product cost. Because the purchasing department can play a key role in cost reduction, supplier selection and order allocation are the most important functions of purchasing

DOI: 10.4018/978-1-60566-856-7.ch005

management. In view of its complexity, we will focus especially on the final selection stage that consists of determining the best mixture of suppliers and allocating orders among them so as to satisfy different purchasing requirements and recent developments (new integrated models) in supplier selection and order allocation process in this chapter.

The contents of the other sections are also summarized in introduction part. In the second part; supplier selection process (different stages and characteristics) are explained. The tangible/intangible criteria used for performance evaluations are discussed and several multi-criteria methods used for pre and/or final selection stage are introduced to evaluate these tangible and intangible criteria, some of which may conflict. The differences among these methods, the advantages and disadvantages of them are also discussed in detail in this part.

In recent years, many researchers used integrated approaches for supplier selection and order allocation. They combine multi-criteria approaches such as AHP/ANP and linear programming (LP), mixed integer programming (MIP), non-linear programming (NLP), mixed integer non-linear programming (MINLP) and goal programming (GP) with different achievement scalarizing functions. In the third part, these integrated models are introduced. The constraints, variables, and goals/objectives of these models are explained in detail.

Many real-life supplier selection and order allocation problems as well as the proposed models in the literature involve more than one objective. In the fourth part, the authors will focus on the solution procedures of multi-criteria and multi-objective supplier selection and order allocation models. Multi-objective optimization models such as ε-constraint, Tchebycheff Metric-based Scalarizing Methods, interactive methods (Reservation Level Driven Tchebycheff Procedure-RLTP), GP with different achievement scalarizing functions (Archimedian, Preemptive, Minmax), Conic

Scalarization Method (CSM) are introduced to readers in this part.

In the last part, a comparative study is performed for the recent integrated models in the literature so; the readers can understand the advantages and disadvantages of these integrated models.

SUPPLIER SELECTION PROCESS

As reported by De Boer et al. (2001), several decision-making steps make up the supplier selection process. At first, a preparation step is achieved by formulating the problem and the different decision criteria. After that, prequalification of potential suppliers and final choices are successively elaborated. De Boer et al. (2001, 2003) present an interesting overview of the literature on supplier selection models. It specifies the published works treating every stage of the selection process for every purchasing situation. In this section, every stage of the selection process (problem definition, decision criteria formulation, pre and final selection of potential suppliers) is demonstrated.

Problem Definition

Due to shortened product life cycles, the search for new suppliers is a continuous priority for companies in order to upgrade the variety and typology of their products range. On the other hand, purchasing environments such as Just-In-Time, involve establishing close connections with suppliers leading to the concept of partnership, privileged suppliers, long-term agreement, etc. Thereby, decision makers are facing different purchasing situations that lead to different decisions. Consequently, in order to make the right choice, the purchasing process should start with finding out exactly what we want to achieve by selecting a supplier.

Decision Criteria Formulation

Depending on the purchasing situation, selecting the right suppliers is influenced by a variety of factors. This additional complexity is essentially due to the multi-criteria nature of this decision. As reported by Aissaoui et al. (2007), the analysis of this aspect has been the focus of multiple papers since the 1960's. Cardozo and Cagley (1971), Monczka et al. (1981), Moriarity (1983), Woodside and Vyas (1987), Chapman and Carter (1990), Tullous and Munson (1991) propose diverse empirical researches emphasizing the relative importance of different supplier attributes. Among works that are a reference for the majority of papers we distinguish Dickson's study (1966). Based on a questionnaire sent to 273 purchasing agent and managers from United States and Canada, it identified 23 different criteria evaluated in supplier selection. Among these, the price, delivery, and quality objectives of the buyer, as well as the abilities of the suppliers to meet those objectives, are particularly important factors in deciding how much to order from the available suppliers. In the same way, Weber et al. (1991) observed that price, delivery, quality, production capacity and localization are the criteria most often treated in the literature. Although the evolution of the industrial environment modified the degrees of the relative importance of supplier selection criteria since the 1960s, the 23 ones presented by Dickson still cover the majority of those presented in the literature until today.

A series of experimental studies was conducted by Verma and Pullman (1998) to examine how managers effectively choose suppliers. The empirical results reveal that they perceive quality to be the most important attribute in the selection process. Nevertheless, the same sample of managers assign more weight to cost and delivery performance than quality when actually choosing a supplier. Cusumano and Takeishi (1991) note as well that the choice of criteria may differ from one culture to another.

Generally, two basic types of criteria are dealt with when deciding which suppliers to select: objective and subjective ones. These former can be measured by a concrete quantitative dimension like cost whereas the latter cannot be like the quality of design. Another factor complicating the decision is that some criteria may conflict each other. Wind and Robinson (1968) identified possible contradictions such as the supplier offering the lowest price may not have the best quality, or the supplier with the best quality may not deliver on time. As a result, it is necessary to make a trade-off between conflicting tangible and intangible factors to find the best suppliers. Observe that in compensatory models, a poor performance on one criterion (generally represented by a score) can be compensated by a high performance in another one whereas in non-compensatory models, different minimum levels for each criterion are required.

Regarding available methods, there is a lack in the purchasing literature for the formulation of criteria and their qualification. As for the previous phase, it consists essentially of applying qualitative methods that include tools for visualizing and analyzing the decision-maker's perception of a problem situation and tools for brainstorming about possible alternative solutions. In the survey proposed by De Boer et al. (2001), only two applications are mentioned and some operational research methods such as Rough Sets Theory (Slowinsky, 1992; Pawlak and Slowinsky, 1994), and Value Focused Thinking (Keeney, 1994) are proposed as suitable alternatives for criteria identification and selection.

Regardless of the method used, supplier selection criteria formulation affects several activities including inventory management, production planning and control, cash flow requirements, product/service quality (Narasimhan, 1983). Therefore such decision must be made under the consensus of a multidisciplinary group of decision makers with various points of view and representing the different services of the company (Dyer and Forman, 1992; Mobolurin, 1995; Benyousef et al., 2003).

Pre-Selection of Potential Suppliers

Today's co-operative logistics environment requires a low number of suppliers as it is very difficult to manage a high number. Therefore, the purpose of this process's stage is to rule out the inefficient candidates and reduce the set of all suppliers to a small range of acceptable ones. This process may be carried out in more than one step. However, the first step always consists of defining and determining the set of acceptable suppliers while possible subsequent steps serve to reduce the number of suppliers to consider. Basically, pre-selection is *sorting* process rather than a *ranking* process. However, the difference between sorting and ranking is often not explicitly made in the purchasing literature (De Boer et al., 2001). Some methods could be used in the final selection stage but their sorting nature makes them more suitable for pre-selection:

Hwang and Yoon, (1981) have used Conjunctive, Disjunctive and Lexicographical Screening to support pre-selection stage. In Conjunctive Screening a supplier is acceptable if the supplier equals or exceeds a minimum score on each criterion. Similarly, in Disjunctive Screening a supplier is acceptable if the supplier at least equals or exceeds a minimum score on one criterion. According to Lexicographical Screening criteria are ranked in order of importance. Suppliers are first evaluated on the most important criterion. Suppliers that pass this criterion are then evaluated on the second criterion and so on (De Boer et al., 2001).

Timmerman (1986) have used Categorical methods a kind of qualitative models. Based on historical data and the buyer's experience current or familiar suppliers are evaluated on a set of criteria. The evaluations actually consist of categorizing the supplier's performance on a criterion as either 'positive', 'neutral' or 'negative'. After a supplier has been rated on all criteria, the buyer gives an overall rating, again through ticking one of the three options. In this way, suppliers are sorted into three categories.

Another method, Cluster Analysis (CA), is a basic method from statistics which uses a classification algorithm to group a number of items which are described by a set of numerical attribute scores into a number of clusters such that the differences between items within a cluster are minimal and the differences between items from different clusters are maximal. Obviously, CA can also be applied to a group of suppliers that are described by scores on some criteria. The result is a classification of suppliers in clusters of comparable suppliers. Hinkle et al. (1969) were the first to report this, followed some 20 years later by Holt (1998). Nowadays, classification studies of suppliers attract more attention (Wang et al., 2009).

Data Envelopment Analysis (DEA) is built around the concept of the 'efficiency' of a decision alternative. The alternatives (suppliers) are evaluated on benefit criteria (output) and cost criteria (input). The efficiency of a supplier is defined as the ratio of the weighted sum of its outputs (i.e. the performance of the supplier) to the weighted sum of its inputs (i.e. the costs of using the supplier). For each supplier, the DEA method finds the most favorable set of weights, i.e. the set of weights that maximizes the supplier's efficiency rating without making its own or any other supplier's rating greater than one. In this way the DEA method aids the buyer in classifying the suppliers (or their initial bids) into two categories: the efficient suppliers and the inefficient suppliers. Weber has primarily discussed the application of DEA in supplier selection in several publications, see Weber and Ellram (1992), Weber and Desai (1996) and Weber et al. (1998). Apart from just categorizing suppliers, Weber shows how DEA can be used as a tool for negotiating with inefficient suppliers. Other publications featuring DEA in supplier selection are Papagapiou et al. (1996) and Liu et al. (2000) an extended version of Weber and Desai's research. Later, Talluri and Narasimhan (2003) stated that multi-factor supplier evaluation methods such as DEA have primarily relied on evaluating suppliers based on their strengths and failed to incorporate their weaknesses into the selection process. They also added that such approaches would not be able to effectively differentiate between suppliers with comparable strengths but significantly different weaknesses. Consequently, the authors proposed an approach based on *min–max* productivity methods that estimates supplier performance variability measures, which are then used in a non-parametric statistical technique in identifying homogeneous supplier groups for effective selection. In this way, buyers are provided with effective alternative choices within a supplier group. This allows the buyer to base the final decision on other intangible factors that could not be incorporated into the analysis. Readers can be found more detailed information about DEA in the Cook and Seiford's study (Cook and Seiford, 2009).

Case-based-reasoning (CBR) systems fall in the category of the so-called artificial intelligence (AI) approach. Basically, a CBR system is a software-driven database which provides a decision-maker with useful information and experiences from similar, previous decision situations. CBR is still very new and only few systems have been developed for purchasing decision-making. Ng et al. (1995) developed a CBR-system for the pre-selection of suppliers.

Final Selection

At this stage, the ultimate supplier(s) are identified and orders are allocated among them while considering the system's constraints and taking into account a multitude of quantitative and/ or qualitative criteria. The state-of-art decision models available at present for the final selection stage are covered by several researchers in their review papers (Aissaoui et al., 2007; De Boer et., 2001).

De Boer et al. (2001) listed all studies of researchers according to their methods (Linear Weighting, Analytic Hierarchy Process-AHP, Analytic Network Process-ANP, Mathematical Programming Models, Statistical Models, Artificial Intelligence Based Models)

Aissaoui et al. (2007) classified all methods used in final selection stage by researchers according to the nature of problems (single/ multiple sourcing, single/multiple item, single criterion/multi-criteria, single/multi period).

Another stream of research suggests considering both quantitative and qualitative measures to better model the multi-criteria nature of decision. These integrated models are achieved in two phases. At first phase, a supplier evaluation is elaborated using a multicriteria tool (AHP or ANP). The AHP is applied to make the trade-off between tangible and intangible factors and calculate the ratings of suppliers. ANP is also a new theory that extends the AHP. With the ANP it is recognized that there is feedback between the elements in different levels of the hierarchy and also between elements in the same level, so the decision elements are organized into networks of clusters and nodes. ANP deals systematically with all kinds of feedback and interactions (inner and outer dependence). When elements are linked only to elements in another cluster, the model shows only outer dependence. When elements are linked to the elements in their own cluster, there is inner dependence. Feedback can better capture the complex effects of interplay in human society (Saaty, 2001).

The second stage of these integrated approaches consists of effectively selecting the suppliers and allocating orders using mathematical programming to take into account the system constraints. Thereby, calculated ratings are applied as coefficients of an objective function in a mathematical programming model such that the total value of purchasing becomes a maximum or total cost of purchase becomes a minimum.

In this chapter, we will cover in detail the state-of-art integrated models available at present in the third section.

INTEGRATED SUPPLIER SELECTION AND ORDER ALLOCATION MODELS

First publications on vendor selection can be traced back to the early 1960s. Although the problem of supplier selection is not new, quite a few researchers treat the supplier selection issue as an optimization problem, which requires the formulation of an objective function (Wang et al., 2004). Since not every supplier selection criterion is quantitative, usually only a few quantitative criteria are included in the optimization formulation. To overcome this drawback, Ghodsypour and O'Brien (1998) proposed an integrated approach for supplier selection and order allocation problem. The authors combined analytic hierarchy process (AHP) and linear programming to take into account tangible as well as intangible criteria and to solve order allocation problem among suppliers. They are achieved in two phases. At first, a supplier evaluation is elaborated using a multi-criteria tool.

The second stage of these global approaches consists of effectively selecting the suppliers and allocating orders using mathematical programming to take into account the system constraints. Thereby, in Ghodsypour and O'Brien's study (1998), calculated ratings are applied as coefficients of an objective function in a linear program such that the total value of purchasing (TVP) becomes a maximum. This single period single item model was constrained by the demand, capacity and quality requirements. Their single period model contains two different objectives: maximization of TVP and minimization of defect rate. They used ε-constraint method to solve the multi-objective problem. By following this study; Wang et al. (2004) developed an integrated AHP and preemptive goal programming (PGP) ap-

proach based on multi-criteria decision making methodology to maximize TVP and to minimize the total cost of purchasing. In Xia and Wu's paper, an integrated approach of analytical hierarchy process improved by rough sets theory and multi-objective mixed integer programming is proposed to simultaneously determine the number of suppliers to employ and the order quantity allocated to these suppliers in the case of multiple sourcing, multiple products, with multiple criteria and with supplier's capacity constraints (Xia and Wu, 2007).

Although time-horizon was not considered in the previous studies (Demirtas and Ustun, 2008; Ghodsypour and O'Brien's, 1998; Wang et al., 2004; Xia and Wu, 2007), time can not be neglected in real life problems. To eliminate this drawback, Ustun and Demirtas (2008a) proposed ANP and Multi-objective Mixed Integer Linear Programming (MOMILP) Model to solve multi-period supplier selection and order allocation problems. Demirtas and Ustun (2006) used ANP and goal programming approach for multi-period lot-sizing with supplier selection. Ustun and Demirtas (2008b) have also used the integration of ANP and achievement scalarizing function to solve multi-period order allocation problem.

In recent years, many integrated approach have proposed for solving the supplier selection and order allocation problems (Ho, 2008). These integrated models are used for single/multi product, multiple suppliers, volume discount environment, single/multi period, zero inventory level/ inventory handling and backlogging. Lead times, transportation and quality constraints are also included to these models. Supply chain performance is directly related to supplier selection and order allocation decisions due to evaluation criteria. Enterprise Information System such as Enterprise Resource Planning System supports managers by providing fast and accurate information.

A general structure of the integrated supplier selection and order allocation process can be shown as in Figure 1.

Figure 1. The flow chart of the selection and allocation stages

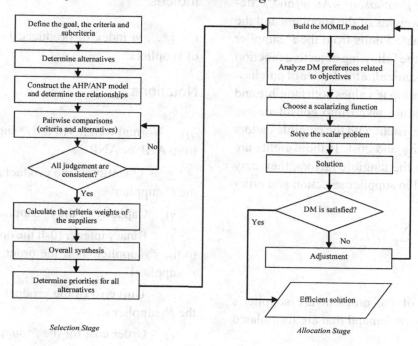

In this section, these integrated models are introduced and the constraints, variables, and objectives of these models are explained.

Order Allocation Model with Single Period, Single Product and Multiple Suppliers

One of the order allocation models with Single Period, Single Product and Multiple Suppliers has been recently proposed by Demirtas and Ustun (2008). The objective functions and the constraints of this model are as follows:

Indices

$i = 1,\dots, n$ index of suppliers

Notations

w_i: Normal weights of the ith supplier obtained from AHP or ANP.

x_i: Order quantity for the ith supplier

v_i: Capacity of the ith supplier

y_i: Binary integer (0-if the order is not given to the ith supplier, 1- if the order is given to the ith supplier)

c_i: Unit cost for the ith supplier

o_i: Order cost for the ith supplier

D: Demand for the period

q_i: Defect Rate of the ith supplier

Objective Functions

Cost - The sum of material cost and order cost should be minimized; therefore,

$$\min f_1(X,Y) = \sum_{i=1}^{n} c_i x_i + \sum_{i=1}^{n} o_i y_i$$

Defect Rate - q_i is the defect rate of the ith vendor, this objective should be minimized; therefore,

$$\min f_2(X) = \sum_{i=1}^{n} q_i x_i$$

Total value of purchasing - As w_i and x_i denote the normal weights of the suppliers and the numbers of purchased units from the ith supplier respectively, and the following objective function is designed to maximize the total value of purchasing. While calculating w_i values both tangible and intangible factors are taken into consideration; hence w_i's are consistent with the tangible factors of quality, capacity and cost. If the weights are inconsistent with the tangible factors, they may play no role at all in supplier selection and order allocation.

$$\max f_3(X) = \sum_{i=1}^{n} w_i x_i$$

Constraints

The constraints of the problem are supplier's capacity and buyers demand that are formulated as follows:

Capacity constraints- As supplier i can provide up to v_i units of the product and its order quantity (x_i) should be equal or less than its capacity, these constraints are;

$$x_i \leq v_i y_i \ i = 1, 2, \dots, n$$

Demand constraint- As sum of the assigned order quantities to n suppliers should meet the buyer's demand;

$$\sum_{i=1}^{n} x_i \geq D$$

Nonnegativity and Binary Constraints

$$x_i \geq 0 \ i = 1, 2, \dots, n,$$
$$y_i = 0 \text{ or } 1 \text{ integer } i = 1, 2, \dots, n.$$

Order Allocation Models with Single Period, Multi Product and Multiple Suppliers

The model for a single product proposed by Demirtas and Ustun (2008) can be generalized for multi-product environments as follows:

Indices

$i = 1, \dots, m$ index of products; $j = 1, \dots, n$ index of suppliers.

Notations

w_j : Normal weights of the jth supplier obtained from AHP or ANP.

x_{ij} : Quantity of the product i ordered from the jth supplier

v_j : Capacity of the jth supplier

y_j : Binary integer (0-if the order is not given to the jth supplier, 1- if the order is given to the jth supplier)

c_{ij} : Unit cost of the product i ordered from the jth supplier

o_j : Order cost for the jth supplier

D_i : Demand of the product i for the period

q_{ij} : Defect rate of the product i ordered from the jth supplier

pt_{ij} : Unit production time of the product i for the jth supplier

Objective functions

Cost - The sum of material cost and order cost should be minimized; therefore,

$$\min f_1(X, Y) = \sum_{i=1}^{m}\sum_{j=1}^{n} c_{ij} x_{ij} + \sum_{j=1}^{n} o_j y_j .$$

Defect Rate - q_{ij} is the defect rate of the product i ordered from j^{th} supplier, this objective should be minimized; therefore,

$$\min f_2(X) = \sum_{i=1}^{m}\sum_{j=1}^{n} q_{ij} x_{ij} .$$

Total value of purchasing - As w_i and x_{ij} denote the normal weights of the suppliers and the numbers of purchased product i units from the jth supplier respectively, and the following objective function is designed to maximize the total value of purchasing.

$$\max f_3(X) = \sum_{i=1}^{m}\sum_{j=1}^{n} w_j x_{ij}$$

Constraints

The constraints of the problem are supplier's capacity and buyers demand that are formulated as follows:

Capacity constraints- As supplier *j* can provide up to v_j production time and its total production time of orders from the supplier *j* should be equal or less than its capacity, these constraints are;

$$\sum_{j=1}^{m} pt_{ij} x_{ij} \leq v_j y_j, j = 1,2,\ldots,n$$

Demand constraint- As sum of the assigned order quantities to *n* suppliers for each product should meet the buyer's demand;

$$\sum_{j=1}^{n} x_{ij} \geq D_i, i = 1,2,\ldots,m$$

Nonnegativity and binary constraints

$x_{ij} \geq 0 \; i = 1, 2,\ldots, m; j = 1, 2,\ldots, n.$
$y_j = 0$ or 1 integer $j = 1, 2,\ldots, n.$

Order Allocation Model in Volume Discount Environments with Single Period, Multi Product and Multiple Suppliers

The model for a single product becomes more complicated when business volume discount exist (Xia and Wu, 2007). The objective functions and the constraints of this model are as follows:

Indices

$i = 1,\ldots, m$ index of products; $j = 1,\ldots,n$ index of suppliers; $r = 1,\ldots,m_j$ index discount intervals.

Notations

S_i : Set of suppliers offering product *i*,

K_j : Set of products offered by supplier *j*,

w_j : Normal weights of the *j*th supplier obtained from AHP or ANP.

R_j : Set of discount interval of supplier *j*,

m_j : The number of discount intervals in supplier *j*'s discount schedule,

r: Discount interval, $1 \leq r \leq m_j$,

b_{jr} : Upper limit in interval *r* of supplier *j*'s discount schedule, $0 = b_{j0} < b_{j1} < \ldots < b_{j,mj}$

d_{jr} : Discount coefficient associated with interval *r* of supplier *j*'s discount Schedule,

p_{ij} : Unit price of the product *i* quoted by supplier *j*,

q_{ij} : Defective rate of the product *i* offered by supplier *j*,

Q_i : The buyer's maximum acceptable defective rate of the product *i*,

t_{ij} : On-time delivery rate of the product *i* offered by supplier *j*,

T_i : The buyer's minimum acceptable on-time delivery rate of the product *i*,

C_{ij} : Maximum supply capacity of the product *i* offered by supplier *j*,

D_i : Demand of the product *i*,

x_{ij} : Quantity of the product *i* ordered from the *j*th supplier,

V_{jr} : Business volume purchased from *j*th supplier in discount interval *r*,

$y_{jr} = 1$, if business volume purchased from *j*th supplier falls on the discount interval *r* of its discount schedule; 0, otherwise.

There are three criteria considered for supplier selection such as price, defects and delivery in the model proposed by Xia and Wu (2007).

Objective Functions

Total value of purchasing - As w_i and x_{ij} denote the normal weights of the suppliers and the numbers of purchased product *i* units from the *j*th supplier respectively, and the following objective function is designed to maximize the total value of purchasing.

$$\max f_1(X) = \sum_{i \in K_j} \sum_{j \in S_i} w_j x_{ij}$$

Cost - Considering suppliers' cumulative price breaks, the buyer makes decision to minimize the total purchase cost. The sum of purchasing cost should be minimized; therefore,

$$\min f_2(V) = \sum_{j \in S_i} \sum_{r \in R_j} (1 - d_{jr})V_{jr},$$

where

$$\sum_{r \in R_j} V_{jr} = \sum_{i \in K_j} p_{ij} x_{ij}, \quad j \in S_i,$$

Defect Rate - q_{ij} is the defect rate of the product i ordered from j^{th} supplier, this objective should be minimized; therefore,

$$\min f_3(X) = \sum_{i \in K_j} \sum_{j \in S_i} q_{ij} x_{ij}.$$

On-time Delivery - For production going on wheels, the buyer expects to maximize the number of items delivered on time. The objective function can be stated as

$$\max f_4(X) = \sum_{i \in K_j} \sum_{j \in S_i} t_{ij} x_{ij}$$

Constraints

The constraints of the problem are supplier's capacity and buyers demand that are formulated as follows:

Capacity constraints - As supplier j can provide up to C_{ij} units of item i and its order quantity X_{ij} should be equal or less than its capacity, these constraints are;

$$\sum_{i \in K_j} x_{ij} \le C_{ij}, \quad j \in S_i,$$

Demand constraint - As sum of the assigned order quantities to available suppliers for each product should meet the buyer's demand;

$$\sum_{j \in S_i} x_{ij} = D_i, \quad i \in K_j,$$

Quality constraint - Since Q_i is the buyer's maximum acceptable defective rate of item i and q_{ij} is the defective rate of supplier j, the quality constraint can be shown as;

$$\sum_{i \in K_j} \sum_{j \in S_i} q_{ij} x_{ij} \le Q_i D_i$$

Discount constraint - Business volume V_{jr} from supplier j should be in appropriate discount interval r of discount pricing schedule and only in one interval. It can be stated that;

$$b_{j,r-1} y_{jr} \le V_{jr} \le b_{j,r} y_{jr}, \quad j \in S_i, r \in R_j,$$
$$\sum_{r \in R_j} y_{rj} \le 1, \quad j \in S_i,$$

Delivery constraint - Since T_i is the buyer's minimum acceptable on-time delivery rate of item i and t_{ij} is the on-time delivery rate of supplier j, the delivery constraint can be shown as;

$$\sum_{i \in K_j} \sum_{j \in S_i} (1 - t_{ij}) x_{ij} \le (1 - T_i) D_i,$$

Nonnegativity and binary constraints

$x_{ij} \ge 0 \, i \in K_j; j \in S_i.$
$V_{rj} \ge 0, r \in R_j; j \in S_i.$
$y_{rj} = 0$ or 1 integer $r \in R_j; j \in S_i.$

Order Allocation Models (*No Backlogging*) with Multi Period, Single Product and Multiple Suppliers

Multi period Order Allocation Models requires more complex decision-making to determine inventory levels and capital budgeting according to time dimension (Ustun and Demirtas, 2008a). The objective functions and the constraints of this model are as follows:

Indices

$i = 1, \ldots, n$ index of suppliers; $t = 1, \ldots, T$ index of time periods.

Parameters

D_t: Demand of the product in period t.
  h_t: Holding cost of the product in period t.
  o_{it}: Order cost for supplier i in period t.
  q_{it}: Expected defect rate of supplier i in period t.
  v_i: Capacity of supplier i.
  c_{it}: Purchasing price of the product from supplier i in period t.

w_i: The overall score of the supplier i obtained from ANP Model.

Decision Variables

x_{it}: Number of the product ordered from supplier i in period t.

$y_{it} = 1$ if an order is placed on supplier i in time period t, 0 otherwise.

Intermediate Variables

I_t: Inventory of the product, carried over from period t to period $t + 1$. (We assume that $I_0 = 0$)

U: The maximum cost in each period.

Objective Functions

Total Cost - The sum of the periodic material cost, periodic order cost and holding cost should be minimized; therefore,

$$\min f_1(X,Y) = \sum_{t=1}^{T}\left(\sum_{i=1}^{n} c_{it}x_{it} + \sum_{i=1}^{n} o_{it}y_{it} + h_t I_t\right)$$

Total Defect Rate - q_{it} is the expected defect rate of the ith vendor in period t, this objective should be minimized; therefore,

$$\min f_2(X) = \sum_{t=1}^{T}\sum_{i=1}^{n} q_{it}x_{it}.$$

TVP- As w_i and x_{it} denote the normal weights of the suppliers and the numbers of purchased units from the ith supplier in period t respectively, and the following objective function is designed to maximize the total value of purchasing.

$$\max f_3(X) = \sum_{t=1}^{T}\sum_{i=1}^{n} w_i x_{it}.$$

Balancing the total cost among time periods- in order to balance the total cost among the periods maximum periodic cost should be minimized; therefore,

$$\min f_4(X,Y) = \max_{t=1,\dots,T}\left\{f_{4t}(X,Y) = \sum_{i=1}^{n} c_{it}x_{it} + \sum_{i=1}^{n} o_{it}y_{it} + h_t I_t\right\}$$

The objective function $f_4(X,Y)$ is nonlinear and non-differentiable so the following linear expression equivalent to $f_4(X,Y)$ is more usable for optimization.

$$\min\left\{U \in R \,\middle|\, U \geq f_{4t}(X,Y), t = 1,\dots,T\right\}.$$

Constraints

The constraints of the problem are formulated as follows:

Capacity constraints-As supplier i can provide up to v_i units of the product and its order quantity in period t (x_{it}) should be equal or less than its capacity, these constraints are;

$$x_{it} \leq v_i * y_{it} \; i = 1,2,\dots,n; \; t = 1,2,\dots,T.$$

Demand constraint- As sum of the assigned order quantities to n suppliers and carried quantities from the preceding period should meet the buyer's demand;

$$I_{t-1} + \sum_{i=1}^{n} x_{it} \geq D_t \; t = 1,2,\dots,T.$$

Material balance equations

$$I_t = \sum_{i=1}^{n} x_{it} - D_t + I_{t-1} \; t = 1,2,\dots,T.$$

Nonnegativity and binary constraints

$$x_{it} \geq 0 \; i = 1, 2,\dots, n; \; t = 1, 2,\dots, T,$$
$$I_t \geq 0 \; t = 1, 2,\dots, T,$$
$$y_{it} = 0 \text{ or } 1 \text{ integer } i = 1, 2,\dots, n; \; t = 1, 2,\dots, T.$$

Order Allocation Models (*Backlogging Allowed*) with Multi Period, Single Product and Multiple Suppliers

We can obtain the order allocation model with backlogging by introducing the positive variables I_t^+ and I_t^- to Ustun and Demirtas (2008a)'s model as on-hand inventory and backorder position, respectively, at the end of period t. Then the net inventory position is $I_t = I_t^+ - I_t^-$.

Order Allocation Models (*Backlogging Allowed*) with Multi Period, Multi Product and Multiple Suppliers

Ustun and Demirtas (2008a)'s model can be generalized situations that inventory handling and backlogging are allowed for multi-product environments. The objective functions and the constraints of this model are as follows:

Indices:

$i = 1,..., n$ index of products; $j = 1,..., n$ index of suppliers, $t = 1,...,T$ index of time periods.

Parameters:

D_{it}: Demand of the product i in period t.

   h_{it}: Holding cost of the product i in period t.

   π_{it}: Backorder cost of the product i in period t.

   o_{jt}: Order cost for supplier j in period t.

   q_{ijt}: Expected defect rate of product i from supplier j in period t.

   v_j: Capacity of supplier j.

   c_{ijt}: Purchasing price of the product i from supplier j in period t.

   w_j: The overall score of the supplier j obtained from AHP or ANP Model.

   pt_{ij} : Unit production time of the product i for the jth supplier

Decision Variables:

x_{ijt}: Number of the product i ordered from supplier j in period t.

   $y_{jt} = 1$ if an order is placed on supplier j in time period t, 0 otherwise.

Intermediate Variables:

I_{it}^+: Inventory of the product i, at the end of period t.

   I_{it}^- : Backorder position of the product i, at the end of period t.

U: The maximum cost in each period.

Objective Functions

Total Cost - The sum of the periodic material cost, periodic order cost, holding cost and backorder cost should be minimized; therefore,

$$\min f_1(X,Y) = \sum_{t=1}^{T}\left[\sum_{j=1}^{n}\sum_{i=1}^{m}c_{ijt}x_{ijt} + \sum_{j=1}^{n}o_{jt}y_{jt} + \sum_{i=1}^{m}(h_{it}I_{it}^+ + \pi_{it}I_{it}^-)\right]$$

Total Defect Rate - q_{ijt} is the expected defect rate of the product i from supplier j in period t, this objective should be minimized; therefore,

$$\min f_2(X) = \sum_{t=1}^{T}\sum_{i=1}^{n}q_{it}x_{it} .$$

Total Value of Purchasing - As w_i and x_{ijt} denote the normal weights of the suppliers and the numbers of purchased units from the jth supplier in period t respectively, and the following objective function is designed to maximize the total value of purchasing.

$$\max f_3(X) = \sum_{t=1}^{T}\sum_{j=1}^{n}\sum_{i=1}^{m}w_j x_{ijt} .$$

Balancing the total cost among time periods- in order to balance the total cost among the periods maximum periodic cost should be minimized; therefore,

$$\min f_4(X,Y) = \max_{t=1,...T}\left\{f_{4t}(X,Y) = \sum_{j=1}^{n}\sum_{i=1}^{m}c_{ijt}x_{ijt} + \sum_{j=1}^{n}o_{jt}y_{jt} + \sum_{i=1}^{m}(h_{it}I_{it}^+ + \pi_{it}I_{it}^-)\right\}$$

The objective function $f_4(X,Y)$ is nonlinear and non-differentiable so the following linear expression equivalent to $f_4(X,Y)$ is more usable for optimization.

$$\min\left\{U \in R \mid U \geq f_{4t}(X,Y), t = 1,...,T\right\} .$$

Constraints

Capacity constraints- As supplier j can provide up to v_j production time capacity and its production time should be equal or less than its capacity, these constraints are;

$$\sum_{i=1}^{m} pt_{ij} x_{ijt} \leq v_j * y_{jt} \; j=1,2,\ldots,n; \; t=1,2,\ldots,T.$$

Demand constraint- As sum of the assigned order quantities to n suppliers and carried quantities from the preceding period should meet the buyer's demand;

$$I_{i,t-1}^+ - I_{i,t-1}^- + \sum_{j=1}^{n} x_{ijt} \geq D_{it}, \; i=1,2,\ldots,m; \; t=1,2,\ldots,T.$$

Material balance equations

$$I_{it}^+ - I_{it}^- = \sum_{j=1}^{n} x_{ijt} - D_{it} + I_{i,t-1}^+ - I_{i,t-1}^- \; i=1,2,\ldots,m; \; t=1,2,\ldots,T.$$

Nonnegativity and binary constraints

$$x_{ijt} \geq 0 \; i=1,2,\ldots,m; j=1,2,\ldots,n; t=1,2,\ldots,T,$$
$$I_{it}^+, I_{it}^- \geq 0 \; i=1,2,\ldots,m; \; t=1,2,\ldots,T,$$
$$y_{jt} = 0 \text{ or } 1 \text{ integer } j=1,2,\ldots,n; \; t=1,2,\ldots,T.$$

The given models in this section are multi-objective optimization models. These multi-objective models are formulated in such a way as to simultaneously determine the number of suppliers to employ and the order quantities allocated to them so as to concurrently minimize or maximize the objectives, while satisfying the constraints. In the multi-objective models, solution concept is different from single objective models.

Let S be the feasible region in decision space of the multi-objective order allocation model. A point $x^0 \in S$ is called an efficient solution of the model if there is no other point $x \in S$ such that $f_k(x) \geq f_k(x^0)$ for $k=1,2,\ldots,s$ with strict inequality holding for at least one component. The image $f(x^0)$ of an efficient solution x^0 in the objective space is called a non-dominated solution.

These models have many efficient solutions according to the trade-off between conflicting criteria. Hence, multi-objective methods are required to reach a decision for decision maker.

MULTI-OBJECTIVE OPTIMIZATION METHODS

In this section, we will concentrate mainly on works that employ operations research and computational models. Many real-life supplier selection problems as well as the proposed models in the literature involve more than one objective. Thereby, we will focus on the main properties of the multi-objective supplier selection and order allocation models and its solution procedures. Over the last decade, various interactive methods and decision support systems have been developed to deal with multi-objective programming (MOP) problems. In the same period, a variety of scalarization methods have been developed to find efficient solutions of MOP's. Scalarization means combining different objectives to a single one such that the obtained single objective optimization problem allows to find (all) Pareto (or properly) efficient solutions of the initial multi-objective problem. There are many scalarization methods for combining different objectives to a single one (see, for example, Chankong and Haimes, 1983; Ehrgott, 2005).

Reservation Level Driven Tchebycheff Procedure (RLTP)

An approach to reducing the set of nondominated solutions within a Tchebycheff framework is a RLTP proposed by Reeves and Macleod (1999). This approach uses RL based upon decision maker responses for objective space reduction. This RLTP is shown to be more flexible than the original Interactive Weighted Tchebycheff Procedure (IWTP), while producing solutions of similar high quality Reeves and Macleod (1999). Tchebycheff metric based approaches have become popular for sampling the set of nondominated solutions in an interactive search for a most preferred solution in multiobjective decision making situations. These approaches systematically reduce the set of nondominated solutions which remain available for identification and selection from one iteration to the next. One of the Tchebycheff metric based approaches is RLTP. This approach uses RL based upon decision maker responses for objective space reduction. ε-constraint method can also use RL to solve non-convex MOP's. Because of nonconvex nature of the problem and RL, ε-constraint and RLTP methods are more suitable than goal programming techniques.

RLTP can be described in terms of an initialization phase followed by one or more iterations. Iterations consist of sampling, solution, and adjustment.

Step 1. Initialization

Specify the number of solutions, P, to be presented to the DM at each iteration, where $P \geq s$.

Compute a reference objective vector, z, where $z = \max\{f_k(x)|\ x \in S\} + \varepsilon_k$ and the ε_k values are small positive scalars, for use in solving the Tchebycheff programs.

Set $RL_k = -\infty$, $k = 1, \ldots, s$, where RL_k is the RL for the kth objective.

The maximum number of iterations could be prespecified also, if desired, as part of the initialization process.

Step 2. Sampling

Generate a group of $2P$ dispersed weight vectors,

$$\Delta = \{\lambda \in R^s \big| \lambda_k \in (0,1), \sum_{k=1}^{s} \lambda_k = 1\}.$$

Step 3. Solution

Solve the associated Thebycheff program for each weight vector

$$\min \{\alpha - \rho \sum_{k=1}^{s} z_k\}$$

s.t.

$$\alpha \geq \lambda_k(z_k^{**} - z_k) \quad k = 1, \ldots, s,$$
$$f_k(x) = z_k \qquad\quad k = 1, \ldots, s,$$
$$z_k \geq RL_k \qquad\quad k = 1, \ldots, s,$$
$$x \in S.$$

where ρ is a small positive scalar. Present the

P most different of the resulting objective vectors to the DM. If the DM wishes to continue to search for an improved solution, proceed to step 4. Otherwise, have the DM select his/her current most preferred solution and stop.

Step 4. Adjustment

Have the DM partition the current solutions into more preferred and less preferred subsets,

$$MPWV_k - r(MPWV_k - CSWV_k) \qquad (I)$$

adjust the RL and return to step 2.

DM participates more actively in this procedure only at step 4 of each intermediate iteration and step 3 of the final iteration. At these iterations DM try to partition current solutions into more preferred and less preferred subsets and choose most preferred solution. RL are adjusted based upon the objective values of the current more preferred and less preferred solutions. The RL can be adjusted automatically by the RLTP, rather than by the DM, as a default option. The following default objective space reduction is suggested by Reeves and Macleod (1999).

Let $CSWV_k$ and $MPWV_k$ be the worst values for the ith objective over the set of all current solution and the subset of most preferred current solutions, respectively. RL_k could be specified as equation I, where r is a reduction factor between 0 and 1. Smaller values for r would correspond to faster rates of objective space reduction.

Additionally, giving DM, the option of adjusting some or all of the RL does allow them to participate more actively in the interactive solution process, if they choose to do so.

On the other hand readers can find methods for generating dispersed weight vectors at step 2 in Steuer's studies (Steuer, 1983; Steuer, 1986). The suggested range for the parameter at step 3 is from 0.0001 to 0.01 given in Steuer (1983). Methods for reducing the number of trial solutions generated at step 3 down to the P most different are discussed in Steuer's studies (Steuer, 1983; Steuer, 1986).

Several experiments were conducted to compare the performance of the RLTP and IWTP by Reeves and Macleod (1999).

Demirtas and Ustun (2008) and Ustun and Demirtas (2008a) proposed RLTP to solve single period and multi period order allocation problems, respectively.

ε-Constraint Method

In ε-constraint method, introduced by Haimes et al. (Chankong and Haimes, 1983), one of the objective functions is selected to be optimized and all the other objective functions are converted into constraints by giving an upper bound for each of them. ε_k values can be assumed equal to RL_k values.

Now the problem to be solved is in this form:

$$\min f_j(x)$$
$$\text{s.t. } f_k(x) \leq \varepsilon_k \text{ for all } k = 1,\ldots,s; j \neq k \ (\varepsilon_k = RL_k)$$
$$x \in S.$$

Ghodsypour and O'Brien (2008) proposed the ε-constraint method to solve their multi-objective order allocation model. Demirtas and Ustun (2008) and Ustun and Demirtas (2008a) have also used the ε-constraint method to compare results with RLTP.

Preemptive Goal Programming (PGP)

On the other hand, measuring the relative importance among objectives in an ordinal scale usually results in a preemptive priority ranking, which divides the objectives $f_1,\ldots,f_s$ into L priority classes, $1 \leq L \leq s$. Each class is associated with the quantity $P_l, l = 1,\ldots, L$, signifying that the lth class has lth priority. Preemptive priority ranking is in the same spirit as that used in the lexicographic ordering. Although it is not necessary to assign any numerical value to each P_l, it is convenient to think of $P_1,\ldots, P_L$ as a sequence of numbers with the property $P_l \gg P_{l+1}$ for each $l = 1,\ldots, L$-1.

The analytical structure of a PGP model is the following:

$$\min \sum_{l=1}^{L} P_l \left(\sum_{k \in J_l} (w_k^+ d_k^+ + w_k^- d_k^-) \right),$$
subject to
$$f_k(x) - d_k^+ + d_k^- = t_k, k = 1,\ldots,s,$$
$$d_k^-, d_k^+ \geq 0 \text{ and } d_k^- . d_k^+ = 0, k = 1,\ldots,s,$$
$$x \in S,$$

where J_l is the set of indices of objective functions in the lth priority class, t_k is target level for kth goal, d_k^- and d_k^+ are negative and positive deviations from target value of kth goal respectively. w_k^- and w_k^+ are weights of the negative and positive deviations from target value of kth goal respectively.

Preemptive achievement functions imply a non-compensatory structure of preferences. In other words, there are no finite trade-offs among goals placed in different priority levels. Wang et al. (2004) proposed PGP to solve the order allocation model with single product, single period and multiple suppliers.

If there are finite trade-offs among goals placed in different priority levels, Archimedean Goal Programming (AGP) is applied to solve the order allocation model. In the other hand, if a decision maker wants to balance the unwanted deviations, Min-max Goal Programming is more desirable than others. For a usage of any combinations of these type of GP, achievement scalarizing functions proposed by Romero (2004). Demirtas and Ustun proposed the AGP and achievement scalarizing function for solving the multi period order allocation models (Demirtas and Ustun, 2006, Ustun and Demirtas, 2008b).

Conic Scalarization Method (CSM)

The CSM suggested by Gasimov (2001). Gasimov introduced an explicit class of increasing convex functions which serve for combining different objectives to a single one without any restrictions on objectives and constraints of the problem under consideration, such as convexity and/or boundedness. These functions were used to characterize Benson proper efficient solutions of non-convex multiobjective problems in terms of saddle points of scalar Lagrangian functions introduced in the paper. Besides, this approach preserves convexity, if the initial problem has such a property. Note that it has successfully been applied to a multi-objective 0–1 faculty course assignment problem studied by Ozdemir and Gasimov (2004) and multi-objective 1.5 dimensional assortment problem studied by Gasimov et al. (2007).

The scalarizing function of the CSM is the following:

$$\min_{x \in S} \left\{ \alpha \sum_{k=1}^{s} \left| f_k(x) - a_k \right| + \sum_{k=1}^{s} w_k \left[f_k(x) - a_k \right] \right\}$$

The weights vector $\{\alpha, w_1, \ldots, w_s\}$ must be selected from the set $W := \{(\alpha, w) \in R \times R^s \mid 0 \leq \alpha < \min\{w_1, \ldots, w_s\}\}$. The parameter a_k is reference point for kth objective. It is reflected a aspiration level of decision maker for kth objective to the model.

Although some of the methods work well only on problems with concave objective functions and a convex feasible region, the order allocation models have discrete variables, so the set of nondominated solutions for these problems is not convex. Weighted sums of the objective functions do not provide a way of reaching every nondominated solution. Besides supported nondominated solutions, there exist unsupported ones—solutions that are dominated by convex combinations of other nondominated solutions. Tchebycheff metric-based scalarizing programs and Conic scalarizing programs have the advantage over weighted-sums programs of being able to reach, not only supported, but also unsupported nondominated solutions. These achievement functions were designed to have a significant advantage over goal programming by producing only nondominated, or pareto-optimal solutions.

COMPARISON OF THE INTEGRATED MODELS

All integrated approaches discussed in this chapter are listed according to their characteristics such as the supplier selection procedure, product type, discount type, time dimension, inventory handling and backlogging, objectives or goals, constraints and scalarization methods in Table 1. The advantages and disadvantages of these models can be easily shown by their related characteristics. For example, main advantages of Ustun and Demirtas's study (2008a) are to consider the time dimension and nonconvex nature of the mathematical model by using RLTP. It also provides more flexible decision-making process joining with decision maker. On the other hand, it does not consider product types, discount types and variability of the parameters.

This chapter is based on recent developments in supplier selection and order allocation process. The integration of the suppliers and main firms is discussed according to the supplier selection and order allocation point of views. The integrated approaches selected in literature are also given in detail. Also some generalizations of these models are proposed in sections 3.2, 3.5 and 3.6. Unlike the traditional cost-based optimization techniques, the proposed approach considers both quantitative and qualitative factors and also aims at maximizing the benefits of deliverer and customers.

FUTURE TRENDS

In this chapter, after the stages of supplier selection process are explained, these new integrated models are introduced and their constraints, variables, and goals/objectives of these models are explained in detail. Then the solution methods of these integrated models are given. Finally, different integrated models are compared by considering their advantages and disadvantages. The Enterprise Information System (EIS) integration of the

Table 1. The characteristics of the integrated approaches

Characteristics / Study	Wang et al. (2004)	Xia and Wu (2007)	Demirtas and Ustun (2008)	Demirtas and Ustun (2007)	Ustun and Demirtas (2008a)	Ustun and Demirtas (2008b)
Suppliers Evaluation Method	AHP	AHP improved by Rough Sets Theory	ANP	ANP	ANP	ANP
Product Type	Multiple	Multiple	Single	Single	Single	Single
Discount Type	No	Volume Discount	No	No	No	No
Time Dimension	Single Period	Single Period	Single Period	Multi-period	Multi-period	Multi-period
Inventory Handling and Backlogging	No	No	No	Inventory handling	Inventory handling	Inventory handling
Objectives / Goals	TVP, Total Cost of Purchase.	TVP, Total Purchase Cost, Defective Product, Delivered on Time.	Cost, Defect Rate, TVP.	Budget, Aggregate Quality, TVP, Demand.	Total Cost, Total Defect Rate, TVP, Balancing.	Total Cost, Periodic Budget, Total Aggregate Quality, Periodic Aggregate Quality, Total Shipment.
Constraints	Capacity, Demand.	Capacity, Discount, Demand, Quality, Delivery.	Capacity, Demand.	Capacity, Material Balance.	Capacity, Demand, Material Balance.	Capacity, Demand, Material Balance.
Scalarization Methods	PGP	-	RLTP, ε-Constraint.	AGP	RLTP, ε-Constraint, PGP.	Additive Achievement Scalarizing Function.
Case Study / Numerical Example	Illustrative Example	Numerical Examples	Numerical Example	Numerical Example	Numerical Example	Numerical Example

suppliers and main firms in SMEs can be studied other perspectives such as logistic firm and route selection, competition policy, production planning and control systems, warehouse, facility planning and design, management information systems design, etc. To solve the mathematical models which represents these real life systems, meta-heuristics can be applied to solution procedure. The AHP or ANP can be integrated with these meta-heuristics, including simulated annealing (SA) and tabu search (TS), Artifical Neural Network (ANN), Genetic Algorithms (GA). Because the meta-heuristics are more efficient in solving hard optimization problems than the exact algorithms, the combined approaches can be applied

to solve the combinatorial optimization problems with multiple criteria. On the other hand, SMEs need the classification systems to evaluate the worldwide suppliers. Data mining techniques can be integrated to EIS of SMEs for this purpose.

REFERENCES

Aissaoui, N., Haouari, M., & Hassini, E. (2007). Supplier selection and order lot sizing modeling: A review. Computers & Operations Research, 34, 3516–3540. doi:10.1016/j.cor.2006.01.016doi:10.1016/j.cor.2006.01.016

Benyoucef, L., Ding, H., & Xie, X. (2003). *Supplier selection problem: Selection criteria and methods*. INRIA, Rapport de recherché no. 4726.

Cardozo, R. N., & Cagley, J. W. (1971). Experimental study of industrial buyer behavior. JMR, Journal of Marketing Research, 8, 329–334. doi:10.2307/3149571doi:10.2307/3149571

Chankong, V., & Haimes, Y. Y. (1983). *Multiobjective decision making: Theory and methodology*. New York: Elsevier Science Publishing.

Chapman, S. N., & Carter, P. L. (1990). Supplier/customer inventory relationships under just-in-time. Decision Sciences, 21, 35–51.

Cook, W. D., & Seiford, L. M. (2009). Data envelopment analysis (DEA)-thirty years on. European Journal of Operational Research, 192, 1–17. doi:10.1016/j.ejor.2008.01.032doi:10.1016/j.ejor.2008.01.032

Cusumano, M. A., & Takeishi, A. (1991). Supplier relations and management: A survey of Japanese, Japanese-transplant, and U.S. auto plants. Strategic Management Journal, 12, 563–588. doi:10.1002/smj.4250120802doi:10.1002/smj.4250120802

De Boer, L., Labro, E., & Morlacchi, P. A. (2001). Review of methods supporting supplier selection. European Journal of Purchasing and Supply Management, 7, 75–89. doi:10.1016/S0969-7012(00)00028-9doi:10.1016/S0969-7012(00)00028-9

De Boer, L., & Van der Wegen, L. L. M. (2003). Practice and promise of formal supplier selection: A study of four empirical cases. Journal of Purchasing and Supply Management, 9, 109–118. doi:10.1016/S1478-4092(03)00018-9doi:10.1016/S1478-4092(03)00018-9

Demirtas, E. A., & Ustun, O. (2006). Analytic network process and multi-period goal programming integration in purchasing decisions. Computers & Industrial Engineering. doi:10.1016/j.cie.2006.12.006.

Demirtas, E. A., & Ustun, O. (2008). An integrated multiobjective decision making process for supplier selection and order allocation. *Omega - The International Journal of Management Science, 36*, 76-90.

Dickson, G. W. (1966). An analysis of supplier selection: systems and decisions. Journal of Purchasing, 1, 5–17.

Dyer, R. F., & Forman, E. H. (1992). Group decision support with the analytic hierarchy process. Decision Support Systems, 8, 99–124. doi:10.1016/0167-9236(92)90003-8doi:10.1016/0167-9236(92)90003-8

Ehrgott, M. (2005). *Multicriteria optimization* (2nd ed.). Berlin, Germany: Springer-Verlag.

Gasimov, R. N. (2001). Characterization of the Benson proper efficiency and scalarization in nonconvex vector optimization. In M. Koksalan & S. Zionts (Eds.), Multiple criteria decision making in the new millennium (pp. 189-198). Berlin, Germany:Springer-Verlag.

Gasimov, R. N., Sipahioglu, A., & Sarac, T. (2007). A multi-objective programming approach to 1.5 dimensional assortment problem. European Journal of Operational Research, 179, 64–79. doi:10.1016/j.ejor.2006.03.016doi:10.1016/j.ejor.2006.03.016

Ghodsypour, S. H., & O'Brien, C. (1998). A decision support system for supplier selection using an integrated analytic hierarchy process and linear programming. International Journal of Production Economics, 56-57, 199–212. doi:10.1016/S0925-5273(97)00009-1doi:10.1016/S0925-5273(97)00009-1

Hinkle, C. L., Robinson, P. J., & Green, P. E. (1969). Vendor evaluation using cluster analysis. Journal of Purchasing, 5, 49–58.

Ho, W. (2008). Integrated analytic hierarchy process and its applications – a literature review. European Journal of Operational Research, 186, 211–228. doi:10.1016/j.ejor.2007.01.004doi:10.1016/j.ejor.2007.01.004

Holt, G. D. (1998). Which contractor selection methodology? International Journal of Project Management, 16, 153–164. doi:10.1016/S0263-7863(97)00035-5doi:10.1016/S0263-7863(97)00035-5

Hwang, C. L., & Yoon, K. (1981). *Multi attribute decision making*. New York: Springer.

Keeney, L. R. (1994). Creativity in decision making with value-focused thinking. Sloan Management Review, 35, 33–41.

Liu, J., Ding, F. Y., & Lall, V. (2000). Using data envelopment analysis to compare suppliers for supplier selection and performance improvement. Supply Chain Management: An International Journal, 5(3), 143–150. doi:10.1108/13598540010338893doi:10.1108/13598540010338893

Mobolurin, A. (1995). Multi-hierarchical qualitative group decision method: Consensus building in supplier selection. In *Proceedings of the International conference on applied modeling, simulation and optimization,* USA (pp. 149-152).

Monczka, R. M., Giunipero, L. C., & Reck, R. F. (1981). Perceived importance of supplier information. *Journal of purchasing and Materials Management, 17,* 21-29.

Moriarity, R. T. (1983). *Industrial buying behavior*. Lexington, MA: Lexington Books.

Narasimhan, R. (1983). An analytic approach to supplier selection. Journal of Purchasing and Supply Management, 1, 27–32.

Ng, S. T., & Skitmore, R. M. (1995). CPDSS:Ddecision support system for contractor prequalification. Civil Engineering Systems: Decision Making Problem Solving, 12(2), 133–160.

Ozdemir, M. S., & Gasimov, R. N. (2004). The analytic hierarchy process and multiobjective 0–1 faculty course assignment. European Journal of Operational Research, 157(2), 398–408. doi:10.1016/S0377-2217(03)00189-9doi:10.1016/S0377-2217(03)00189-9

Papagapiou, A., Mingers, J., & Thanassoulis, E. (1996). Would you buy a used car with DEA? OR Insight, 10(1), 13–19.

Pawlak, Z., & Slowinsky, R. (1994). Rough set approach to multi-attribute decision analysis. European Journal of Operational Research, 72, 443–459. doi:10.1016/0377-2217(94)90415-4doi:10.1016/0377-2217(94)90415-4

Reeves, G. R., & MacLeod, K. R. (1999). Some experiments in Tchebycheff-based approaches for interactive multiple objective decision making. Computers & Operations Research, 26, 1311–1321. doi:10.1016/S0305-0548(98)00108-7doi:10.1016/S0305-0548(98)00108-7

Saaty, T. L. (2001). *Decision making with dependence and feedback—the analytic network process* (2nd ed.). Pittsburgh, USA: RWS Publications.

Slowinsky, R. (1992). *Intelligent decision support: Handbook of applications and advances of the rough set theory*. Dordrecht: Kluwer Academic Publishers.

Steuer, R. E. (1986). *Multiple criteria optimization*. New York: Wiley.

Steuer, R. E., & Choo, E. U. (1983). An interactive weighted Tchebycheff procedure for multiple objective programming. Mathematical Programming, 26, 326–344. doi:10.1007/BF02591870doi:10.1007/BF02591870

Talluri, S., & Narasimhan, R. (2003). Vendor evaluation with performance variability: A max–min approach. European Journal of Operational Research, 146, 543–552. doi:10.1016/S0377-2217(02)00230-8doi:10.1016/S0377-2217(02)00230-8

Timmerman, E. (1986). An approach to vendor performance evaluation. Journal of Purchasing and Supply Management, 1, 27–32.

Tullous, R., & Munson, J. M. (1991). Trade-offs under uncertainty: implications for industrial purchasers. International Journal of Purchasing and Materials Management, 27, 24–31.

Ustun, O., & Demirtas, E. A. (2008a). An integrated multi-objective decision making process for multi-period lot-sizing with supplier selection. *Omega - The International Journal of Management Science, 36*(4), 509-521.

Ustun, O., & Demirtas, E. A. (2008b). Multi-period lot-sizing with supplier selection using achievement scalarizing functions. Computers & Industrial Engineering, 54(4), 918–931. doi:10.1016/j.cie.2007.10.021doi:10.1016/j.cie.2007.10.021

Verma, R., & Pullman, M. E. (1998). An analysis of the supplier selection process. Omega, 26, 739–750. doi:10.1016/S0305-0483(98)00023-1doi:10.1016/S0305-0483(98)00023-1

Wang, G., Huang, S. H., & Dismukes, J. P. (2004). Product-driven supply chain selection using integrated multi-criteria decision-making methodology. International Journal of Production Economics, 91, 1–15. doi:10.1016/S0925-5273(03)00221-4doi:10.1016/S0925-5273(03)00221-4

Wang, S. Y., Chang, S. L., & Wang, R. C. (2009). Assessment of supplier performance based on product-development strategy by applying multi-granularity linguistic term sets. *Omega - The International Journal of Management Science, 37*(1), 215-226.

Weber, C. A., Current, J. R., & Benton, W. C. (1991). Supplier selection criteria and methods. European Journal of Operational Research, 50, 2–18. doi:10.1016/0377-2217(91)90033-Rdoi:10.1016/0377-2217(91)90033-R

Weber, C. A., Current, J. R., & Desai, A. (1998). Non-cooperative negotiation strategies for vendor selection. European Journal of Operational Research, 108, 208–223. doi:10.1016/S0377-2217(97)00131-8doi:10.1016/S0377-2217(97)00131-8

Weber, C. A., & Desai, A. (1996). Determination of paths to vendor market efficiency using parallel co-ordinates representation: A negotiation tool for buyers. European Journal of Operational Research, 90, 142–155. doi:10.1016/0377-2217(94)00336-Xdoi:10.1016/0377-2217(94)00336-X

Weber, C. A., & Ellram, L. M. (1992). Supplier selection using multi-objective programming: A decision support system approach. International Journal of Physical Distribution & Logistics Management, 23(2), 3–14. doi:10.1108/09600039310038161doi:10.1108/09600039310038161

Wind, Y., & Robinson, P. J. (1968). The determinants of vendor selection: Evaluation function approach. *Journal of Purchasing and Materials Management, August*, 29-41.

Woodside, A. G., & Vyas, N. (1987). *Industrial purchasing strategies*. Lexington, MA: Lexington Books.

Xia, W., & Wu, Z. (2007). Supplier selection with multiple criteria in volume discount environments. *Omega - The International Journal of Management Science, 35*, 494-504.

Chapter 6
Complex Information Technology–Intensive Firms:
A New Paradigmatic Firm–Theoretical Imperative! (Or a Pragmatically Impractical Interpretation of the Nature of the Virtualized Firm?)

Jonatan Jelen
Parsons The New School for Design, USA

Marko Kolakovic
Ekonomski Fakultet Zagreb, Croatia

ABSTRACT

In its late 20th century incarnation, information technology has affected our economic structures not only more intensely but all around differently than in its previous heydays when it brought us language or print. The objective of the present research is to identify if and to what extent IT has transformed society's very crown jewel of productivity, the firm. IT has impacted every parameter and variable of the firm's character, its strategy, structure, scale, scope, and social position in such fundamental ways that we may be in the presence of a truly new nature of the firm. The resulting complex information technology-intensive firms are much altered from the original nature of the firm as it was envisaged by Ronald Coase and his fellow New Institutionalists. Through empirical research the authors are trying to identify and model some elements of a new framework of why and how firms are intended, designed, and created.

INTRODUCTORY FRAMEWORK

Many of the new phenomena of the information and information technology-centric new economy and network society are presenting formidable interpretive and conceptual challenges for the information systems (IS) discipline. This is driving novel constructs and frameworks for its more prominent productive elements, i.e. firms.

We focus one such specific phenomenon: The impact of information technology IT on the design

DOI: 10.4018/978-1-60566-856-7.ch006

elements of firms, which is giving rise to complex information technology-intensive (CITI) firms.

The objective of this research is to identify if and to what extent the current wave of IT has affected the *design elements* used to conceive and construct firms. We have discovered that IT in its most recent forms is transformational in nature and is no longer limited to transactional effects. We show how this transformative effect manifests itself in a particular segment of the new economy, associated with social networking, community, and wiki models. This segment is exemplified by the emergence of such well-known firms as Google, YouTube, Face Book, Craig's List, Amazon, and eBay, and such little known firms such as jamspire.com (a website in New York connecting artists and the art world for varied projects) and HJenglish.com (a Shanghai-based website primarily dedicated to creating communities for Chinese foreign language learners).

Our contribution will be to show how profoundly the design elements of firms have been affected by the current version of IT and to propose elements of a framework that resiliently accommodates such effects. This framework can guide the practitioner designer for further refinements in the conception of CITI firms. The discoveries and framework elements are the result of our grounded theory methodology study in which executives, professionals, practitioners, entrepreneurs, and high-level decision-makers from a variety of firms participated.

A brief note on research methodology

Notwithstanding the theoretical character of this concept paper, the uncovered dimensions and framework elements are the result of a grounded theory methodology study in which sixteen executives, professionals, practitioners, entrepreneurs, and high-level decision-makers from a variety of firms in New York, Shanghai, China, and Zagreb, Croatia, were tape-interviewed over a eight–month period in 2007-2008.

We first take up the elements of the above stated research objective in turn.

1. The current impact of information technology

From an economic perspective, our new economy is sometimes labeled "information economy" or "knowledge economy". This label is erroneous, as every economy was an information or knowledge economy (Foss, 2001). Information and knowledge were always important in the economic productive process. IT as a productive technology always coexisted with other technologies of productions, such as transformation, transportation, energy-generation, energy-distribution, coordination, collaboration, and transaction technologies. Over time, operating under different conditions and environments, these technologies took turns moving to the foreground. IT itself had played a lead role at several junctures – for example, as we entered the era of print culture, then electronic culture, and now as we move into the photonic age.

From an IS perspective, IT was originally considered important for its transactional contributions. We moved from automating to informating to strategically leveraging the knowledge of the firm to operate cheaper, faster, better. Firms *adopted* IT and *adapted to* IT in order to enhance their activities, their decision making, and their positions as economic actors. Firms controlled the absorption and integration of IT and the ensuing effects on the firms' functioning.

The dynamics of the underlying change in the IS discipline were pragmatically captured by the interactionist perspective and structuration theory (Orlikowsky, 1993), for example, kept fixed the parameters of the organizational paradigm.

However, we have uncovered additional truly transformational effects deserving of increased attention today. Unlike previous technologies that had to be practiced to manifest themselves, information and knowledge with their cognitive characteristics, simply exist, whether used in the productive process or not.

In this research we have identified the extent of this property specific to information and IT and how it affects the model of the firm, its design elements, and ultimately its character, possibly redefining the nature of at least one cluster of firm type. It is this perspective that will inform the scope of this research.

2. The design elements of firms

In order to demonstrate our proposition, we first separate the pragmatic from the paradigmatic aspect of the firm.

From a *pragmatic* vantage point, firms are practical productive assets. Their purpose is value creation, their activity is production of products and services through processes, their objective is profits. Call this the business *mode*.

But firms also have also a *paradigmatic* aspect. They represent our most sophisticated business *model* for productive assets to date, elegantly sidestepping some of the infamous shortcomings of individual production, peer-production, statism, and markets. The business model can be broken down into its functional components on one hand (Afuah, 2003, Afuah and Tucci, 2002), and what we will label its design elements that define the "nature of the firm" on the other hand. Originally, this latter terminology was proposed by Ronald Coase (Coase, 1937) and further refined by the ensuing New Institutionalist school of economic thought (Williamson and Winter, 1991). Coase used it to identify the particular capabilities of firms to make superior decisions about their scope of activities than markets would. He avert that the firm's predisposition to control which activities it would integrate or release back into the market, based on transaction cost associated with such integration - rather than on production cost - was the true nature of it. Since markets already assumed production cost-allocative decisions, a novel justification for the co-existence of firms with markets became necessary. And Coase delivered.

Subsequent work by Chandler expanded on the defining elements of the model, adding scale to scope, and including strategy and structure. And most recent work has identified social position through the creation of culture and social value (e.g. Arakji and Lang, 2007; Hughes and Lang, 2006) as an element of the model in its own right.

We hold that these elements of scale, scope, strategy, structure, and social position are not only constitutive of the firm as a model that can be used to describe and analyze the firm in terms of its outcomes, behaviors, and change processes, but are also design elements in their own right that can be used to generate new firm designs. Since we are interested in very young, utterly novel, and turbulently emergent firms in a very volatile and fast-paced environment, we are not interested in these variables as a result of an evolutionary bottom-up process upon being impacted by IT. Rather it is their reinterpreted character under the new realities of IT for purposes of a top-down design act for the CITI firm that informs our research. We then hold that certain combinations of these newly defined elements may yield firm designs beyond the interpretive and integrative capacity of the current framework. In this research we identify how IT's influence may generate such combinations and how the framework may have to evolve to accommodate them. We find that the current framework unduly limits itself to studying the formative forces on firms from an experiential, too epistemologically grounded bottom-up approach, and with the elements studied separately rather than integratively. Recognizing the possibilities of a more cognitive and ontological top-down design approach would provide greater insights and benefits.

We are encouraged by similar developments that expanded our understanding of the firm paradigm previously: Porter's (1996) value chain idea was extended to include the value shop and the value network; bureaucratic hierarchical organizations were joined by flat network structures; and finally the initial construct of productive organizations based on fairly rigid mechanistic forms evolved into recognizing a continuum between mechanistic and organic structures. It is this last example that particularly informs our research proposition.

The research on general Taylorian organizational (productive) or Weberian bureaucratic (administrative) structures identified five definitional variables of organizations or bureaucracies: specialization (division of labor), departmentalization (compartmentalization of like activities), chain-of-command (hierarchy), authority-responsibility linkages (reporting relationships), and span of control (size of the organizational subunits or groups to be commanded). Originally there was a tendency to interpret these variables strictly. Over time, however, understanding relaxed to allow for flexible, responsive, and nimble application. And if all of them are relaxed at the same time, an entirely new concept emerges, the organic form of the organization, creating the new continuum. In this scenario, organizations could choose where to position themselves rather than having to gravitate towards the mechanistic form or to be conflicted when departing from it.

We add our research to this movement. We identify the five variables -- scale, scope, strategy, structure, and social position -- as our design elements for firms. We evaluate evidence for how the advent of IT is enabling a more *a priori*-combination of these to generate firm designs not previously apparent.

3.   The construct of the complex information technology-intensive (CITI) firm

One possibility of new paradigmatic design is the case of the complex information technology-intensive (CITI) firm, especially in the form of the social networking sector, but also including the search sector (e.g. Google), the barter and exchange sector (e.g. eBay, Craig's List), and the sector of cultural goods creation through transmutability models (Hughes and Lang, 2006).

Intriguing anecdotal evidence and intuitive reasoning readily suggest a much greater level of complexity in describing these firms. Important questions arise: How were they created? What are the antecedents, consequences, and replicable results of these efforts for future entrepreneurs and decision-makers? These firms are challenging conventional wisdom and are curiosities in many respects: Their market valuation is high, and their growth is rapid, suggesting high levels of value creation. Yet it remains uncertain what exactly drives revenues and profits, how sustainable their position is, and how it will be translated into wealth. Their business models seem experimental and unfinished, their purpose and mission changing and unresolved, their product blurred. Their customers are not their users; that is, the users are not the paying party. Their industry or sector classification is unclear and their organizational structure incomplete. Yet, they have grown to become dominant players in our new economy.

We admit that 'CITI' is a rather liberally labeled and proprietary construct. Its purpose is to limit the scope of this research by contrasting CITIs to other modern firms that are simple information technology-intensive (SITI) constructs and merely a result of the patently necessary and natural increased adaptation to and adoption of IT.

But while the emergence and existence of the CITI firms is recognized for their intriguing activities and curious attributes, we suggest that their design, for its elements, influences, and consequences, merits a more ontological treatment.

THE EFFECT OF IT ON THE COMPONENTS OF THE FRAMEWORK

In the following we trace the effect of IT on the five design variables of the firm: strategy, structure, scale, scope, and social position.

The Impact of IT on Strategy

The notion of strategy has long been a challenging concept with fuzzy contours. Its breath in definition and depth in meaning resulted in some inconsistencies in interpretation and ambiguities in rationale.

In a narrow sense for example, in terms of the firm, it is the action plan that relates the purpose of value proposition to the goal of wealth creation. It translates this motivation into executable measures for three distinct levels, enterprise (corporate), business (unit), and product (individual products) and along two major dimensions, internal capabilities (resources and competencies) and external responsiveness (environmental fit).

At the other end of the spectrum, as a broader idea held by some strategy comprises the entire complex associated with purpose, mission, goal, policy, and actionable tactics of the firm as a productive economic and social actor.

Both perspectives, however, remain historically grounded in Greco-military principles. Strategy, in both its introverted and extroverted interpretation therefore evolved unchallenged as an adversarial paradigm with competitive advantage as its central premise. It was not until 1996 that the edge was taken off a little by Brandenburger's and Nalebuff's intervention labeled "co-opetition" (Brandenburger and Nalebuff, 1996).

The somewhat elastic and sometimes misconstrued purpose of strategy along with its contentious character resulted in some distinctly opportunistic practices over time. Strategy was highly combative, divisive, and aggressive. It was excessively focused on short-term profits at the expense of long-term customer loyalty. Inconsistently it was obsessive about competitor action while at the same time isolationist, secretive, and protective of proper intellectual property. Particularly for public firms increasingly dependent on external financial resources it was biased towards shareholders in neglect of cultivating a wider stakeholder community.

Under the impact of the current version of IT the complications associated with our understanding of strategy are taken to a new level. In fact, the current conditions created by IT challenge the purpose, the premise, and the practice of conventional strategy concurrently and in multiple aspects. It is around these three themes that we coded our contributors' comments.

1.   Strategy's new reason for being

It has created some unique conditions that warrant to examine if and to what extent the central tenets of strategy have shifted. As some describe it: "There is no entropy on the Web. Information only proliferates. There is no consumption of information, only obsolescence. There is no moment when the system will collapse because its major resource has been depleted. Information cannot be traded like conventional goods. There is no production-consumption dichotomy any longer, only production and more production and sharing. That changes the fundamental flow. The question then becomes, how then do we drive people to create it, share it, and spend their time with it without monetary benefit."

"It's not like you're dealing with selling something to people", notes another of our contributors. "You're involving users, giving them something to do." Others shared in this new perspective on strategy: "The objective is to create a service for them wherein they can become the service." "You have to empower people, give them a sense of autonomy, individuality."

These select albeit unsystematic, crude, and reductive statements of mainly practitioner entrepreneurs are indicative of how new context brought about by the uniqueness of information determines a new reason for being of strategy: it is transformational, and it is concerned primarily with the human condition.

Conventional strategic wisdom was highly transaction –centric. It was about out-selling and out-pacing the competitor through cheaper, better, and faster products and processes, based on superior rational decision-making and excellent execution. This particularly defining property of strategy has shifted substantially. While it certainly doesn't cease to need transactions to generate revenue and above-average returns or profits for purposes of expansion of beneficial productive activity, this needn't be the primary focus any longer. In fact, the associated problems are either already structured or at least programmable, thus solved or solvable. Therein lies little value. Much more valuable is the newly discovered transformational property of strategy.

In their transactional capacity strategy supported the firm either as part of the problem, part of the solution, or part of the landscape. It rationally processed conditions from the environment to optimize the firm's position with respect to a set of multiple constraints. The purpose of strategy was mostly to provide responsive, reactive, and defensive mechanisms.

The transformational aspect of strategy allows it now to proactively and preemptively either be the entire landscape and/or to move entire landscape and/or to move between landscapes. Case in point is Amazon. It didn't aspire to become just another participant in a larger market of bookseller but elevated itself to a marketmaker in its own right, actively shaping the entire book-trading environment. Strategy does radically change nature from a mere (action) planning paradigm to become agenda. The purpose of strategy is to make value-based choices, enact policy, cause movement of entire systems, not merely aspire to rationally best respond to the largest possible set of environmental economic and/or social conditions.

Secondly, while transactions are task-oriented, transformation is people-oriented. The human condition becomes thus the direct and primary determinant of the strategic purpose. The purpose of strategy is no longer to drive transactions, but to facilitate, create, leverage experiences. Strategy's purpose is no longer the repetitive completion of technical cycles involving products and processes,

production for consumption, but to maintain human interaction, perpetuate movement and change in the relationships between different economic actors.

2. The strategic premises revisited

Strategy is no longer preoccupied with managing the path to traverse between value proposition and wealth creation but to create, maintain, and solidify the relationships that exist between the many social and economic participant. The purpose is to weave a socio-economic web wherein participants take on different roles and functions of production based on the socio-economic occasion. This fundamentally affects the conventional basic premises of strategy.

These basic premises were originally formalized most elegantly by Michael Porter in his "Five Forces Model" (Porter, 1998), the power of buyers, power of suppliers, intensity of new entrants, intensity of rivalry, and availability of substitutes. In this context, strategy is predicated on a combative or defensive position to absorb, withstand, or overcome those forces. It is thus aggressive.

Furthermore, it presupposes that the opponent, the competitors are known or identifiable, and that the means are accessible and practical. It is thus highly technical and analytical in nature as represented by the famous SWOT analysis framework.

Finally, a necessary precondition for formulating strategy is a clear and widespread understanding of the ends to be obtained. Without these ends in view, it is argued, action is purely tactical and can quickly degenerate into nothing more than a flailing about. Strategy then has no existence apart from the ends sought. The formulation of strategy is thus highly deterministic, in fact categorical with respect to the complete span between the framework that provides guidance for actions to be taken and, at the same time, is shaped by the actions taken and the crystal clarity of the goal.

All three of these premises however seem contradicted by the realities of the complex information technology intensive firm framework.

i.   The assumption of integration

CITIs seem first and foremost very integrative or, at least, ambivalent in their approach to other firms, customers, clients, other stakeholders, to the extent of virtually humbling the original frameworks of co-opetition, virtual networks, cluster models, and select episodic collaborative efforts limited in scope and periodic in frequency.

On the one hand, the original outsiders, i.e. customers, are being involved and engaged to become part of the productive process in their own right. It defines a new context in which the roles of the actors of the firm are being altered. Former external clients or customers are being involved to become responsible co-generators and informed insiders, rather than being confined to their space as consumers. The firm becomes a comprehensive platform enabling customers and internal clients to express themselves rather than a mere internal marketplace merely facilitating exchange between each other. It agitates the context and actively moves the various parties towards each other, assigning them various active roles in turn. The most prominent examples are in the realm of cultural goods creation and digitizeable entertainment and creative content via the construct of transmutability.

The purpose is not the product anymore, and the means is not the process, but the way information is organized by the firm to provide this platform for co-generation that becomes the very mission. Rather than having precise products in mind a priori, it is from the interactions that firms will allow the products and processes to evolve.

On the other hand, there seems to be no room left for competition in similar industries. In fact, the various firms representative of our study almost instantaneously emerged as near-monopolies for their respective activities. They specialized to such extremes so as to leave little room for others to imitate, while at the same time necessitating others to occupy distinct complementary activities, translating into unprecedented levels of monopolistic competition. But this new division of roles doesn't seem to be happening in an aggressively adversarial manner of past technological cycles. IT seems to uncover an almost endless yet unoccupied space for activities of intermediation and market making between the universe of already existing simple information technology-intensive firms wherein specialization almost naturally happens and at the same time requires a myriad of new connections and relationships between the nodes to generate and maintain the ever more complete and complex outcomes of the experience-economy. Thus contrary to past experiences the new strategy is predicated to be inclusive, integrative, conciliatory, rather than distributive, divisive, isolationist.

ii.   The new premise of generative boldness

Secondly, strategy has become increasingly action-biased, de-emphasizing the analytics of planning. It may seem rather counterintuitive, however, to cast strategy as more immediately action-biased in a world that with its increasing complexity requires the processing of an increasing number of varying parameters. But it may be the very information overload resulting from the many new dimensions of this environmental complexity that prompted a shift to more bold early action and more cursory and loose planning. It seems that the aspirations of the CITI firms are just much too important at a socio-economic level to be delayed by the disciplined rational optimization process perfected in past technological cycles. In their favor plays the resource abundance of information and the associated needlessness of obsessing over efficiency. Effectiveness of action takes precedence.

iii.   The improvisational side of strategy

Finally, the traditional almost recipe-like premise of strategy is giving way to a much more sophisticated normative stance. Strategy is an agenda, certainly, but it is also very resilient, improvisational, adaptable. While the new strategy is predicated on agitation and movement as its principal outcome, ends and means may not be specific, explicit, and consistent. The example repeatedly cited by our respondents is the continuously morphing strategy of Mark Zuckerberg for Facebook.

3.   New strategy practices

Our respondents repeatedly noted three profound changes in how the practice of strategy presents itself in the context of the CITI firms: strategy is more than just a result of brilliant, rational, deliberate collective decision-making, it is intimately attributable to a specific leader as a person, indeed dependent on that individual, their personal value systems, and characterical idiosyncracies; second, strategy is no more issue of a strictly rational, formal process, but seemingly ad-hoc, irrational, visionary, discontinuous, and highly reflective of the eclecticism of the decision-makers' personalities; lastly, strategy does no longer organize a series of the revered win-win situations between participants, but a game to which many parties are invited.

i.   The leadership imperative

The dependence of strategy on personal leadership is not revolutionary per se, as evidenced by the many captains of industry of past economic cycles, such as Henry Ford for example. One of our respondents critically noted that in fact historically "groundbreaking new change, fundamental shifts will always be done by people who are different and who do things differently all the way, all throughout." But while originally only the initial impetus for a venture may have intimately hinged on such leaders actions and involvement, the continuity of the enterprise didn't. In fact, one dominant aspect of previous leadership situations was to quickly operationalize the idea of the leader into an industrial, repetitive process that would take on a life of its own, as in the Ford Motor Company today. And their leadership was symbolic. But it also was very emblematic. "Von Siemens, Krupp, and others all approached society in such a novel way that it touched a whole new generation." Their innovations were movements at social level, not merely firm level.

The leaders in CITI firms have a much different role. They are not fixtures of just the initial entrepreneurial idea, but continuously, actively, and directly involved in shaping strategy. While Jack Welch is a distant myth at GE, Steve Jobs is a mentor at Apple every day. Leaders of the new strategy directly impress upon it and infuse it with their non-linear and non-standard personal value systems. Two concerns arise from such an intimate relationship between strategy and leader: For one, strategic identity crises evolve in tandem with personal crises, such as the ups and downs at Dell, or the long way to maturity at Apple demonstrate. Secondly, These firms are at present hard to imagine without these specific leaders at the helm, what would Amazon be without Jeff Bezos, Apple without Steve Jobs, Google without Page and Brin, and Facebook without Mark Zuckerberg? Such dependence of leadership may thus also be setting us up for un unprecedented crisis in successorship questioning the framework of the firm as a 'going concern' and reducing it to a leader's life project.

ii.   The irrational side of strategy

An extension to the de-emphasis of formal, deliberate, and rational a prori planning is the insight that so many of the ideas about the products and processes to support the IT experiences are in fact irrational at core. Many of them seem impractical, improbable, outrageous, and immature at first: iPhone's virtual keyboard, Amazon's mall-like shopping opportunities, eBay's car auctions, Facebook's indeterminable business model.

While we were honing our left brain for centuries obsessing over efficiency and optimization, we are realizing that the bang for the buck is much bigger when addressing the right brain with an effective experience. While this may be at the expense of more wasteful processes and products, this is easily offset in that information is abundant, networks are resilient, and cyberspace is limitless.

iii.   A new role for game theory

The origins of game theory were grounded in the paranoia of increasingly oligopolizing industry structures. This is not the aspect of games of interest here.

Indeed, in partial conclusion, in conjunction with IT the originally rather defined and focused meaning of strategy has given way to an expanded understanding of the phenomenon. An entire continuum of possible new approaches and interpretations in their own right supports numerous ways in which strategy can be re-imagined as a design variable for the firm to more fully take advantage of the new information-technological realities. In conclusion, our analyzed CITI firms have a very loose understanding and liberal interpretation of strategy, strategic decision making and the requisite principles as acquired during the industrial economy. They are actively reshaping these principles to serve an entirely different dimension of how value propositions are translated into wealth. Partly this could be attributed to the increasingly formalized separation of using and paying parties in the transaction, for example. Since wealth extraction often doesn't happen directly from the users, it can ultimately be determined in a different space at a later point in time. Thus, the formulation and articulation of strategy is disassociated from its immediate practice, and the timing of when,

where, and how a value proposition progresses towards wealth creation.

The Impact of IT on Structure

Similar to its effect on strategy, IT in its current version profoundly affects its immediate correlate, structure. Unlike structuration theory, we are not, however, interested in determining to what extent existing structures are being altered as a process. We are rather interested in the effect of IT on structure as a design variable and to what extent our understanding of structure as a necessary support to strategy has been affected. The many observations that we collected can be aggregated around the following four themes: As for the conventional structure-related labels that float in the media and the literature that are maintained in conjunction with CITI firms they are only of nominal value, i.e. the terminology related to structure does not reflect the actual source, meaning, and definition of structure; next, C ITI firms exhibit a uniquely high level of flat and at the same time open, but only seemingly loose structures; also, structures are designed to favor play, not control; and finally, structure and size are disassociated und unrelated.

1.   The role of nominal structure

While there is some conventional nomenclature associated with describing some of the aspects of structures of CITI firms, terms such as CEO, Board of Directors, Management, Headquarters etc. seem merely an artifact of our only slowly adapting legal underpinnings. In reality, structure is a sophisticated intangible network of conversations, ideas, aspirations, communication patterns, and common values that defy the definitions of traditional hierarchical bureaucracy. The multitude of power sources, commitment mechanisms, and cohesion elements cannot be captured neatly through orgcharts, not even though Mintzberg's dynamic organigram framework (Mintzberg,

1979). The new face of structure is non-bureaucratic, network-based, flat, informal, and implicit. The result of this complete disassociation of structure as a formal element from its practice is that it can now be used rather arbitrarily and discretely as a design variable and can be inserted at different points in the life cycle of the emergent organization for such other purposes like the mentioned legitimization of the corporation for market recognition. This may be necessary because the speed at which those organizations are put together or progress through their life-cycle stages doesn't leave room for an embryonic process. Rather the designers look for components of blueprints in the already existing proven architectures but alter them significantly to reflect their specific needs for resilience, flexibility, nimbleness, adaptability, and preparedness.

2.   The partnership imperative

What leadership is to strategy, partnership is to structures. Partners are rather equals. And such partnering is enabled by a pronounced emphasis on flatness and openness. Traditional thinking on structure was optimizing and glorifying the hierarchical bureaucracy for purposes of control and definition of a distinct, isolated identity for the organization. The impact of IT has exploded that notion. While people can be harnessed in such ways albeit unsustainably for purposes of tangible transactional activities, such modes of control become impractical and impossible for controlling ever evasive and proliferating information. In fact, information appreciates with sharing, and information begets more information only when it is shared. The value of a structure is thus no longer in how tightly it controls its information, but how many connections to other nodes it can manage to enrich the existing information. But while such openness and flatness may be extremely popular during the evolution of information, once this information reaches the knowledge stage, i.e. becomes actionable for purposes of wealth

creation, CITI firms exhibit an entirely different attitude and employ and entirely different mode of containing that information within their structures to only discretely share it via the legal framework of intellectual property protection, especially enhanced since the infamous State Street Bank Decision, that, roughly speaking, added the possibility to protect business process ideas alongside business product ideas. In that sense, rather than relying on the traditional uniform control centric structure CITI firms are pursuing a bimodal approach, extreme openness and flatness on one hand simultaneous with a very protective approach beyond structural ramifications on the other. But this seeming structural looseness is offset by an attractive working environment. Our respondents repeatedly noted the favorable working conditions revered by the employees across those firms and the many complementary collaboration projects in place, evolving, and under consideration between many of those firms.

In the words of some of our respondents: "Any network if first of all based on your ability to connect people. A network is only as powerful as the amount of people linked to it. First of all you have to have the infrastructure for that. The firm is only acting in tandem with the user."

3.   The new structures supportive of play

"The rule for the new firms is: Is the value that the user gives to the firm met with greater value going out of the firm? They have to feel that when they spend their time on the site it is giving them something that's more important, i.e. that it's worth their time." That's why CITI firms are increasingly designing their structures as 'game' platforms. People are very easily attracted to work together when it is organized in the form of a game. Auctions, transmutability, YouTube, MySpace, and Facebook are capturing this natural drive in people towards gaming very effectively. One of our observers commented as follows on the initiative of HJenglish.com: "The most amazing fact about them is that they look like they are playing, not working".

4. Disassociation of structure from size

Finally, a recurring observation was that the traditional - albeit not proportionate - correlation between structure and size is almost eliminated. The case of Face Book's stellar ascent years from startup to a $20b market valuation in only three years is a case in point: The variable of organizational size in terms of occupied space, number of employees, functional units, and locational dispersion seems entirely unrelated to its capitalization potential. The size of Amazon. com is almost unspecifiable. HJenglish aggregated 1.5m paying clients in only 18 months with an estimated 10 million browsing users, but employs consistently about 50 full-time and 200 part-time employees.

Structures are henceforth being regularly designed to accommodate this type of disassociation by incorporating a priori the real options of expansion, contraction, delay, acceleration, and abandonment of their activities. Amazon's platform, for example, and now liberally expand but also shut down explorations into new product and service areas. More than for actual size is the design of structure for supporting an exclusive, near- monopolistic positioning of the firm.

The Impact of IT on the Scale of the Firm

To explain the impact of IT on the notion of the scale of the firm seems simpler than that of the impact on the aforementioned variables strategy and structure. Scale here refers to the size in terms of groupings of like and similar activities. The limits to scale were traditionally functional and structural: The highly physical industrial technologies for example were defined by the concepts of economies of scale and returns to scale.

Clearly the limitlessness of cyberspace, the costlessness of replicating information, and the compression of space and time profoundly affect how we can use the scale variable for new designs.

The scale or size of firms, especially in the previous industrial economy, created physical and cognitive limits. These needed to be carefully optimized through concepts such as economies and diseconomies of scale, diminishing returns, and increasing, decreasing, and constant returns to scale.

In CITIs scale takes arguable an entirely new dimension. From our interviews, we were able to discern at least four distinct shifts with respect to the understanding of scale as a result of the impact of IT. The notion of incrementalism to firm growth has been abandoned. Size is used as a real option to break away from path-dependent decisions. Size is treated as a necessary condition for monopolistic positioning. Size is decoupled from any particular individual metric, such as number of employees, revenue, profit, market valuation or occupied space (virtual market space or physical locational space). The purpose of size is not anymore regulatory capture, defensiveness, or the potential to freeze the environment; size is important so as to create value, i.e. tremendous social value first form which a portion will distill into appropriable private value.

We analyze the evidence for these in turn.

1. Sizing up (or down) is not incremental

For CITIs size is not an incremental issue. While there remain certainly some practical issues such as number of employees, or processing capacity of requests, the practical and cognitive limits of industrial-character firms vis-à-vis size are transcended. Firms are not sized iteratively any longer or at least the previously required time to size them has been utterly compressed. Digital servers in the new economy have manyfold the expansion capacity when compared to the physical servers and tellers of the service economy or the assembly line practices of the industrial economy. In fact, mass manufacturing through assembly lines was additionally complicated by the multiple phase character of each channel notwithstanding the automation efforts through robotics and electro-mechanical servers. Examples would be Goggle's growth in only seven years to rival Wal-Mart's of forty -five years (in terms of market capitalization). For the little incrementalism that there is it remains confined to areas of acquisition of employees and capital equipment. But in terms of capital accumulation, processing capacity (based on light-speed!), market share gain, and market position (in little limited cyberspace after all!) combined with first-mover advantages CITI sizing is of different nature. The result is a serious of overnight successes occupying quickly and unchallenged entire markets. The combination of processing information and information processing based on the tremendous IT capabilities and capacities sidesteps the pragmatic limits imposed on traditional firms and allows for an entirely new understanding of how scale and sizing need to be designed, implemented, and managed.

2. Size as a real option

Size is considered a real option. In the finance disciplines, real options theory has long recognized the inadequacy of traditional incremental cash flow-based estimation models to capture some of the value creating phenomena exhibited by IT based firms. Especially, the finance discipline was grappling with comparatively risky decisions by managers vis-à-vis net present value calculations. It seemed as if managers made decisions based on some hidden knowledge, some instinctive and intuitive elements not properly captured in the cash-flow and discount rate estimates. Enter real options theory. While net present value calculations need all a priori information and result in a path-dependent and conservative decision model, managers realize that they have options subsequent to launching a project to expand, delay, contract,

abandon, and accelerate. These are valuable in addition to the initial cash flow estimates. Thus, building into the decision model immediately the possibility of such options increases the value of the project. For CITIs, size is such a variable. It needs to be designed into the project *ex ante* so as to truly provide the insurance that the entire space of the niche that it targets can be occupied quickly. So the life cycle of the CITI shapes very differently firm the traditional life cycle of a firm. It exhibits a deeper curve in terms of negative cash flows (outlays) during a longer introductory period in which the immediately large-size project is built; it then exhibits much steeper and longer growth curves before leveling off into maturity.

3. The importance of monopolistic positioning

The actual objective for the CITI, however, is not size directly. It is its monopolistic position vis-à-vis the newly founded niche. Size is used as a tool to acquire that position. The monopolistic position is partly a necessity, and partly a result in an economy with IT as the predominant form of technology. Since IT products are costlessly replicated and distributed, the variable cost is near-nonexistent and fixed cost is the actual total cost of the project. That forces potential providers into a game of lowering prices to virtually zero that would ultimately always only leave the best capitalized to take the entire market. Which on the other hand is possible absent cognitive or practical limits on the number of processing transactions that can be supported thanks to the rapid accessibility and availability of IT hardware and software. The result is a run to monopolize each market segment quickly, and not merely become a substantial participant. Respectively eBay, Amazon, Google, Yahoo, YouTube and Facebook have done exactly that. And the aspiring newcomers are closely imitating this phenomenon. HPenglish.com, for example, has acquired 1.5 million users in 18 months.

4. Meaningless traditional metrics

Traditional metrics for size are meaningless for CITIs. Size variables are unrelated with each other; so, for example, there is no correlation between profits, market valuation, number of employees, revenue, occupied building space, or similar variables. Google with one tenth of employees of Wal-Mart has the same market capitalization for example. If some standardization were possible in the future, new metrics such as transaction processing capability, electricity consumption through servers, number of servers, or represented locations should be taken into account.

5. Corollary functions of size

Size, however defined, traditionally had some corollary functions. If sufficiently large firms could protect themselves to some extent easier from competitors, regulators, and a changing environment. Firms could virtually freeze the environment (such as AT&T froze development in telephony for decades), engage in regulatory capture or arbitrage and fend off competitors (such as Microsoft currently can given its market share and cash position).

The new meaning of size, however, is that serves as a base for value creation. Related to our findings below with respect to social position, the objective of scale is to generate movement, attention, even through costless transactions by the immediate end-user (such as our all searches on Google) to form a large base of activity. Ultimately, it is this tremendous number of 'eyeballs' that can then be leveraged at an entirely different level of transactions. The current level of reach and richness to that end is only possible as a result of the capabilities provided by IT. But while this latter capability has been recognized previously, it is the manner in which scale is used as a design variable to disassociate the immediate end-user from the ultimate revenue generation function that supports a distinctly new character of the firm.

We thus find some substantial evidence for a necessary new perspective on scale as a design variable. Even if we may not yet even know how to properly capture and define scale, it needs to be built into firms immediately as much as necessary to achieve quickly and securely monopoly status; and it needs to be used for a large user base, not necessarily revenue base.

The Impact of IT on Scope

In examining the evidence with respect to scope as a design variable we find that the notion has undergone enlargements and enrichments in several directions beyond the original Cosian understanding.

Coase's original understanding of scope as truly defining of "the nature of the firm" is being revisited in several respect.

The original understanding was that while markets were already solving production cost problems through their allocation mechanisms, the very essence of the firm was justified by its ability to solve transaction cost problems vas its decision mechanisms to integrate or to outsource related upstream and downstream activities. It is through this decision about its scope that the firm was able to distinguish itself from the market and from other firms.

This today seems to insufficiently characterize the role of scope in firm design. This question of the determination of the identity of the firm via its chosen activities has already been partially addressed by some, such as Brusoni's (Brusoni and Tronchetti-Provera, 2005) work on modular networks and Clemons's (1993) work on the boundary of the firm.

We are grouping the additional and novel evidence collected for the present study into four areas: modularity, fractionality, adaptability, and imitability.

We are grouping the observations as follows:

1. Modularity

CITIs don't limit the variable of scope to make temporary static decisions about which activities to integrate to then subsequently operate them, albeit for a defined timeframe. Traditionally, this decision has a path-dependent aspect to it, i.e. the determinants of future outcomes are known at the time of the projection and don't change.

Rather, analogously to real options theory, firms are designed to support continuous modularity, they morph their boundary dynamically. For most of the examples given this has also been characterized as a monotonically integrative process, i.e. any CITI examples cited mostly exhibited absorptive bias by integrating an increasing number of upstream and downstream activities in the spirit of related diversification; some, however, were also interpreted to demonstrated conglomerative tendencies engaging in unrelated diversification, such as Google's telephony and electricity initiatives.

2. Fractionality

Firms are designed as incomplete, i.e. fractional firms. Not only do firms continuously change their composition of related upstream and downstream activities (see (a) above), they also do so with respect to their very core (be it value chain, value network, or value shop configuration) primary and support activities. While the traditional perspective required for completeness of a firm to have a well-defined set of activities surrounding the central marketing, operations, and finance activities, it seems that the CITI dispenses with this requirement. The scope of the CITI can very well be limited to just a subset of previously activities that previously thought to have to exist more comprehensively and cohesively. Indeed, in many cases the operations and production function along with related activities such as quality control, and in certain cases design, and transportation and logistics have been readily outsourced. Though

appearing as producers of certain activities and services, CITIs in many cases are in reality limited to being the mere coordinators of these, such as in the Case of eBay, Amazon, and Apple for example. While this is not new, since traditionally more industrial firms such as Dell have broken ground for such practice, it seems remarkable to what extent the CITIs are able to do it for mere experience-level, i.e. fully intangible products and dematerialized outcomes.

This particular tendency had originally been interpreted very differently by proponents of socalled 'modularity theory'. In fact, according to advocates of modularity, it was the markets that were moving in on firms as products were becoming increasingly modular. Markets were absorbing some of traditional firm activities as hierarchies were becoming impractical and limited vis-à-vis too much complexity. But, as Brusoni (2005), argues in his interpretation of engineering design activities, irrespective of the extent of the market there are cognitive limits to the division of labor. "[…][c]oordinating increasingly specialized bodies of knowledge, and increasingly distributed learning processes, requires the presence of knowledge-integrating firms even in the presence of modular products. It is firms, not markets, that exhibit the requisite 'authority' to "indentify, propose and implement solutions to complex problems" (Brusoni, 2005).

3. Adaptability

The notion of scope was traditionally associated with a defined industry affiliation for each firm. Firms integrated activities that reiterated their location within a particular industry (and didn't integrate otherwise). The practice of CITIs, however, is to explode this notion by simultaneously and sequentially playing across various, sometimes rather unrelated industries.

Especially our Chinese respondents reiterated that in fact, it must be this very capability and competence that drives their valuation beyond common comprehension. In the mind of some of the interviewed business owners of the predominantly industrial Chinese economy the activities of such examples as Facebook, Google, and You-Tube are - at their base - merely temporary and unsustainably irrational. Our interviewees were conflicted about their own Baidu, indeed thought of as ill conceived and controversial by some. They accorded, however, that the capacity to "industry-hop", to immediately adapt to conditions and rules of a new industry, and to seamlessly morph and migrate across industries may ultimately be extremely valuable in its own right.

4. Imitability

While the New Institutionalist role of scope was to determine the firm as a distinct entity with respect to market, competitor firms, and consumers (clients, customers, users), the opposite seems to be practiced by CITIs. CITIs indeed link their activities across these other entities. They are able to imitate or rightout supplant markets, such as in the case of Amazon. They intertwine their activities so strongly with consumers so that it becomes unclear who is consuming and who is producing and when, such as is the case with YouTube and Facebook. They continuously vary their loyalties, affinities, affiliations, and relationships increasingly generating co-opetitors for subsets of their activities such as the attempts between Google and Yahoo for example.

The understanding of the design variable scope is vastly expanded when compared to its traditional Cosian notion. The ways in which it is being used and in which it can be used are demonstrated by CITIs in various respects. While parts of the idea are not entirely new, nor entirely specific to CITI firms, it remains that we are at a very unique juncture in the way scope is put into practice by those firms by simultaneously deconstructing and reconstructing every single of its traditional aspects almost entirely transcending economies and diseconomies of scope.

The above perspective is also different from the already existing notions of virtualization, clusterization, and the networked firm. The latter were a result of economic transitions and transformations of existing firms taking advantage of IT and the associated new possibilities of combinations with existing industrial technologies. These were pragmatic processes of adoption and adaptation, i.e. attempts to harness the boost that IT would provide when injected in already existing industrial automated processes. The result was however not in terms of firms of different character and nature, but a mere increase in efficiency and effectiveness of pre-existing activities, optimized control structures, and maximized communication and coordination mechanisms. Our perspective, while probably utterly impractical for much needed organizational situations of transition and necessary industrial transformations, is on the original design of new firms that can take advantage of the redefined design variables immediately and without needing to compromise by accounting for existing organizational constraints and conditions.

At the time of this writing many established industries (banking, automobile, housing, heavy shipbuilding) are hardpressed to complete such major transformations under conditions of an ever faster changing environment and under conditions of extreme volatility. While our framework is still extremely focused in many respects on the small category of CITI firms, it may serve as a template for major redesigns of entire industry sectors to supplant the current disintegrating designs.

The Impact of IT on the Social Position of the Firm

Societies are based on two complementing environments: A socio-political one that sustains them intellectually, spiritually, and morally. And an economic one that sustains them materially. All actors (firms predominantly as producers;

individuals or households, and government primarily in their role as consumers) are participants in both of those spheres.

By "social position" of the firm we are referring to the particularly challenging situation of the firm as a simultaneous social and economic entity. Firms are pursuing social goals with economic means and vice versa. In addition to their original economic nature, their design thus needs to take into account their relationship to society at large. This wider perspective has already been manifesting itself for several decades in the guise of the social responsibility movement: Firms certainly need to be economically and legally responsible, i.e. they must not do certain 'bads'. But furthermore, firms are also held to a standard of responsibility to all stakeholders in society in an affirmative manner: they must contribute to weaving the social fabric by positively doing good.

Under conditions of industrial technologies this equated to a trade-off: more activities diverted to social value meant less support for private profits. Firms were hard pressed to strike a delicate balance between these two extremes of the economically indicated minimalist and the socially demanded maximalist solutions. They often failed and resolved to so called socially "responsive" solutions by discontinuing contentious activities upon experiencing social pressure, for example.

Thus the context of IT is seemingly complicating this already very exigent situation for the firm yet. Paradoxically, however, firms now seem to more comfortably negotiate the balance between those two extremes. In fact they seem to be able to meet and exceed the related challenges concurrently. A prominent example is Google. While the social value deriving to users seems tremendous, Google is still a highly profitable company.

We note "seemingly", however, as there is yet another side to this newly found socio-economic identity. Since "there is no free lunch", as the infamous business adage goes, our respondents were more conflicted about how IT affects the social position of the firm. This is in stark contrast to the enthusiasm with regards to the previous four design variables where our respondents seemed inclined to more readily and more positively interpret a broadened meaning, definition, and space for each.

We may be able to partly reconcile this apparent controversy via the changing nature and definition of value in general and the definition of social value in particular on one hand. To that end we revisit and reinterpret the dimension of intentionality of social impact, question the associated condition of specific and explicit goals for social change, and propose to accommodate a larger set of social-value generating activities to qualify as such under this definition.

On the other hand, our respondents also admitted to the "dark side" of the new social position of the firm. It comes at a new price, a new social cost: Extreme protectiveness and control of intellectual property.

1. A new definition of social value

Economic goods are conventionally defined by two dimension: rivalrousness and excludability. Private gods are both, rivalrous (scarce and desirable) and excludable (one's consumption precludes another one's); public goods are neither, impure public goods are rivalrous but not excludable; and commonpool resources are excludable but not rivalrous. The important consequences of this careful distinction is that the universe of beneficial and valuable economic goods is significantly larger than just the quadrant of private goods with which we most immediately associate, especially since Adam Smith formalized it in his "Wealth of Nations".

Somehow naturally resulted a separation of concerns in that private goods are provided by private enterprise, while social value in form of the other three economic goods categories is created by socalled social enterprises, enterprises on the public service or interest, government, and not-for-profit entities.

But under the current conditions of IT social value creation seems not the exclusive domain of the above assumed type of 'social' ventures. Other forms of production as well as private value initiatives have been advanced to also generate socially – and not only economically – valuable products, such as in the case of transmutability (Hughes and Lang, 2006).

Initially, the apparent distinction between such ventures and our original social venture category rests on the intentionality and quality of the outcomes related to social impact and change. While conventional social ventures pursue social outcomes as an essential, indeed defining part of their purpose and mission, the highly general social value-generating new ventures produce such outcomes rather unintentionally as by-products and without an explicit perspective related to social change or otherwise social impact.

In contrast to the above is the parallelism of the structure of transactional relationships: So called new ventures and original social ventures alike exhibit a high degree of separation of transactional concerns: users, consumers, subscribers, paying parties, and producers may all be shifting from being entirely disparate at some point all the way to becoming identical entities at another. This varies over time and depending on the occasion of the transaction. At some point producers may also become simultaneous consumers of the network externalities, for example.

Such a conciliatory approach to these two apparently incongruent paradigms may have practical consequences and yield valuable implications for purposes of social venture capital formation, for example. In particular, we may be able to suggest that current social ventures re-focus their original capitalization process to include parameters stemming from their (should we say 'hardcore') private market-economic counterparts. In fact, we suggest that, if social ventures can cast their originally very specific and narrow explicit objectives in a broader context, they may benefit from an increased tangible value assessment and attract capital providers from unexpected corners of the socioeconomic spectrum.

2. New processes for social value creation

Representative of the idea of social value creation through the recent phenomenon of social networking is Hughes' and Lang's work on transmutability (Hughes and Lang, 2006). Firms have emerged that enable simultaneous consumption and production of culture goods by the same entities through digital technologies and the process of transmutation unlike what was (im)possible in the locked and frozen environments of analogue goods. They thus produce new digital culture goods that are in fact socially valuable.

More anecdotal examples are Google's various opportunities for users (search, maps, e-mail) at no cost and seemingly unrelated to the real purpose of producing increased attention and traffic for featured and, paying, but also simply listed business as results of a search.

Another example is the explosive popularity of Facebook based on its production of connections between people. The almost immediate and widespread adoption of the paradigm by users, the overwhelming popularity and the time and attention committed by users is a case in point of tremendous benefits. Furthermore, considering that the environment was transformed into a mineable database that can be exploited by advertisers, for example, speaks to its immediate financial feasibility.

But the resulting potential for social value, however intuitively compelling, is, still difficult to measure. Especially difficult to resolve are issues of properly quantifying the value, capturing its sustainability, and measuring the appropriate allocation of revenue, cost, and profit between the participants. While valuations of Facebook fluctuate between \$ 15 b to \$ 20 b after only roughly 40 months of existence of the venture, it is still difficult to imagine how this value will be appropriated. Consequently it seems impractical to solicit capital commitments in a wider market, under conditions of transparency and efficiency with such an opaque valuation. Microsoft's recent acquisition of a small percentage of the venture for the astronomical price of $ 240m[1], while seemingly rational, may just as well prove a very irrational assessment at any future point. Who is to say?

What can't be measures, can't be understood. And what can't be understood, can't be managed. While the craft-like production of social value through networks has existed for a long time, we are only at the beginning of defining its contours for future successful replication. Encouraging, however, already at this point is the enthusiastic acceptance and immediate adoption by users and implementation by IT providers of the necessary solutions.

3. The impractical condition of intentionality of outcomes

While we may have ascertained so far that – at least perceived - social value may be generated by other than explicit social ventures, our reasoning has not yet considered the quality and nature of such social value with respect to the creator. It seems that the conventional definition of social value is inclusive of both, the producer's and consumer's perspectives on what constitutes social value.

In the case of the above examples, however, especially with regards to the social networking model, there may be an incongruent definition of value creation between the parties. The producer may not in fact *intend* to create social value after all, but only wants to create an illusion of it, consciously and intentionally generating indeed private value, for which the materialization is simply delayed in time and redistributed in space (to paying parties other than the immediate user, such as advertisers, for example).

But, while this distinction may be ontologically important, it may not be relevant for the result of the ensuing transactions. Value is in fact measured in the eyes of the appreciating party, not necessarily including the creator's intentions. If users perceive value that they are appropriating as part of a community they are appreciating social value, however defined at the producer level.

It seems therefore that this incongruence only persists at the philosophical level of the definition of the social value-creating paradigm, but dissolves at the practical level of consumption. This would legitimize the structures and processes to be transposed for application for social ventures and allow them to accumulate a much broader base for capital commitments.

New opportunities from the analogy between Complex Information Technology-Intensive Firms and social ventures

The properties of complex information technology-intensive firms transpose quite easily to social ventures. Both share the simultaneous multiplicity and identity of the transacting parties as well as the strong decoupling between them. They both have a tendency to disengage revenue from profits in time and over various degrees of aggregation, i.e. experienced as a community rather than at individual level. They both rely on a collective appreciation of the absorbed value. They both offer opportunities for the individuals to realize that are as yet undefined in terms of their goals and only partially defined in terms of purpose and mission at the time the interactions are experienced. They both rely on rather large communities for the value to be considered existing in the first place. And they are analogous in their lack of properly pricing the interaction opportunities.

In conjunction with the above analyzed opportunities, this leads us to suggest that social ventures could greatly benefit in terms of their capital formation efforts, for example, to adopt strategies that deemphasize the purpose-centric, narrow, and specific perspective of a social value definition bound by the congruent understanding and simultaneous exchange of such value in favor of a broader experience of what constitutes such value..

While it seems that this is currently still a central defining moment for social entrepreneurship, it is also its ultimate limitation with respect to funders. Already it is very difficult to source risk capital, for funders must be convinced of the feasibility, realism, and reasonability of a project, let alone reducing the number by requiring them to also share entirely the associated motivation and intention of social impact.

The original strict social value approach also seems rather un-strategic in that it works its way backwards to purpose and mission once the target of social impact is set. This locks them into a rather self-centered, inward-focused, and operations-optimizing attitude and leaves no time and energy to aspire to growth. Indeed, if strategy is forward looking, it is embracive of changes along the way. The cited complex information technology-intensive firms have taken that to an extreme level. In creating much undetermined value (opportunities) up front they pave the way for future resilience and nimbleness.

4.   The new cost of the new social position

The explosive growth of IT based business process patents since the famous State Street Bank decision indicates an increased intensity to protect intellectual property by firms. It is especially noteworthy in CITIs. Our respondents advanced this with concern. It is indicative of a ambivalent image of the CITI that compromises some of the very positive contributions in terms of design opportunities and especially with respect to it is a priori generative social position. The latter comes at a possibly high price. CITI are unreasonably locking in near trivial business processes and locking out many, if not all others, from enhancing their position in the foreseeable future. Cases in point are Amazon's Once-Click-Stop-Shop, and Google's Relevancy component in

their search engines. This seems counterintuitive to the Internet's open source base, the freedom of information, and initiatives of intense cooperation and co-opetition. The competition between CITI firms has shifted to the squatting of patents on ideas to the detriment of their proliferation. It ultimately translates into raising the cost of interaction rather than lowering of it. In the eyes of our contributors this seemed also an underestimated, too quiet revolution, drowned by the hype of the tremendous quantity of value apparently appreciated users.

CONCLUDING REMARKS AND SUGGESTIONS FOR FURTHER RESEARCH

The foregoing represents and attempts to capture the nature, context, and to frame a new breed of a priori highly successful firms that are in many respects defying conventional wisdom. We labeled these firms Complex Information Technology-Intensive (CITI) firms. Our findings come with several caveats.

From the point of view of our immediate assumptions those firms seem to be a result of a fundamental the impact of IT on their design variables, which we identified to be strategy, structure, scale, scope, and the social position. This may be an incomplete framework. Further research could affirm or disprove the accuracy of such an assumption, i.e. to interpret those variables as design variables.

From the point of view of the timing of the underlying research, the relevancy of our findings is probably time-sensitive. As the world economy experiences testing challenges in 2008, further research will have to validate the generalizeability of our findings over time.

From the point of view of the addressed firm segment, we acknowledge a very narrow perspective. CITIs are still emerging, their contours are fuzzy, and their numbers are hard to measure.

We also acknowledge that with its high degree of specificity and focus on this particular segment, our findings do not address many of the imminently pressing problems of transitioning, and transforming economies. For example, the politically and economically most prominent problems in Croatia (wherefrom this research originated) at the time of this writing were of industrial nature, such as assuring the viability and continuity of the ship building sector that accounts for a large portion of employment. Our research subsequently spanning the globe and elevating the discussion to the level of the CITI firms via only the most prominent examples seems rather esoteric to these problems at hand. But we hope that further research can contribute to transpose elements of our framework if not in its entirety.

REFERENCES

Afuah, A. (2003). *Business models: A strategic management approach.* New York: McGraw-Hill/Irwin.

Afuah, A., & Tucci, C. L. (2002). *Internet business models and strategies: Text and cases.* New York: McGraw-Hill/Irwin.

Arakji, R. Y., & Lang, K.-R. (2007). Digital consumer networks and producer-consumer collaboration: Innovation and product development in the digital entertainment industry. In *Proceedings of the 40th Annual Hawaii International Conference on System Sciences (HICSS'07).*

Brandenburger, A. M., & Nalebuff, B. J. (1996). *Co-opetition.* New York: Currency Doubleday.

Brusoni, S., & Tronchetti-Provera, S. (2005). The limits to specialization: Problem solving and coordination in 'modular networks'. *Organization Studies*, *26*(12), 1885–1907. doi:10.1177/0170840605059161

Clemons, E. K. (1993). *Information technology and the changing boundary of the firm: Implications for Restructuring* (Research Report). Wharton School.

Coase, R.H. (1937). The Nature of the Firm. *Economica*, 4(N.S.):386-405.

Foss, N. J. (2001). Misesian ownership and Coasian authority in Hayekian settings: The case of the knowledge economy. *The Quarterly Journal of Austrian Economics*, *4*(4), 3–24.

Hughes, J., & Lang, K.-R. (2006). Transmutability: Digital decontextualization, manipulation, and recontextualization as a new source of value in the production and consumption of culture products. In *Proceedings of the 39th Annual Hawaii International Conference on System Sciences (HICSS'06).*

Mintzberg, H. (1979). *The structuring of organizations.* Upper Saddle River, NJ: Prentice Hall.

Orlikowski, W. J. (1993). CASE tools as organizational change: Investigating incremental and radical changes in systems development. *MIS Quarterly*, *17*(2), 309–340. doi:10.2307/249774

Porter, M. E. (1996). What is strategy? *Harvard Business Review*, *74*(6), 61–79.

Porter, M. E. (1998). *Competitive strategy: Techniques for analyzing industries and competitors.* New York: Free Press.

Whitford, J. (2005). *The new old economy: Networks, institutions, and the organizational transformation of American manufacturing.* New York: Oxford University Press.

Williamson, O., & Winter, S. (Eds.). (1991). *The nature of the firm: Origins, evolution and development.* New York: Oxford University Press.

Williamson, O. E. (1981). The economics of organization: The transaction cost approach. *American Journal of Sociology, 87*(3), 548–577. doi:10.1086/227496

Yin, R. K. (1989). Research design issues in using the case study method to study management information systems. In J.I. Cash Jr. & P.R. Lawrence (Eds.), *The information systems research challenge: Qualitative research methods* (pp. 1-6). Boston: Harvard Business School Press. [1] Reported on cnet's news.com on Oct 24, 2007 for example; http://www.news.com/8301-13577_3-9803872-36.html (accessed January 15, 2008)f

Chapter 7
A Methodology for the Auditing of Technological Knowledge Management

Enrique Paniagua Arís
Universidad de Murcia, Spain

Belén López Ayuso
Universidad Católica San Antonio de Murcia, Spain

ABSTRACT

This work presents a methodology for auditing technological knowledge management that allows the proposed solution to be aligned with the competitive strategy of organisations, as well as with their processes, key competences, and the associated knowledge resources. That enables the solution to be technologically oriented and to be applied to different types of business, from SOHO and SME to large companies. Firstly, the authors will present their view regarding knowledge management, which is a technological perspective; they will specify the context of application and their objectives. Secondly, the authors will analyse the characteristics of knowledge as the object to be managed and will identify, analyse and criticise the most relevant knowledge management approaches, models and methodologies related to their objectives, then outlining the requirements that technological knowledge management must meet. Thirdly, the authors will present the components of the model on which the methodology is based, and they will describe its stages and tasks. Then the authors will analyse the advantages of the model and methodology regarding other proposals. Finally, the conclusions and future lines of work will be presented.

DOI: 10.4018/978-1-60566-856-7.ch007

INTRODUCTION

Within literature related to Knowledge Management there is a great diversity of models, which can be classified within the following dimensions or approaches: a) knowledge resources (Leonard-Barton, 1995; Sveiby, 1997), b) knowledge activities (Alavi, 1997; Leonard-Barton, 1995; Nonaka, 1994; Szulanski, 1996; Wiig, 1993) and c) factors of influence (Andersen & APQC, 1996; Szulanski, 1996). While the first approach attaches importance to the sources of knowledge themselves and gives as its main purpose the measurement of the value of knowledge for the organisations where it is placed, the second focuses on the possibility of the evolution of knowledge and has as its main objective increases in creativity and innovation in organisations. Finally, the third approach is aimed at the structure of organisations and mainly investigates the adaptation of knowledge to their strategic objectives.

A second way of classifying the proposed approaches and models, complementing the first, is according to their dependence on technology, including the following categories: a) knowledge evaluation, b) knowledge management and c) technological knowledge management. While the first approach is aimed solely at the assessment of the intangible assets of organisations, regardless of whether their sources are people or information systems (Sveiby, 1997), the second focuses on the management processes of said knowledge, which may be independent of technology (e.g. the creation of a training plan) or dependent on it (e.g. creating a document based project management system) (Leonard-Barton, 1995; Nonaka, 1994; Szulanski, 1996; Wiig, 1993), and the third focuses its attention on the management, mainly through processes and computer systems, of the knowledge of organisations (Alavi, 1997; Andersen & APQC, 1996).

According to Holsapple & Joshi (2002), none of the mentioned models covers all of the specified dimensions. On the other hand, it can be seen that the group of models oriented mainly towards technological knowledge management is relatively small.

To better understand technological knowledge management, it is very useful for us to analyse the Conceptual Model of the Knowledge Management System proposed by (Kerschberg & Weishar, 2002), that is based on his Model of Knowledge Management Processes (Kerschberg, 2001) in which the author attempts to connect processes with data and their representation. The aforementioned conceptual model, based on three layers (the data layer, the knowledge management layer and the presentation and creation layer), proposes the modelling of a portal that is used as a vehicle to create, share and search for knowledge in organisations. If we observe the group of services defined in the middle layer, and taking into account the business model of organisations and the goals established by their strategic management, it can be divided into two sub-groups: a) Services Based on Unstructured Knowledge and Information and b) Services Based on Standardised Processes and Structured Information (Paniagua, 2007).

The services of the first sub-group are those that are aimed at the organisation's needs relating to its competitive knowledge: business intelligence for the monitoring and management of processes; knowledge engineering for the modelling of intensive knowledge processes and the culture of the organisation, management of the unstructured or semi-structured information of the organisation that amounts to 80% of all of the available information, and work in group processes, containing a certain degree of automation of the workflow.

Therefore, a technological knowledge management model must take the following requirements into account:

- To find a technological strategy, composed of a group of solutions, for the knowledge management of the organisation,
- To be composed of a group of services based on knowledge and unstructured information, and which must be integrated

Table 1. Knowledge models

Sort of Knowledge	Type of Knowledge
By Its Accessibility	Tacit, Explicit, Embedded, Passive, Active
By Its Representation	Declarative, Semantic, Procedural, Episodic
By Its Cognitive Focus	Application, Resolution of Problems
By Its Nature	Factual, Conceptual, Expectational, Methodological

into the services based on standardised processes and structured information.

- Said services must apply the appropriate activities of knowledge transformation to the identified and evaluated knowledge, from their competitive knowledge resources, which are part of their key skills and tasks,
- To support the implemented competitive strategy,
- And to be applicable to the structure and type of the organisation.

Taking into account this group of requirements, the two principal objectives that we set ourselves are the following:

- To design a technological knowledge management model in accordance with the identified requirements.
- To design a knowledge auditing methodology based on the proposed model.

KNOWLEDGE MANAGEMENT APPROACHES AND MODELS

The Importance of Knowledge in Companies

Before analysing the different Knowledge Management approaches and models it is helpful to place the importance of knowledge in companies into context.

For companies, knowledge can be defined as the information that possesses value to be able to act, in other words, information that allows companies to generate a competitive advantage; either to satisfy market needs or to exploit opportunities through the use of the various skills of its resources. The different categories of useful knowledge for companies are:

- **Tacit/Explicit:** This is the knowledge that the human and physical resources of the organisation have, categorised according to its accessibility.
- **Observable:** This is the knowledge that is reflected in the products and services offered by the organisation.
- **Positive/Negative:** This is the knowledge generated by the R+D area in the development processes for new products or by innovation in processes, divided into discoveries (positive) and useless approximations (negative).
- **Autonomous/Systemic:** This is knowledge that generates value without the need to apply sensitive modifications in the configuration of the organisation (autonomous), or is that related to the value generated by other components of the configuration of the organisation (systemic).
- **Intellectual Property System:** This is the knowledge protected by Intellectual Property Law.

Table 2. Classification of knowledge according to cognitive approach

Sort of Knowledge	Type of Knowledge	Knowledge Sub-Type
According to Cognitive Approach	Application	Domain
		Tasks
		Inferences
	Problem Solving	Methods
		Strategies
		Control

Knowledge Models

Once we are clear about the importance and about the different knowledge categories that a company wishes to manage, and to better understand the different approaches and models of Knowledge Management, we must analyse knowledge as the object that we wish to manage, from the point of view of the different models to which it can be added. In Table 1 we can see a classification of said models.

Regarding its *accessibility*, knowledge can be: a) *tacit*, which are skills, abilities and experience that enable people to carry out a given task and fulfil established objectives; b) *explicit*, which is knowledge that is coded (or precoded) and dumped onto any communication format and which people can learn; and c) *embedded*, which is that intermediate knowledge between tacit and explicit that is not directly accessible, as is the case with tacit knowledge, but which has been intentionally coded to form part of some artificial artefact.

In turn, these types of knowledge can be classified as *active* or *passive*. For example, in the case of tacit knowledge, the active knowledge is that which is present in peoples' memory and the routines that they know how to apply, and the passive knowledge is represented by the facts and examples that they know in order to solve problems. In the case of explicit knowledge, the active knowledge is that which the Knowledge Based Systems (KBS) possess and the active is that which is contained in manuals, books and reports.

Finally, in the case of embedded knowledge, the active knowledge is that which is contained in the artificial systems and the passive, that which forms an implicit part of technology.

Regarding its *representation*, knowledge can be:

- **Declarative:** Declarative representation shows us the knowledge we have over the command of an application, stating the concepts, together with their attributes, and the relationships that are established between them, mainly showing us its ontological character.
- **Semantic:** Semantic representation shows us the internal structure that declarative knowledge has: a) relating concepts, attributes and relationships to parts of the domain; and b) establishing the type of epistemological evaluation (classic logic, nonmonotonic logic, probabilistic logic, fuzzy logic etc).
- **Procedural:** Procedural representation shows us the sequence of actions that the conceptual domain objects use and affect.
- **Episodic:** Episodic representation shows us the examples of use, called "cases", as units of knowledge that unify declaration and procedure, as we can remember them in "specific episodes" of problem solving.

In Table 2 we show the categories of knowledge according to their *cognitive approach* (Schreiber,

Akkermans, Anjewierden, de Hoog, Shadbolt, Van de Velde, & Wielinga, 1999). Regarding said classification criteria, there are two sorts of knowledge: a) of application and b) problem solving.

On one hand, *Domain Knowledge* is composed of the concepts, attributes and relationships (at an ontological level) of the relevant parts of the model that we are attempting to represent and upon which we wish to base our argument (at a meta-ontological level), *Task knowledge* is composed of the hierarchical breakdown of the task processes that we wish to model, and *Inference Knowledge* is composed of the basic reasoning processes through which the task is constructed (in more detail than in the hierarchical breakdown).

On the other hand, *Method knowledge* is that which is applied when we have various alternatives in problem solving, *Strategy knowledge* is the group of inference patterns that we apply when we solve problems, and *Control knowledge* is what we use to monitor and decide on the course of action during the process of problem solving.

According to its *nature,* knowledge can be classified into the following categories:

- **Conceptual:** This knowledge is composed of personal or shared points of view, including shared experiences or approaches that are universally accepted, on models about the application domain (related to the ontological and meta-ontological levels, declarative and semantic representations and domain knowledge).
- **Factual:** This knowledge is composed of the facts of a domain application known by people, which can be composed of personal observations, shared experiences, scientific texts or models (related to semantic, procedural and episodic representations, and to domain knowledge).
- **Expectational:** This knowledge is composed of the value judgements, beliefs, hypotheses and priorities that are established during problem solving (related to

semantic, procedural and episodic representations, and to strategy and control management).

- **Methodological:** This knowledge is composed of intuitive notions, expert strategies, and generic methodologies used in problem solving (related to semantic, procedural and episodic representations, and to task, inference, strategy and control knowledge).

Technological Knowledge Management

What makes organisations competitive is its set of intangible resources, that is, the abilities of their resources (human and artificial), which are based on the knowledge that they possess. Therefore, the competitive advantage of an organisation is greater when its abilities are different and difficult to imitate. Hence, the importance of Knowledge Management in organisations, although first we should clarify said concept.

According to Davenport & Prusak (1998), Knowledge Management is a systematic process of searching for, organising, filtering and presenting information with the objective of improving peoples' comprehension in a specific area of interest. According to Malhotra (2001) is the organisational process that searches for the synergic combination of data processing and information through the capabilities of Information and Communication Technology (ICT) and the capabilities of peoples' creativity and innovation. And according to Sveiby (1997) is the art of creating value using the intangible assets of an organisation.

The different points of interest that are proposed in Knowledge Management can be seen in these definitions. For Davenport & Prusak it is the process of managing knowledge (information that enables organisations to achieve an objective) that gives organisations a better understanding of its environment (internal and external); for Malhotra it is the technological process that increases creativity and innovation (sources of competitive advantage) in organisations; and for Sveiby it is simply the identification of the value of knowledge (intangible assets) in organisations.

From our point of view, "(Technological) Knowledge Management is the set of (computer) processes and systems that enable organisations to generate competitive advantage that is sustainable over time, by means of the efficient use and application of their knowledge".

Knowledge Management Models

The different Knowledge Management approaches are embodied in a set of models, which we will describe and analyse below.

The Nonaka Model

The Knowledge Management model of Nonaka (1994), is based on processes of knowledge transformation, that is, on the various phases that it passes through and which transform it, so that it can be used by organisations. From this approach, if we take into account the aforementioned models, Nonaka deals with the accessibility of knowledge, that can be of two types: tacit and explicit.

The proposed model is a process of dynamic and continual interaction between tacit and explicit knowledge. This is composed of a spiral that defines the permanent ontological transformation of knowledge, developed over four stages: socialisation (tacit), externalisation (explicit), combination (explicit) and internalisation (tacit).

The Wiig Model

According to Wiig (1993), knowledge is composed of facts, concepts, judgements, expectations and methodologies, that is, Know-How. Said knowledge is accumulated and added and is stored for long periods of time and is available to solve specific situations and problems. Information solely consists of facts and information that is

organised and used to describe particular situations or conditions.

Using this approach, Knowledge Management focuses on those functions (or activities) that enable organisations: creating, displaying, using and transmitting their knowledge based on the so-called Pillars of Knowledge Management, which we could summarise as identification, evaluation and management.

The Leonard-Barton Model

The Knowledge Management model of Leonard-Barton (1995) is based on two basic components: a) the basic capabilities of organisations, and b) their knowledge creation activities.

The basic capabilities of organisations are the knowledge management sources and activities that allow organisations to strengthen their knowledge: a) the physical systems and the knowledge and skills of employees; b) the management and regulatory systems. The first two are the sources, and the last two are the management activities.

The knowledge creation activities are those, mainly aimed at the development of products that generate new knowledge in organisations. These are divided into four activities: a) problem solving (shared or creative) to produce current products; b) the implementation of new methodologies and techniques (and integration) to optimise current processes; c) experimentation and the creation of prototypes to innovate and create new capabilities in organisations, and d) the acquisition, importing, and absorption of external technology.

The KMAT Model

The Knowledge Management model of Andersen & APQC (Andersen & APQC, 1996), is based on the processes of knowledge management (creation, identification, compilation, adaptation, organisation, application, exchange) that organisations can use, applied to organisational knowledge. In said model, a series of instruments are considered (which we will call factors of influence) that positively or negatively influence the setting up of said processes.

Four facilitators that help Knowledge Management in organisations are also considered. These are:

- **Leadership:** To establish the mission of an organisation and the strategy to improve its different abilities.
- **Culture:** To establish the mechanisms and actions that support innovation and knowledge management in an organisation.
- **Technology:** To establish the role and importance of technology as a support to knowledge management in an organisation.
- **Measuring:** To establish the indicators of Intellectual Capital and the distribution of resources to strengthen knowledge, in order to improve the competitiveness of an organisation.

Based on said model, Andersen & APQC propose two Knowledge Management systems using Information Systems: knowledge sharing networks and "packaged" knowledge systems. The first consists of supplying organisations with environments for access to and the sharing of knowledge in the so-called "practical communities", the second strategy consists of supplying organisations with environments for access to standardised knowledge about the organisation (best practices, methodologies, tools, …).

The KPMG Model

The Knowledge Management model of KPMG Consulting (Alavi, 1997) focuses on those knowledge management processes aimed at improving customer service in organisations, using the Web as a storage and consultation environment. The

knowledge management processes that are carried out as sequences are:

- **Acquisition of knowledge:** In this process, knowledge related to experiences and lessons learnt from projects executed with clients is created and developed.
- **Indexing, Filtering and Linking:** In these processes, the typical activities of library management are carried out, such as the emission, classification, addition and interconnection of knowledge from different sources from those from which it has been acquired in the process of Acquisition.
- **Distribution:** In this process, the grouping and delivery of knowledge is carried out through Web pages (a problem of structure and design).
- **Application:** In this final process, the knowledge that has been acquired, compiled and delivered is used, to produce improvements in the products and services of the organisation.

The Szulanski Model

The Knowledge Management model of Szulanski (1996), focuses on the analysis of organisations' internal structures, to evaluate the difficulty in the transfer of internal knowledge. In a similar way to the model of Andersen & APQC, both the knowledge transfer processes and the factors of influence in the organisation on said processes are analysed. The knowledge transfer processes are as follows:

- **Beginning:** At this stage, a need for knowledge for the organisation is recognised, that requires a search for said knowledge and the transfer of said knowledge to satisfy the need.
- **Implementation:** At this stage, the transfer of the knowledge is carried out. Said

Table 3. Factors of influence in the KM model of Szulanski

Factor of Influence	Threats
Knowledge Transfer	Causal Ambiguity
	Lack of Knowledge Verification
Source of Knowledge	Lack of Motivation
	Instability
Recipient of the Knowledge	Lack of Motivation
	Small Capacity for Assimilation
	Small Capacity for Retention
Organisational Context	Difficult Relationships
	Barren Context

process requires the identification of the source of knowledge, and the route that it must follow to the client (or recipient).

- **Increase:** At this stage, the recipient uses the transferred knowledge, applying it to problems not previously solved, after they have been identified and classified.
- **Integration:** At this final stage, the transferred knowledge, after being used successfully, is institutionalised and becomes a routine within the organisation.

The factors of influence are those negative characteristics (and which must be evaluated and reduced) related to the transfer processes and components of the transfer of knowledge. Table 3 shows said factors of influence and their dangers.

The Sveiby Model

The Knowledge Management model of Sveiby (1997), focuses on identifying and evaluating the intangible assets of organisations. The model is composed of three parts:

- **External structures:** Composed of the relationships with clients, suppliers, brands and reputation.
- **Internal structures:** Composed of the models, concepts, patents, ICT resources,

organisational infrastructure and culture.
- **Employee skills:** The aptitudes and knowledge bases of the individuals inside organisations.

The Holsapple & Joshi Model

The Knowledge Management model of Holsapple & Joshi (2002) is an attempt to unify the different approaches that we have seen above. To this end, the authors identify three dimensions that appear to be fundamental in Knowledge Management: a) the knowledge resources; b) the activities of knowledge management; and c) the factors of influence.

In the study by Hoslapple and Joshi, it is shown that none of the models that we have seen so far include all of the three specified dimensions. What can be seen is that each one of them is interested in a specific dimension, focussing methodology towards resources, activities or the factors of influence.

Regarding the knowledge resources, the Leonard-Barton model is the only one that considers them in a special way, classifying them into two types: employee knowledge and knowledge from physical systems.

Regarding the activities of knowledge management, the majority of the models explicitly consider said activities. However, a very strong focus can be seen (as is the case of Nonaka or Leonard-Barton),

Table 4. Components of the Hoslapple & Joshi KM model

Dimension	Component
Knowledge Resources	Knowledge of the Agents (people, physical systems)
	Culture of the organisation (regulations, principles, rules)
	Infrastructure (functional level, operational level)
	Artefacts (products, services)
	Strategy (mission, positioning, competitive strategy)
	External Resources (shared, acquired)
Knowledge Activities	Acquisition of Knowledge
	Selection of Knowledge
	Internalisation of Knowledge
	Use of Knowledge
Factors of Influence	Influence of the Agents
	Influence of the Management
	Influence of the Environment

along with a very weak focus (as is the case of Andersen & APQC, Wiig, and Szulanski).

Regarding the factors of influence, only some of the models explicitly recognise them (as is the case of Andersen & APQC, Leonard-Barton, and Szulanski). However, only the Szulanski model analyses the dangers (although only in the activity of the transfer of knowledge).

From the study carried out, Holsapple & Joshi establish a model of three levels (or dimensions):

- **Knowledge Resources:** These are the sources of knowledge in organisations.
- **Knowledge Activities:** These are the processes that establish the handling of knowledge.
- **Factors of Influence:** These are the elements of organisations that could support or hinder the knowledge activities in organisations.

In Table 4 we show the components of the three dimensions of Knowledge Management from the Holsapple & Joshi model.

From the analysis of these three components (or dimensions) we obtain a match with the three principal technological strategies of knowledge management: a) orientation to people; b) orientation to documents; and c) orientation to business.

Engineering and Technological Knowledge Management

Kerschberg (2001) presents a Model of Knowledge Management Processes to establish a structure of three layers: A Layer of Knowledge Representation, a Layer of Knowledge Management and a Layer of Information (Figure 1).

The Model attempts to connect the different Processes (Activities) of Knowledge Management with Information (Knowledge Resources) and finally their Representation. The Processes are:

- **Acquisition:** In this process, Knowledge Engineers capture knowledge from experts in a domain, by means of interviews, case studies, etc.
- **Refinement:** In this process, knowledge from various sources is captured,

Figure 1. Model of knowledge processes

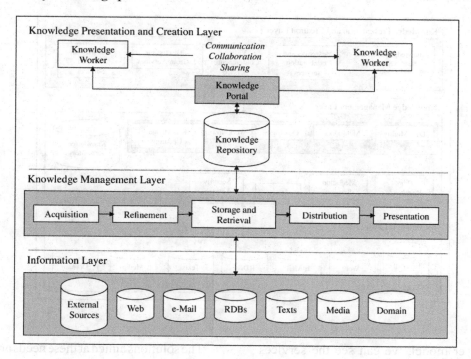

like Relational Databases (RDBs) or Object Oriented Databases (OODBs), Transactions, E-Mail, etc. Said knowledge is identified, classified and listed, establishing the meta-information needed for the concepts and relationships of the domain.

- **Storage and Retrieval:** The information obtained is stored and indexed to achieve rapid consultations, based on concepts, key words, etc.
- **Distribution:** The knowledge can be distributed through a Corporate Portal, Electronic Messenger or Subscription Services.
- **Presentation:** The knowledge must be presented taking into account the interests of each user, and allowing their collaboration so that they can share tacit knowledge and combine it with explicit knowledge in problem solving.

Based on said Model of Processes, Kerschberg & Weishar (2002), proposes a Conceptual Model

of a Knowledge Management System (Figure 2), also based on three layers:

- **A Presentation and Creation of Knowledge Layer:** In this layer, the knowledge workers can obtain personalised information through the Portal, make search requests about specialised information, collaborate on the creation of new knowledge and transform tacit knowledge into explicit knowledge through discussion groups.
- **Knowledge Management Layer:** In this layer, the *middleware* services associated with the indexing of knowledge and the Information Integration Services can be found.
- **Information Layer:** This layer contains all the information sources of the organisation.

In Figure 3, based on the Conceptual Model of Kerschberg & Weishar, we show the components of a *Corporate Knowledge System*. Using

Figure 2. Conceptual model of a knowledge management system

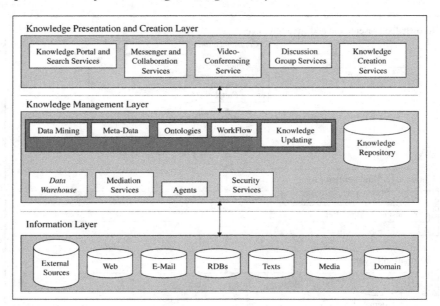

the three layer model, we can see the services that are defined in the middle layer, based on the *Business Model* and the goals established by the *Strategic Management*, which we can divide into two subgroups: *Services Based on Knowledge and on Unstructured Information,* and *Services Based on Standardised Processes and Structured Information.* Within each of the subgroups we can find the following services:

- **Knowledge Based Services and Unstructured Information (KBS-UI).** These services are aimed at the needs of organisations relating to knowledge: the *Business Intelligence* for the monitoring of competitive processes, the *Knowledge Engineering* for the modelling of the intensive knowledge processes and the culture of organisations, as well as the management needs of the *unstructured information*, which is usually 80% of the total in an organisation, and finally, the *Work in Group* processes (and a certain amount of automation based on the Work Flow).

The solutions aimed at these needs are *Decision Support Systems* (DSS) and *Data Mining* for Business Intelligence; *Knowledge Based Systems* (KBS) and *Knowledge Engineering* (KE) to manage the intensive knowledge processes (*Intelligent Agents* in Generic Tasks), the culture of the organisation (*Corporate Reports*), and developing *Intelligent Agents* that can be used for *Learning, Information Retrieval Systems* (IRS) combined with *Document Based Management Systems* (DBMS) to optimise the use of unstructured information in organisations, and *Collaborative Work Systems* (CWS) to support the group processes within organisations.

- **Services Based on Standardised Processes and Structured Information (SBSP-SI).** These services are aimed at the needs of organisations relating to standardised processes: *Finance, Customer Relations, Production, Logistics* and *Products*; using automation through the *Work Flow*, as well as the multi-platform of the *WEB* environment. All of this based on the *structured information* of organisations.

Figure 3. Elements of a corporate knowledge system

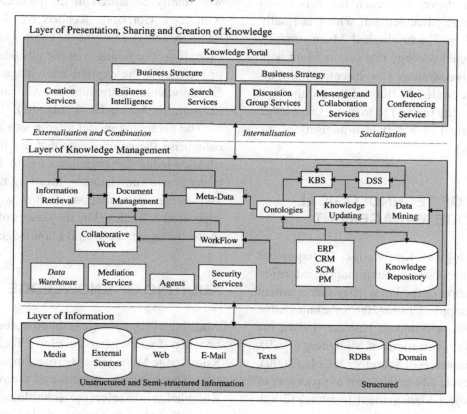

The solutions aimed at these needs are *Enterprise Resource Planning* systems (*ERP*) for Production management and its connection to Finance, *Customer Relationship Management* systems (*CRM*) to manage communication between organisations and their clients or shareholders, Supply *Chain Management* systems (*SCM*) to manage Logistics, and *Product Management* systems (*PM*) to manage the life cycle of each product developed by organisations.

From the point of view of *Knowledge Engineering*, the *Knowledge Based Services and Unstructured Information* are the most relevant for organisations. Leaving the second subgroup, that of *Services Based on Standardised Processes and Structured Information* for *Information Technology Engineering*. In any case, the second group has a supporting role to first, providing the necessary information about the standardized processes of the organization.

Therefore, we understand *Technological Knowledge Management* to be the vision, the mission, the business models, and the strategy that globally solve information management (and knowledge management) in organisations; and *Knowledge Engineering* to be the fundamental knowledge and methodologies related to *Information and Communication Technology* (ICT) that allow organisations to use and integrate technological systems and solutions that meet said requirements.

As Pávez states (2000), *Knowledge Management* establishes the direction to be followed, while *Technological Knowledge Management* (by means of *Knowledge Engineering*) develops the ways to move in said direction. The services in the Presentation Layer – Creation and Sharing of Knowledge – can be grouped into the four Activities of Knowledge Transformation of Nonaka: Socialisation, Externalisation, Combination and Internalisation.

From the above, we reach the conclusion that Knowledge Management, which is finally implemented in "Technological Management", must have a methodology that is consistent with the competitive strategy (the direction) and allow the appropriate handling of the technological resources (the tactics) to manage knowledge (the capabilities) of a certain organisation (the configuration).

A MODEL OF TECHNOLOGICAL KNOWLEDGE MANAGEMENT

The Technological Knowledge Management model that is proposed is a combination, extension and qualification of the knowledge management model of Holsapple & Joshi (2002), the knowledge transformation activities of Nonaka (1994), the taxonomy of organisations of Mintzberg (1979), the knowledge assets of Schreiber & Cols. (2000), and the life cycle and breakdown of processes of the PMI (Project Management Institute) (2000, 2001), taking into account the strategic management models of Ansoff, (1965), Bueno, (1987), López (2007), and Porter (1980).

In Table 5 we show the resource components, transformation activities and factors of influence of our Technological Knowledge Management model.

In Figure 4 we can see the relations that are established between knowledge resources, the knowledge transformation activities and the factors of influence in Technological Knowledge Management.

It can be observed that the knowledge resources (agents and physical systems), which are the tacit and explicit sources of knowledge (structured, semi-structured and unstructured) respectively, socialize knowledge (sharing experiences or experts), either through informal systems or with the support of ICT (Collaborative Work Environments or Knowledge Access and Transfer Environments), externalise knowledge, which

will finally be stored in the physical systems (Ontology, Corporate Reports and Knowledge Bases Systems), combine the explicit knowledge, extending it or fusing it in the physical formats, or internalise the explicit knowledge (Learning Environments, Tutorship, and Consultation, or Information Access Environments).

The presented model attempts to define and categorise the components that are the sources of knowledge for organisations, to be able to manage said knowledge by means of the model's knowledge transformation activities, which will be supported or hindered by the factors of influence in the management of said knowledge.

AUDITING OF KNOWLEDGE

Auditing of Knowledge is the first step that must be taken if you wish to develop a Technological Knowledge Management project in an organisation. The principle objective of the Auditing of Knowledge is to select the technological strategy and define the key factors and indicators of the future Technological Knowledge Management project that will have to be implemented in the organisation. The results obtained from the Auditing of Knowledge will be the admissions (or requirements) to develop the project. The various objectives of the Auditing of Knowledge are summarised as:

- To have the components of the Technological Knowledge Management model identified, classified and evaluated.
- To have the Opportunities and Threats that present themselves identified and evaluated, and to have the internal capability analysed (Strengths and Weaknesses) to achieve or reduce them, respectively.
- To have the objectives of the Technological Knowledge Management defined and specified.

- To have the Technological Knowledge Management strategy selected.
- To have the Key Factors and indicators available, which will allow evaluation of

the Technological Knowledge Management project that implements the strategy.

Table 5. Components of the technological knowledge management model

Dimension	Component	Element
Knowledge Resources	Knowledge of the Agents	People and Core, Experience
		Physical Systems, Information
	Culture of the organisation	Principles, Regulations and Rules
	Infrastructure	Functional Level
		Operational Level
	Artefacts	Products
		Services
	Strategy	Mission and Vision
		Strategic Positioning
		Competitive Strategy
		Key Factors of the Competitive Strategy
	External Resources	Component (Shared, Acquired)
Knowledge Transformation Activities	Socialisation of Knowledge	Sharing of Experiences
		Identification of Experts
	Externalisation of Knowledge	Identification and Classification
		Evaluation
		Selection
		Formalisation
	Combination of Knowledge	Fusion
		Extension
	Internalisation of Knowledge	Learning
		Access to Experiences
Factors of Influence in Knowledge Management	Influence of the Agents	Motivation
		Instability
		Inertia
		Skills
	Influence of the Management	Coordination Mechanism
		Level of Grouping
		Type of Centralisation
		Level of Leadership
		Core or Key Element
	Influence of the Environment	External Agents: (Clients, Suppliers, Competitors, Social Actors) Climate: PEST analysis

Figure 4. Relations between the knowledge transformation activities and the factors of influence of the technological knowledge management model

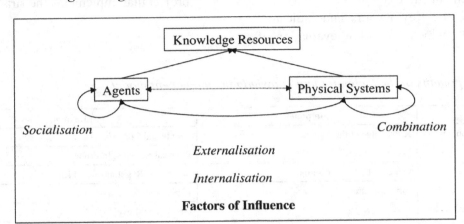

Stages of the Auditing of Knowledge

In Figure 5, the breakdown of the task of the Auditing of Knowledge is shown. The main stages are as follows:

- **Analysis of Knowledge:** In this first stage, the studies and analysis needed to identify the sources of knowledge of organisations, the knowledge transformation activities used (or that need to be used) and the factors of influence that could support or hinder the appropriate Technological Knowledge Management are carried out.
- **SWOT Analysis:** In this second stage, the threats and opportunities in the Technological Knowledge Management are identified, and the strengths and weaknesses of organisations are evaluated to be able to achieve or reduce them, respectively.
- **Definition of Objectives:** In the third stage, the desired objectives for the organisation are established, based on SWOT analysis, defining them as accurately and realistically as possible.
- **Selection of Strategy:** In the fourth stage, a standard solution is selected that is specified in a Technological Knowledge

Management strategy. Said standard solution is related to the three dimensions of the Technological Knowledge Management model.

- **Definition of the Key Factors for Success:** In the fifth and final stage, the key factors of the of the TKM are defined, which will enable success, and the indicators and values that will enable the TKM team to carry out the monitoring and evaluation of the project are established.

Knowledge Analysis

In the first stage of the Auditing of Knowledge, we must carry out an exhaustive analysis of the organisation, with the objective of identifying the sources of knowledge and identifying and classifying the various factors of influence in Technological Knowledge Management. To this end, this first analysis is broken down into the following activities:

- **Definition of the Mission and Vision of the organisation:** In this activity, the mission of the organisation is defined (what products and services it offers) and how the organisation wishes develop itself in

Figure 5. Structure of the auditing of knowledge task

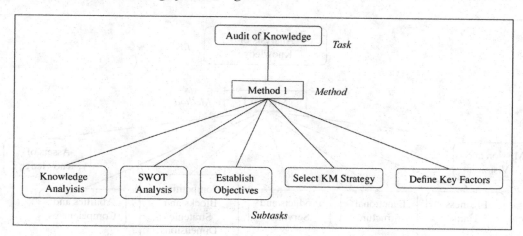

this environment in the future, allowing it to specify the associated Competitive Strategy.

- **Description of the Business Units:** Each of the products or services that the organisation offers is described in terms of the environmental parameters in the second activity.
- **Description of the Functional Structure:** In this third activity, the organisational and functional structure of the organisation is described, which will be of great use in the analysis of the allocation of resources to the processes that are carried out.
- **Description of the Products/Services, WBSs, OBSs, and Processes:** In the fourth activity, the Work Breakdown Structures (WBS) of each product or service that the organisation offers are described, along with their associated Organisational Breakdown Structure (OBS). This is a process that enables us to connect the operational level (Life Cycle of the Product, Chain of Value, Tasks) to the functional level (Functional Organisation Chart, Allocation, Roles).
- **Identification of the Competitive Blocks and Strategic Dimensions:** The definition of the competitive blocks and strategic

dimensions that the organisation uses is very important, since they will allow us to focus on the sources of knowledge needed to achieve the appropriate competitive advantage. Said process allows the analysis of the consistency between the established Competitive Strategy and the organisation's behaviour and the client's external vision. It also allows the analysis of the consistency with the key tasks of the WBS.

- **Identification of Abilities and Competencies:** In the sixth activity, the available abilities and competencies are identified to be able to carry out each of the WBS processes, identify which are different competencies, and the agents that they have in the OBS.
- **Identification of Knowledge Assets:** In the seventh and final activity of this stage, the sources of knowledge and their nature are identified, which are used in the abilities and competencies to competitively carry out the WBS processes.

Figure 6 shows the breakdown of the Analysis of the Knowledge of the Organisation.

Figure 6. Structure of the subtask of analysis of the knowledge of the organisation

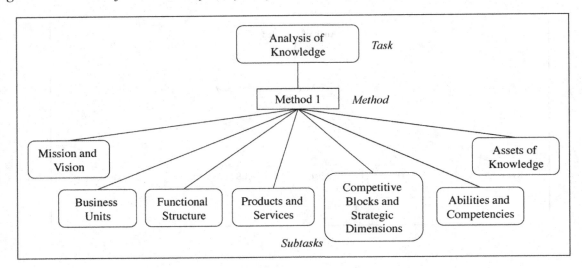

SWOT Analysis of Knowledge

Now that we have an exhaustive and detailed description of the, mission, vision, business units, functional structure, competitive strategy, competitive blocks and strategic dimensions, the WBSs and OBSs of the products and services of the organisation, the components, stages and tasks, the competences, abilities and assets of knowledge, it is the time to analyse and categorise all this information to identify the Threats and Opportunities related to the Technological Knowledge Management in organisations, and evaluate if their Strengths and Weaknesses will allow us to carry out said management successfully or not.

Regarding the Opportunities, we can define them, in relation to the Technological Knowledge Management, as those Assets of Knowledge (internal or external) that are different competencies within the key processes of organisations, and as those Knowledge Transformation Activities that can be applied to said assets to obtain a sustainable competitive advantage.

Regarding Threats, we can define them as those Assets of Knowledge (mainly internal) that

belong to threshold competencies (or deficient ones) within the key processes of organisations, and which therefore make them less competitive in their environment, or as those Knowledge Transformation Activities that organisations do not possess or do not know how to use appropriately to manage or improve said assets.

Considering these sets of Opportunities and Threats, we can define Strengths as those Factors of Influence of organisations that support or facilitate the development of TKM strategies to achieve appropriate management of the Assets of Knowledge, and the Weaknesses as those Factors of Influence that do nor allow or hinder the development of said TKM strategies. We can see said relationships in Figure 7.

In Figure 7 we can see that a Knowledge Objective can be an opportunity (to be achieved) or a threat (to be eliminated or reduced) for organisations. And that these opportunities or threat can be either assets of knowledge that make organisations more competitive (or less competitive), or knowledge activities that organisations could apply to the assets (or which they do not know how to apply). We can also observe how the factors

Figure 7. Relationships between the assets, activities and factors of influence

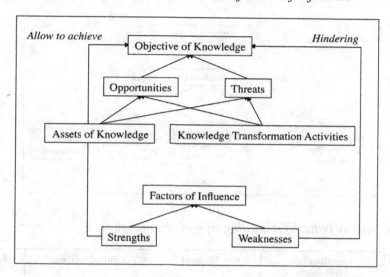

of influence can support or hinder the knowledge activities and its assets. The structure of the SWOT analysis task is as shown in Figure 8.

Establishment of Objectives

From the SWOT Analysis, organisations only select those Opportunities and Threats that they can face with guaranteed success and which are priorities, that is, those that for organisations have the necessary Strengths to begin a TKM strategy and that generate (or recover) a considerable competitive advantage.

Taking the objectives from the TKM Objectives Table, organisations must organise them by order of priority and accept only those whose evaluation is positive or very positive. In general TKM projects present a high risk in their development, both because of the nature of the knowledge, and because of the knowledge transformation activity that organisations wish to apply, and the factors of influence of organisations that affect the TKM. Therefore, it is better to adopt a conservative strategy, only accepting those objectives that show a high or very high degree of success.

Selection of Strategies

Once the TKM objectives have been selected that are of higher priority and that offer a high degree of success, we must select those TKM Strategies that best match said objectives.

In Table 6 are shown the different knowledge transformation activities, and, in Table 7, the strategies of technological knowledge management. These depend both on the definition of Opportunity (or Threat), and the Strengths of the organisation (the basic types of business and political organisation have been eliminated).

If we use the nature of the Assets of Knowledge as a parameter, we can find three types of TKM Strategy: orientation towards people, orientation towards business and orientation towards documents (Table 8).

Definition of the Key Factors

Once the TKM Strategies have been selected, organisations have to establish what the Key Factors will be that will enable them to evaluate the development of the TKM Project. In this final stage of the Auditing of Knowledge, we should

Figure 8. Structure of the SWOT analysis task

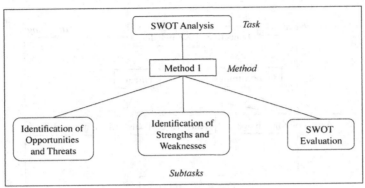

Table 6. Knowledge activity patterns regarding type of organisation

Organisation Type	Coordination Mechanism	Key Element	Centralisation	Knowledge Activity
Entrepreneurial	Direct Supervision	Strategic Group	Centralised	Internalisation
Machine	Standardisation of Work	Technological Group	Horizontal Decentralisation (limited)	Externalisation, Combination and Internalisation
Professional	Standardisation of Skills	Operations Group	Horizontal Decentralisation	Socialisation
Diversified	Standardisation of Outputs	Intermediate Group	Vertical Decentralisation (limited and parallel)	Externalisation and Internalisation
Innovative	Mutual Adjustment	Support Group	Selective Decentralisation	Socialisation and Internalisation
Missionary	Standardisation of Norms	Culture	Decentralised	Internalisation
Political	None	None.	Various	Socialisation

Table 7. TKM strategies applicable to organisations.

Knowledge Asset	Knowledge Activity	Organisation Type	TKM Strategy
Explicit	Internalise	Entrepreneurial	Document Based Management Systems, Information Retrieval Systems Data Mining
Tacit	Socialise	Professional	Collaborative Environments, Expert Management
Tacit Explicit	Externalise, Combine, Internalise	Machine	Knowledge Based Systems, Corporate Reports, Document Based Management Systems, Data Mining
		Diversified	Corporate Reports, Data Mining
Tacit Explicit	Socialise Internalise	Innovative	Collaborative Environments, Corporate Reports, Document Based Management Systems, Information Retrieval Systems, Data Mining Desktop Agent
Explicit	Internalise	Missionary	Corporate Reports, Desktop Agent
Tacit	Socialise	Political	Collaborative Environments,

Table 8. Assets of knowledge and TKM strategies.

Asset of Knowledge	TKM Strategy Type	TKM Strategy
Tacit	Orientation towards People	Collaborative Environments, Expert Management
Explicit Structured	Orientation towards People	Desktop Agents
Explicit Structured	Orientation towards Business	Knowledge Based Systems, Corporate Reports
Explicit Unstructured	Orientation towards Documents	Information Retrieval Systems
Explicit Structured or Semi-structured	Orientation towards Documents	Document Based Management Systems Data Mining

indicate those factors that will represent the benefit that the TKM project will contribute to the organisation, and the indicators that will be used for their measurement.

CONTRIBUTIONS OF THE MODEL OF TECHNOLOGICAL KNOWLEDGE MANAGEMENT

The comparison that we are going to carry out of the proposed model is going to be principally applied to the model of Holsapple & Joshi (2002), since this compares and include the previous models of Knowledge Management. In a first general comparison, we can identify the following contributions:

Regarding the *resources of knowledge*, our model, as well as considering the different components of resources in the model of Holsapple & Joshi (2002), studies the knowledge of the agents through the analysis of the key element of the organisation (Mintzberg, 1979), and in all those parameters related to the strategy: mission, vision, positioning, competitive strategy, competitive blocks, strategic dimensions and key factors. Regarding the *knowledge activities*, instead of using a management process model, we use a knowledge transformation model in which the types of knowledge activity are adapted to the accessibility of knowledge (Nonaka, 1994), and we connect said activities to the typology of the organisation (Mintzberg, 1979). Finally,

regarding the *factors of influence*, we study the different components of organisational configurations; coordination mechanisms, levels of grouping, types of centralisation, levels of leadership and key elements (Mintzberg, 1979), to identify possible strengths and weaknesses when starting a Technological Knowledge Management project.

And in a second detailed comparison:

Within the stage of the Analysis of Knowledge of organisations: firstly, we add the strategic analysis of organisations (Bueno, 1987; López, 2007), analysing the consistency between the vision, the positioning (Ansoff, 1965), the competitive strategy (Porter, 1980), the competitive blocks and the competitive dimensions (Johnson & Scholes, 2001). Secondly, we add methodology techniques from Engineering Projects such as the Life Cycle of Products, WBSs and OBSs (PMI, 2001), and from Strategic Management, such as the Chain of Value (Porter, 1980) for the functional and operational analysis of organisations, identifying the key tasks and resources within the different stages of the life cycle of products that must agree with the strategic analysis of organisations previously carried out. Thirdly, we analyses competencies, connecting them to their importance within WBSs and their assets of knowledge to the model of knowledge oriented towards the cognitive approach (Schreiber, Akkermans, Anjewierden, de Hoog, Shadbolt, Van de Velde, & Wielinga, 1999). Finally, at the stage of the Strategy Selection, we orient the strategies of technological knowledge management towards the assets of knowledge, the applicable knowledge activities (Nonaka, 1994) and the type of organisation (Mintzberg, 1979).

CONCLUSIONS AND FUTURE LINES OF WORK

Firstly, the approach of Knowledge Management that is applied to this work has been defined, aimed at the selection of strategic technologies. Then, the object to be managed, the internal knowledge of the company and the different models of knowledge that need to be considered have to be analyzed, taking into account the inter-relations between them. Then, a critique of the different approaches and models of Knowledge Management has been made, and finally the dimensions and components of our model have been established, based on which, a methodology for the auditing of technological knowledge management in companies has been designed.

The presented model enables organisations to select a technological strategy for knowledge management in companies, composed of a group of services based on unstructured knowledge and information that must be added to the services based on standardised processes and structure information. Said services apply the appropriate knowledge transformation activities to the identified and evaluated knowledge, from its competitive knowledge resources, belonging to their key competencies and tasks, and the proposed technology supports the competitive strategy implemented in the company and is applicable to different organisational types.

The approach used in the analysis of the assets of knowledge is based on a model oriented towards the cognitive approach, strongly influenced by Knowledge Engineering, which principally considers the ontological and epistemological levels of knowledge.

Regarding the modelling of knowledge at a computer level, this presents a series of problems: the Problem of Tacit Knowledge, the Problem of Communication and the Problem of the Representation of Knowledge (Musen, 1993). When dealing with the first and third problems, Newell (1982) states that the Level of Knowledge does not show any law of composition. Lecoeuche, Catinaud and Gréboval (1996), question said "pure absence" of structure, identifying that the major modelling methodologies of knowledge divide the level of knowledge through a process of "rationality in two steps" (Van de Velde, 1993): a) structuring of knowledge into a knowledge level model and; b) filling said model by using knowledge.

Regarding the structuring of knowledge, two lines of future work could consist of: a) developing semantic categories of knowledge that needs to be structured, taking into account the meaning for the interpretant (the knowledge resource of the company), based on the works of Pierce; and b) based on the works of Morris, developing categories of behaviour in the light of said meanings, which would enable expectational and methodological relationships to be established in the representation of knowledge.

REFERENCES

Alavi, M. (1997). *KPMG Peat Marwick U.S.: One giant brain* (Report Nr. 9-397-108). Boston: Harvard Business School.

Andersen, A., & APQC (American Productivity and Quality Center). (1996). *The KM assessment tools: External benchmarking version. Winter.*

Ansoff, H. I. (1965). *Corporate strategy.* New York: McGraw-Hill.

Bueno, E. (1987). *Dirección estratégica de la empresa: Metodología, técnicas y casos.* Madrid, Spain: Pirámide.

Davenport, T. H., & Prusak, L. (1998). *Working knowledge: How organizations manage what they know.* Cambridge, MA: Harvard Business School Press.

Holsapple, C., & Joshi, K. D. (2001). Knowledge management: A three-fold framework. *The Information Society, 18*(1), 47–64. doi:10.1080/019722402528818225

Johnson, G., & Scholes, K. (2001). *Exploring corporate strategy.* Hemel Hempstead, UK: Prentice Hall.

Kerschberg, L. (2001). Knowledge management in heterogeneous data warehouse environments. In Y. Kambayashi, W. Winiwarter, & M. Arikawa (Eds.), *Proceedings of the Third International Conference on Data Warehousing and Knowledge Discovery, DaWaK 2001* (LNCS 2114, pp. 1-10). Munich, Germany: Springer-Verlag.

Kerschberg, L., & Weishar, D. (2002). Conceptual models and architectures for advanced information systems. *Applied Intelligence, 13*(2), 149–164. doi:10.1023/A:1008340529122

Lecoeuche, R., Catinaud, O., & Greboval-Barry, C. (1996). Competence in human beings and knowledge-based systems. In *Proceedings of the 10th Knowledge Acquisition for Knowledge-Based Systems Workshop: Vol. 2.,* Banff, Canada (pp. 38-1:38-20).

Leonard-Barton, D. (1995). *Wellsprings of knowledge: Building and sustaining the sources of innovation.* Boston: Harvard Business School Press.

López, B. (2007). *Modelado de la planificación estratégica a nivel de conocimiento.* Murcia, Spain: Universidad de Murcia.

Malhotra, Y. (Ed.). (2001). *Knowledge management and business model innovation.* Hershey, PA: Idea Group Publishing.

Mintzberg, H. (1979). *The structuring of organizations: A synthesis of the research.* Englewood Cliffs, NJ: Prentice-Hall.

Musen, M. A. (1993). An overview of knowledge acquisition. In J. M. David, J. P. Krivine, & R. Simmons (Eds.), *Second generation of expert systems* (pp. 405-427). Berlin, Germany: Springer Verlag.

Newell, A. (1982). The knowledge level. *Artificial Intelligence, 18,* 87–127. doi:10.1016/0004-3702(82)90012-1

Nonaka, I. (1994). A dynamic theory of organizational knowledge creation. *Organization Science, 5*(1), 14–37. doi:10.1287/orsc.5.1.14

Paniagua, E. (Ed.). (2007). *La gestión tecnológica del conocimiento.* Murcia, Spain: Universidad de Murcia, Servicio de Publicaciones.

Pávez, A. A. (2000). *Modelo de implantación de Gestión del Conocimiento y Tecnologías de Información para la Generación de Ventajas Competitivas.* Valparaíso, Chile: Universidad Técnica Federico Santa María.

PMI (Project Management Institute). (2000). *Guide to the project management body of knowledge, a (PMBOK® guide).* Sylva, NC: PMI Publishing Division.

PMI (Project Management Institute). (2001). *Practice standard for work breakdown structures.* Sylva, NC: PMI Publishing Division.

Porter, M. E. (1980). *Competitive strategy: Techniques for analyzing industries and companies.* New York: Free Press.

Schreiber, A. Th., Akkermans, J. M., Anjewierden, A. A., de Hoog, R., Shadbolt, N. R., Van de Velde, W., & Wielinga, B. J. (1999). *Engineering and managing knowledge. The CommonKADS Methodology.* Cambridge, MA: The MIT Press.

Sveiby, K. E. (1997). *The new organizational wealth*. San Francisco: Berrett-Koehler.

Szulanski, G. (1996). Exploring internal stickiness: Impediments to the transfer of best practice within the firm. *Strategic Management Journal, 17*, 27–43.

Van de Velde, W. (1993). Issues in knowledge level modelling. In J.M. David, J.P. Krivine, & R. Simmons (Eds.), *Second generation expert systems* (pp. 211-231). Berlin, Germany: Springer Verlag.

Wiig, K. (1993). *Knowledge management foundations: Thinking about thinking – how people and organizations create, represent and use knowledge*. Arlington, VA: Schema Press.f

Chapter 8
E–CRM and CMS Systems:
Potential for More Dynamic Businesses

Silvia Brito Fernandes
University of Algarve, Portugal

ABSTRACT

Any change in customer's behaviour affects the customer's value. In addition, profitability and economic viability also change. Most companies still do not know entirely their customer base characteristics. They find difficult to define criteria that segment their customer base to find high-value customers. They need to focus on target selections to carry on with marketing campaigns which involve high investments. Given the potential of e-CRM and CMS as powerful tools to guide customer-oriented understanding and analysis, greater attention is required. Several companies, operating within the same business and having access to the same information and technology, differ in e-CRM performance. Without sufficient evidence, managers are prone to making investment decisions that are neither efficient nor effective. So it is imperative to base the decision of e-CRM and CMS adoption, on not only their analytical power, but also on economic viability criteria for sustainable business dynamics.

INTRODUCTION

The environment of modern enterprising is ever changing. Typical examples of such changing factors are: shorter life cycles, management focus, relationship marketing, online features. In the 19th century the life cycle of a product or business idea was often 50 years or more. With competition the life cycle shortened to 20 years in the 1950's (until the beginning of the 1980's). Now they are often 3-5 years and even 3-6 months as for a mobile phone (Philipson, 2008). The lowering of variable costs was the result of continuous management efforts to stay competitive. New costs have come to focus as relationship marketing has led to cooperation between economic agents, which often replaces competition (Gummesson, 2002). This is related with the need of finding smarter solutions to fundamentally change the pace of development.

DOI: 10.4018/978-1-60566-856-7.ch008

Modern drivers of change have led to new patterns or features for sustaining business competitiveness: virtual enterprises, design management, intellectual assets, interactive and mobile platforms. These responses require IT-based processes and imply the increase of information content. Any commercial enterprise that wants to optimise its success in the information society must have a basic awareness and a strategy for dealing with this new environment. A virtual enterprise is the generalisation of the ongoing differentiation of complex value chains and the market as an encompassing principle in organising all economic activity. The relative stability of the early industrial value chain has contributed for the relations between companies to evolve at a slow pace. With the shortening of life cycle and time to market these relations have to evolve with a pace that approaches a need for real time creation of such relations (Philipson, 2008). The internet brings critical new functionalities to virtual enterprises by real time business dynamics and relations. A virtual enterprise is not necessarily a contrasting model to big business which can use it as a mode of activity.

One significant aspect of virtual enterprising is giving small companies the possibility to access economies of scale. It also contributes for small businesses to access complex intellectual assets. As many IT start-ups in the late 1990s have collapsed, online retailers have realized that the rules of traditional marketing may also apply to the online business. They create their online stores as places to sell products as well as to provide service and enhance long-term customer relationships (Wang and Head, 2007). This contemporary approach is based on the premise that building consumer satisfaction and long-term relationship lead to repeat visit and purchase. These are chain effects of IT-enabled services affecting online business performance (Ayanso et al., 2008). Many online firms are then investing in the implementation of IT-enabled tools to enhance their online service and website interactivity.

This article emphasises the business potential of e-CRM (electronic Customer Relationship Management) and CMS (Content Management) systems as an integrated approach to identifying, acquiring and retaining customers. It acknowledges that a commitment to e-CRM with dynamic content requires from managers to analyse customer data and use a combination of financial and customer based metrics for e-CRM effectiveness. CRM helps business use technology and human resources to gain insight into the behaviour of customers and their relative value. This constitutes the heart of today's businesses success, so a correct implementation of e-CRM platforms can have a positive impact on the efficiency of their whole activity. By enabling companies to manage and coordinate customer interactivity across multiple channels, departments, lines of business, e-CRM helps them maximize the value of every customer interaction and drive high corporate performance.

BACKGROUND

Electronic CRM (e-CRM) is customer relationship management over the internet and extranet platforms. Most CRM systems have one or more web-based applications for selling to or supporting the customer, so the terms e-CRM and CRM are used interchangeably. If this is combined with a CMS which enables building web sites and powerful online applications with a very high level of content organization, many competitive aspects including efficiency and flexibility are achieved. For example *Joomla*, a very popular content managing tool and open source (freely available), has been used for government applications, corporate extranets, organizational web sites, community-based portals, e-commerce and online reservations. A content management system keeps track of every piece of content on a web site, much like a local public library keeps track of books and stores them. Content can be simple text, documents, photos, music, video or other types of data. A major advantage of using a CMS is that it requires almost no technical skill or knowledge to manage, since it manages all the content. The core *Joomla* framework enables developers to quickly and easily build:

- inventory control systems;
- data reporting tools;
- application bridges;
- custom product catalogs;
- integrated e-commerce systems;
- complex business directories;
- reservation systems;
- communication tools.

Recent studies have examined the direct impacts of multiple channel strategies on relationship marketing (Wallace et al., 2004). Among several tools that firms apply on their websites are e-CRM and CMS. CRM has been defined in different ways, but there are two main approaches to define it: management and information technology. For the management focus, which is emphasised in this work, CRM stands for customer relationship management as an integrated approach to identifying, acquiring and retaining customers. By enabling organizations to manage and coordinate customer interactivity across multiple channels, departments, lines of business, CRM helps organizations maximize the value of every customer interaction and drive high corporate performance. CRM is a strategy used to learn more about customers' needs and behaviors in order to develop stronger relationships with them. CRM helps businesses use technology and human resources to gain insight into the behaviour of customers and the value of those customers, which constitutes the heart of today's business success (Roh, 2005). Thus e-CRM plays an important role in the process of managing the activity of e-commerce websites.

Correct implementation of information technology in e-commerce websites design can have a positive effect on not only data processing,

but also on the efficiency of their whole activity (Ellatif, 2007). e-CRM features range from advanced applications, such as database-driven product customization tools, to simple ones as a line of contact information on a webpage. e-CRM can effectively provide better service, make call centers more efficient, cross sell products more effectively, help sales staff negotiate faster, simplify marketing and sales processes, increase customer revenues, discover and retain customers. And CMS systems can contribute to enhance the potential of personalization that these online features can entail. Their focus is on content management, which combines technology and business processes to effectively manage and deliver large amounts of diverse information to different media (Forsyth, 2004). This kind of systems determine the structure of a website, its appearance and the site navigation provided to users. This involves a holistic approach to building websites in order to match their businesses to what business partners and customers want by providing the dynamic creation, distribution and publishing of information on the website. Features like online forums, live chats, social networking are explored in order to enhance the shopping experience of customers and strengthen long-term relationships with them (Piccoli et al., 2004). CMS can build a motivating force for consumers to purchase and return to the website in the future.

Internet interactive applications and web technologies have changed the way of doing processes in all business, especially in the e-commerce websites industry. Due to its information intensive nature, e-commerce websites design can benefit greatly from the internet. This platform offers firms new opportunities to enhance customers' satisfaction and gain competitive advantage by providing their needs through internet-based services. As e-CRM integrates all customer-related processes through the internet, it helps leverage integrated information on customers and improve customer acquisition, development and retention by managing deep long-lasting relationships. Firms can understand customer behaviour and anticipate customer preferences more easily than before through better online tracking and analysing. For instance, analytical CRM is viewed as a continuous process with the intention of identifying and understanding customer demographics pattern of purchasing in order to create new business opportunities.

Issues and Controversies

It is not clear how exactly e-CRM and CMS systems improve customer satisfaction and business performance. Recent studies have provided some empirical evidence that describes direct and indirect effects of these systems on customers' satisfaction and sales performance (Ayanso et al., 2008; Ellatif, 2007). These works examine the linkages between online features and consumer decision to purchase and repeat visit to a website. The existing literature in online retailing classify the essential online features in two main categories: customer service management and content management. Customer satisfaction is the mediating force in the relationship between those two categories of IT-enabled services and online sales performance. A large set of literature focus on strategies to help online businesses improve the quality and creativity of their products and services in order to increase customer loyalty. In modern web-based retailing these strategies are implemented around IT-enabled services related with: information content management, search mechanisms, service quality and website interactivity (Chu et al., 2007). Customer service management and content management are among the key issues emphasised in the research on e-service quality. According to Collier and Bienstock (2006) credibility, usability and content are the main indicators used to measure service quality on a website. The content dimension is related to the site's management of accurate product information and personalization. The credibility dimension is related to the quality of customer

service. These authors also refer the award for the world best websites which has identified content and customer service functions as key dimensions of online business dynamics.

Technology can play an important role in enhancing customer shopping experience. With the increasing competition in the online retail market, e-commerce has shifted its focus beyond the technological factors of business to the approach that better understands customer's behaviour and experience (Moe and Fader, 2004). One of the goals of implementing IT-enabled services is to add value for customers, derived from online features such as product information, visualization and search tools. Most of the features now designed to improve online businesses are related to content management systems such as: interactive catalogs, customization, multimedia and personalization tools. However, several mentioned authors acknowledge that there is few empirical evidence of how these online features really impact on consumer decisions and drive sales performance. Jun et al. (2004) argue that most important factors that make customers return to a retail website are its dynamic and accessible content in a well structured layout which form a central building block of a content management system. Also online customer management systems are crucial to the success of online retailers. The responsiveness of online customer services is among the most important attributes valued by consumers (Griffith and Krampf, 1998). The Ayanso et al. (2008) study, based on real data from a large number of top performing web retailers, gives empirical evidence that the effort to improve customer service and content management systems is positively related to both customer loyalty and online sales performance. An important step in building more dynamic businesses is to employ innovative strategies based on the use of modern information and communication technologies. Especially the presence of IT-enabled customer service and content management functions creates a dynamic business environment, as reflected in customers' decision to spend more and frequently visit websites that deploy these two functions (Ayanso et al., 2008). The specific functionalities mentioned so far may not represent an exhaustive list of online features implemented by all web retailers. There are other aspects designed to improve customer service management and content management systems.

For example, the Ratio One with WebtraffIQ is a tool for web analysis/metrics that specially captures benefits of combining e-CRM with CMS functions. It verified that by putting these two skill sets together, a fuller service emerges. They then offer a tremendous opportunity to develop products and services in line with changing customer needs. With the increased use of integrated web systems and information systems, it is apparent that more sectors require robust online features that are flexible enough to operate with them easily and creatively. Then many organizations will adopt similar process integration as more useful data becomes available on time. It is crucial to know and respond to how clients navigate and interact with internet, intranet, extranet and related technologies in order to deliver even more cost effective services at an even higher standard. The worth of information system's investment lies in knowledge rather than in technologies or systems. Those combined functionalities help people find, use and manipulate this knowledge more effectively in order to improve productivity. The next table shows some impacts and benefits of applying or combining e-CRM and CMS systems from real cases:

Based on the comparison of real cases and experiences, a very important aspect to consider is the time spent in parametrizing the system and training employees. This should take 6 to 9 month, however if it takes more it is necessary to evaluate the investment using some economic indicators like ROI (return on investment) together with tools of web metrics/analytics like WebtraffIQ. There is a general obstacle related with some resistance to change, as some employees prefer

the previous system as they were used to it, even with all its inefficiencies. Other obstacles refer to some dependence on the firm that supply the system, implement and support it (such as SAP, ORACLE, etc.). One tendency that tries to overcome this limitation is the increasing development and application of tools like agile methods and UML (unified modelling language). Their aim consists on embedding code in the architectural objects that create and relate the system's functions with the business entities through data and procedure fluids. This gives the manager and his collaborators a simple and easy tool to understand and develop the system without depending only on specialized firms. The main advantage is its dynamic structure based on several easy diagrams (behaviour, communication, interaction diagrams) in order to help simulations that generate automatically the code that perform the routines designed in those diagrams.

Solutions and Recommendations

Successful organizations have to manage a lot of data. This exists in many forms and must be accessible to more people in an organization. Most of this data is also very time-sensitive and security-sensitive. Today, decision-making processes in companies are characterised by the fact that an increasing amount of information must be acquired, analysed and interpreted in lesser time. According to surveys by the Gartner Group, the information quantity in a company increases annually by approximately 20 percent. Company-wide content management is necessary to channel this flood of information and process it in a goal-oriented manner. Company data can include website content, billing data, calendars, project folders and files, computer file servers for storing important documents and forms, and email programs for storing messages and contact lists. With the sheer volume of this data increasing exponentially, the need for every person in an organisation to have some level of access to the data also increases. Juggling all of this electronic data and paper can lead to lost information, missed communication, many small notes and pieces of paper, and a lack of good customer service and employee accountability. It also requires more meetings to get employees refocused on the tasks at hand. Frequent meetings are sometimes impractical for companies that have several offices in different locations. However, meetings without tracking and accountability are also less productive.

If they don't constantly invest in improving their process of managing their data, they would quickly become paralysed. Building custom software systems to accomplish this can become so large and complex that the software and hardware requires an 'army' of engineers and consultants to manage it. The cost of this type of solutions is staggering. Small to medium businesses also need a way to organise and manage their important data, but on a smaller scale and without the expense of hiring costly consultants or paying for maintenance contracts. Unfortunately, the approach of building and managing a custom software solution is financially out of reach for small to medium-sized companies, and is also not practical. Therefore companies are moving to web-based software as it can eliminate the need to purchase and manage computer servers, firewalls, routers, and software servers just to run the application. A broadband (high-speed) connection to the Internet is recommended for sustaining a design in a very modular way, which allows for tremendous flexibility in building intranets that meet the needs of a particular industry. Modules can be mixed and matched to meet a particular need as they keep the intranet free from clutter because firms configure just the features they wish in their intranets. The applications built in a modular way can be combined to form an application suite which is best used as a company intranet. Unlike most websites that are publicly accessible, an intranet is a website that is for use within a company, and is secured with password-protected group and user level access,

SSL encryption or IP filtering. This allows control over which computers or which users have access to the system. Intranets can be configured to be accessible from anywhere in the world using a web browser, cell phone, or a PDA (personal digital assistant). In order to explore the business potential and competitive advantage of e-CRM and CMS systems, firms are integrating these functionalities into their intranets. The increasing demand on modern management systems like ERP, CRM, SCM and CMS go far beyond simple information management. Nowadays, the integration of applications and processes in a personalized environment is state of the art. Mobile ubiquitous platforms, based on e-CRM features, are the emergent way of doing innovative sustainable business. The next table shows the main strategic and technological differences between CRM and e-CRM:

FUTURE TRENDS

Revolution in Business Dynamics

Having solved their back-end problems through ERP systems and data warehouses, many companies are now focusing on solving their front-end problems with e-CRM. Based on Table 1 one can recognise e-CRM as a new generation of CRM systems (Chandra and Strickland, 2004) with advances that definitely improve business dynamics and competitiveness:

- a single integrated service and view of each customer across all touch-points (e-mail, fax, sms, phone, web, etc.);
- effectively 'know your customers' to effectively satisfy and respond to their current and future needs;
- make effective business decisions/intelligent recommendations to further enhance the customer-centric decisions;

Table 1. Cases with positive impact in combining e-CRM and CMS (Source: own)

Cases / Systems	Benefits of combining e-CRM and CMS
WebtraffIQ	web analytics and measurement email tracking real-time visitor tracking higher portfolio of services
EasyConsole	integrated service and view across all touch points (email, fax, sms, phone, web) flexible, open and customisable structures granular client-specific transaction request
Enterprises: AFC (real estate); Algarsonic (Tele-communications); Freie Universität Berlin (learning and webpresence); Gesundheit Nord (clinics); Hannover Re (reinsurance); Yamaha Holding Europe (music); among others	uniformity and standardization of information and process integration of activities in the same platform higher efficiency and agility in resource management and higher business dynamics, services and products better articulation of strategies (internally and with partners) total tracking of products, stocks and documents from their origin until their supply to stores or clients total automation of business analysis and business reporting

- efficiently gauge the ideal timing for new service introduction, drive increased customer satisfaction in the service centre and generate incremental revenue with intelligent service cross-sell and up-sell at the point of service;

Table 2. Main differences between CRM and e-CRM (Source: Adapted Chandra and Strickland, 2004; Vrechopoulos, 2007)

Aspect	CRM	E-CRM
	Strategic Differences	
Objective	Development and maintenance of mutually beneficial long-term relationships with customers	Uses digital processes, data and applications to integrate customer information at every touch-point in the context of multichannel retailing
Initial contact	Customer contact initiated through traditional means: retail store, telephone or fax	Contact initiated through the internet, e-mail, wireless, mobile or PDA access
Perspective	It is more a system strategy: emphasis on operational and technological aspects of CRM	It is more a business strategy: integrates a firm's entire supply chain to enhance customer value; aligned with customer strategies and marketing plan
Focus	Designed around products and processes (internal). Web-enabled applications are designed around one department or business unit	Designed around customer's needs (external). Enterprise wide portals are designed and not limited to one department or business unit
	Technological Differences	
Interface	Works with back-end applications through ERP systems	Designed for front-end applications which interface with back-end through ERP systems and data warehouses
Functionality	Web-enabled applications require a client computer to download various applications	No such requirement; the browser is the customer's portal to e-CRM
Customization	Different audiences require different types of information. But personalized views are made through programming	Highly individualized views based on preferences are possible. Each audience individually customizes the views
Implementation	Is longer; management is costly as the system is situated at various locations and several servers	Less time and cost involved; system can be managed in one location and on one server

- inspire greater brand, service and corporate awareness;
- low cost of ownership through a flexible, open architecture and productive implementation tools.

An e-CRM which in turn integrates a CMS can combine the features of the company intranet with sales force automated mobility, project management, relationship marketing, document management, messaging, news, calendars, all in one easy to use interface. Enterprise content management software with an innovative, intuitively operable user interface offers an enormous potential to demanding content management projects through the integration of data, applications and processes in web-based information portals. But only direct access to all important resources achieved in this way makes it possible to fully use the potential of a content management solution. Flexible and extensive personalization and access control functions enable the implementation of customized dynamic portals. CMS should integrate with existing IT infrastructures as users continue to use office applications they are comfortable with to create and edit all types of content. The consistent use of open standards and the support of open-source web technologies make content management solutions more scalable having a long-term perspective as they protect the investment in future. The CMS open interface ensures a more effective communication with applications vital for the company such as ERP and CRM systems. e-CRM is the application of e-business digital activities that require open interface-based processes, data and applications. This is an increasing requirement as it integrates customer information collected at every customer touch-point in the context of multi-channel retailing (internet, web, mobile, call centres, sales force, PoS at the physical store, digital interactive TV). e-CRM with CMS are designed to align business strategy with information system and marketing strategies. A solution based on e-CRM with CMS

can have a great potential for enterprises in modern dynamic businesses: instead of 'pushing' products it can support long-term customer relationships, as it allows firms to leverage their resources by applying them disproportionately to the most profitable customers.

Focus on profitable customers is not new, what is new is that information/communication technologies allow firms to identify high-value customers and respond with customized offers in real-time. Focus on acquiring new customers, which is more expensive, gives place to retaining and building business with fewer loyal high-value customers through:

- reduced promotion costs;
- higher response rates to promotional efforts;
- effectiveness of sales teams that know customers better;
- loyal customers that cost less to service;
- increasing up and cross selling.

According to Vrechopoulos (2007), e-CRM could be the 5th 'P' of marketing mix (besides price, place, product, promotion) because of its emphasis on long-term relationships and one-to-one interactions through communication channels. The main results that justify its importance are:

- Increase order size through more effectively targeted cross-sell promotions;
- Expand wallet share by increasing the variety of products and categories customers buy;
- Better tracking and tracing of products;
- Move overstocks by knowing which customers will buy them at least price to avoid deep discounting;
- Enable multi-channel coordination of field sales, inside sales, e-commerce and direct mail through relevant product recommendations for each customer interaction.

Today, business activity is very high volume with increasingly rapid and global distribution channels. Companies launch a wider variety of often more complex products what results in shorter product life cycles. These trends are increasing the potential impact on economic stability as well as the threat to product brand value. As globalisation continues, entrepreneurs are deploying new, higher functionality business systems that can provide a 'single system of record'. However, without more highly automated tracking and tracing integrated to this single system of record, it will lack the accuracy and robustness to pass the corporate risk-mitigating due to diligence of businesses today. The system should have the ability to monitor the functioning of all online platforms and it should include tested interfaces to other systems such as control, production management, ERP and data warehouse management. It should be able to download product and label information without manual intervention, from a business system to the factory system. And it should be capable of automatically generating product and shipping reports. In addition, it must support high data collection and real-time operations. The system software require facilities to support client-specific data customization and regulation. Finally, the system should have fully automated enterprise-wide product change management through CMS systems.

Factors to Consider in e-CRM Adoption

There are some aspects to consider that slow e-CRM adoption and explain the existing heterogeneity among countries. One is related with several features of e-commerce websites quality (trust, response time, security, usability, payment protection, etc.). Even if the adoption of electronic communication tools is relatively fast throughout Europe, the practices of consumption still evolve slowly. When European citizens were asked why they don't order goods or services via internet,

between 25% (Denmark) and 90% (Portugal) of the individuals surveyed answered that they preferred to go shop in person and to see the product. This is the most frequently given reason, regardless of the country observed. Between 10% (Latvia) and 70% (Finland) worry about security problems on Internet and are reluctant to disclose their credit card number online. Noticeable differences also occur when it comes to the supply of personal details over the internet: whereas in Portugal, this reason is mentioned by 52% of those internet users that never bought anything over the web, it appears only to be the case for only 5.4% in Denmark (Eurostat, 2007). These three elements are the main concerns in the individual countries. Conversely, internet 'non-buyers' rate worries about not receiving the ordered goods at home or concerns on returning goods at a much lower level.

The use of a website by enterprises is a step forward in e-business, as it involves a more active role than just using an internet connection. The overall percentage of enterprises in the EU with a website is 61%, but notably higher for larger enterprises with 90% for large and 79% for medium-sized enterprises. The same analysis of adoption levels for the existence of a website shows that all European countries appear to be in the fast progressing phase of the technology diffusion. Even leader countries Sweden and Denmark seem to be still in this zone of the S-shaped adoption curve. It appears that some progress can be expected in the adoption of websites, especially for smaller enterprises. But internet and websites are not enough for e-business. Enterprises need to use more of the technological potential in order to reap all the benefits. When it comes to using the internet and other external computer connections for doing business, the most prominent activity is e-commerce. The percentage of enterprises which placed orders via computer networks was particularly high in the UK, where half of the enterprises did so. Germany, Ireland and Sweden followed, all with 41%. Overall, 24% of enter-

Figure 1. Percentage of enterprises' total turnover from e-commerce

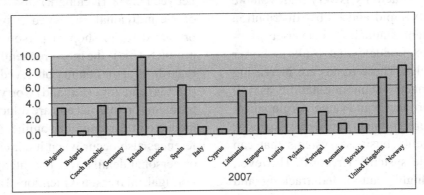

prises in the EU were making purchases online. When looking at online sales, there is a marked difference. Only 12% of enterprises engaged in that activity. Adoption of online sales can be more complex than purchases, as it can entail a new business model for the enterprise. This aspect reflects on other differences between countries, such as the percentage of enterprises' turnover from e-commerce:

The benefits of the use of information and communication technologies by enterprises in running their business go beyond making purchases or sales online. The use of computer networks internally in the enterprise is believed to yield potential gains in productivity. The adoption of internal computer networks is a first step towards the computer integration of business processes. Analysis of the adoption curve for Local Area Networks (LANs) indicates that all EU countries are in the fast growing zone of the curve. This reflects the fact that adoption levels are still low among small enterprises (60%), as for medium-sized and large enterprises the percentages already reach 85% and 95% respectively. An intranet is a specific application of the internal computer network which serves as a communication tool within the enterprise. Around one third of enterprises in the EU use an intranet, ranging from 13% in Hungary to 46% in Belgium. This is half of those which

have an internal computer network. The sectoral pattern for the adoption of LANs and intranets are not very different. The use of these technologies is particularly frequent among enterprises engaged in service activities. In the business services sector, the rate is 77% of enterprises for LANs and 45% for intranets.

One of the most important applications of computer networks is to integrate business processes. Such process integration potentially streamlines and boosts the efficiency of the enterprise. There are several ways in which business processes can be integrated. One of them is the automatic linking of different processes, information systems or business functions of the enterprise. In order to measure internal integration of business processes (business processes within the enterprise, as opposed to external integration, where several enterprises are involved), the Eurostat community survey measures automatic linking between computer systems to manage orders (placed or received) and three other internal systems: re-ordering of replacement supplies; invoicing and payment; and management of production, logistics or service operations. Around one third of enterprises in the EU automatically link their computer system to manage orders with at least one of those three systems. However, there are marked differences between enterprises of dif-

Figure 2. Percentage of enterprises with an intranet

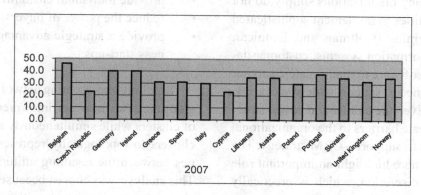

2007

ferent sizes: 68% of large enterprises in the EU integrate internally, while less than half of small firms are doing so.

Approach to Measuring e-CRM Effectiveness

Other important factor to consider is related with what Coltman and Dolnicar (2007) have analysed about the heterogeneity of e-CRM performance at the individual firm level. For instance they verified that it differs between organizations that operate within the same line of business and have access to the same information and technologies. Given the potential of e-CRM as a powerful tool to guide customer-oriented thinking and analysis,

greater empirical attention is required. Without sufficient evidence, managers are prone to making investment decisions that are neither efficient nor effective. One of the problems with measuring e-CRM is that the concept often means different things to different people. And other is that these investments have items that are quite different from other assets, resources and capabilities investments. As CRM systems provide techniques to customize relationships, the operational goal of treating customers differently is achieved as they know their different levels of relationship development. This enables the firm to pitch marketing programs at target customer markets. However, in many cases related IT investments have proven to be a source of intense frustration

Figure 3. Percentage of enterprises with internal integration of business processes

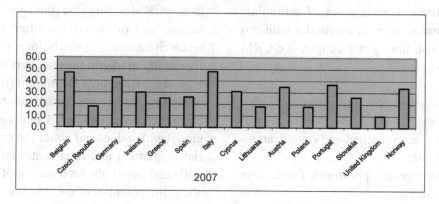

2007

to managers. Many organizations simply do not have the capabilities to implement sophisticated marketing programs (Coltman and Dolnicar, 2007). Their information systems, customer databases and the software to manipulate customer data is not designed to support widely accessible customer data. Even the culture and power structure can also create barriers to the organizational change required to support e-CRM strategy. The aspects pointed here highlight an important role for managerial discretion, which is practically relevant to the e-CRM payoff.

According to Vrechopoulos (2007) the features and tools that firms can increasingly manipulate are those attributes controlled by the retailer (customer service through call centres, personalized marketing campaigns, individualized selling proposals, loyalty scheme programs, time to answer incoming mails, integration with ERP systems, promotional programs, etc.). And the dependent variables are those attributes that refer to consumer behaviour (sales, revisit rate, share of wallet, number of new customers referred from partner sites, campaign response, rate of customer recovery, prospect conversion rate, customer up and cross-sell rate, average order value, satisfaction, loyalty, trust, perceived service quality, time spent within the store, current customer retention cost, number of low-value customers move to high value, etc.).

To understand how the role of managerial discretion plays out in determining e-CRM performance, Coltman and Dolnicar (2007) measured managerial beliefs against a set of attitudinal questions related to various external conditions and internal constraints. For example, if e-CRM implementation would:

- receive support by managers in other departments;
- face major technological and organizational constraints;
- provide joint profit opportunity for the firm and customers;

- provide individual customization;
- reduce the power of buyers;
- provide a strategic advantage over e-business start-ups.

Topology-representing networks were used to group the cases (answers) into a predefined number of clusters while simultaneously arranging those clusters to topologically represent the similarities between the resulting attitudinal segments. This analysis was chosen because it outperforms alternative partitioning algorithms in an extensive comparison using artificial data sets. The results obtained by Coltman and Dolnicar (2007) in their study confirm the importance of implementation constraints and organizational assets to financial and operational performance. They also highlight differences in the type of relationship exchange that appear to explain why managers in a certain segment have strong reservations about the strategic potential in e-CRM. This indicates that managerial judgement is an important competence that is under emphasized in the literature. If an organization does not have the skills and mind-set to execute an e-CRM strategy, then it is better to choose another option.

This analysis is consistent with recent works like the one by Nohria et al. (2003) about the role of strategy against implementation. These authors have tested that it matters less which strategy is picked by a firm as long as implementation is successfully achievable. Indeed, environments like e-CRM where the linkages and between actions and outcomes are often uncertain, the research framework must be increasingly explicit. Especially marketing researchers have access to a set of measurement techniques (discrete choice modelling, structural equations for measuring consumer behaviour, etc.) that can be used to model and understand better the role of managerial judgement and organizational culture. This will shed new light on a source of relevant data about the potential of e-CRM for more dynamic businesses and how firms can effectively succeed on exploiting e-CRM for new business models and opportunities.

CONCLUSION

Today's competition is tough and global, and that especially holds true for internet offerings. It is therefore vital to continuously reach out to prospects, convert them into customers, and finally to ensure their loyalty in the long run. Meeting and mastering these challenges is essential to maintaining a long-term competitive edge. Content management systems (CMS) and electronic customer relationship management systems (e-CRM) put enterprises in a position to develop simple but comprehensive solutions to ensure customer loyalty that help realize synergies between their IT systems for greater efficiency and effectiveness. This high-tech approach is neither high-maintenance nor high-priced. A hosted e-CRM service eliminates much of the start-up, maintenance and upgrade fees of its on-premise counterparts. Rather it offers a cheaper, faster and easier means of tracking consumers.

In a rapidly changing global business marketplace, it is realized that there are subtle and complex changes in relationship marketing directly impacting the brand equity, owing mainly to an unprecedented glut in communications and information channel like the internet. Add to this the typical consumer's desire to move across media while expecting seamless, consistent services. It is a deep challenge to attract, serve and retain the consumers profitably today. Essentially, e-CRM helps in enabling a customer oriented organization to deliver an extended infrastructure to customers and partners in new ways: to proactively learn customer needs, design new added values, gain new economies in scale/time/costs, reach new customers, and deploy innovative retention strategies. Like many of its predecessors, e-CRM is a term that is tied to a great deal of hype and con-

fusing messages. This article attempts to provide a framework for understanding it, especially that a commitment to true CRM implies the ability to analyse customer data and to use a combination of financial and customer based metrics for decision-making. Back office applications such as ERP require the same types of tools. The developments that streamline online shopping provide a rich source of information just waiting to be mined for business advantage. With every click, consumers provide information about themselves. Internet sites, web browsers and databases help in determining the most worthwhile business practices by giving important details such as product needs, spending patterns and shopping habits.

For example, in 2006 US retail websites enjoyed $102.1 billion in sales from consumers, reflecting a 24% increase over 2005's figures. Web-based technologies offer a wealth of sales opportunities. Without e-CRM and CMS firms are just selling themselves short. In this pace consumer is not the passive target of a sales pitch designed to provoke a desired response. Today's internet shopping experience represents a flipping of conventional roles. Customers act rather than react, voluntarily initiating the transactions. Although a firm's products or services are at the fingertips of potential customers actively searching for them, so are those of every other online company. To survive in this fiercely competitive scene, firms must understand, embrace and exploit this virtual reality. Intranets and the internet have taken on strategic importance for many enterprises. That goes hand-in-hand with mounting demands related to quality, currency and efficiency and an increasing volume of electronic content that can only be handled using content management systems or solutions that do an optimal job of modelling individual requirements and goals. CMS with online editing system support customers throughout the process of selecting, customizing and developing additional components, rolling the system out and providing ongoing support. Thus these systems are the foundation of intranet or internet presence portals with personalized content for increased acceptance and success.

The contribution of e-CRM and CMS can only be realized by understanding the driving factors behind them. In today's competitive world, maintaining direct and interactive communication with customers is crucial. Better customer services provide opportunities for increasing revenue from existing sources as well as new. By creating innovative ways to make new relationships and persuading old ones to buy online, a company can greatly improve its revenue base. A possible after-effect of this action is the chance to bypass any intermediary points of contact. Companies are always on the lookout for ways to cut internal information processing costs. Companies can pass on low value tasks like creating and updating of databases to their customers through use of an efficient e-business technology system.

Technology has not diminished the importance of maintaining a personal relationship with every customer. In fact, cyberspace offers buyers so much freedom of choice that a meaningful buyer-seller bond is what sets successful businesses apart from their rivals. Meaningfulness differs among customers but by recording, analyzing and retrieving important data, e-CRM and CMS offer communication and information on the right topic, in the right amount and at the right time to fit the customer's specific needs. Gaining and retaining customers is imperative for all businesses. Unlike traditional methods, with e-CRM and CMS the ways to gain and retain customers take another shape: these include online promotion campaigns, online customer database and customer profiling, sending interactive customer feedbacks and tracking visitor behavior on websites. A company can succeed if it has a better understanding of its consumers, their needs and the value they generate. Organizations may also include several e-business methods for identifying and interacting with customers. These might include the creation of communities of interest, offers of special conditions, personalization of customer communication, use

of customer feedback and personalized customer support. With e-CRM companies can now offer more products and services by cross-selling and up-selling. By analyzing customer preferences, companies can create customized service bundles. This can be exemplified by considering travel websites: apart from selling travel services, they can also sell various side products like travel books, insurance, hotel rooms, hire cars and much more. This certainly can not happen through traditional CRM where the main task is to sell tickets. Better pricing and post-sales service support are other benefits arising from implementing e-CRM. The internet's dynamic nature has the potential to capture customer concerns and frustrations in real-time, ultimately helping companies to respond effectively.

Overall business goals must be kept in mind when choosing an e-CRM application. The application's compatibility with people and processes that support those goals is of utmost importance. Choosing an e-CRM application is not a simple task, but there are several yardsticks with which to measure the productiveness of an application: within a company, tracking information on individual customers and making it accessible through various levels is crucial to building customer loyalty. Automating customer interaction can help companies to handle customer requests and complaints effectively and efficiently. Any CRM system should be able to systemize these processes to ensure consistently high service levels, quick response times, full accountability and prompt problem resolution. A successful CRM application provides analysis of customer data to help with the optimal allocation of personnel and other resources to encourage a customer-centric corporate culture. Applying e-CRM, a company can better analyze new opportunities for revenue growth and cost cutting, determine where its best customers come from, how to keep them and how to find more.

REFERENCES

Ayanso, A., Lertwachara, K., & Thongpapanl, N. (2008, July). *The effect of customer service and content management on retail sales performance: The mediating role of customer satisfaction.* Paper presented at the 15th International Conference on Advances in Management, Boston, USA.

Chandra, S., & Strickland, T. (2004). Technological differences between CRM and eCRM. *Issues in Information Systems, 2*, 408–413.

Chu, S., Leung, L., Hui, Y., & Cheung, W. (2007). Evolution of e-commerce websites: A conceptual framework and longitudinal study. *Information & Management, 44*, 154–164. doi:10.1016/j.im.2006.11.003

Collier, J., & Bienstock, C. (2006). Measuring service quality in e-retailing. *Journal of Service Research, 8*(3), 260–275. doi:10.1177/1094670505278867

Coltman, T., & Dolnicar, S. (2007). eCRM and managerial discretion. *International Journal of E-Business Research, 3*(2), 41–56.

Ellatif, M. (2007). *A cluster technique to evaluate effect of eCRM on customers' satisfaction of e-commerce websites.* Egypt: Mansoura University, Faculty of Computers and Information.

Eurostat. (2007). *Internet use in Europe: Security and trust* (Community survey on ICT usage and e-commerce in enterprises). Brussels, Belgium: European Commission.

Forsyth, K. (2004). Content management: A prerequisite to marketing and sales effectiveness. *International Journal of Medical Marketing, 4*(3), 228–234. doi:10.1057/palgrave.jmm.5040169

Griffith, D., & Krampf, R. (1998). An examination of the Web-based strategies of the top 100 US retailers. *Journal of Marketing Theory and Practice, 6*(3), 12–23.

Gummesson, E. (Ed.). (2002). *Total relationship marketing.* Burlington, MA: Butterworth-Heinmann.

Jun, M., Yang, Z., & Kim, D. (2004). Customers' perceptions of online retailing service quality and their satisfaction. *International Journal of Quality & Reliability Management, 21*(8), 817–839. doi:10.1108/02656710410551728

Moe, W., & Fader, P. (2004). Capturing evolving visit behaviour in clickstream data. *Journal of Interactive Marketing, 18*(1), 5–19. doi:10.1002/dir.10074

Nohria, N., Joyce, W., & Roberson, B. (2003). What really works. *Harvard Business Review, 81*(7), 42–50.

Philipson, S. (2008, July). *A specification of an environment for modern product development.* Paper presented at the 15th International Conference on Advances in Management, Boston, USA.

Piccoli, G., Brohman, M., Watson, R., & Parasuraman, A. (2004). Net-based customer service systems: Evolution and revolution in website functionalities. *Decision Sciences, 35*(3), 423–455. doi:10.1111/j.0011-7315.2004.02620.x

Roh, T. (2005). The priority factor model for customer relationship management system success. *Expert Systems with Applications, 28*, 641–654. doi:10.1016/j.eswa.2004.12.021

Vrechopoulos, A. (2007). *Digital marketing and eCRM.* Athens, Greece: University of Economics and Business, Eltrun Research Centre.

Wallace, D., Giese, J., & Johnson, J. (2004). Customer retailer loyalty in the context of multiple channel strategies. *Journal of Retailing, 80*(4), 249–263. doi:10.1016/j.jretai.2004.10.002

Wang, F., & Head, M. (2007). How can the Web help build customer relationships? An empirical study on e-retailing. *Information & Management, 44*(2), 115–129. doi:10.1016/j.im.2006.10.008

Chapter 9
Integrating Production Planning and Control Business Processes

Rui M. Lima
University of Minho, Portugal

ABSTRACT

Organizations have production planning and control (PPC) processes supported by systems that execute, mainly, repetitive calculations. Based on these calculation results, decisions are taken by production managers. These decision processes make the connection between different levels of aggregation of information and could benefit from the increment of the level of automation. An increased level of application of business process modelling languages is proposed in order to contribute to increment the level of process automation and the detail of business analysis. Thus being, concepts of integration of production management processes, specifically of production planning and control processes are presented. These concepts, the application of business process modelling language (BPML) and some solutions of PPC integration compose the core content of this work. Additionally, criteria for evaluation of these processes of integration are identified and discussed. Finally, the presentation of an industrial case will be supported by BPML model.

INTRODUCTION

The incessant search of improvement of productivity and competitiveness business indices is a fundamental issue addressed by production management processes. It is broadly accepted that one way of improving these indices is to increase the integration between management processes. This integration could be based on business process modelling contents that are being expanded to different industrial areas and functions within companies. In a recent study of Palmer (2007) involving 74 companies, an analysis of the current involvement in industry initiatives regarding business processes is made, including: modelling, analysis, management and automation of business processes. According to this study, functional areas where there is a greater resistance to the introduction of these techniques,

DOI: 10.4018/978-1-60566-856-7.ch009

with a larger frequency of answers "no plans" are: research and development with 68% of replies; risk management with 58% of replies; production with 54% of replies. It should be noted that these areas are very distant from the area following which presents a relative frequency of 45% of replies "no plans".

The production of products and services is led by management processes that must be adapted to the existing organizational conditions. These processes must adjust to the implemented company production system. Among the most common activities of management, the following production planning and control activities can be identified: determination of the demand in some planning horizon, determination of the resources necessary to satisfy the demand, determination of the activities to execute, execution of production activities, control of processes and finally, analysis of the results and eventually a change in the procedures. All these processes are based on information and their integration enables the increase of the system performance. It is intended to contribute to the following objectives through the application of business process modelling languages:

- Recognition and analysis of production planning and control main processes.
- Characterization and evaluation of production planning and control integration processes.

Some published works report the utilization of business process modelling (BPM) techniques for enterprise modelling. Rahimifard & Weston (2007) used the established CIMOSA (Computer Integrated Manufacturing Open System Architecture - Vernadat, 1996) modelling framework linked to simulation models to analyse a case company. This work refers improvement results in lead time reduction. Monfared, West, Harrison, & Weston (2002) also used the CIMOSA modelling framework to analyse and represent, mainly, a design process and project management involving

several entities. These authors realized that BPM is helpful to capture knowledge that is essential for enterprise processes understanding. Furthermore there was a recognized impact on cost assessment and managing changes. Quiescenti, Bruccoleri, La Commare, Noto La Diega, & Perrone (2006) applied the Process Description Capture Method IDEF3 (Integration Definition for Function Modelling) to represent both processes of design and implementation of an enterprise resource planning (ERP) system. Xu, Besant, & Ristic (2003) used XML (Extensible Markup Language) to build a business process model for a collaborative exception handling process in production planning and control. Cuenca, Ortiz, & Vernadat (2006) present a methodology to create CIMOSA partial models from data flow diagrams and unified modelling language (UML). Although there is a high level representation of the PPC model, the main work is related with a service process definition. These works reinforce the main idea of utility and performance increment based on the application of BPM languages to enterprise processes. Furthermore, it also contributed to recognize the lack of works relating BPM, production planning and control and integration of production management processes, emphasizing the need to evaluate the applicability of combining these business areas.

The integration is related with the incorporation or adaptation of elements between them, and can be seen in this context as the interdependence relationship between different production management processes. Production of a physical article or service requires a relationship between people, departments, management processes, design processes and execution of production activities. The focus of the present article is on the interdependence aspects between different production management processes, and between management processes and execution of production activities. According to this, it is intended to discuss a classification framework for integration. After this, there will be a short presentation on some business modelling languages. Both this topics will form a foundation for integration concepts and modelling integration processes. Information requirements for hierarchical production planning and control will form the base for integration characterization and for the industrial case description.

BACKGROUND

Integration processes require the incorporation of new elements or the adjustment of existing elements to each other, building up an interdependence relationship between different processes. The part or services production requires a relationship between people, departments, management processes, process design and execution production processes.

The correct perception of the company's mission, the capacity and responsibility to make decisions and arrange for appropriate forms of communication will enhance the chances of success of integration within the company. These concepts are referred by Vernadat (1996) and can be summarized in a set of basic principles. Human resources tend to do the right thing if they realize the vision or broader task of the company, if they are responsible for some objectives, and also if resources and the correct information are available. Moreover, if collaborators are empowered and have a good leadership, they will have the desire to participate in decision-making. In order to be able to have the correct information, there must be an understandable and effective communication system, enabling the distribution of knowledge and information, providing openness and trust that allow the individual to feel the power to affect the real problems. Thus, information sharing between people empowered and motivated to make decisions will distribute the decision-making through the organization. This whole process of sharing and transmitting information over the network in all directions without distinction by the position in the organization enables the Integrated Enterprise to be truly integrated.

These concepts draw upon a set of a few key ideas:

- Explaining the vision and objectives leads collaborators to proper decision-making.
- Collaborators with power have the desire to participate.
- Distributing information by organizational units reduces discrimination and can contribute to the desire of decision-making.
- Sharing information with empowered and motivated collaborators will contribute to the distribution of the decision-making process.
- Distribution of decision-making can contribute to the integration process.

Types of Integration

Integration can be classified regarding the following aspects: concepts, flow of materials, information and decision; boundaries of the system considering physical limits, applications or organizations.

It is important to consider, although it is not an addressed topic in this article, that technological solutions of integration may be classified according to three types of solutions: replacement, translation and encapsulation. In the first case, functions of a particular subsystem are replaced by new systems. In the second case, forms of translation are used, based on translation focused processes, or in neutral data formats. In the third case, a wrapper is used to encapsulate the functions of a particular subsystem.

Integration of Concepts

The integration process of different systems may have to deal with one of the following situations in relation with concepts: similar concepts can have different names; similar concepts can have different definitions; a particular concept of a system cannot exist. In regard to this, Vernadat (1996) presents a distinction between a weak integration and a full integration. The first is characterized by different definitions with the existence of semantic gaps, requiring the establishment of procedures for the translation of concepts. The second is characterized by shared concepts definitions that simplify the process of integration. For example, it can be noted that integration may have to exist between departments of the same company with a different or shared product notion.

Flow Integration

Production of goods or services is based on the flow between materials or information processing activities. So, flow integration between these processes is mandatory in order to deliver products or services. Vernadat (1996) calls this type of integration a horizontal integration and the integration of flows of decision is classified by the same author as a vertical integration. Horizontal integration could be generalized, extending it to internal information service providers, which may include, for example, monitoring activities.

Integration Boundary

According to Vernadat (1996), integration can be classified in relation to the boundaries of the system, namely relating to communication means, relating to the information processing application system and relating to the business processes coordination. In this article the boundary integration classification is generalized according to: means of communication; logical processes for information transformation; organizational units' interaction. The means of communication may include computer networks, data protocols, or physical means of communication between people. Interoperability between software processes could be achieved through: distributed processing environments; common services (IT), open application program interfaces, standard data formats. The interaction between organizational units is carried

out through coordination of business processes, that is, by shaping the rules of operation within the company or between companies.

Processes and Data Integration

In a company, one can usually find knowledge divided by different information databases and software, which are used by processes associated with various organizational units that can even perform overlapping functions. Thus, according to Scheer (1994) processes and data integration can be classified according to the following scenarios: information and activities completely separated by organizational unit; shared databases with totally separated processing activities; common data and activities functionally integrated.

Business Process Modelling Languages

Business Processes can be seen as a series of linked enterprise tasks with the intention to create a specific output. The end product of the business is the required output, which will be used by customers of the process. This method of modelling is used, in a very broad sense, to build enterprise models and has the advantage of enabling a focused analysis about the value chain of customer service. The aim is to make business processes more meaningful for the organization and to use those representations to understand and connect multiple functions in a more effective way.

With the use of business processes modelling it is possible to represent the business activity and contribute to the following objectives:

- Store the organization knowledge.
- Improve the performance through organizational changes.
- Support the certification process.
- Determine procedures costs.
- Manage implementation and customization procedures of software systems.

Although this work is based on the utilization of BPML (Business Process Modelling Language) a short insight to more than one BPM language specification is helpful to generalize their fundamental concepts and to understand their applicability. So, this section presents a short introduction to three BPM language specifications, namely: YAWL (Yet Another Workflow Language) as a workflow modelling language; ARIS (Architecture of Integrated Information Systems) and the correspondent BPM language specification; BPML (Business Process Modelling Language) a standard for BPM language specifications.

YAWL – "Yet Another Workflow Language"

Workflow is one of the main areas of knowledge related to the modelling of business process. A workflow diagram represents a series of operations, which may be associated with the work of one person, work of machines, or work of people within an organization. Any form of interrelation between work activities can be seen as a representation of the workflow. In these streams of work it is possible to combine resources, information and activities flow in a process representation that can be documented. Thus, workflows describe a set of activities with a goal that may be to carry out some sort of physical transformation, service delivery or information processing. Each of these activities will have inputs, outputs and implementing rules. Two examples of workflows could be: the flow of items through manufacturing work stations into a product; processing service requests with intensive processing of information and documentation.

The workflow patterns initiative, initiated in 1999 by *Wil van der Aalst* e *Arthur ter Hofstede*, has worked to specify a formal set of patterns of flow - WPI (2007). Van der Aalst & Hofstede (2005) presented the 20 most common patterns classified into 6 categories. These patterns have been used as a basis for comparison between dif-

ferent workflows modelling systems. Based on the results of the modelling systems evaluation a decision was taken in order to create a modelling language called YAWL - "Yet Another Workflow Language".

This modelling language for workflows is based on the Petri net modelling language that allows representing networks of tasks and also allows processing changes of state of the system - Proth & Xie (1997). Although the YAWL language is based on Petri Nets it has a complete new language specification with independent semantics - Van der Aalst & Hofstede (2005). YAWL is composed by Extended Workflow Nets (EWF) with a hierarchy. The tasks or activities can be atomic (single) or composite. Each composite task refers to a EWF-net of a lower level in the hierarchy.

The basic symbols of the YAWL language, according to YAWL (2007a) and YAWL (2007b), include conditions that correspond to states of the process. In these conditions a distinction is made between entry and exit conditions, that is, start and completion of the process. In addition to the condition elements of the language, it is possible to represent atomic and composed activities (tasks), of a single instance or multiple instances. In certain situations you can perform multiple instances of a task in parallel, for example one can mention the task of monitoring project teams, which can be made by a different element for each team. The connection between different streams of work can be done using *join* tasks: AND - join; XOR - join; OR - join. The split of flows can be made through *split* tasks: AND - split; XOR - split; OR - join.

ARIS – "Architecture of Integrated Information Systems"

Scheer (1999) describes the "Architecture of Integrated Information Systems" (ARIS) based on a modelling language with multiple graphic elements, allowing the representation of business processes in which several types of flow can be included, namely:

- Control Flow - the logic execution of processes through events and messages.
- Output Flow - output flow of materials or services.
- Information Flow - processes use of information.
- Material Output Flow - flow of materials between different processes.
- Resource and Organization Flow – resources required and responsible entities for business processes.

The functional flow is represented through the sequence of activities and the representation of entities responsible for them. In this case you must represent the activities called "function" under the ARIS framework. This flow may also include conditional logical operators to represent the separation or the connection of flows. The events can trigger a process or can result from a process. This type of functional flow is primarily based on networks of processes based on the EPC ("Event-driven process chain") model. The sequence of processing is represented by connection lines between the graphic elements.

The overall ARIS model of business processes includes a clear distinction between results, that is, between materials and services, and between the control flow and the associated events. In this general model, the control flow results from tasks (activities) execution triggered by events, which can be external or may have resulted from the execution of other internal processes. Output flow allows modelling material networks and / or information derived from services. The use of information stored in databases is shaped by information flows between tasks and external data. The representation of goals is modelled in each activity in which there is the intention to monitor and to evaluate the performance. This reference architecture also allows modelling organizational

units, human resources, machinery, computers and the software applications required to carry out the activities.

BPML – "Business Process Modelling Language"

The non-profit industry consortium OMG (Object Management Group ") aggregates several cooperating organizations in the development of standards for the integration of businesses. Among the most adopted standards are the following: Unified Modelling Language (UML), Common Object Request Broker Architecture (CORBA), Model Driven Architecture (MDA), and Business Process Modelling Language (BPML). The BPML is, according to White & Miers (2008), a modelling language composed by the following four basic categories of elements:

- Objects of Flow: Events; Activities; Gateways.
- Objects of Connection: Sequence Flow; Message Flow; Association.
- Swimlanes (graphic elements for aggregation of activities): Pools; Lanes.
- Artifacts (graphic elements to add additional information about the processes): Data Object; Group; Annotation.

Swimlane objects are used for layout organization of activities networks, with the main objective of interpretation clarification. Pool objects are used for representing internal and external entities and the corresponding activities. Lane objects are used to group internal participants' activities in order to facilitate analysis process. Artifacts are used to add information to the model, using data objects, comments, and group activities within the same category.

Figure 1 represents the nuclear BPML flow objects. The events are represented by circles, single line, double line or thick line in case of the representation of the initial, middle or final

Figure 1. BPML – graphic elements – flow objects - OMG (2008)

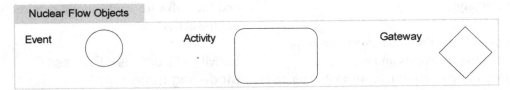

events, respectively. The activities are represented by rounded rectangles, which is a symbol used for this purpose in various languages of modelling, namely in ARIS and UML- OMG (2008).

Logical conditions, called gateways, are objects used to control sequence flow, and are represented by diamond shapes. The exclusive gateway allows splitting the flow by selecting only one of the objects following the flow or joining the flow based on any one of the previous flow objects. The inclusive gateway allows selecting one to all of the objects following the flow, based on the completion of one to all preceding flow objects. This gateway is generally used in pairs to split and join the flows. The complex gateway can create complex conditions for joining or splitting of the flow. The parallel port allows synchronizing all of the preceding flows activating all of the following objects without a restricting condition.

The nuclear connecting objects in Figure 2 represent the flow sequence in the network of activities, the sending of a message, and the association of activities with artifacts.

PRODUCTION PLANNING AND CONTROL PROCESSES INTEGRATION

To enable the integration and coordination of the organization processes we need, on one hand, a platform of integration consisting of means allowing the communication of objects (hardware and software) between systems, and on the other hand, a model that works as a common semantic reference, allowing mutual understanding between different systems.

An organization can be seen as a set of cooperating business processes executed by functional entities (resources) that contribute to the objective of the company. A model of the organization relevant to our system allows: creating a uniform representation; improving the understanding of the company; supporting the project or the redefinition of the processes; creating systems to control and monitor the activities of the company.

Production management relies on the performance of production planning and control processes, applying appropriate procedures and techniques to each organization. One of the most

Figure 2. BPML – graphic elements – connecting objects - OMG (2008)

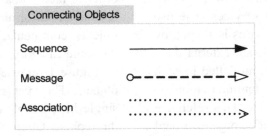

common PPC business problems is the integration of different functions, and a solution should be based on the common knowledge, of all stakeholders, about PPC objectives and concepts. In this section some of the most common processes and procedures for PPC are described, and some of the fundamental issues of modelling and integration within the Production Management processes are discussed.

Base Information for Production Planning and Control Processes

The founding information for production planning and control systems (SPCP) is composed of product information, production processes and resources used by the production system. The representation of information about the products and all his components is made through bill-of-materials (BOM). All material items of the organization, i.e. articles, can have simultaneously different roles, from raw materials to end products. For instance, an article can act simultaneously as an end product delivered to a customer, and as a subassembly item consumed by production processes of parent items.

The bill-of-materials is a list of all raw materials, intermediate articles, and sub-assemblies that supply an end product, indicating the required quantity of each item to produce one unit of each parent. You can even say that it is a list of all the materials needed to make a production series of an end product.

A product multilevel bill-of-materials already includes partial information about the processing sequence of articles in order to produce the final product. Each item corresponds to a state of the product that results from the implementation of a series of operations. This means that, at least, every article results from the execution of one type of operation. However, most articles result from the implementation of various types of operations. Articles result from the implementation of these production operations during a predetermined

time. This means that information about operations can be organized in interdependence networks, representing routing production processes to deliver each article.

To characterize processing operations it will be necessary, at least, to register an identifier, a description and resources that can perform these types of operations. In addition it will be necessary to relate them with articles that result from the operation and consumed articles. Associated with this relation there must exist a record about the amount of work associated with the production of each article.

In the process of modelling a production system, you must include the production resources and their capacities. The restrictions on the use of resources can be modelled using the following information:

- Amount of work, not negative, of a specific operation type that must be executed by some organization resources of production in order to produce an article.
- Available amount of work that each resource can execute on specific operation types

Production Planning

Production planning is the PPC function responsible for defining quantities of end products to be available in order to satisfy demand in each period over a time horizon. So, this is a function that links production to customers through demand management. In the scope of this function, the manager must deal with high levels of uncertainty over the medium to long range planning horizon and a low level of uncertainty over the short range planning horizon. To deal with different levels of uncertainty, production planning will be based on different levels of aggregation of information.

Aggregated and Master Production Planning

Aggregated and Master Production Planning functions are those that define the output of the production system, i.e. define quantities and dates of delivery to the customers' organizations. Aggregated Production Planning (APP) defines quantities of product families to be delivered to customers in extended periods and horizons, according to forecasts or contracts - Heizer & Render (2004). So, there is aggregation of information on products, periods of time and horizons in a medium to long range planning. This information is valuable for resource planning and for the analysis and definition of strategies to meet demand.

Master Production Scheduling (MPS) function defines which products, at what dates and in what quantities should be available to meet customers' needs. This definition should take into consideration the efficiency of the use of available resources in the organization, whose utilization generic strategy was defined under the Aggregated Production Planning function. Aggregated Production Planning function defined this strategy considering the objectives specified in conjunction with the Business and Financial management functions.

The definition of a master production plan that meets the aforementioned requirements is characterized by a variable complexity that increases with the variety of the production strategy and supply of products, including:

- Delivery of products that behave like commodities, i.e., that are purchased from suppliers and sold without any further internal processing.
- Production of goods to satisfy orders, in which the acquisition or the processing of raw materials begins after the order confirmation with the final customer.
- Production of goods for stock in an effort to increase customer satisfaction by

an high degree of availability of required products.
- Production or assembly of products, from existing stocks, after confirmation of an order.

Depending on the organization, aggregated planning can provide direct information input for the master production planning. In these cases, based on information about quantities of products, aggregated or not, to be produced in aggregated time periods, like weeks or months, it is necessary to define the quantities of final products to be produced in less aggregated periods, usually days or weeks. In order to validate this production plan it is necessary to ensure the availability of acquired materials and production capacity. Although the determination of the quantity of material and capacity is, in most cases, carried out from the MPS, there are limited situations that must be met under the terms of APP. For example, it may be necessary to carry out orders for materials over the medium term, either for reasons of distribution time, whether for reasons of production time. The definition of these orders will depend, in these situations, mostly on demand forecasts.

Companies should have enough information to link production planning with the customer orders management, integrating information on planned production, ordered quantities and quantities available for orders from customers. In the example presented in Table 1, demand information related with product P1 is related with forecast information, an order ORD202 and a production planned order PO113 for another article.

In general terms, meeting PO113 could be seen as a way of fulfilling demand generated by a parent article *customer*. In this example, to establish the demand quantity in each period, the maximum between the orders total and the forecast is considered. This is the defined quantity to be delivered in each period for meeting customers demand for this product. Forecasts result from the application of qualitative or quantitative

Table 1. MPS example – demand analysis

Product P1	1	2	3	4	5	6	7	8	9	10
Forecast								10	10	
PO113									20	
ORD202								30		20
Demand								30	10	40

techniques on historical data. Furthermore, it may be necessary to analyze the demand for variant option or add-on option to reach the final outcome of the demand analysis.

Information Requirements for Integration of APP and MPS

In this section and others that follow, the intention is to summarize the information used in different situations of integration between PPC processes. Although these are exhaustive lists, there was not an intention to present complete lists, because different companies have different processes and ways of modelling the information, which create different requirements to integration. However, this is a view supported by hierarchical models of production management - McKay, Safayeni, & Buzacott (1995) - and some industrial cases. The requirements will stem from the context of previous sections of the text and will be presented in the form of a listing in order to serve as reference for analysis and reflection in the context of production planning integration.

The demand analysis is one of the basic procedures for carrying out production planning, which should be considered in the integration between different levels of the Production Planning. Thus, between levels of aggregated and master production planning it is required to consider the following types of information:

- *Demand analysis*: forecasts; customer orders; planned production orders; product variant options; product add-on options.

- *Aggregated production planning*: product families; planned production quantities; planning time periods; planning horizon of time; product families disaggregation rules; demand fulfill strategy; strategic objectives.

- *Master production planning*: master level items (products); planned production quantities; planning time periods; planning horizon of time; available stock; minimum stock quantity; lot size procedures; scheduled receipts.

Material and Capacity Planning

The production execution requires availability of capacity and materials in the quantities needed for their implementation. To ensure this availability it is necessary to implement materials planning processes based on a production plan to determine the materials requirements quantities:

- Compute quantities and dates on which it is necessary to produce or purchase items in order to meet the demand.
- After you make the calculation it is necessary to issue purchase or production orders, depending on the case of items that are raw materials, finished products or intermediate articles in the manufacturing process, while ensuring their availability at the time set.

The materials requirements planning (MRP) is the most common procedure used for materials

Table 2. MRP partial example

Product A		Periods				
LT = 1		1	2	3	4	5
GR - Gross Requirements			5	20	15	5
SR - Scheduled Receipts		30				
AS - Available Stock	5	35	30	10	25	20
NR - Net Requirements					5	
PO - Planed Orders				30		

planning. This procedure creates suggestions on which items to buy or produce by setting their amounts and dates. This information is used by managers to make decisions about the release of production orders, which could accept the suggestions of the procedure or make changes.

Materials Requirements Planning Basic Concepts

The procedure of calculating needed quantities through the MRP technique, deeply described by Vollmann, William, Whybark, & Jacobs (2005) or Plossl (1995), is usually represented by tables like the one presented in Table 2. In this technique, based on the bill of materials, the component quantities needed for production of each parent article and lead times for each article, the calculation of material requirements are made following each level of the product structure. In MRP procedure, from gross requirements (GR) of the article, net requirements (NR) are computed for each period of time "*i*". In this procedure of calculation, the scheduled receipts (SR) and the planned available stock (AS) are used according to the following equation: $NR_i = \text{Max} [0; GR_i - (SR_i + AS_{i-1})]$. Applying appropriate techniques of lot sizing net requirements are transformed in production planned orders (PO) release suggestions for the managers to analyse before taking the decision to launch those orders.

The main MRP records may be defined as follows:

- **GR - Gross Requirements:** represent quantities of each item that must be available in each period. These quantities must satisfy demand associated with production orders from parent items and also demand associated with customer requirements.
- **SR - Scheduled Receipts:** represent the arrival of purchase orders or the completion of production orders in each period.
- **AS - Available Stock:** represent the projected stock under each period depending on the initial stock, scheduled receipts, planned orders and consumption represented by gross requirements.
- **NR - Net Requirements:** represents the minimum quantity of each item that must be available in each period, as a result of production or purchase orders.
- **PO - Planed Orders Release:** represents suggestions to release purchase or production orders for the item in each period, in order to satisfy specific net requirements out in time.
- **LT - Lead Time:** represent the amount of time from release until delivery of production or purchase orders.
- **L - Lot:** represent, in this case, a fixed lot quantity.

The calculation of quantities and indexing of information requires a much more extensive record of information for each item, as described by Plossl (1995). Table 3 presents an example of an expanded registry. In this record you can identify the source of gross requirements, the storage location for stock and the date of release and receipt of planned orders.

There is an important distinction between planned orders and scheduled receipts. The receipts are purchase orders with a scheduled delivery date or are open production orders, which have material booked and are already running. The planned receipts do not affect the gross requirements calculation of components of the article,

Table 3. Example of an expanded MRP record for one item - partially based on Plossl (1995)

Product A LT = 1	L=30	Periods				
		1	2	3	4	5
GR - Parent Article ZZ				10		5
GR - Parent Article YY			5	10		
GR - Order WW					15	
GR - Gross Requirements Total			**5**	**20**	**15**	**5**
SR - Running Production Order 115		15				
SR - Purchase Order 123		15				
SR - Scheduled Receipts Total		**30**				
SR - Storage Location 001		20	10	10	10	10
SR - Storage Location 002	5	5	5	5	15	10
AS - Available Stock Total	**5**	**35**	**30**	**10**	**25**	**20**
NR - Net Requirements Total					5	
PO - Planed Orders Reception					30	
PO - Planed Orders Release				**30**		

because there are already associated components, i.e. reserved or even moved.

Information Requirements for Integration of Materials Planning Processes

This function of PPC uses production plan information on the need for provision of end products in certain periods. The process of implementation of MRP will rely on the existence of the following information:

- Master production plan; requirements origin; articles information; bill of materials; articles stock by storage location; scheduled receipts; lot size rules; where used data.

Based on this information MRP process will generate or change information about:

- Planned orders; open orders; firm planned orders; scheduled receipts; gross requirements; net requirements; available stock; indexing records.

Capacity Planning Basic Concepts

Capacity Planning (CP) processes determine the capacity required to implement the master production plan, open orders and planned orders. This computed capacity is compared with the installed capacity to ensure the availability of resources for the implementation of plans and orders for production. Using information about the production operations associated with the bill of materials, capacity requirements are computed in order to satisfy material plan outputs from MPS and MRP processes.

It is not the purpose of this text to thoroughly describe the techniques of CP that can be found at Vollmann, William, Whybark, & Jacobs (2005). There is only an interest in realizing their information needs. Based on MPS it is possible to apply the following techniques: Capacity Planning using Overall Factors (CPOF); Capacity Planning using Capacity Bills (CPCB); Capacity Planning Using Resource Profiles (CPRP). These techniques require information on the quantities of final products to be delivered by period and on different forms of aggregated time used to produce those final products.

CPOF uses the total time for producing a product including its components and make a distribution by different work centres based on historical data percentage use. It is a simple method that does not consider the current demand mixture or the time of each article operation by work centres, or the distribution of those times by several periods.

In the CPCB, the time of each article operation by work centres is used to determine the capacity lists with the total time of the product in each work centre. From these lists the capacity requirements by work centre are computed, which, however, does not consider the distribution during several periods of production. Thus, it concentrates all capacity requirement in the period defined in the MPS to deliver the end products.

In CPRP, the time of each operation of the articles is used to build product resource profiles, with the time of use of work centres distributed by the periods in which this capacity will be needed for the production of components. This is the most detailed capacity planning technique based on the MPS, and therefore with greater computational effort. Nevertheless, it does not yet consider the possible existence of articles in stock to reduce the need for capacity.

The MRP process has considered the existence of stocks to determine the planned orders. Thus, using this information, capacity requirements can be computed closer to the current state of the system. The technique Capacity Requirements Planning (CRP) performs the calculation of necessary capacity in a work centre in a given period according to planned or open orders that use this centre in that period. Therefore, it distributes the capacity requirements for several periods of production of articles considering available stocks because it uses as input the material requirements defined by production orders. As can be easily inferred, this technique requires more computational effort because it requires the execution of the MRP before being applied. After running the MRP, the technique is quite simple to apply.

The capacity planning procedures analysed here are based on the hierarchical production planning and control model that relies on infinite load concept to build material production plans. The analysis of this information may lead the manager to adjust capacity and production plans. A possible representation of this decision process in BPML is illustrated in Figure 3. In general terms, for each production resource, if capacity load exceeds limits, then capacity compensation scenarios should be created. If some of these scenarios are acceptable it should be implemented, otherwise production plans must be altered.

Information Requirements for Integration of Capacity Planning Processes

Depending on the used technique, this function of PPC requires the production plan or information

Figure 3. Process extra capacity requirement illustration

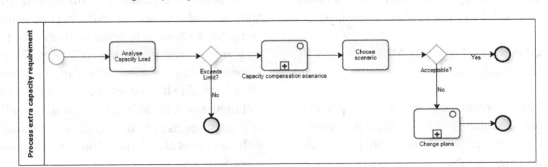

from production orders, which set out the need for delivering articles in certain periods. The implementation of capacity planning will rely on the existence of the following information:

- Master production scheduling; open, planned and firm planned production orders; bill of materials; production processes for each article; resources to use in each operation; time needed for each operation by each available resource; resources availability.

Production Execution

From the planned orders, the system suggests the release of production orders or purchase orders. These orders can be accepted as they are and sent to the manufacturing environment or to suppliers. Many of the production execution activities of a production manager are related with the analysis of MRP output and the decision making about production orders. In particular, suggestions of the system can be accepted, or dates and quantities of orders can be changed. Furthermore, as described by Plossl (1995), managers may have to release planned firm orders to avoid the uncertainty of demand.

It must be noted that planned orders affect gross requirements of components and are transformed in open orders when there is assurance of the existence of materials and capacity. Traditionally, the MRP system deals with these orders assuming they will be released in the current period, and only at that moment move on to the state of execution and reserve stock of components, leaving to affect gross requirements of these articles. According to Plossl (1995) some of the processes of the production manager are:

- Release, cancel or change quantities of production orders or purchase requisitions.
- Reschedule dates of open or firm planned orders.
- Request to change dates of purchase requisitions.
- Approve reduction of non planned stock reduction.

For the purpose of illustrating one of these processes, Figure 4 represents the process of releasing production orders based on planned orders of one specific article. In general terms, if a planned order exists in the current execution period, then if required materials are ready and capacity is available, the production order can be released. Otherwise, if material is not ready or capacity is not available, planned orders should be rescheduled.

Production Monitoring and Control

As already mentioned, based on production plan and on materials requirements plan, production orders are created for the items to be produced within

Figure 4. Releasing production orders based on planned orders of one specific article

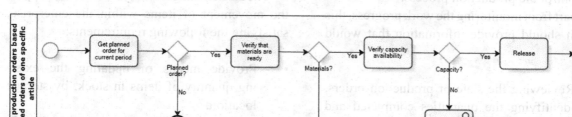

the organization. Once created, having guaranteed the existence of the necessary components for its execution, the production orders are released into production. From this point, each production order will result in a set of work operations relating to the execution of the production process of the article. Each of the work operations, depending on the utilization of production lots, should be associated to work centres of the organization and monitored. The monitoring system should be composed of equipment and data acquisition networks able to:

- Provide relevant information about the operations being run, identifying materials, tools, resources, time, quantities and conditions for the production execution.
- Register time used in each executed operation.
- Store information on resources used in the execution of operations and their time.
- Register information about non-productive operations, such as maintenance, machine setup, training of workers, troubleshooting and so on.

To comply with these requirements it will be necessary for the monitoring system to allow information registering about the company's production resources. These resources can be used individually or grouped into work centres or production cells or lines. They should be allocated to each production order operation and adequate equipment must be used to collect information and control the production process.

Apart from monitoring the work progress, this system should provide information that would allow:

- Reviewing the state of production orders, identifying the quantities completed and the state of the operations.
- Analyzing the actual time used for each production order in relation to standard time.

- Analyzing time spent on operations, productive or not, by machines and workers.
- Calculating efficiency of machines and workers.
- Evaluating the effective use of available capacity and recognizing and classifying non-productive time.
- Reviewing and comparing the amount of time actually spent in relation with the predefined time.

In addition to the aforementioned goals, this type of monitoring system can also be integrated with stock management systems for automatic update of inventories and with scheduling systems through the introduction of dispatching rules.

Stock Management

The Stock Management function is responsible for supporting the registration of stocks in storage and shipment of finished products to satisfy customer orders. Furthermore, it must also allow registering all material items during the production process, to adequately support the production planning and control system. The implementation of a stock management system is essential for supporting some of the processes related to the production planning and control. Depending on the desired objectives, this system could support the implementation of procedures for the classification of suppliers, purchase of materials, and entrance control of raw materials and movement of articles.

The stock management system should support the movement of items within the enterprise, satisfying the following requirements:

- Provide means of updating the existing quantity of items in stock, by storage location.
- Allow making entrances and exits of stock, by storage location, integrated with PPC system. Thus, it should allow linking the

movement of articles with the corresponding production orders, or other unplanned transactions.

- Provide means to support movement or shipment of the quantities of items needed to meet the demand associated with production orders or customer orders, on the requested dates.
- Provide means of control and analysis of actual consumption of items in each production order, which allows comparing the actual cost of materials with calculated cost.

Following purchases of items to suppliers, it is essential to control the entries in stock of such items. It will be necessary to ensure means of implementation of the following procedures:

- Receipt of purchased items controlling the quantities and characteristics of items ordered from suppliers.
- Traceability of items, enabling to connect end products with the items acquired. While there may be differences between different types of industry or businesses, traceability requirements can go as far as to identify the supplier, the collaborators who approved the delivery, delivery date, the date of production or conditions of distribution.
- Updating the classification of suppliers, depending on the price of the acquisition, compliance with deadlines, quantities and other conditions of delivery.

Information Requirements for Integration of Production Execution Processes

As can be inferred from the previous description production execution processes are mainly focused on production orders management, which can be planned, firm planned, open or running, and will use or transform the following information:

- Production orders state, including the level of compliance with their requirements.
- Information on articles, bill of materials and operations of production orders.
- Jobs of the production orders corresponding to instances of types operations.
- Resources to be used in each operation.
- Required time per operation per used resources.
- Availability of resources per period.
- Availability of material components.
- Operations and non-productive work.
- Classification of suppliers.
- Stock by storage location.
- Input and output of stock and related orders or requisitions.

PRODUCTION PLANNING AND CONTROL INTEGRATION CHARACTERIZATION

As stated before, hierarchical production planning and control is based on the existence of several levels of aggregation. Initial stages of PPC are based on aggregated information about families of products, production resources and planning periods. This is important in order to reduce complexity and deal with lack of information. As time passes, production planning starts to deal with less aggregated information about products (master level items) demand, capacity of production resources and planning periods. On a short term basis, those processes must deal with all product items (components, materials and subassemblies), with types of operations and jobs, and short planning and execution periods of time.

All levels of aggregation of production items and operations must be represented and interconnected in order to integrate production planning and control business processes.

Figure 5 presents an illustrative example of PPC integration levels. Rectangular shapes with rounded corners represent Petri nets, in which each organization object (circles with the refer-

Figure 5. PPC integration levels illustration

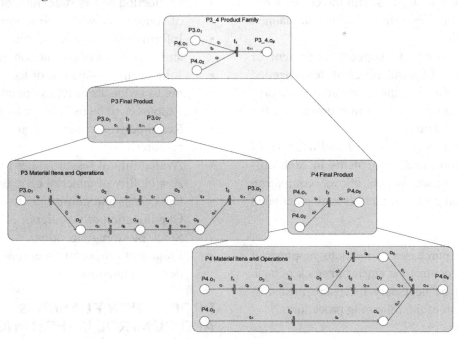

ence *o#*) corresponds to a material article, and where each transformation (bars with reference *t#*) is related to production activities necessary to deliver products. It should be noted that the indices numbering have a meaning only within each of the networks. These networks represent activities in a single level of decision that may however be influenced by decisions at different levels.

In this example, the higher network is associated with a family that includes the final products P3 and P4. At this level, materials and resources decisions are taken for medium or long term with highly aggregated information. At the level immediately below, the networks are associated with the end products P3 and P4, at which material and capacity decisions are taken from short to medium term, without aggregation of final products, but with aggregation of intermediate articles and needed resources. At the lower level, decisions are associated with more detailed information about intermediate articles and resources, in a short decision horizon.

Production planning and control integration is, most of the times, characterized by the need to integrate different levels of information aggregation, related to different levels of PPC business process. Different types of integration, presented upfront, could be used to classify and analyse PPC process integration requirements. Nevertheless, PPC levels characteristic is, simultaneously, mainly related with flow integration and integration boundary. This means that there is a vertical flow integration between different decision levels, and boundaries of integration cross different business processes.

A production planning and control integration process, as any PPC process, can be evaluated by the impact on production system performance measures. According to Wiendahl, Cieminski, & Wiendahl (2005) the main PPC measures are: throughput time, schedule reliability and utilization. Of course these are all related with the work in process (WIP) level, which is also a known used measure. Furthermore, the assessment of the integration of these processes can be based on several additional performance measures associated with production management and related improvement techniques, such as flow time, identification of constraint resources, identification of waste and identification of adding and non-adding value activities. Nevertheless, the integration process can also be evaluated by its direct impact. So, the following criteria can also be used: process execution time; number of errors; functionality. Reducing the process execution time and number of errors, and augmenting the functionality of the integration process will contribute for performance improvement of production managers. This can result from reduction of the number of involved information systems, increase of process automation and increase of computer aided decision processes.

In this section industrial cases were analysed and adapted in order to demonstrate the applicability and utility of business process modelling for the integration of production planning and control processes.

Industrial Case - Integration Between Different Planning Levels

Matos (2007) describes a problem of lack of integration between systems and planning processes.

This problem was identified in a car multimedia systems manufacturer. Based on the description presented in that work, a BPML diagram is proposed in Figure 6 in order to illustrate the integration process. Analysing this diagram it is possible to recognise the process of production planning as being dependent on the interaction between different systems: EVA, a proprietary system; APO, advanced planning system from SAP software enterprise; R3, ERP system from SAP. This interaction occurs through manual procedures that allow combining and processing information in Excel worksheets. The definition of the quantities produced runs through the analysis of short-term orders received in the EVA system compared to the aggregated amounts recorded in the APO system, which includes forecasts and contract orders. Analysis of these quantities, existing stocks and the minimum stock plan allows establishing, in a biweekly review schedule, production plans for 12 months. These plans have yet to consider the available aggregated capacity. This integration process, mainly based on manual procedures, increases the complexity, the running time and the occurrence of errors for the implementation of several manual steps. The

Figure 6. Production planning process example

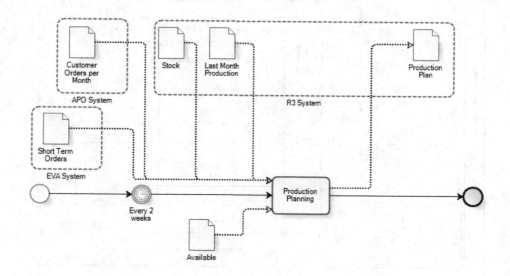

simple automation of the worksheet procedures performed in the planning process reduced the planning time by 25%.

Industrial Case - Integration of Production Planning Processes

Duarte & Lima (2008) described an integration problem in an automotive industry company. The daily production planning process in this company is composed of a set of manual procedures, which require access to several software systems. This process is slow and prone to errors. Thus, a proposal for integration was presented, first based on analysis of the planning process and of the used system and then on an assessment of anticipated advantages.

The daily production plans act like links between production demand and the sewing line collaborators, so that these productions lines are geared to meet the needs of the client. Development of these plans, in this company, follows a logical sequence.

The sales manager creates internal orders for the intermediate items according to customers' needs. These orders act as internal production orders for the cutting section and sewing section. This mechanism of internal orders is similar to a process of creating gross requirements for intermediate articles in the MRP technique. These requirements are transformed into daily production plans for cut and sewing sections. The sewing sections has yet to consider the "timings" of cutting plans to set priorities and to establish the order sequence for the execution of production plans.

The development of these plans is made in accordance with the process representation in Figure 7. This process representation is simplified in sake of diagram clarity, and among other, does not include data information.

Analysis of client demand for each product part is required to establish priorities for production. Demand for each product part is required because production is organized by teams, and only one part can be allocated to each of them by project

Figure 7. Daily production planning process

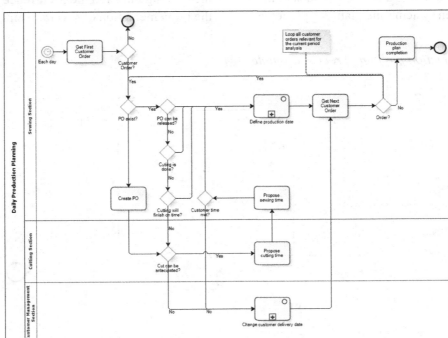

reasons. Information about these teams' characteristics is available in a proprietary developed system (SYS1). Orders for sewing section and cutting plan must exist before priorities can be assigned to the teams. If orders don't exist they must be created. If the order exist and is ready to start, then it should start running into production. If there is an order and the production order is not available, the cutting section must be alerted to prepare, if possible, the needed quantities as soon as possible, so that shipping to the client does not fail.

For the development of the plan it is necessary to check the daily orders for manufacturing, the cutting plan and the customer needs by piece. These needs will be taken from the AS400 company management system. Integration process get capacity of resource teams from SYS1 and time for each piece operation from a proprietary SYS2 system. So, this integration process requires utilization from three different systems of the organization. Figure 7, allows inferring that the integration process deal with the interrelation of two PPC levels, respectively: end product quantities to deliver (MPS) and component production order release. It can also be inferred that there exist at least three participants responsible for taken decisions, one for each section. As stated before, this integration process is mainly based on non automated analysis and decisions. Improvements could include actions to increase the automation of the process and reductions of the number of participants responsible for decisions.

Examining the represented production planning process of this company, it is possible to identify relations between two levels in the hierarchical production planning and control model. The production plan is obtained after analysing the end products demand from master production planning, followed by procedures of capacity and materials requirements plans verification. If customer data delivery can be satisfied then production dates are defined and combined into the daily production plan.

CONCLUSION

Production planning and control on small and medium enterprises are mainly based on the hierarchical model and this model is the most implemented one in enterprise resource planning software. Knowledge about this model processes for production planning and control are fundamental for their integration. Description of these processes has been a large part of this article. It was not intention of this article to describe PPC techniques or procedures, but to describe data requirements and the interrelation between different production levels. This interrelation is fundamentally restricted by decisions that must be taken between different aggregation levels, eventually crossing organizational boundaries. Production system evaluation metrics can be used for evaluation of processes of integration. Furthermore, a few more criteria directly related with processes of integration are proposed to evaluate performance of the solution, namely: process execution time; number of errors; functionality.

Business process modelling languages form a less explored road for the integration of PPC processes. This work makes a contribution in the way of clarifying some of the possibilities of using BPML for achieving this objective. This contribution was done in two distinct ways: (1) linking general PPC processes and proposing their integration characterization; (2) modelling more detailed integration processes from industrial cases.

Fundamental trends of application of business process modelling languages for processes of integration are related with decision process modelling, process automation, application of workflows patterns and definition of PPC integration patterns. Decision taken by production managers are, most of the time, less formalized, contributing for reduction of clarity, transparency and acknowledgement by production stakeholders. Process automation will, undoubtedly, contribute for PPC integration processes time and errors reduction. Furthermore this could contribute for augmenting integration with enterprise software. Finally, utilization of patterns will contribute for reduction of business process design effort and simultaneously for reutilization of this integration processes.

REFERENCES

Cuenca, L., Ortiz, A., & Vernadat, F. (2006). From UML or DFD models to CIMOSA partial models and enterprise components. *International Journal of Computer Integrated Manufacturing, 19*(3), 248–263. doi:10.1080/03081070500065841

Duarte, C. S. R., & Lima, R. M. (2008, 2008.09.02-2008.09.04). *Proposta de Melhoria do Processo de Gestão de Células de Fabrico de Coberturas para Assentos Dedicados à Indústria Automóvel [portuguese]*. Paper presented at the 5° Congresso Luso-Moçambicano de Engenharia (CLME'2008), Maputo - Moçambique.

Heizer, J., & Render, B. (2004). *Operations management* (7th ed.). Upper Saddle River, NJ: Prentice Hall.

Matos, M. (2007). *Redefinição de procedimentos de integração para planeamento da produção e redefinição de processos de gestão de produtos em fim de vida na indústria de auto-rádio [portuguese]*. Universidade do Minho, Guimarães.

McKay, K. N., Safayeni, F. R., & Buzacott, J. A. (1995). A review of hierarchical production planning and its applicability for modern manufacturing. *Production Planning and Control, 6*(5), 384–394. doi:10.1080/09537289508930295

Monfared, R. P., West, A. A., Harrison, R., & Weston, R. H. (2002). An implementation of the business process modelling approach in the automotive industry. *Proceedings of the Institution of Mechanical Engineers -- Part B -- Engineering Manufacture, 216*(11), 1413-1427.

OMG. (2008). *Business process modeling notation, V1.1*. Retrieved June 30, 2008, from http://www.omg.org/spec/BPMN/1.1/PDF

Palmer, N. (2007). *A survey of business process initiatives* [Electronic Version]. Retrieved July 1, 2008, from http://www.wfmc.org/researchreports/featured_research.htm

Plossl, G. (1995). *Orlicky's material requirements planning* (2nd ed.). New York: McGraw Hill.

Proth, J.-M., & Xie, X. (1997). *Petri Nets: A tool for design and management of manufacturing systems*. New York: John Wiley and Sons.

Quiescenti, M., Bruccoleri, M., La Commare, U., Noto La Diega, S., & Perrone, G. (2006). Business process-oriented design of Enterprise resource planning (ERP) systems for small and medium enterprises. *International Journal of Production Research, 44*(18/19), 3797–3811. doi:10.1080/00207540600688499

Rahimifard, A., & Weston, R. (2007). The enhanced use of enterprise and simulation modelling techniques to support factory changeability. *International Journal of Computer Integrated Manufacturing, 20*(4), 307–328. doi:10.1080/09511920600793220

Scheer, A.-W. (1999). *ARIS - business process frameworks* (3rd ed.). Berlin, Germany: Springer-Verlag.

Van der Aalst, W. M. P., & Hofstede, A. H. M. (2005). YAWL: Yet another workflow language. *Information Systems, 30*(4), 245–275. doi:10.1016/j.is.2004.02.002

Vernadat, F. (1996). *Enterprise modeling and integration: Principles and applications*. London: Chapman & Hall.

Vollmann, T. E., William, L. B., Whybark, D. C., & Jacobs, F. R. (2005). *Manufacturing planning and control for supply chain management* (5th ed.). New York: McGraw-Hill.

White, S. A., & Miers, D. (2008). *BPMN modeling and reference guide: Understanding and using BPMN*. Lighthouse, FL: Future Strategies.

Wiendahl, H.-H., Cieminski, G. V., & Wiendahl, H.-P. (2005). Stumbling blocks of PPC: Towards the holistic configuration of PPC systems. *Production Planning and Control, 16*(7), 634–651. doi:10.1080/09537280500249280

WPI. (2007). *About the workflow patterns*. Retrieved July 2, 2008, from http://www.workflow-patterns.com./about/index.php

Xu, H. Q., Besant, C. B., & Ristic, M. (2003). System for enhancing supply chain agility through exception handling. *International Journal of Production Research, 41*(6), 1099–1114. doi:10.1080/0020754021000049826

YAWL. (2007a). YAWL editor 1.5: User manual. Retrieved July 2, 2008, from http://yawlfoundation.org/yawldocs/YAWLEditor1.5UserManual.doc

YAWL. (2007b). YAWL lexicon. Retrieved July 7, 2008, from http://www.yawlfoundation.org/resources/lexicon.html

Chapter 10
Environments for Virtual Enterprise Integration

Maria Manuela Cruz-Cunha
Polytechnic Institute of Cávado and Ave, Portugal

Goran D. Putnik
University of Minho, Portugal

ABSTRACT

The Virtual Enterprise model relies on dynamically reconfigurable collaborative networks, with extremely high performances, strongly time-oriented while highly focused on cost and quality, in permanent alignment with the market, and strongly supported by information and communication technology. Networking and reconfiguration dynamics are the main characteristics of this model, which claim for enabling and supporting environments, assuring cost-effective integration in useful time and preventing the risk of leakage of private information about products or processes. Some existing technologies and Internet-based environments can partially support this organizational model, but the reconfiguration dynamics can only be assured by environments able to manage, control, and enable virtual enterprise creation/operation/reconfiguration. Several environments are introduced in the article, and particular focus is given to the Market of Resources, an environment coping with the requirements of the Virtual Enterprise model.

INTRODUCTION

The new requirements of the business environment, in permanent change, claim for dynamically reconfigurable global networked structures, with extremely high performances, strongly time-oriented while highly focused on cost and quality, permanently aligned with business opportunities, and strongly supported by information and communication technology, dictating a paradigm shift face to the traditional organizational models. The leading organizational model traducing these characteristics is the Virtual Enterprise (VE) organizational model.

Virtual Enterprise Integration is one of the most important requirement for making VE a real, competitive, and widely implemented organizational and management concept. It is virtually the most important requirement (Putnik, Cunha, Sousa, & Ávila, 2005).

VE creation, operation, and reconfiguration must be supported by environments, managed and maintained by third parties, able to assure the VE requirements of high reconfiguration dynamics and business alignment, overcoming the VE reconfiguration disablers as transaction costs and leakage of private information on products or processes. The authors have been working on the concept of Market of Resources, detailed in the article.

Other examples of third party entities acting as VE enablers (Market of Resources alike concepts, services, and products), include the new generation of high value–added electronic marketplaces, Electronic Alliances (Malhotra & Gosain, 2005), Virtual Organization Breeding Environments (Camarinha-Matos & Afsarmanesh, 2004; Romero, Galeano, & Molina, 2007), Electronic Institutions (Cardoso & Oliveira, 2004; Rocha, Cardoso, & Oliveira, 2005), Virtual Enterprise Cluster (Zhang, Gao, Zhang, & Chang, 2008), Virtual Industry Clusters (Molina & Flores, 1999), brokerage services (Ávila, Putnik, & Cunha, 2002; Mejía & Molina, 2002) and "guilds."

It is expected that these environments will be in a near future the regular environments for VE integration, reconfiguration dynamics, and operation.

Considering that the VE concept aims to represent a new organizational paradigm for enterprises in general, and, in that way, permeating virtually the whole economy and even society (through the concept of Virtual Organizations), we could talk about the social costs of ineffective and inefficient integration of VE. However, many authors recognize that the present solutions for VE integration are either inexistent or insufficient.

Therefore, there is a need for further effort by the community toward satisfactory and competitive solutions.

This article intends to be part of this effort. It discusses the VE reconfigurability requirement and the requirements of reconfiguration dynamics; introduce some of the most recent developments and environments to cope with these requirements; and presents the Market of Resources as part of a new generation of electronic marketplaces, a tool for managing, controlling, and enabling networking and dynamics in VE integration at low transaction cost and preserving the firms' private knowledge.

The article makes two contributions: (1) to industry managers, it highlights the importance of dynamic organizational models, as the ultimate paradigm; and (2) to information systems professionals, it alerts to the development of a new generation of environments, able to effectively and efficiently cope with the VE model.

REQUIREMENTS FOR VIRTUAL ENTERPRISE INTEGRATION

Several VE definitions and similar models exist and many similar and sometimes overlapping designations are used: collaborative networks, collaborative supply chains, networked enterprise, star alliances, agile/virtual enterprises, and so forth. These are all forms of virtual enterprises, in a broad sense. What makes the distinction is the duration and the links established or intended to establish, the legal formalities, scope, sharing of responsibilities and results, coordination, reconfiguration dynamics, and so forth.

Concerning duration, such networks can be established on a temporary or a long-term basis. Temporary organizations seem to better fit the dynamics of the market and the typically short duration of business opportunities, whereas long-term organizations better cope with the trust building process and the investment on common

Figure 1. Evolution of product life cycle

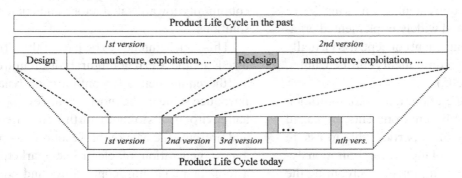

infrastructures and practices. However, we will not be concerned with the particularities of these labels, their overlapping and differences in structure, organization or operation.

Most definitions of Virtual Enterprise (VE) in broad sense incorporate the idea of extended and collaborative outsourcing to suppliers and subcontractors to achieve a competitive response to market demands (Webster, Sugden, & Tayles, 2004). As suggested by several authors (Browne & Zhang, 1999; Cunha & Putnik, 2005, Cunha, Putnik, & Ávila, 2000; Davidow & Malone, 1992), a VE consists of a network of independent enterprises (resources providers) with reconfiguration capability in useful time, permanently aligned with the market requirements, created to take profit from a specific market opportunity, and where each participant contributes with its best practices and core competencies to the success and competitiveness of the structure as a whole. Even during the operation phase of the VE, the configuration can change, to assure business alignment with the market demands, traduced by the identification of reconfiguration opportunities and constant readjustment or reconfiguration of the VE network, to meet unexpected situations or to keep permanent competitiveness and maximum performance.

The implementation of the VE model should assure the required networking and reconfiguration dynamics. However, the main factors against networking and reconfiguration dynamics are the reconfiguration costs and the leakage of private information. The reconfiguration dynamics requirement is dependent of (1) the reduction of reconfiguration costs and effort, that is, requires a balancing between reconfiguration dynamics and reconfiguration time and costs, and (2) the capability to preserve the firms' private knowledge on products or processes.

Shaping the virtual enterprise is complex but not if resources providers are found and can be integrated, the question is whether this can be done cost effectively, on a reasonable time frame, and preventing the risk of leakage of private information.

Networking and Reconfiguration Dynamics: The VE Enablers

For the past few years, global competition has strengthened the significance of a company's ability to introduce new products, while responding to increasingly dynamic markets with customers rapidly changing needs, and thus claiming for shortening the time required to design, develop, and manufacture, as well as for cost reduction and quality improvement. In the past, a product could exist without great changes (adaptations, redesigns). Faced with the challenges of today, besides the shorter duration of a product, it usually suffers several redesigns to be competitive, that is, aligned with the market demands, as shown in Figure 1.

These trends requires enterprises the capability to incorporate into their products or processes the best resources available in the market, and to dynamically adjust its inter-organizational structure to keep its maximum alignment with the business opportunity.

Multiproduct companies, that is, those whose organisational model consists of the production of various products, present different performance levels for the different products, as a consequence of the different performances of its resources in the execution of the different operations of a given product. In general, the operations performed with larger efficiency correspond to the core competencies of the company. Contrarily, under the concept of a networked organisation, it is possible to conceive a new physical structure of the production system for each new product (one network created for each product), where all the processes to produce a product are decomposed in operations performed by partners of the network. For each operation the partner presenting the highest possible performance is selected to optimise overall performance of the network (ideally 100%).

But the changing business environment requires also the permanent adaptation of the network (VE), to assure its alignment with business opportunities, with the market. By alignment, in this context, we mean the actions to be undertaken to gain synergy between a market opportunity, and the delivery of the required product, with the required specifications, at the required time, with the lowest cost and with the best possible return (Cunha & Putnik, 2005).

Reconfiguration, meaning the substitution of resources providers, generating a new instance of the network, can happen mainly from four reasons:

1. Reconfiguration during the network company life cycle is a consequence of the product redesign in the product life cycle, to keep the network aligned with the market requirements, that is, to deliver the right product.

2. Reconfiguration as a consequence of the nature of the particular product life cycle phase (the evolutionary phases of the product).

3. Reconfiguration can happen also as a consequence of the evaluation of the resources performance during one instantiation of the network, or a consequence of voluntary contract rescission by a participating resources provider, willing to disentail from the network.

4. Reconfiguration can also be a consequence of fluctuation in the demand side, or even a consequence of the so-called bull-whip effect phenomenon in the supply chain, where a little fluctuation in end customer demand can be dramatically amplified at the upstream company, requiring a fast adaptation for a short period of time. Supply chain dynamics is a strong cause of possible and unexpected reconfiguration needs in the VE, originating a new instantiation of the VE, substituting or reinforcing the provision of any resources, which is independent from the integrated resources performance, or from the product or business lifecycle.

A dynamic organisation is a reconfigurable network in transition between states or instantiations (physical configurations) along time, as represented in Figure 2. A VE is a dynamic organisation and in this context dynamics means precisely the intensity of change the VE is subject of.

A high reconfiguration dynamics, or the ability of fast change and adaptation face to the unpredictable changes in the environment (market), is, thus, a requirement of the VE model. This requirement implies the ability of (Putnik, 2000):

Figure 2. Networking dynamics considers a succession of network's states along the time (source Cunha & Putnik, 2005)

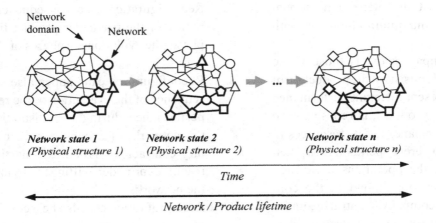

1. Flexible and almost instantaneous access to the optimal *resources* to integrate in the enterprise;
2. Design, negotiation, business management, and manufacturing management functions independently from the physical barrier of space; and
3. Minimisation of the reconfiguration and integration time.

In Cunha & Putnik (2006a, 2006b, 2008), the authors propose two parameters of reconfiguration dynamics: the number of requested reconfigurations per unit of time (reconfiguration request frequency) and the time to reconfigure (reconfiguration time). Reconfiguration dynamics is directly proportional to the number of requests and inversely proportional to the time to make operational the reconfiguration (selection, negotiation, and integration of resources in the VE).

Ideally, reconfiguration time should tend to zero, and stable configuration durations should be dictated by business alignment needs, to keep VE performance at its maximum level.

Transaction Costs and Leakage of Private Information: The VE Disablers

The main factor against reconfigurability dynamics, that is, the main factor disabling reconfiguration frequency is reconfiguration cost and time, reducing dynamics by increasing the duration of stable and sometimes less performing configurations.

The costs of outsourcing are composed of both the explicit cost of carrying out the transaction as well as hidden costs due to coordination difficulties and contractual risks. The major costs associated with outsourcing include (1) the transaction costs, and (2) the leakage of private information.

In dynamic organisations, *transaction costs* are the firm reconfiguration costs, associated to partners search, selection, negotiation, and integration, as well as permanent monitoring and the evaluation of the partnership performance (Cunha & Putnik, 2006a).

A firm's private information is confidential, and gives a firm an advantage in the market. This private information often is a core competitive advantage that distinguishes a firm from its competitors. Networking or partitioning tasks among resources providers increases the risk of losing control of such type of information, which only through complete contractual agreements could be safeguarded, or through an environment assuring trust and accomplishment of the duty of seal.

The implementation of dynamic organisations requires the existence of tools and environments that overcome these two disabling factors, allowing dynamics as high as required to assure business alignment.

ENVIRONMENTS FOR VIRTUAL ENTERPRISE INTEGRATION

Value chains have been supported by a wide variety of technologies to communicate, but the pace of competition requires more intelligent and effective information and communication systems and technologies. Literature suggests that "traditional" Internet-based tools (such as Web search engines, directories, e-mail, catalogue-based e-Marketplaces, agents, etc.), can support some activities of VE integration, helping from procurement processes to the search of partners for a partnership, including electronic automated negotiation, electronic contracting, and market brokerage services (Ávila, Putnik & Cunha, 2005; Cunha, Putnik, & Gunasekaran, 2003; Dai & Kauffman, 2001; Dogac, 1998; Hands, Bessonov, Blinov, Patel, & Smith, 2000; O'Sullivan, 1998; Wang & Benaroch, 2004).

The new VE paradigm claims for intelligent support for transactions, new effective methods for finding partners, intelligent support to virtual teams, knowledge management support systems, negotiation (automated to personalised), reliable decision support in VE design/configuring/reconfiguring, effective tools for information filtering and knowledge acquisition, and support in the identification of reconfiguration opportunities and the best configurations to keep the network competitive.

This section introduces some examples of the recent generation of electronic marketplaces, the collaborative e-Marketplaces, and introduces the concepts of breeding environments, virtual industrial clusters, electronic institutions, and the Market of Resources. We will dedicate a different section to the Market of Resources, a solution proposed by the authors, to fully support VE implementation, operation and management, which is deeply documented in Cunha and Putnik (2006c) and Cunha, Putnik, and Ávila (2008).

Electronic Marketplaces

To contribute to the reduction of search time in procurement and engineering, and to reduce transaction costs, manufacturers in several industries created electronic marketplaces (e-Marketplaces), to pool their purchasing power and to develop technology platforms to exploit networked technologies. E-Marketplaces like *Covisint* (http://www.covisint.com) or *SupplyOn* (www.supplyon.com) in the auto industry, *Aeroxchange* (www.aeroxchange.com) in the aviation industry, *Bizipoint* (www.bizipoint.com) in electronics and electrical products, *MfgQuote* (www.mfgquote.com) in manufacturing industry, or *Elemica* in the chemicals (http://www.elemica.com), provide environments to help collaboration, networking and at a certain extent, could support the VE model.

Covisint, officially announced in December 2000 as an independent company, created by Ford, Chrysler, General Motors, Renault, Nissan, and a number of development partners, was projected to be a one-stop-shop for the automotive supply chain. The service encompasses the complete interaction between suppliers or suppliers and their customers, and includes procurement transactions, pre-production collaborative engineering, and exchange of information during production or for supply chain management (Covisint, 2009a). At present, Covisint says it exists because they "deliver a trusted, on-demand collaboration platform worldwide" (2009b).

Elemica was founded in August 2000 by 22 of the world's largest chemical firms. It was the premier global neutral information network built to facilitate the order processing and supply chain management, offering an integrated suite of product solutions that enable buyers and sellers of chemicals to streamline their business processes and collaborative development (Elemica, 2005). It is able to connecting up the chemical industry by offering integration of participants' ERP systems and providing a fully connected operational framework (Elemica, 2009). Collaboration e-Marketplaces are expected to benefit participants by reducing the costs and increasing the quality of multiparty information exchange (Christiaanse & Markus, 2003).

The neutral e-Marketplace Manufacturing Quote (http://www.mfgquote.com) was founded in 1999 and facilitated its first online sourcing transactions in February 2000. It is an online Sourcing Management System with automated supplier discovery and a global network of independent participating suppliers. MfgQuote connects buyers with suppliers of manufacturing services while facilitating the request for quotations or proposals process, supplier discovery, engineering data exchange, revision control, collaboration, due diligence, analytics, and supplier management. Buyers using MfgQuote are typically Original Equipment Manufacturers (OEM's) requiring the services of contract manufacturers and job-shops (2009).

Another crucial example of an electronic marketplace is given by the European Union through EURES—European Employment Services (http://europa.eu.int/eures/home)—with the project "The European Job Mobility Portal." The service is pretended as "the easy way to find information on jobs and learning opportunities throughout Europe," where both jobseekers and employers can meet and personalize the service according to their individual needs. EURES offers a human network of advisers to provide the information required by jobseekers and employers through personal contacts. This field of intervention is also fundamental when we are addressing VE dynamics.

The SEEMSeed project, funded by the European Commission-Information Society Directorate-General in the frame of the "Policy-orientated Research" priority, intends to introduce a Single European Electronic Market (SEEM) "accessible and affordable to all businesses, organisations and individuals of any nature, size and geographic location, with no technological, cultural or linguistic restraints" (European Commission-Information Society Directorate-General, 2005). SEEM will allow the dynamic creation and operation of collaborative structures, to trade goods, services or work, in a peer-to-peer manner. The SEEM concept is driven by the changing work paradigms in business.

In fact, several technologies and valuable applications have been developed that can partially support activities of the VE model; however, they do not cope with the requirements of the VE model.

Virtual Industry Clusters

A Virtual Industry Cluster (VIC) is a functional entity collection of independent component organization correlated with a certain industry, with well-defined and focused competences, with the purpose of gaining access to new markets and business opportunities by leveraging their resources (Flores & Molina, 2000). The intention of the formation of VIC is to enable search and selection of partners for the formation of Virtual Enterprises. VE Brokers are intermediaries that possess the ability to look for core competences in a VIC and to integrate the competences of partners into successful VE (Mejía & Molina, 2002).

Electronic Institutions

An Electronic Institution is a framework that, based on communication network, enables automatic transactions between parties, according to sets of explicit institutional norms and rules, ensuring the trust and confidence needed in any electronic transaction (Rocha, Cardoso & Oliveira, 2005; Cardoso & Oliveira, 2008). The Electronic Institution is a meta-institution, which is a shell for generating specific electronic institutions for particular application domains. The meta-institution includes general modules related to social and institutional behaviour norms and rules, ontology services, as well as links to other institutions (financial, legal, etc.). The main goal of a meta-institution is to generate specific electronic institutions through the instantiation of some of these modules that are domain dependent according to the current application domain.

Breeding Environments

The Virtual Organization Breeding Environment (Camarinha-Matos & Afsarmanesh, 2004) represents a long-term cluster/association/pool of organizations that are supported and facilitated for the establishment of virtual organizations and other forms of dynamic collaborative networked organizations. If traditionally, such clusters were established in a given geographic region, having a common business culture and typically focused on a specific sector of the economical activity of that region, today, the challenge is the replacement of these clusters by a new "support-environment" called a breeding environment by the authors. This environment is supposedly based in effective information and communication infrastructures to provide common grounds for collaboration, facilitation of the establishment of virtual organizations and assisting its operation.

Market of Resources

The Market of Resources is an institutionalised organisational framework and service assuring the accomplishment of the competitiveness requirements for VE dynamic integration and business alignment. The operational aspect of the Market of Resources consists of an Internet-based intermediation service, mediating offer and demand of resources to dynamically integrate in an VE, assuring low transaction costs and the partners' knowledge preservation. The next section will detail this environment.

MARKET OF RESOURCES FOR VIRTUAL ENTERPRISE INTEGRATION

The Market of Resources appears as an alternative to existing tools and solutions, which were developed to support isolated activities like procurement and partners search and selection, negotiation, and enterprise collaboration in supply chains, but without the purpose of responding to the VE requirements.

Virtual Enterprise Integration Using the Market of Resources

The section explains the main activities involved in VE creation or VE reconfiguration using the Market of Resources. The activities to perform in order to create or reconfigure a VE are the following:

- *VE Request*: involves the negotiation with the Market of Resources, broker allocation, and VE Design. The VE Design complexity is function of product complexity and required time to answer (by the Market). The resources needed to completely design the VE (creation or reconfiguration) are broker time, knowledge, and effort (human and computational). VE design consists of a number of instructions and specifications that will drive the search, negotiation, and integration and is associated with a degree of complexity. VE Design is an activity to be undertaken by the Client of the Market

Table 1. Description of VE creation/reconfiguration activities

Activity	Activity Description
VE Request	
- *Request negotiation*	- Registration of the VE owner, specification of the request, broker allocation and contractualisation with the Market.
- *VE Design*	- Computer-aided VE design, with specification of the resources requirements and of negotiation parameters; - The broker validates the VE project, or supports the design in complex products or when complex negotiation methods are required.
Resources Search and Selection	
- *Eligible Resources Identification*	- Identification of the subset of the Market of Resources knowledge base where it is intended to perform the search (focused domain); - Focused domain filtering – automatically, from the requirements for VE Design to identify Eligible Resources (eligibility is automatically driven from the catalogues / resources providers database)
- *Negotiation*	- Computer aided (more or less automated) negotiation with the eligible resources providers, to identify the candidate resources for integration; we distinguish between automatic search, inverse auction and direct negotiation.
- *Selection*	- Computer-aided and broker mediated decision-making for final selection of resources to integrate; sorting of the negotiation results and identification of the best combination of resources providers, followed by confirmation with the selected ones. Depending on the complexity, it involves more or less Broker dedication.
VE Integration	
- *Contractualisation*	- Automatically, when a selected resources provider confirms its participation; - Selection of the adequate contract from a standardised collection (for request formalisation, integration, …); - The Market also offers integration procedures, not considered here.

(or VE owner) and after validated by the Broker of the Market of Resources, or in alternative, undertaken interactively by the Client and the Broker, depending of the request complexity, or of the Client ability / knowledge to define the VE Project.

- **Resources Search and Selection**: Search, negotiation, and selection consist of several steps: the identification of potential resources providers, separation of eligible resources, negotiation within these to the identification of candidate resources, and finally the selection among these and find the best combination for integration. The identification of the potential resources and, within this set, the separation of the eligible ones is made automatically by the Market from its knowledge base, and without intervention of the Client. In the Market, the negotiation can be done using different approaches (automated, reverse auction and direct negotiation). The final selection is a computer-aided activity, controlled by the broker, with an eventual intervention of the VE owner if necessary.

- **VE Integration**: In this activity we have consider only the contractualisation aspect. The Market of Resources assures an automated contractualisation.

These activities are systematised in Table 1.

The Market of Resources Structure

The overall functioning of the Market of Resources is represented by an IDEF0 diagram[1] in Figure 3. It consists of the creation and management of the Market of Resources itself (Process A.1.), as the environment to support the design and integration of the VE (Process A.2.) that, under the coordination of the environment, operates to produce

Figure 3. IDEF0 representation of the global process for the creation of a Market of Resources and for VE design, integration and operation

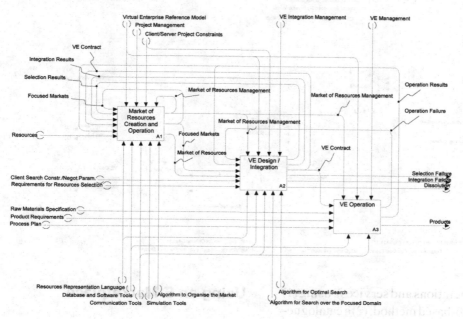

Table 2. Mechanisms and controls in the representation of the market of resources

Mechanisms	- Resources Representation Language: normalized description of the entities (Clients, resources providers, and resources) - Database and Software Tools - Communication Tools - Simulation Tools: to simulate alternative combinations of search patterns, to improve the performance of the Market of Resources - Algorithm for Search over the Market of Resources - Algorithm for Search over the Focused Market - Algorithm for Optimal Search
Controls	- Virtual Enterprise Reference Model: corresponds to the "hierarchical multilevel model for the enterprise /manu-facturing system control" (BM_VEARM) proposed by (Putnik, 2000) - Project Management: management procedures for creating the Market of Resources (Process A.1.) - Client/Server Project Constraints: constraints concerning the possible combination of resources - VE Integration Management: management of the integration of the selected resources in the A/V E - Market of Resources Management: (already defined)

a product to answer to a market opportunity (Process A.3.). The Market offers technical and procedural support for the activities of identifying potential partners, qualifying partners, and integrating the VE, as well as coordination and performance evaluation mechanisms.

VALIDATING THE MARKET OF RESOURCES

To analyze and validate the suitability of the Market of Resources, the authors have conducted several experiments, with different degrees of complexity. Experiments consisted of finding resources providers (providers of products,

Figure 4. IDEF0 representation of Process A.2.–VE Design and Integration

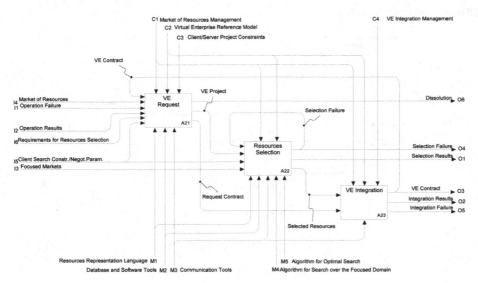

manufacturing operations and services), using (1) a "traditional" Web-based method; (2) a catalogue-based e-Marketplace where applicable; and (3) a prototype of the Market of Resources.

With the achieved results the authors have parameterized a cost and effort analytical model for the first and third tools, as e-Marketplaces differ to match from each other to be framed into a mathematical model.

The next subsections explain the utilization of the three tools, emphasizing the Market of Resources.

Using the "Traditional" Web-Based Method

The "traditional" method to find suppliers on the Web, consists of searches on the Web to identify potential resources, visit the Web pages of some of these to verify its eligibility, followed by contacts and negotiation of conditions using e-mail, until the selection of the best solution (that can consist of one or more suppliers, depending of the availability and other parameters).

Using an E-Marketplace

Using an e-Marketplace consists of selecting a suitable e-Marketplace from a directory like Zallah (2005) or eMarketServices (2008), and performing a search using the specifications of the required products or services.

Using a Prototype for the Market of Resources

The process of VE design and integration (Process A.2. in Figure 3) consists of three activities: (1) a request to create/reconfigure a VE (A.2.1), (2) resources search selection (A.2.2.) and (3) VE integration (A.3.3.).

Resources search and selection involves the design of the VE that matches the requirements to produce the desired product, negotiation and the search for the "best" combination of resources that will be integrated in the VE. Search is performed in particular subsets in which the Market knowledge base is organized (Focused Markets). The redesign or reconfiguration of a VE, implying

Figure 5. IDEF0 representation of Process A.2.1.–VE Request

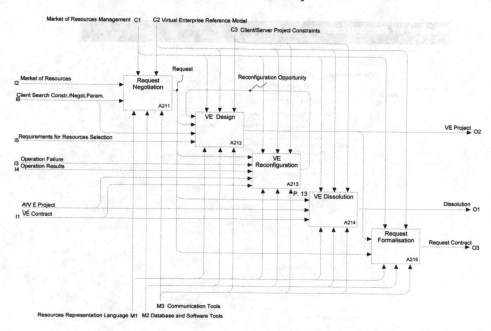

the substitution or integration of new resources providers is also considered in this process, as well as the dissolution of the VE.

Integration consists of formalising the VE (contractualisation) and of establishing procedures regarding the integration of the participants and the implementation of management and evaluation techniques.

Process A.2. (VE Design and Integration) is detailed in Figure 4.

Process A.2.1., Request for VE Creation (or reconfiguration or dissolution), is composed by Request Negotiation, VE Design (or VE Reconfiguration or VE dissolution) and Request Formalisation, and is the more effort consuming for the Client in the specification of the VE requirements. Process A.2.1. is detailed in Figure 5.

The prototype of Figure 6 partially represent the Negotiation of VE Creation Request (Process A.2.1.1.), where in the first step the overall aspects of the required project are defined, client search constraints, overall negotiation parameters and a first attempt to fit the project in one or more

focused markets (to facilitate the identification of a Broker) and in the second step (Figure 7) the Broker is allocated. At this phase, the Client could require an estimation of the cost of the service he is requiring, but the exact cost can only be calculated after the conclusion of the VE Design.

The Request for VE Creation continues with the VE Design (Process A.2.1.2.) where, for each of the required resources, in two steps, the Client specifies the Requirements for Resources Selection and Negotiation Parameters (Figure 8) followed by second step with the VE project validation. The Broker can *chat* with the Client to provide guidance in the design process.

Finally, after the validation of the project, the request for the service of creating a VE according to the project can be formalised.

CONCLUSION

The full potential of the VE model can only be achieved through supporting environments, such as those presented in the chapter.

Figure 6. Request negotiation for VE Creation–Step 1

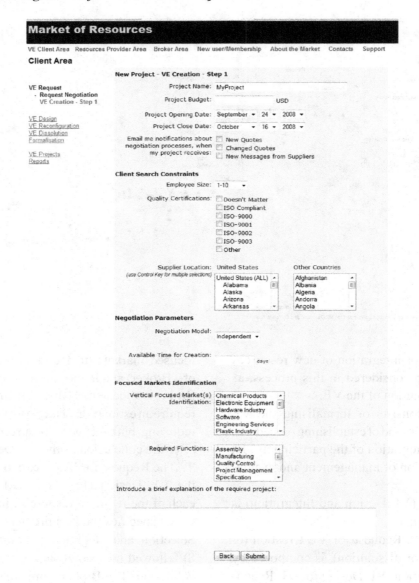

The study undertaken by the authors to validate the ability of the Market of Resources to support the high dynamics intrinsic to the VE model, based on an analytical cost and effort model and on the prototype of the Market of Resources, revealed its high performance when compared with the traditional Internet-based solutions like Web search engines.

Based on analytical simulation results, the authors identified the domain of opportunities for the Market of Resources, in function of the number of required resources and of the search domain dimension. This search domain is the number of potential resources identified with the "traditional" Internet-based tools or the number of results potential resources providers provided by the Market, after the Client specification of the VE project, with whom will be undertaken the negotiation process.

Figure 7. Request negotiation for VE Creation–Step 2

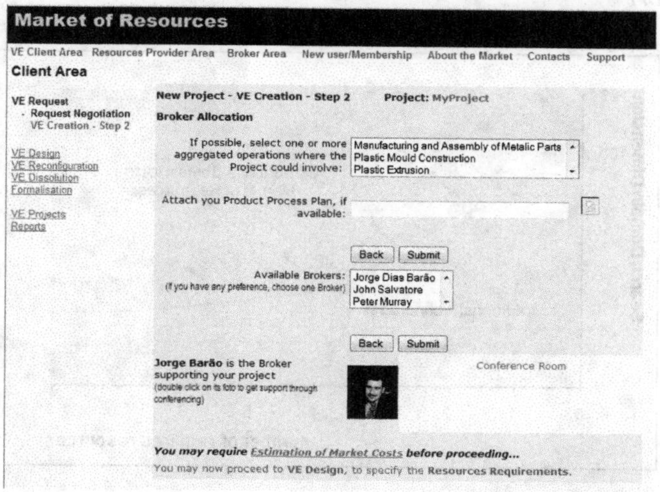

Figure 8. VE Design–Step 1

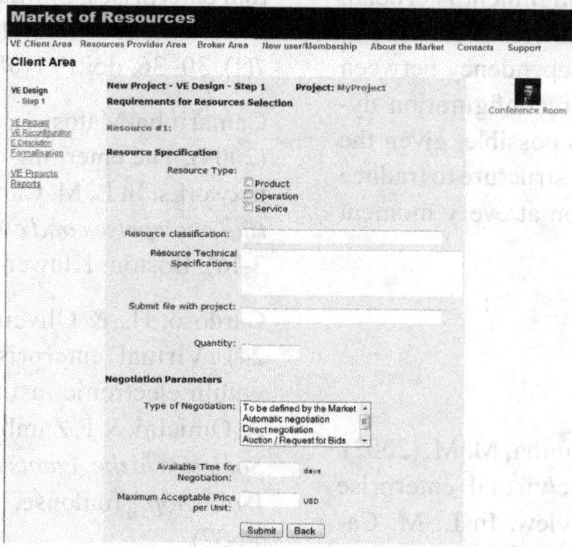

Figure 9 identifies the region where the Market of Resources presents increased efficiency.

The Market of Resources revealed the ability to support higher reconfiguration requirements than the "traditional" tools (due to the more reduced reconfiguration time and cost it allows) and its suitability increases with product complexity (traduced by the number of required resources). Traditional tools only support simple products (one at each time) and do no support dynamics. By reducing reconfiguration time and cost, the Market of Resources is an enabler of reconfiguration dynamics, an enabler of dynamic organizational models as the Virtual Enterprise one.

Obviously, dynamic organisational models are not general and "all-purpose" solutions. This model represents and adequate solution for highly customised products, with small series, in

Figure 9. Break-even points between "traditional" technologies and the Market of Resources based on search and selection effort

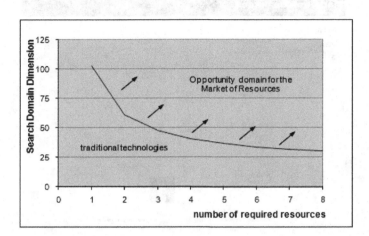

highly competitive and changing environments where permanent business alignment is crucial, that is, situations where partnership stability is low (sometimes very low), dependency between partners is very weak and reconfiguration dynamics should be as high as possible, given the permanent monitoring of the structure to traduce the most competitive solution at every moment of the product life cycle.

REFERENCES

Ávila, P., Putnik, G. D., & Cunha, M. M. (2002). Brokerage function in agile/virtual enterprise integration - a literature review. In L. M. Camarinha-Matos (Ed.), *Collaborative business ecosystems and virtual enterprises* (pp. 65-72). Boston: Kluwer Academic Publishers.

Ávila, P., Putnik, G. D., & Cunha, M. M. (2005). Broker performance for agile/virtual enterprise integration. In G. D. Putnik & M. M. Cunha (Eds.), *Virtual enterprise integration: Technological and organizational perspectives* (pp. 166-185). Hershey, PA: Idea Group Publishing.

Browne, J., & Zhang, J. (1999). Extended and virtual enterprises: Similarities and differences. *International Journal of Agile Management Systems*, *1*(1), 30–36. doi:10.1108/14654659910266691

Camarinha-Matos, L. M., & Afsarmanesh, H. (2004). The emerging discipline of collaborative networks. In L. M. Camarinha-Matos (Ed.), *Virtual enterprises and collaborative networks* (pp. 3-16). Boston: Kluwer Academic Publishers.

Cardoso, H., & Oliveira, E. (2004, October 20-24). Virtual enterprise normative framework within electronic institutions. In M.-P. Gleizes, A. Omicini, & F. Zambonelli (Eds.), *Engineering Societies in the Agents World V: 5th International Workshop*, Toulouse, France (LNCS 3451, pp. 14-32).

Cardoso, H., & Oliveira, E. (2008). Electronic institutions for B2B: Dynamic normative environments. *Artificial Intelligence and Law*, *16*(1), 107–128. doi:10.1007/s10506-007-9044-2

Christiaanse, E., & Markus, M. L. (2003, January 6-9). Participation in collaboration electronic marketplaces. In *Proceedings of the 36th Hawaii International Conference of Systems Sciences (HICSS 03)* (Vol. 7, pp. 178-185).

Covisint. (2009a). Covisint-services–portal & collaboration services. Retrieved January 2009, from http://www.covisint.com

Covisint. (2009b). *Collaboration portals, Web messaging and security delivered as a service–covisint.com.* Retrieved January 2009, from http://www.covisint.com/services/portal/

Cunha, M. M., & Putnik, G. D. (2005). Business alignment requirements and dynamic organizations. In G. D. Putnik & M. M. Cunha (Eds.), *Virtual enterprise integration: Technological and organizational perspectives* (pp. 78-101). Hershey, PA: Idea Group Publishing.

Cunha, M. M., & Putnik, G. D. (2006a). On the dynamics of agile/virtual enterprise reconfiguration. *International Journal of Networking and Virtual Organisations, 3*(1), 102–123. doi:10.1504/IJNVO.2006.008787

Cunha, M. M., & Putnik, G. D. (2006b). Identification of the domain of opportunities for a market of resources for virtual enterprise integration. *International Journal of Production Research, 44*(12), 2277–2298. doi:10.1080/00207540500409947

Cunha, M. M., & Putnik, G. D. (2006c). *Agile/virtual enterprise: Implementation and management support.* Hershey, PA: Idea Group Publishing.

Cunha, M. M., & Putnik, G. D. (2008). Market of Resources–a cost and effort model. In G. D. Putnik & M. M. Cunha (Eds.), *Encyclopedia of networked and virtual organizations* (pp. 891-888). Hershey, PA: IGI Reference.

Cunha, M. M., Putnik, G. D., & Ávila, P. (2000). Towards focused markets of resources for agile/virtual enterprise integration. In L. M. Camarinha-Matos, H. Afsarmanesh, & H. Erbe (Eds.), *Advances in networked enterprises: Virtual organisations, balanced automation, and systems integration* (pp. 15-24). Berlin, Germany: Kluwer Academic Publishers.

Cunha, M. M., Putnik, G. D., & Ávila, P. S. (2008). Market of resources for virtual enterprise integration. In G. D. Putnik & M. M. Cunha (Eds.), *Encyclopedia of networked and virtual organizations* (pp. 918-925). Hershey, PA: IGI Reference.

Cunha, M. M., Putnik, G. D., & Gunasekaran, A. (2003). Market of resources as an environment for agile/virtual enterprise dynamic integration and for business alignment. In O. Khalil & A. Gunasekaran (Eds.), *Knowledge and information technology management in the 21st century organisations: Human and Social Perspectives* (pp. 169-190). Hershey, PA: Idea Group Publishing.

Dai, Q., & Kauffman, R. (2001). *Business models for Internet-based e-procurement systems and B2B electronic markets: An exploratory assessment.* Paper presented at the 34th Hawaii International Conference on Systems Science, Maui, HI.

Davidow, W. H., & Malone, M. S. (1992). *The virtual corporation-structuring and revitalising the corporation for the 21st century.* New York: HarperCollins.

Dogac, A. (1998, March). *A survey of the current state-of-the-art in electronic commerce and research issues in enabling technologies.* Paper presented at the Euro-Med Net 98 Conference, Electronic Commerce Track, Nicosia, Cyprus.

Elemica. (2005). *Elemica overview.* Retrieved April 2005, from http://www.elemica.com

Elemica. (2008). *Top chemical company selects Elemica's business process network to automate global procurement.* Retrieved January 2009, from http://www.elemica.com/News-Events/Press-Releases-and-News/page.aspx?cid=153

eMarketServices. (2008). *Directory of electronic marketplaces.* Retrieved March 2005, from http://www.emarketservices.com/start/eMarket-Directory/index.html

European Commission-Information Society Directorate-General. (2005). *Report of the SEEM-seed workshop held at the European Commission in Brussels on May 30, 2005.* Retrieved from http://www.seemseed.org/default.aspx

Flores, M., & Molina, A. (2000). Virtual industry clusters: Foundation to create virtual enterprises. In L. M. Camarinha-Matos, H. Afsarmanesh, & H. Erbe (Eds.), *Advanced Network Enterprises, Virtual Organizations, Balanced Automation, and Systems integration* (pp. 111-120). Deventer, the Netherlands: Kluwer B.V.

GlobalSources. (2009). *Global sources overview.* Retrieved July 25, 2009, from http://www.corporate.globalsources.com/PROFILE/BGROUND2.HTM

Hands, J., Bessonov, M., Blinov, M., Patel, A., & Smith, R. (2000). An inclusive and extensible architecture for electronic brokerage. *Decision Support Systems, 29,* 305–321. doi:10.1016/S0167-9236(00)00080-4

Laubacher, R., & Malone, T. W. (2003). Inventing the organizations of the 21st century. In T. W. Malone, R. Laubahcer, & M. S. S. Morton (Eds.), *Inventing the organizations of the 21st century* (pp. 3-14). Boston: MIT Press.

Malhotra, A., & Gosain, S. (2005). Absorptive capacity configurations in supply chains: Gearing for partner-enable market knowledge creation. *MIS Quarterly, 29*(1), 145–187.

Mejía, R., & Molina, A. (2002, May 1-3). Virtual enterprise broker: Processes, methods and tools. In L. M. Camarinha-Matos (Ed.), *Proceedings of the IFIP Tc5/Wg5.5 Third Working Conference on infrastructures For Virtual Enterprises: Collaborative Business Ecosystems and Virtual Enterprises* (pp. 81-90). Deventer, the Netherlands: Kluwer B. V.

MfgQuote. (2009b). *MFG.com corporate profile.* Retrieved January 2009, from http://www.mfg.com/en/about-mfg/mfg-corporate-profile.jsp

Molina, A., & Flores, M. (1999). A virtual enterprise in Mexico: From concepts to practice. *Journal of Intelligent & Robotic Systems, 26,* 289–302. doi:10.1023/A:1008180621733

O'Sullivan, D. (1998). Communications technologies for the extended enterprise. *Int. Journal of Production Planning and Control, 9*(8), 742–753. doi:10.1080/095372898233515

Putnik, G. D. (2000). BM_Virtual enterprise architecture reference model. In A. Gunasekaran (Ed.), *Agile manufacturing: 21st century manufacturing strategy* (pp. 73-93). New York: Elsevier.

Putnik, G. D., Cunha, M. M., Sousa, R., & Ávila, P. (2005). Virtual enterprise integration: Challenges of a new paradigm. In G. D. Putnik & M. M. Cunha (Eds.), *Virtual enterprise integration: Technological and organizational perspectives* (pp. 2-33). Hershey, PA: Idea Group Publishing.

Rocha, A. P., Cardoso, H., & Oliveira, E. (2005). Contributions to an electronic institution supporting virtual enterprises' life cycle. In G. D. Putnik & M. M. Cunha (Eds.), *Virtual enterprise integration: Technological and organizational perspectives* (pp. 229-246). Hershey, PA: Idea Group Publishing.

Romero, D., Galeano, N., & Molina, A. (2007). A conceptual model for virtual breeding environments value systems. In L. Camarinha-Matos, H. Afsarmanesh, P. Novais, & C. Analide (Eds.), *Establishing the foundation of collaborative networks* (pp. 43-52). Boston: Springer.

SupplyOn. (2009). SupplyOn for successful supply chain management. Retrieved January 31, 2009, from http://www.supplyon.com

Wang, C. X., & Benaroch, M. (2004). Supply chain coordination in B2B electronic markets. *International Journal of Production Economics, 92*(2), 113–124. doi:10.1016/j.ijpe.2003.09.016

Webster, M., Sugden, D. M., & Tayles, M. E. (2004). The measurement of nanufacturing virtuality. *International Journal of Operations & Production Management, 24*(7), 721–742. doi:10.1108/01443570410542019

Zallah, S. (2005). *Significant e-marketplaces report.* Retrieved from http://www.emarketservices. com/clubs/ems/artic/SignificanteMarkets.pdf

Zhang, Z., Gao, M., Zhang, R., & Chang, D. (2008). Symbiotic virtual enterprise cluster ecological balance model and stability analysis. In *Proceedings of the Fourth International Conference on Natural Computation (ICNC '08),* Jinan, China (pp.251-255). Washington, DC: IEEE Computer Society.

ENDNOTE

[1]   IDEF stands for ICAM DEFinition methodology (ICAM – Integrated Computer-Aided Manufacturing). IDEF diagrams illustrate the structural relations between two processes and the entities present in the system. The processes (represented as boxes) transform the *inputs* into *outputs* (respectively the left and the right arrows of a process), using the *mechanisms* for the transformation (the bottom arrows of a process) and constrained by *controlinformation or conditions* under which the transformation occurs (the top arrows).

This work was previously published in The International Journal of Enterprise Information Systems 5(4), edited by A. Gunasekaran, copyright 2009 by IGI Publishing (an imprint of IGI Global).

Section 2
Supporting Technologies and Tools

Chapter 11
Tool–Support for Software Development Processes

Marco Kuhrmann
Technische Universität München, Germany

Georg Kalus
Technische Universität München, Germany

Gerhard Chroust
Kepler University Linz, Austria

ABSTRACT

Software development projects are complex. The more complex a project is, the higher are the requirements related to the software development process. The implementation of a process is a great challenge. This, in part, has to do with human factors (acceptance, etc.) as the benefits of a formal development process might not be obvious immediately and it may take a while until the process becomes the lifeblood of a team. A crucial step towards implementing, enacting and enforcing a process is to provide tool support for the many activities the process asks for. Tool support is necessary to guarantee efficiency in the project, to do the housekeeping and to minimize the "overhead" of the process. This chapter describes challenges and options for supporting process models by tools. Furthermore it describes concrete samples and shows how tool chains can be created with commercial tools as well as with open source tools.

SOFTWARE ENGINEERING ENVIRONMENTS

The quality demands on to-day's software together with the demands on the development processes are increasing due to the growing complexity of today's software products. In answering these demands the guidance of software development by a software development process model and the support of all activities by tools has nowadays become state-of-the-art, leading to so-called *software engineering environments* (SEE). Due to increased awareness of project risks and cheaper software and hardware, the utilization of SEEs becomes interesting not only for large but also for small and medium enterprises (SME). Traditionally tools always supported software development for certain development tasks like code-generation, design support etc. The understanding that the development process needs also to be incorporated and supported has brought

DOI: 10.4018/978-1-60566-856-7.ch011

about tools to support and enforce the enactment of software processes. Especially for a SME the choice of the right process and appropriate tools is difficult. A highly dynamic project environment, agile development practices, strict time-to-market requirements etc. are common in SMEs. Nonetheless, SMEs might find themselves in situations that necessitate and justify the introduction of a more formal process instead of only being agile. Such situations could be:

- In the last years, capability maturity models (e.g. CMMI (Chrissis, Konrad, & Shrum, 2006)) have gained popularity. Along with that development, many customers nowadays demand their suppliers to use standardized, certified processes.
- A company or a team could grow to a size that makes it hard to apply a purely agile development methodology.
- Distributed development with teams being geographically dispersed asks for more explicit structure in the development process (Raghvinder, Bass, Mullick, Paulish, & Kazmeier, 2006).

In this chapter we discuss options, limits and challenges of process enactment. We discuss what to consider when implementing processes in organizational environments with respect to organization-structure, users and tools. We then list options of process/tool-integration. Topics of interest are capabilities of software development processes, options for bringing together processes and tools and finally the area of process-aware tools. A central question in this area is: "What is adequate tool-support for a development process?" Finally in this chapter we give two real world examples using common and widely spread collaboration and development tools. The examples concentrate on two points of view in a software development project: The first example targets the management as user audience and the second one aims at supporting developers. A more general

discussion of options for integrating standard and open source tools completes this section.

Terminology and State of the Art

Tool support always existed for certain development tasks (editors, compiler, flow charters etc.). With the growth of the complexity of software products and the necessary development processes also other tools had been introduced. Up until quite recently, software development processes were mostly described verbally in the form of books or articles. The implementation of a verbally defined process had to rely heavily on educating project members. Little to no tool support was available and would have been hard to realize because no machine-understandable description of the process was available. Much of the enactment and enforcement of a process thus had to be done manually by the people in a project.

Two schools of thought can be roughly distinguished since several years:

- One proclaims the post-bureaucratic age and relies on agile methodologies such as XP (Beck & Andres, 2004; Cockburn, 2001) and Scrum (Schwaber & Beedle, 2008). These lightweight processes contain a couple of core concepts and leave much of the details of a project unspecified. The rationale being that a software development project is so full of uncertainties and subject to change that an a priori process will be hard to follow anyway.
- The other one has driven forward the evolution of heavier processes – up to a level where these processes are described in a formal model. Examples for this kind of development processes (or process frameworks) are the German V-Modell XT (Koordinierungs- und Beratungsstelle der Bundesregierung für Informationstechnik in der Bundesverwaltung, 2008), the OPEN Process Framework (OPF)

(Firesmith & Henderson-Sellers, 2001), the Microsoft Solutions Framework (MSF) (Turner, 2006) and the Software Process Engineering Meta-Model (SPEM) (Object Management Group, 2008) and processes based on it, such as the Rational Unified Process (RUP) (Kruchten, 1998) and the Eclipse Process Framework (EPF) (Eclipse Foundation, 2008).

Both viewpoints are not mutually exclusive (Chroust, Kuhrmann & Schoitsch, 2010): Agile processes are being formalized where necessary to provide for tool support and formal process models are designed to accommodate flexibility and agile methodologies.

The less stringent a process is the more important are the people in the project. With only a couple of concepts and rules in lightweight processes, there is not as much to enact and to enforce by tools as in more stringent processes. The tool infrastructure for lightweight processes often does not (have) to include much more than task management and communication facilities. In the rest of this chapter we therefore put a little more emphasis on supporting formally defined processes. What and how much is actually needed then depends on the specific requirements of the project and the kind of its process.

We can contend that a formal process tends to be easier to implement in software than a verbally defined process because of its machine-readable and unambiguous description. With fully formal process descriptions being relatively young, integrated tool support that covers a complete project lifecycle is still in its infancy. The majority of tools that exist today focus on supporting a particular sub-process such as bug tracking or project planning. We provide examples for integrated and loosely coupled tools in the section "Concrete Samples".

Implementing Software Development Processes

First and foremost a development process model describes the way people should work together. This includes organizational structures, interaction and the definition of artifacts, how and when these shall be worked on and not at least tools. All those points depend on each other. Hence, all organizational aspects have to be considered together.

When defining a process or adapting an existing one and to automate it where possible, one has to consider:

The **Organization** itself constitutes the frame for the process. It defines goals, standards, regulations and IT-strategies. One therefore has to:

- Analyze organizational goals and their consequences for the process. For example: Is it a goal to reach or keep a certain CMMI level or some other kind of process certification?
- Collect rules, regulations, strategies, etc. For example: Are we part of a larger organization and does the parent organization demand the use of a certain language or is there an IT infrastructure that has to be used?
- Examine past and ongoing projects and analyze processes there.

People work according to the rules of an organization. Usually they are organized in groups with different competences. When integrating and supporting processes, one firstly has to find out what users really do. What are the duties and responsibilities of a person? How would these correspond to roles as prescribed by the process? What tools are used to fulfill the tasks? Are there tasks that could be supported better? Steps that have to be done here are:

- Analyze people's organization.
- Analyze people's real work and relate it to roles required by the process. Is there a role defined in the process that would stay unfilled?
- Analyze people's tool-usage behavior.

The **Tool infrastructure** is often set up rather pragmatically according particular project's or individual's needs (ignoring organizational structures). Often, several tools are used to perform one type of task. For a process to unfold its full potential, tools have to be harmonized, possibly discontinuing the use of existing tools and/or introducing new tools. Steps that have to be done here are:

- Analyze existing tools. Which tasks are they used for and how?
- Analyze which tools are suitable for process-support. Can the tools be adapted or extended?
- Analyze how tools work together. Are there tools that do not fit into the landscape well?
- Analyze technological barriers. Are there for example multiple technological platforms that have to be supported? How could such a technological gap be bridged?
- Analyze which tool supports what sub-process. Are there sub-processes that have to be carried out manually but could be automated or aided by a tool?

It should have become clear from the (incomplete) collection above that a lot of thought can and shall go into the implementation of a process in an organization. It is also quite obvious that there hardly is a "right" or "optimal" approach. Some of the questions above may lead to contradictory answers that have to be weighed against each other to find a process implementation strategy that suits the organization best. Furthermore, in order to answer those questions, often several aspects have to be considered together such as the

tool landscape and the organization itself. This is why process improvement projects always need management support (Standish Group, 2004).

The introduction of a formal process and to make it lived by the team are particularly challenging tasks. Some reasons for that are:

- The appropriate process has to be defined in accordance with the teams, the anticipated tasks and the culture of the software developing organization.
- Team members have to be educated to understand and to be able to follow the process, which can be time-consuming.
- The process might be seen as overhead taking away from productivity instead of adding to it. Documents have to be finished "just for the sake of the process", keeping the developers away from "what's really important". A typical attitude towards well-defined processes is "we don't have time for this".
- Software development is a highly creative task. A process could be seen as limiting the individual developer's freedom, his flexibility and his creativity.
- A good process makes developments in the project transparent. This is also true for unfavorable developments and mistakes in the project. Developers might fear that their mistakes become visible and exposed for example through a bug tracking system.
- A process is meant to separate *what* is done in a project from *how* it is done and by *whom*. A process that establishes a culture of independence from people could be seen as a threat to the individual team member.
- Ad-hoc changes to work products are inhibited - if not forbidden - with a defined change management process. A working style such as "I've already found the bug, let me just fix that line and I'll send you the binary in a minute" is not possible with a well-defined process. A process could thus be seen as slowing down the team.

Some of the obstacles faced when introducing a formal process are of psychological nature (Chroust, 2007). But many can be overcome by making it as easy as possible for the team to follow the process. This can be done by automating the process where sensible and by supporting it with tools. The support of a process by automation and tools is often called *process enactment*.

Organization-Specific Process Tailoring

The activity of organization-specific process tailoring is usually understood as the customization, adaptation and optimization of a process to the organization's needs. Often the customization is only aimed at the organization itself, the people and their work. In our mind the consideration of better infrastructure or tool environment support is an integrative part of this activity. Tool support already starts at the organization-level. The organization has to decide, whether

- Existing tools should be reused or customized, or
- Existing tools should be disposed or replaced, or
- New tools should be obtained or developed.

Process tailoring is usually done including practitioners of all affected teams. They can provide valuable input about the tools they are currently using and about their usage behavior. People actually working with the tools know best about requirements regarding the tools, shortcomings in the IT-infrastructure, platform preferences, etc. With respect to tools, the process tailoring should therefore include the following steps:

- Examine used and missing tools.
- Consider tools during the process design.
- Consider processes while (re-)design tool-infrastructure.

The tailoring should result in a specific process that is consistent from its high-level definition (organization-level) down to the enacted process in a project.

PROVIDING TOOL-SUPPORT FOR SOFTWARE DEVELOPMENT PROCESSES

In this section we discuss concrete challenges and options for supporting development processes by tools. We therefore first take a closer look at some important aspects of software development processes. Some structural concepts and content that can be found in any formal process model are examined for possible tool support. We then shed some light on different user perspectives on a development process (often *phases* in correlation with specific tasks or workflows, refer Figure 1). Project members usually deal with only a small section of the process depending on their responsibilities or qualifications. This also means that they possibly only use a subset of the overall tool infrastructure in the organization. Because the tools needed by a project member depend on his/her role in the project, the process and tools have to be considered side by side. Finally process-aware tools are of interest. Process-aware tools usually support one or more disciplines of a project. So we focus on their capabilities to be included in a tool-chain for process enactment.

Software Development Processes

Software development process models provide rich support for managers as well as for developers. They consist of documentation, samples, templates, etc. Furthermore, they contain structure definitions for the project itself and for the system under development (what entities exist and how are they related?). The technical as well as the organizational content and structure has to be enabled for being used by tools.

Figure 1. Phases of a development project (Eclipse Foundation, 2008)

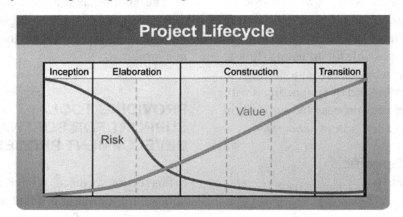

Navigating Guidance and Knowledge

Process models usually contain a substantial amount of documentation – the RUP (Kruchten, 1998) or V-Modell XT (Koordinierungs- und Beratungsstelle der Bundesregierung für Informationstechnik in der Bundesverwaltung, 2008) documentation each consist of several hundreds of pages. People applying a process need intuitive access to this knowledge. Compared to older process models, such as the V-Modell 97 (Dröschel & Wiemers, 1999), which was only available as printed book (often ignored, so-called "shelfware"), modern process models contain documentation as a HTML-based site collection. This improves navigability as one can start at any topic and can follow hyperlinks to associated information. Here formal processes are of advantage, again. Because they are designed as collection of process elements and relations in a machine-readable form, tools can evaluate this structure and can provide an automatically generated, navigable documentation (see RUP or V-Modell XT). When thinking about enacting a process, electronic documentation is of clear advantage. Project members do not need to have a book available but only a Web Browser. Only the required information can be retrieved and it is usually quicker to find with electronic search than

by browsing a book. Currently several techniques to provide electronic documentation are available. Simple interlinked HTML-sites are one solution. Also very popular are Wiki-based systems. Using such distribution channels, process documentation can be centrally (by an organization or a project) provided and maintained. Process-aware tools could use such a central documentation repository to cross-reference artifacts etc. with the respective process documentation similar to the context-sensitive help in Microsoft Visual Studio.

Deliverables and System Structure

Every project ends with one or more deliverables. In software development, the main deliverable is a software component or system. Because software systems are complex in general, process models specify a concept for system decomposition and usually also hints and methods for doing the decomposition in a decent fashion. Several aspects of system structure and decomposition are interesting for tool support:

- There are relationships and dependencies *within the system* between the decomposed parts. The parts and their interrelationships together constitute the whole system. Many of these relationships are inherent in the deliverables themselves for example through method-call dependencies. Some dependencies might not be so obvious, for example when using remote procedure calls (RPC) and late bound components. The system model as seen by the process model should adequately represent the *real* system model, which is why development process models define some kind of relations and dependency structures between particular outcomes and deliverables (e.g. software components). These relations between deliverables (on a process level) should be navigable in the tool infrastructure supporting the process.

- There are many ways how and in which order the parts of a decomposed system can be realized. Some parts may be realized in parallel, others might build on one another etc. In any case, complex systems are developed in several steps. Typical strategies for ordering the steps are incremental or iterative development. For the successful implementation of any strategy, there has to be a mapping between the system components and the project plan or schedule. This mapping has to be expressed in tools.
- There are other dependencies between system components and *outside* deliverables: (Functional) Requirements relate to system components; as do test cases, bug reports, change requests, etc. In an ideal tool infrastructure, all these relationships would be traceable.

To put all together: A tool supporting process-based software development should enable its users to trace the whole system. This goes from requirements, over architecture models and code, to test cases, bug reports, project schedules and team member assignment (who is working on what?) Since process structures related to deliveries are defined, dependencies (defined by the process and implemented by the tool) enable e.g. release managers to create a release.

Support for Collaboration, Scheduling and Management

Process models define artifacts, activities and roles and also interrelations between these entities. The relations state for example which role is responsible for which artifact and which activity affects which artifact. This is of special importance at project runtime, where process elements are no longer abstract. Artifacts become concrete work products; roles are assigned to real people, activities become scheduled tasks, etc.

As mentioned above, dependencies are the key to realize a tracing over the system structure. But they cannot only be used to realize tracing. During project runtime dependencies state, which concrete artifacts have to be instantiated at what point in time. These artifacts can be scheduled and assigned to a project member. The assignment is of special interest: Tools supporting collaborative work have additional requirements with regards to:

- Rights management
- Accessibility
- Availability

Rights management is very critical since in distributed environments, sensitive data may be exchanged. This includes requirements, designs, architecture, code and any other mission critical data that has to be visible to many project members. All these artifacts have to be (securely) available to project members.

The work on artifacts will eventually have to be scheduled. With the assignment of artifacts to project members, an implicit mapping between the delivery structure and the organizational structure is established. If the process model supports synchronization of delivery structure and process/schedule (e.g. the V-Modell XT), a tool can make use of this knowledge to provide workspaces for the sub-teams according to the artifacts they are or will be working on.

Tools and Processes

As outlined above, there are several areas of software development process models that could benefit greatly from tool support. Only a very few people in a project need to have an overview over the whole project and process. Most of the project members only need a window onto the process according to their role in the project. We therefore firstly list some different viewpoints and how these affect the tool infrastructure. The second point to be considered is the style of the desired tool infrastructure, meaning integrated vs. self-made and loosely coupled tool chains. Finally one has to discuss whether simple reactive controlling mechanisms as provided by so-called Software Project Control Centers are suitable or if more sophisticated tool support is wished for.

Viewpoints on Tool-Support

A development process can only be effective if the whole team follows it. But the aspects of a process that are relevant to team members differ quite largely depending on their role in the team. Generally speaking, a developer is interested in different artifacts than a tester or a project manager and may want or need to use different tools. A tool landscape should respect the different views onto a project and ideally targets different audiences in the team individually.

- *Requirements engineers* need tools for collecting requirements. The collection of requirements is quite difficult: requirements have to be collected, prioritized, and connected to each other and if possible to be assigned to outcomes and deliverables. Depending on how the requirements are written down, the tools required often include case tools for graphical representation of e.g. scenarios or use cases.
- *Architects* use tools that provide modeling capabilities. Such tools can be based on several modeling languages, nowadays e.g. UML (Booch, Jacobson, & Rumbaugh, 2000; Pilone & Pitman, 2005) or so-called *Domain-specific Languages* (DSL) (Fayad & Johnson, 1999). Those usually provide graphical notations (other than e.g. mathematical models) and so tools for architects often include graphical editors. Modeling tools are often coupled with code generators. The generators produce source code (templates) from the architecture models. Sophisticated tools also provide so-called round-trip-engineering. This additionally allows for "the way back" from source code to the model. The model will reflect the changes in source code and vice versa.
- *Developers* are closer to IDE-tools and do not have a great interest in management issues. They tend to prefer straightforward task lists, compile- or build statistics, code-analysis reports and the similar artifacts.
- *Testers* have to address a wide audience. Depending on the degree of a system's integration and completeness, different tasks have to be performed. For example on the code-level, unit tests (Astels, 2003) are an accepted method for automated software test. On the application-level integration or performance test have to be performed. Most actual IDEs implement test capabilities or there are additional frameworks exist to support testing. There are also a whole lot of standalone tools for software testing.
- The *management* usually needs options for planning, controlling and storing documents. Relevant processes are e.g. management, controlling or reporting. Managers are familiar with (project) management and office tools. They are usually interested in cost, schedule and overall project state and trends and not so much in implementation details such as design diagrams, source code and so on.

One of the challenging questions is how to create a tool landscape that does not treat the individual views on a project separately but rather as different angles on the same subject. If there is one tool for requirements management, one for system design and one for project planning but they cannot interact, much of the desirable automation and support cannot be realized.

Integration vs. Loose Coupling

The implementation approaches of a tool infrastructure in an organization can be classified on a scale between two extremes: On the one hand, there are many different tools that are loosely coupled or cannot interact at all. On the other hand there is a tightly integrated solution, often from only one tool vendor. Both approaches have their advantages and drawbacks and the optimum is usually found somewhere in between. Generally, high integration of tools is desirable. But highly integrated solutions from commercial vendors can be inappropriate in a project for several reasons. We discuss the alternatives more deeply in section "Concrete Samples". There we also provide sample configurations of tools chains based on commercial as well as open source tools.

Are Software Project Control Centers Enough?

A relatively new trend is the concept of the Software Project Control Centers (SPCC). Such tools should support management to have full control over the project. The idea behind SPCC (Münch & Heidrich, 2004) is to visualize project status and trends. This should help project members to detect und react to unfavorable developments in a project as they occur. For that purpose a SPCC collects, measures, interprets, analyzes and visualizes data of a project. A SPCC always displays on-line information about the project, which can be done for example by integrating the necessary data collection and interpretation in a nightly build.

Input data for a SPCC can come from various, heterogeneous sources, such as the project plan, quality models of system architecture and source code, test statistics, bug statistics, the process model and many more.

For supporting the whole development project, SPCCs are not enough. A SPCC is a passive, observing tool – mostly aimed at supporting the management. Tasks such as design or coding are not directly supported. Although a SPCC may contain measurements that display how well the development process is implemented, it does not by itself enforce the process. Tool support can – and has to – go further than pure visualization of project status.

Process-Aware Tools

Process-aware tools support or implement (whole or sub) processes. As opposed to a simple task list for example, a process-aware tool has "knowledge" of the process model that the project is following. This enables tools e.g.

- to display on-line process documentation
- to cross-reference artifacts according to the process model
- to enact and enforce the process

To enable process-awareness, we can identify a couple of minimum requirements that tools and the process model have to fulfill. Furthermore we give an impression of tools for selected disciplines e.g. project management or development.

Options and Requirements for Processes-Aware Tools

Beyond the above basic and fundamental considerations with some hints at integration options we now want to condensate that information to outline core requirements and options for process/tool-integration.

- Process-aware tools *have* to provide open and/or standardized data exchange formats. This is necessary to establish loosely coupled tool-chains.
- In addition to open formats, process-aware tools should provide defined APIs. The APIs should provide capabilities for controlling the imported process either at runtime or to make more detailed configurations.
- Processes *have* to provide an explicit meta-model. The meta-model describes the structures and relations of the process that have to be imported by the tools.
- A basic requirement according to process-aware tools is the capability to execute processes. Usually workflow engines or complete process players can be found to fit this requirement.

After the selection of one or more tools realizing these requirements, appropriate mappings have to be defined. Concrete processes have to be translated related to the selected tools capabilities.

Project Management and Collaboration Tools

The first discipline we want to cover is project management. Often project management is reduced to using Microsoft Project. But project management contains disciplines that are not covered by this particular tool. There also exist several comparable tools (for different platforms). Commonly project management tools should at least provide the following features:

- Planning/scheduling a project
- Planning resources
- Controlling
- Task management for particular project members
- Reporting
- Communication support

Project management tools are often tightly integrated with collaboration environments that provide the communication features. A good example for a tightly integrated management and collaboration platform is the combination of Microsoft SharePoint Server, Microsoft Project and Microsoft Outlook.

These tools are still quite generic. For specific situations or processes, specialized tools exist. We take the *Getting Things done*-method (GTD) (Allen, 2002) as sample. GTD is a compact method for organizing people's tasks. Originally designed for self-management (according to the *Personal Software Process* (PSP) (Pomeroy-Huff, Mullaney, Cannon, Sebern, & Mark, 2008)), this method also scales up to for small teams. This method is supported by specialized tools (Figure 2). Those tools integrate contacts, mail and (public) calendars. Another example are tools to support *Scrum* (Schwaber & Beedle, 2008). Scrum is a lightweight, agile project management method. It contains only a very small amount of basic concepts. Tools for Scrum are at most simple communication and development-related tools. The so-called Scrum backlog for instance can easily be managed using Microsoft Excel-sheets; unit and integration testing can be done using unit testing tools, e.g. NUnit (Astels, 2003) (NUnit. org, 2008).

Case and Design Tools

Case and design tools are available in several forms. At first, a huge market for commercial tools can be found. Here big players such as IBM/ Rational provide complex solutions e.g. *Rational Rose* (Quatrani, 1999) for UML modeling. There are also exist lots of open source tools e.g. for the Eclipse platform. Such tools address UML modeling, too. But other techniques related to DSLs, e.g. *AndroMDA* (AndroMDA Team, 2008), are also available. Of importance is the question of data exchange and model reuse. Firstly for model exchange, the *Object Management Group* (OMG)

Figure 2. iGTD as sample for compact task and time management tool for PSP-sized projects

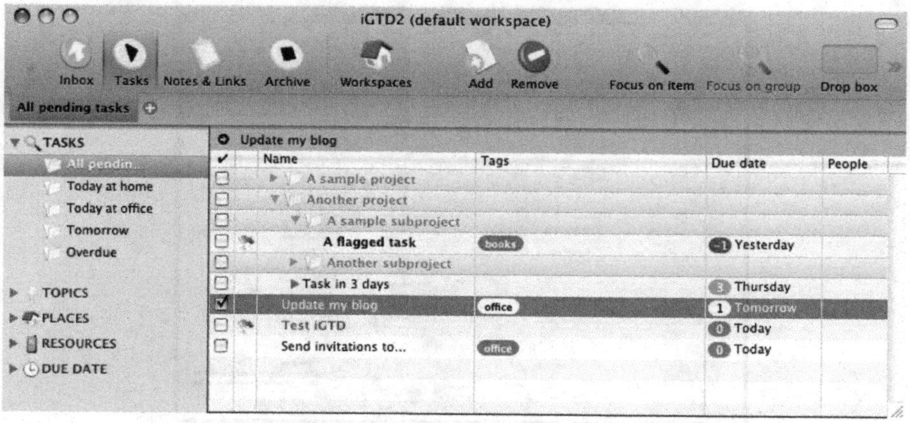

(Object Management Group, 2008) defined *XML Metadata Interchange* (XMI) (Object Management Group, 2007) for that purpose. The support of such a standard might be of advantage, but most tool vendors only partially support those standards. So if evaluating case and design tools, one should have a clear imagination what the final tool-chain should look like. This is necessary to ensure that all other tools, which have to interact with the case tool, understand the data exchange formats. The next point of importance is – if considering data exchange – the reuse of the information contained in the model. Often development tools are of interest. As mentioned above, codes or test cases can directly be generated from models. That's why code-related modeling (e.g. class modeling) is often integrated in development environments such as Eclipse or Visual Studio.

Integrated Development Environments

An Integrated Development Environment (IDE) is a software tool that provides a harmonized container for several development(-related) tools. Usually IDEs consist of:

- Code (Text) editors
- (Graphical) designers
- Frontends for compilers or debuggers

- Management tools for source code control or build management

In Figure 4 a sample for an Integrated Development Environment is shown. IDEs became popular during the last years as they provide a fully-fledged framework for development and development-related tasks. There exist many software vendors that provide plug-ins e.g. for modeling (Figure 4) or source code control etc. The most popular IDEs today are Eclipse (mainly used in the Java area) and Visual Studio (mainly used in the Microsoft-related area).

Configuration Management Tools

Configuration management tools (CM) have to be seen in context. The context is given from the current phase of a project's life cycle. So for example if a project is in very early stages, CM-support might be a shared, backed-up system drive of a shared web-folder. Later, during development, CM-support might be given by source control systems as CVS (Cederqvist, 2002), Subversion (Pilato, Collins-Sussman, & Fitzpatrick, 2004) or ClearCase (Bellagio & Milligan, 2005). After the development project is finished and the system's rollout was performed, a configuration management e.g. CMDB from ITIL (Office of Government Commerce, 2008) will be used.

Figure 3. Sample integrated development environment: Microsoft Visual Studio

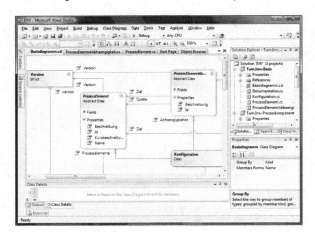

CONCRETE SAMPLES

In this section we want to show two examples of process/tool-integration. Furthermore, we discuss options of tool support and what should be considered when thinking about a tool-chain in an organization. Shall the tools be tightly integrated or loosely coupled? Should highly integrated standard software products be used? Is a more flexible solution required, possibly for the price of loosing integration? These questions are discussed at the end of this section.

Selected Settings

We outlined several roles participating in a project (Sect. "Viewpoints on tool-support"). To provide an appropriate tool-support for the disciplines it is first necessary to define the settings/roles that shall be supported. We therefore chose two different sample settings (Kuhrmann, Kalus, & Diernhofer, 2008; Kuhrmann, Kalus, 2008), one focusing on project management only and the other one providing support for projects with development parts. The requirements (repetition from before) roughly are:

- The *management* usually needs options for planning, controlling and storing documents. Relevant processes are e.g. management, controlling or reporting. Managers are familiar with (project) management and office tools. They are usually interested in cost, schedule, task assignment and overall

Figure 4. A sample workflow from Team Foundation Server based on V-Modell XT

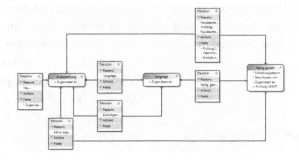

project state and trends and not so much in implementation details such as design diagrams, source code and so on.

- *Developers* are closer to IDE-tools and do not have a great interest in management issues. With respect to planning a project they tend to prefer straightforward task lists, compile- or build statistics, code-analysis reports and the similar artifacts.

Sample: Management Support

To provide tool-support with focus on the management, we chose Microsoft SharePoint 2007 (Murphy & Perran, 2007) as platform. SharePoint is a web-based collaboration infrastructure tightly integrated with the Microsoft Office product family. It is sometimes also called Office Server because it offers facilities for creating a centralized repository for all types of office documents. Besides document sharing, project team members can share calendars and task-lists, link-lists and much more. Wikis, discussion boards and Blogs are also part of SharePoint.

Another feature of SharePoint is its powerful API that lets application developers change almost every aspect of a SharePoint portal. The process tool integration can thus be realized by programming directly against that API.

We assume that the V-Modell XT was selected as the process model since it has suitable properties for being tool-supported. The meta-model of that process provides the necessary type information needed for automatic data imports. The data format exposed through the programmable API of SharePoint acts as target data format. Principally a model transformation (Kuhrmann, Kalus, & Diernhofer, 2008; Kuhrmann & Kalus, 2008) from the process model to the tool data model has to be performed. The information to be extracted from the tailored V-Modell XT is defined using the selected scenario. With the focus on management or generally projects without development activities, we want to provide simple mechanisms

to manage project artifacts and some capabilities to coordinate a team. We therefore only need a small subset of the information contained in the whole process model. In fact we actually need work product templates, some process description, task lists and some information to be able to create reporting data.

- *Work product templates*: The V-Modell XT contains lots of descriptions related to products being created during the project. The description of those is available in a formal structure. Furthermore there already exist exporters that create concrete document templates (Word, RTF, ODT) from the descriptions. To use and provide those templates, we take the given content and include it to a SharePoint's document library.
- *Process description*: Each element of the V-Modell XT is self-describing. We take the documentation relevant to the process elements that are imported into SharePoint to provide on-line reference. If for example a particular task is generated in the SharePoint website that needs to be described, the corresponding documentation is generated in place so that it is immediately available.
- *Task lists*: Based on the initial schedule that can be set up when planning a V-Modell XT project, we generate initial tasks in SharePoint. These are cross-referenced with the artifacts that they belong to. The initial set of tasks can be immediately assigned to project members and the task list shows project progress at a central place (see also techniques like Scrum Task Boards (Schwaber & Beedle, 2008)).
- *Reporting data*: To provide status information to the team, data to be measured has to be defined. In this setting, we chose e.g. the work products' finished state flag as simple metric for creating a traffic-light-indicator.

The broad idea here is to extend SharePoint elements such as tasks, lists, document libraries etc. to accommodate process model metadata. This metadata is then used to realize cross-references between elements, for reporting and to enable process-awareness in general.

Sample: Development Support

For the tool-support related of projects with development parts, we chose Microsoft Team Foundation Server (TFS) (Microsoft Corporation, 2007). TFS is a server backend for Microsoft Visual Studio, providing features such as source code control, web portals, report-systems, work item tracking and Microsoft Office integration. In contrast to the SharePoint-setting, the focus is on the developers and their tasks (Kuhrmann, Kalus, & Diernhofer, 2008). Usually developers don't care about process. So the process integration has to be realized as transparent as possible. Secondly it has to be realized, that the target environment is completely different, compared to SharePoint. To implement a process using TFS, special so-called *process templates* have to be created. Since those templates only allow declarative contents (no computed links, no active content etc.) some limitations have to be considered.

Respecting the limitations and the needs from developers, we decided to provide only a flat process documentation, specialized work item types (data structures for tracking issues) that also contain micro-processes (Figure 5). Those micro-processes are derived from the V-Modell XT process and ensure that tasks are executed according to the process's needs. As work items are fully automated concepts, developers don't have to do paperwork. A welcome side effect is the availability of data appropriate for reporting (e.g. state, work performance etc.). In addition, work product templates are also provided as in SharePoint. In addition to the reference micro-processes we also defined so-called controlling work items. These are work items used for estimating and determining

projects' states. Samples are *activities* that provide containers for simple tasks as well as they can be used for planning issues.

Integrating Standard Software

Another point that has to be considered is the type of tool-chain to be created. In principle two categories can be distinguished: Integration of standard software and secondly open source tools, which we cover in the next section, can be the matter of interest.

Standard software related to development projects refers to standard development and development-related tools. Samples are standard development environments e.g. Visual Studio for development or Doors (IBM Corporation, 2008) for requirements elicitation and management. Standard software usually consists of highly integrated tools. Using Microsoft tools as an example, we will shortly describe an integrated tool-chain based on standard products:

A second sample would be a collection of (classic) tools related to RUP with an association to the RUP-phases (refer Figure 1):

All products listed in the tables are tightly integrated and are able to communicate and to exchange data with each other. Such integrated tool-chains have advantages as well as disadvantages. Of advantage is the high degree of integration. The tools can cooperate since data exchange formats are well known. Another point is that those are harmonized according to e.g. user experience what reduces costs of training.

Costs are the main disadvantage: Standard tools as shown above are very expensive. If a company thinks of procuring such a tool-chain actually some 10,000 €/$ of investment are necessary! Furthermore, if the tool vendor does not provide solutions for particular processes, additional tools from 3rd party vendors have to be bought, too. This increases the costs and will result in media-breaks if data formats or user experiences are not harmonized. Thinking of the tools listed in the first table, no

Table 1. Sample tool-chain: selected Microsoft infrastructure

Tool	Discipline	Description
Windows Server	-	Backend infrastructure
Exchange	Collaboration & Communication	Provides the basic communication structure e.g. Mail or Calendar services
SharePoint	Collaboration & Communication	Provide extended infrastructure for sharing documents, task list, calendars or to-do lists. Provides web-based access
SQL Server	Configuration Management, Business Intelligences (Reporting)	Provides services related to data storage (documents, codes, empirical project data etc.)
Office	[several]	Basis infrastructure for frontend desktops containing, word processors, calculation or Email. Contains also tools e.g. Project for management and planning
Visual Studio	Development	Contains code editors, compiler-, test- and build-integration
Team Foundation Server	Development Collaboration & Communication	Contains components for process enactment e.g. micro-processes by work item tracking, source control, project statistics

support for requirements elicitation is provided. So additional tools are necessary. Looking at the second table, not operating system support is provided by default so that additional software has to be bought.

Integrating Open Source Software

Another option is the usage of open source tools. Open source tools are an accepted alternative to commercial products. They are available for several areas and largely cover all relevant disciplines needed in development projects. We give again a sample tool chain, which is based on open source products.

As shown in the table, numerous tools are available. We can further observe that for each type of tool variants and alternatives exist. Organizations that built up their tool infrastructure based on open source tools have a huge pool available. This is an advantage as well as a disadvantage. It is challenging to identify tools that meet the requirements. Furthermore data interchange might be difficult since each tool has it own formats. As there is no central vendor for open source, organizations, which decide to use open source tools, have to invest into integration. For some cases vendors exist that provide specialized solutions, e.g. Novell with SuSE-Linux (Novell, 2008) or

Red Hat (Red Hat, 2008). The software itself stays free but the related consulting effort is expensive. So the advantage with respect to cost might be lost. Usually open source tools are free (or at least cheap). If there is no investment necessary for buying the software, costs for trainings have to be calculated, too. Other than using an integrated platform (where training activities are also necessary), open source training activities could result in increased cost-effort. If a tool infrastructure is created using several tools (from different sources/ vendors), different trainings have to be organized (in contrast the integrated approach, where a single vendor can provide integrated trainings).

We refrain from giving advice regarding the use of either commercial or open source software to build up a process-supporting tool chain. The selection of appropriate tools depends on several aspects, which have to be determined during the implementation of an organization-specific process. First it has to be determined what philosophy the particular organization stands for. If an organization strictly follows an open source strategy, commercial tools are of no relevance. The second question to be answered is the philosophy/strategy of the (core) customers. If for example customers prefer Microsoft .NET solutions, Java-related tools are not of interest (and

Table 2. Sample tool-chain: selected RUP-related tools by IBM

Tool	Discipline/Workflow	Description
Rational Rose	e.g. Business Modelling, Requirements, Analysis & Design, Implementation	Visual modeling of business processes, requirements artifacts or round-trip-engineering
RequisitePro	Requirements	Elicitation of requirements and its management
ClearCase	Configuration & Change Management	Management of project artifacts, management and tracing of changes within the artifact database
ClearQuest	Deployment, Project Managment	Tracing of bugs and changes related to project management
Windows Server or Linux	-	Backend infrastructure
Windows, Mac or Linux	-	User frontend for office and operating systems
Eclipse	-	User frontend for working with the tool chain (integration framework)

the other way round). Another question is related to support. As open source tools are available in source code, so that each user could in principle create an own, individualized and specialized tool-set, the question of professional support, licensing etc. is nevertheless of importance. If a selected tool is buggy and no support/no vendor is available, the bug will stay unfixed, which may result in quality issues.

CONCLUSION

When thinking about the installing of a development process in an organization, the tool infrastructure cannot be left unconsidered. Current state of the art with the existence of formally defined, machine-readable process models opens the door for extensive tool support. Yet, the set-up of an integrated infrastructure covering a whole project's lifecycle is anything but simple. A first step is the analysis of status quo: What are requirements and constrains of the organization? What does the existing tool infrastructure look like? The

Table 3. Sample tool-chain: selected Open Source tools

Tool	Discipline	Description
Linux Server	-	Backend infrastructure, including user management, mail services etc.
Wiki	Collaboration & Communication	Shared, editable web sites (requires additional tools for storing data, e.g. Subversion)
MySQL or PostGres	Configuration Management	Database backend for storing data including capabilities related to reporting etc.
CVS or Subversion	Configuration Management	Provides configuration management, specially for source code-intensive projects, including merging, history, baselining etc.
Open Office	[several]	Provides infrastructure in the frontend including word processors etc. additional tools e.g. mail clients might be necessary
Eclipse	Development	Provides a framework for many aspects of the development (coding, debugging, design, clients for e.g. CVS etc.) Compilers have to be separately integrated, so e.g. a standalone Java or C-compiler might be necessary. But there also exist integrated packages
BugZilla or Mantis	Development support	Implementation of micro-processes related to bug-tracking or common work item tracking (can bi integrated via specialized clients e.g. into Ecplise)

examination of the process to implement is the next step. We outlined some potentially rewarding areas for tool support:

- Process documentation.
- Requirements analysis and verification.
- The system structure with its interrelationships and dependencies to other artifacts in the project.
- Project planning and scheduling.

By looking at a couple of different project roles, one can see that a one-size-fits-all solution is often not desirable because of the sometimes almost disjoint tool requirements of these roles. Generally, the options for a tool landscape lie somewhere between a highly integrated solution and a set of loosely coupled tools. Software project control centers are a step towards better controlling in a project but are mostly passive in their nature. (Pro-)active process-aware tools can go beyond pure display of project status. How and to what extent a tool is affected by the process and can be enabled for process-awareness is discussed by outlining some common categories of tools and their place in the overall process.

The chapter provided a list of examples for both integrated solutions and candidates for a loosely coupled tool infrastructure. Both options are discussed.

Based on the previous considerations, we presented two example implementations – one targeting project management as user audience and the other one meant to support developers.

REFERENCES

Allen, D. (2002). *Getting things done: The art of stress-free productivity.* New York: Penguin.

Andro, M. D. A. Team. (2008, April 21). *AndroMDA.* Retrieved November 24, 2008, from http://www.andromda.org/

Astels, D. (2003). *Test driven development: A practical guide.* Upper Saddle River, NJ: Prentice Hall.

Bargiel, B. (2008). *iGTD2 online portal.* Retrieved November 26, 2008, from http://www.igtd.pl/iGTD/iGTD2/

Beck, K., & Andres, C. (2004). *Extreme programming explained: Embrace change.* Boston, MA: Addison-Wesley.

Bellagio, D. E., & Milligan, T. J. (2005). *Software configuration management strategies and IBM rational ClearCase: A practical introduction.* Armonk, NY: IBM Press.

Booch, G., Jacobson, I., & Rumbaugh, J. (2000). *OMG unified modeling language specification.* Retrieved November 24, 2008, from http://www.omg.org/docs/formal/00-03-01.pdf

Cederqvist, P. (2002). *Version management with CVS.* Network Theory Ltd.

Chrissis, M. B., Konrad, M., & Shrum, S. (2006). *CMMI: Guidelines for process integration and product improvement.* Boston, MA: Addison-Wesley.

Chroust, G. (2007). Psychologische widerstände bei der einführung computer-gestützter vorgehensmodelle. In *Proceedings of the Workshop der Fachgruppe WI-VM 2007 der GI.* Garching b. München, Germany.

Chroust, G., Kuhrmann, M., & Schoitsch, E. (2010). Modeling software development processes. In M. M. Cruz-Cunha (Ed.), *Social, managerial and organizational dimensions of enterprise information systems.* Hershey, PA: Business Science Reference.

Cockburn, A. (2001). *Agile software development.* Boston, MA: Addison-Wesley.

Corporation, I. B. M. (2008). *Telelogic doors.* Retrieved November 24, 2008, from http://www. telelogic.com/products/doors/index.cfm

Danube. (2008). *ScrumWorks Pro.* Retrieved November 26, 2008, from http://www.danube. com/scrumworks

Dröschel, W., & Wiemers, M. (1999). *Das V-Modell 97. Der standard für die entwicklung von IT-systemen mit anleitung für den praxiseinsatz.* München, Germany: Oldenbourg.

Eclipse Foundation. (2008, August 13). *Eclipse process framework.* Retrieved November 24, 2008, from http://www.eclipse.org/epf/

Fayad, M. E., & Johnson, R. E. (1999). *Domain-specific application frameworks: Frameworks experience by industry.* New York: John Wiley & Sons.

Firesmith, D., & Henderson-Sellers, B. (2001). *The OPEN process framework: An introduction.* Boston, MA: Addison-Wesley Professional.

Koordinierungs- und Beratungsstelle der Bundesregierung für Informationstechnik in der Bundesverwaltung. (2008). *V-Modell XT online portal.* Retrieved November 24, 2008, from http://www.v-modell-xt.de/

Kruchten, P. (1998). *The rational unified process.* Boston, MA: Addison-Wesley.

Kuhrmann, M., & Kalus, G. (2008). Providing integrated development processes for distributed development environments. In *Proceedings of the Workshop on Supporting Distributed Team Work at Computer Supported Cooperative Work (CSCW 2008).*

Kuhrmann, M., Kalus, G., & Diernhofer, N. (2008). Generating tool-based process-environments from formal process model descriptions - concepts, experiences and samples. In *Proc. of the IASTED International Conference on Software Engineering (SE 2008).* ACTA Press.

Microsoft Corporation. (2007). *Team development with visual studio team foundation server.* Redmond, WA: Microsoft Press.

Münch, J., & Heidrich, J. (2004). Software project control centers: Concepts and approaches. *Journal of Systems and Software, 70.*

Murphy, A., & Perran, S. (2007). *Beginning SharePoint 2007: Building team solutions with MOSS 2007 (programmer to programmer).* New York: Wrox Press.

Novell. (2008). *openSUSE.* Retrieved November 24, 2008, from http://en.opensuse.org

NUnit.org. (2008). *NUnit – home.* Retrieved November 24, 2008, from http://www.nunit.org

Object Management Group. (2007). *MOF 2.0 / XMI mapping specification.* Retrieved November 24, 2008, from http://www.omg.org/technology/documents/formal/xmi.htm

Object Management Group. (2008). *Software process engineering meta-model.* Retrieved November 24, 2008, from http://www.omg.org/technology/documents/formal/spem.htm

Object Management Group. (2008). *The object management group.* Retrieved November 24, 2008, from http://www.omg.org/

Office of Government Commerce. (2008). *Official ITIL website.* Retrieved November 24, 2008, from http://www.itil-officialsite.com/home/home.asp

Pilato, C. M., Collins-Sussman, B., & Fitzpatrick, B. W. (2004). *Version control with subversion.* Sebastopol, CA: O'Reilly Media, Inc.

Pilone, D., & Pitman, N. (2005). *UML 2.0 in a nutshell*. Sebastopol, CA: O'Reilly Media, Inc.

Pomeroy-Huff, M., Mullaney, J., Cannon, R., & Sebern, M. (2008, March 26). *The personal software process (PSP) body of knowledge*. Retrieved November 24, 2008, from http://www.sei.cmu.edu/publications/documents/05.reports/05sr003.html

Quatrani, T. (1999). *Visual modeling with rational rose 2000 and UML*. Reading, MA: Addison-Wesley Professional.

Raghvinder, S., Bass, M., Mullick, N., Paulish, D. J., & Kazmeier, J. (2006). *Global software development handbook*. Boston, MA: Auerbach Publications.

Red Hat. (2008). *Red Hat enterprise Linux 5*. Retrieved November 24, 2008, from http://www.redhat.com/rhel/

Schwaber, K., & Beedle, M. (2008). *Agile software development with scrum*. Upper Saddle River, NJ: Prentice Hall.

Standish Group. (2008). *CHAOS*. Standish Group International Inc.

Turner, M. S. (2006). *Microsoft solutions framework essentials: Building successful technology solutions*. Redmond, WA: Microsoft Press.

Chapter 12
Enterprise Tomography:
An Efficient Approach for Semi-Automatic Localization of Integration Concepts in VLBAs

Jan Aalmink
Carl von Ossietzky University Oldenburg, Germany

Jorge Marx Gómez
Carl von Ossietzky University Oldenburg, Germany

ABSTRACT

Enterprise tomography is an interdisciplinary approach for an efficient application lifecycle management of enterprise platforms and very large business applications (VLBA). Enterprise tomography semi-automatically identifies and localizes semantic integration concepts and visualizes integration ontologies in semantic genres. Especially delta determination of integration concepts is performed in dimension space and time. Enterprise tomography supports software and data comprehension. SMEs, large scaled development organizations and maintenance organizations can benefit from this new approach. This methodology is useful for tracking database changes of business processes or coding changes within a specific domain. In this way root cause analysis is supported.

INTRODUCTION

This chapter covers an interdisciplinary approach for an efficient Application Lifecycle Management of Very Large Business Applications (VLBA) and Enterprise Platforms.

To be more precise, Enterprise Tomography is primarily seen as a new methodology for supporting distributed software engineering teams in their incremental business development tasks and during their enterprise software maintenance phases. We regard enterprise software along with its meta-data, business data and contextual data as an abstract information source. In this extended abstract data universe our approach semi-automatically identifies semantic coherent entities of interest. We propose an algorithm for tracking the changes in this data universe in the dimension time and space. In contrast to Web 2.0 search engines, we apply advanced indexing techniques. To meet developers and maintainers needs to the greatest extent possible, we take integration ontology extraction

DOI: 10.4018/978-1-60566-856-7.ch012

algorithms into consideration, enable controllable domain-specific indexing, apply delta analysis based on indices and visualizes search results of the Delta-Operator in semantic categories. Furthermore, Enterprise Tomography includes sharing of integration knowledge from individual integration experts across the enterprise development and maintenance community.

In Enterprise Software Industry development and maintenance of VLBAs and Enterprise Platforms is getting more and more complex. Large and distributed teams are involved, teams are changing and division of labor proceeds. Agile development methods assume efficient development and maintenance means for software and business data evaluation.

Without knowing the semantic integration of enterprise software it is inherently difficult to control and orchestrate large scaled development and maintenance processes. Domain-specific enterprise integration knowledge, coded in enterprise software, is normally not instantaneously available for development teams. Lack of precise knowledge of integration concepts in development and maintenance phases results in erroneous software, is risky and might have negative business impact for both the software manufacturer and the consumer.

In this paper we present a semi-automatic environment for Application Lifecycle Management of VLBAs and Enterprise Platforms based on enhanced standard scientific algorithms. In accordance with medicine diagnostics, we utilize the metaphor Enterprise Tomography for scanning, indexing, identifying, visualization and delta visualization of enterprise integration knowledge containing in enterprise software conglomerates. Based on the results of the Enterprise Tomograph the operating teams are in the position to make efficient decisions and have a reliable foundation for incremental steps of the development and maintenance life cycle.

The Enterprise Tomograph represents a central ecosystem for sharing domain specific integra-

tion knowledge across the development teams. Because of sharing and socializing of integration knowledge across SCRUM teams, the Enterprise Tomography approach can be incorporated in the Enterprise 2.0 initiative.

In the research area VLBA (Very Large Business Applications) located within business informatics, Application Lifecycle Management is the center of attention (Grabski, et. al, 2007). A real life VLBA, in dimension time, is in a permanent flux: Gradual development to meet business requirements, continuous improvements to exploit innovation, continuous maintenance to keep consistent business processing, horizontal connection of software systems to scale data processing and to extend business scope, recombination of loosely coupled services to exploit new business functionality, re-configuration and personalization, data evolution resulting from service calls and business transactions and background processing, just to name a few.

VLBAs are not usually built from scratch and deployed in an immutable stadium (Opferkuch, 2004; Ludewig & Opferkuch, 2004). VLBAs are not monomorphic. Some of the characteristics of VLBAs are: Complexity, a long life-cycle, huge continuous development and maintenance efforts, large user groups, inter- and intra-enterprise coupling.

Today, in business reality, VLBAs are conglomerates of inter-operating software systems. Technical and semantic integration are the 'DNA' of a VLBA. Integration can cross both system and system boundaries. In this chapter we want to propose and outline a generic algorithm that makes this VLBA integration visible and tangible from different perspectives in different semantic genres. Moreover, a delta operator is supposed to make the integration difference between points of time t_0 and t_1 visible. Having in mind that VLBAs consist of heterogeneous constituents, we need to have an abstract holistic view on the normalized integration aspects. Beyond software, we also take persistent data, meta data, system logs, business process activity journals, virtual and transient data, solution databases, model databases and so forth into consideration. So, we not only take the software of the Enterprise Platform itself into consideration but the business data and meta data and contextual data as well.

Integration is a polymorphic topic. We regard integration on different levels of granularity. For instance, on a low level of granularity, dynamic method calls can be seen as an integration aspect. On a medium level of granularity, cross component service consumption can be seen as an integration aspect or security as a cross cutting integration scattered in a VLBA. Registered integration content (e.g. message routing rules of integration hubs in enterprise service bus) is to be regarded as high level integration. Logistical quantity flow, accounting value flow and financial data flow are also prominent examples of integration on high granularity level. Workflow, Webflow and Process Integration can be regarded as integration on high granularity level as well.

Developer teams and maintenance teams have different perspectives on VLBAs in their daily work: Developers are primarily assembly focused (bottom up), whereas maintainers have the inverted top down view on a VLBA: Maintainers are thinking rather in error symptoms and ontologies provoking the error symptoms (Abdullah, 2001). For example, they need to find out for a given (inconsistent) production order id the involved coding and meta data, the header and items in the persistency layer, material consumption, confirmation items, models, relevant documentation etc. In this example we regard integration as a semantic join between those concepts. It is valuable information to see the delta of this semantic join between points of time t_0 and t_1. So one can track the evolution of the integration of a VLBA. A comparison of VLBAs (e.g. modified code clones) will be possible with our algorithm as well. So it might be very interesting to evaluate the software Add-On between two releases or the delta in the business data.

In accordance to tomography in medical diagnostics, we utilize a similar metaphor: The Enterprise Tomograph. It is supposed to diagnose integration aspects of a complex VLBA, perform indexing of all scanned information, and provide time efficient access to the assembled scanned data from different semantic perspectives. Especially the integration aspect delta is supposed to be made available for large maintenance and service teams. Based on this information maintenance teams can locate real error symptoms in a VLBA more easily and they are in a better position to assess the consequences of any change in the VLBA software and therefore mitigate the risk of inconsistent data processing.

In the scope of this chapter we assume that in an enterprise software factory the construction procedure of a VLBA is very similar to that of the building industry. The first step is requirement specification, architecture modeling, review and acceptance, construction and finally continuous maintenance. The construction procedure in both industries is quite similar: If architecture models are in place, the construction procedure starts bottom up: Beginning from the foundation and ending in the construction of the roof, not vice versa.

Traditional top down model driven approaches of Software Engineering do not necessarily meet the needs of service and maintaining teams in the context of VLBAs adequately. Models are important, but usually those models are not linked to the VLBA software. To bridge this technical gap, the Enterprise Tomograph comes into place with multiple phase iteration: The Enterprise Tomograph knows three phases. The first phase in concerned with scanning of the VLBA, the intermediate phase constructs and prepares indices for efficient access and the third phase provides access to integration data.

During the time-consuming scanning procedure (parallel crawling of VLBA), the Enterprise Tomograph orchestrates concept mining algorithms. The mining algorithms extract models, software fragments, links of software fragments, business objects, technical objects, meta data, solution databases and transforms those to standard ontology representations that are grammar compliant. The resulting ontology is the integration knowledge representation. We take a subset of the ontology representation standards into consideration: The concept mining algorithms are supposed to map the integration ontology to rooted unordered labeled trees. The set of rooted unordered labeled trees are to be indexed and stored in PAT Arrays (PAT Array as a space efficient and access optimized data structure of Patricia Tries and suffix trees; PAT Arrays are well known in genetic engineering and information retrieval).

One theme of the Enterprise Tomograph will be the Enterprise Introspector. It generically calculates the footprint of a business transaction execution in the persistency layer, the footprint of a service call or the footprint of a message choreography process instance between t_0 and t_1, or the delta between two database schema in a specific domain area.

The basis algorithm of the Enterprise Tomograph is a modified DC3-algorithm (difference cover modulo 3 known in information retrieval (Dementiev, 2006; Burkhardt, 2006). It constructs PAT Arrays and stores textual suffixes in a compressed manner. The set of resulting PAT Arrays are organized in a genre-layered tenancy concept allowing independent user groups working on the global index and updating it in a concurrent polychronic way. There will be defined a quasi algebra on the set of PAT Arrays: Delta operator, plus operator, pseudo inverse operator.

For instance the plus operator merges 2 indices (PAT Arrays) resulting in one encompassing PAT Array.

Integration deltas are determined by modified tree distance algorithms (Lu, et. al., 2001) and displayed in a structured textual manner.

Typically integration concepts are best known by individual developers and maintainers of the VLBA community. They may want to register additional concept mining algorithms to the integration

ecosystem of the Enterprise Tomograph. In this way the integration knowledge of a few integration experts can be shared across the community. The Enterprise Tomograph provides a domain-specific search UI and displays the integration aspects. The output can be iteratively refined and may serve as input/workload for the Enterprise Engineer for further processing. For example, refactoring, navigation, semantic tagging, search & replace within integration genres, multiple breakpoints, code & data compare, undo.

The Enterprise Tomograph itself is dedicated for service enabling and can be hosted in a VLBA side-by-side mode. It provides high efficient logarithmic access to integration concepts of a VLBA in the space time continuum.

Enterprise Tomography is a proposed collaborative index-snapshot based and domain-specific approach for efficient incremental development and maintenance of VLBAs in the enterprise software industry.

Figure 1 outlines the Enterprise Tomography approach in the context of cross-organizatorial VLBAs. The Enterprie Tomograph crawler extracts integration ontology forests from VLBAs, Enterprise Platforms and databases. In-memory indices and delta indices are created. Via search UI a full domain-specific search is possible. In the Delta Monitor changes of integration concepts can be traced.

Enterprise Tomography - Use Cases and Scenarios

First of all Enterprise Tomography supports program comprehension in maintenance and development phases of VLBAs and Enterprise Platforms. Views from different semantic perspectives can be projected on a domain or area of expertise. These views can incrementally be refined to a set of integration concepts of interest. In this way a dynamic model is derived from the enterprise software and its contextual data. Maintainers and developers are in the position

Figure 1. Enterprise tomography for VLBAs and enterprise platforms

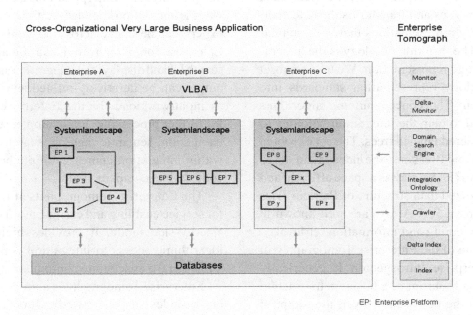

to make assessments for side effects of software changes and enhancements.

Furthermore, Enterprise Tomography supports refactoring of Enterprise Platforms and VLBAs in software engineering development phases. Cross-system where-used lists of integration concepts can easily be generated. Textual search and replace functionality based on the where-used lists can be provided. The search result list of the Enterprise Tomograph serves as workload for refactoring tasks. In-place navigation to software fragments and contextual data enables software engineers to drill down into the software and business data universe.

The Enterprise Tomograph can be seen as an abstract navigation tool for software fragments, entities and business data. Depending of the search criteria a launch pad can be generated. This launch pad points to the appropriate entitiy-associated operations. In contrast to Page-Rank prioritization in Web 2.0 search, the Enterprise Tomograph prioriztizes integrations concepts in search result list based on reuse frequency. This

means integration concepts with highest reuse frequency appears first. Because of global impact in VLBA software, changing of those integration concepts requires highest attention.

Regarding real world VLBAs and Enterprise Platforms there is normally no semantic linkage between coding fragments, metadata, models, configuration data, business data, corrections, consulting documents, documentation, process journals, system logs, training material, and contextual data. Taking those information sources into consideration, the Enterprise Tomograph joins development and maintenance relevant information and provides ubiquituous search and delta tracking functionality. Integration ontologies serves as an interlingua for the participating systems. Integration ontology extracting algorithms generate normalized ontologies. With a generic search UI software engineers can locate and visualize cross-cutting concerns.

In Test Driven Development (TDD) software engineers needs to reiterate business processes. A generic inverse operator for business processes is advantageous. Enterprise Introspection as a spezialization of Enterprise Tomography is focused on business data and configuration data of VLBAs and Enterprise Platforms respectively. The Enterprise Introspector visualizes the data delta (database footprint) of a business process, of a business transaction or of a service call sequence in a domain.

Based on the delta index the Enterprise Introspector enables restoring the business process data to its former condition. The business process chain can be executed again.

Traditional IDEs support debugging functionality. Breakpoints can be set directly in coding. Conditional breakpoints and watchpoints can be defined. Typically, in enterprise software industry software maintainer are not the authors of the coding they are responsible for. This means it is very difficult for software maintainer to identify appropriate breakpoints, not to mention to define complex conditional breakpoints. With refinement technique, the Enterprise Tomograph supports software engineers to find appropriate software fragments. The contextual data for finding appropriate locations is taken into consideration.

Along the lifecycle of VLBA and Enterprise platforms, quality management engineers need indicators for quality assessment purposes. Software metrics and architecure metrics are appropriate means for that purpose. The Enterprise Tomograph attach metric figures to integration ontology concepts or generates virtual metric entities in tree based formats. Delta tracking of the metric figures on a domain is facilitated by the Enterprise Tomograph.

Integrated exception handling and alerting are efficient functions for setting up regulator circuits in software engineering.

Enterprise software often is deployed in releases. Codelines are the pendants in software logistics. Development teams are focused on areas of expertise or domains respectively. Taking functional upward-compatibility into consideration, functionality of lower releases is a subset of functionality of higher releases. To put it in other words: release n+1 = release n + delta. Typically the codbase of delta is significant smaller than the codbase of release n. Release n+1 and release n are similar code clones and nearly identical. The Enterprise Tomograph serves as a engineering environment for controlling the code clones: Incremental deltas can be tracked with the delta monitor. The delta can be visualized in semantic genres. E.g. new service calls, new code fragments, new reusables, new business objects, new UI Objects, new metadata or new configuration data between code clone A and code clone B. Corrections to be made in lower releases have normally to be upported to the latest release. This is a prominent example when code clones comes into play: the delta ist the correction of release 1..n. . The same applies for downports of funktionality to lower releases.The Enterprise Tomograph supports to add the delta to each individual release.

Sharing integration knowledge amongst SCRUM teams and within SCRUM teams is an essential use case. The Enterprise Tomograph serves as a SCRUM environment. It provides an infrastructure for sharing integration knowledge to be categorized in semantic genres. A full search in a genre and a search on delta in a genre allows efficient location of involved integration concepts. This supports comprehension of Integration in Enterprise Platforms and VLBAs.

Generic operations and navigation based on the located integration concepts allow further development of the enterprise software. This includes mass processing on the worklist provided by search result of the Enterprise Tomograph.

Changes and enhancements made by the SCRUM teams can be visualized instantaneously. In the delta monitor the results can be verified.

Figure 2. Application lifecycle management with enterprise tomograph

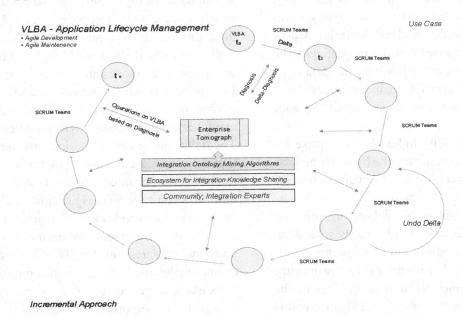

Enterprise Tomography - Placement in Agile Development and Agile Maintenance

In Enterprise Business Engineering the evolution of VLBA integrity is to be regarded in a holistic way. In Application Life Cycle Management the VLBA software itself cannot be taken isolated into consideration; there are multiple correlations between the VLBA software, the business data, the contextual data like documentation, solution databases, e-training databases and model databases, just to name a few. In our approach we extract Enterprise Integration Ontologies out of this holistic data universe, map the retrieved ontologies to a hierarchical textual representation, perform parallel indexing on the textual representation, organize the indices on abstract domain levels and make the integration knowledge available for development and maintenance teams via a search engine. The main contribution of our approach is an efficient algorithm for delta determination of Enterprise Integration Ontologies.

Figure 2 illustrates the embedding of the Enterprise Tomograph in the SCRUM development process. SCRUM teams are concerned with refactoring, error detection and functional enhancement of VLBA software. For the sake of consistent change of the software, SCRUM teams need during their operations permanently an actual view on the integration concepts in a domain of a VLBA software. SCRUM development is inherently an incremental approach. The software engineers needs to track the progress of their teamwork between subsequent point of times and verify their enhancements and modifications. The Enterprise Tomograph provides extended domain-based search capabilities to identify the integration concepts of interest. For instance when executing a business transaction on the Enterprise Platform the Enterprise Tomograph visualizes the footprint (data delta) on the database between two points of time. Beyond that the Enterprise Tomograph visualizes software changes and documentation changes model changes amongst others. The Enterprise Tomograph abstracts the technical data sources of the enterprise data universe and makes integration knowledge accessible.

The Enterprise Tomograph can be fed with integration ontology mining algorithms. In real world scenarios those algorithms are provided by few integration experts. In this way the integration knowledge is shared by the SCRUM teams using the Enterprise Tomograph. The Enterprise Tomograph functions as a generic domain-specific search engine based on registered ontology mining algorithms.

To make our approach applicable for real world VLBAs and Enterprise Platforms we assume the existence of a dendrogram and an enumeration of the dendrogram nodes. According Figure 3 a dendrogram categorizes the software and contextual data fragments in domains (sub-trees in the dendrogram). A dendrogram sub-tree bundles semantic related entities of a VLBA. The dendrogram must cover the complete VLBA software. A visitor enumerates the dendrogram nodes. Ontology mining

algorithms operate on dendrogram nodes. Indices are created and organized in multidimensional grids spanned by axis of integration genres and dendrogram nodes.

Moreover we assume that the dendrogram can be processed randomly and independently. This implies that the nodes are the basis granularity for parallel processing of ontology mining.

For instance in SAP Enterprise Platforms the package hierarchy or application component hierarchy are representatives of a dendrogram.

In a typical scenario software maintainers are starting with error symptoms of a VLBA and are interested in the involved integration concepts and the related entities. For instance a production order 4711 has inconsistent confirmations on consumed components. The maintainer would start with a node of the manufacturing domain. The Enterprise Tomograph in this case would explode the associated sub-tree and merge the attached indices to a domain index. The resulting index

Figure 3. Dendrogram of a VLBA

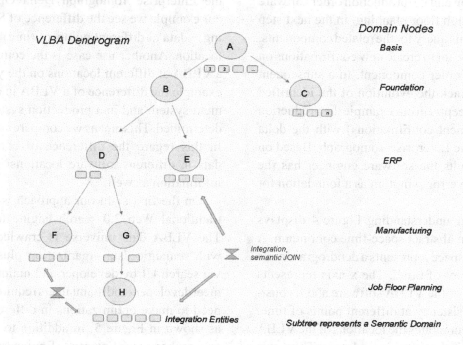

Figure 4. VLBA data universe

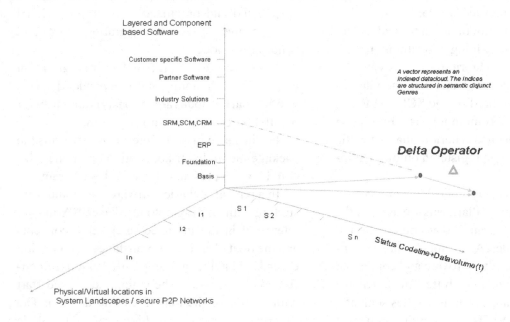

can be queried with the production order id. As a result he gets the data structure of the production order, the production order instance, persistency, documentation and the production order software fragments of job floor planning. In the next step he can refine his query for the related components. Now he may want to create new confirmations on a production order component. In a subsequent step he can track the evolution of the identified ontology concepts (in our example the production order component confirmations) with the delta operator of the Enterprise Tomograph. Based on the delta results the software engineer has the context of the error symptom as a foundation for his diagnosis.

For deeper understanding Figure 4 displays a VLBA in an abstract space-time continuum. A vector in this space represents a dendrogram node index at a point of time . The x-axis represents the instances of the VLBA software and its business data persistency at different points of time. The y-axis enumerates the locations of the VLBA software within the software landscape. The z-axis enumerates the domains of the dendrogram path beginning from root node to leaf node.

The difference of 2 vectors is calculated by the Enterprise Tomograph Delta Operator. In our example we see the difference of SCM (coding + data at different points of time) on a fixed location. Another use case is the comparison of a VLBA at different locations on the y-axis. For example the difference of a VLBA in a development system and in a production system can be determined. This means we compare code clones. In this regard the difference of configuration data in different software locations is valuable information as well.

On the first sight our approach is similar to traditional Web 2.0 search engine techniques. The VLBA data universe is crawled, indexed with semantic data organization plus querying via search UI by developer and maintainers. To meet developers and maintainers requirements, we need to make optimizations in different aspects as shown in Figure 5. In addition to traditional approaches, in the Enterprise Engineering context

Figure 5. Design principles of the enterprise tomograph

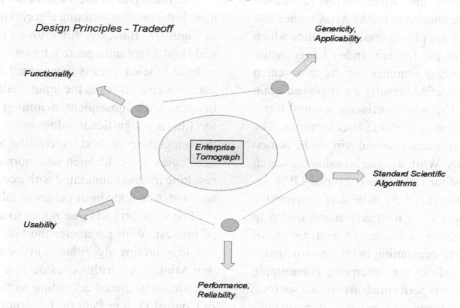

we need to focus on domain specific search refinements and a flexible delta calculation based on domains. Generic operators on generic in memory data representations are the main focus of this scientific paper.

Enterprise Tomography is focused on integration ontologies and their evolution. It can be regarded as a special case of ontology integration (Abels, et. al., 2005; Nicklas, 2005).

Enterprise Tomograph - Building Blocks and Data Flow

The Enterprise Tomograph is divided in building blocks for time consuming tasks (data extraction and data organization) and building blocks for time efficient tasks like querying, index merging, and visualization. Figure 6 illustrates the anatomy and high level architecture of the Enterprise Tomograph. First of all the VLBA dendrogram is determined. Based on a dendrogram the Enterprise Tomograph starts the VLBA crawling for containing nodes. For each node and for each semantic

genre an Ontology Mining Algorithm is executed. It supplies rooted unordered labeled trees. Those trees are sequenced. The skewed algorithm DC3 (difference cover modulo 3) is performed on the sequenced data. The resulting index and the original sequenced data is compressed and in-memory organized in an 2 dimensional node-genre grid. Each element of this grid points to a compressed PAT Array and its associated sequenced data. Based on a VLBA dendrogram this procedure can be repeated for different data sources, i.e. for different VLBA locations or for different point of times. Later on the data sources can be compared with the Enterprise Tomograph Delta Operator.

When the developer needs to perform a search in a domain, he selects a dendrogram node. The node sub-tree is exploded and all node-associated PAT Arrays together with sequenced data are decoded. The PAT Arrays are merged. The results are published in the Domain Index Layer. A Query Engine executes queries based on the domain index. Monitor 1 visualizes the search results. Now the developer may want to refine the search results.

The search results are sequenced and re-indexed with DC3 Algorithm. A new PAT Array comes into being, is coded and placed into a data source which is published to the Domain Index Layer again. The Query Engine searches for the new search pattern and the refined results are displayed again in Monitor 1. This search-refinement round-trip is depicted in Figure 6 with the circular arrow. The phases of the refinement round-trip can be started asynchronously: While the user is evaluating search results on Monitor 1, the time consuming PAT Array construction via DC3 can be started in parallel as preparation for the next refinement query. In this way the user is not aware of interruptions of subsequent time consuming index construction.

In delta mode of the Enterprise Tomograph, delta calculation is performed on two data sources. As explained later on in more detail, domain indices of source m and source n are merged together with watermark data. Delta trees of both tree sets are determined. Monitor 1 serves for displaying of delta trees of source m in full version whereas Monitor 2 displays delta trees of source n in full version. The edit scripts of the delta trees are visualized in Delta Monitor.

The main part of the VLBA crawling mechanism is the ontology mining algorithm as outlined in Figure 7. Basically for a given dendrogram node and a semantic genre a forest of rooted unordered labeled trees is determined. The VLBA data universe serves as the input. Data extraction happens with subsequent stemming algorithms for filtering significant information relevant to the integration context. According to rule sets, ontologies are calculated and normalized. The resulting trees are annotated with tree hash values and with tree node hash values as labels.

The view projects tree nodes to the node set of interest. With parameter the behavior of the ontology mining algorithm is influenced. Ontology Mining Algorithms reside in a framework and are orchestrated according to the Inversion of Control Design Pattern. Integration ontology mining algorithms can be registered by integration experts.

Rooted unordered labeled trees are used for representing integration concepts. An exemplary integration ontology instance is displayed in Figure 08. Here the business object instance relations, coding fragments, data persistency, APIs amongst

Figure 6. Anatomy and high level architecture of enterprise tomograph

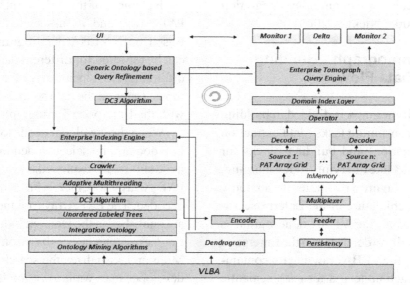

Figure 7. Integration ontology mining

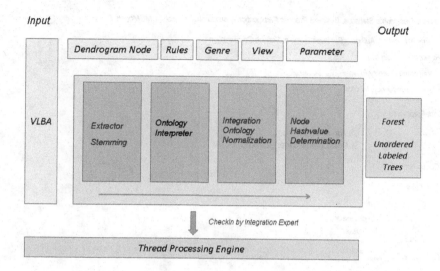

others are highlighted. Trees containing the integration concepts are sequenced to a textual data, that is indexed with DC3 algorithm.

Enterprise Tomograph - Delta Operator

In this chapter we want to examine the delta determination and delta visualization of enterprise integration ontologies. Tree distance algorithms generated considerable interest in the research community within the last years. Assuming there are 2 ontology trees originating from different data sources as depicted in Figure 9. Each node is annotated with a label, i.e. with a hash value calculated by the ontology mining algorithm mentioned before. Now the question arises which minimal set of operations need to be performed on tree F to retrieve tree G. This minimal set of operations is called edit script. The minimal number of edit operations is called edit distance. The edit script serves as a basis for visual mapping of tree F into tree G in the Enterprise Tomograph Delta Monitor.

It is worth noting that as of today delta determination for rooted unordered labeled trees is considered as NP-complete. Delta determination of ordered labeled trees is much more efficient. Because of paging in the Delta Monitor, it is not mandatory to determine all tree deltas at a time. Although extremely time consuming procedure for large trees, delta determination for reasonable sized unordered labeled trees can be performed efficiently on demand at visualization time.

In contrast to the original definition of labeled trees (Shasha, 1992), we take non-unique labeled trees into consideration. We assume that delta determination for unordered non-unique labeled trees is a relaxative or similar problem in comparison to delta determination for unique labeled trees. A proof for this can be made with Simplex Algorithm known in Dynamic Programming (Bille, 2005). This issue is not detailed in this paper.

In the next section we want to enlighten the skewed DC3 algorithm for PAT Array construction. As explained in Figure 10, PAT Array construction means an indirect lexicographical sort of semi-finite suffixes of a given string. In (Burkhardt, 2006) is is proven that this construction consumes linear operations. The DC3 Algorithm is a skewed divide & conquer algorithm. Basically the steps mentioned in Figure 10 are executed. A detailed

Figure 8. Example for integration ontology

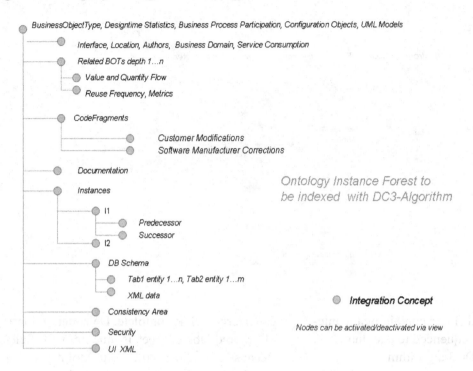

Figure 9. Tree distance visualization with edit script

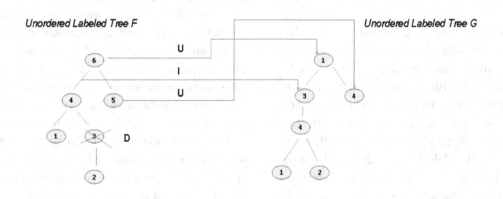

pseudo algorithm and a concrete implementation of DC3 is given in (Burkhardt, 2006).

PAT Arrays are space efficient data structures containing indirect hierarchical lexicographic sort order according to Patricia Tries. Extended PAT Arrays accelerates the search procedure. Longest Common Prefix LCP can be skipped during search (Abouelhoda, et. al., 2005). A drawback of the extension is the additional space consumption in PAT Array.

PAT Arrays in the context of Enterprise Tomograph are advantageous because PAT Arrays can be merged in linear time.

A PAT Array is the basis for logarithmic indirect search. Assuming all semi-finite suffixes with prefix = search string are to be identified. A' points to semi-finite suffixes. A' is divided in 2 intervals: [left bound...medium] and [medium... right bound]. Medium serves as a basis for indirect comparison: if search string is lower than semi-finite suffix of medium then the new right border:= medium otherwise new left border:=medium. The new medium is determined in the middle of the

new interval. This procedure is re-iterated until border convergence.

All lexicographical neighbors can be found in a row direct behind the location identified previously via indirect logarithmic search.

The Delta Operator of the Enterprise Tomograph is concerned with detecting Delta Trees of two forests originating from different data sources. As shown in Figure 12 the intersection represents integration ontologies existing in both data sources A and B. A subset of this intersection are delta integration ontologies and needs to be identified and visualized according to Figure 09. The delta identification algorithm is explained in the next section in more detail.

The basic idea for identifying delta trees is to integrate watermarks into the sequenced forest text content. As outlined in Figure 12 a watermark is assembled of a 4 fixed-lenght tuple with hash value of TreeID, hash value of tree, the location of the tree and the offset of the sequenced tree. Watermark integration is done for all trees in both forest A and B. PAT Array construction is done for

Figure 10. DC3 algorithm for PAT array construction

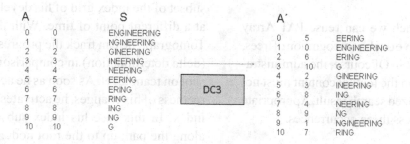

Indirect lexicographical sort of suffix pointers

A[ ] = integer array; components pointing to semi-finite suffixes of string S=ENGINEERING

Figure 11. PAT array search

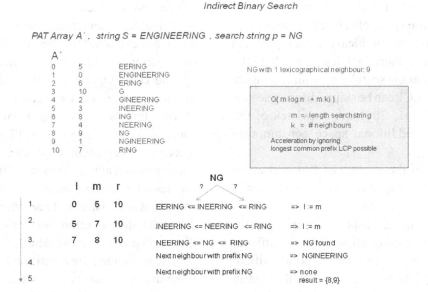

the textual content of A and B each. The resulting PAT Arrays are merged. On this constructed PAT Array a binary indirect search is performed for the tag <WATERMARK>. Watermark neighbors can be found in a sequence. Iterating over this sequence we can easily determine trees located in A only, in B only, trees in A and B, and delta trees in A and B. Delta trees have a common prefix '<WATERMARK>Hash Value TreeID' with different hash value tree in consecutive PAT Array positions.

With this approach we can reuse PAT Array algorithms for negative doublet recognition of trees, i.e. delta tree detection. Of course, the administrative data integrated in the textual content must not be part of any visualized search result. Appropriate measures can suppress these occurrences.

Enterprise Tomograph - Index Organization

In large-scaled VLBA development and maintenance projects numerous organizational entities on different granularity levels are involved. Entities

are potentially performing changes on the VLBA data universe. The aim is to keep the index up-to-date without complete re-indexing after each change made.

We assume that the project organization is hierarchical. Figure 14 reflects this situation. The root node represents the global index. Each development location may redefine subsets of the global index. A user for example works in a user-specific workspace. He may want to redefine a subset of the index grid of his development team at a different point of time. With the Enterprise Tomograph he can track the progress of his work (delta determination) in comparison to the snapshot on team level. As soon as he accepts the correctness of his changes, he activates user-specific index. In this case his index subset is updated along the path up to the root node. After this all predecessor entities can access the user specific changes. A lock mechanism during redefinition phase circumvents conflict resolution.

This collaborative index update policy ensures a consistent index without the need for re-indexing the whole VLBA data universe.

Figure 12. Delta trees

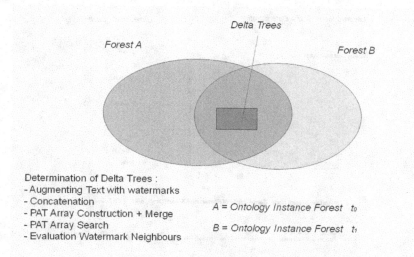

Determination of Delta Trees :
- Augmenting Text with watermarks
- Concatenation
- PAT Array Construction + Merge
- PAT Array Search
- Evaluation Watermark Neighbours

A = Ontology Instance Forest t_0

B = Ontology Instance Forest t_1

Generic Operators in Maintenance Networks

Enterprise software manufacturers normally provides maintenance services for their customers. They are granted access to their individual customers for detailed root cause analysis. In fact, the code bases of the individual deployed enterprise software may be modified or enhanced. Such individual changes may result in error symptoms. To make modifications and enhancements visible, the Inter-Delta Operator of the Enterprise Tomograph comes into place. E.g. enterprise software manufacturer SAP provides an encoded index of a domain of its Enterprise Platform (reference index) into a P2P network. The customer can calculate

Figure 13. Delta tree determination

Text augmentation with fixed length 4- tuple:

(*)

<WATERMARK> Hash Value TreeID, Hash Value Tree , Location, Offset</WATERMARK>
+
Serialization: text sequence of Unordered Labeled Tree

1.   FOR EACH *Tree* IN *Forest A* INTEGRATE WATERMARK (*)   *Loc = A or B*

2.   FOR EACH *Tree* IN *Forest B* INTEGRATE WATERMARK (*)   *Off = length of sequenced tree*

3.   CONSTRUCT *PAT Array A, PAT Array B*

4.   MERGE *PAT Array A* AND *PAT Array B* INTO *PAT Array C*

5.   SEARCH *PAT Array C:* FIND ALL WATERMARK TAGs *<WATERMARK>*

6.   EVALUATE *lexicographical ordered watermark sequence* IN *PAT Array C :*

7.   FOR ALL *Hash Value TreeID* IS COMMON PREFIX AT POSITION *i* AND *i + 1* DO

     IF *Hash Value Tree* ARE DIFFERENT AT POSITION *i* AND *i + 1*

     THEN *TreeID is a Delta Tree,* APPLY *Tree Distance Algorithm*

Figure 14. Enterprise tomograph index organization

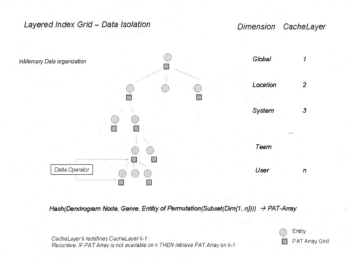

the delta of its changed enterprise software and the decoded reference index. In semantic genres the modifications and enhancements are listed. Now the maintainer semi-automatically can assess and estimate, if the error symptom relates to modifications and enhancements made by the customer.

Another meaningful operator in maintenance networks is the align operator. Assume the enterprise software manufacturer wants to deploy a best practice. This best practice (delta) can be added to customers configuration. In this case, adding a delta is equivalent to aligning configuration in a domain.

The align operator can also be applied for code bases. In this way updates of enterprise software can be provided.

The locate operator performs concept location in integration ontologies. This operator can be iteratively be applied for refinement purposes. Based on the result other orthogonal operators can be applied e.g. multiple break-point operator, launch operator, modify operator. The locate operator is the basis for refactoring purposes.

In the P2P network the sender of the encoded domain index is the owner of the key. Enterprises

knowing this key are able to decrypt and use the domain index only. The domain index is divided into n fragments. These fragments are redundantly encoded and the resulting amount of encoded fragments $m = n + k$ is distributed to the peers of the network. The retrieval of the encoded index happens according to an implementation of a distributed hash table (DHT).

With Reed Solomon Codes, retrieval of arbitrary n of m fragments suffices for reconstruction of the original domain index (Grolimund, 2007). The basics behind is the fundamental theorem of algebra (Korner, 2006). If a fragment is damaged, or not transmitted consistently, the retrieval of an additional encoded fragment may be triggered (n different consistent encoded fragments are necessary for reconstruction of the original domain index).

The independent fragment retrieval approach ensures an efficient upload and download of large Enterprise Tomograph domain indices because n (n of m) arbitrary encoded fragments can be retrieved in parallel for reconstructing the original domain index (Grolimund 2007).

In addition, with RS-Codes (Reed Solomon Codes) damaged or not consistently transmitted

Figure 15. Generic operators in maintenance network

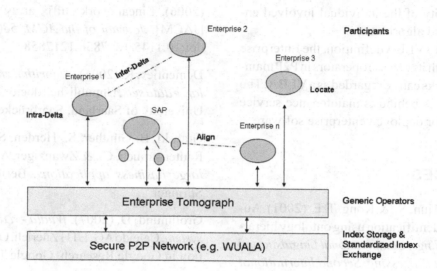

encoded fragments can be reconstructed with high reliability. Encoded fragments contains attached redundant information (polynom). With polynom division the correctness can be evaluated. With help of RS erasure codes damaged fragments can be repaired (Forward Error Correction).

Figure 15 outlines the interplay of the generic operators in the P2P maintenance network.

RELATED WORKS

Enterprise Tomograph with its delta operator has similarities to ontology versioning in ontology management frameworks (Noy & Musen, 2004). Integration concept location is related to identifying cross-cutting concerns in enterprise software. Ontology mining relates to static and dynamic aspect mining in a more abstract sense (Krinke, 2006). Techniques used in (Hollingsworth & Williams, 2005) can be seen as a special case of Enterprise Tomography.

Semantic Integration in VLBAs is covered in (Brehm & Haak, 2008). In Enterprise Tomography

integration ontologies are derived from VLBAs. Integration ontologies as an intermediate dynamic model are used for ontology integration.

Ontology concepts are also used as model for program comprehension in combination with technical unrelated artifacts (Panchenko, 2007).

CONCLUSION

Enterprise Tomography is an efficient approach for Application Lifecycle Management of VLBAs and Enterprise Platforms. It supports development and maintenance teams to track incremental changes of integration concepts in VLBA software, business data and contextual data. Full domain-specific search of integration concepts, refinement search and delta search and its visualization is realized with enhanced standard scientific algorithms. Interchangeable enhanced PAT Arrays, PAT array based delta tree recognition, tree distance algorithms and tree mappings based on dynamic programming are the main algorithms used in Enterprise Tomography. Complexity calculation for Enterprise Tomography can easily be derived from complexity of the individual involved enhanced standard algorithms.

According to VLBA definition, the Enterprise Tomograph with its generic operators in P2P maintenance networks can be regarded as a VLBA. The business process behind is maintenance service provisioning for deployed enterprise software.

REFERENCES

Abdullah, R., Tiun, S., & Kong, T. E. (2001). Automatic topic identification using ontology hierarchy. In *Proceedings, Computational Linguistic and Intelligent Text Processing, Second International Conference CICLing,* Mexico City, Mexico (pp. 444-453). Berlin, Germany: Springer.

Abels, S., Haak, L., & Hahn, A. (2005). Identification of common methods used for ontology integration tasks. Interoperability of heterogeneous information systems. In *Proceedings of the first international workshop on Interoperability of heterogeneous information systems,* Bremen, Germany (pp. 75-78). New York: ACM.

Abouelhoda, M. I., & Kurtz, S. (2005). Replacing suffix trees with enhanced suffix arrays. *Journal of Discrete Algorithms, 2,* 53–86. doi:10.1016/S1570-8667(03)00065-0

Bille, P. (2005). A survey on tree edit distance and related problems. *Theoretical Computer Science, 337*(1-3), 217–239. doi:10.1016/j.tcs.2004.12.030

Brehm, N., & Haak, L. (2008). Ontologies supporting VLBAs: Semantic integration in the context of FERP. In *Proceedings of the 3rd International Conference on Information and Communication Technologies: From Theory To Applications, ICTTA 2008,* (pp. 1-5).

Burkhardt, S., Kärkkäinen, J., & Sanders, P. (2006). Linear work suffix array construction. [JACM]. *Journal of the ACM, 53*(6), 918–936. doi:10.1145/1217856.1217858

Dementiev, R. (2006). *Algorithm engineering for large data sets.* Unpublished doctoral dissertation, University of Saarland, Saarbrücken.

Grabski, B. Günther, S., Herden, S., Krüger, L., Rautenstrauch, C., & Zwanziger, A. (2007). *Very large business applications.* Berlin, Germany: Springer.

Grolimund, D. (2007). *Wuala - a distributed file system.* Caleido AG, ETH Zuerich. Online Publication in Google Research, Google TechTalks.

Hollingsworth, J. K., & Williams, C. C. (2005). Automatic mining of source code repositories to improve bug finding techniques. *IEEE Software Engineering, 31*(6), 466–480. doi:10.1109/TSE.2005.63

Korner, T. E. (2006). On the fundamental theorem of algebra. *Journal Storage, 113*(4), 347–348.

Krinke, J. (2006). Mining control flow graph from crosscutting concerns. In *Proceedings of the 13th Working Conference on Reverse Engineering (WCRE): IEEE International Astrenet Aspect Analysis (AAA) Workshop,* Benevento, Italy (pp. 334-342).

Lu, C. L., Su, Z.-Y., & Tang, C.-Y. (2001). A new measure of edit distance between labeled trees. In *Proceedings of the Computing and Combinatorics, 7th Annual International Conference, Cocoon 2001,* Guilin, China (pp. 338-348).

Ludewig, J., & Opferkuch, St. (2004). *Softwarewartung - eine taxonomie.* Softwaretechnik-Trends, Band 24 Heft 2, Gesellschaft für Informatik.

Nicklas, D. (2005). *Ein umfassendes umgebungs-modell als integrationsstrategie für ortsbezogene daten und dienste.* Unpublished doctoral dissertation, University Stuttgart, Online Publication, Stuttgart.

Noy, N. F., & Musen, M. A. (2004). Ontology versioning in an ontology management framework. *IEEE Intelligent Systems, 19*(4), 6–13. doi:10.1109/MIS.2004.33

Opferkuch, St. (2004). *Software-wartungsprozesse - ein einblick in die industrie.* Fachbericht Informatik, Nr. 11/2004, Universität Koblenz-Landau.

Panchenko, O. (2007). Concept location and program comprehension in service-oriented software. In *Proceedings of the IEEE 23rd International Conference on Software Maintenance: Doctoral Symposium, ICSM,* Paris, France (pp. 513–514).

Shasha, D., Statman, R., & Zhang, K. (1992). On the editing distance between unordered labeled trees. *Information Processing Letters, 42,* 133–139. doi:10.1016/0020-0190(92)90136-J

Chapter 13
Workflow as a Tool in the Development of Information Systems

José Luis Leiva
University of Malaga, Spain

José Luis Caro
University of Malaga, Spain

Antonio Guevara
University of Malaga, Spain

María de los Ángeles Arena
University of Veracruz, Mexico

ABSTRACT

This chapter proposes a cooperative methodology for information system (IS) development, focusing on the end user's collaboration in the process, providing the training and tools required to obtain the characteristics of the processes in which he/she is involved and actively integrating the user in the IS development team. Each of the steps involved in IS development is coordinated by a meta-CASE tool based on a workflow management system (WfMS). An important characteristic of the authors' methodology is the utilization of tools that allow to realize functions of reengineering to adapt existing systems allowing to add new functionalities or modifying the already existing ones. This methodology provides a high degree of reliability in the development of the system, creating competitive advantages for the organization by reducing times and costs in the generation of the information system (IS).

INTRODUCTION

Across the time, the organizations have improved according to new technologies, therefore it's been necessary to invest large amounts of money in the acquisition of computer products, undoubtedly this has brought along many advantages, however, not like it would be expected, because in the majority of these organizations it's been automatized an amount of ordinary tasks in isolated ways, in other words, these are not interconnected, which leads to

DOI: 10.4018/978-1-60566-856-7.ch013

a non – optimal productivity in the organization. To avoid these kinds of problems it is necessary to make an adequate analysis and automatization process, which take us to a total integration from the processes conforming a unique automatized information infrastructure, and perfectly coordinated processes and resources, with the sole purpose to offer better services to the clients and to increase in this form the productivity of the business.

The complexity of <u>information systems</u> (IS) for business has now increased considerably, due to customer demands for a better quality of service. For IS to meet all the necessary quality requirements, their development must be based on a method guiding the whole process of development. Different tools, techniques and models have been created to facilitate system generation while attempting to prevent common problems associated to quality, cost and development time; to mention just a few: Métrica, RUP (Rational Unified Process) (Arlow & Neustadt, 2005; Booch, Jacobson & Rumbaugh, 2004), UML (Unified Modelling Language) (Booch, Rumbaugh & Jacobson, 2005), MDA (Model Driven Architecture) (Kleppe, Warmer & Bast, 2003). IS must satisfy the necessary quality requirements, for which their development must be based on a method guiding the entire process, from the definition of their requirements, a fundamental aspect of all IS, to their implantation. There is a growing need for information systems and technologies with the sufficient flexibility to adjust to the constant changes demanded by the environment. The new technologies must focus on managing large volumes of information from management systems integrated in a corporate platform, providing a global information model of the organisation and thus defining cooperative work models. It is very important to create cooperative methods to guide IS development in order to obtain high-quality, error-free and easy-to-maintain software tailored to the customer's needs, in which all the agents involved use the same tools to understand the entire product. Although there are some models, they do

not fully satisfy all the aspects of cooperative IS development, such as work teams including the end users and models enabling easy understanding of communications between different parts of the system, among others. The purpose of this chapter, then, is to present a cooperative methodology for IS development, using different technologies which can be linked to help companies guarantee customer satisfaction by providing the best possible service. We aim to active involve all the system's users, from managers to operators. Also, due to the rapid evolution of computer systems, the appearance of new platforms and the logical needs of future <u>workflows</u>, many systems either become aged or at least require maintenance to adapt them to organizations' needs. Software maintenance is not always possible, due to multiple difficulties, such as:

- Size and storage space constraints.
- The tools with which the system was created are no longer used.
- The changes made to the information system to adapt or improve it have made it less structures and less consistent with current specifications.
- Impossibility of contacting with the engineers who developed the system.
- Having used a traditional software engineering method based on supposedly correct specifications.

One solution for the problem is the use of <u>re-engineering</u> and <u>reverse engineering</u> techniques, examining and reconstructing the system in order to guarantee satisfactory communications between the users and the experts. Our method involving the user in system design and analysis, to adapt the specifications to current requirements and help both users and experts to obtain specifications of the system's external design and to define the workflows or functions involved.

The technology workflow and the systems of management workflow (WFMS) stems from several disciplines between which it is necessary to emphasize CSCW (Cooperative Work Supported by Computer) and OIS (Systems of Information in the Office). Workflow includes a set of technological solutions that allow to automate the processes of work developed in an organization. Implant workflow is adapted in any type of environment, being used principally for (Caro, Guevara & Aguayo, 2003):

- to coordinate and to manage the work of groups of agents,
- to direct automatically the processes of work between the agents,
- to take a control of the processes of work, there being obtained a global vision of the state of the complete process,
- to improve, by reengineering, the processes of work and to obtain a more rapid service and better quality,
- to reduce the costs of the developed processes,
- to accelerate the cycles of development of products and processes.

The chapter is organised as follows. The first section presents some related methodologies, followed by a proposed cooperative method centred on the system's end user; we then suggest a Meta-CASE tool based on WfMS to coordinate the different CASE (Computer-Aided Software Engineering) tools. Later, we study the language for the representation of workflows and describe a tool for the description of user's interfaces and, finally, present our conclusions and projects which may arise from this proposal.

BACKGROUND

The following sections present a set of IS development methods, providing an overview of the current state of the art and generating the methodology proposed in this chapter.

Bottom-Up -- Top-Down Iterative Collaborative Methodology

The primary objective of this method is for users to actively collaborate in the development of the information system, assuming that they have the know-how and must provide solutions for their own demands, with technicians compiling, coordinating and unifying their proposals. This cooperative methodology (Caro, Guevara & Aguayo, 2003; Guevara, Aguayo, Falgueras & Triguero, 1995; Falgueras, Guevara, Aguayo, Gálvez & Gómez, 1997) comprises the following five phases.Phase I. Definition of the problem and viability study.- This phase includes defining the current state of the system, establishing objectives, estimating costs and identifying the company members whose cooperative participation is required. This phase ends with the system's division into subsystems, which can in turn be divided into other subsystems.Phase II. System analysis.- The objective of this phase is to define the requirements to be satisfied by the information system. The users of each subsystem cooperatively plan how their subsystems will operate. Basically, this phase involved defining requirements (logic model), creating a process model and creating an integration plan for the two. The users also design the subsystem interfaces, taking control and security requirements into account.Phase III. System design.- This phase includes the physical design of the architecture and described the interfaces with other systems. The physical design of the data is also defined.Phase IV. System construction.- The objective of this phase is the construction and testing of the system's components, generating the code, implementing the database and performing integration tests.Phase V. Implementation and maintenance.- This phase consists of global testing and the design of an implementation plan.In general, the method proposes initial decomposition into subsystems to the smallest unit (top-down), in which the expert user is responsible for defining the input, processes and output of the different processes performed; once they have been analysed, designed and encoded, they are iteratively integrated into higher level systems (bottom-up) to create the global information system (Guevara, Aguayo, Falgueras,& Triguero, 1995).

AMENETIES

AMENETIES (A MEthodology for aNalysis and dEsign of cooperaTIve systEmS) (Garrido, 2003; Gea, Gutierrez & Cañas, 2003). The objective of this methodology is to provide systematic support for the analysis and design or cooperative systems, facilitating subsequent software development with special emphasis on group behaviour. This methodology includes several general phases: system analysis and definition of requirements; cooperative system modelling; cooperative model analysis; system design and software development. It also involves a series of models: requirement model, cooperative model, formal model and software development model. Within the cooperative model, AMENETIES describes the cooperative system from four perspectives: Organisation view.- It described how groups are structured in the organisation, considering aspects such as: participant adjustment, work loads, group evolution, etc. Cognitive view.- It represents the knowledge of each member of the organisation by describing the functions he/she can perform. Interaction view.- This perspective refers to communication between participants, either when performing common functions or activities indirectly affecting other group members.Information view.- It is responsible for representing data such as documents and messages by which information is transmitted in a more or less structured manner. The AMENETIES methodology structures an organisation in roles and breaks down functions in order to work as a team, and is therefore more focused on dynamic aspects.

MPlu+a, Usability and Accessibility Engineering Process Model

The primary objective of this methodology (Granollers, 2004) is to implement highly usable and accessible interactive systems, involving multidisciplinary development teams.It is based on three basic elements: software engineering, prototyping and evaluation in an iterative process. The phases involved are:Analysis of requirements. It applies user-oriented requirement analysis techniques as the quality of the software system is determined by its consistence with and accomplishment of the established requirements. Design. This stage involves the design of the activity, which is directly related to the functional requirements, the technology and the possibilities available for users. In other words, it fills the gaps between the functionalities and the interface. The design of the information supports the perception, interpretation and comprehension of the system data. Implementation. This stage includes encoding the specifications defined in the analysis and design and establishing connections between the modules and devices. At the start of this stage, it is advisable to build prototypes to be evaluated by the end users. Finally, heuristic evaluations are required to verify the global consistence of the system.Launch. The system is installed for the testing stage, in which users' remarks are used to introduce improvements. This is followed by a new testing period until they are fully satisfied. Prototyping. The users are involved in the system's development in this phase, in which designers can use different tools to simulate the operation. A prototype can be constructed from the start of the project with a view to obtaining users' impressions.Evaluation. This phase uses techniques to obtain feedback from expert users. It is applied throughout the development process, improving the solutions evaluated and correcting errors.

GRAI

The GRAI (Groupe de Recherche en Automatisation Intégrée) (Merlo & Girard, 2004) method is based on system theory, hierarchical theory and activity theory. The objective of the GRAI methodology is to improve the performance of the designed product, which first requires an understanding of its present status in order to identify its strong points and weaknesses. The new system is subsequently designed according to the organisation's strategic plan. This method comprises a conceptual (GRAI) model, graphic formalisms and a generic structure. The system is thus divided into three subsystems: technology, decision-making and information. The phases of the GRAI methodology are: 1st phase. It consists of an initial meeting with the company manager: information and training in the method, definition of targets and fields of study, definition of different groups involved in the study. 2nd phase. Modelling the existing system to diagnose the improvements required. 3rd phase. Design for modelling the new system and for the specification of the new information system which will provide the technical support required to design the coordination.

Cooperative Methodology for Information Systems (COMIS)

To achieve our goal of an integral automatization, it is necessary to include a work frame that improves the processes of software development, that's why we proposed a cooperative methodology that involves inside the development team to the end users to the information system, trying to break the hierarchic structures of the organization and conforming cooperative work teams between all the interested parts.

This cooperative methodology for the development of information systems is supported by three different technologies:

- **Software Engineering:** Systematic application, disciplined and method – measurable, for all the software development process, in other words, it indicates the order of the processes to follow and inside each one of these, all the activities to follow to obtain a quality product.

- **Workflow:** With this technology, it is possible to model the executable processes used inside the organization. Starting from here, in case it's necessary, to improve this processes, which will bring an improvement in the products and services, along with a reduction of the costs and a competitivity increase. Once all the processes have been modeled and analyzed, it is possible to obtain the software requirements, because we will have information from: the executed processes, the agents involving every one of the processes, the necessary information and the sequence to execute them, whether it's parallel or serial.

- **Teamwork:** The cooperative work is indispensable to achieve the goals in the organization, accordingly to systems development it is necessary to participate along with the development team all the direct users of the processes, because they are the carriers of the necessary knowledge to execute the processes, that's why it's proposed the conformation of work teams (specialists in systems development and specialists in the automation of processes), whom it can be obtained since the workflow maps, because in those are indicated the people involving in every one of the processes.

The creation of an IS requires a method which contemplates process specification, means of communication and how groups collaborate to reach their objectives. Each phase of development has to include verification processes to prevent errors being discovered in the final stages, generating

Figure 1. Development model

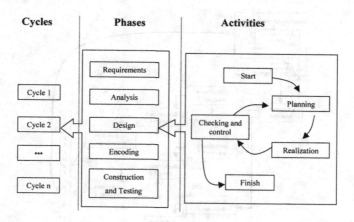

high correction costs. The COMIS (Cooperative Methodology for Information Systems) method follows an incremental iterative model (Jacobson, Booch & Rumbaugh, 2004), comprising three workflows (Oktaba, 2005): cycles of development, phases of a cycle and activities of each phase (Figure 1).

Cycle of development: It is the set of phases through which the IS progresses to obtain a deliverable version.

Phases of a cycle: Set of activities aimed at obtaining one or several elements of the Information System (IS).

Activities of each phase: Set of operations or tasks, in this case pertaining to project administration.

Before to initialisation the development process is necessary a formation process that provide the end user the general knowledge in order to do his functions inside the team of development, as well as a training in the tools to facilitate his participation. The purpose is that the end user consider really part of the team, collaborating in a voluntary and active way, allow us to extract his knowledge of the different processes that he perform in the organization. Following is a description of each of the phases (Figure 2) in a COMIS methodology cycle.

This phase includes a definition of the IS and a development plan, in which the members of the organisation should be cooperatively involved in order to specify each of the processes in detail and the relationships between them. The Cooperative Methodology proposed considers that end users should actively participate in IS development, although the members of the organisation have always been separate from the developers. This requires a training plan in which roles are assigned to the work team members and tools are created to facilitate their participation (Leiva, Guevara & Caro, 2006). Another essential aspect is the workflow design, a powerful tool for representing an organisation's processes, supplementing these diagrams with the information required to perform each process and identifying the users actively involved, thus generating the Interaction Model, consisting of a triplet containing the three following models:

- Organisational: The agent/s, who are the members of the organisation involved in the process, with at least three different levels: executive, management and operation (Oktaba, 2005; Rialp, 2003).
- Process: The description of the set of activities to be performed to attain an objective,

Figure 2. Phases of COMIS

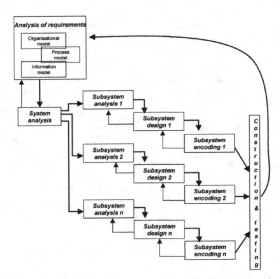

which is the point connecting the other two elements (Caro, 2003).

- Information: The data required for each process to be performed (Gálvez, 2000).

Figure 3 shows in detail how the processes are run by the agents in the organisation and where they obtain the information. There can be different interactions on all levels, such as:

- Different people cooperate to run a given process.
- One person can be involved in different processes.

- The same data store can be used in different processes.

The workflow is defined as we move down from the executive to the operation level, where most of the process takes place, so we are able to generate an IS moving in the same direction as the organisation's strategic plan. With the active participation of the members of the organisation, the diagrams will contain the functions performed, which must be easily interpreted in order to confirm that the required functionalities have been correctly understood.

Analysis: Once the requirements have been defined, the processes, agents and information

Figure 3. Interaction model

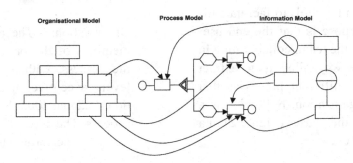

Figure 4. Division of the IS into Subsystems

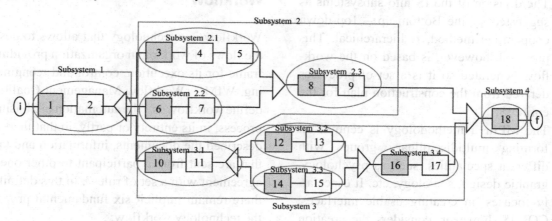

involved in each one are determined, followed by an analysis to form subsystems.

Division of the IS into subsystems The IS is divided into subsystems by considering the basic block partition algorithm (Aho, Sethi & Ullman, 1998), with each subsystem being a basic block, as follows: A set of leading processes is determined 1: The first process is a leader, and all processes immediately following the connection between two or more processes are also leaders (they are shown in grey on figure 4. For each leader, the basic block (subsystem) comprises the leader and all the subsequent processes up to the process prior to the following leader. An example of the division is shown on figure 4, generating 9 subsystems.

Each subsystem is assigned to a group of people comprising the direct users of the processes in which they are involved, as shown in figure 3. A conceptual model is defined for each of the subsystems, refining and structuring the established requirements, analysing uses and identifying the classes involved and describing the interactions. Once the analytical classes have been defined, responsibilities, attributes and the relationships between them have to be identified. This phase also includes a subsystem construction plan, considering the functional dependence between them.

Design: The design phase is responsible for generating a physical model for each subsystem, defining the architecture, design classes and re-

lationships between objects and identifying their attributes and operations.

Encoding: This phase contemplates the implementation of the design classes of each subsystem, forming components and assigning them to their respective nodes. It also includes individual or unit testing.

Construction and testing: The final step is incremental integration according to the construction plan established in the analysis, with integration and system testing to ensure that the system works properly with the new increment. The proposed methodology is focused on the active participation of the users throughout IS development. It takes some elements from the methods described earlier, making certain adjustments to improve the result, such as:

• Unlike the AMENETIES method, which is based on four perspectives (organisation, corresponding to the organisational model; cognitive, which is the relationship between the organisational and process models; interaction, referring to communication between participants, or the relationship between the three models; and, information, corresponding to the information model), COMIS only generates one model showing the interactions between agents, processes and information.

- The division of the IS into subsystems as suggested by the Bottom-up – Top-down cooperative method, is hierarchical. This proposal, however, is based on the work-flow generated so it is a set of processes derived from the construction plan for the entire IS.
- The MPIu+a methodology is centred on forming multidisciplinary groups with different specialities, such as psychology, graphic design, sociology, etc. It especially focuses on creating usable interfaces. COMIS, however, considers the creation of teams including the end users of the IS, who have to provide their knowledge about the processes they perform.
- The GRAI methodology proposes the participation of the members of the organisation, dividing it into 3 subsystems. What COMIS proposes is the participation of all levels, from the executive level to operations, so the IS is consistent with the strategic plan, thus meeting the organisation's objectives.

As we mentioned earlier, the method contemplates forming work teams involving the end users of the IS, so an end user-oriented cooperative CASE tool is required to provide the necessary facilities to simply obtain the know-how of users with no knowledge of system development. A CASE tool to guide the development process according to a given method is certainly good support for developers. Although there are different tools, most of them do not support teamwork (Caro, Guevara & Aguayo, 2003; Post & Kagan, 2000). Teamwork requires a standard support, which is another tool responsible for coordinating teams throughout the development of the IS. A WfMS would solve this problem, operating as a Meta-CASE controlling the activities of the teams during the different phases of development.

Workflow

Workflow is a technology that allows to design the flows of work of an organization providing a frame for its execution, control and reengineering. WfMC (Workflow Management Coalition) define workflow as, "the automation of a business process, in its entirety or partly, in that there are described the documents, information and tasks that are sent from a participant to other one, in agreement with a set of rules". In this definition there remain implicit six fundamental props of the technology workflow:

- **Routes:** with them there are defined the ways that follow the objects in an organization. Objects can be documents, information, forms, …
- **Rules:** the technology workflow is based on a series of rules that the agents must follow for the correct accomplishment of the work.
- **Roles:** the work is realized by agents who possess a series of skills and characteristics that form a part of the flowchart of the organization.
- **Processes:** they are the tasks.
- **Policies:** the declarations of how they must be treated the processes.
- **Practices:** This one is the way (not documented) current of work that is realized in the organization.

Though the principal area of application of this technology is placed in the managerial world, many authors prefer extending this area to any situation in which cooperative processes are realized. Workflow can be defined as the set of activities that there includes the coordinated execution of multiple tasks developed by different entities to come to a common aim.

One of the basic elements of a system of management workflow is the form to shape formally the reality. To be able to implement a WFMS the use of a design methodology, which will facilitate the following functions:

- Identification, representation and comprehension of the processes,
- analysis and simulation of processes and mechanisms of demonstration, to detect the possible necks of bottle, to evaluate costs, ...
- communication between processes,
- documentation to assure the quality,

We define for system workflow (Swf) to the set of elements so much physical as necessary logicians to manage of efficient form a work destined for the attainment of a final aim. We can divide in: the general aim of the general process of the system (Obj), set of resources (R), model of organization (OM), process map workflow (Mwf) and workflow management system (WFMS).

$$Swf= Obj \cup R \cup OM \cup Mwf \cup WFMS \quad (1)$$

Later, we will define the components of the workflow system

<u>General aim</u>: the general aim represents the mission to realizing with the workflow. It will be said that the system has finished successfully if all the sub-aims Sobj_i are fulfilled.

$$Obj= Sobj\_1 \cup Sobj\_2 \cup \ldots \ldots \cup Sobj\_n \quad (2)$$

Resources: it is denoted by set T, to all the necessary objects of the system to realize the process of the system workflow. We will classify the resources under assets or with capacity of process and liabilities, that is to say, those that are used by the previous ones.

Organizational model: The organizational model (OM) gathers the environment in the one that will develop the work. It includes agents, tools, groups, categories, departments and the existing relations between them.

The definition of the organizational model will depend on the organization, being indicated the levels of grouping (Glev) and the existing relations (Rdep) between them.

$$OM= Glev \cup Rdep \quad (3)$$

We define level of grouping (Glev) each of the organizational structures that compose the organization in the one that will implant the workflow. Examples of these are the sections, departments, groups, ...

On the other hand, Rdep will establish a net that will represent the relations of the different levels of grouping. The application Rdep (A, B) where A, B $\in$ Glev, have value 1 if relation of subordination exists (being B the level of grouping dependent of A) and 0 y 0 in another case.

$$Rdep:Glev \times Glev \rightarrow \{0,1\} \quad (4)$$

Workflow Management System

The workflow management system WFMS is a system " that defines, creates and manages automatically the model the execution of workflow by means of the use of one or more coordinated engines that take charge interpreting the process definition, interacting with the agents and, when it is needed, to invoke the use of the systems of information implied in the work". Therefore, it is the software that supports all this structure of the workflow system. A WFMS it is composed by other modules as: tools to define workflows, tools to design and define specifications for workflow, applications clients, inherited applications, administrations tools, reengineering tools, ...

Workflow Map

The system Workflow map (Mwf) take the specification of the tasks to realizing to obtain the aim Obj. A workflow map will design the set of all the models workflow of all the tasks to realize. Each workflow model has the next characteristics:

Name: Name or identifying of the workflow in the system.

Sobj: Aim of the workflow.

Cli: Agent or customer who orders or can arrange the instance of the workflow.

Svr: Agent who orders the instance of the workflow.

Dis: A trigger is the event that activates the development of a workflow. We can distinguish between:

- **Manual (m):** the activity or workflow is activated of manual form. For example, an agent.
- **Automatic (a):** the activity or workflow is activated of automatic form. For example, when an activity finishes, the following one is activated.
- **Temporal (t):** the activity or workflow is activated when an event happens.
- **Predicate (p):** the activity or workflow is activated when the predicate P is true.
- **External (e):** the activity or workflow is activated when an external event (not belong to the system) happens.
- **R:** set of resources of the system that are necessary for the correct execution of the workflow. If one of these resources the system will stay to wait of being able to obtain it and, therefore, it will not continue in its execution.
- **E:** in the specification of the model there will be described all the operations necessary for the correct attainment of the workflow. This attribute is the one that describes how it is necessary to realize the workflow that is defined. The specification of the model will be empty when there is described the map of a primitive task.

Workflow's Specifications

The model workflow that we propose allows to specify the flows of work in four differentiated levels:

- **Management level:** It is the level used by the high-level users. In this level the granularity will be indicated so much of specification as transaction (Caro, Guevara &Aguayo, 2003). Finally there is desirable the utilization of graphical interfaces that represent the flows of work on temporary fibers.
- **Formal level:** The specifications of this level it is expressed by equations in which the flows of work will be specified to a detailed and formal level.
- **Automation level:** In this level the flows of work represent with a language of specification workflow that will be used as internal representation by the engine workflow.
- **Demonstration level:** Translation to a temporary logic for the automatic demonstration of properties.

It is very important to think that all levels are directly translatable to the most expressive level (up-down). Though understanding itself equivalent in every area at the moment of the specification workflow they can be used by different types of designers (managers, high-level users, and experts in the system,…).

Meta-Tool

The Meta-CASE tool (Costagliola, Deufemia, Ferrucci & Gravino, 2006; Sorenson, Findeisen & Paul, 1996) is driven by a WfMS, which is responsible for iteratively completing all the phases defined in the cooperative methodology, ending when all the defined functionalities have been implemented. This WfMS (Fig. 5) basically

Figure 5. General meta-CASE workflow

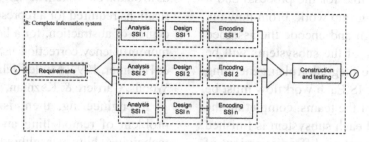

comprises the following components:Process definition tool, responsible for obtaining the specifications to generate the workflow map for subsequent implementation.Model of the organisation, defining the agents and their organisation in the system. This model is referenced by the workflow processes, which are assigned to different agents according to their profiles and work loads.CASE tools, interacting with the workflow. In this case, they support the development of the IS and are all the traditional CASE tools involved and used by the agents.Work list manager, responsible for controlling interactions between users and assigning the tasks and tools to be used. Workflow engine, the principal component, which interprets and controls the different instances of the processes, manages the work list and controls all the IS development processes. The components interact as follows: the process definition tool tells the workflow engine which processes are to

be followed; the organisation model shows who will be involved; the CASE tools indicate what will be used to perform these tasks and the work list manager controls when the process will be assigned and to whom (the specific agent in the organisation model).The processes to be developed by the agents involved in the development of the IS are described by a process description language. The different workflows involved in the previous methodology are represented in figures 5 and 6.

In the requirements phase, the tool generates an interaction model comprising the organisation model, the process model and the information model, with which the requirements of the IS can be defined.

In the following phase, Analysis, the IS is divided into different information subsystems, performing an analysis for the creation of work teams including the expert user (member of the

Figure 6. Requirements phase workflow

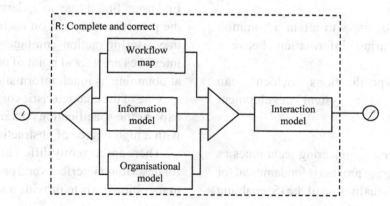

organisation responsible for the process) and a training plan for the group work. From now on, each team will design and encode the assigned subsystem and some of the subsystems will be added according to the integration plan, generating a new version of the IS.Each workflow must be performed by each of the teams, completing the cycles required until each subsystem is finished and correct, thus generating different versions of the system.

Language for the representation of workflows

One of the tools that we have designed and that it allows to design the flows of works is EXINUS Tools (Extraction of information of the user-Interaction computer-human), who allows to define flows of work of an organization. With EXINUS it is possible design the interfaces of the system and its functionalities. EXINUS obtains a specifications and primitives compatible with the proposed methodology. In this section we are going to treat both the primitives and the language

The primary objective of the EXINUS tool is to help end users and experts to obtain appropriate specifications with which to obtain a new system that satisfies users' needs. It is a cooperative tool based on the following principles:

- Users have most information about the IS; they are aware of its functionalities, where there is room for improvement and what will be required in the near future.
- Ease of use so that users become involved in the process.
- Cooperation of users to attain a common objective, sharing information between them.
- Obtaining specifications which can be exported to a system development environment.

The use of reverse engineering techniques as part of the reengineering process is fundamental for obtaining the conceptualisation of the IS, enabling

us to obtain the system design and workflow specifications required for a representation with a high degree of abstraction, for a better quality IS with more efficiency, correction, usability, etc. (Champy & Hammer, 1994; Müller, Jahnke & Smith, 2000; Woods, Carriere & Kazman, 1999).

Reengineering, then, is a solution to the problem of remodelling an application. These techniques, however, although they obtain high quality applications with major advantages, can generate programs which do not fully satisfy the user's requirements (Carrillo, Falgueras & Guevara, 2006; Di Lucca, Fasolino, Face, Tramontana & De Carlini, 2002; Leiva, 2003). We therefore suggest that the user should provide the information required to obtain the necessary present and future interface design and workflow specifications. The method is based on providing the user with the simple tools required to create an external (interfaces) and internal (workflows) of the IS, so that users are involved in the development of the new system (Leiva, Caro, Guevara & Arenas, 2008).

EXINUS is based on a model enabling the specification of workflows on several levels: management level (use of primitives), automation (XML language) and demonstration (temporal modal logic) (Caro, Guevara, Aguayo & Leiva, 2004).

User Interfaces as a Descriptive Focal Point

End users find it easy to understand and describe the processes they run on each of the interfaces they use(Interaction computer-human), so user interfaces are a focal point of our method, aimed at obtaining as much information as possible.

One of the characteristics of EXINUS is that it exports the specifications obtained in a language with a high degree of abstraction.

There are currently different types of language for describing interfaces and processes. Their primary objective is to provide a simple description

Figure 7. User participation in EXINUS.

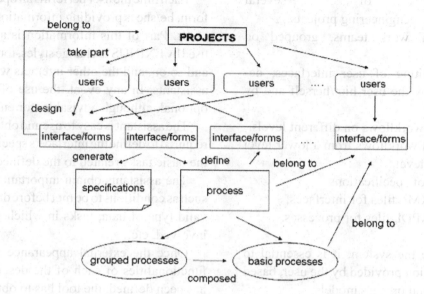

of the structure of the interface, with a high level of abstraction, so that this specification can be used to generate the final user interface.

Declarative languages are independent from and unrelated to any specific programming language. The fact that they are independent of context is a great advantage, as the interface can thus be created in any programming language and will be capable of creating interfaces on any device (PC, PDA,).

We have conducted a study of different languages, including AAIML, AUIML, UML, XIML, XUL and XFORMS and concluded that we need a language with the following characteristics:

- It must be able to describe the interfaces and processes involved.
- It must enable the definition of systems designed in different environments, regardless of the platform, programming language, etc.
- It must clearly distinguish elements from the previous and future system. In other words, it must be capable of defining interfaces and processes of both the present

system and the system to be constructed.
- It must be flexible enough to enable us to generate prototypes in any programming language.

Figure 7 shows how users participate in the design process and how the focal point of our model (Leiva, Guevara & Caro, 2006) is the interface, from which not only do we obtain specifications of the interfaces themselves but also of the functions that the user performs between them.

Each user involved in the project can define and design different interfaces, with some of them being shared by several users, so the tool has to allow for <u>cooperative</u> work, enabling one user to consult and change other users' forms providing he/she has the appropriate permission to do so.

Each interface designed by the user defines a set of processes which can be basic (pertaining to the designed object) and grouped on different levels. In turn, processes can belong to one or several interfaces (Leiva, 2003).

Following is a general description of the main features provided by the EXINUS tool, showing how powerful it is. Its basic features include:

- Creation of several engineering/reengineering projects.
- Creation of work teams, grouped on levels.
- Creation-Editing of user interfaces, defined both by the user him/herself and by other users.
- Creation of workflows on different levels.
- Grouping of workflows from a lower level on a higher level.
- Generation of specifications.
- Obtaining XML files for interfaces.
- Obtaining XPDL files for processes.

To restructure the system, it is essential to compile information provided by the user, based on the interface and process models.

Once the external appearance of the interface has been designed, the data related to its functionality is collected in order to obtain the required workflow diagrams.

The application provides control of the interfaces created in the current project from a single window, from which we can create new interfaces or change, eliminate or share existing ones. There is also a visor showing a picture of the interface, so they can be easily identified.

Besides creating forms, the tool enables the creation of tasks aimed at grouping together the interfaces involved in the same process. The tasks can be described when the design of an interface is completed.

For users to describe different interfaces, they are supplied with an easy-to-use toolbar with different objects (text fields, labels, lists, checkboxes, option buttons, command buttons, etc.).

The environment is attractive enough for all users to actively participate. Each defined object will have a series of properties, some related to their external appearance (size, colour, position) and others with their individual behaviour (for instance, a given command button remains disabled until a certain value is entered in given text fields, etc.)

Each time the user performs an operation on the form, he/she is providing information of different kinds. Part of this information is automatically used by EXINUS to change styles, fonts, positions, and so on, and the other interacts with the tool's assistants. In any event, the use of assistants is optional, although advisable, for end users.

The assistant is easy to use and obtains all that is required to define the interface's specifications and the basic tasks related to the defined objects.

The assistants obtain important information, such as conditions to be met before data is entered, valid type of data, tasks in which given data is involved, etc.

Once the external appearance and intrinsic functionalities of each of the described objects has been defined, the tool has to obtain information about workflows in order to define their specifications. It has to distinguish between the workflows in the present IS and the changed or new workflows in the new system (Müller, Jahnke & Smith, 2000).

The user can define two types of task:

- Tasks performed on several interfaces.
- Tasks performed on a single interface.

The core of the tool is the definition of tasks in 'bottom-up' mode, based on basic or intrinsic tasks of the form's objects, which are grouped in others on a higher level. For each form designed, the tool shows the set of primitive tasks related to the objects used in the design. The end user this groups tasks into others on a higher level and so on.

The following figure shows the primitives (Leiva, Guevara, Caro & Arenas, 2008) which will form part of the workflow diagrams obtained with the tool:

Following are the characteristics of each of the primitives which will form part of the workflow diagrams generated with EXINUS:

Figure 8. Workflow description primitives

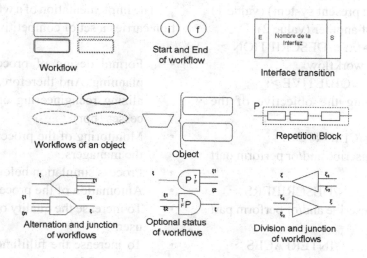

- Workflow component: each workflow represents a sub-task which forms part of the workflow. The flows represented with dotted lines show that this flow is not in the present system but required in the future; double line flows show that the task is primitive and not divided into more sub-tasks, whereas single line workflows can be broken down. Continuous line flows are current workflows.

- Interface transition: this component is used to indicate the changeover from one interface to another. In the transition, there may be a parameter step, either input (E), output (S) or both (E/S).

- Object: representation of each of the objects forming part of the interface. The description mat involve a list of preconditions and/or post-conditions which must be met before and/or after the appearance of said object on the interface

- Workflows of an object: represented in the same way as the previous workflows, except that we use an ellipse instead of a box.

- Start and end: start and end of the workflow.

- Alternation and junction of workflows: these components indicate the possibility of running several workflows simultaneously. A basic workflow is divided into several sub-flows, of which one or several may be run.

- Division and junction of workflows: these constructors refer to the parallel running of workflows, creating new sub-flows of undetermined duration which will at some time become synchronised by the junction constructor.

- Optional status of workflows: this component runs one of the flows, depending on the result of predicate P.

- Repetition block: set of workflows which will be repeated as long as condition P is met.

An XML structure is defined for each workflow, to store the following properties:

<TYPE>...</TYPE>:

Type of workflow

<NAME> ... </NAME>:

Name of workflow

<MODE> ... </MODE >:

It indicates whether the workflow defined pertains to the current system (value 0), the future system (and not in the present system) (value 1) or is in replacement of another (value 2)

<DESCRIPTION> ... </DESCRIPTION >: Description of the workflow

<OBJETIVE > ... </OBJETIVE >: Predicate describing the objective of the workflow

<CLIENTS > ... </CLIENTS >: Set of users who describe and/or perform part of the workflow

<DESCRIBERS> ... </DESCRIBERS >: Set of users who describe and/or perform part of the workflow

<INTERFACES> ... </INTERFACES >: Set of interfaces involved in the tasks defining the workflow

<RESOURCES> ... </RESOURCES >: The set of resources required

<CODE> ... </CODE >: Description of the workflow. Translation of the workflow diagram. The code is divided into three sections, task imports, definition of variables and body of instructions.

```
<CODE>
<IMPORT>
FROM...................
</IMPORT>
<VARAIBLES>
...........................
</VARIABLES>
<BODY>
..........................
</BODY>
</CODE>
```

FUTURE TRENDS

The application of the technology workflow allows to realize a formal design of the processes, and offers a computer support for its execution. In addition, it is a support adapted for the coopera-tive work developed by agents both human and not human processors.

The implementation of a wfms in an organiza-tion carries a set of competitive advantages:

- Formal design of processes for a better planning. And therefore, possibility of re-alizing reengineering on the shaped pro-cesses (bpr).
- Monitoring of the processes on the part of the managers.
- Process simulation before implanting it.
- Automation of the process execution.
- To increase the quality of the service to the user.
- To increase the fulfillment of the require-ments of the client.
- Integration of inherited systems of information.

CONCLUSION

Organisations must adopt new technologies to enable them to face new challenges, and they therefore need to change the way they operate and adopt cooperative, flexible models based on team work, using new computing environments where several applications can be integrated in computing networks.Cooperative IS development methods are guides for all involved: developers, users, clients, executives, and so on. Together, they can obtain a high quality product. This paper thus proposes a cooperative methodology directly involving the members of the organisation, from executives down, throughout the IS development process. The active participation of different members of organization, with previous formation in the methodology, will assure that the system's requirements are fulfilled and oriented towards the organization's strategic plan.

The use of techniques and <u>cooperative</u> tools in the Information System development, facilitate the participation and communication of all the members of the development equipment, assigning the appropriate tasks to each one of the participants, establishing the communication mechanisms to share the necessary information and using a language easily interpreted by all.

It is important to provide support and project management tools in order to automate the proposed methodology, supplying the facilities required for end users to provide all their know-how in a simple manner, monitoring, controlling and auditing the entire IS development process by means of a WfMSSICUMA group of the University of Malaga has some tools to support tasks like: CBD (Cooperation in Data Base) to generate from forms to Data Base scheme and a tool to model Workflow. EXINUS to generate workflows and design interfaces… As future works, we have to design other tools to automate tasks that support to COMIS methodology, like an automatic division of subsystems from workflow, automatic generation of the plan of subsystems integration, control of the activities of administration project, among others.

REFERENCES

Aho, A. V., Sethi, R., & Ullman, J. D. (1998). *Compiladores: Principios, técnicas y herramientas*, Mexico: Addison Wesley Longman.

Arlow, J., & Neustadt, I. (2005). *Uml 2.0 and the unified process*. Reading, MA: Addison Wesley.

Booch, G., Jacobson, I., & Rumbaugh, (2004). *El proceso unificado de desarrollo de software*. Reading, MA: Addison Wesley.

Booch, G., Rumbaugh, J., & Jacobson, I. (2005). *The unified modeling language user guide*. Reading, MA: Addison-Wesley.

Caro, J. L., Guevara, A., & Aguayo, A. (2003). Workflow: A solution for the cooperative development of an information system. *Business Process Management*, *9*(2), 208–220. doi:10.1108/14637150310468407

Caro, J. L., Guevara, A., Aguayo, A., & Leiva, J. L. (2004). *Communication based workflow loop formalization using temporal logic of actions (TLA)*. Paper presented at the 6th International Conference on Enterprise Information Systems, ICEIS 2004, Porto, Portugal.

Caro Herrero, J. L. (2003). *Metodología de modelado de procesos cooperativos en ingeniería de software*. Unpublished master's thesis, University of Málaga, Spain.

Carrillo, A., Falgueras, J., & Guevara, A. (2006). *GDIT: Tool for the design, specification and generation of goals driven user interfaces*. Paper presented at the 8th International Conference on Enterprise Information Systems ICEIS, 2006, Paphos, Cyprus.

Champy, J., & Hammer, M. (1994). *Reengineering*. Ed. Norma.

Costagliola, G., Deufemia, V., Ferrucci, F., & Gravino, C. (2006). Constructing meta-CASE workbenches by exploiting visual language generators. *IEEE Transactions on Software Engineering*, *32*(3), 156–175. doi:10.1109/TSE.2006.23

Di Lucca, G., Fasolino, R., Pace, P., Tramontana, P., & De Carlini, U. (2002). *WARE: A tool for the reverse engineering of Web applications*. Paper presented at the *6th* European Conference on Software Maintenance and Reengineering, IEEE Computer Society, Budapest, Hungary.

Falgueras, J., Guevara, A., Aguayo, A., Gálvez, S., & Gómez, I. (1997). *El interfaz de usuario en el diseño participativo de sistemas de información*. Cádiz, Spain: III Jornadas de Informática.

Gálvez. S. (2000), *Participación del usuario en el diseño cooperativo de bases de datos. Metodología y Herramientas*. Master's thesis, University of Málaga, Spain.

Garrido, J. L. (2003). *AMENITIES: Una metodología para el desarrollo de sistemas cooperativos basada en modelos de comportamiento y tareas*. Unpublished master's thesis, University of Granada, Spain.

Gea, M., Gutiérrez, F. L., Garrido, J. L., & Cañas, J. J. (2003). *Teorías y modelos conceptuales para un diseño basado en grupos*. Paper presented at the IV Congreso Internacional de Interacción Persona-Ordenador, Vigo, Spain.

Granollers. (2004). *MPIu+a. Una metodología que integra la ingeniería del software, la interacción persona-ordenador y la accesibilidad en el contexto de equipos de desarrollo multidisciplinares*. Unpublished master's thesis, University of Lleida, Spain.

Guevara, A., Aguayo, A., Falgueras, J., & Triguero, F. (1995). *Metodología métrica y utilización de técnicas cooperativas (CSCW) en el desarrollo de sistemas de información*. Paper presented at the IV Jornadas sobre Tecnologías de la Información para la Modernización de las Administraciones Públicas. TECNIMAP'95, Palma de Mallorca, Spain.

Guevara, A., Aguayo, A., Triguero, F., & Falgueras, J. (1995). User participation in information systems development techniques and tools. *ACM SIGOIS Bulletin, 16*(1), 68–78. doi:10.1145/209891.209908

Kleppe, A., Warmer, J., & Bast, W. (2003). *Mda explained: The model driven architecture: Practice and promise*. Reading, MA: Addison-Wesley

Kruchten, P. (2003). *The rational unified process: An introduction*. Reading, MA: Addison Wesley Professional.

Leiva, J. L., Guevara, A., & Caro, J. L. (2006). *Aplicación del Modelado workflow a la reingeniería de sistemas de información basándose en interfaces de usuario*. Paper presented at the 1ª Conferencia Ibérica de Sistemas y Tecnologías de la Información, CISTI 2006, Esposende, Portugal.

Leiva, J. L., Guevara, A., Caro, J. L., & Arenas, M. A. (2008). *A cooperative method for system development and maintenance using workflow technologies*. Paper presented at the 10th International Conference on Enterprise Information Systems, ICEIS 2008, Barcelona, Spain.

Merlo, C., & Girard, P. H. (2004). Information system modelling for engineering design co-ordination. *Computers in Industry, 55*(3), 317–334.

Ministerio de Administraciones Públicas. (2000). *Métrica versión 3*. Retrieved from http://www.csi.map.es/csi/metrica3/

Müller, H. A., Jahnke, J. H., & Smith, D. B. (2000). *Reverse engineering: A roadmap*. Paper presented at the Future of Software Engineering Track at the 22nd International Conference on Software Engineering-ICSE 2000, Limerick, Ireland.

Oktaba, H. (2005). *Modelo de procesos para la industria del software. Versión 1.3.* (NMX-059/01-NYCE-2005). Ciudad de México: Organismo nacional de normalización y evaluación de la conformidad.

Post, G., & Kagan, A. (2000). OO-CASE tools: An evaluation of rose. *Information and Software Technology, 42*(6), 383–388. doi:10.1016/S0950-5849(99)00099-3

Rialp, A. (2003). *Fundamentos teóricos de la organización de empresas*. Pirámide Ediciones.

Sorenson, P. G., Findeisen, P. S., & Tremblay, J. P. (1996). Supporting viewpoints in metaview. In *Joint proceedings of the second international software architecture workshop (ISAW-2) and international workshop on multiple perspectives in software development (Viewpoints '96) on SIGSOFT '96 workshops*. San Francisco: ACM Press.

Woods, S., Carriere, S. J., & Kazman, R. (1999). *A semantic foundation for architectural reengineering and interchange*. Paper presented at the International Conference on Software Maintenance-ICSM- 99, Oxford, UK.

Workflow Management Coalition. (1995). *The workflow reference model, DN:TC00-1003 (Versión 1.1)*. Retrieved from http://www.wfmc.org/standards/docs/tc003v11.pdf

ENDNOTE

[1] A leading process is the first process in a basic block

Chapter 14
Designing Open–Source OMIS Environment for Virtual Teams to Support Inter–Enterprise Collaboration

Kam Hou Vat
University of Macau, Macau

ABSTRACT

Today companies large and small have taken to open source as a way to increase collaboration, reduce development costs, provide a friendly platform for their products and services. Underlying this movement is a set of concerns related to the initiative to allow knowledge workers across different enterprises to participate in joint project work, resulting in some inter-organizational processes of knowledge sharing, to be modeled and followed by other enterprises of interest. This formulation, in terms of discovering business mutual benefits, could be considered as the open source philosophy behind an enterprise's co-operation with other counterparts. In the specific context of establishing enterprise information systems (EIS) to enable organizations (especially small and medium enterprises) to integrate and coordinate their business processes, the stakes can be high in light of maintaining a company's competitive advantages. Whether open source will work at any company depends on both the capabilities of the company and the maturity of the open source processes and hence the software to support them. This article investigates the context of knowledge networks among virtual teams of professionals as the case-in-point discussion on a specific type of open source knowledge environment based on the Wiki technology, called organizational memory information system (OMIS) to support people working within and across organizational boundaries with technology. The issues of trust and shared understanding among organizations using the relevant OMIS environment is also deliberated in the discussion alongside the technology alignment and process adaptation for managing the OMIS-based collaboration among members of the knowledge networks.

DOI: 10.4018/978-1-60566-856-7.ch014

INTRODUCTION

Today, the scope of open source has grown beyond basic development tools (Fogel, 2006) to become a top-to-bottom infrastructure for computing of all stripes, including development environments, databases, operating systems, web servers, application servers, and utilities for all types of data center management. By open source (Woods & Guliani, 2005; Golden, 2005), we are referring to software that has source code available to its users. It can be downloaded at will and used or modified as desired, as long as its license requirements are observed. Typically, commercial software licenses reflect the rights of the creator to control how the software is distributed. They protect the intellectual property of the creator(s). Yet, open source licenses differ significantly from commercial software licenses. Commercial licenses restrict the use of the software as much as possible, to enhance the possibility of selling many licenses. In contrast, open source licenses are written with the aim of encouraging widespread use, with very few restrictions placed on the use of the software. Also, open source software is often distributed at no cost. This makes sense because it reflects the reality of source code availability. Thereby, a clear model of how open source for the enterprise (Woods & Guliani, 2005) comes to life is crucial to understand the life cycle of open source development for enterprise information systems (EIS) (Dunn, Cherrington, & Hollander, 2005) and its attendant processes, which have incrementally become essential in the process of organization development in the Internet age. Of critical concern here is the electronic medium (such as the Web) to support knowledge sharing (Vat, 2006) referring mainly to the activities that define expectations, enable empowerment, or verify performance of the people or units involved. In the specific context of competitive advantages, the transformative impact of an open source effort on the intellectual and social capital of an enterprise is not to be ignored (Stewart, 1997). Our discussion centers on conceiving specific EIS whose open source design relates to the practical rendering of IS (information systems) support for virtual teams within and across enterprises, for such purposeful organizational activities as collaborative project work and knowledge sharing for given areas of responsibilities (Vat, 2005, 2002). The framework of analysis employed should accommodate the configuration of an organization's value profile in cyberspace as exemplified in today's digital economy (Tapscott, 1997). This framework puts in perspective many an enterprise's efforts to nurture intra- and inter-organizational knowledge environments to support the value shop model of organizational memory (OM), mostly known as the OMIS, the organizational memory information system (Vat, 2008, 2001), in which value is created by configuring and applying specific knowledge to problems of interest to customers. The chapter concludes by elaborating on the issues behind open source for the enterprise OMIS, providing a sense-making perspective on the challenge to overcome barriers to knowledge sharing among virtual teams distributed throughout any network of business collaboration.

THE CONTEXT OF ENTERPRISE INFORMATION SYSTEMS

The idea of an enterprise information system (EIS) could be understood from the context of the two terms: enterprise and information system. The former could be defined as an organization (Hall, 2002) established to achieve a particular undertaking involving industrious, systematic activity. Today, whether the undertaking of an enterprise is profit driven or charity motivated, the enterprise needs an information system to support its activities. An information system (IS) is often defined as the network of all communication channels used within an organization (Dunn, Cherrington, & Hollander, 2004, pp. 1-2). This IS definition is quite consistent with the view (Checkland &

Holwell, 1998) that an organization is often seen at core as a social process, essentially a conversational process in which the world is interpreted by organizational members in a particular way which legitimates shared actions and establishes shared norms and standards. Indeed, organizations are also regarded as networks of conversation or communicative exchanges in which commitments are generated (Ciborra, 1987; Winograd & Flores, 1986). And IS support could be thought of as making such exchanges easier – the exchange support systems. Certainly computer technology is an important component of most modern IS; namely, any paths by which enterprise employees and business partners impart and receive information are included in the EIS. Typically, an EIS provides a technology platform that enables an organization to integrate and coordinate her business processes. It comprises different pieces integrated into a whole system that is central to the organization and ensures that information can be shared across all functional levels and management hierarchies. Put more simply, an EIS can be defined as a set of communication channels in a business organization, combined together in such a way as to form one network by which information is gathered and disseminated.

DEFINING EIS FOR LEARNING ORGANIZATION

In today's knowledge economy (OECD, 1996), many an organization is being compelled to question their entire existing operation and try to redesign it in a way that uses new technology to serve their organization better. Indeed, the excitement brought about by the Internet and the corresponding changes in organizational behavior, has prompted speculation about what the future generations of EIS support will look like for knowledge work, which is essentially subjective, eclectic, individual, context-specific and often one-off making it traditionally the most difficult

to support with technology. Meanwhile, amidst the learning organization movement (Vat, 2003; Gregory, 2000; Jashapara, 1993; Garvin, 1993; Senge, 1990) towards empowering responsible organizations (and their human members) to create innovative IS support to meet the challenges of the knowledge-intensive organizations, there is a strong need to share knowledge in a way that makes it easier for individuals, teams, and enterprises to work together to effectively contribute to an organization's success. Therefore, enterprises are often confronted with the question of how to design EIS in support of the learning expected of today's organizations (King, 1996; Levine, 2001). Example support could include such features as structured and unstructured dialogue and negotiation among colleagues; creative synthesis of knowledge in integrating working and learning; documentation of data, information and knowledge as it builds up; and retrieval of recorded data, information and knowledge, as well as access to individuals with the necessary knowledge resources. To this end, the acronym "LOIS" (Learning Organization Information System) (Williamson & Lliopoulos, 2001) as applied to an organization is often used as a collective term representing the conglomeration of various information systems, each of which, being a functionally defined subsystem of the enterprise IS, is distinguished through the services it renders. An example to be discussed in this chapter is the organizational memory information system (OMIS) whose purpose is to facilitate organizational knowledge transfer within and without an enterprise. Collectively, a LOIS can be considered as a scheme to improve the organization's chances for success and survival by continuously adapting to both the internal and the external challenges. Consequently, we stand a better chance of increasing social participation and shared understanding within the enterprise, and thus foster better learning. Although we believe that this positioning of EIS represents a significant vision of a future generation of information systems, there are serious questions to be addressed in connection with design approach used to characterize knowledge capture and sharing within the enterprise (Tabaka, 2006). All these have consequences for enterprise transformation (Rouse, 2006) in such areas as strategies, structures, processes, systems and people.

THE KNOWLEDGE POTENTIAL OF LOIS-BASED NETWORKS

In a world of growing competitive pressures and accelerated transformation of economies (Hamel & Prahalad, 1994), knowledge is increasingly recognized as an important source of value generation in modern organizations. In particular, the ability to create knowledge and move it from one part of the organization to another is the basis for competitive advantage (Inkpen, 1996; Jashapara, 1993). Modern information and communication technology (ICT) has played a central role in this by making it easier for small and medium-sized companies to form network links (Figallo & Rhine, 2002) and by facilitating the transformation of hierarchical organizations into ones based on networks of EIS (Malone & Laubacher, 1998). Yet, the central domain of an enterprise is often considered as the social network (Badaracco, 1991) that absorbs, creates, transforms, and communicates knowledge taking advantage of any LOIS blueprint of the organization. Indeed, this network concept has been approached in different ways (Nohria, 1992). While some approaches focus more on the structural aspect of networks, others tend to emphasize the processes of or relations within or between networks. One frequently quoted definition from Mitchell (1969, p.2) is this: a network is a specific set of linkages among a defined set of actors, with the additional property that the characteristics of these linkages as a whole may be used to interpret the social behavior of the actors involved. Consequently, the term knowledge network can be interpreted as a social relationship between actors. And ac-

tors in a social network of knowledge sharing can be persons, groups, collectives of organizations, communities or even societies. Today, hardly any industry remains unaffected by the evolution of network-like relationships within and between organizations (Fleish, 2000; Lodge & Walton, 1989). The term 'knowledge networking' is often used to describe the assembling of people, resources, relationships and communication technologies in order to accumulate, transfer and use knowledge for the purpose of creating value. Knowledge resources are continuously augmented by knowledge gained from learning situations, and therefore knowledge networks should be regarded as dynamic structures rather than static institutions. Thereby, in order to enhance the interaction of network members, it is necessary to examine their relationships, which are considered as the platforms for knowledge exchange, in which relationships can vary in duration and intensity, as well as in terms of frequency of interactions. But, they imply personal involvement, commitment, care and the optimum use of communication tools. Still, the flow of knowledge in the network is subject to such factors as the size and characteristics of the network, entry barriers, participation difficulties, as well as peculiar ownership issues.

POSITIONING TEAMWORK IN KNOWLEDGE NETWORKS

In the context of knowledge creation, whether the objective is to develop a new product or service or to design and implement a new organizational technology, such as a new ICT system, the key resource that is required is unquestionably knowledge such as that of the markets and customers, that of the available technologies, and that of materials. These different types of knowledge must be brought together so that new knowledge is created which leads to the development of the new product, service or organizational process. Typically, this diversity of knowledge will not be possessed in a single individual, but rather will be dispersed both within the organization, say, across functional groups, and across organizations, say, with consultants or suppliers. Thus, knowledge creation, within the context of an organization or knowledge network, is typically the outcome of an interactive process that will involve a number of individuals who are brought together in a project team or some other collaborative arrangement. The successful completion of project tasks will often depend on selecting team members with appropriate knowledge, skills and expertise, so teams ideally will be chosen so that their members have a mix of knowledge and capabilities. We can refer to this as the intellectual capital of the team, or what Nahapiet and Ghoshal (1998, p. 245) call the "knowledge and knowing capability of a social collectivity." In fact, intellectual capital and its mix across the team, is important because in any group-based project work, team members are not likely to have all the relevant knowledge and expertise required, either to design the system, product or service per se or to ensure that it is accepted and implemented by all those for whom it is intended. Rather, team members will need to network with a range of other individuals in order to appropriate the necessary knowledge. In doing this, they will be drawing upon their collective social capital, defined by (Nahapiet & Ghoshal, 1998, p.243) as the "sum of actual and potential resources within, available through, and derived from the network of relationships possessed by an individual or social unit." Thereby, knowledge creation needs to be seen as an interactive teamwork process – one which involves a diverse range of actors with different backgrounds, cutting across organizational boundaries, and combining skills, artifacts, knowledge and experiences in appropriate ways. It is no doubt that teamwork should lead to more creative solutions than would arise if individuals (or individual organizations) worked alone or in sequence on a particular project. Still, effective teamwork must be cultivated, especially when the team members come from different backgrounds

and have different disciplinary knowledge bases. The key is trust to be developed. This is seen to be perhaps the most critical issue for effective teamwork in knowledge sharing.

EMPOWERING KNOWLEDGE NETWORKING THROUGH VIRTUAL TEAMS

Knowledge is often considered as an objective commodity that is transferable independently of person and context. In light of this, many an organization has tried to solve problems and enhanced knowledge sharing by improving the information flow through the intensive use of modern technologies such as intranet-based yellow pages, knowledge maps and information warehouses. The potential of these technologies is undisputed. Nevertheless, what is also required is an integrated approach that includes both explicit and tacit knowledge where and how it is created and transferred. In practice, in order to make effective use of knowledge, networks must incorporate and make available the knowledge and experience of employees in their daily context of organizational working, learning, and innovating (Brown & Duguid, 1991). Working is traditionally seen as the production and delivery of products or services. Oftentimes, attention is focused on the efficiency with which this is achieved; so, working is frequently resistant to modification. Understandably, learning is explicitly regarded as the absorption of new knowledge, though the focus is typically on individual employees' acquisition of knowledge, rather than on encouraging them to learn how to learn, and how to interlink areas of knowledge. This tends to obstruct the conversion of new knowledge into working skills (Seufert & Seufert, 1999). Meanwhile, innovating is often associated with revolutionary proposals developed in a research and development context. Admittedly, this form of innovation is an important part of change in general, but it is just one end of a continuum of innovations that also take the form of improvements in daily business, such as continuous process improvements. Consequently, taking too narrow a view of working, learning, and innovating can possibly lead to the strengthening of various barriers: functional and hierarchical barriers; barriers to customers, suppliers and cooperative partners; and mental barriers that impede the generation, transfer, and application of new knowledge. These could not only hinder the short-term flow of knowledge, but in the long term can also damage the organization's innovative and learning capabilities. Thereby, knowledge networking must render a conceptual framework to rethink the knowledge sharing model, with which knowledge barriers can be overcome by networking, and knowledge islands could be cross-linked to stimulate the evolution, dissemination and application of knowledge. In the peculiar context of inter-organizational collaboration, the openness and richness of OMIS to support virtual teams over knowledge networks are believed to offer fertile environment for the creation of new knowledge as well as the acceleration of innovation (Powell, Koput, et al., 1996). Importantly, to be considered virtual to some degree, a team must have some basic attributes (Gibson & Cohen, 2003): Firstly, it must be a functioning team – a collection of individuals who are interdependent in their tasks, share responsibility for outcomes, see themselves and are viewed by others as an intact social unit embedded in one or more social systems, and collectively manage their relationships across organizational boundaries (Hackman, 1987; Alderfer, 1977); Secondly, the members of the team are geographically dispersed; Thirdly, the team relies on technology-mediated communications rather than face-to-face interaction to accomplish their tasks. It is the degree of reliance on electronic communication that increases virtuality often thought of as a spectrum from slightly virtual to extremely virtual. In fact, where a team exists on this spectrum is a function of the amount of dependence on electronically mediated communication and the degree of geographical dispersion.

OMIS – AN ORGANIZATIONAL LEARNING AND KNOWLEDGE TRANSFER MECHANISM

The success of today's enterprises, measured in terms of their ability to learn and to apply lessons learned, is highly dependent on the inner workings and capabilities of their information technology (IT) function. This is largely due to the emergence of the digital economy (Ghosh, 2006; Turban, Leidner, McLean, & Wetherbe, 2005), characterized by a highly competitive and turbulent business environment, inextricably driven by the intra- and inter-organizational processes and the associated knowledge processing activities they support. One visible consequence is the increase in organizations' efforts to deliberately manage knowledge (Tapscott, 1997), especially the intellectual capital (Stewart, 1997; Menon, 1993) of their employees, which necessarily deals with the conceptualization, review, consolidation, and action phrases of creating, securing, combining, coordinating, and retrieving knowledge (De Hoog, et al, 1999). In a knowledge-creating company (Nonaka & Takeuchi, 1995), such efforts must be instrumental to enable the organization to launch and learn. Meanwhile, employees are expected to continually improvise, and invent new methods to deal with unexpected problems, and share these innovations with other employees through some effective communication channels or knowledge transfer mechanisms. The key is collaboration, implying that organizational knowledge is created only when individuals keep modifying their knowledge through interactions with other organizational members be it within or without the organization. The challenge that organizations now face is how to devise suitable information systems (IS) support to enable such collaboration, namely, to turn the scattered, diverse knowledge of their people into well-documented knowledge assets ready for reuse to benefit the whole organization or her affiliated knowledge network. This important context of employee-based collaboration through the design of specific IS support constitutes the core of the organizational memory information system (OMIS) (Vat, 2008, 2005).

Defining Organizational Memory

By organizational memory (Walsh and Ungson 1991), we are referring to various structures within an organization that hold knowledge in one form or another, such as databases and other information stores, work processes, procedures, and product or service architecture. As a result, an organizational memory (OM) must be nurtured to assimilate new ideas and transform those ideas into action and knowledge, which could benefit the rest of the organization (Ulrich, Von Glinlow, & Jick 1993). Through understanding the important components of the OM (Vat, 2006, 2002, 2001), an organization can better appreciate how it is currently learning from its key experiences, to ensure that relevant knowledge becomes embedded within the future operations and practices of the organization. In practice, creating and using an OM is a cooperative activity, necessarily involving many members of the organization. If those individuals are not adequately motivated in contributing to the OM initiative, and the organizational culture does not support knowledge sharing (Orlinkowski, 1992), it is not likely to turn the scattered, diverse knowledge present in various forms, into well-structured knowledge assets ready for deposit and reuse in the OM.

Differentiating OM and OMIS

Operationally, it is important to distinguish between the organizational memory (OM encompassing people) and the OMIS that captures in a computational form only part of the knowledge of the organization. The OM captures the knowledge of the organization. The associated OMIS makes part of this knowledge available either by providing direct access to it (for example, codified knowledge assets such as experience reports),

or indirectly by providing knowledge maps (for example, tacit knowledge assets such as personnel with specific expertise). Managing the OM deals first of all with the question of "Which knowledge should go into the OMIS?" Answering this question requires determining what knowledge is owned by the members of the organization, what knowledge is needed now, what is going to be needed in the future and for what purposes. This helps the organization to define not only a strategy for acquiring the needed knowledge, but also to establish validation criteria in relation to the defined goals. Besides, we also need to deal with "who needs the knowledge, when and why," as well as the policies for accessing and using the OMIS. This contextualization of the OMIS with respect to the organization's ability to learn is essential to implement the mechanisms of organizational knowledge transfer, examples of which are discussed in (Vat, 2006). In fact, in this modern age of information technology and swift change, learning has become an integral part of the work of an organization run along principles intended to encourage constant reshaping and change. An OMIS-based organization can be characterized as one, which continuously transform herself by developing the skills of all her people and by achieving what Chris Argyris has called double-loop learning (Argyris 1992), which helps transfer learning from individuals to a group, provide for organizational renewal, keep an open attitude to the outside world, and support a commitment to knowledge. One of the missions of the OMIS is to facilitate and bring about the fundamental shifts in thinking and interacting and the new capabilities needed in the organization.

Designing Services for OMIS

When designing an OMIS to nurture an organization's ability to learn (Vat, 2001; 2002), of particular interest are the following modes of learning behavior: 1) individual, 2) group, and 3) repository. Individual learning is characterized by knowledge being developed, and possibly the result of combining an insight with know-how from other sources in the organization, but it is often not distributed and is not secured for reuse. Group learning is centered about the concept of communication in two possible modes: supply-driven, or demand-driven. The former is characterized by an individual who has found a way to improve the work process and communicates this to one's co-workers. The latter refers to a worker who has recognized a problem in the current process and asks fellow workers whether they have a solution for this problem. In each case, knowledge is developed, distributed, and possibly combined with knowledge from other parts of the organization, but it is seldom secured. In repository learning, the communication element is replaced by collection, storage and retrieval of knowledge items. Namely, it is typified by storing lessons learned in some information repository so that they can be retrieved and used when needed. Overall, in repository learning, knowledge is developed, secured, distributed, and is possibly the result of knowledge combination. It is convinced that the requirements of an OMIS design should be formulated in terms of some typical usage scenarios. Namely, an OMIS should facilitate individual workers to access the knowledge required by combination, to submit a lesson learned, and to decide which of the co-workers would be interested in a lesson learned. Also, there should be criteria to determine if something is a lesson learned, how it should be formulated and where it should be stored, and how to distribute some newly asserted knowledge piece to the workers in need. The perceived technical issues, nevertheless, could include the following: How are we to organize and index the OM to enhance its diffusion? How to retrieve relevant elements of the OM to answer a user request or proactively push relevant elements towards users? How to adapt the answer to users, in particular to their tasks, according to the knowledge contexts? These problems are largely related to the OM framework for knowledge distribution, whose goal is to improve organizational learning, with the aid of some innovative OMIS support the discussion of which, through the idea of service-orientation could be found in (Vat, 2008).

FUTURE TRENDS OF OPEN-SOURCE OMIS DEVELOPMENT

To collaborate is to work in a joint intellectual effort, to partition problem solving to produce a synergy such that the performance of the whole exceeds that of any individual contributor. The central issue in OMIS-based collaboration for inter-organizational knowledge networking is how individual learning is transferred to the organizational level and beyond. In this regard, the use of open source Wiki technology (http://www.wiki.org) as a collaborative tool within an organizational setting renders an excellent example. Yet, only with a clear understanding of the transfer process can we manage learning processes consistent with organizational goals, issues and values. If this transfer process were indeed actualized in the design and practice of the OMIS, we could well have a knowledge organization which has the capability of capturing learning in its different paths and incorporating that learning into the running of its daily operations.

The Design Aspects of Wiki Technology

Wiki is an open source technology. The software that operates any Wiki is called a Wiki engine (Kille, 2006). A variety of free Wiki engines (also known as Wiki clones) are available from the Web (http://www.wiki.org). There are also Wiki hosts offering Wiki service with a minimal fee, such as the Seedwiki (http://www.seedwiki.com), and JotSpot (http://www.jot.com). The first Wiki application invented by Ward Cunningham in 1995 was to publish information collaboratively on the Web (Leuf & Cunningham, 2001), and this first Wiki Web site (http://c2.com/cgi/wiki) is still actively maintained today. Leuf and Cunningham define a Wiki (Hawaiian word meaning quick) as a freely expandable collection of interlinked Web pages, a hypertext system for storing and modifying information (Leuf & Cunningham, 2001, p14). Cunningham's original vision was to create a Wiki as the simplest online database that could possibly work. Today, Wikis are interactive Web sites that can offer numerous benefits to users (Wagner, 2004), in the form of a simple editing and publishing interface that can be used and understood easily. Anyone can create a new Wiki page, add or edit content in an existing Wiki page, and delete content within a page, without any prior knowledge or skills in editing and publishing on the Web. In fact, the major distinguishing factor between Wikis and regular Web sites is the ability of Wiki users to easily edit all aspects of a Wiki Web site. Fuchs-Kittowsk and Kohler (2002) interpret a Wiki as an open author system for a conjoined construction and maintenance of Web sites (p.10). They suggest that Wiki technology can facilitate cooperative work and knowledge generation in such contexts as content management system, discussion board, and other innovative forms of groupware. Indeed, members of a Wiki community can build and develop meaningful topic associations by creating numerous links among Wiki pages. To make the Wiki technology useful for collaborative work in organizations, Wagner (2004) suggested eleven principles that govern the functional design of a Wiki application (p.270):

- **Open:** If a Wiki page is found to be incomplete or poorly organized, any reader can edit it as he/she sees fit.
- **Incremental:** Wiki pages can cite other pages, including pages that have not been written yet.
- **Organic:** The structure and text content of the site is open to editing and evolution.

- **Mundane:** A small number of (irregular) text conventions will provide access to the most useful but limited page markup.
- **Universal:** The mechanisms of editing and organizing are the same as those of writing, so that any writer is automatically an editor and organizer.
- **Overt:** The formatted (and printed) output will suggest the input required to reproduce it.
- **Unified:** Page names will be drawn from a flat space so that no additional context is required to interpret them.
- **Precise:** Pages will be titled with sufficient precision to avoid most name clashes, typically by forming noun phrases.
- **Tolerant:** Interpretable (even if undesirable) behavior is preferred to error message.
- **Observable:** Activity within the site can be watched and reviewed by any other visitor to the site. Wiki pages are developed based on trust.
- **Convergent:** Duplication can be discouraged or removed by finding and citing similar or related content.

The Knowledge Potential of Wiki as a Collaborative Tool

According to Wagner (2004) and Raman, Ryan and Olfman (2005), the use of Wiki technology can address some knowledge management goals for collaborative work and organizational learning. Here, a knowledge management system refers to any IT-based system that is developed to support and enhance the organizational processes of knowledge creation, storage, retrieval, transfer and application (Alavi & Leidner, 2001, p. 114). In particular, any Wiki clone can be designed to support such basic functions as searching and indexing capabilities for effective retrieval and storage of knowledge attributes. The most often cited benefits of using Wikis to support collaborative work thereby include the simplicity of learning and working with the technology, and the free download through the Wiki engines all the necessary knowledge items of interest throughout the organization. More importantly, Davenport and Prusak (1998) provide three essential reasons why organizations need such a technology to implement its knowledge management systems: 1) to enhance visibility of knowledge in organizations through the use of maps, hypertexts, yellow pages, and directories; 2) to build a knowledge culture, namely, to create avenues for employees to share knowledge; and 3) to develop a knowledge infrastructure, not confined solely to technology, but to create an environment that permits collaborative work. Promisingly, if designed and implemented effectively, Wiki technology can support a large portion of an organization's collaboration and knowledge management requirements – specifically, knowledge sharing, storing, and support for the communication process within organizations. A key advantage of using Wikis to support knowledge management initiatives is that the technology is free. Nonetheless, issues such as sufficient user training, the availability of resources and skills to support the technology, and effective customization of Wiki features must be considered before the value of using the technology to support collaborative work within and across any organization is to be realized.

REMARKS OF CONTINUING CHALLENGE FOR VIRTUAL TEAMS

Teams in general and virtual teams in particular, are complex social forms whose effectiveness is often the result of multiple practices (Gibson & Cohen, 2003; Lipnack & Stamps, 2000). To promote the working of virtual teams, it is important to create the conditions that support their effectiveness. This in turn requires to identify the many design and implementation factors, such as the organizational context (selection, training, and rewarding of team

members), task characteristics, technology use, team member skill profiles, as well as work and team processes. Besides, the degree of virtuality amplifies the challenges that such teams face. As teams become more virtual, they confront greater uncertainty and complexity, increasing the difficulty of the information processing and sense-making tasks that they do. Meanwhile, since virtual teams are typically composed of members representing different disciplines, functions, professions, business units, organizations, countries, and cultures, the greater the number and depth of differences that need to be managed, the greater are the barriers to team effectiveness. Thereby, virtual teams must be designed, supported, and nurtured in a careful manner to be successful. Nonetheless, even though the working of virtual teams is yet to be readily smooth, the reality is that virtual teams have the potential to amplify the benefits of teamwork; namely, they could enable the best talent regardless of location to be applied to solve different business problems, create products, and deliver services. Cross-organizational teams can be set up to capitalize on each enterprise's unique competencies. When knowledge networks comprise virtual teams with people from different perspectives and knowledge bases (high degree of differences), innovation is more likely to occur (Pinchot, 1985), such that problems can be framed in ways that allow people to apply knowledge from one domain to another. Besides, relying on electronically mediated communication reduces the cost of coordination, and hence, the benefits of efficiency, as an important competitive advantage. Yet, what are the enabling conditions to harness the potential of virtual teams? According to Gibson and Cohen (2003, p. 8-10), there are three enabling conditions that need to be established: shared understanding, integration, and mutual trust.

- **Shared Understanding:** It is important for virtual team to develop shared understanding (or common perspective among members of the team, concerning some specific object of interest, such as project goals or difficulties) about what they are trying to achieve (their goals), how they will achieve them (work and group processes), what they need to do (their tasks), and what each team member brings to the teamwork (member knowledge, skills, and abilities). When teams involve people from different disciplines, business units, organizations, and cultures, their members will have different ways of perceiving their tasks, key issues, and making sense of their situation. Dougherty (1992) used the term "thought worlds" to describe new product development team members because of such differences. By developing shared understandings, virtual teams learn how to bridge the chasm between thought worlds.

- **Integration:** It is important to establish ways in which different parts of an organization can work together to create value, develop products, or deliver services. This is the idea behind integration; however, the parts of the organization(s) represented by virtual team members are likely to be peculiarly differentiated in response to global competitive pressures and changing business environments. This differentiation across organizational units means that they are likely to have different policies, organizational structures, and systems of operation. Such differences can hinder effective collaboration in virtual teams both directly or indirectly. In a more subtle way, business unit policies, structures, and systems influence employee behaviors, providing incentives for some such as more company-wide collaboration and disincentives for others such as less cross-organizational conversations. The greater the degree of differentiation in an organization, the greater is the need for integration. The formation of

virtual team is one mechanism to encourage integration. Other examples could include: access to communication channels, social coordination through agreed norms, providing individuals with particular role responsibilities for linking individuals together, assigning authority and control to particular individuals, careful selection of individuals to ensure an appropriate mix of skills and expertise, and utilizing incentive systems.

- **Mutual trust:** Trust is defined in different ways in the literature (Rousseau, Sitkin, Burt, & Camerer, 1998; Cummings & Bromiley, 1996), although two issues seem quite relevant: first, that trust is about dealing with risk and uncertainty; and second, that trust is about accepting vulnerability. Namely, to trust someone there must be a situation of uncertainty in which there is an element of perceived risk on the trustee's part: "the willingness of a party to be vulnerable to the actions of another party based on the expectation that the other will perform a particular action important to the trustor, irrespective of the ability to monitor or control that other party" (Mayer et al., 1995, p. 172). In the context of virtual team, mutual trust is a shared psychological state characterized by an acceptance of vulnerability based on expectations of intentions or behaviors of others within the team. Luhmann (1988) sees trust as an attitudinal mechanism that allows individuals to subjectively assess whether or not to expose themselves to situations where the possible damage may outweigh the advantage. Teams that have established mutual trust are safe environments for their members, who are thereby willing to take risks with one another and let their vulnerabilities show. There are, however, many sources of vulnerabilities that may be at risk in collaborative situations, such as reputation and self-esteem, especially when members of virtual teams are geographically dispersed, and are of different backgrounds having diverse experiences and cultures. Typically, people tend to trust those whom they perceive as similar to themselves, but electronically mediated communication lacks the interpersonal cues essential for trust building. Likewise, it is often necessary to install special measures to establish trust in virtual teams, examples of which can be found in (Gibson & Manuel, 2003).

CONCLUSION

One of the most obvious characteristics of human beings is our readiness to attribute meaning to what we observe and experience in the world outside ourselves. If information is interpreted as what we get when human being attribute meaning to data in a particular context, then an enterprise information system (EIS), in the full sense, will be a meaning attribution system in which people select certain data out of the mass potentially available and get them processed to make them meaningful in a particular context in order to support those engaged in purposeful action (Checkland & Holwell 1995; Checkland & Haynes, 1994). Thus, if we wish to create an appropriate OMIS in the exact sense of the phrase, we must first understand how people in the specific situation conceptualize their world. We must find out the meanings they attribute to their perceptions of the world and hence understand which action in the world they regard as sensible purposeful action, and why. Having obtained that understanding we shall be in a position to build some of the purposeful models, and use them to stimulate debate aimed at defining some human activity systems (HAS) (Wilson, 2001) widely regarded by people within

the situation as truly relevant to what they see as the required real-world action. Once an agreed truly relevant system has emerged, the use of HAS-based system development requires us to ask of each activity in the model the following questions: What information would have to be available to enable someone to do this activity? From what source would it be obtained, in what form, with what frequency? Besides, we need to be aware of what information would be generated by doing this activity? To whom should it go, in what form, with what frequency? In this way, an activity model may be converted into an information-flow model. Given the information-flow model, which is agreed to be a necessary feature of the situation studied (say, virtual teamwork), we may then ask: What data structures could embody the information categories that characterize such information flows? It is only then that we could start the design of a suitable information system, which should yield the information categories and information flows required by the structured set of activities regarded as truly relevant to the real-world action (say, inter-enterprise collaboration) that is itself relevant according to the meanings which people in the situation (virtual teams) attribute to their world as a result of their worldviews. Hence, those engaged in the tasks of building LOIS (or OMIS) support are involved in the delicate business of creating, within the organization, a conglomeration of different human activity systems (HAS) using the term from soft systems thinking (Checkland & Scholes, 1999). To create an entirely new organizational dynamics of OMIS to support virtual teamwork across any knowledge network, through the HAS's actually requires effort and commitment on the part of everyone involved, as well as a good imagination in the mind of the persons charged with directing its implementation.

REFERENCES

Alavi, M., & Leidner, D. E. (2001). Review: Knowledge management and knowledge management systems: Conceptual foundations and research issue. *MIS Quarterly, 25*(1), 107–136. doi:10.2307/3250961

Alderfer, C. P. (1977). Group and inter-group relations. In J.R. Hackman & J.L. Suttle (Eds.), *Improving the quality of work life.* Palisades, CA: Goodyear.

Argyris, C. (1992). *On organizational learning.* Cambridge, MA: Blackwell Business.

Back, A., von Krogh, G., & Seufert, A. (2006). *Getting real about knowledge networks: Unlocking corporate knowledge assets.* New York: Palgrave.

Badaracco, J. (1991). *The knowledge link.* Boston: Harvard Business School Press.

Brown, J. S., & Duguid, P. (1991). Organizational learning and communities of practice: Toward a unified view of working, learning and innovation. *Organization Science, 2*(1), 40–57. doi:10.1287/orsc.2.1.40

Checkland, P., & Haynes, M. (1994). Varieties of systems thinking: The case of soft systems methodology. *System Dynamics Review, 10*(2-3), 189–197. doi:10.1002/sdr.4260100207

Checkland, P., & Holwell, S. (1998). *Information, systems, and information systems: Making sense of the field.* Chichester, England: John Wiley and Sons.

Checkland, P., & Scholes, J. (1999). *Soft systems methodology in action.* Chichester, England: Wiley.

Ciborra, C. U. (1987). Research agenda for a transaction costs approach to information systems. In R. J. Boland & R. A. Hirschheim (Eds.), *Critical issues in information systems research.* Chichester, England: John Wiley and Sons.

Cohen, S. G., & Bailey, D. E. (1997). What makes team work: Group effectiveness research from the shop floor to the executive suite. *Journal of Management, 23*(3), 239–290. doi:10.1177/014920639702300303

Cummings, L. L., & Bromiley, P. (1996). The organizational trust inventory (OTI): Development and validation. In R.M. Kramer & T.R. Tyler (Eds.), *Trust in organizations: Frontiers of theory and research.* Thousand Oaks, CA: Sage.

Davenport, T. H., & Prusak, L. (1998). *Working knowledge: How organizations manage what they know.* Boston, MA: Harvard Business School Press.

De Hoog, R., van Heijst, G., van der Spek, R., et al. (1999). Investigating a theoretical framework for knowledge management: A gaming approach. In J. Liebowitz (Ed.), *Knowledge management handbook* (pp. 10-1). Berlin, Germany: Springer-Verlag.

Dougherty, D. (1992). Interpretive barriers to successful product innovation in large firms. *Organization Science, 3*(2), 179–202. doi:10.1287/orsc.3.2.179

Dunn, C., Cherrington, J. O., & Hollander, A. S. (2005). *Enterprise information systems: A pattern-based approach.* Boston, MA: McGraw-Hill.

Figallo, C., & Rhine, N. (2002). *Building the knowledge management network: Best practices and techniques for putting conversation to work.* New York: Wiley Technology Publishing.

Fleisch, E. (2000). *Das netzwerkunternehmen: Strategien und prozesse zur steigerung der wettbewerbsfahigkeit in der networked economy.* Berlin, Germany: Springer.

Fogel, K. (2006). *Producing open source: How to run a successful free software project.* Sebastopol, CA: O'Reilly.

Fuchs-Kittowsk, F., & Kohler, A. (2002). Knowledge creating communities in the context of work processes. *ACM SIGCSE Bulletin, 23*(3), 8–13.

Garvin, D. A. (1993). Building a learning organization. *Harvard Business Review, 71*(4), 78–91.

Ghosh, R. A. (2006). *CODE: Collaborative ownership and the digital economy.* Boston: MIT Press.

Gibson, C. B., & Cohen, S. G. (Eds.). (2003) *Virtual teams that work: Creating conditions for virtual team effectiveness.* San Francisco, CA: Jossey-Bass.

Gibson, C. B., & Manuel, J. A. (2003). Building trust: Effective multicultural communication processes in virtual teams. In C.B. Gibson & S.G. Cohen (Eds.), *Virtual teams that work: Creating conditions for virtual team effectiveness* (pp. 59-86). San Francisco: Jossey-Bass.

Golden, B. (2005). *Succeeding with open source.* Boston, MA: Addison-Wesley.

Gregory, V. (2000). Knowledge management and building the learning organization. In T.K. Srikantaiah, & E.D. Koenig (Eds.), *Knowledge management: For the information professional* (pp. 161-179). ASIS: Information Today, Inc.

Hackman, J. R. (1987). The design of work teams. In J.W. Lorsch (Ed.), *Handbook of organizational behavior.* Upper Saddle River, NJ: Prentice Hall.

Hackman, J. R. (1990). Work teams in organizations: An orienting framework. In J.R. Hackman (Ed.), *Groups that work (and those that don't): Creating conditions for effective teamwork.* San Francisco: Jossey-Bass.

Hamel, G., & Prahalad, C. (1994). *Competing for the future.* Boston: Harvard Business School Press.

Inkpen, A. C. (1996). Creating knowledge through collaboration. *California Management Review, 39*(1), 123–140.

Jashapara, A. (1993). The competitive learning organization: A quest for the holy grail. *Management Decision, 31*(8), 52–62. doi:10.1108/00251749310047160

Kille, A. (2006). *Wikis in the workplace: How Wikis can help manage knowledge in library reference services.* Retrieved December 11, 2006, from http://libres.curtin.edu.au/libres16n1/Kille_essayopinion.htm

King, W. R. (1996). IS and the learning organization. *Information Systems Management, 13*(3), 78–80. doi:10.1080/10580539608907005

Leuf, B., & Cunningham, W. (2001). *The Wiki way: Quick collaboration on the Web.* New York: Addison Wesley.

Levine, L. (2001). Integrating knowledge and processes in a learning organization. *Information Systems Management,* (Winter): 21–32.

Lipnack, J., & Stamps, J. (2000). *Virtual teams: People working across boundaries with technology* (2nd ed.). New York: Wiley.

Lodge, G. C., & Walton, R. E. (1989). The American corporation and its new relationships. *California Management Review, 31,* 9–24.

Luhmann, N. (1988). Familiarity, confidence, trust: Problems and alternatives. In D. Gambetta (Ed.), *Trust: Making and breaking cooperative relations* (pp. 94-107). New York: Basil Blackwell.

Malone, T. W., & Laubacher, R. J. (1998). The dawn of the e-lance economy. *Harvard Business Review, 76*(5), 145–152.

Mayer, R., Davis, J., & Schoorman, F. (1995). An integration model of organizational trust. *Academy of Management Review, 20*(3), 709–719. doi:10.2307/258792

Menon, A. (1993). Are we squandering our intellectual capital? *Marketing Research: A Magazine of Management, 5*(3), 18-22.

Mitchell, J. C. (1969). *The concepts and use of social networks*. Manchester, UK: Manchester University Press.

Nahapiet, J., & Ghoshal, S. (1998). Social capital, intellectual capital and the organizational advantage. *Academy of Management Review, 23*(2), 242–266. doi:10.2307/259373

Newell, S., Robertson, M., Scarbrough, H., & Swan, J. (2002). *Managing knowledge work*. New York: Palgrave.

Nohria, N. (1992). Is a network perspective a useful way of studying organizations? In N. Nohria & R. Eccles (Eds.), *Networks and organizations*. Boston, MA: Harvard Business School Press.

Nonaka, I., & Takeuchi, H. (1995). *The knowledge creating company: How Japanese companies create the dynamics of innovation*. Oxford, UK: Oxford University Press.

OECD. (1996). The knowledge-based economy. *Organization for Economic Cooperation and Development*. OCDE/GD(96)102, Paris.

Orlikowski, W. J. (1992). *Learning from notes: Organizational issues in groupware implementation* (Working paper #3428). Boston: MIT Sloan School of Management.

Pinchot, G., III. (1985). *Intrapreneuring*. New York: HarperCollins.

Pinchot, G., & Pinchot, E. (1994). *The end of bureaucracy and the rise of intelligent organization*. San Francisco: Berrett Koehler.

Powell, W., Koput, K., & Smith-Doerr, L. (1996). Inter-organizational collaboration and the locus of innovation: Networks of learning in biotechnology. *Administrative Science Quarterly, 41*, 116–145. doi:10.2307/2393988

Quinn, J. B. (1992). *Intelligent enterprise*. New York: Free Press.

Raman, M., Ryan, T., & Olfman, L. (2005). Designing knowledge management systems for teaching and learning with Wiki technology. [JISE]. *Journal of Information Systems Education, 16*(3), 311–320.

Rouse, W. (2006). *Enterprise transformation: Understanding and enabling fundamental change*. Hoboken, NJ: Wiley-InterScience.

Rousseau, D. M., Sitkin, S. B., Burt, R. S., & Camerer, C. (1998). Not so different after all: A cross-disciplinary view of trust. *Academy of Management Review, 23*(3), 393–404.

Schrage, M. (1990). *Shared minds*. New York: Random House.

Senge, P. M. (1990). *The fifth discipline: The art and practice of the learning organization*. London: Currency Doubleday.

Seufert, A., & Seufert, S. (1999). The genius approach: Building learning networks for advanced management education. In *Proceedings of the 32nd Hawaii International Conference on System Sciences*, Maui, HI.

Stewart, T. (1997). *Intellectual capital: The new wealth of organizations*. New York: Doubleday.

Tabaka, J. (2006). *Collaboration explained: Facilitation skills for software project leaders*. Boston: Addison Wesley.

Tapscott, D. (1997). *The digital economy: Promise and peril in the age of networked intelligence*. New York: McGraw Hill.

Turban, E., Leidner, D., McLean, E., & Wetherbe, J. (2005). *Information technology for management: Transforming organizations in the digital economy*. New York: John Wiley & Sons.

Ulrich, D., Von Glinlow, M., & Jick, T. (1993). High-impact learning: Building and diffusing a learning capability. *Organizational Dynamics, 22*, 52–66. doi:10.1016/0090-2616(93)90053-4

Vat, K. H. (2001, November 1-4). Towards a learning organization model for knowledge synthesis: An IS perspective. In *CD-Proceedings of the 2001 Information Systems Education Conference (ISECON2001)*, Cincinnati, Ohio, USA. Association of Information Technology Professionals.

Vat, K. H. (2002). Designing organizational memory for knowledge management support in collaborative learning. In D. White (Ed.), *Knowledge mapping and management* (pp. 233-243). Hershey, PA: IRM Press.

Vat, K. H. (2003). Architecting of learning organizations: The IS practitioners' challenge in systems thinking. *Information Systems Education Journal (ISEDJ), 1*(26). Retrieved from http://isedj.org/1/26/

Vat, K. H. (2005). Designing OMIS-based collaboration for learning organizations. In M. Khosrow-Pour (Ed.), *Encyclopedia of information science and technology* (pp. 827-83). Hershey, PA: Idea Group Reference.

Vat, K. H. (2006). Knowledge synthesis framework. In D. Schwartz (Ed.), *Encyclopedia of knowledge management* (pp. 530-537). Hershey, PA: Idea Group Reference.

Vat, K. H. (2008). OMIS-based collaboration with service-oriented design. In M. Khosrow-Pour (Ed.), *Encyclopedia of information science and technology, 2nd edition* (pp. 2875-2881). Hershey, PA: Information Science Reference.

Wagner, C. (2004). WIKI: A technology for conversational knowledge management and group collaboration. *Communications of the Association for Information Systems, 13*, 265–289.

Walsh, J. P., & Ungson, G. R. (1991). Organizational memory. *Academy of Management Review, 16*(1), 57–91. doi:10.2307/258607

Williamson, A., & Lliopoulos, C. (2001). The learning organization information system (LOIS): Looking for the next generation. *Information Systems Journal, 11*(1), 23–41. doi:10.1046/j.1365-2575.2001.00090.x

Wilson, B. (2001). *Soft systems methodology: Conceptual model building and its contribution*. New York: John Wiley & Sons, Ltd.

Winograd, T., & Flores, F. (1986). *Understanding computers and cognition*. Reading, MA: Addison-Wesley.

Woods, D., & Guliani, G. (2005). *Open source for the enterprise: Managing risks, reaping rewards*. Sebastopol, CA: O'Reilly.

TERMS AND DEFINITIONS

Collaboration: To facilitate the process of shared creation involving two or more individuals interacting to create shared understanding where none had existed or could have existed on its own.

Double-Loop Learning: Together with single-loop learning, they describe the way in which organizations may learn to respond appropriately to change. Single-loop learning requires adjustments to procedures and operations within the framework of customary, accepted assumptions, but fails to recognize or deal effectively with problems that may challenge fundamental aspects of organizational culture, norms, or objectives. Double-loop learning questions those assumptions from the vantage point of higher order, shared views, in order to solve problems.

Knowledge Management: The broad process of locating, organizing, transferring, and using the information and expertise within the organization, typically by using advanced information technologies.

Learning Organization: An organization which focuses on developing and using its information and knowledge capabilities in order to create higher-value information and knowledge, to modify behaviors to reflect new knowledge and insights, and to improve bottom-line results.

OMIS: An information system supporting the development of organizational memory, whose design philosophy is often organization-specific. An example philosophy is to consider the OMIS as a meaning attribution system in which people select certain resource items out of the mass potentially available and get them processed to make them meaningful in a particular context in order to support their purposeful actions.

Organizational Learning: A process of leveraging the collective individual learning of an organization to produce a higher-level organization-wide intellectual asset. It is a continuous process of creating, acquiring, and transferring knowledge accompanied by a modification of behavior to: reflect new knowledge and insight, and produce a higher-level asset.

Organizational Memory: A learning history that tells an organization its own story, which should help generate reflective conversations among organizational members. Operationally, an organizational memory has come to be a close partner of knowledge management, denoting the actual content that a knowledge management system purports to manage.

Wiki Technology: This technology is based on open-source software in the form of a Wiki engine. The Hawaiian word "Wiki" means quick, with the connotation that this technology is easy to use once installed. Wikis run over the World Wide Web and can be supported by any browser. The technology is governed by an underlying hypertext transfer protocol (HTTP) that determines client and server communication. Wikis are able to respond to both requests for data (GET) and data submission (POST), in a given Web front, based on the HTTP concept.

Chapter 15
Information Systems Planning in Web 2.0 Era:
A New Model Approach

José Sousa
IBMC – Instituto de Biologia Molecular e Celular, Portugal

ABSTRACT

Since the early development in the 90's, organizations had been growing in a rapid way, becoming each more difficult to manage. Organization business cycle changed from 7 years in 1970-1980 to 12-18 months in the 90's, and is even shorter in our time. This addressed the organizations world to a new and complex reality. To be able to deal with this reality, organizations set a big pressure in information access and information turn out to be the most valuable organization asset. Nevertheless, this asset, the information object, has some main characteristics like, exists in larges quantities, has many different forms, is very volatile and it also must have confidentially, integrity and availability and all this together can be very hard to manage. It's clear that the management of this information reality is only possible with the adoption of information technologies and planning that adoption and implementation is a central need in order to get the correct solution for the organization ecosystem.

INTRODUCTION

Organizations had been growing in an accelerated manner since the beginnings of 90's decade, becoming each more complex to manage. This growing, compressed the business life cycle and organizations development, and droves (and drives) to high needs in the information access and management.

In face of this central need, organizations have been defining information has their most valuable asset. But when information exists in a great amount, is very volatile and diverse makes fundamental the adoption of information technologies in its management.

This took to the evolution of information technologies according to organizational needs.

If in the beginning the use of technology could be a competitive advantage, due to high investment cost, functional complexity and the need to use a

DOI: 10.4018/978-1-60566-856-7.ch015

Table 1. Information system development periods - based on (Hsu, 1995)

	Period	Characteristics
60's	Data processing (DP)	Stand alone computers, fare from users, cost reduction function
70's & 80's	Information Systems Management (ISM)	Distributed processing, interconnected, business support, user oriented
80's & 90's	Strategic information systems (SIS)	Networked integrated systems, user functional and available, business strategic related, business development oriented
20th/21st century	Information Security (IS)	Dynamic management of all information flow, security oriented

large amount of human resources, today, with a small investment is possible to get technology with the same functionality of bigger systems.

This trivialization of technology, makes clear that, this demand to information access, only can be supported with the correct quality and efficiency, using the correct characterization of organization information systems (André Vasconcelos, 1999), been able to evaluate not only the acquiring and processing of information, as happened on the firsts years of information systems, but clearly point a parallel information systems path within the organization development, being able to at each time supply the correct and needed information.

Defining this relationship, where organization information needs are mapped into the adoption of correct information technology has been the main goal of information systems planning.

In order to have suitable technology, at each organization development moment, information systems planning models were developed. By this way it was created a benchmark for the organization characterization and consequent translation into technology. The development of these models has been associated to specific phases, characteristics and needs of organizations development and also aligned with the development of the information systems solutions and technology.

Table 1, illustrates the different phases of information systems development and their fundamental concerns also showing information systems planning challenges and the characteristics of expected needs and targets.

With a compressed life cycle, dynamic organizations face now, a deep change in how interactions are made with the elements that define its development.

Organizations suffered the first impact with the Internet arrival, known as World Wide Web and that can be defined as WEB 1.0, and its possibility to have availability of information in a new and innovative way. However, technology continued development allowed the potentiality grow of Internet and leaved to the development of new ways of information availability. In the last three years, this evolution is been centered in the WEB 2.0 (Reilly, 2005) paradigm . With this new paradigm, the information world migrates from a "*network is the computer*" to "*networked user*" vision.

This networked user, using technological ubiquitous tools and interacting in many different ways, produces networked centered knowledge according to some predetermined preferences and goals. So, is possible to see an accelerated growth of this kind of knowledge, and some examples like Facebook, Flick or the more well known, YouTube can be pointed out.

Despite this, the full value of networked knowledge was present in the development of two primary Web 2.0 examples, the open-source software and Wikipedia, that in their form reflect the new way of organizational development and show the path to the collaborative ecosystem creation.

This ecosystem can be defined as "*unique combination of integrated "things" where information flows in order to promote maximization*".

Organizations are trying to create value with focus on this new ecosystem, using this new paradigm as resource. This collaborative ecosystem, puts organizations and their capability to adopt this new functional reality in a way that empowers and integrates their development in this networked centered economy (Don Tapscott, 2006), to the test.

For organizations, this integration puts a new set of challenges at information security and availability. In this collaborative ecosystem, the guarantee of information characteristics is fundamental, since the availability of organization information is sustained by a fundamental key element, reliability. Information security is not any more only information access management, whose objective is guaranteeing availability, integrity and confidentiality but becomes a built-in characteristic of information, being part of how information ecosystem development occurs. As well as information as to be secure to be reliable, is wanted that this information availability must allow the achievement of a certain organizational effect.

Organizations have to assure conditions to guarantee the achievement of the wanted effect.

Allowing organizations to add this new paradigm and guarantee information security at the same time as the wanted information effects is only possible with the right informational ecosystem characterization, and there is only a way to do this, planning.

The correct information ecosystem planning, is today, as it was in the past, the great challenge for the correct management of the organization information (Hsu, 1995).

Current information systems planning models, still only worried about organization internal aspects and how systems can be implemented, developed and improved, having as center goals, organizational functional support, the so called strategic alignment.

The ecosystem concept allows an evolution to the integration of new external elements in the actual systems and with that information interaction develop organization informational effect.

On the actual information systems planning models is wanted a strategic alignment between organization and IT, oriented to value creation, developing of organization processes or integration of differentiate technology. The current word, when we talk about information system planning is then "*strategic alignment*". This strategic alignment is hard to do in an information systems world where functional context is in permanent change leaving to the complete malfunctioning between information systems and organizations.

Information system planning models have frequently as focus only a certain information life cycle, wherever it's financial, productive, etc. However, collaborative reality that we see in the information ecosystem, demands the creation of an information system with an architecture able to manage information flow, from the physical world (data) to the cognitive world (knowledge) having as middle tier the information creation process.

Organization are in a global and competitive world where the phrase "*think global act local*" (Anna H. Perrault 2000) has been replaced by "*think global act global*" (Don Tapscott, 2006).

It becomes necessary, that information system planning moves from the standard and usual strategic alignment to the development of a collaborative ecosystem and with that, been able to, at each moment supply suitable information systems architecture conditions to organizational development needs. Actual organization challenges are presented at Figure 1.

In face of these challenges, a need of developing a new information systems planning model that integrate this new reality, information ecosystem, emerged. This planning model must guarantee the wanted information effects, without which information has no value, and also confidentiality, integrity and availability of information, translated into a guarantee of information security, without which informa-

Figure 1. Organization paradigms Braga Square

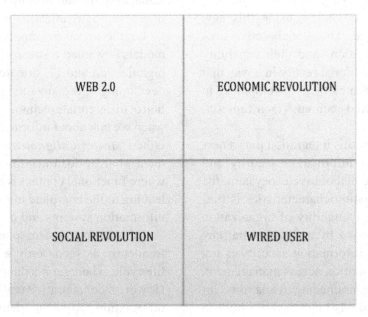

tion can't add value and the achievement of the wanted effect is uncertain.

Information, as organizations most valuable asset, it should be protected according to its importance, but what we see, in traditional information systems planning, is that information security is essentially a technological problem and developed after information systems implementation.

On this chapter is presented a new planning model, for this new information ecosystem, oriented to information effects, that aims to be able to address the actual needs of information at organizations, adding as information characteristic, the effect and security.

A change of paradigm is proposed, going from strategic alignment to information effect with integrated information security as information characteristics. On this logic, this model makes organization effects characterization, and from there, characterize which consequences, effects have, at the development of support elements.

With focus on the major element of organization, information, and applying information war concepts, is presented the model ability to suite

information security needs for the wanted effects and in the information flow. This model definition absorbs the information needs and security, translating its complexity and volatility into the modeling process.

So, using the information war military planning, from the model effect oriented (Nunes, 2006) and adding two new elements, prioritization (Leffingwell D., 2000) and interdependency (Robertson, 1999), from software engineering to manage effects, its aimed to achieve a model that understands organizational ecosystem and empowers the achievement of a certain effect, been fundamental guarantee information security flow, without which, the wanted ecosystem effect could be put at risk.

Each organization is seen, as parte of an ecosystem using cause/effect processes relationship in which owned information would always be an ecosystem element and which usability goal, is guarantee that organization survives in this collaborative ecosystem.

A NEW MODEL APPROACH FOR INFORMATION SYSTEMS PLANNING IN WEB 2.0 ERA

Web 2.0 for a Collaborative World

Information systems context, has been, since its geneses, constantly challenged. In the first stage, the challenge was to support the automation process, rapidly developed to organizational support and the creation of strategic value was the next step. As a consequence, now we have a completely technology reliant society with a continued functional and structural pressure over IT.

Information systems planning models are a clear example of that evolution process, supported by the technology evolution.

Information technology evolution made available tools and architectures that allow functional ecosystems creation in a simple manner and where information is available to interested users consideration and development of any kind of activities. We are becoming a *wikinomics* society (Don Tapscott, 2006). This society, user networked centric and with collaborative platforms, is today for organizations a usability challenge, in the sense that, each organization have at their doors a great number of potential co-workers.

These co-workers have already grown in the net-generation (Don Tapscott, 2006), and they assume that Internet is a commodity with e-mail as a tool from the past, using instant messaging and P2P as preferred communications tools.

Co-workers attraction and their integration, forces organizations to expose is structure and as consequence its information systems, to these new challenges. Now, organization information systems are parte of an external reality that they do not control and on which they depend. Organizations are forced to integrate information systems that were not created with security, sharing and collaboration as a goal, in this new collaborative reality and for that organizations must change the way they interact with this reality.

Normally defining local policies, using think global act local (Anna H. Perrault 2000), they try now to adjust complex regulatory rules, with think global act global, in mind.

Collaborative networks, when possible their integration, allow the use of the institutional repository in a way that interested users can analyze the possibilities of available information and add value.

We are now using Internet, not only for publication, supported by WEB 1.0, but as a computational mean, we are at WEB 2.0 era. The Internet becomes a programmable network infrastructure, creating space for the development of new applications, new business models, and promoting and creating competitive differentiation.

We can notice that organizations have to change, and some of them already did it, their information management concepts and planning.

Information needs to be supplied not only to direct collaborators and employees, but also to the outside of organizations borders, in order to make possible the motivation of knowledge networks that are at the organization boundaries. These knowledge networks, when transformed in collaborative networks, increase the way organizations, persons and things can interact, using Internet as mean.

Traditional departments will be the guardians of standards, center for specialists training, will not be the place where the work is done. The work will be done, essentially, in specialized large teams geographically distributed (Drucker, 2001). WEB 2.0 tools are allowing the integration of world-distributed teams, in a way that organizational departments will only have teams management . One of the startup examples of this collaboration was Lotus Notes that in the first years of the 90's used workflow tools, supported by an e-mail application server, to add new management ways to organization processes. In 2005 with the boom of P2P, new tools, made sharable all kinds of information, becoming the first spot of knowledge networks development.

Despite this organizations need to change, competitiveness continues a fundamental goal. So, collaboration demands a correct implementation, in the business context. So, it must be viewed, like an ecosystem, where the result not only depends on organizations actions but also on competitors and context, becoming a dynamic system with no linear results.

It's clear that WEB 2.0, supported by an Internet that has availability and characteristics that allow the integration of new kinds of functionality, making possible the new collaborative paradigm implementation, demands something completely new for organizations, the openness. This new need, openness, is truthfully actually, the most important element in actual development of organizations.

This new platform and characteristics are clearly defined by Tim O'Reilly, considered the father of this new web. "*WEB 2.0 is not a technology, but a new collaborative attitude, integrating technology, attitude and philosophy*" (Reilly, 2005; Roman Hoegg, 2007).

WEB 2.0, whose real development started after Tim O'Reilly conference, about Media WEB in 2004, becomes certain.

The WEB 2.0 architecture can be represented, in a simple way, by the model in Figure 2. From there is possible to understand that WEB 2.0 is also philosophy and not only a technology, whose goal is common knowledge empowerment of participants. WEB 2.0 is in that way a philosophy to common intelligence maximization that adds value for which participant using sharing and knowledge creation in an informal way (Roman Hoegg, 2007).

This collective intelligence is joined together in communities and is not associated to any innovative or specific technology. From the technical point of view, WEB 2.0 is only a unique combination of protocols and computer languages. Available functionality and associated communities, allow the following functional classification (Panada, 2007):

- *Blogs* e *blogosphere*;
- *Wikis*;
- *Podcasts*;
- *Social networks;*
- *Social bookmarking* e *Folksonomies*;

These communities create knowledge according to different areas of interest, and they can, when correctly integrated on organizations, create value by promoting development and change (Mikroyannidis, 2007).

The migration from the WEB publication and information-linking concept, WEB 1.0, is definitively made, now we have a collaborative and dynamic structure, WEB 2.0.

According to Tim O' Reilly (Reilly, 2005), "*WEB 2.0 is a business revolution in computer industry, made, using the internet as platform and an attempt to understand success rules for this new platform*". This new platform supports a great set of software tools that are characteristic of WEB 2.0 and some examples are illustrated in Figure 3.

This set of software applications and also web sites that are now in the WEB 2.0 concept consolidation phase, of which Wikipedia is perhaps the best example of collaborative paradigm, gives organizations the perception of the potential advantages, in case of been able to translate this, to business development. Napster and BitTorrent represent other examples of software applications. In the traditional voice communication area, Skype allowed VOIP to rapidly grow in user use, putting under pressure organizations, for use, develop and adoption of those solutions.

The collaborative paradigm and available tools are creating conditions for organizations to use co-workers, collaborative workers. The organization limits are now completely transparent organization had become border less.

In any case, since Tim O' Reilly WEB 2.0 presentation, the way that users use those concepts have been irrational and sometimes even with a real exuberant approach. Beside that, this

Figure 2. WEB 2.0 effect – based on (Roman Hoegg, 2007)

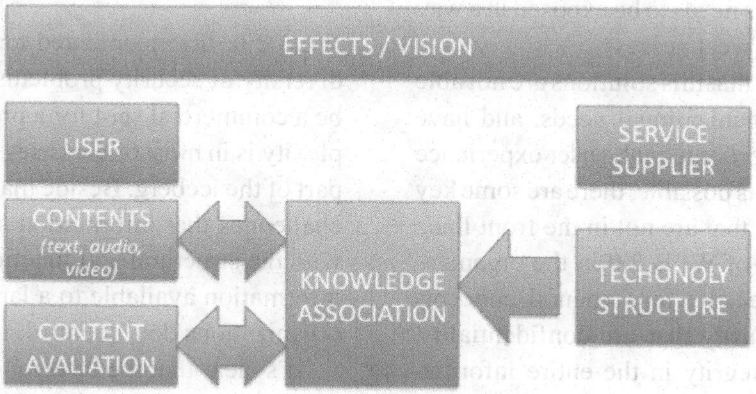

new WEB can add value to organizations in three different ways:

- Creation of committed communities, based on social computing, that don't search directly for financial valor;
- Content and data access expands innovation networks, supported on knowledge networks allow complex searches and data combination;
- Effective commitment as differentiation element for competitiveness, and for that, organizational information should be completely reliable.

In order to be able to add, by this way, value and make a transparent integration of communities, WEB 2.0 uses technological tools supported in:

- Information integration with availability as central focus;
- Social computing, making available communication and sharing;
- Process flow support, using the collaborative platform.

WEB 2.0 has at its disposal a set of solutions whose goal is to optimize and to attract users to collaboration.

Organizations should have the notion that WEB 2.0 is not a solution for all organizational development needs, since (Hammond, 2007):

- WEB 2.0 is not made and is not prepared for the more complex applications;
- Service availability is a preposition of all or nothing;
- Is very hard to hide weak processes and applications.

Figure 3. Tools examples in collaboration era

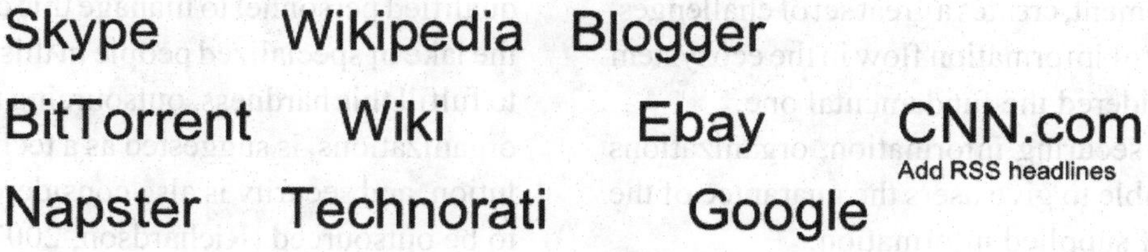

So, the information that exists in organization information systems needs to be exposed in a way that prevents those weaknesses.

In the same way that this solutions are not able to deal with all organizational needs, and have been developed in order to make user experience the most agreeable as possible, there are some key aspects as security, that are not in the front line.

The integration of WEB 2.0 in the organization must guarantee the fundamental concepts of information security that are confidentiality, availability and integrity in the entire information ecosystem.

Its fundamental for organizations that the integration of those knowledge networks in there own information systems is done in a way that feats organizational challenges and needs and for that there are set of elements such as, copyright, authorship, identity, ethics, tastes, rhetoric, management, privacy, commerce, love, family and in limit ourselves, should be rethought.

This change creates opportunities and the collaborative paradigm, centered on the development model of WEB 2.0, will bring a sustained and disruptive development to business.

Organizations that can create value with this integration will achieve to attract vibrant and enthusiastic knowledge communities, putting a definitive and fundamental accelerating focus in innovation. These organizations will have conditions to win the organizational race to WEB 2.0.

Machines will be the "*individual*", digital text and "*hypertext*" will not only be associated information. The WEB 2.0 not only joins information, it joins people in personal relations, business and collaboration.

This new ecosystem, for organizations innovation development, creates a great set of challenges, and security of information flow in the ecosystem can be considered the fundamental one.

Without securing information, organizations will not be able to give users the guarantee of the reliability of supplied information.

Security in a Collaborative World

WEB 2.0, if implemented tomorrow, presents a diversity of security problems, today. This could be a commercial spot for a problem whose complexity is in most of the cases the under the water part of the iceberg. Beside that, this translates the challenges that information systems face today, with the structural and functional needs to make information available to a large set of users that organizations don't control.

It's clear that the integration of collaboration paradigm is only possible if it's done in a secure way, where security of information becomes a complete transversal element to the development of this new collaborative ecosystem.

Information systems security in often mentioned as a standard subject when information systems are the center talk, but its fundamental to make the correct context and characterization of information systems security. For that, a fundamental source can be Computer Security Institute (CSI) 2007 report.

In the 2007 report, it's obvious that systems security is the element of organizations information systems where investment is stable. It's also clear the importance, in terms of investments, that information systems managers give to security. In 2007 that value razed in a significant way in the middle values from, 3% to 5% of global information systems investments (Richardson, 2007).

On this report the security of information is seen as a technological issue. If this perspective doesn't change it will not be possible to protect user centric organizations, the new collaborative organizations, since user interacts with the information in a complete ubiquitous manner.

Frequently, organizations associate their difficulties to manage change, to the hardness to get qualified personnel to manage this change, due to the lake of specialized people in this area. In order to fulfill this hardness, outsourcing to specialized organizations, is suggested as a technological solution, and security is also considered as possible to be outsourced (Richardson, 2007).

Despite these, organizations consider that personnel that belong directly to organization must do this task but for that, organizations must guarantee complementary formation to their employees, or hire specialist, to maintain information secure.

The security of information can be measured, using a simple metric, such as, the number of identified attacks. In the means of attack, a set of pointers can be identified as fundamental for security characteristics:

- 59% of attacks are made from outside the organization, and are user centric;
- 52% are viruses (despite the fact that the origin is not mentioned, in general, internet is defined as most frequent);
- 50% were portable equipments steal, user centric;
- 26% was Phishing, user centric;
- 25% was misuse of instant messaging, a user centric attack.

Despite the fact that information security is a central concern and associated investment is been done in technological solutions, the user, the center of collaboration development and the common element of presented information security risks, is not getting all the needed attention.

We are not only dealing with organization information users that are outside organizations, but also with the large number off them that use corporate facilities.

For there so, is possible to verify that security must add, to the analyze spectrum, the human behavior, taking in consideration the way users interacts with the information ecosystem.

Another characteristic is the increase in the number of undetermined attacks cases, meaning that organizations, don't know methods of security analyze and that's a problem, or organizations are protecting that type of information and that's also a problem. Once more, information security investment increases, but the knowledge that organizations have of their security state decreases.

Fraud appears in the top of the list of security issues, while web sites changes introduced by WEB 2.0 are at the bottom of the list.

If, in a first stage, vulnerability exposure was a question of self-proud, now organizations feel that fraud is the main goal and has been present, for instance, in pop-up boxes with malicious code, and also in Phishing, with large media coverage.

However, viruses introduced vulnerabilities are in the top of the list in value of financial losses and theft of identities is becoming the leader in very different ways. Its necessary to put emphasis that virus, is not a problem that came with WEB 2.0, is an older problem that had been the center of attention in security procedures for a long time and whose financial cost increases every year, without an alteration in security perception.

This makes clear that despite the fact that investment had increased, there is no significant reduction in the number of security incidents, and the investment is been addressed to antivirus solutions, firewalls, VPN and anti-spyware tools.

This type of security investment is been made in the organization boundary, and since this is becoming more and more difficult to define, the fragilities of these solutions, to assure information security, are becoming more often visible.

Some Technological solutions like NAC, that could protect the users access inside organizations, where is possible to produce more damages, area putted aside or in the last places of the investment list or even suffer some investment cut.

Normalization procedures have been presented as a fundamental way to increase information security. Its possible to verify that 25% (Richardson, 2007) of respondents totally disagree with that. This value is almost more than the double when compared with the number of respondents that totally agrees making believe that when organization information systems managers implements normalization, this is done with the purpose to apply markets rules to organization and not to, with effectiveness, add value to information security management.

Normalization is also presented as an element for increase organizations technological potential management, adding some buzzwords like governance or e-governance used according to the implementation context. However, the number of responders that completely disagree with the fact that regulations, taking as example Sarbannes-Oxley, increase governance is three times more than those that completely agree. For that fact, normalization, at least the example and that had been in the center of the normalization process, does not seem to be able to manage information security integration in a way that the ecosystem characteristics demands and needs.

This report (Richardson, 2007) reflects the stat of art in information security and show the path that organizations should trace to provide and manage security in the organization ecosystem. Nevertheless, if some problems come from the past, like virus and the understanding that security is technology, organization information needs are now at the turning point to a new era.

Security Impact of Web 2.0

To the actual problems in information system security development and implementation was added the development and integration of WEB 2.0. This in the limit, can take to the transformation of organization perimeter in a border less zone, encouraged by the migration to the information ecosystem.

This integration, of knowledge communities, in the actual information system, in order to create an organizational information ecosystem, makes information systems security a more serious problem.

WEB 2.0 tools usability goal is to have a simple and easy RIA often done by grouping a set of different solutions and products. Due to the context development these solutions have the same problems of actual software solutions, promoting usability in expense of security.

For that, the security of this border less organization, the information ecosystem, faces problems that can put at risk even societies development. One example of that can be XSS based attack, which explores, using malicious programming code injections and their execution in the user web browser, a great number of browser vulnerabilities.

Beside that, Internet continues to be crammed with blogs and e-mail menaces. Attacks of DOS, SPAM, web browser bugs exploration and other vulnerabilities exploits continue to be possible.

In Table 2 are illustrated two examples of attacks against two of the most representative sites of WEB 2.0 era, where is possible to verify their vulnerabilities and insecurity.

In Table 3 is possible to verify some of the vulnerabilities on one of the most popular sites and how can be exploited.

Table 2. Two attack examples of WEB 2.0 era

Yamanner	Samy & Spaceflash
• Yahoo e-mail as main goal • Relates malicious JavaScript code to standard HTML image tag • User doesn't need to do any click to be infected • Auto-flow while gets e-mail addresses	• MySpace as a goal

Table 3. MySpace characteristic and vulnerabilities exploit

MySpace	Samy, Spaceflash
• Sixth world most popular WEB site in English language • Sixth most popular WEB site in any language • Third most popular WEB site in the United States	• Alters user profile in order to add author as a friend • URL Redirection to a Macromedia flash file with malicious code • Malicious Quick Time files change user profiles in order to promote phishing

Table 4. Vulnerabilities and exploits

Vulnerabilities	Exploits
• Cross-site scripting using AJAX[1] and XML[2]	• AJAX is executed on the client side allowing exploit due to the use of malicious scripts
• XML poisoning	• It can take to a DOS or functional logic break
• Malicious AJAX code execution using XM-LHTTPRequest	• Cookies can take to a lost of confidential information
• RSS/Atom Injection (XML 1.0 based)	• Feeds with JavaScript injection in order to allow attacks using the client browser
• WSDL[3] enumeration and search	• Web services language definition can have open unnecessary services or methods • This file gives key information about exposed services, protocols, doors, functions, methods, execution processes, etc
• AJAX function validation on the client side	• Its possible to bypass validation and make new requests to the solution (i.e. SQL[4] Injection, LDAP[5] Injection, etc.)
• Web services routing problems	• If the routing nodes where compromised, access to SOAP[6] messages can be possible
• Parameters manipulation trough SOAP	• Services variables can be manipulated
• XPATH[7] injection on a SOAP message	• XPATH is the computer language used to make XML questions to documents being normal software solutions to allow inputs that can lead to injection
• Binary manipulation of RIA thick client (using reverse engineering)	• Functionalities such us flash, activex controls or applets are used on UI[8] of RIA as primary interface for the web applications what can lead to security problems

WEB 2.0 collaboration paradigm stands on the shoulder of the user and reach the user and discover the path to information access that exists in the ecosystem, from inside, became the primary goal (CIO, 2006), and that is made clear in Table 2 and 3.

The exploit of security vulnerabilities appears in a way that is not pointed to the systems that supports the ecosystem itself, but to the user of that ecosystem, that after been compromised, allows the access to information systems from inside. This kind of access is always most flexible and permissive to the use of other types of attacks, which potential damage is greater when compared with outside attacks.

Its also clear that, exists a traditional way of vulnerabilities exploit, they are exploited according to the visibility of the element to compromise, and in the WEB 2.0 era, a way to verify that visibility is by the number of registered users. As any tool, WEB 2.0 solutions have vulnerabilities, that in this case affect the user and some of which are presented in the Table 4 where is presented the relation between the vulnerabilities and the consequence of vulnerabilities exploit.

These vulnerabilities are outcome of the technological use of WEB 2.0 platform. However, traditional and critical information systems vulnerabilities persist and to which, the use of technological solutions such as AJAX, bring a new and dangerous dimension.

To exploit these new characteristics a new set of malicious software applications emerged. JITKO is the example of that type of applications. Something that started as a search software application for web vulnerabilities it can be integrated in the aggressor site or injected in a trusted web site. It can then discover various types of security holes and connect to his remote controller in order to get instructions of which web sites to attack and what variables to search. An example of that kind of search using JITKO, is presented in Table 5.

Traditional information systems integration on this new paradigm adds other vulnerabilities, such as, composite documents exploit. Standard and well-known documents, produced in ERP standard solutions or others that use standard names for reports, where transformed on the best structured attack ever see. For that had been used actual reports names and valid e-mail address as

Table 5. JITKO working example

Example	Result
var encodedText = *"dW5lc2NhcGUoIiV1OTA5MCV1OTA5MCIp...";* *var decodedText = decode(encodedText);* *document.write(decodedText);* *decode(input) {* *...* *}*	*var shellcode =* *unescape("%uyadd%uayad%udaya%uddaa");* *var nop_sled = unescape("%u9090%u9090");* *while(nop_sled.length <= 40000)* *nop_sled += nop_sled;* *var myArray = new Array();* *for(var i=0; i<300; i++)* *myArray[i] = nop_sled+shellcode;*

well, acquired by unauthorized means (Panada, 2007).

When a software solution is fully transversal to organization, presents problems, due to their use level this is a difficult problem to address that affects virtually all web sites in the world.

For instance, Adobe Reader vulnerabilities to XSS attack in which, when supplying the link for a local PDF, allows JavaScript execution on the local zone.

This kind of attack surprises by simplicity and whose format is clear in the following sentence:

http://www.xzy.com/whatup.

pdf#javascript:alert('test');

Table 6 presents some of the most popular 2007 software applications available for WEB 2.0 and some of the associated vulnerabilities.

As illustrated in Table 6 vulnerabilities affect a quit different set of software solutions and have continued development. In order to address that, information security of the ecosystem should be a dynamic process that includes the possibility of constant review, reformulate and change of all ecosystem model security aspects, in order to manage all information security aspects (Richardson, 2007).

There is a clear need for an information security culture centered not in technology but in the users in a world where technological complexity rises every day and where the merge between the mobile and fixed communications, the ubiquitous computation foundation, is one example.

Organization are also reformatting their software solutions for services oriented architecture, supported by WEB 2.0 tools, trying to get competitive advantage, but simultaneously creating a swamp of new vulnerabilities very hard to manage and control (Richardson, 2007).

In the past, the battle was between IT professionals and hackers, having in common the technology factor, but WEB 2.0 posts a more serious problem, since attackers put their attention in users. If we limit information security to firewall and anti-virus status quo, information security in organizations will suffer a great deal of decrease.

The task of creating an information ecosystem to manage information in a way that can be translated to the creation of an organization ecosystem is a very difficult, complex and hard task. Security management of that information raises even more, the complexity level.

Normalization that is frequently presented as the solution for everything and explicitly Sarbanes-Oxley, is not seen as been able to address information systems security planning.

Despite the fact that security is a fundamental problem in the mind of all intervenes in the process of ecosystem creation, its clear that securing information only with technological investment has been perfectly incomplete, even more now, with the addressing of collaboration and border less organization.

This barriers removal gives to the three fundamental elements of information security (confidentiality, integrity and availability) a human dimension, which enrollment is desirable, but whose control, if possible, can be a dysfunctional threat. Ecosystems integration leave to integrated problems that flow

Table 6. More frequent WEB 2.0 software solutions and associated vulnerabilities

Software	Version	Suggested solution	Vulnerabilities nature
Yahoo! Messenger	8.1.0.239 and following	Upgrade to 8.1.0.419	Buffer overflow allows arbitrary code execution using unspecified vectors
Apple QuickTime	7.2	Correct	Diverse vulnerabilities allow arbitrary command execution and Applets Java and URL codification
Mozilla Firefox	2.0.0.6	Upgrade to 2.0.0.7 for some corrections	Allow execution of arbitrary commands using special URL codification
Microsoft Windows Live (MSN) Messenger	7.0, 8.0	Upgrade to 7.0.08.20 or 8.1	Heap-based buffer overflow allows remote attacks with user assistance and the execution of arbitrary code using unspecified vector that uses video connections managed by live web cam sessions
EMC Vmware Player (and other products)	2.0, 1.0.4	Upgrade to 2.0.1 or 1.0.5	Allow a remote attacker to execute arbitrary code using malformed DHCP packets that activates a stack-based buffer overflow or corrupts a stack memory
Apple iTunes	7.3.2	Upgrade to 7.4	Buffer overflow that allows to remote attacks finish the application or execute arbitrary code using a music file with change in the cover art
Intuit QuickBooks Online Edition	9 and following	Upgrade to 10 or correction	Several stack-based buffer overflows in activex control allows to remote attacks the execution of arbitrary code using unspecified vectors
Sun Java Runtime Environment (JRE)	1.6.0_X	Not available	Buffer overflow in Java Web Start allows to remote attackers to have unknown impact with the use of arguments calls inside methods
Yahoo! Widgets	4.0.5 and before	Upgrade	Stack-based buffer overflow allows the execution of arbitrary code using unexpected arguments in a methods call from remote attack
Ask.com Toolbar	4.0.2.53 and before	Not available	Stack-based buffer overflow in ActiveX and Ask Toolbar that allows remotes code execution
Broadcom wireless device driver as used on Cisco Linksys WPC300N Wireless-N	3.50.21.10	Driver upgrade	Stack-based buffer overflow allows to remote attackers the execution of arbitrary code in a response frame from 802.11 that contains SSID long field
Macrovision (formerly InstallShield) Install-FromTheWeb	All versions	Not supported	Multiple buffer overflows that llow to attackers the execution of arbitrary code using HTML documents

from layer to layer demanding a complete knowledge of the ecosystem information flow.

To be able to maintain organization information on this border less information world, confronted with quicker development and functional pyramids growing, is the challenge of this innovative information ecosystem planning model. Some numbers help to understand the dimension of these collaborative platforms and in face of the vulnerabilities presented on Table 5, understand the problem dimension:

- 74% of CIO consider that WEB 2.0 adds insecurity (Bradbury, 2007);
- 67,000 is the number of blog entries in which hour (Sifry, 2006);
- 12% is the number of North American on-line consumers that use RSS (Jupiter, 2006);
- 12 millions was the number of podcasts subscriptions (Forrester, 2006);
- 52.4 millions was the identified number of podcasts in August 2006 (Sifry, 2006).

Information security shouldn't be something that inhibits improvement but the platform that chains persistent innovation.

Information Systems Planning Model

The increase of technology as incorporated element of organizations and the possibility that easily acquire small systems, with the same level of functionality of big systems, but with significant lower costs, as well as the availability of easier use operating systems, the argument that technology is the key differentiate element is put down to hearth.

So, its fundamental to change the way how organizations relate with technology, the correct relation should not be, what can technology do for organizations but what technology organization need and with that achieve organizational development with wanted effects while using information elements.

With the change from technological to collaboration paradigm the old models are not the right solution or tool to allow a global vision of information and are not able to cover all information life cycles with the integration of information security in the information flow, making visible information interactions happening in the ecosystem. Security of information flow can't be seen anymore at his own light or methodology it should be considered as information characteristic and should have the tools to support the development of another information characteristic, the effect.

The use of this two fundamental information characteristics, security and effect, compels to the definition of an information systems planning model that can handle this life cycle of information flow in the organizations ecosystem.

With the presented model, it is intended to develop a new planning approach allowing the integration of traditional planning in system conception, being able to develop the information flow concept and also guarantee the correct relationship between information and effect.

The developed model is supported by the information effect, concept developed in the information war. In order to be possible to define the information effects role, two additional variables where added to the model, interdependency and prioritization.

With border less organizations, its fundamental that information security is not only a set of technological solutions at the actual organization perimeter, but something that is at the heart of information. When security is considered a fundamental characteristic of information, it can and should change according to the information life cycle. The must frequent information security control is access control, that is static along all information life cycles, where each user has a set of definitions and privileges that allows the use of some set of data. This type of solution, controls information availability but not the flow, so, after the information been released by the access validation it can be compromised.

On the actual stage of WEB 2.0 development, this access control is clear insufficient and doesn't give the set of mechanisms needed to protect information ecosystems.

The organizations ecosystem must be correctly defined in order to guarantee the collaboration layer and the desired trust level in information security flow.

This model is supported on the definition of five strategic rings characterized according to the order presented in Figure 4.

Each one of these rings can be defined as follow:

- **Head**: available resource to produce a certain type of effect;
- **Essential systems**: fundamental elements that make possible the development of a certain effect;
- **Infra-structures**: set of physic elements that allow the operation of the essential systems;

Figure 4. Strategic rings

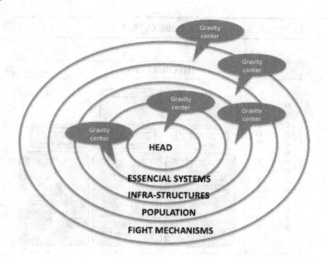

- **Population**: set of entities that can be the target of the effect or that can do any kind of interaction with the effect;
- **Fight mechanisms**: set of elements that can guarantee that certain effect is executed without been compromised.

In the information ecosystem and when compared with other forms of organization, a set of elements as presented in Table 7 can be found.

Each ring is developed using as starting point, three elements of analyze, in order to discover needs associated to each effect, and there are:

- **Critical capacities (CC)**: fundamental capacities of certain effect;
- **Critical needs (CN)**: resources that allow the capacities development;

- **Critical vulnerabilities (CV)**: vulnerabilities that are part of the resource.

From these elements derives model architecture presented in Figure 5.

Figure 5 illustrates in a simple way the elements of the information ecosystem effects based planning. The information security that will allow the correct effect achievement is completely integrated in the critical needs identified for each effect. The implementation of the supporting element of each effect is more or less relevant and depends or not on other ecosystem elements. Because of that, prioritization and interdependency are integrated in a transversal manner being able to gather all elements that allow effect development.

Effects orientation planning is not a new concept but the innovation of this model is how this

Table 7. Information ecosystem strategic rings comparative definition

Strategic Rings	Individual	Organizations	Information Ecosystem
Head	Brain	Directors Board	Information
Essential System	Eyes, heart, lungs	Financial, Human resources, production systems	Protocols
Infra-structures	Blood vases	Production systems	Hardware, Software, Communication systems
Population	Cells	Markets	Electronic equipments
Fight Mechanisms	Immunity system	Regulatory systems	Information systems planning moelssistemasinformação

Figure 5. Model architecture

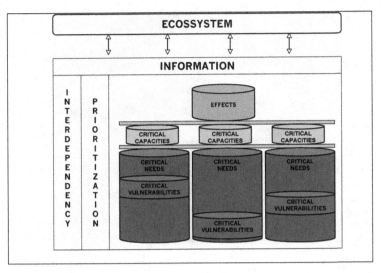

concept is extended to the sustained development of an information systems architecture where the development of each element strongly depends from the network interaction, defined by the organization ecosystem and with that allowing a big jump from a strategy centered on operational support to ecosystem centered.

It's very hard to choose a unique definition for this vision, fundamentally due to the origin of the subject, essentially from military source and centered on the way to do war.

However, the effect foundation definition for the information system-planning model based on effects is sustained as been: *"the set of coordinated actions that seek to constrain the state of a system through the integrated implementation of instruments of power, so cross-spectrum of the effect, considering the effects of actions in the achievement of objectives. Actions are planned, implemented, evaluated and adjusted using a holistic knowledge of the problem and the area in which it is developed, aimed to constrain the conduct of actors"*(Vicente, 2007).

Is therefore possible to consider that planning should do a ecosystem cross analyze, understanding capacities our sources of power, vulnerabilities and weakness, bringing to the top, vulnerable nods

and also the ideal forms of actions execution, aimed to change effect behavior.

The effects refer to *"a range of results, events, or consequences of actions, which may arise from any instrument. Effects are a cross-cumulative consequence to the strategic environment from one or more actions"*(Vicente, 2007).

In order to improve effects understanding, it's necessary to classify the different types of effects, as direct or indirect effects. The basic distinction between them is that the direct effect *"results from actions without a middle mechanism between action and result"*. Indirect results are difficult to predict and take a long time to complete, contributing or not to obtain the expected result.

Direct effects can be:

- **Physical**: physical change on the object of development;
- **Functional**: affects working on capability with degradations of operation;
- **Psychological**: that result from an action that induce emotions, reasons and in last consideration systems behavior;
- **Collateral**: results that occurred beyond intentions, with positives or negatives consequences to goal achievement.

Indirect effects can be:

- **Psychological**;
- **Collateral**;
- **Functional**;
- **Cumulative**: the results of direct and indirect effects action against a system;
- **Cascade**: indirect effects that cross different systems;
- **Systemic**: influence a specific operation of systems.

In order to obtain a complete understanding of effects that result from a possible action, it's necessary to have a holistic knowledge considering the existing relationships between the different systems that compose the ecosystem.

During the planning process are firstly recognized the information wanted effects.

In order to be able to identify the importance of effect and as consequence define its implementation, it was adopted on this model, prioritization, whose origin comes from software engineering.

The role of prioritization is to establish a relation of criticality between developing effects.

"The challenge is to select the "right" effects from a set of candidate effects in order that different interests, technical limitations and preferences of the different actors are watched over"(Ruhe G., 2002).

This prioritization development is supported on the following variable definitions (Berander & Andrews, 2005):

- **Importance**;
- **Penalties**;
- **Cost**;
- **Time**;
- **Risk**;
- **Volatility**;

That variables definition should also consider:

- **Abstraction layer**;
- **Reprioritization**;
- **Functionality**;

The quantification of those variables should be as isolated as possible, and can be used a different set of methods to obtain that goal (Berander & Andrews, 2005), such as:

- **AHP** (Analytical Hierarchy Process);
- **100 dollar test**;
- **Grouping**;
- **Classification**;
- **Top-ten**;

The result of prioritization suggests effects that should be implemented and in what order. Like any other evaluation method, the result should be appreciated and adjusted by the decision maker who detains the knowledge and not only simply accepted. This knowledge can also be grabbed from the network using a collaborative model.

The effects can also be self-related in many different ways, and its influence can have many aspects, such as the fact of been able to limit others effects development, affect the cost of implementation or increase/decrease the satisfaction level of other effects (Dahlstedt & Persson, 2005).

Effects interdependency can influence a set of development activities and decisions, at the planning phase, in management changes, in implementation and design characteristics, in testing and reuse of effects.

The knowledge about the existence and consequence of effects interdependency is essential in order to prevent potential mistakes that can be associated to a higher cost or even additional vulnerabilities that put effects at risk. Identifying interdependency characteristics allows effects traceability during all life cycles. For a certain effect, it makes possible to trace the development path and the role of the effect in the development of other effects.

Figure 6. Interdependency fundamental characteristics

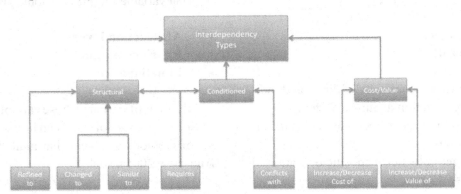

The interdependency presents a set of characteristics as illustrated on Figure 6.

Structural interdependencies is related with the fact that, given a specific set of effects, they can be organized in a structure where relationships are of hierarchal type, as well as transverse, and can be separated in three categories:

- **Refined to**: the effect is detailed to a determinate number of more specific effects;
- **Changed to**: change from one effect to another if a new version of that effects replaces the older one;
- **Similar to**: an effect is declared similar or overlaid by one or more effects.

In Figure 6 are also illustrated conditioned interdependencies that define the way some effects can limit others. This conditioning is defined by:

- **Requires**: the execution of an effect depends from the execution of another effect. To depend, on this case, means that one or more detailed effects are needed, this is, they are not optional, in order to complete the higher level effect;
- **Conflicts with**: effect conflicts with another and can't exist simultaneously or if the fulfillment of one decreases the other fulfillment;

The third type of interdependency illustrated in Figure 6, is the cost/value interdependency. The type cost/value interdependencies is related with the related cost in the implementation and that effect added value, and can be defined in the following way:

- **Increase / decrease cost of**: if an effect is chosen for implementation the other effect cost increase or decreases;
- **Increase / decrease value of**: if an effect is chosen for implementation then the value of another effect will increase or decrease.

The exponential grow of information technology use, according to Moore Law (Kopp, 2002; Moore, 1965) and current collaboration paradigm, with WEB 2.0 tools, act as collective knowledge strength multiplier for organizations.

These concepts flow trough frontiers as if there where none. Today, more than ever, the hourly spindles are more important than frontiers (Wriston, 1997). States, companies and individuals are now connected to a global commerce, by media, by transportation and by communication technologies. We are living in a networked economy era, centered in information ecosystem, where information effects are each time more important.

From this good perspective, allows to any individual, in any part of the globe the access to knowledge (Alberts, 2003).

The software replaced the importance of the hardware function.

From a collaborative paradigm perspective, supported by WEB 2.0 tools, the information perimeter has no limits, becoming each more a multidimensional space, where prevails upon the spatial dimension catalyzed by the time/velocity aspect.

It's in this complex context that the information ecosystem concepts based on effects comes to live, as a model for achieve information security at organization, obtaining the correct architecture for supporting the information life cycle, and creating a sustainable and healthy ecosystem.

With the integrating of information systems war concepts and their development in a information ecosystem, the model gives, in the rings definition, an illustrate and integrated vision of the ecosystem.

This model also uses actual concepts of information sharing, allowing the characterization of the fundamental elements of its development making available the informational state of network reliable connections and the shared knowledge.

With the identification of the wanted effects in the development phase of the ecosystem, making the characterization of the three support elements is created a model that will be able to follow all the organization development cycle.

The integration of critical vulnerabilities guarantees that the security analysis is not a process of information access analyze but an effect support characteristic that reflects the importance of associated effect.

CONCLUSION

It's clear that is happening a deep change in way how organizations interact with their working environment. The IT is a fundamental element for this change and WEB 2.0 in particular, gives the concepts that allow the change empowerment.

Despite this fact is recurrent to see titles like "IT doesn't matter" that follow the idea that been IT so ordinary, that is, been parte of actual organizations development, it's completely useless as differentiate element and in competitiveness raise.

This vision puts information systems department under pressure, in order to reduce investment value and also to do more with less, something clear in the last few years and even more now in this crises.

IT can be able to express its importance in an innovative manner, not trough the universal support of organizations but as developer of new ways of thinking organizations integration and information ecosystem.

MySpace shows a development of 2 Millions users each month, Facebook is used by 85% of all American students and one blog is born at each second, this is the reality.

This is not about putting information on-line. It's about the use of mass collaboration tools as production mean and in that way been the key element of a fundamental change in the way innovation is made.

Organizations traditional model presents a closed hierarchy in this new model we have an open organization, fundamentally centered in the network and people, not in capital.

However, this change in organization model only has now available conditions to be developed, and they are:

- **Correct technology**;
- **Demography**;
- **Economy**;
- **Society**.

The set of technology tools capable to support this new dynamic and whose name is WEB 2.0 is not anymore a set of static links and only useable on a PC, uses all equipments able to implement any kind of communications.

The use of this dynamic and ubiquitous world, allows the integration of different formats and solution that make the user experience each more interactive. This new dynamic allows environment based computing and the element that interacts with the organization ecosystem is the *thing*.

In face of this scenario, the development of information systems planning is each more complex. This complexity is also a consequence from the way manufactures understand technology, from the way organizations integrate technology and for last, from the way how human resources develop, integrate and use that resources.

With the emergence of the Internet, providing a new mean of communication and development, organizations developed a set of tools to empower this new channel, such us electronic commerce.

The electronic commerce arrived in a massive manner to organizations, integrating with existing information systems and developing on-line ordering systems, workflow methods and promoting the evolution of mobile communication platforms.

Communications evolved, allowing the ubiquitous connection of organization and with that organization made available to their workers tools for on-line access to organization using essentially VPN solutions. With the increase of use, communications velocities continued to grow, reflecting once more the Moore law (Moore, 1965).

This communications evolution supplied conditions that allowed each more interactive solutions integration, the application developer, didn't have to be worried about velocity optimization, not been necessary deep communication knowledge to develop a working application.

WEB 2.0 applications appeared each more, with well developed graphical ambient and interactive, implementing solutions from simple sharing personal relationships to knowledge sharing.

In the advent of this technological development, supported in WEB 2.0 the information system become each more exposed to the sharing need, in order to promote organization innova-

tion development and in the limit, guarantee that organizations will be able to survive.

However, traditional information systems planning models still giving only organizations internal visions, they still closing organizations inside the four walls.

This structure reflects the form how organizations think their information security. Typically having a firewall that protects perimeter and allows access to certain organization functionality, however organization commitment happens with more complexity and cost inside the organization LAN.

This problem is even more serious with the integration need of doing and thinking of WEB 2.0, moving from the LAN knowledge centric world to WAN knowledge.

The only way that organization has to prepare themselves in order that, this ecosystem can be the innovation support and development, is guaranteeing that they have knowledge about the way how organization information flows and in which form.

The presented model allows a new approach, since de early phase of the first effect development until the development of the organizational ecosystem, with conditions to minimize the problems and the impact of unpredictability in organizational development.

The information is the element that flows in this ecosystem and organizations must be able to create conditions that allow the knowledge communities integration in a way that they can empower organization development and survival in this num world of global competitiveness.

Organization must understand that agility depends less and less from how produced information is protected, but from how information is made available with the reliability stamp.

Information is not the final product but the raw material for organizations development that all organizations want to convert in knowledge. For each elementary information notion, it becomes necessary to translate the wanted effect.

It's them fundamental that organization understands the consequence and capabilities of the use of that information during all the transformation process.

This planning model is presented as an approach to this problem, creating conditions for the organizational knowledge and developing organization ecosystem concepts.

If when modeling we have the possibility to create this ecosystem dynamic reality, despite its complexity, we will have conditions to understand complexity.

WEB 2.0 challenges are clear, more and more collaboration but for organization this paradigm adoption is only possible if reliable change of information is guaranteed and for that were presented some fundamental characteristics.

It was also presented that this integration, in order to really empower organization is extremely complex, since exposes organization structural systems and makes available new tools developed in order to supply a good user experience not to put up with organization integration with security in mind.

Existents information systems associated problems and these new tools enlarge even more the problems on this safe ecosystem creation, as illustrated in presentation of the different problems associated to each one of the actors in this form of interaction.

This model wants to integrate the WEB 2.0 challenges, presenting a way to achieve a suitable orientation to these networked users.

Considered as the start point in the way to creating a steady and dynamic ecosystem, capable to guarantee, wherever information is, that collaborative innovation, will be more an more rapidly integrate in organization.

WEB 2.0 is the treasure of organization development and innovation, and this information system planning model will be the map to X spot.

FUTURE WORK

As further development and based on effects planning model the main goal is to achieve the definition of the semantic flow of information integrating WEB 2.0 concepts, creating conditions for defining associated ontology.

For collecting searched information that will be mapped into the semantic model a plug-in agent development could be a solution. That agent will collect user interactions with information that then will be reflected on organization semantic information flow and ontology.

This semantic flow according to user needs will point the information that organization needs to produce the wanted effects and with that point out the model of information systems.

This semantic will also allow the creation of organization effects context and user context and with that being able to produce a model of organization ecosystem.

One idea of the model is presented in Figure 7.

Everybody is talking about that, but nobody is doing nothing.   Mark Twain

Figure 7. Effects Model Ontology architecture

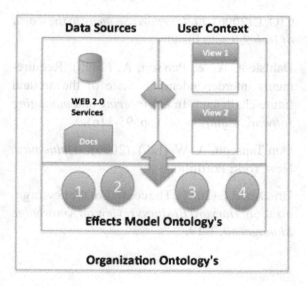

We should accept the future, because will be past quickly. However we should respect the past because was the human possible Saint-Exupery

REFERENCES

Alberts, D. S. H., & Richard, E. (2003). Power to the edge: Command...control...in the information age. In C. f. A. C. & Technology (Eds.), *Information age transformation series*. Center for Advanced Concepts and Technology.

André Vasconcelos, A. C., Sinogas, P., Mendes, R., & Tribolet, J. (1999). *Arquitectura de sistemas de informação: A ferramenta de alinhamento negócio / sistemas de informação?* Lisboa, Portugal: Fundação Portuguesa de Ciência e Tecnologia, programa POSI, FEDER.

Anna H. Perrault, V. L. G. (2000). Think global, act local: The challenges of taking the website global*. *INSPEL, 34*.

Berander, P., & Andrews, A. (2005). Requirements prioritization. In *Engineering and managing software requirements* (pp. 69-94).

Bradbury, D. (2007). Web 2.0 - beyond the buzz words. *Computer Weekly*.

CIO, I. (2006). *Field report: Security in the world of Web 2.0*. Cio Insight.

Dahlstedt, Å., & Persson, A. (2005). Requirements interdependencies: State of the art and future challenges. In *Engineering and managing software requirements* (pp. 95-116).

Don Tapscott, A. W. (Ed.). (2006). *Wikinomics*. New York: Portfolio.

Drucker, P. F. (2001). The coming of the new organization. *Harvard Business review on Knowledge Managment*, 1-19.

Forrester, R. (2006). *Preparing For the new IT ecosystem — building the foundation*. Forrester Research.

Hammond, J. (2007). Developing enterprise Web 2.0 applications. Forrester Research.

Hsu, S. P. C. (1995). *Strategic information systems planning: A review*. Paper presented at the Information Resources Management Association International.

Jupiter, R. (2006). *Jupiter RSS consumption March 2005* (Research report). Jupiter Research.

Kopp, C. (2002, Jan). *Moore's law and its implications for information warfare*. Paper presented at the The 3rd International AOC EW Conference, Zurich.

Leffingwell, D. W. D. (2000). *Managing software requirements – a unified approach*. Upper Saddle River, NJ: Addison-Wesley.

Mikroyannidis, A. (2007). *Toward a social Semantic Web*. Washington, DC: IEEE Computer Society: Moore, G. (1965). Cramming more componentes onto integrated circuits. *Electronics, 38*(8).

Nunes, P. V. (2006). *Planeamento operacional baseado em efeitos (PEBE)*. Paper presented at the Sociedade em rede: competição e conflito no dominio da informação.

Panada, F. (2007). *The emerging thread*. Armonk, NY: IBM Global Services.

Reilly, T. O. (2005). *What is Web 2.0?* Sebastopol, CA: O'Reilly.

Richardson, R. (2007). *2007 - computer crime and security survey*. Computer Security Institute.

Robertson, S., & Robertson, J. (1999). *Mastering the requirements process*. London: ACM Press.

Roman Hoegg, R. M., Meckel, M., & Stanoevska-Slabeva, K. (2007). *Overview of business models for Web 2.0 communities.* Institute of Media and Communication Management.

Ruhe, G. E. A., & Pfahl, D. (2002). *Quantitative WinWin – a new method for decision support in requirements negotiation.* Paper presented at the Proceedings of the 14th International Conference on Software Engineering and Knowledge Engineering (SEKE'02), Ischia, Italy.

Sifry, D. (2006). State of the blogosphere. *Technorati.*

Vicente, J. (2007). Operações baseadas em efeitos: O paradigma da guerra do século XXI. *Jornal Defesa e Relações Internacionais.*

Wriston, W. B. (1997). Bits, bytes, and diplomacy. *Foreign Affairs (Council on Foreign Relations),* 76(5), 11.

ENDNOTES

[1]   Ajax (asynchronous JavaScript and XML), or AJAX, is a group of interrelated web development techniques used for creating interactive web applications or rich Internet applications

[2]   The Extensible Markup Language (XML) is a general-purpose specification for creating custom markup languages

[3]   Web Services Description Language (WSDL) is an XML-based language that provides a model for describing Web services

[4]   Structured Query Language

[5]   Lightweight Directory Access Protocol, or LDAP, is an application protocol for querying and modifying directory services running over TCP/IP

[6]   SOAP (Simple Object Access Protocol) is a protocol for exchanging XML-based messages over computer networks, normally using HTTP/HTTPS

[7]   XPath (XML Path Language) is a language for selecting nodes from an XML document

[8]   User Interface

Section 3
Managerial and Organizational Issues

Chapter 16
Identifying and Managing Stakeholders in Enterprise Information System Projects

Albert Boonstra
University of Groningen, The Netherlands

ABSTRACT

This article focuses on how managers and sponsors of enterprise information system (EIS) projects can identify and manage stakeholders engaged in the project. This article argues that this activity should go beyond the traditional ideas about user participation and management involvement. Also suppliers, customers, government agencies, business partners and the general public can have a clear interest in the ways that the system will be designed and implemented. This article proposes to apply identification, analysis and intervention techniques from organization and management disciplines in the IS field to enhance the changes for the successfulness of enterprise information system implementations. Some of these techniques are combined in a coherent method that may help implementers of complex IS projects to identify and categorize stakeholders and to consider appropriate ways of involvement during the various stages of the project.

INTRODUCTION

Information system implementation projects traditionally affect a number of parties, including managers, developers, and users. The notion that managers and developers allow users to participate in system development has been a core topic of IS research and practice since the 1960s. Mumford is one of the main advocates of this notion, by arguing that "people at any level in a company, if given the opportunity and some help, can successfully play a major role in designing work systems" (Mumford, 2001, p. 56). Main reasons for participation are the assumed link between participation and system success in terms of system quality, user satisfaction, user acceptance, and system use (Markus & Mao, 2004). Mintzberg (1994) argues that people who have been consulted and have participated in the process will better understand the trade-offs between project benefits and disadvantages and have greater trust. Consequences of neglecting participants, on the other hand, may lead to system failure and resistance towards the system (Gonzalez & Dahanayake, 2007).

During recent decades, however, the traditional notion of users has been eroded by new trends in IS development, such as package installations, outsourcing, enterprise systems, and systems that cross organizational boundaries, and has changed the nature of IS practice. These trends indicate that modern information systems are increasingly complex since they affect a broader range of stakeholders both from within and from outside the organization. This wider group of stakeholders is also becoming an integral part of EIS implementation and is part of the 'sociology of technology.' Depending on the impact and scope of the system, these stakeholders may include suppliers and customers, business partners (such as banks), providers of IS/IT services, competitors, government agencies, and, in some cases, may well extend to the press and the general public. Information systems tend to increase the scope from smaller, internal, and functional areas to enterprise wide systems (such as ERP-systems) and systems that cross company boundaries and may well impact on personnel from different countries, with their own language and different value and legal systems.

This means that system development is increasingly an undertaking where many different people believe that they can affect or can be affected by the process or the outcome of the system. Many of these people will respond to system proposals according to their interests and their perception of the impact, the function and the objectives of the system (Rost, 2004). If project managers and others, responsible for the development and the implementation, are not prepared to take into account these wider requirements, they will be reactive rather than proactive. In such circumstances, as Boonstra (2006) elucidates, the progress will be shattering and shocked by all kinds of unexpected actions and responses from a variety of stakeholders during the various stages of the project.

To take into account such considerations and be proactive, a systematic stakeholder management is needed in the more complicated information system projects. Stakeholder management means that stakeholders around EIS (Enterprise Information System) projects are identified and analyzed so that appropriate actions are taken in ways that support the project (McElroy & Mills, 2003). To address this need for stakeholder management, the objective of this article is to propose a coherent set of techniques that can be used to identify and categorize stakeholders and stakeholder relations in EIS projects as well as to define appropriate actions towards stakeholders.

Of course methods exist for stakeholder identification and categorization. However, these methods are diverse in focus and nature and not specified to EIS development and implementation. Some exclusively focus on identification of stakeholders (Vos & Achterkamp, 2006), others on assessing their relative importance (Mitchell, Agle, & Wood, 1997) or on ways to involve them (Bryson, 2004). The contribution of this article is that it will specifically focus on stakeholders within complex enterprise IS projects and that it combines various theories and approaches into a practical and consistent method.

The article is structured as follows. It begins with some theoretical backgrounds of the stakeholder management approach. This section will briefly discuss literature on stakeholders and its most important findings. The next section discusses the seven activities of the method and combines these activities into a coherent method. The details of the proposed method will be illustrated by a case study. The discussion section examines the extent to which the method contributes to solving the stakeholder identification, categorization and intervention problem in IS contexts. Finally, the conclusion section will discuss the strengths and limitations of the method, by providing some suggestions for further work and by suggesting some guidance for practitioners.

BACKGROUND

Orlikowski (1992) proposes that the results of information systems depend on the interaction of both technology and people over an extended period. Information systems are both a product of human action and an influence of human action. People initiate, design, and use an IT system. Designers construct the system according priorities and expectations. Then, various stakeholders, such as users and managers, react in different ways, for example, by welcoming, rejecting, or adapting it. In doing so, they socially construct the technology in the sense that these reactions may become features of the system. This continuing interaction means that the results eventually obtained are different from those, which were originally expected. Orlikowski also suggests that stakeholders around the system can modify technologies during design, implementation, and use, since people and technology interact. Because of this, information systems are not primarily technical systems but social systems and their design, implementation, and use involve dynamic social and political processes in articulating interests, building alliances, and struggling over outcomes (Levine & Rossmoore, 1994). To understand how a system functions in a business, we must understand the nature of the relationship between various stakeholders and their interactions with the system. Stakeholder management should be based on such an understanding.

According to Mitchell et al. (1997), stakeholders can be defined in many different ways. Different kinds of entities can be stakeholders, such as persons, groups inside as well as outside

an organization. Within this research, Freeman's classical definition is a useful starting point. He defines stakeholders as follows: "A stakeholder is any group or individual who can affect or is affected by the achievement of the organization's objectives" (Freeman, 1984, p. 46). In the case of an EIS project, this implies that any person or group who can affect or is affected by the EIS system is a stakeholder. Stakeholders' interests can be very diverse, since information systems affect many aspects of the business, including strategic position, cost-effectiveness, job satisfaction, security, customer satisfaction, and commercial success. This implies that many parties around an EIS project can be stakeholders.

McLoughlin (1999) adds an important perspective to the definition of Freeman by arguing that stakeholders are "those who share a particular set of understandings and meanings concerning the development of a given technology." He emphasizes the interpretive nature of stakeholders. Stakeholders are groups or individuals *who believe* that they can affect or are affected by an information system. This means that stakeholders are determined by perceptions and not by objective realities. This is in line with social constructivist (Pinch & Bijker, 1997) and interpretive (Walsham, 1993) views on reality and technology. Walsham argues that people act according to subjective interpretations of their world, "our knowledge of reality ... is a social construction by human actors ... there is no objective reality which can be discovered by researchers and replicated by others" (1993, p.5). Stakeholders interpret the existing context and may act to change it to promote personal, local, or organizational objectives (Boddy, 2004). This implies that stakeholders are potential actors—people or groups with the power to respond to, negotiate with, and change the specifications and eventually impact the success of the system. Project managers and other promoters of new information systems have the responsibility to manage this process of stakeholder activity by creating a context for dealing with stakeholders

Figure 1. Stakeholder management activities

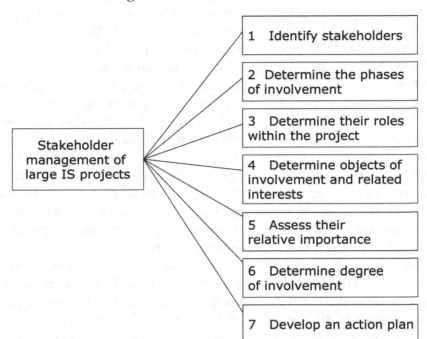

in effective ways. The method as presented in this article is developed to facilitate the creation of this context.

STAKEHOLDER MANAGEMENT ACTIVITIES

Figure 1 briefly describes the method as presented in this article by seven activities that can be conducted to form the basis for sound stakeholder management. These activities are 1) identify stakeholders, 2) determine the phase of involvement, 3) determine their roles within the project, 4) determine objects of involvement and related interests, 5) assess the relative importance of stakeholders, 6) determine the degree of involvement, and 7) develop an action plan. Each activity will be explained in more detail in the following paragraphs.

The order of these activities will depend on the preference of the user of the method and the

specific project characteristics. The order as presented in Figure 1 can be followed at the start, but often activities have to be reconsidered, given the results of subsequent activities. Mintzberg also argues that stakeholder management should be "… an ongoing and adaptive process …" (1994, p. 74). Therefore, the activities of stakeholder management are often interactive and dynamic (see Figure 2). When time elapses, stakeholder managers may come to new insights, often caused by unexpected actions of stakeholders or because stakeholders influence each other, which may lead to redoing certain activities and to an adaptation of the action plan to manage stakeholders (Activity 7).

Identify Stakeholders

An important activity of deliberate stakeholder management is to identify relevant players. Identifying stakeholders comes in essence to the question "who are they?" For dealing with this question, stakeholder literature offers a variety of

Figure 2. Enterprise information system stakeholder management as an interactive and dynamic activity

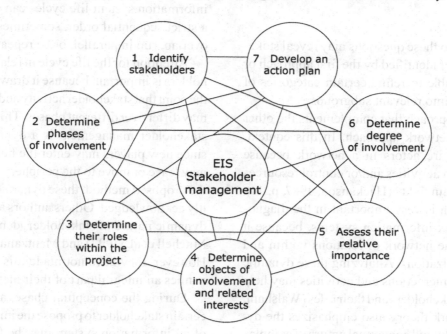

classification models (Mantzana, Themistocleous, Irani, & Morabito, 2007; Mitchell et al., 1997; Pouloudi & Whitley, 1997; Vos & Achterkamp, 2006; Wolfe & Putler, 2002).

Identifying stakeholders around IS means that a stakeholder mapper makes a subjective interpretation about who affects and who will be affected by a new information system. This means that groups or individuals have to be identified and that boundaries have to be drawn. There are various approaches to identify stakeholders, which can be regarded as complementary.

One is to use frameworks (Mantzana et al., 2007), often in the form of checklists relevant to the generic types of stakeholders, such as "customers, suppliers, competitors, users, managers, and developers" (Cummings & Doh, 2000). Such checklists can be adapted to make them more suitable for particular industries, for example, *doctors, patients, pharmacies, pharmaceutical companies*. They can then be used to determine which specific groups of stakeholders are impor-

tant in relation to the information system. For example, *neurologists, patients with neurological diseases, pharmacy A, Merck*. This way of identifying stakeholders is quite generic but could serve as a useful starting point.

A second approach is posing questions concerning the information system and its nature. Relevant questions that may help to identify relevant groups and individuals in this context are (Cavaye, 1995; Pouloudi & Whitley, 1997):

- Who are the initiators of the system?
- Who are the sponsors of the system?
- Who have to adopt the system and make it work?
- Who are the intended users?
- Who will receive the output of the system?
- Who are the intended developers and operators of the system?
- Who will be impacted and affected by the system?

- Who will win or lose by using the system?

Answers to these questions may reveal stakeholders not yet identified by the first approach or make it possible to refine certain categories of stakeholders into relevant subgroups.

A third approach that complements the other ones is the network approach. In this context, stakeholders are actors in a network because they "perform activities and/or control resources within a certain field" (Håckanson, 1987, p. 14). This approach is very important in the diagnosis of complex information systems, because it focuses on the network of relations within and among organizations. Analyzing these dynamic networks of interactions and activities may help to identify stakeholders and their roles (Walsham, 1993). Network theory also emphasizes the dynamic, flexible, and contextual nature of complex information systems. This implies that it is not possible to draft one static stakeholder map. Stakeholders depend on a specific context that may change in time. In addition, stakeholders are related and may influence each other and therefore they cannot be viewed in isolation. Perceived interests and power of stakeholders are interactive and they may change over time (Pouloudi & Whitley, 1997).

Determine the Phases of Stakeholder Involvement

An information system follows a life cycle that begins when the system is conceived and ends when it is no longer available for use. Various authors have proposed phases that can be distinguished in this life cycle (e.g., Markus. Axline, & Petrie, 2000; Turner, 2006). A typical IS life cycle includes a concept stage, a development stage, an implementation stage, an operation and maintenance stage, and a termination stage. However, in practice, these processes can be quite different

and more complicated (Boonstra, 2003). Some information system life cycles can take place in a strict sequential order, sometimes phases will overlap, run in parallel, or be repeated.

Attention for the life cycle in relation to stakeholders is important because it draws attention to the point that stakeholder activity and involvement may differ over different phases. This implies that stakeholder management is a dynamic process since new players may enter the field and others may leave or move to the periphery over time. In the proposed method, these dynamics are explicitly acknowledged. Others authors also stress the dynamic nature of stakeholder identification are Mitchell et al. (1997) and Mantzana et al. (2007). However, they have not made this essential dynamics an integral part of their methods.

During the conceptual phase, a reason for a certain stakeholder to propose the implementation of an information system may be that a system may strengthen its position in the organization or in the value chain, e.g. by providing more reliable information and transparency. Other stakeholders may interpret the availability of such information as a threat. During the development phase, a stakeholders' main concern is to shape the system to fit its interests. The implementation phase can be used by stakeholders to support implementation activities or to hinder these, depending on its specific interests. During the operational phase, the main concern is to align the system with the stakeholders' going concerns. Actions of stakeholders may also vary during the various stages, from dormant to very active and vice versa. For stakeholder managers, this may imply that it can be important to involve stakeholders actively in phases that they are dormant, to prevent for upright opposition during later stages.

Determine Stakeholders' Roles within The project

Within complex EIS projects, different stakeholders will often have different roles. For an under-

Table 1. Stakeholders roles in EIS projects

Owner:	Who provides resources to develop or buy the system;
Project manager:	Who monitors the performance of the project and takes action if the project does not achieve the desired progress;
User:	Who will use the system by entering data or by retrieving information from it;
Developer:	Who designs, develops, or adapts the system; this includes consultants who contribute to the IS project;
Decision maker:	Who will be involved in decisions with regard to the scope and design of the system;
Passively involved:	Who will be affected by the consequences of the system but is not willing or able to play one of the above mentioned roles.

Table 2. Objects and related issues within EIS projects

	Objects	Related Issues
1.	Scope of the system	Goals and business advantages of the system
2.	Business model	Work flow model and business processes
3.	Functioning enterprise	Inputs and outputs of the system
4.	System model	Human interface architecture
5.	Technology model physics	Presentation architecture
6.	Component configuration	Security of the system, compatibility
7.	System Project	Project performance, time, money

standing of stakeholder attitudes and responses toward EIS initiatives, it is important to attach such roles explicitly to stakeholders. Roles and responsibilities that people have are a determining factor of attitudes and responses to initiatives and change ideas. Based on Turner (2006), Vos and Achterkamp (2006), and Mantzana et al. (2007), Table 1 lists the possible roles among the stakeholders in EIS projects.

Vos and Achterkamp (2006) also distinguish stakeholders in being directly involved or being represented. In relation to EIS projects, this is relevant since many stakeholders are often represented by others who formally may act on their behalf. In practice, stakeholders can play different roles at the same time and roles also may change in time or during subsequent phases. For example, a project manager of a large information system project can also be business manager who eventually has to work with the system.

Determine Objects of Possible Involvement and Related Interests

Stakeholders are generally interested in certain objects of the system. It is important to identify those objects as well as their interests. Objects can vary from the scope and objectives of the system to programming issues and from security to consequences for work and employment. Zachman (1999) provides a useful contribution for identifying relevant objects of involvement with his work on information system architectures. Based on this work, Table 2 identifies the objects and related issues.

In many EIS projects, decision makers, such as business managers, tend to focus mainly on the first three objects, whereas developers are more directed to objects 3–6. Users, on the other hand, tend to be interested in objects 2–4. For effective stakeholder management, it is important to identify objects that are relevant for each group of stakeholders to keep them interested.

When these objects are identified, it is important to determine the specific interests that are at stake in relation to these objects of the information system. Freeman (1984) uses the term "stake" interchangeably with "interest." Stakes or interests motivate stakeholders and are important determinants of stakeholders' priorities.

Stakeholders do often have different interests and different priorities among shared interests. Interests can also be conflicting (e.g., some stakeholders may be in favor of central decision making, while others may strive towards local autonomy). Besides, it may be possible that certain interests are not realistic, meaning that they cannot be realized by the system. Because of this, stakeholders tend to follow different agendas to achieve their goals.

Examples of interests of stakeholders in enterprise information systems (e.g., Doherty, King, & Al-Mushayt, 2003; Müller & Turner, 2007; Saarinen, 1996; Shenhar, Levy, & Dvir, 1997) are that the system:

- promotes the realization of strategic objectives of the company or the business unit (scope);
- delivers a positive return on investment of the system (scope);
- will strengthen business process performance (business model);
- provides good value and quality of information (functioning enterprise);
- is easy to use and user friendly (system model and presentation architecture);
- promotes work satisfaction (system model);
- promotes employment (functioning enterprise);
- has a good technical performance, maintainability and security (technology model physics);
- project will be completed in time and within budget (system project).

The objects in which stakeholders are interested imply criteria to which they will assess EIS projects. These criteria will often by highly related to the roles that these stakeholders may have (Fowler & Walsh, 1999; Wolfe & Putler, 2002). For example, top managers (a function) will often have roles as owner/decision maker. Given this function and these roles, they will be interested in the objects, scope and business model and will generally assess EIS projects against the criteria strategy, return on investment, business process performance, and project performance. Users of the system, on the other hand, will be focused on objects like business model and functioning enterprise and will be interested in issues like work satisfaction, employment, and user friendliness. If customers of the implementing organization are users (e.g., in case of a Web site for ordering goods or services), they may assess the system against criteria such as compatibility with their own systems, ease of use, and attractiveness of the system compared to those of alternative suppliers. These examples show that it is important to understand the roles that stakeholders play, the objects in which they have an interest, and the specific interests that they may have, as a consequence of those roles.

Assess Their Relative Importance

It is also useful to categorize stakeholders by their relative salience during the various stages of the project. Salience is the degree to which managers may give priority to stakeholder claims. For classifying stakeholders, Mitchell et al. (1997) developed the stakeholder salience model. Stakeholder salience theory (Mitchell et al., 1997) categorizes stakeholders against the possession of three relationship attributes: power, legitimacy, and urgency (see Figure 3).

A group has *power* to the extent it has access to coercive, utilitarian, or normative means for imposing its will in the relationship. *Legitimacy* is a social good and more over-arching than in-

Figure 3. Stakeholder salience model (Mitchell et al., 1997)

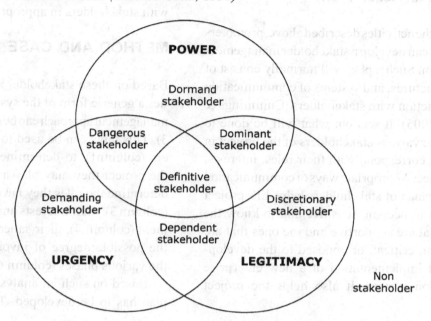

dividual self-perception and is shared amongst groups, communities, or cultures. *Urgency* is based on time sensitivity and criticality. Combining these attributes generates eight types of stakeholder: dormant, discretionary, demanding, dominant, dependent, dangerous, definitive, and non-stakeholder (Mitchell et al., 1997). Stakeholder salience theory suggests that the amount of attention attributed to these categories should not be equal and that it can be used to give priority to competing claims of stakeholders.

Determine Degree of Involvement

Promoters of an EIS project should think about a successful project by considering the interests and relative importance of stakeholders to realize a balance of pluralist and sometimes contrasting perceived interests and power. Whether this negotiation is explicit or not, the stakeholders and their interests have to be managed to move forward and to achieve the objectives. Thus, once a decision has been made about involving a stakeholder on a certain object, the degree of involvement should be clarified. Many managers will let this

depend on the salience of the stakeholder during a particular phase of the project and the interests, roles and expertise of that stakeholder. Degrees of engagement can vary (Bryson, 2004):

- *inform* (stakeholder is provided with information on the system without further real influence);
- *consult* (stakeholder and project members exchange information and opinions and there is real openness for advice);
- *involve* (stakeholder has a main influence on the development and implementation of one or more objects of the information system);
- *collaborate* (stakeholder becomes co-responsible for the development and implementation of one or more objects of the information system);
- *empower* (stakeholder is responsible for the development and implementation of one or more objects of the information system).

Develop an Action Plan

Based on the activities described above, promoters of the EIS can develop a stakeholder management action plan. Such a plan will normally consist of ideas, structures, and systems of communication and interaction with stakeholders (Cummings & Worley, 2005). It sets out what will be done to engage the various stakeholders of the project in ways that correspond with their roles, interests, and salience. Appropriate ways of communication with the range of stakeholders helps EIS project managers to become sensitive and to know the parties that are supportive and the ones that are indifferent, critical, or opposed to the development and implementation of a new enterprise information system. It also helps the project leader to become credible and to communicate with stakeholders in appropriate ways.

METHOD AND CASE STUDY

Based on these stakeholder management activities a generic form of the systematic stakeholder management approach can be developed (see Table 3). This table can be used to identify stakeholders (column1), to determine in what phases of the project they may play a role (column 2), to determine the roles they have within each phase (column 3), their interests and objects of involvement (column 4), their salience (column 5), and the possible degree of involvement throughout the various phases (column 6).

Based on such an analysis, a specific action plan has to be developed. Table 3 implies that

Table 3. Stakeholder management method

1	2	3	4		5	6	7
Stakeholder	Involvement in phase	Roles	Objects of involvement & related interests		Relative importance	Degree of involvement	Specific action plan
Pouloudi & Whitley (1997) Vos & Achterkamp (2006) Bryson (2004) Mantzana et al. (2007)	Markus et al. (2000)Turner (2006)	Turner (2006) Vos & Achterkamp (2006) Mantzana et al. (2007)	Zachman (1999) Shenhar et al. (1997) Saarinen (1996) Doherty et al. (2003) Müller & Turner (2007)		Mitchell et al. (1997)	Burke (1997) Bryson (2004)	Cummings & Worley (2005)
Name of individual, unit, or organization	*Phases:* Concept Development Implementation Operation Maintenance Termination	*Roles:* Owner Project manager User Developer Decision-maker Passively involved Direct involved or Representative	*Objects:* Scope of the system Business model Functioning enterprise System model Technology model physics Component configuration System project	*Interests:* Strategy Return on investment Business process performance Work satisfaction and employment User friendliness Technical performance and security Quality of information Project performance	*Sailence is based on:* Legitimacy Urgency Power *Stakeholder can be:* Dormant Discretionary Demanding Dominant Dependent Dangerous Definitive or Non stakeholder	*Modes of Involvement:* Inform Consult Involve Collaborate Empower	

some stakeholders can become participants during certain phases. Participants are subsets of stakeholders who are actually given the chance to participate in concept, development, implementation, or operation activities (Markus & Mao, 2004). Other stakeholders may only be informed or consulted. Some groups may be more able and willing to participate in certain stages than others. Project managers will tend to provide opportunities to participate to the more salient stakeholders (column 5). Involvement and participation activities (column 7) may differ throughout the various phases and can be more and less intensive. Examples of such activities are discussion meetings, requirements generation, testing, training sessions, information sessions, and brainstorming sessions. Various methods and techniques can be used to engage stakeholders, such as working via prototypes, Joint Application Development (JAD), brainstorming sessions, and forums.

The following case study shows how the method has been applied during the development of an electronic patient record in a regional health care system. The description does not intend to provide a complete stakeholder management approach; it only gives an impression of how the method can be used in practice

This electronic patient record was proposed by the management of a large hospital. The system was intended to enable hospital doctors, hospital departments, GPs, and pharmacies to share medical data. Within this concept, authorized users could access patient data from any location, and the system would conduct automated checks for drug and allergy interactions, record clinical notes and prescriptions, schedule appointments, and distribute laboratory data. The hospital's Information Systems (IS) department would manage the system; costs would be shared; and a representative council would provide control. Since the management of the hospital felt that this would be a complex project, not only from a technical viewpoint but also from a contextual perspective, they decided to explore in depth how

this context is in terms of stakeholders by using the method as explained above.

Promoters of the system first identified the most relevant stakeholders by using a combination of methods that are described in the previous section. These promoters included a manager of the hospital responsible for information systems, the IS director, and an external consultant. For each stakeholder group, the other cells were also completed, in most cases per phase or per object. This led to a preliminary action plan (column 7 of Table 4 references specific action plans). (Table 4 only shows a part of the table to give an impression of the use of the method.)

Completion of this table led to extensive discussions about the identification of stakeholders (who are they), but also interests, power, roles, and ways to include their interests in the concept and development of the system. During the concept phase, two sessions of 2 hours were held to develop this table and make a first sketch of an action plan (consisting of references to ideas of stakeholder involvement, see column 7 of Table 4). This plan was used by the project manager, who was appointed at a later stage.

During the use of the method, the project manager discovered that power and interests of some stakeholders were sometimes assessed in ways that proved to be inadequate. In other cases, certain stakeholders received too much attention from the project manager, which led to a degree of influence that did not match with their actual degree of salience. This led to adaptations of the plan throughout the project. During the activity "identification" promoters ignored the general public (and potential patients) and perceived them as "non stakeholders." For that reason, the general public did not have a place in the stakeholder management table and were ignored by the project manager. However, press coverage in a regional newspaper paid attention to the development of an electronic patient record. Based on those articles, a patient organization asked about the reasons for the system and about privacy issues. During an

Table 4. Stakeholder management plan for electronic patient record system

Stakeholder management plan for Electronic Patient Record						
1	2	3	4		5	6	7
Stakeholder	Involvement in phase	Roles	Objects of involvement & related interests		Relative importance	Degree of involvement	Specific action plan
Hospital directors	Concept	Owner / decision maker	Scope of the system Business model Functioning enterprise	Strategy Return on investment	Definitive	Empower	Ref 1
	Development	Decision maker	Business model Functioning enterprise	Business process performance Project performance	Dominant	Involve	Ref 2
	Implementation		Functioning enterprise	Project performance System use		Consult	Ref 3
	Operation	Passively involved	Functioning enterprise	Quality of information	Dormant	Inform	Ref 4
IS department of hospital	Concept	Passively involved	Business model	Technical feasibility	Demanding	Consult	Ref 5
	Development		System model Technology model physics Component configuration		Dependent		Ref 6
	Implementation	Decision maker	System model Technology model physics Component configuration	Technical performance and security	Definitive	Involve	Ref 7
	Operation	Owner	Functioning enterprise System model Technology model physics Component configuration			Empower	Ref 8
Project manager	Development & implementation	Project manager	System project	Project performance	Dependent	Collaborate	Ref 9
External consultancy	Development	Developer	Business model Functioning enterprise	Business process performance Project performance	Dependent	Collaborate	Ref 10
Hospital doctors	Concept	Decision maker	Scope of the system Business model Functioning enterprise	Quality of work Autonomy Financial consequences Quality of information	Definitive	Involve	Ref 11
	Development		Business model Functioning enterprise				Ref 12
	Implementation	User	Functioning enterprise				Ref 13
	Operation					Collaborate	Ref 14
General practitioners	Concept	Passively involved	Scope of the system Business model	Autonomy Financial consequences Quality of work and information	Discretionary	Inform	Ref 15
	Development						Ref 16
	Implementation	User				Involve	Ref 17

evaluation, project managers agreed that a more pro-active approach to the public by providing information brochures and advertisements would have prepared the public supported the project.

DISCUSSION

The method as described combines various theories and brings them together into a practical approach for managing stakeholder relationships that can be used by managers to consider stakeholders in a systematic manner. The method helps users to link stakeholder identification and analysis with influence and intervention. The method also goes beyond traditional ideas of user participation, since it suggests identifying all affected parties around a project. Using the method raises attention for developing strategies of managing stakeholder relationships: for example, engaging the participation of powerful supportive stakeholders and simultaneously attempting to deal with opponents through processes of negotiation, communication, and education.

It is important to recognize the dynamic nature of the stakeholder map, which means that the actual stakeholder approach has to be reviewed. This is because stakeholders depend on a specific context, which may change over time in ways that are difficult to predict in advance (Pouloudi & Whitley, 1997, p. 5). One reason for this dynamic nature of the stakeholder environment is that stakeholders are often inter-related, and the effects of these relationships are hard to predict. For that reason, it is not possible to design a complete stakeholder map if only the relations between stakeholders and the project are considered and the effects of the project on their mutual relationships are ignored.

In the illustrated case, one specific group of hospital doctors (dermatologists) was not cooperative in the attempt to develop one electronic patient file. They preferred to use their own system. When other specialists became aware of this resistance of the dermatologists, they also tended to become less cooperative. As a consequence, representatives of all specialties had to become involved in the development process, instead of one representative for all. That meant a major change in the stakeholder management process. This example shows how stakeholders can influence each other in unexpected ways, which may have an impact on the development process.

Another reason to review a stakeholder approach is changing circumstances. For example, when project costs or project duration become higher or lower than expected initially, attitudes of stakeholders may change. In the case of the electronic patient file, hospital directors became more critical towards the system once they discovered the increasing costs of the development and the growing resistance from many other stakeholders. This led to a review of the relations around the system and to other stakeholder management approaches. The project leader had to "empower" directors again during the development process to make decisions about the further course of actions.

Despite the issues mentioned above it still may be useful to design a preliminary plan on how to deal with stakeholders at the start of an EIS project. Such a plan can be used to establish stable communication structures and to identify the issues to be dealt with as well as the status of the meetings, for instance informative, consulting, or for making decisions.

The method has been applied by more than 50 managers, responsible for IS projects, as well as by general managers who were a decision maker of such projects. During feedback sessions, these managers generally commented that the method helped them to consider the stakeholder environment and stimulated them to think in advance as well as during the project about stakeholders and appropriate actions. However, data analysis about their experiences is not yet sufficiently advanced to evaluate the effectiveness of the method.

FUTURE TRENDS

An agenda for further research can be directed at specifying how certain degrees of stakeholder involvement can lead to effective action plans (Activity 7). The approach as described in this article leaves this issue quite open. However, it is very relevant to include effective action plans into the method, which can be related to the various degrees of involvement throughout the various stages of the life cycle. Another interesting piece of future work is to address the question whether stakeholder analysis does help to produce desirable (or better) information systems. Finally, there is limited literature of how stakeholders around information systems are interrelated. Such research should provide suggestions about implications of inter-relatedness for action plans of stakeholder involvement.

CONCLUSION

Since information systems do increasingly affect interests of many parties, it is essential for management to focus on these parties by identifying them and by assessing their interests and their capabilities to influence the design, implementation and use of the proposed system. It is a common mistake to rush the implementation of a complex information system and to ignore the interests of various parties or to take them for granted. This may lead to system failure, troubled relations with parties or other undesirable effects. IS development in complex environments is often a situation where no one is fully in charge and many are involved, affected, or have certain responsibilities (Bryson, 2004). In such a diffuse situation, it is essential to think about policies and actions that promote effective development and implementation activities.

The main contribution of this article is that it suggests a practical method that helps managers to identify stakeholders as well as their interests and power and to develop possible actions to involve them or include their interests in the specifications of an information system. Taking deliberate steps to diagnose EIS initiatives and to involve relevant parties and divide benefits among stakeholders prior, during, and after implementation may prevent failure and disappointment. The method may help managers to be sensitive for their environment and to shift from a one dimensional, technological, and linear approach to system development to a multiple perspective assessment.

The method is flexible and acknowledges and addresses the time dimension of stakeholder management. Stakeholders may come and go during the process and interests and power positions may change during the design and implementation process. Because of this, the method should be used on a continuous basis to revise and monitor the positions and interests of stakeholders.

A limitation of the method is that it does not address the philosophies that project managers may have towards stakeholders. Some emphasize normative, moral, or ethical views on stakeholder management (Yuthas & Dillard, 1999; Gibson, 2000), while others hold a more instrumental view that emphasizes a contingent relationship (Donaldson & Preston, 1995). Independent of those views, managers can use the method as an integrated approach that combines theories on stakeholder management and is intended to help implementers and managers think systematically about how to deal with various social groups that affect or are affected by the system. It emphasizes instrumental, pragmatic, opportunistic, as well as normative, views on stakeholder management (Hirschheim & Klein, 1989).

REFERENCES

Achterkamp, M. C., & Vos, F. J. F. (2006). A Framework for making sense of sustainable innovation through stakeholder involvement. *International Journal of Environmental Technology and Management*, *6*(6), 525–538. doi:10.1504/IJETM.2006.011895

Boddy, D. (2004). Responding to competing narratives: Lessons for project managers. *International Journal of Project Management*, *22*(3), 225–234. doi:10.1016/j.ijproman.2003.07.001

Boonstra, A. (2003). Structure and analysis of IS decision making processes. *European Journal of Information Systems*, *12*(3), 195–209. doi:10.1057/palgrave.ejis.3000461

Boonstra, A. (2006). Interpreting an ERP implementation from a stakeholder perspective. *International Journal of Project Management*, *24*(1), 38–52. doi:10.1016/j.ijproman.2005.06.003

Bryson, J. M. (2004). What to do when stakeholders matter. Stakeholder identification and analysis techniques. *Public Management Review*, *6*(1), 21–53. doi:10.1080/14719030410001675722

Cavaye, A. L. M. (1995). User participation in system development revisited. *Information & Management*, *28*(5), 311–326. doi:10.1016/0378-7206(94)00053-L

Cummings, J. L., & Doh, J. P. (2000). Identifying who matters: Mapping key players in multiple environments. *California Management Review*, *42*(2), 83–105.

Cummings, T. G., & Worley, C. G. (2005). *Organization development and change*. Mason, OH: Thomson.

Doherty, N. F., King, M., & Al-Mushayt, O. (2003). The impact of inadequacies in the treatment of organisational issues on information systems development projects. *Information & Management*, *41*(1), 49–62. doi:10.1016/S0378-7206(03)00026-0

Fowler, A., & Walsh, M. (1999). Conflicting perceptions of success in an information systems project. *International Journal of Project Management*, *17*(1), 1–10. doi:10.1016/S0263-7863(97)00063-X

Freeman, R. E. (1984). *Strategic management, a stakeholder approach*. Boston: Pitman.

Gibson, K. (2000). The moral basis of stakeholder theory. *Journal of Business Ethics*, *26*(3), 245–257. doi:10.1023/A:1006110106408

Gonzalez, R., & Dahanayake, A. (2007). Responsibility in user participation in information system development. In M. Khosrow-Pour (Ed.), *Managing Worldwide Operations and Communications with Information Technology* (pp. 849-851). Hershey, PA: IGI Publications. Håckanson, H. (1989). *Corporate technological behaviour: Co-operation and networks*. London: Routledge.

Hirschheim, R., & Klein, K. (1989). Four paradigms of information system development. *Communications of the ACM*, *32*(10), 1199–1217. doi:10.1145/67933.67937

Levine, H. G., & Rossmoore, D. (1994). Politics and the function of power in a case study of IT implementation. *Journal of Management Information Systems*, *11*(3), 115–134.

Mantzana, V., Themistocleous, M., Irani, Z., & Morabito, V. (2007). Identifying healthcare actors involved in the adoption of information systems. *European Journal of Information Systems*, *16*(1), 91–102. doi:10.1057/palgrave.ejis.3000660

Markus, M. L., Axline, S., & Petrie, D. (2000). Learning from adopters experiences with ERP: Problems encountered and success achieved. *Journal of Information Technology*, *15*(4), 245–265. doi:10.1080/02683960010008944

Markus, M. L., & Mao, J. Y. (2004). Participation in development and implementation—updating and old, tired concept for today's IS contexts. *Journal of the Association for Information Systems*, *5*(11-12), 514–544.

McElroy, B., & Mills, C. (2003). Managing stakeholders. In R. J. Turner (Ed.), *People in project management* (pp. 99-118). Aldershot, UK: Gower.

McLoughlin, I. (1999). *Creative technological change*. London: Routledge.

Mitchell, R. K., Agle, B. R., & Wood, D. J. (1997). Toward a theory of stakeholder identification and salience: Defining the principle of who and what really counts. *Academy of Management Review, 22*(4), 853–886. doi:10.2307/259247

Müller, R., & Turner, J. R. (2007). Matching the project managers' leadership style to project type. *International Journal of Project Management, 25*(1), 21–32. doi:10.1016/j.ijproman.2006.04.003

Mumford, E. (2001). Action research: Helping organizations to change. In E. Trauth (Ed.), *Qualitative Research in IS: Issues and trends* (pp. 46 - 77). Hershey, PA: Idea Group Publishing.

Orlikowski, W. J. (1992). The Duality of Technology: Rethinking the Concept of Technology in Organisations. *Organization Science, 3*(3), 398–427. doi:10.1287/orsc.3.3.398

Pinch, T. J., & Bijker, W. E. (1997). The social construction of facts and artifacts: Or how the sociology of science and the sociology of technology might benefit each other. In W. E. Bijker, T. P. Hughes, & T. J. Pinch (Eds.), *The Social Construction of Technological Systems* (pp. 17-50), Cambridge,MA: MIT Press.

Pouloudi, A., & Whitley, E. A. (1997). Stakeholder identification in inter organisational systems: Gaining insights for drug use management systems. *European Journal of Information Systems, 6*(1), 1–14. doi:10.1057/palgrave.ejis.3000252

Rost, J. (2004). Political reasons for failed software projects. *IEEE Software, 21*(6), 104–107. doi:10.1109/MS.2004.48

Saarinen, T. (1996). An expanded instrument for evaluating information system success. *Information & Management, 31*(2), 103–118. doi:10.1016/S0378-7206(96)01075-0

Shenhar, A. J., Levy, O., & Dvir, D. (1997). Mapping the dimensions of project success. *Project Management Journal, 28*(2), 5–13.

Turner, J. R. (2006). Towards a theory of project management: The nature of the project. *International Journal of Project Management, 24*(2), 1–3. doi:10.1016/j.ijproman.2005.11.008

Vos, F. J. J., & Achterkamp, M. C. (2006). Stakeholder identification in innovation projects: Going beyond classification. *European Journal of Innovation Management, 9*(2), 161–178. doi:10.1108/14601060610663550

Walsham, G. (1993). *Interpreting information systems in organizations*. Chichester, UK: John Wiley & Sons.

Wolfe, R. A., & Putler, D. S. (2002). How tight are the ties that bind stakeholder groups? *Organization Science, 13*(1), 64–80. doi:10.1287/orsc.13.1.64.544

Yuthas, K., & Dillard, J. F. (1999). Ethical development of advanced technology: A postmodern stakeholder perspective. *Journal of Business Ethics, 19*(1), 35–49. doi:10.1023/A:1006145805087

Zachman, J. A. (1999). A framework for information systems architecture. *IBM Systems Journal, 38*(2/3), 454–471.

Chapter 17
Industrialism:
Reduction Either Complexity Patterns

Rinaldo C. Michelini
PMARlab, University of Genova, Italy

Roberto P. Razzoli
PMARlab, University of Genova, Italy

ABSTRACT

The chapter discusses the wealth generation mechanisms of the industrialism from its intrinsic cultural start, associated with the western-world stile. The prospected remarks single out several characterising features, in opposition to the east-Asia habits and cultural marks. Among other points, noteworthy remarks lead to prise complexity, instead of exploiting the reductionism. This is recognised as the robot age sign, opposed to the industry age patterns. The all discussion does not provide full solutions, rather suggests looking at the industrialism founding motivations (up to the cultural backing), in view to devise worthy alternatives.

INTRODUCTION

The nations' wealth build-up is conquest (or myth) brought forth with the industry patterns, when the transformation efficiency applies to the natural resources, obtained from earth fields, extensively changed in marketable goods, for widespread enjoyment, but at the expenses of waste and pollution increase. The designation conquest leads to the *affluent society*, founded on ceaselessly replacing items, to always remain at the front edge of technologies, and brings to distinguish the communities on their

innovation rates, still assuming the *industrialism* as the wishful target, towards which the *developing* countries should aim. The definition myth is frequent criticism of sceptical guesses, emphasising the irreversibility of the material transformations, making illusory the linked affluence, or, more correctly, predatory, turning the profit to temporary elites, with impoverishment of all the others (future generations, included). The picture leads to the *thrifty society*, founded on resources sparing and consumption lessening, through the *parsimony* way, or pace-wise decrease of waste and pollution.

Actually, the development defines as "the process through which the men achieve their per-

DOI: 10.4018/978-1-60566-856-7.ch017

Figure 1. Typical industry deployment features

> - the «industry» revolution beginning, within the tangibles transforms efficiency minimalism, out of decay bookkeeping;
> - the complexity/reductionism dilemma, showing the alternative approaches to make out describing causality relationships;
> - the conceptualisation habits in inferring classifications, to single out ordering taxonomies, also, in the current languages;
> - the community/individuals relationship, and the social-political appreciation of competition and democratic confrontation;
> - the preference of abstract reasoning, up to "physical laws" or "scientific work organisation", as *static* reference patterns;
> - the opponent logic to single out sharp statements, and to eliminate the knowledgeable fuzziness of entangled situations;
> - the competition, up to the *free market* axiom, as self-explaining idea, to *simplify* the lawful ethical behaviour of people.

sonal upgrading, with benefit in enhanced life conditions". The wealth expansion is the material side; the successfulness, nonetheless, should deal with the humanity in its integrity, and this is not the case, if the natural capital shrinks, while the waste and pollution amplify. The industry patterns wellbeing (even out of political implications) is temporary, and the growth for ever is cheating prospect. Then, affluence decrease is the only non-swindling scenery, while the conscious eco-logic behaviour shall turn to parsimony habits. That attitude leads to better *safe* than *sorrow*: the safety needs to refrain from pollution (and genetic modified organisms); the sore is subtle question, as *a contented mind is a perpetual feast*, notably, if the spendable riches are taken away from the yet-to-be generations.

The industrialism economics, on that picture, today is, perhaps, looking for relief from value chains in intangibles, with resort to the to de-materialise axioms of the knowledge entrepreneurship. The way out, most obviously, does not build on *contented mind*, or totally risk-safe *cautious headway*. It comes from the pioneering spirit of adventure, to discover new transformation economy processes, perhaps, with resort to the *cognitive* breakthrough, exploring the to re-materialise axioms, based on *bio-mimicry* and the genetic engineering.

- the industry revolution beginning, within the tangibles transforms efficiency minimalism, out of decay bookkeeping;
- the complexity/reductionism dilemma, showing the alternative approaches to make out describing causality relationships;
- the conceptualisation habits in inferring classifications, to single out ordering taxonomies, also, in the current languages;
- the community/individuals relationship, and the social-political appreciation of competition and democratic confrontation;
- the preference of abstract reasoning, up to "physical laws" or "scientific work organisation", as *static* reference patterns;
- the opponent logic to single out sharp statements, and to eliminate the knowledgeable fuzziness of entangled situations;
- the competition, up to the *free market* axiom, as self-explaining idea, to *simplify* the lawful ethical behaviour of people.

In the present chapter, we intend to study the industry patterns conquest (or myth) as specific and localised happening in the mankind history, to figure out lessons about likely breakthroughs, at any rate, as cultural phenomenon. Within the sketched premises, the chapter organises discussing topics, such as the ones collected in the Figure 1, which help understanding some industry features, through roughly arbitrary choice of characterising operations.

The Affluent Society Through Industry Patterns

The industry patterns are comparatively recent achievement in the mankind history, having their start with the UK industrialism two centuries ago, and characterise by rather localised deployment, being typical of the western world lifestyle, instigated by the European culture. The industrialism reaches the full effectiveness by the rather peculiar capitalism, where some socio-political sceneries (*free-market, economic global assent*, etc.) join with special scientific and technological knowledge, to promote (what is now named) the *industrial* revolution. The time and space narrow setting bears special import, and the industrialism, we know, needs to be understood as temporary success, not to last in time, and to spread out of bounded regions. Now, the *sustainable* growth (as if *sustainability* could assure indefinite increase) or the *developing* countries (as if the *affluent society* might repeat everywhere) are terms quite often repeated, not without ambiguities or even hypocrisy, because the outcomes, basically, refer to special mankind parentheses, and many reasons lead to the conjecture that a new revolution is necessary to keep the growth going on.

Besides, the industrialism we know is recognised to be defective in terms of entropy, energy and materials balance. With the entropy, if we believe in the physics laws, there is little to do. With the energy, we already trust in outer *natural* sources (chlorophyll synthesis, etc.) and hope in *artificial* extensions. With the materials, the reverse logistics provides limited recovery, and we shall look after totally new processes, e.g., the *artificial* life transformation of bio-mimicry. This motivates the parallelism between the *artificial* energy of the *industrial* revolution and the *artificial* intelligence trends of the (imaginative) *cognitive* revolution to come. By now, however, no certainty exists that the industry patterns might find *durable* alternatives into knowledge patterns, through value chains in *intangibles* and productivity in *artificial* life synergies.

Indeed, the *artificial* energy path aims at series of daring inventions, such as the replication of star nuclear fusion. The *artificial* intelligence path is associated with bio-mimicry, and the systematic resort to the ordering property, carried out by the living entities generating codes, to exploit the artificial life, for effective re-materialisation processes. We, already, have the bio-fuels (from bio-masses); and bio-engineering and genetic manipulation could open unhoped-for prospects. The long terms falls-off cannot be forecast, because the technologies have still to be developed, and they clang against the precaution principle. The fact of operating on living beings poses lots of questions. The pragmatic approaches incline to imply correspondences with the old *agricultural* revolution, when the man tamed sets of animals and vegetables, for better usefulness. Anyway, if no certainty exists about the successfulness, no evidence is given that the *artificial* changes are worse than the *natural* evolution, notably, under the *artificial* intelligence pace wise monitoring.

On these premises, to struggle for the *growth* challenge, either to *cautiously* oppose to risky falls-off is question of entrepreneurial mind and cultural background, and it might be worthy to understand a little more these aspects, compared with the recent *industrialism* deployments. Undoubtedly, these correspond with specific capitalism forms, at the nation-state level, to make feasible the sufficient backing-up (as compared with the earlier city-state capitalism), to establish imperialist hegemony, to forcedly open the market to the protected manufacture business. The history remembers the "*long global assent*", ruled for almost a century by the British empire, and the "*short global assent*", at the end of XX century, leaded by the USA. The *no-global* opposition combines the ecologic *caution* and the cultural position against technology-driven development and entrepreneurial competition. In these views, the *sustainablegrowth* is deceptive propaganda, used by the multi-national companies to support their hegemony, when the nation-state backing (even at the USA sub-continental level) is no more sufficient, to dominate the world-wide.

The *global/no-global* dilemma is unsolved quarrel of the beginning of the XXI century, at least, as for the underlying cultural positions (out of the, certainly highly biasing, political contexts). When the attention is moved, from the developed, to the developing countries, the said dilemma has quite different flavour, and the industrialism, as an all, is not without surprising outcomes.

Reductionism and Technical Deployment

The European cultural background, with the encyclopaedism and before, is putting the man in the central position, assuming, basically, the belief in the anthropic superiority, authorising the earth exploitation, whenever benefits are obtained. The technology-driven opportunities motivate the idea of progress, and the hope in growth sustainability. The approach has to look at knowledge set-ups, capable to trigger off and to feed the *revolution*, each time barriers to the development appear: the ancient *agricultural*, the recent *industrial* and the imaginary *cognitive* revolutions are just example outcomes. Indeed, no certainty exists about prospects on the physical world, unless that we have full trust on the models we are using to describe it, to have complete confidence on what we extrapolate from these models about possible future evolutions.

The last statement sounds, today, obvious (if not to all, for sure) to many persons. Apparently, this was not the case some three centuries ago, and the *industrial* revolution was typical western world prerogative. There is no reason to believe in the superiority of one or the other world population; on the contrary the fear exists that some internal contradictions of the western societies may hinder the progress to factual achievements (as it has been the case for, otherwise, advanced societies at the beginning of the *industrial* revolution). Anyway, the birth of the technical knowledge is somehow

a curiousness, being in progress generated into so a restricted world area, the Europe, due to in reality peculiar cultural conditions. Several interpretations can be devised, starting from the individualism, leading to the independence of actions and commitment, so that each human being is the author of his own success or failure. On these premises, the man is forced to find series of principles, such as the assessment of identity, the causal attribution, the logical reasoning, and so on, in view to build simplified necessary and sufficient conditions to oppose to the competing fighters, as fixed truths, not to be modified, thus permitting to reach his personal achievements.

The science, accordingly, develops along the reductionism paradigms, namely, the assertion that models exist, capable to describe the universe where we live, providing a self-consistent relational framework. This is the same as to declare that the world might be reduced to lists of (permanent) properties, and that the complexity can always be reduced into elementary constituents. The analysis is powerful instrument, allowing to reach the roots of all the situations. Of course such scientific spirit is not enough by itself; it has to be connected with the inclination towards action, so that the technology build-up occurs by trial-and-error tracks or activity-and-correction devising. With the standard *a posteriori* reasoning, assessing the outcomes and looking for the sources, one moves to a series of driving elements, providing the religious, linguistic, economical and political stimuli, Figure 2, biasing the western cultural style, towards mastering the personal fortune, even out of the originally recognised peculiarities. This means that the European common approach to the people wealth build-up demands the simultaneous individual/social, guidance/ collaboration and cultural/planning levels, each time putting the personal responsiveness, as the primary motivation.

• the belief in causal orders, culminating in the transcendent reliance on the originator

Figure 2. The Western style intellectual priorities

> - the belief in causal orders, culminating in the transcendent reliance on the originator (single) God, whose necessary and sufficient assessment is obtained by the ontological proof;
> - the learning of syntactically built rhetoric schemes and communication languages, in which the sentences orderly distinguish names, adjectives, verbs and complements;
> - the training requiring ways of life extensively based on the confrontation with competitors, so that the resort to laws is worthwhile opportunity and vital safeguard;
> - the culture to the syllogism, forced by the individualism habits, based on the socio-psychological requirements of the formal logic, as driver of communities and nations ruling.

(single) God, whose necessary and sufficient assessment is obtained by the ontological proof;

- the learning of syntactically built rhetoric schemes and communication languages, in which the sentences orderly distinguish names, adjectives, verbs and complements;
- the training requiring ways of life extensively based on the confrontation with competitors, so that the resort to laws is worthwhile opportunity and vital safeguard;
- the culture to the syllogism, forced by the individualism habits, based on the socio-psychological requirements of the formal logic, as driver of communities and nations ruling.

The mixing of the mentioned driving motivations along the three operation levels is conveniently expanded to encompass, one by one, in the foreground, the citizens' lifelong efforts to achieve the personal fulfilment and objective benefit, from, in the background, the everlasting quandaries of the mankind civilisation to give a rationale to the current demands. The foreground challenges concern each people as front end responsible of his destiny, e.g., addressing:

- the communication habits, say, the distinguishing features of the daily used languages;
- the competition standards, say, the common prised ways to create wealth and establishment.
- the static being opposed to the becoming, chiefly, when the interpretation models are built on the experimental evidence, and exploited as the reference truth;
- the dialectic opposed to the dialecticism, notably, each time the doubt becomes non-avoidable worry, and a single decision is important opportunity;
- the competition opposed to the fairness, particularly, when the socio-political issues are basic concern, and the personal success is current goal.

The background conditions gather the funding concepts, whose acknowledgment distinguishes the wise men in the European, either in the Far-east Asia nations. The example behavioural dilemmas show, Figure 3, permanent impasses, discerning the alternative features. The subsequent discussion summarises introductory hints, to assert that the western world approach to the industrial revolution

Figure 3. Main Western/Eastern behavioural dilemmas

> - the static «being» opposed to the «becoming», chiefly, when the interpretation models are built on the experimental evidence, and exploited as the reference truth;
> - the «dialectic» opposed to the «dialecticism», notably, each time the doubt becomes non-avoidable worry, and a single decision is important opportunity;
> - the «competition» opposed to the «fairness», particularly, when the socio-political issues are basic concern, and the personal success is current goal.

Figure 4. Basic actions of the causal analysis

> • to define the problem, listing the facts/ideas to be considered, with the all pertinent details;
> • to declare the theories/procedures that might be suited, according to the selected hypotheses;
> • to describe the methods/algorithms used in the inferences, assessing the related correctness;
> • to discuss the results, motivating why these always match the facts due to the assumptions;
> • to sum up the outcomes, rejecting all opposing deductions (as deviating digressions);
> • to add comments on the exploited references and on the similar proofing/reasoning lines.

cannot be viewed as deployment with no alternative. On the contrary, we now know that it aims at quite an hazardous use of the earth resources, so that the reconsideration of the different impasses can only be noteworthy exercise.

Education Dependence and Complexity Ties

The abilities in the construction of causal reasoning patterns are characteristics of the Europeans, from the ancient Greece world, where the philosophical schools, paradigmatically embodied into the Aristotle's teaching, provide the (still unrivalled) standard models. The causal analysis exploits steady rules, Figure 4, taught along the curricula of the European students, so that, e.g., it is obvious to learn the history connecting the sets of facts, to their originating causes, as if logical links need to be found, and no alternative might ever happen.

The approach is, without fall, worthy, when the action spirit is privileged. The backward model shows the input/output portrait, to assess pieces of evidence from already happened sequences. This might appear subjective or childish, if the fairness spirit is preferred, established on objectives of harmony, where each person is seen as community's member, with no reason/means to acquire independency. The surroundings is conditioning frame, and to singling out limited lists of properties cannot give insight on the actually in-progress processes. Opposite to the Aristotle's teaching, the Tao's one stresses on the becoming as the world's current attribute. Thereafter, it is foolish, to refer to snapshots, inferring general facts,

independent from the context. The chaining of the single portraits never explains the history.

- to define the problem, listing the facts/ideas to be considered, with the all pertinent details;
- to declare the theories/procedures that might be suited, according to the selected hypotheses;
- to describe the methods/algorithms used in the inferences, assessing the related correctness;
- to discuss the results, motivating why these always match the facts due to the assumptions;
- to sum up the outcomes, rejecting all opposing deductions (as deviating digressions);
- to add comments on the exploited references and on the similar proofing/reasoning lines.

Along similar schemes, the Plato's ideas permit to conceive the (abstract) meaningful being from the empirical phenomena, since, at the back, two assumptions are made:

- the universe is static, so that series of characterising features exist (and can be devised);
- the layers can be separated, detaching meaningful attributes, from the neighbouring context.

Together, they bring to the well known paradoxes of the sophists, so as the arrow never reaching the target, making impossible the motion (and the becoming). They lead, as well, at the interest to classify the objects, in view to extract their fundamental properties. In the Taoism, the cataloguing is confusing; the ancient philosopher Zhuangzi explains that:

- "to classify and to restrict the knowledge prevents from achieving true wisdom".

The separation of parts from the whole cannot make any sense; the segmented entities emerge from how they fit in the temporary context: the frame is omitted, the detail is confusing. The alternative approaches correspond, either, to look after a world of objects and characterising attributes, either, to conceive a world of relations and conditioning contexts. The second picture requires to never disregard the inherent *complexity*, so that the standard perception methods follow from the set of liaison patterns, notably, using the concord or association or alliance processes, to guarantee the community harmony. The dependence from the environment lowers the interest to acknowledge attributes, assigned to the individuals and objects, as innate (permanent) properties. Moreover, the focus on the complexity ties induces to preserve the frames and to enable all measures granting the best choral

achievement, because the success belongs to the community, within which the part subsists.

The two approaches are, certainly, mutually exclusives, and the wise man should never follow one or the other, but shall choose in-between paths, according to the current situations. Nevertheless, in the average, the action spirit is deemed to characterise the European (inspired by the Aristotle's teaching); the other side, the harmony mind is typical of the Chinese (motivated by the Tao's teaching). The remark has several possible explanations, maybe starting from the differences in the language that the people use to communicate.

- the Far-east Asia languages are basically context-driven: a phoneme has several meaning and is worthless out of given linguistic location; the English terms are easily listed in the dictionary, with their definitions, since the interpretation, moved out of the sentence, is current habit;
- the Indo-European languages have the standard option to wording abstract entities, adding suited suffixes to real objects attributes (e.g., whiteness); the Chinese philosophers never theorised Plato's abstraction procedures, and no similar option exists in the language;

Figure 5. Typical language characteristic features

- the Far-east Asia languages are basically context-driven: a phoneme has several meaning and is worthless out of given linguistic location; the English terms are easily listed in the dictionary, with their definitions, since the interpretation, moved out of the sentence, is current habit;
- the Indo-European languages have the standard option to wording abstract entities, adding suited suffixes to real objects attributes (e.g., whiteness); the Chinese philosophers never theorised Plato's abstraction procedures, and no similar option exists in the language;
- the nominal sentences are usual in English, not in Chinese; the sentence: "squirrels eat nuts" distinguishes from "my squirrel is eating a nut" has no Chinese equivalent, and only the context gives evidence if or not general assertions are stated;
- the English is subject prominent language, and even impersonal sentences require the subject (it is raining); the Chinese is topic prominent, and the sentences, typically, start from the framework, and give the object in the defined context (in Switzerland, it is nice skiing);
- in Europe, the entity decides the action; in the Far-east Asia, the action is enabled in concert with others or is the outcome of impersonal accidents. The European speech is agentive (he made the item to fall); the Chinese, non-agentive (the occurrence happened to make the item drop off).

- the nominal sentences are usual in English, not in Chinese; the sentence: "squirrels eat nuts" distinguishes from "my squirrel is eating a nut" has no Chinese equivalent, and only the context gives evidence if or not general assertions are stated;
- the English is subject prominent language, and even impersonal sentences require the subject (it is raining); the Chinese is topic prominent, and the sentences, typically, start from the framework, and give the object in the defined context (in Switzerland, it is nice skiing);
- in Europe, the entity decides the action; in the Far-east Asia, the action is enabled in concert with others or is the outcome of impersonal accidents. The European speech is agentive (he made the item to fall); the Chinese, non-agentive (the occurrence happened to make the item drop off).

The Indo-European languages are syntactically structured, with the subject-verb-object-complement lay-out, where the stress is made on the parts' characterisation, with series of adjectives. The Mandarin language coding orients the stress on the becoming, favouring attention on the verb prominence, to emphasise the relations that rule the world. Further example features are listed in the Figure 5.

There is no reason saying that the language originates the habits, either that the brain adjusts the communication means; anyway, the children, since when they start speaking, are fostered along one or the other approach. The education and learning, in any case, play essential role in the

shaping of the citizens' mind. The way that the Aristotle's either Confucius's ideas are preferred, becomes the lifelong unconscious cultural and behavioural reference.

People Self-Sufficiency and Wealth Growth

The centrality of the individual, either of the communitarian, responsiveness, is supplementary characterising figure. For instance, the majority of the US citizens is ready to subscribe standard propositions, Figure 6, which show that the personal autonomy is basic expectation.

- each person has distinguishing marks, and is proud to be singled out because of these;
- each one deems to control his life, and feels pleased if he can orient the others' conduct;
- the success is main objective, and the multitude ties are feared as hazardous hindrance;
- the personal trust is main requisite, and achieved records are ground for pride in the society;
- the interpersonal relations on equal are chosen, otherwise, top-down hierarchy is favourite;
- the same rules ought to apply to everyone, and no privilege shall be allowed out of the merit.

The individual believes to operate on the surroundings with active conduct, having the optimism to positively affect his future. The

Figure 6. Example personal autonomy patterns

- each person has distinguishing marks, and is proud to be singled out because of these;
- each one deems to control his life, and feels pleased if he can orient the others' conduct;
- the success is main objective, and the multitude ties are feared as hazardous hindrance;
- the personal trust is main requisite, and achieved records are ground for pride in the society;
- the interpersonal relations on equal are chosen, otherwise, top-down hierarchy is favourite;
- the same rules ought to apply to everyone, and no privilege shall be allowed out of the merit.

statements bring to think up alternative human organisations:

- on one side, the enterprises, say, institutions aimed at making easier the achievement of pre-set scopes: the competition is main capacity, and the success is necessary stipulation;
- the other side, the communities, say, people gathering because of shared identities and civic belonging: friendly behaviour is principal glue, and harmony fundamental prerequisite.

The USA corporation looks at the effective work-organisation, as basic step for optimal results. The Japanese company requires the workers concern, as featuring means of the business success. These recent years have shown that the western world effectiveness is not the only entrepreneurship rule, and the participation govern might become the winning alternative, when, in a not far away future, the organisation complexity could not, any more, be tackled through the reductionism procedures. In recent years, the Toyota's intelligent task planning opposes to the Ford's scientific job allotment.

The relational intricacy emphasis brings to say that the operators' feeling, state of mind, reactions, etc. cannot be disregarded, and, might, on the contrary, rise to utmost level for the entrepreneurial settings. The remark is here mentioned, to suggest that lots of western world thoughts might deserve revisions, so that existing considerations represent temporary appraisals. We have to acknowledge, nonetheless, that the people independence practices, shown by list of propositions, has granted, not only, the economical growth of the industrialised countries, but has been, as well, the winning spur of the technological advance, up now, acquired. What about the *"better safe than sorrow"* mind ?

In the western world mind, the reductionism principle is fundamental assumption, because of the innate belief to be able to model the material transformations into algorithmic procedures. In fact, the trust on the causal inference is well posed into the static universe, where the regularities that come out from the experimental testing, are transformed into the laws of the physics. The process is supported by the falsification rule, logically taken from the non contradiction principle, as a statement cannot be, at the same time, "true" and "false". The belief is equivalent to the identity principle, which assumes the situation coherence: "A is A, independently from the context".

The laws of the physics, in the recent views, do not necessarily ascend to absolute frames, or belong to transcendent domains; nevertheless, the falsification rule, on the recalled supports, is sufficient to grant their factual worthiness for all the practical applications (notably, at engineer concern). The connection between the technical knowledge deployments and the people autonomic attitude about the action spirit is lucid issue of backward reasoning, founded on pictures we are accustomed to use describing the western world successfulness during the last centuries.

- the end of the opportunistic economy (management of necessities, based on what is picked-up in the wild nature) started the agrarian age, where the land produce and livestock come of farming and breeding, due to wild vegetable cross and wild animal taming;
- the swap to the transformation economy (management of necessities, with involvement of human labour) leads to the industry age, with systematic exploitation of the earth stocks, where the staples are manufactured goods built from raw materials, turned in pollution and waste;
- the end of the affluent economy (wealth, with squander of non-renewable tangibles) might give rise to the robot age, where artificial *life* joins to artificial *intelligence*, to widen the tangibles by intangible enablers,

Figure 7. Mankind acknowledged divides

> - the end of the opportunistic economy (management of necessities, based on what is picked-up in the wild nature) started the «agrarian age», where the land produce and livestock come of farming and breeding, due to wild vegetable cross and wild animal taming;
> - the swap to the transformation economy (management of necessities, with involvement of human labour) leads to the «industry age», with systematic exploitation of the earth stocks, where the staples are manufactured goods built from raw materials, turned in pollution and waste;
> - the end of the affluent economy (wealth, with squander of non-renewable tangibles) might give rise to the «robot age», where «artificial *life*» joins to «artificial *intelligence*», to widen the tangibles by intangible enablers, with resort to *regenerative* bio-mimicry processes.

with resort to *regenerative* bio-mimicry processes.

The sketch brings to suggest that the mankind history characterises by turning points (revolutions), when the previous life conditions could not anymore supply sufficient, safe and reliable provisions for subsistence. The list, Figure 7, shows that the industry age is short relative to the agrarian age, and the robotic age is epoch to come, with no certainty on how and how long it will expand. The divide between the industry age and the robot age is foretold by several warning signals, and the discussion is looking at the main cultural options, to suggest hints on get rid from impasses that characterise the industry economics. The reductionism is industry age feature; the robot age is typically related with the complexity preservation mode. There is no reason to believe that the switch, from Eastern world style, to the Far East Asia habits, is winning. Anyway, the alternative, whether functional, needs to be considered, and further deepening is useful for better forecasts.

The Universe of States and Transforms

The scientific approach with explaining motivations systematically derived from general principles is Greek concept; the unveiling of the speculative backstage was motive of high gratification; the Greek word "schole" means

happy hours, say, the time, free from work, to be spent developing the knowledge according to the personal whims. In the Confucius' doctrine, the happiness, far from putting individual quirks before social obligations, consists in getting pleasure from the harmonic participation to the country life, in the allocated social network. The Chinese citizen was conscious to belong to his family, village and nation; the protective community automatically requires exact and strict obligations, while giving all ethical instructions of civil behaviour. Within the hierarchical social group, the discussion is useless, being the roles accepted to achieve the ordered continuance of the collective life. This should not be confused with conformism; Confucius, states the prominent citizen is the one distinguishing himself by the achievement of harmonic fairness.

The Chinese wise man was not interested into speculative science; the masterworks, more relevant than the ones of the ancient Greco-Roman world, covered many areas: from irrigation, well drilling, chinaware, (magnetic) compass, to quantitative map-making, biological immunisation means, etc., always aiming at case-driven solutions, with no interest in theoretical implications. In a different way, the Greek philosophers were looking at the originating explanations of the natural phenomena, so that, when the empirical evidence was misleading, there was no fear to conceive abstract models (Plato's ideas), provided that these better satisfied the devised theory.

The identity principle is recalled, to allow separating any *object* from the *background*, to single out unit elements, easy to investigate, having removed the disturbing effects. Along these lines, Democritus hypothesised the "atomic" theory, to trim down every *object* into elemental *atoms*. We mention the method, not the frame; similarly, the Aristotle's physics offers worthy schemes, with erroneous binding laws. Indeed, the hypothesised frameworks today are *childish*, and the Tao's distrust of the simplifying reductionism results wise. The context-driven picture brings to holistic views, and, whether the sought relational complexity could uniformly be portrayed by distributed effects, so to predict the "field" theory, assigning the pertinent *field* intensity, to each *point* of the space. However, in the modern science the two views are complementary, and no clear evidence exists to support the holistic approach.

Indeed, the today physics accepts the "atomic" and the "field" views; we, quite obviously, deal with "photon" either the "field" description of the light (and electromagnetic waves). Are still *childish* these models? One either the other, or both, as they lead to equivalent pictures? The answer is not straightforward, and is highly affected by how we consider the physical laws truth or trustfulness. Anyway, out of consistent responses, it is deemed imperative to look after the frameworks required by the scientific knowledge build-up, notably, to lead to the technologies. In that perspective, we have to refer, along with the physical laws legitimacy, to the disputes on the *invariants*, say, the (dimensional) coefficients binding the physical quantities, that happen to be characteristic constants, should we live in the static universe (where the devised laws are permanently true). Of course, the disputes are useless, if we only perceive changing frames, and the laws are passing acronyms.

Among the laws of the physics, the entropy decay is thought to have strong proof (according to the falsification rule). Certainly, it is possible to think up experiments where the reversibility

exists: in the kinetics theory of the (ideal) gasses, the "Maxwell imp" acts at the microscopic level, in view to override the macroscopic set-up, moving the system to the original state. More general reasoning leads, in the macroscopic thermodynamics, to define state functions, say, physical quantities that do not depend on the actually covered paths and are defined by the locally reached state. They are clever constructs, to create context-free changes, so that the transformations universe is, always, reduced to the technically correspondent universe of states, where, positively, the entropy decay is correctly accounted by equivalent assessments.

The ability of separating permanent constructs, suppressing the links with the conditioning context, requires to take out the non essential perturbations and to invent the original patterns (like Plato's ideas). These are risky procedures, if accomplished without continuous (and reliable) experimental checks, in order to reject the false models and to adapt the in progress assumptions. The other way, the acceptation of the complexity might paralyse the talent to figure out possible reductions and underlying taxonomies. Is it virtue or foolishness ? The wise man, in the Tao's view, is the one who acknowledges the person, the society and the environment all around, assuring the highest harmony, in agreement with the inherent becoming, which makes unwise trusting on instant snapshots, not conditioned by the (changing) cross-coupling.

We might hypothesise that the universe of context dependent transformations has an inherently high complexity, so that it would be childish to imagine quantitative models, unless if further 'reduction' is recognised. The western style way to the technical knowledge follows such hypothesis, due to the typical individualism mentality of people with active conduct concerning the personal affairs and the surroundings matters. In the scientific areas, this is recognised in the many causal frames, e.g., the symmetric Hamilton's formalism, permitting the backward time solutions with no worry on the energy conservation, or even the Fourier's transform analyses on sampled transient signals, with tiny concern about the spectral (infinite) repetition.

In the technical areas, the active conduct brings in even higher evidence. The effectiveness, by split-duty allotment paradigms is recognised by Adam Smith (in needle's manufacture), theorised by Frederic W. Taylor (*scientific* labour organisation) and enabled by Henry Ford (flow-shop scale economy). The line of action is deemed to be the industrial revolution winning innovation, bringing forth the exceptional performance of the western way to wealth growth. With some ingenuity, the innovation can be referred as the atomistic segmentation of the human work, as compared with the earlier holistic production management, carried over by the craftsman by mastery manufacturing. Every item is reduced into elements; instead of expert artisans, low wage workers perform the tiny segmented task, so that nothing is left to perturbing changes. In recent times, the Toyota's company replaces the Ford's set-ups by job-shop economy of scope and *intelligent* work organisation, where the operators' commitment is exploited by the total quality schemes, to bring back the holistic order in the production settings.

The being vs. becoming dilemma teaches, among other things, that the ability to extract stable interpretation patterns requires biasing afterthoughts. A bird-eye view picture brings to the (linear) sequencing of states, with inborn hope of the progress. Indeed, the civilisation moves forward, with the ceaseless accumulation of ideas and knowledge, so that, for us, it might be fairly instinctive assuming to be the recipient of incessantly increasing heritages. Quite the reverse, when every thing is unremittingly changing, without making evident progress trends, the complexity becomes chief attribute, forbidding the resort to simplifying hypotheses. Steadiness is apparent, all situations are context conditioned: if the number driving factors is very large, the becoming is *permanent* truth, while the being is useless image.

The man experiments other kinds of "stability": day and night alternation, yearly return of seasons, etc., so that it might be quite instinctive to assume the cyclic character of every phenomenon, with no further addition concerning the (arbitrary) progress. In our interpretation, the "stability" of the growth is characterising feature of the western inclination towards reductionism (and the *scientific* abstraction of laws), and the "stability" of the alternation might be basic attribute of the far-eastern preference of the complexity preservation (and the *intelligent* resort to immanent human faculties).

The Opponent Logic or Mediation Art

Moving ahead with describing the European spirit peculiarities, the role played by the "logics" is directly evident. In China, the Mozi's school properly stated all the fundamental principles; thus, the logic was properly known, still, never was used in factual achievements for suitably deployed inferences. In the ancient Greece, the logics was immediately prised, as the powerful means in the public debates, being the way to impose the individual importance and supremacy through debate, say, *democratic* arguments. The logic, indeed, provides constructs to infer judgements based on the formal evidence only, and the sequences, Figure 8, might happen to be rejected, being untrue.

Now, the logic aims at context-free reasoning, looking after absolute ideas, valid by themselves, so that the inference too is not affected by the chosen contents. The Tao's mind avoids the abstraction and does not worry the compromises. Moreover, the conditioning context, to face the ceaselessly becoming, requires to deal with changing *situations*, for which the abstraction of fixed concepts is subjective (arbitrary). The approach is stated by the dialecticism (compared with dialectics) three propositions, Figure 9, supporting the faith that contrasts are only apparent, existing the liking to believe that "if A is correct neither non-A is wrong",

Figure 8. Example groundless syllogism

> • the natural produces yield crops, having dietetic value to enhance the good physical shape;
> • the tobacco is natural product, farmed and selected with careful harvesting processes;
> • hence, the cigarettes will do good, improving the men's healthiness.

rather than "if A is correct, non-A is wrong". The wisdom to accept negation and conflict clangs against the reductionism to create context-free abstractions, to get rid from uncertainty.

- the natural produces yield crops, having dietetic value to enhance the good physical shape;
- the tobacco is natural product, farmed and selected with careful harvesting processes;
- hence, the cigarettes will do good, improving the men's healthiness.

The way to deal with the measurement errors is very instructive. The scattering of the experimental data brings to the statistical treatment, and to acknowledging the Gauss's distribution, on condition to be subject to independent and unbiased disturbances. With time-varying phenomena, the repeated trials test cannot be used to build the distributions, and the uncertainty reduction cannot be obtained by merely *a posteriori* statistical treatments. The Kalman's filter is well known solution, based on *a priori* probabilistic assumptions: the hidden process is linear Gauss-Markov model and distributions are defined by the covariance parameters; the state updating avails of the transition matrices; and the covariance computation is obtained by iteratively solving the optimal mean-squared problem. The all comes out to a self-sufficient algorithmic construct.

The brilliant outcomes are verified and expressed with the real time assessment of the spacecrafts trajectories, having the cameras, moved to the correct location, ready to film the astronauts landing and getting out. The process uncertainty is fully reduced to algorithmic frames, with suited causal addiction. The model is made to deal with non-linear field effects by time-varying coefficients, and with the insufficient statistics on the initial conditions by adaptive convergence feed-back, or with the biasing coupling drifts by timely re-instantiating the filtering weighs. The computation burden is, maybe, biggest drawback, in front of the context-driven *correction* arbitrariness, since the results validity is factually deferred to backward recognition.

- the *permanent change*: to fix a situation means ignoring the underlying truth, as the reality is permanently fluid;
- the *contradiction rule*: the original fluidity means that contrasts, paradoxes, non-senses, etc., incessantly emerge: the evil and good, the old and new, the weak and strong, etc., are shared attributes, since the opposites are complementary, being integral property together, never to be disjoined;
- the *holistic reliance*: due to change and contradiction, nothing can be segregated from the context; indeed, every detail depends on multitudes of driving sources, which cannot be omitted in the knowledge building.

The *a priori* probabilistic assumptions arbitrariness might suggest to relax the uncertainty models, with resort to the *fuzzy* sets concept. The *membership functions* do not require statistical validation. They, simply, show that sharp values are out of reach (due to measurement errors, or other reasons), and permit to drop some probabilistic models inconsistencies (e.g., vanishing asymptotic density functions). The *fuzzy* logic control systems

Figure 9. Reference dialecticism propositions

> • the *permanent change*: to fix a situation means ignoring the underlying truth, as the reality is permanently fluid;
> • the *contradiction rule*: the original fluidity means that contrasts, paradoxes, non-senses, etc., incessantly emerge: the evil and good, the old and new, the weak and strong, etc., are shared attributes, since the opposites are complementary, being integral property together, never to be disjoined;
> • the *holistic reliance*: due to change and contradiction, nothing can be segregated from the context; indeed, every detail depends on multitudes of driving sources, which cannot be omitted in the knowledge building.

are quite noteworthy achievement, expanding, out of the *deep knowledge* frameworks, the capabilities to deal with context-driven situations, where the A and non-A outcomes co-exist. For computer programming, the situations use object-coding, where the objects assemble: *attributes*, *methods* and *belief*, so that the nominal instantiations join to the current contexts, with the related uncertainty estimates. The *fuzzy* logic control is, certainly, used everywhere, nonetheless with the greatest spreading in Japan, also for current applications, devoid of relevant sophistication.

The *shallow knowledge* frameworks are arrival-issues, when the context-driven situations are dealt with resort to the *expert systems* and knowledge-based mechanisms. The processes are shaped up by singly giving the *declarative* (resources attributes, reference hypotheses, etc.) and the *procedural* knowledge (govern rules, performance criteria, etc.); the context is coded according to rules:

• *if* <antecedent> *then* <consequent> assumptions.

The evolution is performed by the inference engine; the uncertainty estimate follows from the set of plausibility assessments. The situation updating is gained, looking through the coded:

• *if* < .. .. > *then* < .. .. > list of active rules.

The *shallow knowledge* is, anyway, incorporated into causal frames, governed by the action spirit with polydromic falls-out, as the *true/false* opposition is widened, adding the *undecided* out-

comes, possibly, at several range of *belief*, established by the presumed hypotheses and measured by the chosen criteria. The achievements might be considered, as well, as factual issues of the mediation art, promoted by the dialecticism standpoints, because the context-driven situations replace the (absolute) sharp states sequences. The change, not apparent with the probabilistic modelling, is better acknowledged through the *fuzzy* outcomes membership functions, and is fully transparent in the knowledge-based *expert systems*.

The dialectics vs. dialecticism dilemma leads, in short, to distinguish two habits:

• to think positive and to behave competitive in a world, where each one is builder of his destiny;
• to think holistic and to behave wisely, as each individual responds for the whole community fate.

The personal commitment, in the former case, takes profit, aiming at autonomous enterprises, with clear-cut responsiveness that allows rewarding the activity of the best performing operators; in the latter, the perception of liaisons, binding people and surroundings, requires solidarity, assuring protection. The causal inference, with backward attribution of original sources and responsibilities, quite plainly brings about the ideas of abstract models, with, most suitably, algorithmic structure, to grant explicit quantitative mapping to driving inputs and off-setting troubles. The holistic approach, judiciously, preserves the complexity, and acknowledges (apparent) inconsistencies to not indulge in sharp simplifications; the quantitative models, however, show quite higher complication, and are only recent acquisition of the computer engineering advances.

Competing Freedom or Conciliated Fairness

The logic chaining has been recognised to be standard demonstration, displaying the individualism in the political or scientific domains of the western way of life, which, mainly, is the enabling spirit of the industrial revolution. In the physical domains, the universe of states, with causal attributions through sufficient and necessary conditions, permits the clear-cut definition of laws, which offer deterministic evidence on how to construe the world. The way, by explicit or implicit postulations, assumes the centrality of the man, even today, when we know that the earth is totally negligible entity in the cosmos, the life birth, high improbable occurrence, and the intelligence, quite awkward discontinuity.

The claim to build universal laws, by the abstraction of the elemental principles, is amazing, and the positive corroborations are the more astonishing. Nonetheless, the personal independence from the surroundings is fundamental guess, to prise the logical reasoning or the individual actions, finalised, either to the technological knowledge, either to the entrepreneurial commitment. Then, the peoples peculiarities relate with the environmental and social reasons; example remarks, Figure 10, can be used to express the alternative situations.

The holistic/abstraction descriptions cover the same statements, by differently shaping the pictures: concentric diagram either linear chain. The outer shell with the natural surroundings, with inside the social, economic, political and legal layers, the physics/metaphysics guesses and scientific/technical constructs, finally, the kernel of the epistemic structures and learning processes. The linear chain is the trick, permitting to distinguish the sequences, into separate ranges.

- *Natural surroundings* and *socio-economic frameworks*. The China subcontinent characterises by fertile lands, navigable rivers and self-sufficient agriculture, capable to assure the centralised management of the resources under unified ruling; this pushes communities interconnection with harmonic relations, with vertical frames under the village elders, province governors and nation emperors. The (ancient) Greece and, as a rule, the European countries are narrow lands interfaced to the sea with meagre farming, pushing the trading with afar villages, to reach balanced nourishment; the marketing with strangers requires strong attention on the local and personal identity, and, in the same time, widest interest about the foreign people activity, products and habits.

- *Political/legal practices* and *physics/metaphysics conjectures*. While managing the political and official infrastructures, the Chinese citizens always report to authorities and relatives, with utmost importance on bonds and obligations; the habit is to refer to the social universe as diffuse driver yields to look at the world as dim field with context ties. The Greek citizen is forced to focus on the objects and to deal with other individuals, autonomously deciding about his own flock and on what to buy or sell in full freedom; the familiar autonomy habit assumes to be master of his own fortune, and to look at the environment as something that has to be understood and dominated, objectives easier to achieve through steady democratic frames, suitably ruled by positive governing laws.

- *Scientific/technical knowledge* and *wisdom/learning standards*. When the surroundings is permanent overall conditioning context, each one is forced to consider the whole sceneries, without omitting odds and ends; and the learning processes are axed on

Figure 10. Landmark cultural situations and methods

> • *Natural surroundings* and *socio-economic frameworks*. The China subcontinent characterises by fertile lands, navigable rivers and self-sufficient agriculture, capable to assure the centralised management of the resources under unified ruling; this pushes communities interconnection with harmonic relations, with vertical frames under the village elders, province governors and nation emperors. The (ancient) Greece and, as a rule, the European countries are narrow lands interfaced to the sea with meagre farming, pushing the trading with afar villages, to reach balanced nourishment; the marketing with strangers requires strong attention on the local and personal identity, and, in the same time, widest interest about the foreign people activity, products and habits.
> • *Political/legal practices* and *physics/metaphysics conjectures*. While managing the political and official infrastructures, the Chinese citizens always report to authorities and relatives, with utmost importance on bonds and obligations; the habit is to refer to the social universe as diffuse driver yields to look at the world as dim field with context ties. The Greek citizen is forced to focus on the objects and to deal with other individuals, autonomously deciding about his own flock and on what to buy or sell in full freedom; the familiar autonomy habit assumes to be master of his own fortune, and to look at the environment as something that has to be understood and dominated, objectives easier to achieve through steady democratic frames, suitably ruled by positive governing laws.
> • *Scientific/technical knowledge* and *wisdom/learning standards*. When the surroundings is permanent overall conditioning context, each one is forced to consider the whole sceneries, without omitting odds and ends; and the learning processes are axed on complexity, without extracting single entities. The other side, if the individual is get used to autonomic views, he tries to single out the objects, figuring out behavioural rules and models by the abstraction procedures of logic inference and causal association. The alternative approaches consistently lead to human set-ups, either aiming at the harmonic fairness and diffused mediation, either, prising the individual freedom and competitive behaviour.

complexity, without extracting single entities. The other side, if the individual is get used to autonomic views, he tries to single out the objects, figuring out behavioural rules and models by the abstraction procedures of logic inference and causal association. The alternative approaches consistently lead to human set-ups, either aiming at the harmonic fairness and diffused mediation, either, prising the individual freedom and competitive behaviour.

The fact to differently arrange similar (or, even, the same) statements means that the acknowledged differences might direct towards series of alternative views and approaches, Figure 11. The alternatives are not one better than the other. On the contrary, there is ground to expect that better achievements are reached, in general, whether both standpoints are taken in proper notice.

When, in particular, the industry age alone is investigated, the European style alternative seems to be the winning one, to the wealth assemble, up to the affluent society. The straightforward, maybe simplistic, evaluation brings to prise the

competing freedom effectiveness, and to despise the conciliated fairness inefficiency. The appraisal is, though, to revise, when the growth sustainability cannot anymore be confined to the earth raw materials exploitation, according to the reductionism patterns of the industrial efficiency. Alternative ways, built on the complexity continuation, might become winning prospects, and need to be considered. The competition vs. fairness dilemma ought to be revised. The effectiveness in the spendable riches creation, through the competitive *free market* of the affluent world, is worth in a society of equals, where each person has the equivalent defence and opposition opportunities, established by the interplay of (representative) democratic governments. The unbounded exploitation of the natural stocks means to take out from the future generations potential sources, without allowing protection and resistance. Now, the parliamentary democracies respond to the in progress electorate, and the voters' current interests are not directly concerned by the blurred fairness demands, having unclear attribution to citizens to come.

To conclude the remarks, we might point out that the parliamentary democracies have proved to be the most effective enabler of the industrialism. Today, they might happen to be, maybe, structurally inadequate to involve in protecting the (non voting) future generations. However, no evidence exists that other political organisations offer better guarantees. The supranational authorities setting is considered with especial attention, so that the growth sustainability (when planned) could come into the imperative survival requirements, not to be object of opportunistic deals.

CONCLUSION

The industrial revolution is paradigm change in wealth availability, grounded on the transformation efficiency of the earth stocks, to feed the manufactured goods market, later dropped into wastes and pollution. The amount of spendable riches discerns the world countries in terms of the industry levels, and the affluence is directly linked to the consumed raw materials. The manufacture market build-up is quite recent achievement, and it happens to be the western world innovation, based on industry patterns that, originally, permit reaching efficacy by the *scientific* work organisation, with job-allotment after *reduction* to elemental duty sequences.

- in the explanatory constructions, the Asian way prioritises the relational connections,

the European style prefers classes and taxonomies;

- in the universe conception, the intricacy ties suggest looking at fields and frameworks; the reductionism aims at objects with absolute native properties;

- in the implicit assumptions about evolution either steadiness, the first choice needs holistic closure patterns, the second permits repeated trials and probability distribution functions;

- when the outer world is considered, the becoming stresses on the stranger fancifulness, to be assimilated; the being mood trusts the competition and controllability measures;

- in the unfolding models, the complexity recommends the resort to groups and networks; the abstraction allows to define causal frames and physical laws, to be supportively exploited as problem-solving means;

- with resort to the reasoning means, the fuzzy logics is nice with the contrasts mediation, the true/false logic is powerful un-biasing tool;

- in the public/civil concerns, the median mindedness bring to peace the quarrelling partners, the competition spirit brings to defeat the contrasting opponent;

Figure 11. Alternative western and oriental views and approaches

- in the explanatory constructions, the Asian way prioritises the relational connections, the European style prefers classes and taxonomies;
- in the universe conception, the intricacy ties suggest looking at fields and frameworks; the reductionism aims at objects with absolute native properties;
- in the implicit assumptions about evolution either steadiness, the first choice needs holistic closure patterns, the second permits repeated trials and probability distribution functions;
- when the outer world is considered, the «becoming» stresses on the stranger fancifulness, to be assimilated; the «being» mood trusts the competition and controllability measures;
- in the unfolding models, the complexity recommends the resort to groups and networks; the abstraction allows to define causal frames and physical laws, to be supportively exploited as problem-solving means;
- with resort to the reasoning means, the fuzzy logics is nice with the contrasts mediation, the true/false logic is powerful un-biasing tool;
- in the public/civil concerns, the median mindedness bring to peace the quarrelling partners, the competition spirit brings to defeat the contrasting opponent;
- in the perception modes, the attention on the context makes easier to look after and to keep the surroundings, while the focus on the objects brings at neglecting the decay and polluting penalties.

- in the perception modes, the attention on the context makes easier to look after and to keep the surroundings, while the focus on the objects brings at neglecting the decay and polluting penalties.

The chapter presents an original interpretation of the vexed question of the industry patterns bias, with profit of the western world style, reviewing reductionism *vs.* technical deployment, education dependence *vs.* complexity spirit, people self-ruling *vs.* physical laws, states *vs.* evolution spaces, opponent logic *vs.* mediation art, competing freedom *vs.* conciliated fairness, or, likewise, looking at the main cultural marks, which bring to explain why the industrial revolution is issue, linked to given civilising contexts.

The list of dilemmas can be used to identify typical European viewpoints (to provide an explanatory model, the Aristotle's constructs), as compared with similar level of sophistication ones (say, the Tao's constructs). On these bases, the industry winning style becomes temporary parenthesis, to be closed, if unable to assure further growth. This, surely, does not mean to reject the industrialism (there is no evidence that the *industrial* work organisation shall be removed); rather that the series of reductionism *truths* shall be revised, with in mind that the related cultural marks are just possible construct.

The discussion leads to show that the superiority in terms of the industry levels is doomed to end, if the funding ground plans cease to yield spendable riches, because the earth stocks run out and the environment is squandered. The mankind survival might, then, look after the *cognitive* revolution, rethinking the earlier industry paradigms to include alternative knowledge ones, and exploring, out of the reduction ways, the complexity patterns, namely, the second terms in above the listed dilemmas. The winning entrepreneurship shall not, anymore, follow the earlier *reductionism* patterns (e.g., three-S "*simplify, specialise, standardise*" constraint), on the contrary, *complexity* rules (e.g.,

three-R "*robotise, regulate, reintegrate*" option) have to become standard reference of extended enterprises, oriented towards product-service delivery. This entails the throughout patterns change, making worthy to look at reconsidering the cultural marks, comparing the Tao and Aristotle minds, and devising alternative cultural views, to support new technological achievements.

The technical literature, in the sketched domain, is limited. In fact, focus on references about the work organisation changes already permits to recognise that the *scientific* patterns of the economy of scale are now replaced by the *intelligent* ones of the economy of scope. However, this appears tactical upgrading (e.g., the Taguchi/Toyota features, instead of the Taylor/Ford ones), while the suggested picture looks at full strategic upheaval, and this means rethinking the industrial revolution success, from its cultural foundations, say, with a view on the social psychology, to start looking at the alternatives also in the knowledge market, so to transfer the value added on intangibles. The challenge is especially relevant in the SMEs cases, bringing to the rising of goal oriented knowledge entrepreneurship.

The change of patterns is, perhaps, mandatory demand, in view of *sustainable growth* objectives. In fact, this is today challenge. The knowledge patterns of the (imaginary) *cognitive* revolution to come are, most clearly, linked to the *complexity* preservation, more than to the *reductionism* short cuts. However, the *sustainable* growth is challenge to face with trust in technologies. In the *no-global* views, the opposition does not accept end-less development and strictly avoids *artificial* constructs (notably, the wealth from *artificial* life). The principle of precaution turns to worst-case scenarios, each time depicting dark portraits of any changes, assuming "better safe than sorrow".

Certainly, any action is potentially dangerous; the old warning against walking outside, because of the thunder risk, would lead to never come down a stair to not tumble: the safety margins are not zero. The (fission) nuclear plants, the chemical fertilizers and pesticides, the electro-magnetic fields, etc., all have possible not fully controlled falls-off, as it happens with the genetic manipulations or the greenhouse effects. The psychology "when in doubt, do nothing" might result winning in the political context, but with long terms damages, due to the irresponsible riding of the irrational side of the most sloth conservatisms.

The decision keeping conventions, when risky conditions appear, are related to cultural ranks and institutional frames of each given community or nation. The political class aiming merely at easy consensus, rather than at the effectiveness in view of the people wellbeing, has better way along the "do nothing, when in doubt" track, just referring to the precaution care, in front of possible negative outcomes. With the knowledge society, this anti-scientific restrain is puzzling: it is surely unsafe, with the unveiled threat to stop any chance to the future populations.

In the near future, the prospected cognitive revolution will be the prerogative of minds oriented on the complexity management, rather than on the reductionism ability. The focus is turned to the intelligence: innate gift of the man (and, partially, of other animal), and artificial attribute, to be exploited by computer engineering. The (man) intelligence, indeed, is impressive anomaly in the evolutionism, not separable by each individual, who permits to recognise and classify pieces of information, as abstract entities: the data (coded information) and the knowledge (structured information). What can we infer about the artificial intelligence developed by the individuals and communities of the revolution to come?

REFERENCES

Amin, S. (1990). *Maldevelopment: Anatomy of a global failure*. London: Zed Book.

Bass, G. J. (2008). *Freedom's battle: The origin of humanitarian interventions*. New York: Knopf.

Bhagwati, N. (2004). *In defence of globalisation*. New York: Oxford University Press.

Cahn, E., & Rowe, J. (1992). *Time dollars*. Emmaus, PA: Rodale Press.

Casti, J. L. (1991). *Searching for certainty: What scientists can know about the future*. New York: Morrow.

Chambers, R. (1995). Poverty and livelihoods. *Environment and Urbanization*, 7(1), 173–204.

Chan, C. K., & Lee, H. W. J. (2005). *Successful strategies in supply chain management*. Hershey, PA: IDEA Group Inc.

Charbonneau, S. (2006). *Droit communautaire de l'environnement*. Paris: L'Harmattan.

Crane, D., Kawashima, N., & Kawasaki, K. (2002). *Global culture: Media, arts, policy and globalisation*. London: Rutledge.

de-Shalit, A. (1998). *Why posterity matters*. London: Rutledge.

Diamond, J. (2005). *Collapse: How societies choose to fail or succeed*. New York: Viking.

Easterly, W. (2001). *The elusive quest for growth: Economists' adventures and misadventures*. Cambridge, MA: MIT Press.

Eldredge, N. (2002). *Life on earth: An encyclopaedia of biodiversity, ecology and evolution*. Santa Barbara, CA: ABC-CLIO, Inc.

Ellis, C. D. (2008). *The partnership: The making of Goldman Sachs*. New York: Penguin Press.

Flynn, S. (2007). *The edge of disaster: Rebuilding a resilient nation*. New York: Random House.

Freeland, C. (2000). *Sale of the century: The inside story of the second Russian revolution*. London: Little, Brown & Co.

Friedman, T. L. (2005). *The world is flat: A brief history of the twenty-first century.* New York: Farrar Straus and Giroux.

Goldsmith, E., & Piélat, T. (2002). *Le Tao de l'écologie.* Monaco, Principality of Monaco: Edition du Rocher.

Hillary, R. (2000). *Small and medium sized enterprises and the environment business imperatives.* Sheffield, UK: Greenleaf Pub.

Hitchings, H. (2008). *The secret life of words: How English became English.* London: John Murray.

Hoogendijk, W. (1993). *The economic revolution: Towards a sustainable future by freeing the economy from money-making.* Utrecht, The Netherlands: International Books.

Jones, E. (2003). *The European miracle: Environments, economies and geopolitics in the history of Europe and Asia* (3rd ed.). Cambridge, MA: Cambridge University Press.

Karl, T. L. (1997). *The paradox of plenty: Oil booms and petrol-states.* Berkeley, CA: University of California Press.

Kempf, H. (2007). *Comment les riches détruisent la planète.* Paris: Editions du Seuil.

Kherdjemil, B., Panhuys, H., & Zaoual, H. (1998). *Territoires et dynamiques économiques.* Paris: L'Harmattan.

Kothary, R. (1989). *Rethinking development: In search of human alternatives.* Far Hills, NJ: New Horizons Press.

Latouche, S. (2004). *Survivre au développement: De la décolonisation de l'imaginaire économique à la construction d'une société alternative.* Paris: Mille et une Nuits.

Latouche, S. (2007). *Petit traité de la décroissance sereine.* Paris: Mille et une Nuits.

Lévy, B. H. (2008). *Left dark times: A stand against the new barbarism.* New York: Random House.

Malherbe, M. (1995). *Les langages de l'humanité.* Paris: Robert Laffont.

Meadows, D. H. (2004). *Limit to growth: The 30 years update.* Boston: Chelsea Green.

Mendes, C., & Castoriadis, C. (1977). *Le mythe du développement.* Paris: Seuil.

Michelini, R. C. (2008). *Knowledge entrepreneurship and sustainable growth.* New York: Nova Sci. Pub.

Michelini, R. C. (2009). The *Robot age* changeful *knowledge changeover.* New York: Nova Sci. Pub.

Michelini, R. C., & Capello, A. (1985). *Misure e strumentazione industriali: Segnali e strumenti di misura.* Turin, Italy: UTET.

Michelini, R. C., & Razzoli, R. P. (2000). *Affidabilità e sicurezza del manufatto industriale: La progettazione integrata per lo sviluppo sostenibile.* Milan, Italy: Tecniche Nuove.

Minc, A. (2008). *Une sorte de diable: Les vies de John-Maynard Keynes.* Paris: Grasset.

Muller, E. (2001). *Innovation interactions between knowledge-intensive business services and small-and-medium sized enterprises: An analysis in terms of evolution, knowledge and territories.* Berlin, Germany: Springer.

Myrdal, G. (1968). *Asian drama: An inquiry into the poverty of nations.* New York: Pantheon.

Naess, A. (1989). *Ecology, community and lifestyle: An eco-sophy outline.* Cambridge, MA: Cambridge University Press.

Nandy, A. (1987). *The intimate enemy.* Bombay, India: Oxford University Press.

Ndione, E. (1994). *Réinventer le présent.* Dakar, Senegal: Enda-Graf Sahel.

Needham, J. (1969). *Within the four seas: The dialogue of east and west*. London: Allen & Unwin.

Nisbett, R. E. (2003). *The geography of thought*. New York: Free Press.

Nisbett, R. E., & Ross, L. (1980). *Human inference: Strategies and shortcoming of social judgements*. Englewood Cliffs, NJ: Prentice Hall.

Ostrom, E., & Ahn, T. K. (2005). *Foundation of social capital*. Cheltenham, UK: Edward Elgar Pub.

Partant, F. (1997). *La fin du développement*. Paris: F. Maspero.

Perna, T. (1998). *Fair trade: The ethical defy to the world market*. Turin, Italy: Bollati Boringhieri.

Pezzey, J. (1989). *Economic analysis of sustainable growth and sustainable development*. New York: World Bank, WP 15.

Pin, M. X. (2006). *China's trapped transition: The limits of developmental autocracy*. Cambridge, MA: Harvard University Press.

Polanyi, K. (1957). *The great transformation: The political and economic origin of our time*. Boston: Beacon Press.

Polanyi, K. (1977). *The livelihood of man*. New York: Academic Press.

Polanyi, K. (1991). *The great transformation: The political and economic origin of our time*. Boston: Beacon Press.

Pörsken, U. (1989). *Plastikwörter: Die sprache einer internationalen diktatur*. Stuttgart, Germany: Klett-Cotta.

Prado de las Escosura, L. (2005). *Growth, inequality and poverty in Latin America: Historical evidence and controlled conjectures* (Working Paper n. 05-41). Madrid, Spain: University Carlos III. Retrieved from http://docubib.uc3m.es/WORKINGPAPERS/WH/wh054104.pdf

Putnam, R. D. (2000). *Bowling alone: The collapse and revival of American community*. New York: Simon & Shuster.

Putnam, R. D., Leonardi, R., & Nanetti, R. Y. (1993). *Making democracy work: Civic tradition in modern Italy*. Princeton, NJ: Princeton University Press.

Quadrio-Curzio, A., & Fortis, M. (2005). *Research and technological innovation: The challenge for a new Europe*. London: Springer.

Rawis, J. (1999). *A theory of justice*. Oxford, UK: Oxford University Press.

Redclift, M., & Woodgate, G. (1997). *The international handbook of environmental sociology*. Cheltenham, UK: Edward Elgar.

Riegel, K. F. (1975). *Development of dialectical operations*. Basel, Switzerland: S. Karger AG.

Rist, G. (1996). *Le développement: Histoire d'une croyance occidentale*. Paris: Presse de Sciences Po.

Rist, G. (1996). *Le développement: Histoire d'une croyance occidentale*. Paris: Presse de Sci. Po.

Royce, J. (1976). *The world and the individual*. Gloucester, UK: Peter Smith Publisher.

Sachs, W. (1992). *The development dictionary*. London: Zed Book.

Sachs, W. (1999). *Planet dialectics*. London: Zed Book.

Sahlins, M. (1972). *Stone age economics*. Chicago: Aldine-Atherton.

Said, E. W. (1994). *Culture and imperialism*. New York: Vintage Books.

Sala-y-Martin, X., & Subramanian, A. (2003). *Addressing the natural resources course: An illustration from Nigeria* (NBER Working Paper n. W9804). Retrieved from http://ssrn.com/abstract=420318

Schumacher, F. (1999). *Small is beautiful*. Washington: Hartley & Marks Publishers.

Schumpeter, J. A. (1939). *Business cycles*. New York: McGraw Hill.

Seabrook, J. (1993). *Victims of development*. London: Verso.

Sen, A. (2001). *Development as freedom*. New York: Oxford University Press.

Shiva, V. (1989). *Staying alive: Woman, ecology and development*. London: Zed Book.

Steckel, R., & Floud, R. (1997). *Health and welfare during industrialisation*. Chicago: University of Chicago Press.

Steingart, G. (2008). *The war for wealth: Why globalisation is bleeding the west of its prosperity*. New York: McGraw-Hill.

Stiglitz, J. E. (2007). *Making globalisation work*. New York: W. W. Norton.

Stiglitz, J. E., & Charlton, A. (2005). *Fair trade for all: How trade can promote development*. New York: Oxford University Press.

Stiglitz, J. E., & Greenwald, B. (2003). *Towards a new paradigm in monetary economics*. New York: Cambridge University Press.

Subramanian, A. (2008). *India's turn: Understanding the economic transformation*. Oxford: Oxford University Press.

Sussman, R. (1998). *The biological basis for human behaviour*. Englewood Cliffs, NJ: Prentice & Hall.

Terrasson, F. (2002). *En finir avec la nature*. Monaco, Principality of Monaco: Edition du Rocher.

Teune, H. (1988). *Growth*. London: Sage Publication.

Thurow, L. C. (1985). *The zero-sum solution: Building a world-class American economy*. New York: Simon & Shuster.

Tremonti, G. (2008). *La paura e la speranza: Europa crisi globale che si avvicina e la via per superarla*. Milan, Italy: Mondadori.

Tweed, R. G., & Lehman, D. (2002). Learning considered within a cultural context: Confucian and Socratic approaches. *The American Psychologist, 57*(2), 89–99.

Uchitelle, L. (2006). *The disposable America: Layoffs and their consequences*. New York: Knopf.

Vachon, R. (1988). *Alternatives au développement: Approches interculturelles à la bonne vie et à la coopération internationale*. Montréal, Canada: Centre interculturel Monchanin.

Villar, F. (1996). *Los indoeuropeos y los origines de europa: Language y historia*. Madrid, Spain: Editorial Gredos.

Wang, D. J. (1979). *The history of Chinese logical thought*. Shangai, China: People's Press.

Watkins, K. (2002). *Cultivating poverty: The impact of US cotton subsidies on Africa* (Oxfam Briefing paper n. 30). Retrieved from http://www.oxfam.org/en/files/pp020925_cotton.pdf

Weizsäcker, E. U., Young, O. R., & Finger, M. (2005). *Limit to privatisation: How to avoid too much a good thing*. London: Earthscan Pub.

Whorf, B. L. (1956). *Language, thought and reality*. Cambridge, MA: MIT Press.

Winchester, S. (2008). *The man who loved China: The fantastic story of the eccentric scientist who unlocked the mysteries of the middle kingdom.* New York: Harper Collins.

Wolf, M. (2004). *Why globalisation works.* New York: Yale University Press.

Womack, J. P., Ross, D., & Jones, D. T. (1990). *The machine that changed the world.* New York: Rawson Ass.

Worster, D. (1988). *The end of the earth: Perspectives on modern environment history.* New York: Cambridge University Press.

Zakaria, F. (2008). *The post-American world.* New York: W. W. Norton & Company.

Zanotelli, A. (2006). *Avec ceux qui n'ont rien.* Paris: Flammarion.

Chapter 18
Enterprise Modelling in Support of Organisation Design and Change

Joseph Ajaefobi
Loughborough University, UK

Aysin Rahimifard
Loughborough University, UK

Richard Weston
Loughborough University, UK

ABSTRACT

Enterprises (business organisations) are increasingly operating under uncertain conditions arising from: governments that introduce new regulations; a market place which is shaped by ongoing change in customer requirements; change in capital markets that orient overall market directions; an advancing base of technology; and increasing competition which can arise from a growing number of sources (Monfared, 2000). Consequently, organisations are expected to change rapidly in response to emerging requirements. Classical theories and more recently 'method-based' organisation (re)design and change approaches have been proposed and tried with varying degrees of successes. This chapter contribution discusses the role of enterprise and simulation modelling in support of organisation (re)design and change. The capabilities and constraints of some widely acknowledged public domain enterprise modelling frameworks and methods are reviewed. A modelling approach which integrates the use of enterprise modelling (EM), causal loop modelling (CLM), and simulation modelling (SM) is described. The approach enables the generation of coherent and semantically rich models of organisations. The integrated modelling approach has been applied and tested in a number of manufacturing enterprises (MEs) and one case study application is described.

DOI: 10.4018/978-1-60566-856-7.ch018

COMPLEXITY OF ORGANISATIONS AND THE NEED FOR MODELLING

From a systems engineering perspective an 'organisation' is an entity which consists of functional parts or members that contribute to the achievement of that purpose (Blethyn & Parker, 1990). Farnham & Horton (Mullins, 2005) state that organisations are social constructs created by people to achieve specific purposes by means of planned and co-ordinated activities. Organisations deploy people that work in association with other resource systems to realise well ordered sets of activities that lead to achievement of specified objectives. Martin (2005) identified four common aspects of any organisation:

- a system of coordinated activities
- a group of people & other resources that realise those activities
- defined goal(s)
- leadership

Mills et al (2003) describe an organisation as a system of resources that collaboratively execute coordinated routines so as to realise product & services. Siemienuch et al, (1998) suggest that an organisation is configuration of knowledge, embodied in people and machines, which utilises data to create information (e.g. product data models) and their physical manifestations (products for sale). Conventional means of developing an organisation centres on bringing people together and providing them with a structure (action plans) and technology for doing work (Davis, 1982). Here a common requirement is to realised organised association between people (competences) and jobs (related set of activities) (Vernadat, 1996); thereby developing needed behaviour and constraining unwanted behaviour (Weston 1998) . This leads to a unit of society or 'organisations' that function to realise products and services (Drucker, 1990, Warnecke, 1993, Handy, 1993).

With growing uncertainty in the world most organizations need to operate and compete in a volatile environment (Warnecke 1993, Vernadat 1996, Weston 1998 and Mills et al 2003). Successful organisations can take many forms (such as be large or small, centralized or distributed, manual or automated and transactional or transformationally led). Consequently the process of designing and changing organisations is complex and through their lifetime, various 'organisation design and change' (OD&C) projects are needed to maintain alignment between the composition of the organisation and emerging requirements. This paper is concerned with providing improved means of engineering manufacturing organisations, or so called Manufacturing Enterprises (MEs), that typically realise multiple product types in uncertain quantities for various customers. Those MEs can be considered to be complex for the following reasons:

1. they may deploy large numbers and varieties of system components; including people, electromechanical machines and IT systems that execute their many processes, possibly concurrently, to generate values for their customers;
2. causal and temporal dependencies exist between system components such that changes in one component can impact significantly on the entire ME;
3. complexity arises because of need to deploy various philosophies, methods, frameworks and technologies to integrate the operation of ME components;
4. significant uncertainty arises from the environment in which MEs operate, due to increased global competition, rapid technological changes and product customization (that often necessitate changes in product mix, product properties & production volumes).

Despite their inherent complexity, typically MEs are expected to generate unique behavioural responses such that (a) in the short term, profitable responses are made to changing market requirements and (b) in the long term, the enterprise recomposes and renews itself so that it continues to thrive. Consequently managers and engineers responsible for any given ME should deploy suitable means of defining ME goals and needed leadership and integration mechanisms that will: improve the choice and operation of processes and resource systems (human & technical) leading to quality, timely and cost effective delivery of products and services in response to emerging customer requirements, within constraints of stakeholder desires. It follows that implementing change in any ME requires understandings about and manipulation of complex causal and temporal dependencies between 'strategic intentions'; 'process designs'; 'product (and service) portfolios'; 'resource configurations'; 'departmental boundaries and people reporting structures'; 'manufacturing policies'; 'work-organising methods'; and 'human and technical resource systems' (Zhen & Weston 2006).

OD&C (organisation design and change) necessitates coherent thinking and action-taking amongst groups of people with differing agendas, desires, concerns, roles, affiliations, responsibilities, competencies and experiences related to the organisation and its environment (Ajaefobi et al 2008). Generally OD&C implementation will significantly impact on all ME personnel, such as by changing their status, roles, role relationships, work patterns, use of (personal and group) productivity tools, fitness to fulfil their roles and designated workloads, working conditions, opportunities for personal advancement and remuneration and so forth. Classic approaches to OD&C have previously been developed and applied by industry and academia (Mintzberg, 1989). However, most of those classic approaches are rooted in developing mechanistic views of reality with underlying assumptions that: orderli-

ness and regularity exist in nature; thus there is consistency in terms of causes and effects (Alison et al 2001). Classic organisation theorists: Taylor, Fayol, Urwickand Gulick, Mooney and Reilly and Weber generally focused on the question of organisational structure and their prescriptions tended to reflect mechanistic structural prescriptions for centralisation and specialisation of work (Scott & Mitchell, 1976). With increased uncertainty worldwide this kind of approach, and its assumptions about roles in organisations, has increasingly becoming inadequate. However, the merits of the mechanistic approach to organisation design and change lies in is predictability. By assuming that aspects of activities, jobs, roles & tasks are predictable then their outcomes and performances can in part be predicted and planned. There may for example be specialised systems of roles that are relatively stable over long period of time that have clear reporting relationships. Nowadays, however, increasing rates of change in organisations is affecting the stability of role requirements and thereby the suitability of role incumbents. Consequent upon increasing rates of change, traditional assumptions about stable jobs and thereby roles that are punctuated with periodic changes may become obsolete in some types of ME. Roles in organisations may endure for relatively long periods but role requirements may not (Ashforth, 2001). Though the classic approach (to organisation design and engineering) satisfied the requirements of a steady state business environment (Weston et al, 2001), current business environments may not be deterministic but rather stochastic (Ramenyi, 1998). Furthermore, it has also been observed that classic approaches to organisational design have often led to rigid organisation structures and systems that can not be changed with sufficient regularity. The same structures deliberately imposed to organise targeted behaviours and constrain unwanted behaviours can placed severe restrictions on responses to emerging requirements. Consequently the ability to respond to any new set of requirements or to assimilate the use of new technologies within products and products realising processes may be compromised (Goldman et al, 1995, Barber & Weston 1998). It follows that classic approaches and their solution provision are satisfying a diminishing fraction of present organisational change project requirements. Alternatively stated, MEs adopting improved OD&C practice can have significantly improved competitive advantage over MEs who retain conventional practices. In recent decades, 'method – based' approaches to OD&C have been suggested and tried in industry with varying degrees of successes. Popular 'methods-based' approaches to OD&C include: Business Process Re-Engineering, Continuous Process Improvement, Kaisen, Total Quality Management, Just-In-Time Manufacture, Push-Pull Manufacturing, and Lean and Agile Manufacturing (Hammer & Champy, 2001, Davenport, 1993, Evans & Lindsay, 1993, Womack, et al, 1990). Their underlying structures and concepts 'systemise' and 'focus' OD&C thinking and action taking and are reported to yield beneficial outcomes relative to preceding classic approaches. Generally though, the industrial application of method-based OD&C leads to long lead-times, high costs, poorly justified engineering projects that do not prepare the organisation for future change. These outcomes are to be expected because (1) invariably manufacturing organisations constitute very complex and dynamic systems that naturally require complex design and change processes and (2) current method-based OD&C are not analytically well founded. The present authors argue that unless suitable decomposition and quantitative and qualitative modelling principles are used to underpin method-based OD&C they will remain deficient. Enterprise modelling (EM) and enterprise engineering (EE) can now provide a form for model driven OD&C and many virtual engineering (VE) tools and methods are emerging that will build upon such a foundation to revolutionise the way in which organisations are conceived and engineered.

ENTERPRISE MODELLING: MEANING AND SCOPE

To effectively define complex organisations that give rise to stochastic behaviours, it is essential to think in terms of models. Enterprise Modelling (EM) uses an appropriate language or modelling constructs to describe a complex object such as an enterprise, in a way that the model developed can be read and understood by anyone who knows the modelling language. Thus EM is a means of externalising and formalising knowledge about an enterprise in an unambiguous form; making it possible to be exploited by other enterprise agents and those outside the enterprise boundary. Most enterprise knowledge resides in the minds of people who comprise the enterprise. However, by applying suitable decomposition principles formally by using well defined modelling constructs, holistic models of a complete enterprise can be created to facilitate shared understandings about different aspects of an organisation thereby facilitating organisation design and change. Any model can be viewed as being a useful representation of an object. To improve its utility when modelling a complex object the model will necessarily be an abstraction of reality (universe of discourse) expressed in terms of some formalism or modelling constructs for the purpose of the user (Vernadat, 1996). State-of-the-art enterprise models (EMs) are a graphical & possibly computational representation of the structure, processes, information, resources, people, goals that comprise a subject enterprise, possibly with reference to business, government, social, technical and environmental constraints. EMs can be both descriptive and definitional - spanning what the enterprise is at present (so called 'as-is' models) to what the enterprise could be at some point in time into the future. The role of most EMs is to achieve model-driven enterprise design, analysis, operation and change (Fox, & Gruninger, 1998).

Generally, enterprises have structures, functions and behaviours that can be depicted in different models (Christensen et al, 1995). Modelling an enterprise from a structural perspective involves: (a) developing models of mission, vision, values, culture and (b) modelling the enterprise resources and their relationships. Modelling enterprise functions encompasses developing models of (a) what the enterprise does to create values for its customers (an 'as is' EM) and (b) what the enterprise intends doing in future (possible 'to be' models).

Berio & Vernadat (1999) suggest that Enterprise models should describe among other things:

1. three fundamental types of flows within or across the enterprise, namely:
    a. material flows (physical objects such as products, tools & raw materials)
    b. information flows (documents, data, computer files), and
    c. decision/control flows (sequence of operations)
2. five modelling views:
    a. function view (what the enterprise does)
    b. organisation view
    c. information view
    d. resource view
    e. business rule view (economic)
3. three modelling levels
    a. requirement definition – what the customer wants to model to achieve
    b. desig n specification – to design formally one or more solutions of satisfying set of requirements
    c. implementation description – detailed implementation

Therefore, any given enterprise model is not a monolithic model but is an assemblage of models that represent different aspects of the enterprise. Figure 1 (Verndat, 2004) is an illustrative description of different enterprise aspects that can be captured by EMs.

The development of useful models of MEs requires a modelling architecture (or a framework within which modelised elements are created and integrated using well defined modelling constructs) and a modelling methodology (i.e. a well defined set of modelling stages or steps which the modelling takes to create, integrate and deploy the use of modelled elements). Enterprise modelling architectures are designed to

Figure 1. Main views represented by enterprise model

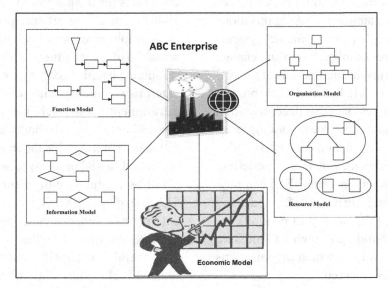

treat enterprises as complex systems that can be designed or improved in a structured and orderly manner. Thereby better results can be achieved relative to the use of an organisation (re)design approach (Bernus, 2003). As previously discussed, real world MEs are complex systems that operate within complex environments. Consequently EM models will invariable be simplified and abstracted representations of complex realities. In theory EM allows the representation of multiple aspects of the enterprise in so called model views. Those views are aspects of the enterprise relevant to multiple model users who will have differing responsibilities for the ME, thereby allowing the user to deploy and possibly develop models of interest without being disturbed by the overall enterprise complexity.

Public domain approaches to EM almost exclusively adopt a process thinking approach to representing, defining, analysing and communicating organisation entities and systems. Such a process oriented approach can facilitate requirements modelling and provides a unifying glue to bring together different aspects (namely: function, information, resources and organisation aspects) of the various ME views required. To deploy EM, so as to facilitate organisation design and change the present authors made the following assumptions:

1. organisations are set of multiple, dependent, concurrent operating business processes: where processes can be conceptualise at various levels of abstraction (suited to model users) in terms of ordered set of value adding activities, inputs, outputs, events (and their associated materials, information and control flows). Related to this assumption is the notion that typically many different instances of these processes need to be organised and resourced so as to realise the products and services created by the enterprise in its life time; and that the qualities, mixes and timings of these process instances will often not be readily predicted.

2. organisations deploy multiple and often interoperating resource systems (human & technical) that need to be modelled in terms of needed resource system attributes, such as competences, capabilities & capacities they can bring to assigned roles, including potential and actual abilities to reach states and change states so as to quantify and qualify relative performances of alternative choices of resource system.

3. organisational processes can be modelled at different layers of granularity to represent value streams, roles, activities and operations that can be explicitly be described in terms of *required competences* to enable marshalling and matching of *available competences* that can be brought to bear on multiple process instants by people and their supporting technical systems in timely and effective ways

4. a suitable integrating infrastructure is needed to link aspects of processes and systems across organisational boundaries to ensure interoperability between processes and resource systems.

Also assumed is that the realisation of those modelling requirements necessitates the use of proven modelling architectures and modelling methods with capabilities to abstract and represent any organisation aspects of different views that suit modeller, user and other stakeholders' requirements. Public domain modelling frameworks were observed to exist that in part provide a viable modelling framework such as: CIMOSA, IDEF0, PERA, ARIS and GRAI/GIM. Most of these frameworks are supported by modelling methods that are designed to systemise enterprise model capture and reuse. They usefully provide means of handling organisational complexity, by offering modelling constructs to decompose (general and specific) process networks into process segments. Also they were observed to provide means of documenting and visualising associated flows of activities, materials, information, controls and so forth. Subsequent sections of this Chapter will briefly review the capabilities of some of these widely known modelling frameworks and methods and suggest reasons why MSI mainly deploy CIMOSA in its modelling ventures.

MODELLING METHODOLOGIES REVIEWED

Structured analysis and design technique (SADT)

SADT was originally designed as a 'blue print' for software engineering and not as complex systems design methodology (Ross & Schoman 1977). However, the scope of SADT has been widened into a full scale methodology for requirements definition, problem analysis and function specification and has since proven useful in many application domains. The strength of SADT lies in its system decomposition principles that uses four modelling constructs, namely: input, control, output & mechanism (ICOM) to model a system. In this way, it provides stakeholders (using the model) with a clear knowledge of the workings of the system being modelled including who and what performs what and necessary operating constraints. But a key limitation of SADT (Vernadat, 1996) is that it cannot sufficiently describe well discrete event dynamic systems (like manufacturing systems) because:

- SADT does not handle flows but focuses on dependences
- SADT provides no dynamic behaviour description e.g. time dependent control flows
- SADT is not precise in its semantics.

IDEF Suit of Methods

IDEF modelling suite was developed in the early 1980's as part of the US Air Force ICAM programme. It is a derivative and further extension of SADT. The IDEF modelling suite consist of (a) IDEF0 for function modelling, (b) IDEF1$_x$ for information modelling and (c) IDEF2 for dynamic modelling. The IDEF suite was designed to model decisions, actions, and activities of a system in a structured graphical manner (Bravoco & Yadav, 1985, Jang, 2003). Figure 2 illustrates the IDEF0 modelling approach. Like its SADT predecessor, IDEF0 adopts a hierarchical decomposition approach to complexity management; thereby decomposing complex problems to lower levels of granularity. It uses the ICOM constructs of SADT to describe the system being modelled. Despite its capabilities, IDEF0 has some widely known limitations especially in terms of its limited time-based capabilities for example, its technique generates ambiguous activity specifications that are essentially static in nature. (Wu, 1992, Jang, 2003). IDEF0 models are static in the sense that they are paper based and are not directly computer executable. Furthermore, IDEF2 which models system behaviours is ill defined requiring the support of other tools such as Petri nets to analyse system behaviours (Vernadat, 1996).

The Purdue Enterprise Reference Architecture (PERA)

PERA was designed to support industry in the development and implementation of integrated manufacturing system (Williams, 1994, Vernadat, 1996). Developed at Purdue University in the USA in collaboration with a consortium of industry collaborators, PERA methodology starts with requirements definition, which is structured in two respective branches, namely: requirement definitions for information and manufacturing systems. Next to this are three compartments that respectively encode: manufacturing system

Figure 2. IDEF0 decomposition principles illustrated

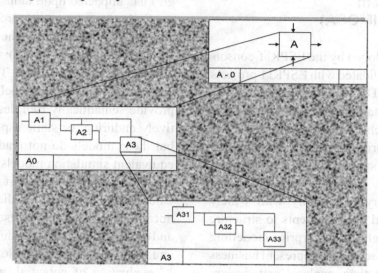

architecture and the information system architecture with human and organisational architecture sandwiched between the two. The human and organisational section provides an architecture for describing organisational structures, human positions, roles and training requirements during the life cycle of MEs. PERA prides itself in comprehensiveness, claiming to cover enterprise life cycle from inception and mission specification to operational and then plant disposal.

Group de Recherché en Automatisation Integrere (GRAI)

GRAI methodology (Domeingts, et al, (1995), Wainwright & Ridgeway, (1994), Vernadat, (1996)) was developed at the University of Bordeaux in early 1980's. GRAI is predominantly a graphical technique using decomposition principle comprising a combination of 'top-down' and 'bottom-up' approaches to define decision centres and information required to make a decision within those centres. GRAI approach is based on three elements: (a) conceptual model, (b) tools & representation rules and (c) application methodology. The conceptual model presumes that as

complex system, an organisation is comprised of three parts namely;

- physical system that comprises technical and human systems, structured work centres and materials that flow through those centres
- operating system that is dedicated to real time control of physical system
- decision system – locus of decisions for the whole organisation via a hierarchical structure organised into decision levels made of decision centres
- the information system that links the other systems with one another and the environment

GRAI uses two graphical tools: (a) GRAI grid used to analyse focused parts of the enterprise and (b) GRAI nets used to analyse decision centres in terms of their activities, resources and mechanisms. GRAI is supported by GIM methodology which extends the capability of GRAI modelling framework to cover the entire CIM systems.

CIM Open System Architecture (CIMOSA)

CIMOSA was developed by the ESPRIT consortium AMICE and validated with ESPRIT projects CIMPRES and CODE in multiple case studies and pilot implementations (Kosanke, 1995). CIMOSA reference architecture supports modelling of complete enterprise life cycle (requirement definitions, design specifications & implementation descriptions). The goal of CIMOSA is to provide the industry community with widely usable and accepted CIM concepts to structure CIM systems; namely: (a) enterprise modelling framework that can accurately represent business operations, support their analysis and design, and lead to executable enterprise models, (b) integrating infrastructure to support application and business integration and (d) a methodology based on CIM system life cycle. CIMOSA views an enterprise as a collection of functional entities processing enterprise objects to realise products and services. CIMOSA modelling methodology adopts systematic and hierarchical approach to complex systems decomposition. At highest level, CIMOSA views an enterprise as a collection of domains, each domain consisting of domain processes (DPs). DPs are core-stand alone processes that interact with one another through exchange of events. DPs can further be decomposed into business processes (BPs), enterprise activities (EAs) and functional operations (FOs). CIMOSA details are summarised in the so called CIMOSA cube and the reader is referred to the references mentioned (AMICE, 1993, Zelm, et al 1995 & Vernadat, 1996).

ENHANCING MODELLING CAPABILITIES OF CURRENT EM SOLUTIONS

Although the emergence of public domain enterprise modelling architectures and methodologies has impacted upon industry with respect to specifying requirements (process models) and structuring and supporting the design of resource systems (human & technical); significant application constraints still remain. The present authors observe that enterprise models created naturally provide semantically rich descriptions of 'relatively enduring' or static aspects of enterprises but those models do not readily transform into equivalent simulation models needed to analyse and thereby to predict short and medium term enterprise behaviours. In reality, however, most if not all enterprise systems are subject to significant and often on going changes during their life cycle and thus necessitate simulation to support 'what-if' evaluation of potential process and system alternatives needed to implement organisational design and change. Standards related to enterprise engineering and integration such as CEN ENV 13550 (model execution services) provide a basis for computer based development and execution but as yet no standard model transformation methods are reported in the public domain literature that allow selected segments of enterprise models to be executed within virtual environments (Zelm, 2003). Table 1 highlights the modelling capabilities and constraints associated with the current enterprise modelling methods (Rahimifard & Weston, 2007).

Researchers at the MSI Research Institute at Loughborough University, UK, have deployed various public domain modelling architectures and concepts to developing coherent models of industrial processes and systems. Those models have supported both large and small scale organisation design and engineering exercises at sites of ME collaborators. In so doing MSI has produced various integrated modelling methodologies including those reported by Monfared et al (2002), Chatha et al (2007); Rahimifard & Weston (2007) and Agyapong-Kodua et al (2008). For most of the integrated modelling methods developed CIMOSA has provided a backbone modelling architecture and representational formalisms for

Table 1. Current EM capabilities & constrains

Capabilities of Current EM Solutions	Primary Modelling Constraints
Can formally and explicitly handle enterprise complexity, decompose complex processes into process segments and their resource systems and related structural dependences.	Resultant models are focused on relatively enduring aspects of MEs and do not encode time dependencies related to process instants and related product flows, control flows, exception instants, and other time dependent causal effects.
Enables attribution of multi-perspective model views to models of process segments and their related resource systems.	Resultant models cannot replicate real ME behaviours, such as in support of model validation.
Can represent and help communicate and visualize unified views about multiple stakeholders.	Resultant models do not provide a basis for prediction of future ME behaviours.
Generates explicit representation of different aspects of ME processes that can inform and support various forms of decision making.	Models created cannot be used to visualise possible future scenarios such as changes in resource systems properties and characteristics.
Has abstraction and generalisation concepts that facilitate the integration and reuse of multi-perspective and decomposed models processes and resource systems.	Models are essentially static and therefore cannot fully capture enterprise stochastic behaviours.
Has life cycle related concepts which coupled with formal decomposition concepts facilitates system integration and interoperation.	Limited integration and interoperability.

graphical capture of relatively enduring aspects of case study enterprises. The choice of CIMOSA as a foundation backbone for MSI's modelling methodologies was made essentially for reasons, which include:

- CIMOSA enterprise modelling architecture and method was through experimental application by MSI researchers considered to provide the most comprehensive public domain architecture available;
- CIMOSA provides a public domain open system architectures that support modelling of different life phases of complex systems from requirements definitions through implementation descriptions (Kosanke, 1995, Gransier & Werner, 1995, Vernadat, 1996);
- CIMOSA provides an extensive set of modelling constructs and representational formalisms (particularly process-oriented constructs) to enable users create particular models of any aspects of enterprise.

The eclectic nature of CIMOSA allows expansion of its modelling capabilities within the con-

fines of general enterprise modelling principles. For example, Monfared et al (2002), described how four types of CIMOSA diagramming template (namely: 'context diagram', 'interaction diagram', 'structure diagram' and 'activity diagram') can be used as a source of enterprise knowledge which can be reloaded using simulation modelling technologies. Those templates support enterprise engineering projects though stages of model development so that modellers and process engineers can move iteratively as they structure and organise:

1. the ongoing capture of coherent and semantically rich picture of dependent processes, in such a way that key dependencies can be explicitly represented;
2. the reuse of multiple coherent views of multi- process models in support of process and system simulation.

The use of these templates was reported to be effective in structuring the capture and coherent representation of multiple static views of enterprise process attributes at needed levels of abstraction. Context diagrams are used to organise process models into interrelated CIMOSA conformant and

Figure 3. Approach used to create CIMOSA enterprise models

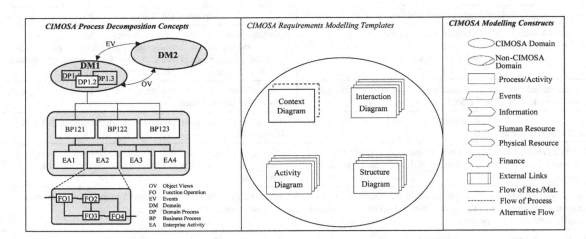

non CIMOSA conformant domains (DMs), the former being the concerned domains. CIMOSA DMs in the context diagrams are further decomposed into more detailed domain processes (DPs). Interactions among the DPs triggered by events typically result in exchange of (informational, material, human, technical and financial) resources amongst DPs and these interactions can be represented using interaction diagrams. Structure diagrams are used to formerly attribute relative enduring organisational relationships that couple business processes (BPs) and enterprise activities (EAs) of a DP while activity diagram templates are deployed to explicitly encode relatively short-lived descriptions of precedence links used to organise the interoperation of BPs and EAs.

Use of CIMOSA 'context', 'interaction', 'structure' and 'activity' diagramming templates enables explicit definition of key structural relationships between DMs, DPs, BPs and EAs. Typically, those structures will indicate process segment ownerships, hierarchical ordering, sequential ordering and precedence relationships, and necessary interchanges of information, material, human resource and finances.

Though the diagramming templates enhanced model creation and descriptions, the models still remained static in the sense that they do not encode

aspects of specific process instants and lack the capability to be used in determining and possibly predicting individual and or collective behaviours of system elements. But such predictions are core requirements for organisation design and change projects in MEs. This is the case because static EMs are focused on an abstract big picture and its decomposition, i.e. on relatively enduring aspects of MEs and do not encode specific time dependencies related to process instants that result as a consequence of product flows, control flows, exception instants and time dependent causal effects that determine factors such as resource utilizations and consumption and associated wastes. On the contrary discrete event simulation modelling however can capture and quantitatively describe aspects of dynamic behaviours including queues, stochastic events, product flows, process routes, resource utilization, efficiencies, break downs, etc, while dynamic systems modelling instrumented by qualitative and quantitative causal loop and continuous simulation models (that can be numerically integrated) can computer execute and predict dynamic behaviours arising from causal dependencies between system variables (Ajaefobi, et al 2008). It follows that to support organisation design and change static models created during enterprise engineering projects will in general need to be re-encoded into dynamic views using suitable simulation techniques with sufficient constructs to represent enterprise systems behaviours and properties. In simulation views, change parameters that can trigger system redesign and change can clearly be observed and different possible solution options tried in a virtual environment. In general the authors' experiences of ME modelling have confirmed the commonly held view that continuous simulation is best suited to modelling dynamic behaviours of either large or small scale systems but with essentially a simplified view of the stochastic nature of products. While discrete event simulation (DES) is best suited to modelling small scale systems in which stochastic behaviours need to be clearly understood. Also observed is that the use of DES can be key when a common resource is used to realise multiple products with a significant product dynamic but that in general the use of DES should be preceded by creating an EM (and possibly causal loop modelling) when supporting enterprise engineering projects.

COMMON ORGANISATION DESIGN & CHANGE (OD&C) TRIGGERS AND THE ROLE OF EM

OD&C projects can be strategically planned or it can come as part of a response to emerging requirements. Generally though, OD&C projects in a given enterprise can be triggered by the need to respond to: perceived opportunities; new requirements and threats; or in anticipation to certain events such as new government legislation, new product launch by a competitor, new customer requirements and technological change (Mullins, 2005). Planned OD&C projects may also constitute a program within an organisation to improve its operational efficiency and current best performance. Practical examples of common triggers that would naturally lead to organisation (re)design and change in a typical production enterprise include:

- bottlenecks generating long queues of WIP
- long lead times and unbalanced workflows
- idle resources (within human or technical systems)
- poor quality jobs or high error rates
- etc.

In theory enterprise modelling has significant potential to support organisation design and change projects because EMs:

a. present interrelated enterprise sub systems as models from different view points

b. models created in respect of (a) 'paint the big picture' of an enterprise by explicitly depicting what the enterprise does and clearly separating this from who/what does what and at what time. This can enhance stakeholder understandings of the enterprise.

c. In dynamic views (where EMs are transformed into models of ME segments using suitable simulation technology), enterprise engineers can observe:

   ◦ throughputs from which assessment can be made as to whether the organisation's performance is acceptable given the available resources and time

   ◦ make informed decision about whether current best performance can still be improved upon, such as by raising work input rates and reducing cycle times by deploying resources with increased efficiency

   ◦ take decisions about what can be changed to improve the quality, quantity and timelines of the work throughput

   ◦ observe production system performance under changing scenarios including the impacts if performance metric of the technical systems and the proficiency with which people use of those technologies are changed

- o assess impacts and observe impacts of changing competences, commitment and motivation of the people
- o assess impacts on performances of alternative resource systems configurations
- o can determine policies for improving interoperability and communications and feedback between people on the shop floor with their managers.

SIMULATION MODELLING (SM) IN SUPPORT OF OD&C

Simulation modelling is an established means of understanding and predicting systems behaviours which has received great attention in literature. Simulation technologies have been widely applied in manufacturing and service organisations (Barber, et al, 2003). Generally, simulated systems imitate real systems. Harrison & Petty, (2002) described why simulation is becoming important tool in science and engineering:

- safety – simulation allows a system to be tested under extreme conditions that could not be justified in a real world scenario
- practicality – with large systems, simulation may be the only practical way of approaching a problem
- simulation allows what if analysis – this allows the physical system to be built and tested under different solution options
- simulation is repeatable
- simulation promotes understanding of systems, particularly if allied with graphics.
- simulation can be used to verify analytical solutions to problems

Though continuous simulation has been usefully applied in manufacturing cases, it is discrete event simulation (DES) technology that has been adopted in the majority of manufacturing studies and applications. Manufacturing variables change at discrete points in time. For example, the time to complete a manufacturing operation may vary each time the operation is undertaken, which can make discrete event simulators more suitable in comparison to continuous simulations. In many production situations orders from customers arrive at unpredictable times and commonly involve uncertain quantities and mixes of product realisation at any point in time. This makes it very difficult to develop equations that adequately characterise different production scenarios which can be solved via numerical integration methods. Whereas DES models can support enterprise systems performance observation and analysis under different possible scenarios where alternative resource configurations are loaded by stochastic order, information and material workflows. Knowledge obtained from such performance analysis could inform and support management decisions about OD&C parameters such as:

1. what needs to be changed, improved or supported amongst the processes & systems deployed by the enterprise to realising specific objectives
2. what control measures are needed to improve systems performances and the appropriate times to put such measures in place
3. how informed decisions can be made about new competences, capabilities and capacities that may be needed by resource systems to improve their throughput and the over all performance of systems
4. what training system operators require and the contents of such training based on current performance and observed gaps
5. needed technology to enhance system performance (software and hardware)
6. how to enhance cost engineering by using value stream maps and activity based costing
7. what wastes, errors and reworks, etc can be reducing thus setting the ground for Lean manufacturing implementation

8. ways of reconfiguring enterprise processes & systems to realised enhanced performance in terms of quality, quantity, timeliness and overall efficiency
9. ways of improving organisation structure and reporting lines can also be observed

To summarise DES models have potential to (a) detect and eliminate problems that otherwise would require cost and time consuming corrective measures during production ramp up, (b) determine optimum times such as processing times, failure times, recovery times, etc, and throughput of the plant, (c) determine size of buffers and numbers of machines with intended throughputs and (d) investigate how failures affect the throughput and the utilisation of resource elements and systems.

However DES models of production situations typically soon become very complex if the reality is closely modelled. Hence the scope of DES models need to be restricted. As a consequence the modeller needs to guard against optimising only a small part of a given ME rather than consider optimising overall ME performance. It follows that EM and SM techniques are complementary with the former designed to provide an explicit structural decomposition of the whole ME and the latter can enable detailed analysis of possible uncertain behaviours in specific segments of the EM where that analysis can be made with the context of the big picture captured by the EM.

For more than two decades, researchers in MSI Research Institute, Loughborough University have collaborated with various industrial partners while developing and deploying coherent and semantically rich ME models drawn from real industrial data. Essentially, MSI's modelling approach unifies the use of: (a) manufacturing enterprise decomposition principles and multi-perspective graphical modelling templates as defined by public domain enterprise modelling (EM) methodologies, (b) causal and temporal relationship modelling notations, provided by

causal loop modelling (CLM) technologies, (c) discrete event simulation models (SM) of selected configurations of workloaded process segments and their underpinning resource systems and (d) mixed reality modelling, based on the use of workflow modelling (WFM) techniques that enable interaction and information interchange between simulation models and real resource systems. Figure 4 is an illustrative description of the modelling approach adopted, which integrates EM, CLM, SM & WFM to create comprehensive, coherent and semantically rich process and system models in support of organisation design and change projects.

This modelling approach is usually realised by taking the following steps:

1. elicit and capture actual plant data from a target organisation, about its process network, product and work flows and its resource systems
2. create 'as is' EM using suitable a enterprise modelling method
3. validate/modify the 'as is' EM
4. encode focused aspects of the 'as is' EM into simulation views using a suitable simulation tool
5. validate/modify the 'as is' simulation models (SMs)
6. develop candidate 'to be' SMs
7. validate/modify the behaviours of the 'to be' SMs
8. integrate the operations of 'to be' and 'as is' SMs to predict an organisation's performance in selected aspects when subjected to alternative strategies/policies and requirements
9. validate and modify as required the integrated SMs
10. recommend and justify improve organisation designs

Figure 4. Illustrative description of the modelling approach

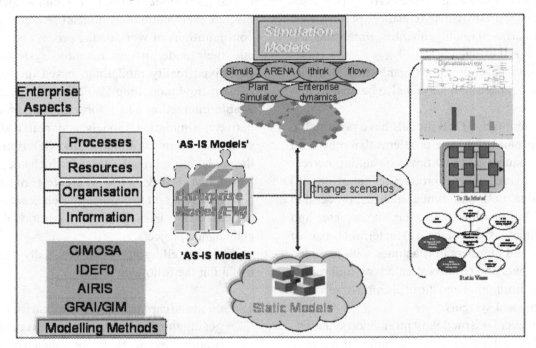

ILLUSTRATIVE CASE STUDY APPLICATION

The modelling approach and steps described in previous sections have been deployed in a wide range of case studies carried out within automotive, machine building, composite and furniture industries. An instance of such applications in a SME furniture making organisation is described in outline in this section to illustrate the complementary natures of EM and SM techniques when used in organisation design and change situations.

Case Study Background & Modelling Requirements

Woodland is a furniture making SME located in East midlands in England. It is a make to order furniture business with over 60 regular workers. Recent increase in market share resulted in management concerns about the company's capacity to cope with increasing customer demands, should the current trend (market share increase) continue. To extend its current market share naturally require continuous performance improvement of its processes and resource systems. Funded by EPSRC in the UK, the authors are collaborating with Woodlands managers in seeking to deploy best industry practices to support the company in reorganising its resource systems to ensure profitability and competitiveness. At the commencement of the project, the following observations were made:

- Woodland's processes were not formerly documented; rather understandings about them existed in the 'minds' of the managers and operators. A Woodland's organisational chart depicted people and their roles, but documented information about people responsibilities was very limited and could not show dynamics associated with roles including 'requirements to perform role', 'inputs to roles', 'role performance outputs', 'resource utilisation' and 'impacts of requirement changes on roles and role incumbents'.

- Woodland's production systems operate in a 'push' production fashion with inputs and outputs of both up & down streams not properly regulated with respect to a give takt time. Consequently during normal operations there is significant WIP and long queues which also results in an untidy working environment and raises questions about conformance to health and safety regulations.

- Woodland's production systems are semi-automated, deploying competent operators to dynamically resource their wood cutting, furniture making machines and work benches as significant fluctuation in customer order is the norm

- Though Woodland currently meets its lead time targets, the management requires further lead time reduction to remain competitive with alternative overseas manufacturers

- Woodland management desires improved resource utilisation and/or better performance without compromising the well being of its resource systems.

Against the backdrop of the observations made, project objectives were agreed as follows:

1. Using suitable EM constructs and representational formalisms to abstract, represent and document Woodland processes and systems, so as to identify who does what and with what competences

2. Encode aspects of Woodland processes and systems in a dynamic (virtual reality) view, thereby better understanding current throughput, performances and resource utilisations

3. Observe and monitor system performance using different resource configurations and

thereafter to suggest improved ways of deploying a finite resource

4. Observe and monitor production system reaction when processing 'cognate' and 'distinct' work item types; so as to analyze and the impact of variations in required quantities of such work items on the system capability and capacity

5. Suggest improved production planning and control methods

6. Investigate the implications of operating a full automated system in comparison with the current semi-automated status quo

7. Suggest alternative ways of running the production system, thereby making it more flexible, lean and agile

8. Suggest possible changes in organisational structure, company policies and management philosophy

Case Study Modelling Approach & Methodology

The modelling approach described was deployed to elicit data and formally decompose and explicitly document three main processes identified in Woodland, namely:

(a) *'production processes'* that on a day to day basis make and deliver furniture to aggregated order

(b) *'new product introduction processes'* that operate annually to develop and introduce new furniture products, replacing around ten percent of products

(c) *'strategy making processes'* that operate as required to conceive and realise improved competitiveness.

The processes identified and modelled correspond to three generic processes commonly found in MEs namely strategic, tactical and operational process types (Pandya et al, 1997). Details of these key processes were modelled using CIMOSA ISO

Figure 5. Top level context diagram showing Woodland domains

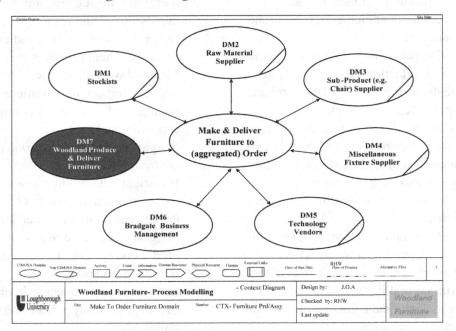

standard modelling techniques. Figure 5 shows a high level context diagram created to model interacting domains identified when Woodland and its supply chain partners realise a 'make and deliver furniture to order' process; while figure 6 is one of the structure diagrams generated to explicitly model elements of business processes and enterprise activities. The domains shown in figure 5 interact with one another at different levels via exchange of information and resources in other to successfully realise 'make & deliver furniture to aggregated order' process

Woodland Production System

Woodlands production system was observed to be a multiple value stream production system. Here, the present authors consider a ***multiple value stream production system*** as being: *"any system which adds value to two or more 'distinctive work item flows'; by realising necessary value adding processing operations through an organised sharing of the (human and technical) resources available to that system"*.

In such systems, work item flows will typically involve flows of raw material, (sub) components, sub assemblies and products. Additional work items flows may take the form of different information types (such as customer order types, works order types, product specification types, etc) which need processing into alternative forms that have increased value in the business context under study. The term 'distinctive work item types' implies that 'significant differences' in processing requirements will be necessary to achieve value addition as different work item types pass through the system. Here it is assumed that:

(A) 'cognate work item types' (such as sub-product and product item types within the same product family) can share a similar value adding process. Therefore also assumed is that for cognate work item types, relatively minor differences between item types (such as dimensional or operation time differences) will need to be accommodated by the assigned production system during process set up and process execution. In such cases, variation within a product family might be accommodated via use of programmable machines and product type sensing mechanisms, or by deploying people with the requisite competencies needed to set up and process all input item types within a family.

(B) 'distinctive work item types' will belong to different product families, in the sense that the sub-product and product item types belonging to different families will each require a distinctive value adding process. Typically this will require alternative processing routes through work centres of production systems, and the various work item flows within each family will likely generate distinctive process dynamics (such as process bottlenecks, inventory level patterns and so forth). Hence production systems used to realise distinctive work item types will likely require correspondingly distinctive work centre processing capabilities and competencies, and distinctive workflow rules and controls. This requirement is also likely to be additional to the need to cope with in-family product variation via the use of flexible resource system elements.

The Woodland project is still on going but the progress reported considers the processing of cognate product types in the assembly shop and how this shop operations could be changed to improve performance. Following the modelling method

Figure 6. Woodland Structure diagram showing some business processes

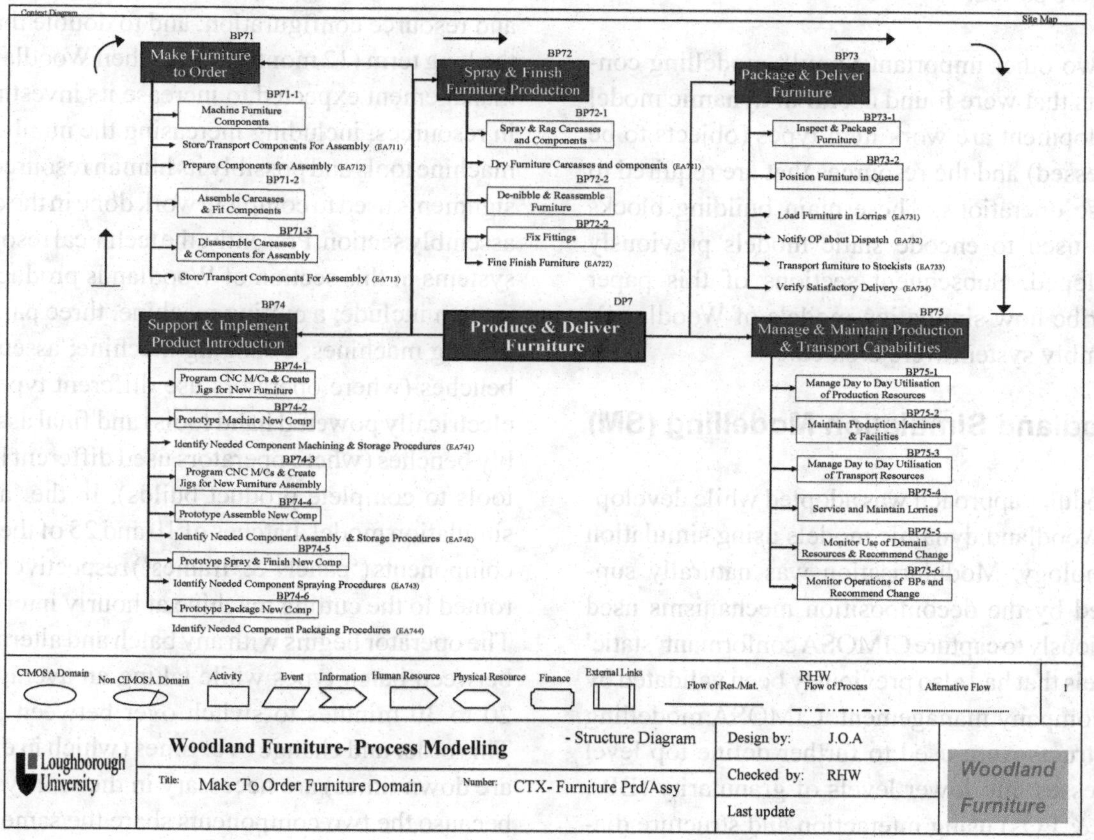

described in section 6, an assembly process model captured using EM technology was re-encoded in a dynamic view using Siml8, a discrete event simulator. The initial objective was to replicate the assembly shop behaviours over time, including how it responds to changing work item types. Simul8 has four basic building blocks namely:

1. Work Entry Points through which work items to be processed enter into the system. The arrival pattern is controlled either to follow a scheduled pattern (deterministic behaviour) or a stochastic (probabilistic) behaviour
2. Queues – hold work items that are waiting to be processed
3. Work centres that perform actual value adding operations under varying probability distribution of processing times and efficiencies
4. Work Exist Points where completed work are stored.

Two other important Simul8 modelling constructs that were found useful in dynamic model development are work item types (objects to be processed) and the resources that are required to realise operations. These main building blocks were used to encode static models previously developed. Subsequent sections of this paper describe how simulation models of Woodland's assembly system were created.

Woodland Simulation Modelling (SM)

A modular approach was adopted while developing Woodland dynamic models using simulation technology. Modularisation was naturally supported by the decomposition mechanisms used previously to capture CIMOSA conformant 'static' models that had also previously been validated by the company management. CIMOSA modelling constructs were used to further define top level processes into lower levels of granularity (BPs, EAs & FOs) using interaction and structure dia-

grams. Figure 7 is an illustrative description of decomposition of a CIMOSA domain into lower level BPs, EAs and FOs.

Here, the rationale was to develop dynamic (simulation) models of different process segments and subsequently to link the modular models into a coherent system model that captures more holistically entire system behaviours. Following this approach, the operations of the door assembly section of the assembly shop were encoded in a simulation view. The 'as is' weekly average throughput of 800 – 900 completed product units was assumed as a benchmark. Resource systems utilisations and queues associated with this throughput were observed based on Woodland's single shift work pattern of 8 hours (excluding break and lunch times). To cope with anticipated customer demands, Woodland management desired that the throughput of this section should be raised to: 1200 units per week in the short term (2-3 months) using the present available resources and resource configuration; and to double that in the long term (12 months time) when Woodland's management expected to increase its investment in resources, including increasing the number of machine tools and possibly its human resource assignments used to complete work done in the door assembly section. Presently, the technical resource systems in this section of Woodlands production system include; a cutting machine, three parallel milling machines, a sanding machine; assembly benches (where operators use different types of electrically powered hand tools) and final assembly benches (where operators used different hand tools to complete product builds). In the 'as is' simulation model, batches of 10 and 25 of the two components ('panels' & 'frames') respectively are routed to the cutting machine at hourly intervals. The operator begins with any batch and alternates between batch types while taking an average of 20 to 30 minutes to switch over between jobs. This order and change over times (which in effect are down times) are necessary in the real system because the two components share the same ma-

Figure 7. CIMOSA hierarchical decomposition modelling approach

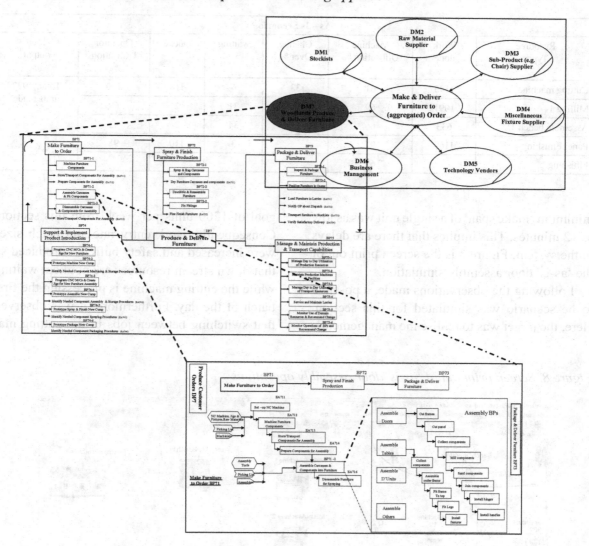

chine for cutting operations and secondly, both components are needed further down stream for subsequent assembling.

From the SM results however, it was observed that the down time due to switching between the two jobs was rather high. The implication here was that the machine spends one third of its production time per day on 'changing over', thereby contributing significantly to under-utilisation of the said machine and its human operator. Furthermore, since the said machine feeds other machines further down stream, delays and under-utilisations of other

related resources were also observed. Similarly it was observed that the human operators working in this section, though apparently were seen to be working all day, their utilisation in terms of time spent on value adding operations was also low. It follows that much time is spent on non value adding operations, which is a trigger for change. Table 2 shows the 'as is' simulation results and observed utilisation of some selected resources.

In summary, 927 product units were assembled and the minimum time spent by a unit in the system was about 60 minutes, even though the

Table 2. Observed 'As - Is' simulation results

As – Is Scenario						
Resource Types	Work done	Machine Utilisation %	Change Over %	waiting	Queue	Operator Utilisation %	Total output
Cutting machine	1145	61	33	6	114	100	Total = 927 units made
Milling 1	1091	69	_	31	2	69	
Assemble bench 1	633	66	_	34	2	43	
Panel Finishing	1169	97	_	3	110	98	
Finishing		69	_				

minimum 'make span' of a single unit was as low as 12 minutes. This implies that there are delays in the system. Figure 8 is the screen print out of the 'as-is' door assembly simulation.

Following the observations made, a possible to be scenario was simulated for this section. Here, the target was to realise the management's goal of 1200 units per week from this section. Consequently, work entry rate and batch sizes were increased and safety buffers introduced so that down stream resources are not kept waiting while the cutting machine is processing the first batch of the day. Furthermore, it was observed that switching between jobs in the cutting ma-

Figure 8. Screen print out of 'as-is' door assembly operations

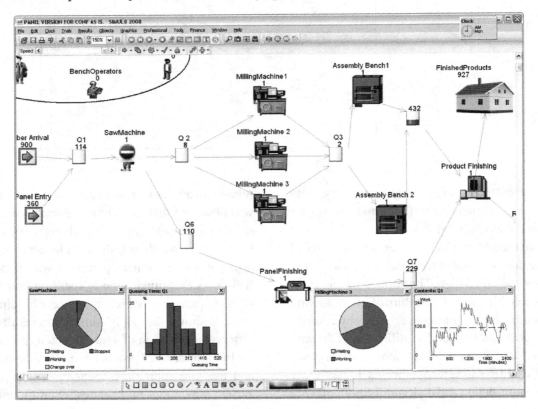

Table 3. 'To - Be' scenario simulation results

Resource Types	Work done	Machine Utilisation %	Change Over %	Waiting Time %	Queue	Operator Utilisation %	Total output
			To – Be Scenario				
Saw machine	1240	66	13	15	0	81	Total =1251 units made % increase = 35
Milling 1	1235	78	–	22	0	78	
Assemble bench 1	745	78	–	22	0	80	
Panel finishing	1178	98	–	2	71	98	
Finishing	1267	79	–	21	268/0	79	

chine could be done in an average of 10 minutes and that the operators had previously been over indulging themselves, hence the new change over time for cutting machine was set between 10 -15 minutes depending on the operator's competences and so called tacit knowledge. The simulation results showed significant increase in throughput from 927 to 1251, representing a 35% increase. Furthermore, queues were significantly reduced especially the queue to the cutting machine. A closer investigation of the behaviour of the queue to the cutting machine showed a rising and falling pattern, with a peak value occurring at mid day. The same pattern is repeated during weekly simulation run with peak at mid week. This possibly captures the mood of the human operator who slows down his pace as the days goes on and then increases after lunch break. Table 3 shows the performance results of some selected resource systems.

Adjacent to the door assembly unit is the table assembly section. This section was also encoded in a simulation (virtual reality) view. Over 3 dozen table types are currently being assembled by Woodland in this unit. However, the authors consolidated them into three broad groups based on the commonality table features; including complexity, routing and processing times. In general, products belonging to the Woodlands table family are assembled from three main components namely; table tops (TT), under frames (UDF) and legs (TLG). The table assemble operations involved produced the tables to a design specification using primary components that are delivered from

Woodland machine shop. Like the case described in the preceding paragraph, the throughput and the resource system utilisations were observed. Following the observations, suggestions were made on how the section throughput and over all performances could be improved by implementation certain OD&C principles observed . Suggestions made were based on consideration of different resource units as components that need for them to interwork to improve the over all performance of the assembly shop. Subsequent section briefly describes the background for component based approach to organisation design and the role of enterprise modelling and engineering.

COMPONENT-BASED ORGANISATION DESIGN AND CHANGE APPROACH

BPR (Hammer & Champy, 2001) advocates a radical approach to organisation design and change, involving fundamental rethinking and radical redesign of business process to bring about dramatic improvement all critical performance measures. Yogesh (1998) however observed that 70% of BPR projects reviewed did not yield the envisaged dramatic results. Essentially, the reason given for failed BPR projects was that BPR focus mainly on organisation's processes leaving other component parts of the organisation unchanged. OD & C project should take a multi perspective view of the organisation. Similarly, OD&C cannot be realised by merely reshuffling of workers followed by changes in organisational structure without changing the process design, procedures and work item flows. It follows that OD&C is not only a radical process reengineering which seeks to change process designs and sequences of operation without change to resource systems compositions, structures and configurations. OD&C projects should take a holistic view of the entire organisation bearing in mind the causal and temporal relationships between all organisation system components. This can be instrumented by EM & engineering concepts, which deploys multi perspective views of organisation (structure, processes, resources & information) and how these views dynamically interact and impact on one another; including the impacts of such interactions on the over all organisation's goals.

In general, a manufacturing organisation is an open system with inputs from the:

- environment (which provides constraints, demands and opportunities)
- resource systems that realise value adding operations to deliver products and services
- mission and strategies that link resource systems to processes, opportunities, constraints and demands so that unwanted behaviours are constrained

Responding to requirement changes which generally will necessitate OD&C is complex and difficult because it implies changes in most if not all the organisation inputs including: strategies, policies, processes, procedures, work organisation structures and resource systems configurations (Nadler, 1993). Weston (1998) suggests that effective and timely responses to change requirements will necessitate change capable organisation systems and structures. Resource systems are integral parts of organisation that are configured in a variety of ways to generate different behavioural responses needed by the organisation to realise specific and emerging business require-

ments. One way of viewing resource systems is that they are building blocks or components with embedded range of attributes and characteristics such as competences/or capabilities that enables them to act individually or collectively to realise specified business requirements. It follows that for organisation design and change to be effective, resource components should be agile and responsive with inherent ability to be reformed or reconfigured so that individual and collective behaviours of organisation system components could rapidly be aligned to meet specific and changing business process needs. This implies that organisations should have:

1. suitable components or building blocks from which high performance systems are to be configured
2. organisational structures and associated mechanisms capable of establishing flexible linkages between different components, so that systems can be configured rapidly and yet have inherent ability to be reconfigured and reengineered in the event of requirement changes
3. means of supporting rapid and holistic definition and redefinition of system behaviours in the form that can be used to help specify, implement, control and change individual and collective behaviours of system components to facilitate organisation design and change.

Generally though, high performing dynamic systems should be built from components by (a) selecting and programming components behaviours and (b) defining and programming system architectures. This will result in composed resource systems that can be defined in terms of their reachable states. To respond to requirement changes; (a) component behaviours are re-selected and re-programmed and (b) system architectures are re-defined and re-programmed, thereby resulting in a re-composed or changed system. It follows that system components of organisations should possess sufficient flexibility characteristics especially 'change capability' and 'change capability rate'. Harrison et al, (2001) present change capability classes and related them to change scenarios that can beneficially be applied as follows:

1. 'programmability': ability to programme system behaviours and or composition so that the system can reach a range of well known states, thereby providing means of addressing changes of predictable nature
2. 'reactivity': ability to react to changes of unpredictable nature by modifying system behaviours or compositions
3. 'proactivity': ability to prepared for modification of system behaviours and compositions

Similarly, the 'change capability rate' includes notions of engineering 'costs and time' when a composed system is moving between states. Change capability rate therefore depends on:

*   the properties of the components (modular building blocks) from which systems are composed, which impact on the ease and extent to which system programming, system reaction and system pro-action could be specified and realised
*   the structure and mechanisms used to integrate various parts of a system as this can enable or constrain subsequent changes to system composition and behaviours
*   the type of change processes and supporting technology that are available to modify system composition or behaviours

Therefore, to design and build change capable organisation systems from system components, the following measures are needed to support improved organisation flexibility:

1. incorporating sufficient redundant capabilities into initial system composition so that possible alternative behaviours could be readily programmed to enable the system reach predictable change of states, possibly on frequent basis
2. structuring the system and its integrating mechanisms in such a manner that its composition could be modified rapidly and effectively in response to change requirements
3. designing and building the organisation in such a way that it can easily and rapidly be decommissioned and or replaced(if need be) in response to change requirements and environmental conditions beyond the scope of the constituting system capabilities

CONCLUSION

Models provide means of abstracting and managing different components of complex organisations. An organisation such as a manufacturing enterprise (ME) has many interacting component parts that can be represented at different levels of granularity. Current business requirements demand that most if not all organisation parts and systems should be responsive and change capable. Models of concerned parts of any given ME make it easier to visualise and analyse characteristic behaviours of alternative configurations of enterprise components thereby supporting production planning and performance monitoring. By so doing, organisation design and change projects are supported. EM and its supporting architectures and methodologies provide solutions to complex systems modelling, thereby facilitating organisation design and change projects. The case study reported described how EM & SM can be used to inform OD&C project via top-down and bottom-up modelling approaches. In the former, Woodland was modelled in context with all the domains that interact to realise 'make furniture to aggregated order' while the later approach described how elemental low level enterprise activities and operations and resource units assigned to execute them can be reorganised to realise improved system performance.

REFERENCES

Agyapong-Kodua, K., Ajaefobi, J.O., & Weston, R.H. (2009). Modelling dynamic value streams to support process design and evaluation. *Int. J. of Computer Integrated Manufacturing*.

Ajaefobi, J. O., Wahid, B., & Weston, R. H. (2008). *Proc. of the ICAM*, Western Michigan University, USA.

Alison, B., O'Sullivia, O.A., Rice, J., Rothwell, A., & Sanders, C. (2001). *Research skills for students*.

AMICE (Ed.). (1993). *Open system architecture for CIM, ESPRIT Consortium* (2nd ed.). New York: Springer-Verlag.

Ashfort, B. E. (2001). *Role transition in organisational life: An identity-based perspective*. Mahwah, NJ: Lawrence Erlbaum Associates.

Barber, K. D., Dewhurst, F. W., Burns, R. L. D. H., & Rogers, J. B. B. (2003). Business-process modelling and simulation for manufacturing management: A practical way forward . *Business Process Management Journal*, *9*(4). doi:10.1108/14637150310484544

Barber, M. I., & Weston, R. H. (1998). Scoping study on business process reengineering: Towards successful IT application . *International Journal of Production Research*, *36*, 574–601.

Berio, G., & Vernadat, F. B. (1999). New developments in enterprise modelling using CI-MOSA. *Computers in Industry*, *40*(2), 99–114. doi:10.1016/S0166-3615(99)00017-2

Bernus, P. (2003). Enterprise models for enterprise architecture and ISO9000:2000. *Annual Reviews in Control*, *27*, 211–220. doi:10.1016/j.arcontrol.2003.09.004

Blethyn, S. G., & Parker, C. S. (1990). *Designing information systems*. Butterworth-Heinemann.

Bravocco, R. R., & Yadav, S. B. (1985). Requirements definitions architecture – an overview. *Computers in Industry*, *6*, 237–251. doi:10.1016/0166-3615(85)90046-6

Chatha, K. A., Ajaefobi, J. O., & Weston, R. H. (2007). Enriched multi-process modelling in support of the life cycle engineering of business processes. *International Journal of Production Research*, *45*(1), 103–141.

Christensen, L. C., Johansen, B. W., Midjo, N., Ornarheim, J., Syvertsen, T. G., & Totland, T. (1995). Enterprise modelling-practices and perspectives. In *Proc. of the ASME 9th Engineering Database Symposium*, Boston, US.

Davenport, T. H. (1993). *Process innovation: Re-engineering work through information technology*. Boston, MA: Harvard Business Press.

Davis, L. E. (1982). Organisational design. In G. Salvendy (Ed.), *Handbook of industrial engineering* (pp. 2.1.1-2.1.29). New York: Wiley & Sons.

Doumeingts, G., Vallespir, B., & Marcotte, F. (1995). A proposal for integrated modelling of manufacturing system: Application to the re-engineering of an assembly shop. *Control Engineering Practice*, *3*(1), 59–67. doi:10.1016/0967-0661(94)00065-O

Drucker, P.F. (1990). The emerging theory of manufacturing. *Harvard Business Review, May-June*(3), 94-104.

Evans, J. R., & Lindsay, W. M. (1993). *The management and control of quality* (2nd ed.). Minneapolis, MN: West Publishing Coy.

Fox, M. S., & Gruninger, M. (1998). Enterprise modelling. *AI Magazine*, 109–112.

Goldman, S. L., Nagel, R. N., & Preiss, K. (1995). *Agile competitors and virtual organisation*. New York: Van Nostrand Reinhold.

Gransier, T., & Werner, S. (1995). Validation of CIMOSA. *Computers in Industry, 27*, 95–100. doi:10.1016/0166-3615(95)00048-0

Hammer, M., & Champy, J. (2001). *Reengineering the corporation, a manifesto for business revolution*. New York: Harper Business.

Handy, C. (1993). *Understanding organisations* (4th ed.). New York: Harmondsworth, Penguin.

Harrison, D. K., & Petty, D. J. (2002). *Systems for planning and control in manufacturing*. Newness, Oxford.

Harrison, R., West, A. A., Weston, R. H., & Monfared, R. P. (2001). Distributed engineering of manufacturing machines. In *Proc. of the Instn. of Mech. Engrs., Vol. 215, Part B Journal of Engineering Manufacture* (pp. 217-231).

Jang, K.-J. (2003). A model decomposition approach for a manufacturing enterprise in business process reengineering. *International Journal of Computer Integrated Manufacturing, 16*(3), 210–218. doi:10.1080/0951192021000039594

Kosanke, K. (1995). CIMOSA- overview and status. *Computers in Industry, 27*, 101–109. doi:10.1016/0166-3615(95)00016-9

Martin, J. (2005). *Organisation behaviour and management* (3rd ed.). Florence, KY: Thomson Learning.

Mills, J., Platts, K., & Bourne, M. (2003). Competence and resource architectures. *International Journal of Operations & Production Management, 3*(9), 977–994. doi:10.1108/01443570310491738

Mintzberg, H. (1989). *Mintzberg on management: Inside our strange world of organisations*. London: MacMillan.

Monfared, R. P. (2000). *A component–based approach to design and construction of change capable manufacturing cell control systems*. Unpublished doctoral dissertation, Loughborough University.

Monfared, R. P., West, A. A., Harrison, R., & Weston, R. H. (2002). An implementation of business process modelling in automotive industry. In *Proc. of the Instn. of Mech. Engineers, Vol. 216 Part B: Engineering Manufacture* (pp. 1413-1427).

Mullins, L. J. (2005). *Management & organisational behaviours* (7th ed.). Upper Saddle River, NJ: Prentice Hall.

Nadler, D. A. (1993). Concepts of management of organisational change. In Mabey, et al (Eds.), *Managing Change* (2nd ed.). PCB Ltd.

Pandya, K. V., Karlsson, A., Sega, S., & Carrie, A. (1997). Towards the manufacturing enterprise of the future. *Int. Journal of Production. Management, 17*, 502–521.

Rahmifard, A., & Weston, R. H. (2007). The enhanced use of enterprise and simulation modelling techniques to support factory changeability. *International Journal of Computer Integrated Manufacturing, 20*(4), 303–328.

Ramenyi, D. (1998). *Doing research in business and management: An introduction to process & method*. London: SAGE Publications.

Ross, D. T., & Schoman, K. E. (1977). Structured analysis requirements definitions. *IEEE Transactions on Software Engineering, SE-3*, 6–15. doi:10.1109/TSE.1977.229899

Siemieniuch, C.E., Sinclair, M.A., & Vaughan, G.M.C. (1998). A method for decision support for allocation of functions and design of jobs in manufacturing based on knowledge requirements. *Int. Journal of Computer Integrated Manufacturing.*

Vernadat, F. B. (1996). *Enterprise modelling & integrations: Principles and applications.* London: Chapman & Hall.

Vernadat, F. B. (2004). *Enterprise modelling & integration: Myth or reality?* France: MACSI/INRIA & LGIPM, University of Metz.

Wainright, C. E. R., & Ridgeway, K. (1994). *The application of GRAI as a framework for manufacturing strategy process, Factory 2000-Advanced Factory Automation, Conference Publication, No. 398.* IEEE Press.

Warnecke, H. J. (1993). *The fractal company - a revolution in corporate culture.* New York: Springer-Verlag.

Weston, R. H. (1998). Integration infrastructure requirements for agile manufacturing systems. *Proc. of Instn of Mech. Engineers., 212*(Part B), 423-437.

Weston, R. H., Clements, P. E., Shorter, D. N., Hodgson, A. J., & West, A. A. (2001). On the explicit modelling of systems of human resources. *International Journal of Production Research, 39*(2), 185–204. doi:10.1080/00207540010001857

Williams, T. J. (1994). The Purdue enterprise reference architecture. *Computers in Industry, 24*(2-3), 141–158. doi:10.1016/0166-3615(94)90017-5

Womack, J. P., Jones, D. T., & Roos, D. (1990). *The machine that changed the world.* New York: Oxford Associates.

Wu, I. L. (1992). *Manufacturing systems design and analysis.* London: Chapman & Hall.

Yogesh, M. (1998). Business process redesign: Business change of mythic proportions? *MIS Quarterly,* 121–127.

Zelm, M. (2003). Towards user oriented enterprise modelling- comparison of modelling language constructs. In R. Jardim-Goncalves, et al (Eds.), *Proc. of the 10th ISPE Int. Conf. on CE: Research and applications.* Madeira Portugal: Swets & Zeitilinger.

Zelm, M., Vernadat, F. B., & Kosanke, K. (1995). The CIMOSA business modelling process. *Computers in Industry, 27,* 123–142. doi:10.1016/0166-3615(95)00018-2

Zhen, M., & Weston, R. H. (2006). Simulating dynamic behaviours in complex organisations: Case study application of a well structure modelling approach. In A. Nketsa, et al (Eds.), *Proc. of the European Simulation and Modelling Conference, Modelling and Simulation (ESM'2006), EUROSIS-ETI,* Toulouse, France (pp. 390-395).

Chapter 19
Communication in the Manufacturing Industry:
An Empirical Study of the Management of Engineering Drawing in a Shipyard

Sigmund Aslesen
Fafo Institute for Labour and Social Research, Norway University of Oslo, Norway

Svein Erik Moen
Fafo Institute for Labour and Social Research, Norway

ABSTRACT

This chapter is based on a case study of one shipyard's effort to make the flow of engineering drawings feeding into its production process more reliable. To construct a ship, detailed drawings of every part of the product is an essential input. For these drawings to be reliable, they must include all relevant information, they have to follow each other in a proper line of order, and they should be released according to production milestones. In the shipyard in this study, an analysis was initiated to explore the management of engineering drawing. The main findings show that the usability of ICT is limited for this purpose, and that to really make an effort in order for engineering drawings to be reliable, a more basic understanding of the interpersonal communication at work in a one-off project environment is fundamental.

"We are stuck with technology when what we really want is just stuff that works" (Adams 2002).

INTRODUCTION

The chapter is based on a case study of one shipyard's effort to make the flow of engineering drawings feeding into its manufacturing production process more reliable. The chapter's interest is with interruptions in this flow caused by technological, organizational and social inadequacies on an intra- and inter-organizational level.

DOI: 10.4018/978-1-60566-856-7.ch019

The rapid development of information and communication technologies (ICTs) has lead to much attention being paid to the impact that the new technology has and will have on the sharing and transfer of information in the workplace. In the manufacturing industry, the use of ICT technologies has contributed to the development of computer aided systems for the modeling of designs and production of drawings, databases and digital catalogues for the capturing and storing of information as well as software systems for the monitoring and integration of processes.

The chapter's main objective is to demonstrate the complex interaction between people, and between people and computer-based technology, in the manufacturing industry. We claim in this chapter that although technological advances in communications are, indeed, welcome in manufacturing enterprises, a more reliable flow of engineering drawings will also depend on a deeper understanding of the interpersonal communication at work in a one-off project environment. A one-off project environment conceptualizes the shipbuilding project as both a temporary production system, and as a set of diversely skilled people working together on a complex task over a limited period of time. As the production system is not stable for very long, and neither is the relationship between many of the people involved, dynamic patterns of communication are developed that may help and sometimes hinder a reliable flow of engineering drawings.

The next section includes a review of relevant literature on topics related to manufacturing production, interpersonal communication, and ICT use. After that follows the analysis section, where the first part contains a discussion upon issues, controversies and problems related to subsequently the engineering drawing as a means of communication, human intervention in ICT application and the relevance of ICT in a one-off project environment. The second part of the analysis involves recommendations and solutions in form of a stepwise approach to a more precise and predictable flow of engineering drawings. The chapter then goes on to examine the adequacy of the emerging trend with digitalization of the building process. The last section concludes the chapter and suggests topics to be elaborated on in future research work.

BACKGROUND

Why focus on the execution of engineering drawings? On the whole, this particular process makes up no more than around three percent of total costs in a shipbuilding project. By comparison, the outfitting part of the production constitutes around two third of all project costs. Nevertheless, there is still a fact that engineering drawings are essential for the building of a ship. Unless these drawings are made available, and include the accurate information, the construction of a ship will not take place. Engineering drawings, as such, is a critical input within shipbuilding. Especially when the ships to be constructed are highly advanced offshore vessels with loads of technology and equipment. Reliable engineering drawings – or having the right drawings, at the right time – are then decisive for a shipbuilding project to deliver on time, and with a high quality of product.

A shipbuilding project is divided in three main phases; design, detailed engineering, and construction. The design phase is when the ship owner communicates with a ship consultant and/ or design company, about ship types and functionalities of the new ship. This is also the phase where a contract agreement is signed between the ship owner and a chosen yard. The contract agreement includes prepared documents concerning specifications of the ship, and rough drawings (general arrangement, tank plan etc.). The detailed engineering phase, which is the primary focus of this chapter, is largely based on the specifications and rough drawings agreed upon as part of the contract. Detailed engineering predominantly occurs ahead of the construction phase, when rough drawings are converted into detailed descriptions of every part of the ship. Detailed engineering moreover also involves the preparing of notifications for the procurement of all heavy equipment. The construction phase involves the production of the ship. It is divided in three; hull construction, outfitting, and testing.

Detailed engineering is far from a straightforward matter. In a recent article concerned with the challenges of supply chain selection in a project environment, containing evidence from UK naval shipbuilding, Sanderson and Cox (2008) put emphasize on the extensive and active role of the end customer in design and specification decisions. Because of the active role played, and for the fact that the ship owner often also exhibits an irregular pattern of demand, it is unlikely that a detailed and complete design will ever be drawn before the commencement of a shipbuilding project (op. cit, p. 18). This means that both the design and engineering phase, as well as the construction phase, are incomplete and subject to on-going change (op.cit, p. 21). Besides, detailed engineering is included as part of a manufacture process that may say to be complex, multi-phase, and multi-actor. It is complex because of the many components, working operations and advanced technological solutions involved, and because of the strong element of craftsmanship still characterizing the manufacturing process (Aslesen 2005, p. 15). It is multi-phase due to the fact that each of the main phases engineering and construction are divided into a number of sequences with many interrelated activities which, in turn, are structured according to several milestones. It is multi-actor in terms of the number of different actors involved in a project, each of which is likely to be pursuing its own agenda, making decisions often politicized and the outcomes sub-optimal from the perspective of the organization as a whole (Pettigrew 1973, Pfeffer & Salancik 1974). Consequently, what appears to be a relatively simple drawing operation is time and again burdened with misunderstandings, delays, stoppages, and abortive work.

This makes communication to lie at the core of what detailed engineering is all about. The particular premise forms the overall starting point for the analysis undertaken in the next section. It derives from an investigation of the building industry carried out more than 40 years ago, by the Tavistock Institute (1966). The report examines the procedures, relationships and interests characterizing communications within the building industry. By introducing the twin aspects of interdependence and uncertainty, the investigation demonstrates the fallacy inherent in the traditional view by each section of the building industry thinking of itself as autonomous in fulfilling a settled sequence of operations. The essence of interdependence in the building process is the relevance of different streams of information to each other in particular contexts, whereas uncertainty arises as a result of these interdependencies, as well as there is uncertainty arising from outside the building process (op. cit, p. 34). It is the authors view that due to interdependence and uncertainty full implications of any decision or action can seldom if ever be forecast with absolute accuracy, and that a communication system which assumes they can will simply not work (op. cit, p. 17).

In cases where the task is complex and cannot be decomposed in detail autonomously, project members must keep interrelating with one another in trying to arrive at viable solutions (Goodman and Goodman 1976, p. 495). Clearly, any technology that directly affects how communication (and information) can be processed, transmitted and understood is thus of considerable importance. This is why the availability and use of information systems and technologies has grown almost to the point of being commodity like in nature, becoming nearly as ubiquitous as labor (Dewett and Jones 2001, p. 313). The rapid development of *information and communication technologies* (ICT) has contributed to a change in the nature of work and how it is organized (Morton 1995, p. 339). To understand ICTs widespread use presupposes a clarification of what these technologies are all about. Dewett and Jones (2001) introduce, in their article on the role of information technology in the organization, a distinction between *information systems* and *information technologies*. Although often inextricably linked, information systems include many different varieties of software platforms and databases, from enterprise-wide systems designed to manage all major functions of the organization to more general purpose database products targeted towards specific uses, while information technologies encompass a broad array of communication media and devices which link information systems and people (op.cit, p. 314). Important technologically based operational tools, such as three-dimensional computer-aided design (3-D CAD) modeling (Rankin and Luther 2006, p. 1538) are here reckoned to belong under information technologies. For the rest of this paper we will refer to these systems and technologies jointly as ICT, apart from when discussing concretely a particular type of system or technology.

In the manufacturing industry, the use of ICT is particularly stressed as part of implementing Concurrent Engineering (CE). CE is a management and operational approach which aims to improve product design, production, operation, and maintenance by developing environments in which personnel from all disciplines (design, marketing, production engineering, process planning, and support) work together and share data throughout all phases of the product life cycle. Information technologies are here regarded important enabling mechanisms in terms of concurrency, by ways of their information processing abilities that help to interlink sequences of information through the different stages of a product's development (Hauptman & Hirji 1996, p. 154). Concurrent Engineering, as such, seems highly relevant for the purpose of improving communications in a shipbuilding project. The extensive use of ICT involved may work to support cross-functional workflow (Monge & Fulk 1995), and make critical information more accessible and transparent to employees and thereby increase the incidence

of problem-solving (Edmondson & Moingeon 1998). Besides, by providing greater information access, across specializations and between levels in an organizational hierarchy, the use of ICT could also contribute to mitigate subunit orientations and may very well result in a flatter organization (Dewett & Jones 2001, p. 330).

ICT then is, without doubt, an important addition to a shipyard's communication infrastructure. Nevertheless, information and communication technologies are, by themselves, just objects, or "simply dead matter" (Poole & DeSanctis 1990; Stephens 2007, p. 486). It is when two or more people interact that ICT becomes an important component in the process of communication (Stephens 2007, p. 486). Interpersonal, and often informal, communication then forms the glue between people and organizations contributing to a project (Emmitt & Gorse 2006, p. 2). Communication is, in this sense, not principally about the transferring of information to another party. Rather, communication concerns the sharing of meaning to reach a mutual understanding and to gain a response, involving some form of interaction between the sender and the receiver of the message (op. cit, p. 3). Of primary concern in terms of ICT use, in order for communication to be efficient and effective, is therefore how different information and communication technologies are interwoven with *interpersonal communication* or, to be more explicit, they ways in which they are used in real life and what recognizes the people and organizations who make use of them.

Past research on information and communication technology use has largely assumed that people use only one ICT per task (Stephens 2007, p. 486). In an article about the successive use of ICTs at work, Stephens asserts that completing a task often requires a mix of ICTs used over time (op.cit, p. 486). Stephens (op.cit) main point is that instead of focusing on the rank-ordering of existing ICTs and attempting to match them to their various uses, one should start by acknowledging that communication efficiency may rest on sequences or combinations of ICTs rather than isolated choices about a discrete medium (Walther & Parks 2002, p. 534). Indeed, an obvious problem in this is that advocating the use of more than one ICT could increase the amount of communication people receives (Stephens 2007, p. 499). Studies continue to show that people are overloaded with messages at work (Thomas & King 2006). However, the ICT succession theory proposes that strategies to maximize modalities, such as oral, visual, and textual modalities, through complementary successive ICT use increases the effectiveness and efficiency of task completion, and that such complementary strategies are particularly helpful when the task involves collaboration or high levels of interaction (Stephens 2007, p. 496-497).

As the completion of a task normally requires a mix of ICTs used over time, complementary successive ICT use could thus increase effectiveness and efficiency of communication. There is nevertheless the problem that people bring differing values, interests and skills into a project team. Research shows that there are many variables that influence ICT use (Stephens 2007). Influences can be grouped into four main groupings: media traits, social influences, organizational influences and individual differences (op.cit, p. 489). In research focusing on media traits ICTs are typically approached from a "matching" perspective, which means that ICTs have certain traits or inherent features that should be, and often are, matched to specific tasks (op. cit, 489). Regarding social influences on ICT use, a social influence model or theory is developed in order to emphasize how other people matter – in two distinct ways. First, enough other people, or a critical mass, must be using the same or compatible ICTs for communication to occur (Markus 1990). Second, group members observe others' behavior, and adjust their own behavior (Fulk 1993). In research on organizational matters in ICT use, the roles and positions occupied by organizational members predict different patterns of ICT use (Rice & Shook

1990) besides a vast list of other organizational variables. Prior research has also uncovered many individual-level differences that play a role in ICT use, such as experience with ICT (King & Xia 1999).

To the point that there are people who produce the information and that many factors influence ICT use, information processing becomes an uncertain undertaking. Not least also because people often make mistakes, especially when working under pressure (Emmitt & Gorse 2006, p. 19). Besides, the ICT itself is developed by humans, and every human tool relies upon, and reifies, some underlying conception of the activity that it is to support (Suchman 1987, p. 3). In an early book about the problem of communication between man and machine, Suchman (1987) examines an artifact built on a planning model of human action. Whereas the model treats a plan as something located in the actor's head, which directs his or her behavior, Suchman argues that the planning model confuse plans with situated actions or actions taken in the context of particular, concrete circumstances (op. cit, p. 3). It is the author's view that plans as such neither determine nor adequately reconstruct the actual course of situated action, and that we therefore have to investigate the basis for interaction between humans and computing machines (op. cit, p. 3). While the technology for information and communication purposes indeed has become much more sophisticated in recent years, research shows that it even now works best when the information required is simple, easy to understand and non-contentious (Emmit & Gorse 2007, p. 19). For addressing contentious issues, problem-solving, conflict resolution and building relationships, face-to-face communication is still fundamental (Abadi 2005).

Ultimately, in the matter of understanding interpersonal communication, as part of executing drawing operations in a shipbuilding project, the use of information and communication technology is self-evident. Not only in order to support collaboration, and sharing and integration of information and knowledge between people. Even more important, it allows great amounts of information to be processed quickly, and the information produced can be easily sent via email, web-based technology or by other operational tools. Since a timely exchange of information is required to enable any process to proceed as planned, be it related to design, engineering or construction, much attention is naturally given to the transfer of information by applying these technologies. However, making information reliable or "robust" is more likely to depend on the ability to employ co-operative attitudes and routines, reliability and other inter-personal skills. This is because information is being produced by people, with varying values, interests and skills. Likewise, even though different information and communication technologies have clearly defined, prescriptive qualities, the information outcome is still uncertain as there are various factors influencing their use. This is especially so when the task to be completed takes place in a one-off project environment. To attain a consistent flow of information under such circumstances, applying computer-based formal procedures to monitor project progress and needs is likely to be insufficient. They must be counterbalanced by informal, conversational acts of people in order to respond to unanticipated situations and to detect and remedy troubles in communication.

COMMUNICATION IN THE MANUFACTURING INDUSTRY

Issues, Controversies, Problems

The analysis that follows next is based on a case study of one shipyard's effort to make the flow of engineering drawings feeding into its manufacturing process more reliable. The shipyard is part of a Norwegian group of companies which moreover includes a design company, several foreign based engineering companies, and an electronic com-

pany. The case study involves a round of in-depth interviews carried out with 15 technical engineers employed at the shipyard's technical department. A seminar with co-coordinators from the production department was otherwise also arranged that particularly addressed the problems of communication between engineering and production. Both the interviews and the seminar were organized in an unstructured way. The main ambition was to come up with as much substance as possible to explore the problem with flow of engineering drawings, whereas little effort was put into collecting data to quantify the problem or to distinguish more accurately its root causes. All the information from the interviews and the seminar were then written down and, in turn, structured according to certain overall subject areas. As part of the analysis, a first presentation of preliminary results was provided to the managers of the different functional groups within the engineering department. This was done to remove ambiguities and to ensure applicability of the final findings presented here.

Paradox 1: Limitations to the Engineering Drawing, as a Means of Communication

In a regular new-building project in the shipyard, around 1200 two-dimensional engineering drawings are produced which are fed into the manufacturing process. Every of these drawings include information about the positioning and identification numbers of different components, as well as information about material types, dimensions and qualities. The engineering drawing is, in this way, an important means of communication. In an old book about the history of engineering drawing, Booker (1963) is concerned with it as a means of communication between designer and constructor[1]. This particular communication must convey not only the qualitative aspects of the design, but also provide the detailed dimensions necessary to realize the design. Booker's concern is otherwise with the developing of multiple drawing techniques. In this development, it is Booker's view that drawing techniques are not replaced, but added to as new problems of communication arise. New practices still arise in the attempt to simplify and accelerate the drawing processes. A major contribution is in this sense three-dimensional computer-aided design (3D CAD). This is a tool that allows for tri-dimensional virtual imaging of not only the end product, but which also opens for 3-D based figurative dissections of the product into smaller parts. As regards design, engineering and construction, 3D CAD represents a powerful visualizing element. In literature on the manufacturability of new products, or to be more specific the designing of products in such a way that they are more easy to manufacture, computer-aided design systems are considered as created to encourage more manufacturable product designs (Nevins & Whitney 1989).

It is particularly against the background of manufacturability that the potential visualizing element of 3D CAD seems not as fully utilized as one might be expecting of a shipyard. While it is widely used both during the design and engineering phase, workers at the shop floor seem to prefer two-dimensional drawings. This is a bit surprising, since three-dimensional, computer-based illustrations are, exactly because of their cubic quality, believed to provide people in production with a fairly well and realistic idea of how to construct a ship. To some extent, it could be about the problem with computers' processing capacity, as this is pointed out by several respondents. At least as important, though, is that it is much more practical for shop-floor workers to take along printed drawings when walking around in the different rooms and sections of a ship, while giving instructions and discussing technical matters. In many of these rooms drawings are also hanged up on a wall, thereby making them immediately available for those who need it. While theoretically, computers could serve the same purpose, it would imply a whole lot of computers exposed to heavy physical strains.

While 3D CAD represents a powerful visualizing element, it only projects the finished product in all its parts and not the manufacturing process that leads to it. Since a great deal of manufacturing knowledge is still experiential in nature, a computerized 3D model will in one way or another be no more than a simplification. What is more, a piece of paper is usually easier to make notes on than a computerized 3D model, for the fact that it happens quite often that information is added to drawings. Production people making notes on drawings moreover bring us to another important point regarding the engineering drawing as a means of communication. It concerns the feedback from production to the technical department. Provided the complexity and high degree of interdependence involved in a shipbuilding project, the frequency of communication and direct contact between technical engineers and production people in a shipyard is likely to be high. This is most certainly true for the shipyard in study, not least for the fact that blue-collar workers may frequently be observed running errands at the offices of technical engineers. However, it seems to lack a well-functioning system for the communication going on between them. One of our respondents thus calls for a better fit between engineering and production dependencies:

We have to sit down with supervisors from construction some time before they actually need the drawings, and discuss. This would make the supervisors more committed than if drawings are just passed on the way they are now, and we could avoid some of their yelling.

One should expect a 3D CAD system, for its visualizing qualities, to work well to support problem-solving activities. While the system is used as a basis for so-called interface meetings between functional groups at the technical department, the meetings are just arranged on an irregular basis. Besides, production people are only occasionally invited to join these meetings.

In terms of communication with, and feedback from, production, a paradox is otherwise that the technical engineers only on rare occasions attend the shop floor. These are the thoughts of one of our respondents in that matter:

Those who have made their thoughts about where to place different things must use the opportunity to follow the whole process – to get out on the shop floor and observe how things look in real life. Then we might also be rid of attitudes among some production people, who look upon us as morons from the technical department.

A pioneer in the developing of engineering drawing was Leonardo da Vinci (1452-1519). Although most famous for his paintings, da Vinci was also valued as an engineer during his lifetime. His approach to science was an observational one: he tried to understand a phenomenon by describing and depicting it in utmost detail[2]. While engineering drawing today has grown into a high-tech field of expertise, its main purpose is still to project a physical object of some sort. In doing this, the power of direct observation is probably as relevant today as it was 500 years ago. Otherwise, to the point negative attitudes towards technical engineers occur among production people; these may also work to obscure facets of communication. In an article on process concurrency, based on an empirical study of 50 cross-functional teams amongst others including the shipbuilding industry, Hauptman & Hirji (1996) stresses the release and use of uncertain and ambiguous information. According to their findings, an upstream group will be less willing to release information early if the environment is hostile (op. cit, p. 154). It is the authors' view that to deal with this problem might implicate a fundamental change of attitude throughout the organization, both upstream and downstream, to enable an integrated problem-solving based on a frequent, two-way flow of information (op. cit, p. 154-155).

Paradox 2: The Problem with Human Intervention in ICT Application

The shipyard uses an ERP (Enterprise Resource Planning) software information system to support its project progress. The system provides an overview of economy and financing, main components, time spending, activities, manning, stock content and so on, in all their projects. The technical department also has an own software system for the management of engineering drawing, which is linked to the overall ERP system. Together, the two systems support a project with detailed information about almost everything that is to be going on, at all times and in the different phases of a project. In addition, a building database exists that is to include all relevant correspondence, external as well as internal, which is going on during the course of a project. Among the advantages by using ERP is that it eliminates the need for external interfaces previously required between systems, that it normally leads to a standardization of procedures, that lower maintenance is needed and that it allows for greater or easier reporting capabilities[3]. In research on the use of information systems by organizations, ERP is claimed to be an imperative for reducing the uncertainties surrounding production and administrative processes (Dewett & Jones 2001).

In the matter of understanding how organizations work, an early, but valuable contribution was made by the political economist and sociologist Max Weber, who analyzed bureaucracy as part of the modern society's movement towards rationalization. In the book *Economy and Society* (1922), Weber outlines the ideal type bureaucratic way of organizing, amongst others embedded in a strong degree of formalization in form of rules and standard procedures. In much the same way as Weber (op. cit) stresses formalization by rules and procedures as determining for an organization's developing of common and shared norms and values, the usability of a company-wide software system such as an ERP system will depend on common, formalized practices regarding the recording and retrieval of information. One of the respondents shares with us the following insightful recognition:

We have to learn to use these data systems, and to report in them on a continual basis. This is our logbook. In order to make it work properly, we have to be verifiable in terms of what is completed and what is not, and what is passed on and what is not. Our remembering is not enough, because the ability to recall varies too strongly between people.

As a point of departure, it then becomes a weak point when people take various routines in their reporting to the system. This is what one respondent say in that matter:

Every one of us has our own way of reporting to the system, and some even avoid reporting on anything. This leads to important information often being left out of the system.

The practice of different reporting routines most certainly serve to lower the trustworthiness of the information, and thereby the usefulness of the whole system. The fact that it appears might be for several reasons. From the interviews, varying skills with concern to ICT use is frequently brought up. Some engineers ask for handbooks, standards and thus like, as well as training programs, to brush up and improve the general level of ICT competence in the department. However, at least as relevant is the problem with complexity-in-use, the way it is pointed out by several of the technical engineers that a too sophisticated and even to some point ill-disposed user interface come in the way for a systematic application. One of the respondents has the following opinion about it:

We seem to work in what might be characterized as a reporting bureaucracy. We should have a more rough reporting system, but which would

include only true information. They way it works now, information is far too detailed and the system too demanding to keep up.

As a rule, the more information is needed to keep a system going, the more demanding is the process of keeping it up. Weber (1922) himself was ambivalent to the increasing element of bureaucratization in modern organizations and societies as a whole. He believed a growing rationalization of human life could trap individuals in a so-called "iron cage", in the meaning a set of rules and laws that we are all subjected and must adhere to (Ashworth, Boyne & Delbridge 2007). Whereas we need common sets of rules and laws to bring social order to society, Weber warns us that an over-bureaucratization amongst others could lead to loss of sensitivity to individuals and individual situations, and to loss of autonomy because actions are being dictated by others (Boucock 2000). In a similar perspective, although a common set of practices is needed regarding ICT use, too much regulation in form of standardized information processing procedures can provide people with some sort of data weariness or, even worse, alienation toward the whole process. This is the expression of deep concern from one our respondents:

There is a danger in that data-based information systems tend to replace a close follow-up of operations. We should do more walking-arounds to follow up on each of the technical engineers.

A somewhat parallel view may say to be taken many years earlier in the previously mentioned investigation of communications in the UK building industry (Tavistock 1966). Although this was conducted long before interactive, computer-based systems were an important ingredient in interpersonal communication, the distinction introduced here between formal and informal control procedures show highly relevant for the purpose of understanding the interaction going on between humans and computing machines. Whereas formal control procedures apply to the formal behavior in setting up and taking the client's interest into the contract, performing cost estimating, time scheduling and designing the project as if the future hold no or little uncertainty, informal control procedures are drawn from direct observation of those at work, from talks about what they are doing, which although undertaken quite consciously and known to all project members are not spoken of on the record (op.cit, p. 46). The authors argue that as a building process progresses, and different irregularities make themselves felt, the application of informal control procedures is determining for the process to function adequately. This is because such procedures, as opposed to formal control procedures that assume those responsible for the building process to be independent and autonomously self-controlling, recognize that the reality holds too much interdependence and uncertainty for the course of a project to be programmable (op.cit, p. 48).

The problem with human intervention in ICT application moreover particularly comes to the surface during planning meetings. The planning meeting is set to co-ordinate processes within and between projects and to make decisions concerning further progress. The setting itself opens for both formal and informal communication and control, the way information collected through different databases tend to form the basis for face-to-face discussions about projects' status, problems and so on. Though a planning meeting is held every second week at the technical department, there is a frustration among several engineers regarding how it works. This is what one of our respondents says in that topic:

Planning meetings must be made more efficient. There is too much rubbish the way they work today. Focus of the meetings should be on what needs to be done, and not on what has already been completed.

Especially in the later stages of a project, when delays start to occur and stresses begin to be felt, the need for immediate, informal actions to adjust to the new situation arises. While this definitely happen, there is seemingly also the tendency among technical engineers to clutch to the formally based ERP system in situations of high uncertainty. For instance, by continuously referring to previous work instead of looking ahead, and maybe for no other reason than to make sure the system still works. If applied to Weber's theory of bureaucratization, this would be a situation where formally based rules and procedures, although claimed to be based on a rationalistic thinking, simply seem to work in an opposite manner. However, even if to some point meaningless, looking back may at least for some provide a kind of confidence when the going gets tough. Because as delays and problems arise, so do normally the tensions between people and organizations involved in the project. As a result, those concerned become increasingly involved in acrimonious attempts to place, or, more usually, to avoid responsibility for these discrepancies (Tavistock 1966, p. 51).

Paradox 3: A One-Off Project Environment Reduces the Relevance of Inter-Organizational ICT

In a recent article concerning information technology and organizational performance within international business to business relationships, Jean et al. (2008) emphasize electronic integration by ways of inter-organizational information systems. In the article, tightly coupled ERP-to-ERP connections or other complementary IT infrastructures are launched as something that facilitates collaborative demand planning and fulfillment in the supply chain exchange relationship (p. 569-570). Electronic integration can in this way be seen as an alternative form of governance structure which reduces transaction cost and provides desired levels of control and flexibility without ownership (Kim & Mahoney 2006). The article ends up by suggesting that information technology capabilities contribute directly to improved supply chain performance, that it works to deter partner's opportunism and that this process is mediated by business-to-business processes (Jean et al. 2008, p. 576). The only difficulty with this line of reasoning is that it cannot be neatly applied to a one-off or low-volume project environment where the project outcome has no directly comparable past and future state (Sanderson & Cox 2008, p. 18).

A shipbuilding project is by definition a temporary system consisting of people and organizations that work together on a complex task over a limited period of time. The temporal limitation of shipbuilding projects, as well as variations with regard to their outcome – the new ship, is what is captured in the term *one-off*. What is emphasized by linking the term to a wider *project environment* is the embeddedness of shipbuilding projects in multiple layers, of networks, localities and institutions. On the one hand, the embeddedness implies a key resource for the performance of projects, and on the other hand it entails multiple perceptions and loyalties of the project members (Grabher 2002, p. 208). It stands to reason that, in managing such a project-specific supply chain, a shipyard will have to promote flexibility and responsiveness by implying a high degree of interactivity and quality of communication (Sanderson & Cox 2008, p. 22).

For the technical department in particular, the effect of being embedded in a wider project environment is most evident when it comes to the acquiring of technical documentation and class approval. Whereas technical documentation on main components is provided by the different equipment suppliers, class approval on drawings is given by a classification company. Since heavy requirements are placed upon the yard regarding the ship's seaworthiness, most drawings in every project will have to be approved. In the matter of getting it at the right time, one of the respondents put it this way:

To have the drawings in time, with the technical documentation included, is fundamental. If this arrives to late then other working operations will also suffer.

The above statement makes clear an inherent variability involved in the execution of engineering drawings. Indeed, the work of the technical department is organized in such a way that it, at least theoretically, allows for many activities to go on in a parallel or overlapping manner. However, due to the element of interdependence involved, the different functional groups on electronics, mechanics and piping, steelwork and hull, outfitting, and furnishing will have to coordinate their drawings. Consequently, delays occurring cause interruptions not solely for the particular functional group that is directly influenced, as nearby functional groups are usually in one way or another also affected. From our interviews with technical engineers it comes clear that the effect of documentation or approvals at a halt can be substantial. Especially, if it concerns one of the "huge" groups, such as that on electronics of which work covers all of the ship and therefore have many interfaces with other functional groups.

To the point interdependence characterizes the definition as well as the accomplishment of a shipbuilding task, project members must keep interrelating with one another. At the same time, interdependence is also a source to uncertainties arising, whether they are engendered by actions of government departments, client organizations or others not directly involved in the building process or stemming from resources like labor, equipment and material since a number of building processes are competing for the same resources (Tavistock 1966, p. 34). The following statement made by one of our respondents is, in this case, illuminating:

The way we are in an order boom we will have to accept a situation of repeated delays. But orders made by the procurement department should not only be based on price, but also on which suppliers have been involved in previous projects. In this way, total costs by preferring one supplier ahead of others will be taken into consideration.

While a shipyard, as the project leader, has the ability to impose upon others the importance of meeting deadlines as well as milestones during the course of a project, these mechanisms alone are clearly not sufficient to prevent participants from being delayed. Even more so, when the delays occurring are the result of high demand, such as in this case, that puts high pressure on the supply system. At the same time, there is the risk that up-coming delays are combined with opportunistic behavior or, to be more concrete, the "incomplete or distorted disclosure of information, especially to calculated efforts to mislead, distort, disguise, obfuscate or otherwise confuse" (Williamson 1985, p. 47). This is because project members have other "homes" before, during and after being involved in a project organization (Lundin & Söderholm 1995, p. 442). Perceptions and loyalty, therefore, are typically founded in their "home" institution as well as being linked to a number of projects and not only one. Whereas applying inter-organizational information systems, by ways of electronic integration, can help monitoring progress throughout the supply chain, it is not likely to prevent neither opportunistic behavior nor multiple perceptions and crossing loyalties. Especially, since a one-off project environment also gives less time for project members to develop trust as a determining factor (Meyerson et al. 1996, p. 171). A more adequate strategy to ensure reliability in a project specific supply-chain is thereby the practice of project organizing shaped both by past experience and affected by the shadow of potential future collaboration (Grabher 2002, p. 209).

Regarding the one-off aspect of every ship, this is particularly reflected through the practicing of change orders. Change orders imply that the ship owner is provided the possibility to make changes in his original requirements practically during all phases of a project, from design to engineering and all the way down to the construction phase. The ship owner's interest in this is because the ship is often ordered a time before a chart is settled with an end user. Only when a chart is gained, such as for instance with an oil company, the ship owner will know the exact uses of the ship and thereby all of its needed functionalities. Change orders imply extra costs for the ship owner's part, but these costs are probably much less than if the ship was to be reconstructed later on. Besides, since the time of delivery of the ship is usually sustained though changes are made, the ship owner does not risk to lose profit in markets where rates are high. For a shipyard, operating with a long window of opportunities for extra orders and adjustments may say to be part of a business strategy. This said, allowing for change orders obstructs the flow in a shipbuilding project. Especially when they are given further out, change orders tend to cause break-downs in the sequential line of operations of not only the construction phase, but also the detailed engineering phase and sometimes even the design phase.

For the technical department, change orders often imply that drawings, apart from being revised, will have to go another round of class approval. Sometimes even, depending on the nature of the order, it will require that new technical documentation should be prepared by a equipment supplier. The consequence of change orders is the source of considerable aggravation in the technical department. This is what one respondent say in that matter:

The general arrangement is constantly changing. There are continual revisions due to better solutions emerging all the time.

As a result of change orders appearing, the execution of engineering drawings becomes very much an off-and-on activity. While ideally, most of the engineering work should be completed at the time when construction starts, it may last by

Figure 1. Communication channels and information flow in the making of engineering drawings

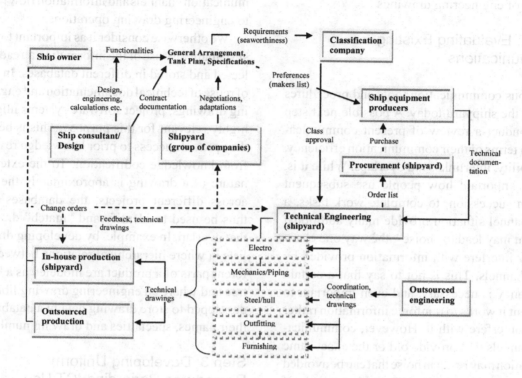

fits and starts all the way to the testing of the ship. As long as change orders continue to emerge in shipbuilding projects, inter-organizational ICT in form of tightly coupled business-to-business information systems is likely to fall short. This is because the handling of such orders depends on a higher degree of flexibility and responsiveness in a supply chain than can be provided through electronic integration.

Solutions and Recommendations

Step 1: Finding the Bottlenecks of Communication

As a first step to attain a more precise and predictable flow of engineering drawings, we suggest to accomplish an analysis of the different communication channels involved in the execution of a drawing operation. We believe that if consistent

decisions are to be taken promptly and meaningfully about the execution of engineering drawings, an investigation is necessary to identify the critical information (and documentation) needed to be exchanged through different channels of communication in order for drawings to be reliable. The idea behind such an analysis would be to find the bottlenecks of communication – whether of technological, organizational or social character – causing interruptions in the critical information flow, and to reduce their influence by increasing the capacity attached to them.

The analysis must be of an operational kind. It has to include representatives that, in one way or another, are involved in the everyday work of executing drawing operations. Only in this way, problems will be exposed for what they really are. As a starting point for the analysis suggested, we hereby present a figure (Figure 1) below based on our preliminary understanding of communication channels and ***information flow*** involved in the making of engineering drawings.

Step 2: Evaluating Existing Communications

Numerous communication tools and procedures exist in the shipyard today. A possible next step is to conduct a review of present communications, in terms of their communication efficiency, adaptability, interlinks, and overlaps. While it is, indeed, important how people use subsequent ICTs, in succession, to complete work tasks, a multichannel situation provide many additional cues that may lead to "noise", the way one channel may interfere with information provided by other channels. This is not to say that a certain redundancy is necessary, and even important to the extent it works to reinforce information rather than to interfere with it. However, communication channels that provide old or the exact same information may result in noise that can be avoided if a more complementary ICT use is applied. Of overall concern is, in this sense, to identify the critical information needed to make appropriate decisions. Too much information may lead to information overload, and result in inability to act. This is because people will have to sort through large amounts of data, thus impeding the aptitude to make timely decisions. Another consideration in relation to existing communications concerns the imbalance between formal and informal control procedures. Today, it seems as if an inappropriate formal control system is coupled with an adaptive, yet to some part non-responsible informal system. In example, while delays in technical documentation from equipment suppliers are registered once they appear, and adjustments are then being made, informal procedures regarding how to follow up on orders seem less developed. As a result, delays are known of later than necessary and succeeding adjustments are often overdue. Generally, we believe that a thorough going over of existing communications, formally as well as informally

based, both will help to reduce and shape up communication channels and information flow related to engineering drawing operations.

We otherwise consider it as important to make systematically use of the information already collected and stored in different databases. In terms of reuse of technical documentation and engineering drawings, project software systems might be highly relevant for this purpose. This is because they provide access to prior knowledge resulting from knowledge codification. To the extent the nature of a drawing is approximately the same across different projects, the databases could thus be used to identify and "match" drawings that overlap. In example, by developing drawing lists in where hierarchical relations between different parts of a product are modeled as a binary tree and where an engineering drawing library is developed to store drawing data in a database by their names, specialties and drawing numbers[4].

Step 3: Developing Uniform Procedures Regarding ICT Use

The human capacity for memory is fallible and subject to erosion and error. This is clearly also the case with ICTs, since their functioning is fundamentally dependent of human intervention. This is why we suggest, as a third step, a training program to apply uniform procedures regarding ICT use. If collectively applied, ICTs will most certainly facilitate the technical department's ability to capture and integrate, store and assimilate information of different kind. But this will only happen if the technical engineers making up the department start to employ a uniform ICT use. A review of existing communications will, in this sense, be determining, the way it may also lead to a clearing up in available user procedures. Besides, when identifying the critical information demanded, it may provide the ICT – such as for instance a project software system – with a more simplistic and user-friendly interface. We believe a training program of some sort will be necessary, in order for ICT procedures to be collectively applied. Since habits are difficult to alter, even when the cause is understood and actions are taken, such a program should include the whole technical department. However, rather than going for a comprehensive educational arrangement, which would have to be repeated on occasions, we believe that a frequent use and systematic co-evaluation of different procedures are the most desirable and effective ways to attain and further develop a uniform practice regarding ICT use.

Applying a New Method for Engineering Drawing Management

As a fourth and last step to achieve a more precise and predictable flow of engineering drawings, we suggest to apply a new method for engineering drawing management. Although the method is new to engineering as part of the shipbuilding industry, a similar method is already successfully applied to the current shipyard's production department (Aslesen & Bertelsen 2008). For more information about the principles behind the method, we would like to refer to Ballard's (2000) outlining of the Last Planner™ system developed to handle production control in the construction industry.

The method has as its basis the phasing of decisions throughout the shipbuilding process. The present situation in the technical department is one in which seemingly safe decisions are taken too early, too finally and too detailed. In face of the uncertainty involved, many decisions could probably with advantage be postponed to a later stage when all the critical information needed to complete a drawing operation is available. However, phasing of decisions cannot be made in a proper manner without identifying the reasons for delay. This is why we introduce that decisions about all drawing operations should be based on a regular investigation of the different prerequisites involved. We believe that only by an orderly control of prerequisites like technical documentation and class approval, can relatively safe and reliable

decisions be made regarding the various drawing operations. In fact, until all prerequisites are in place, no one decision can nor should be taken regarding any drawing operation other than the decision to defer it to a later stage. Furthermore, provided the high degree of interdependence involved in the execution of engineering drawings, decisions should always be taken by cross-references to other nearby functional groups. First and foremost, to avoid that the decisions made of some create intolerable constraint on others.

The phasing of decisions will most certainly, from time to time, break with a rational, sequential decision-making process. We still believe that in many circumstances the consequences of a "wrong" decision made at the right point in time can be much more severe than that of a "right" decision made at a later point. The main idea behind this method is to make each and every of the technical engineers to, on a regular basis, actively seek and transmit information of crucial importance for the reliability of engineering drawings. Included is a genuine sensitivity to the interdependence and uncertainty involved, which is of a practical kind. Instead of making decisions in isolation, and in the next instance being hit to the ground by unforeseen changes, we believe it to be more appropriate to investigate uncertain conditions and make decisions in cooperation with others. This would keep each and everyone on alert and, at the same time, prepared to handle variation of different kind.

We otherwise consider the planning meeting as the most important setting to practice the new method, whereas discussions concerning technical matters and so on do not belong to this meeting. Rather, we suggest the so-called interface meetings, using 3D CAD to explore interfaces, to also be used for technical discussions. Interface meetings should moreover be arranged on a regular basis, they ought to include relevant production people, and some of the meetings could even be arranged as walking-arounds on the shop floor. We think that such meetings may help to reduce some of the uncertainty resulting from the present artificial division between detailed engineering and production in the shipyard.

FUTURE TRENDS

Building Information Modeling – The Digitalization of the Building Process

Building Information Modeling (BIM) is the process of generating and managing building data, during its entire life cycle (Lee et al. 2006). On the one hand, it includes object-oriented CAD systems capable of representing the behavior of common building elements, thereby adding "intelligence" to these objects (Howell & Batcheler 2005, p. 1). Building elements can in this way be displayed in multiple views, as well as they can have non-graphic attributes assigned to them, such as variable dimensions and allocated rules. It likewise permits the representation of complex geometric and functional relationships between building elements (op.cit). On the other hand, BIM includes the coupling of building models with detailed information about a construction project, amongst others involving that the digital design can also be used for cost estimations, simulations, scheduling, fabrication, and erection.

BIM may seem as an adequate approach or method to offer and support the continuous and immediate availability of all critical information needed in the different phases of a shipbuilding project. Provided an integrated digital environment, information will also be up to date and, not least, fully coordinated between phases and functions. As opposed to more traditional methods, in where information is split between design and geometry-related information on the one hand and cost and scheduling information on the other, BIM allows for all critical information to be immediately available so that project-related decisions can be made more quickly and effectively[5].

There are, however, several limitations to BIM. In an evaluation of the potential, success and limitations of BIM, Howell & Batcheler (2005) underlines that the experience to date demonstrates a number of determining factors which complicate achieving the full promise of BIM, such as situational project teams comprising many participants, each of whom has optimized their work processes to use pre-existing technology already deployed in-house; reliance on best-in-class applications from different vendors based on specific project requirements; long-standing delineation of professional responsibility and liability among project participants, and; varying project delivery methods and contractual relationships (p. 3-4). Although BIM is now being used on a number of construction projects around the globe, the industry has yet to reach the tipping point where a critical mass embrace the methodology and its use become commonplace (Sanders 2004). In an article attempting to explain why building information modeling is not yet working, Sanders (op. cit) argues that those who develop the software technology to support BIM base their ideas on manufacturing industries that create mass-produced products. Whereas mass products like cars and planes are the products of an integrated design-build process the way the designer and builder are one and the same entity, this is rarely the case with building design and construction (op. cit). On the contrary, as is also shown in this chapter, creating complex, one-of-a-kind products requires a broadly distributed, specialized work effort and method of decision-making.

Conclusively, BIM has weaknesses and is probably better aligned to the production of design and documentation than to modeling building performance, since a great deal of manufacturing knowledge, whether related to construction or shipbuilding production, is still experiential in nature. Besides, digitalization of the building process will critically depend on the degree of interoperability between different technology software models or tools, in order to represent the building in a consistent way. If interoperability is missing, there is the risk that only scopes of work – be it related to systems, assemblies, or sequences – are included in the building information modeling, thereby supporting a sequential way of thinking throughout the building process.

CONCLUSION

The chapter has presented and discussed main findings from a case study of one shipyard's effort to make the flow of engineering drawings feeding into its manufacturing production process more reliable. The chapter's objective was to demonstrate the complex interaction between people, and between people and computer-based technology, for communication to take place in the manufacturing industry. Our analysis shows that the applicability of ICT is limited for the purpose of making engineering drawings more reliable, for reasons related to the engineering drawing as a means of communication and effects on ICT application of human interaction and project-based way of organizing. A four-step improvement program was in the chapter recommended to attain a more precise and predictable flow of engineering drawings. It includes a more thorough analysis of communication channels and bottlenecks to identify the critical information flow involved in the execution of a drawing operation; a review of existing communications in terms of their communication efficiency, adaptability, interlinks and overlaps; a training program to enhance a more uniform practice regarding ICT use, and; a new method for the management of engineering drawing involving the phasing of decisions and investigation of their prerequisites. At last in the chapter, future communication challenges were directed attention to regarding the trend towards digitalization of the building process.

The main conclusion based on our case study is that usability of ICT depends on the nature of a task. If a task is complex and partly unpredictable, such as with the building of a ship, then the existence of considerable interdependence and uncertainty will necessitate co-operative attitudes and routines among people and organizations in order to respond to unanticipated situations and to detect and remedy troubles in communication. Only by interpreting these interdependencies and uncertainties, as well as their probable causes and consequences, can a proper application of ICT be applied. Otherwise, one is likely to end up with communication procedures and practices that contradict instead of complement each other. The result may, then, very well be disintegrated communications and a disorderly decision-making process, or exact the opposite of what ICT is applied to achieve. From a general point of view, that would be a situation when one is stuck with technology and just want something that works. Though ICT is often an important component in the process of communication, the outcome of this process is principally determined by the people involved, and if they are able to reach a common understanding. To produce reliable information, therefore, interpersonal communication will also in the future be determining. While different information and communication technologies can work to support interpersonal communication, it can never fully replace it provided a one-off project environment.

Our main findings and conclusion regarding communication in the manufacturing industry are based on a case study of one shipyard only. The study is further limited to a shipbuilding process and, in particular, the execution of engineering drawing as part of this process. In terms of the empirical basis, it rests solely on in-depth interviews with a relatively small sample of respondents sharing the same or similar professional background as well as fulfilling some of the same functions. Future research work on the topic should include more than one company, and several lines of business, to make possible comparisons in communications across different types of production and processes. Likewise, to attain a more complete picture of the whole communication process, a multi-level analysis including all phases of a production could be carried out. At last, whereas in-depth interviews work very well to grasp communication problems by their many facets, a more thorough study should also include quantitative material of various sorts to investigate the scale and scope of the different problems emphasized in the chapter.

REFERENCES

Abadi, M. (2005). *Issues and challenges in communication within design teams in the construction industry*. PhD Thesis, Faculty of Engineering and Physical Sciences, School of Mechanical, Aerospace and Civil Engineering, the University of Manchester.

Adams, D. (2002). *The salmon of doubt: Hitchhiking the galaxy one last time*. London: William Heinemann.

Ashworth, R., Boyne, G., & Delbridge, R. (2007). Escape from the iron cage? Organizational change and isomorphic pressures in the public sector. *Journal of Public Administration Research and Theory*, April.

Aslesen, S. (2005). *EU-utvidelsen – mulige tilpasningsstrategier i norske skipsverft*. Fafo-notat 2005:07.

Aslesen, S., & Bertelsen, S. (2008). Last planner in a social perspective – a shipbuilding case. P. Tzortzopoulos & M. Kagioglou (Eds.), *IGLC 16 Proceedings 16th Annual Conference of the International Group for Lean Construction, Manchester, United Kingdom*.

Ballard, H. G. (2000). *The last planner system of production control*. Doctoral thesis submitted to the faculty of Engineering, University of Birmingham, United Kingdom.

Booker, P. J. (1963). *A history of engineering drawing*. London: Chatto & Windus.

Boucock, C. (2000). *In the grip of freedom: Law and modernity in Max Weber*. University of Toronto.

Brownell, H., Pincus, D., Blum, A., Rehak, A., & Winner, E. (1997). The effects of right hemisphere brain damage on patients. *Brain and Language, 57*, 60–79. doi:10.1006/brln.1997.1834

Dankbaar, B. (2007). Global sourcing and Innovation: The consequences of losing both organizational and geographical proximity. *European Planning Studies, 15*(2), 271–288. doi:10.1080/09654310601078812

Dewett, T., & Jones, G. (2001). The role of information technology in the organization: a review model and assessment. *Journal of Management, 27*(3), 313–345. doi:10.1016/S0149-2063(01)00094-0

Edmondson, A., & Moingeon, B. (1998). From organizational learning to the learning organization. *Management Learning, 29*(1), 5–20. doi:10.1177/1350507698291001

Emmitt, S., & Gorse, C. (2006). *Communication in construction teams*. London and New York: Spon Research, Taylor & Francis.

Fulk, J. (1993). Social construction of communication technology. *Academy of Management Journal, 36*, 921–950. doi:10.2307/256641

Goodman, R. A., & Goodman, L. P. (1976). Some management issues in temporary systems: a study of professional development and manpower – the theatre case. *Administrative Science Quarterly, 21*, 494–501. doi:10.2307/2391857

Grabher, G. (2002). Cool projects, boring institutions: Temporary collaboration in social context. *Regional Studies, 36*(3), 206–214.

Hanson, M. T. (1999). The search-transfer problem: The role of weak ties in sharing knowledge across organizational subunits. *Administrative Science Quarterly, 44*, 82–111. doi:10.2307/2667032

Hauptman, O., & Hirji, K. K. (1996). The influence of process concurrency on project outcomes in product development: An empirical study of cross-functional teams. *IEEE Transactions on Engineering Management, 43*(2), 153–164. doi:10.1109/17.509981

Hauptman, O., & Hirji, K. K. (1996). The influence of process concurrency on project outcomes in product development: An empirical study of cross-functional teams. *IEEE Transactions on Engineering Management, 43*(2), 153–164. doi:10.1109/17.509981

Howell, I., & Batcheler, B. (2005). Building information modeling two years later – Huge potential. Some Success and Several Limitations. *Laiserin Letter, 24*. Available at http://www.laiserin.com/features/bim/newforma_bim.pdf

Huber, G. P. (1990). A theory of the effect of advanced information technologies on organizational design, intelligence, and decision making. *Academy of Management Review, 15*(1), 47–71. doi:10.2307/258105

Jean, R.-J., Sinkovics, R. R., & Kim, D. (2008). International technology and organizational performance within international business to business relationships. *International Marketing Review, 25*(5), 563–583. doi:10.1108/02651330810904099

Kim, S. M., & Mahoney, J. T. (2006). Mutual commitment to support exchange: relation-specific IT system as a substitute for managerial hierarchy. *Strategic Management Journal, 27*(5), 401–423. doi:10.1002/smj.527

King, R. C., & Xia, W. (1999): Media appropriateness: Effects of experience on communication media choice. In K. E. Kendall (Ed.), *Emerging information technologies: Improving decisions, cooperating and communication technology* (pp. 194-218). Newbury Park, CA: Sage.

Lee, G., Sacks, R., & Eastman, C. M. (2006). Specifying parametric building object behavior (BOB) for a building information modeling system. *Automation in Construction, 15*(6), 758–776. doi:10.1016/j.autcon.2005.09.009

Lu, T., Guan, F., & Wang, F. (2008). Semantic classification and query of engineering drawings in the shipbuilding industry. *International Journal of Production Research, 46*(9), 2471–2483. doi:10.1080/00207540701737922

Lundin, R. A., & Söderholm, A. (1995). A theory of the temporary organization. *Scandinavian Journal of Management, 11*(4), 437–455. doi:10.1016/0956-5221(95)00036-U

Markus, M. L. (1990). Toward a "critical mass" theory of interactive media. In J. Fulk & C. Steinfeld (eds.), *Organizations and communication technology* (pp. 194-218). Newbury Park, CA: Sage.

Meyerson, D., Weick, K. E., & Kramer, R. M. (1996). Swift trust and temporary groups. In R. M. Kramer & T. R. Tyler (Eds.), *Trust in organizations: Frontiers of theory and research*, 166-195. Thousand Oaks, CA: Sage.

Monge, P. R., & Fulk, J. (1995). *Global network organizations*. Paper presented to the International Communication Association, Albuquerque, NM, May.

Morton, M. S. (1995). Emerging organizational forms: Work and organization in the 21st Century. *European Management Journal, 13*(4), 339–345. doi:10.1016/0263-2373(95)00027-I

Nevins, J. L., & Whitney, D. E. (1989). *Concurrent design of products and processes*. McGraw-Hill.

Pettigrew, A. (1973). *The politics of organizational decision making*. London: Tavistock.

Pfeffer, J., & Salancik, G. (1974). Organizational decision-making as a political process. *Administrative Science Quarterly*, *19*, 135–151. doi:10.2307/2393885

Poole, M. S., & DeSanctis, G. (1990). Understanding the use of group decision support systems: The theory of adaptive structuration. In Fulk, J. and Steinfeld, C. (Eds.), *Organizations and communication technology* (173-193).

Rankin, J. H., & Luther, R. (2006). The innovation process: adoption of information and communication technology for the construction industry. *Canadian Journal of Civil Engineering*, *33*, 1538–1546. doi:10.1139/L05-128

Rice, R. E., & Shook, D. E. (1990). Relationships of job categories and organizational levels to use communication channels, including electronic mail: A meta-analysis and extension. *Journal of Management Studies*, *27*, 195–229. doi:10.1111/j.1467-6486.1990.tb00760.x

Sanders, K. (2004, September). Why building information modeling isn't working… yet. *Architectual Record*. Available at http://archrecord.construction.com/features/digital/archives/0409feature-1.asp.

Sanderson, J., & Cox, A. (2008). The challenges of supply strategy selection in a project environment: evidence from UK naval shipbuilding. *Supply Chain Management: An International Journal*, *13*(1), 16–25. doi:10.1108/13598540810850283

Stephens, K. K. (2007). The successive use of information and communication technologies at work. *Communication Theory*, *17*(4), 486–507. doi:10.1111/j.1468-2885.2007.00308.x

Suchman, L. (1987). *Plans and situated actions: The problem of human-machine communication*. New York: Cambridge University Press.

Tavistock Institute (1966). *Interdependence and uncertainty*. Tavistock publications.

Thomas, G. F., & King, C. L. (2006). Reconceptualizing e-mail overload. *Journal of Business and Technical Communication*, *20*, 252–287. doi:10.1177/1050651906287253

Tushman, M. L. (1977). Communication across organizational boundaries: special boundary roles in the innovation process. *Administrative Science Quarterly*, *22*, 587–605. doi:10.2307/2392402

Van de Ven, A. H., & Ferry, D. L. (1980). *Measuring and assessing organizations*. New York: Wiley.

Walther, J. B., & Parks, M. R. (2002). Cues filtered out, cues filtered in: Computer-mediated communication and relationships. In M. L. Knapp and J. A. Daly (Eds.), *Handbook of interpersonal communication* (529-563). Thousand Oaks, CA: Sage.

Weber, M. (1947). *The theory of social and economic organization*. New York: Oxford University Press.

Williamson, O. E. (1985). *The economic institutions of capitalism. Firms, market, relational contracting*. New York: The Free Press.

ENDNOTES

[1] According to untitled book review by Chilton, D. (1965). *Technology and Culture*, 6 (1), p. 128-130.

[2] http://en.wikipedia.org/wiki/Leonardo_da_Vinci.

[3] http://en.wikipedia.org/wiki/Enterprise_resource_planning

4   In an article about the classification of engineering drawings in the shipbuilding industry, Lu et al. (2008) propose a management method of engineering drawings based on the establishment of classification trees according to different kinds of classifications.

5   http://www.autodesk.com/buildinginformation

Chapter 20
Preconditions for Requisite Holism of Information Bases for the Invention–Innovation Process Management[2]

Matjaž Mulej
University of Maribor, Slovenia

Vojko Potočan
University of Maribor, Slovenia

Zdenka Ženko
University of Maribor, Slovenia

ABSTRACT

Innovation belongs to main open issues of the modern business. Information for the invention-innovation process is an even more open issue, because informed guessing about the future needs of future potential customers is a best case scenario. This is especially true in SMEs with their limited human resources, but the market provides no allowances for them anyway. SMEs are 99% of all organizations in EU or Slovenia. They provide +50% of jobs and +70% of new jobs. But they can hardly survive with no or poor innovation capacity, including a requisitely holistic consideration of the entire invention-innovation-diffusion process. The information system must be adapted to this fact in order to support business quality in line with the demands of the modern rather global than local market. But the usual enterprise information systems cover better the daily routine and past performance than future and innovation issues.

BACKGROUND: THE SELECTED PROBLEM AND VIEWPOINT

The Economist (2007) states that it is time for humankind to stop considering innovation process as an art and to start viewing it as a science. This trend requires a requisitely holistic information system, unlike art. Our experience has confirmed both statements long ago (e.g. Avsec, 1986; Likar, 1998; Mulej et al, 1987; Mulej et al, 1994; Mulej et al, editors of PODIM conferences since 1978; Mulej et al., 1979; Uršič, 1993). An M.A. and

DOI: 10.4018/978-1-60566-856-7.ch020

doctoral program in innovation management has existed at the University of Maribor, Faculty of Economics and Business since 1987, including also the innovation topics as a course in the only MBA program we know of. Here we will not report about this experience, but on findings resulting from it: a dialectical system of viewpoints of the invention-innovation-diffusion process (IIDP), and information support to it, which we have not detected in literature.

We will, of course, apply the Mulej/Kajzer's (1998) law of requisite holism, depicted in Table 1 (Potočan, Mulej, editors, 2007d, and earlier; Mulej, 2007a). A total holism cannot be attained as expected with holism as worldview and existing related methods (Bertallanffy, 1979). This model can well support the innovation-related part of an enterprise information system, especially in its organizational dimension. We do not talk about information as a technological topic, but its organizational and social preconditions, with direct application of technology in order for the organization, such as an SME to attain innovation-based competitiveness. The process is complex, but a requisitely holistic information system can help the innovative part of business to be better integrated in the overall business process.

THE INVENTION-INNOVATION-DIFFUSION PROCESS (IIDP)

Innovation starts with idea that is able, after research, to become innovation in development and marketing/application processes, and then yield benefit to authors, too, not only to users, in a diffusion process.

To create ideas we need to manage the environment for idea creation (Pečjak, 2001). The people - employees who are the most creative have some common characteristics. The creative process has certain features and managers need to know them and respect them.

The process of creating ideas is performed by individual thinkers and supported by their creative cooperation in interdisciplinary teamwork. There are people who were born, raised, developed, educated, and/or trained into more creative person. There are several characteristics of creative spirit (Pečjak, 2001): non-conformism, originality, flexibility, ingenuity, fluidity of thought, elasticity (verbal, associative, ideal, expressive), perseverance, connection between creativity and humor. Some of them may make the co-operation process difficult, before team members learn to listen to each other due to their mutual differences and hence develop their ethic of interdependence (Mulej et al, 2000; Mulej, Kajzer, 1998; Potočan, Mulej, 2007).

Thus, in organizations one needs to encourage, guide and manage creative processes and perform creative activities as guided group activities. The IIDP should be recognized as a complicated and complex process. To overcome one-sidedness and the resulting mistakes we suggest the application of the Dialectical System Theory (DST) as developed by Mulej (1974, and later, including 2008). Thousands of cases have proven its value.

Dialectical system (Table 1, middle part) should be the basis for interdisciplinary co-operation of many different specialists working together on

Table 1. The selected level of holism of consideration of the selected topic between the fictitious, requisite, and total holism

Fictitious holism (inside a single viewpoint)	Requisite holism (a dialectical system, DS, i.e. synergetic network, of essential interdependent viewpoints)	Total = real holism (a system, i.e. synergetic network, of totally all viewpoints)

the solutions of the same problem. To achieve a broad understanding of the problem specialists have to supplement each other's knowledge with their many specialists' precise, deep viewpoints. Most problems are caused by their oversights of crucial attributes and are too often due to one-sided approaches of narrow specialists. They might be lacking interdisciplinary creative co-operation, because they are lacking ethics of interdependence and they fail to attain the requisite holism. We speak of the requisite holism of the human behavior, i.e. observation, perception, thinking, emotional and spiritual life, decision making, and action; it should result in requisite wholeness of insights and other outcomes.

DST helps humans develop their subjective starting points with 10 guidelines concerning the bases of objectives' definition, and further 10 guidelines concerning the objectives' realization by requisitely holistic behavior resulting in requisite wholeness. On this basis, humans understand their need for cooperation; they feel interdependent and complementary to each other, offering and receiving help – in the form of otherwise uncovered viewpoints/views/insights/suggestions and solutions or steps toward solutions . All of them are information, actually, once they make their impact (Rosicky, in Mulej et al, 2000).

There are at least four stages of idea development: preparation, incubation, illumination, verification. Techniques and methods were developed to promote the idea creation processes in order to encourage the IIDP processes. Techniques of creative thinking encourage individuals to produce ideas. According to Pečjak (2001) the American psychologist Alex Osborn started to use Brainstorming and other techniques in industry in 1930's; they became more common after 1960's. Pečjak (2001) lists 42 different

techniques. The more used are also: brainwriting, the craziest idea, free associations, questions technique. Delphi method as a systemic interactive method used in carefully selected group of independent experts is also among them. This method is mainly used for predictions of future marked development trends and forecasting. EU (2004) offers many additional techniques. All of them are aimed to transform data/ideas in information to support IIDP.

According to Drucker (1985) managers should recognize the opportunities and according to them manage their activities in IIDP. The opportunities that should be recognized inside the company or industry include: unexpected occurrences, incongruities, process needs, changes in industry or market. Opportunities outside the company as identified by Drucker include: demographic changes, changes in perception and new knowledge as additional sources of opportunities in company's social and intellectual environment.

Ideas for IIDP might be collected in organizations and if considered by management as promising, they should be further developed into inventions/suggestions. Inventions are possible solutions of complex problems which already exist - are recognized by clients, customers or company managers or require the market need for this invention – product or service to be first developed through marketing activities. Suggestions are recorded inventions and can be forgotten less easily.

Innovating – IIDP – is a very complex and very complicated process toward innovation as its outcome. It is based on preconditions to which the law of requisite holism applies in the simplest case (Mulej, 2007b, and earlier; Mulej, Ženko, 2004); no precondition may be forgotten about

Table 2. Dialectical system of preconditions for innovation to show up

Innovation = (invention X entrepreneurship X requisite holism X management X co-workers X innovation-friendly culture X customers X suppliers X competitors X external (socio-economic) conditions X natural environment X random factors such as good luck).

for success to be attainable, although success is not assured, because they are not deterministic to manage in a linear process (Table 2).

A requisitely holistic – DS – approach to IIP, according to our starting points for this contribution, is depicted in Table 3 in a simplified linear model. In reality, IIP has many feedbacks (Mulej, 2007b).

INNOVATION TYPOLOGY

An additional factor of complexity of requisitely holistic approach to IIDP results from its rich typology (Table 4). For success, every of the 20 types of novelties – inventions, suggestions, potential innovations, and innovations – depends on a specific type of material conditions, knowledge/information and values/culture/ethic/norms. But, first of all, it depends on making preconditions for IIDP to flourish, which depends on innovation of

Table 3. Simplified picture of IIDP from several (networked) essential viewpoints

IIP Phases	Crucial inputs	Usual outputs	Usual output creators	Usual economic situation
Creation of ideas, especially inventions, from knowledge and values of authors	Creative thinking, time and research conditions; information	Promising idea resulting from a part of research, tacit knowledge and values such as interest etc.; information	Inventive and professional humans and groups, (non)-professional researchers	Cost of work and research conditions; no revenue or profit from market/users
Creation of suggestions from inventions	Writing etc. - ones' expression of invention; information	Promising idea recorded (made available); protected / patented perhaps; information	Inventors and advisors about recording the idea	Cost of message preparation; no revenue/profit
Optional diffusion of suggestion/s	Offer to the market of inventions –suggestions inside or outside organization; information	Partly sale, partly giving up, partly transition to development of suggestions; information	Owners of suggestion (authors and/or others) and their co-workers	Cost of offering; revenue / profit from sold suggestions
Creation of potential innovations from suggestions	Creative thinking, time and conditions for development of a suggestion to a potential innovation; information	Usable new product / method / procedure / managerial style / potential market / business item; protected / patented perhaps; information	Inventive and professional humans and groups, (non)-professional researchers and developers (incl. market developers)	Cost of work and conditions of development; no revenue / profit
Optional diffusion of potential innovations	Offer to the market of potential innovations inside or outside organization; information	Partly sale, partly giving up, partly transition to application; information	Owners of potential innovations (authors and/or others) and co-workers	Cost of offering; revenue / profit from sold potential innovations
Creation of innovations from potential innovations	Creative thinking, time and conditions for development of potential innovation to innovation, incl. the entire business operation; information	Beneficially used new market / product / method / procedure / management style / organization / business item – due to users decision and experience; information	Inventive/innovative and professional humans / groups - developers of the novelty and its market, and other professionals, including entire business operation	Cost of offering; revenue / profit from sold innovations (inside or outside organization)
Optional diffusion of innovations	Offer to the market of innovations inside or outside organization, especially to additional customers (after the first ones); information	Beneficially used new market / product / method / procedure / management style / organization / business item – due to users in broader circles; information	Owners of innovations (authors and/or others) and co-workers, especially in marketing and sales, but the entire business process matters equally	Cost of offering; revenue / profit from additionally sold innovations (inside or outside organization)

management (4.1.-4.4. in Table 4) and of culture from the style 'Division in the thinking bosses and the working subordinates' to the style 'We all think and we all work and create, invent and innovate, being bosses and their coworkers with all requisite various and different specializations' (Mulej et al, 1987). The latter includes ethic of interdependence, while the first one includes managerial ethic of independence, and subordinates' ethic of dependence and their resulting irresponsibility due to no permission of thinking and creative and requisitely holistic behavior. The contemporary managerial style and ethic of interdependence of mutually different specialists, who make the organization, is the management part of the DS of preconditions for IIDP and management of it, resulting in excellence, which is very well summarized in Five Pillars of Total Quality (Creech, 1994) in Table 5.

The IIDP needs also a methodological support to flourish. We have recently offered a new one.

APPLICATION OF USOMID/SIX THINKING HATS SYNERGY

The experience with application of the Dialectical systems theory (DST) in non-academic settings soon demonstrated the need for those rather philosophical concepts to be expressed in an organizational technology, i.e. **methodology**. This is why USOMID came about; the acronym reads: Creative Co-operation of Many for an Innovative Work (Mulej, 1082; Mulej et al., 1986).

Creative co-operation can hardly take place if e.g. only hard-systemic methods are used since they are aimed at finding and exposing mechanical, deterministic kinds of relations. They are a very important achievement, if a routine-based behavior is good enough. It is so when e.g. one deals with very technical details of production for all products to be fully equal. It is different when **creativity** is needed. Then, soft-systemic methods become the right choice exposing the probabilistic

Table 4. 24 basic types of novelties - inventions, suggestions, potential innovation and innovations

Three Networked Criteria of Novelties - Inventions, Suggestions, Potential Innovations, and Innovations					
(1) Content of inventions, suggestions, potential innovations, and innovations	*(2) Consequences of innovations*		*(3) On-job-duty to create inventions, suggestions, potential innovations and innovations*		
	1. Radical	*2. Incremental*	*1. Duty exists*	*2. No duty*	
1. Business program items	1.1.	1.2.	1.3.	1.4.	
2. Technology (products, processes, ...)	2.1.	2.2.	2.3.	2.4.	
3. Organization	3.1.	3.2.	3.3.	3.4.	
4. Managerial style	4.1.	4.2.	4.3.	4.4.	
5. Methods of leading, working and co-working	5.1.	5.2.	5.3.	5.4.	
6. Business style	6.1.	6.2.	6.3.	6.4.	

Table 5. Five pillars of total quality

Perfect product	←→	Perfect processes
↕		↕
ORGANIZATION		
↕		↕
Leadership, i.e. management by role-modeling and co-operation	←→	Commitment of coworkers

and possibilistic features/characteristics. Both types of methods are normally needed, of course, in organizations. The provided information must match these different information requirements and specifics expressed by them.

In order for the soft-systemic methods to support a work process the DST authors have developed (and frequently applied) its USOMID method (Mulej, 1982; Mulej et al, 1986). In DST the **human work process** is modeled: it starts from the starting points - a system of five elements:

- The objective, i.e. outer, starting points are the objective 'needs' and 'possibilities'.
- The subjective starting points are 'emotions, values and talents', 'knowledge on contents', and 'knowledge on methods'.

All further process steps depend on them. In USOMID every one of them is reflected:

- Objective needs reflect the law of entropy, which causes the need for the modern innovative society, innovative business and its culture, policy, strategies, tactics, innovation objectives, awards; subjectively, the objective needs are in turn reflected in values and other emotions.
- Values and other emotions are impacted by the objective needs of a modern society in the form of motivation for a deliberate search for many possible changes aimed at creation of inventions, potential innovations and innovations; the motivation for it is created by a well grounded feeling of appreciation for creative co-workers.
- Knowledge on contents is discovered and activated for both purposes said; since more than two thirds of innovations are the incremental ones and have to do with the work processes, and since they can best be produced by the work performers, and since a written insight into processes is usually lacking, especially into the rather

creative partial processes - making this insight in the form of 'programoteque' is the visible informational outcome of USOMID deployment; it is done on a framework level first and then proceeds toward more and more detailed levels, all way to a computer support; it is first a description of the given facts, then comes their 'causes tree' analysis, later one perhaps also innovating.

- Knowledge on methods has a general and a specific part; the specific part is problem/topic dependent; the general part is made of the USOMID/SREDIM procedure of creative work and co-operation.
- The objective possibilities for a creative work and co-operation to take place are made of the USOMID Circles, a version of the Quality Control Circles, with some additions.

The relation between all the quoted elements is double and has the form of information:

- Learning by an initial course, and learning by doing;
- Working out and deployment of the programoteque by a creative co-operation process of the studied job performers and their consultants.

Then, the **innovating** process can follow (thousands of cases since 1969). Hence, in practice the application of DST via USOMID starts with working out the **insight** into the processes under consideration. This is usual, of course; in this case it takes place in the form of working out the programoteque.

On the other hand and in about the same time, the Method of Six Thinking Hats was created by De Bono (2005). It helps to improve the most important human resource: thinking. The greatest obstacle in thinking is confusion. We humans want too much at the same time. Inside of us there are interfering emotions, information, logic, hope and creativity. Like if we were trying to juggle with too many balls.

The Six Thinking Hats is a very simple concept that enables the thinker to perform just one activity at the same time. So she learns to separate emotions from logic, creativity from the provided information, and so on. This is the concept of six thinking hats. When you imagine that you have covered your head with one of these hats, you think in a certain way to match a selected value. Each one of the hats requires a different way of thinking and after applying all six of them we can enormously improve our creativity and achieve good complex solutions.

Six thinking hats encourage us to guide out thinking like the conductor guides the orchestra. At the meetings/sessions participants use different hats to encourage themselves to do different, but focused, thinking about their shared problem on the agenda. The main advantages of this method are its simplicity, readiness and results. The essence of the six hats includes:

- White hat – neutral, objective, facts without interpretation, like a computer;

- Red hat – feelings, emotions, intuition, irrationality, unproved feelings, no justification;
- Black hat – watching out, caution, pessimism, search for danger, doubt, criticism, it all works well against mistakes and weak points of proposals;
- Yellow hat – optimism, search for advantages of proposals, search for implementation ways, sensitivity for benefit of the idea, constructive approach;
- Green hat – energy, novelty, creation, innovation, in order to be able to overcome all obstacles;
- Blue hat – organization, mastering, control over procedure, thinking about thinking.

In (Mulej, M. and N., 2006) we covered a further viewpoint that we now remind of in Table 6. USOMID (Mulej, 1982) and Six Thinking Hats (De Bono, 2005) had been applied in separation for beyond two decades, before we made a synergy to include rational and emotional parts of human personality in IIDP.

Table 6. Synergy of USOMID/SREDIM and 6TH methodologies in procedure of USOMID

SREDIM Phases USOMID Steps inside the SREDIM phases	1. Select problem / opportunity to work on in an USO-MID circle	2. Record data about the selected topic (no 'Why')	3. Evaluate recorded data on the topic ('Why" - is central)	4. Determine and develop the chosen solution/s of the topic	5. Implement chosen solution of the topic in reality	6. Maintain implemented solution for a requisitely long term
1. Individual brain-writing by all in the organisational unit / circle	All 6 hats	White hat	All 6 hats; red, black, yellow, green, first of all	All 6 hats; red, black, yellow, green, first of all	All 6 hats in preparation of implementation	All 6 hats in preparation of mainte-nance
2. Circulation of notes for additional brain-writing by all	All 6 hats	White hat	All 6 hats; red, black, yellow, green, first of all	All 6 hats; red, black, yellow, green, first of all	All 6 hats in preparation of implementation	All 6 hats in preparation of maintenance
3. Brain-storming for synergy of ideas / proposals	All 6 hats	White hat	All 6 hats; red, black, yellow, green, first of all	All 6 hats; red, black, yellow, green, first of all	All 6 hats in preparation of implementation	All 6 hats in preparation of maintenance
4. Shared conclusions of the circle	All 6 hats	White hat	All 6 hats; red, black, yellow, green, first of all	All 6 hats; red, black, yellow, green, first of all	All 6 hats in preparation of implementation	All 6 hats in preparation of maintenance

Thus, the IIDP process runs on a requisitely holistic basis made of the professional and emotional information.

In addition, information must be adapted to the type of market to be served by outcomes of IIDP.

THREE DIFFERENT TYPES OF MARKET FOR NOVELTIES

Application of the requisite holism (Table 1) to the work on innovation to be attained (Table 2) in the IIP (Table 3) may create any type of innovation (Table 4) and attain excellence of it (Table 5) with e.g. the methodology that combines USOMID and 6 Thinking Hats as the rational and emotional parts of the creative work and co-operation process (Table 6). As we see in Table 3, three types of novelties in terms of their finalization per phases show up, for which three different types of market exist (Table 7). In them, the level of profit and other benefit depends on the level of accepted risk of either suppliers of buyer rather than the level of effort or scientific merit of the novelty etc. (Mulej M. and N, in Mulej et al, 2007). Thus, the necessary information is specific: all three markets attract different supplier and different customers.

Yet another type of situation and related information shows up in the diffusion phase of IIDP.

THE DIFFUSION PHASE OF IIDP

Innovation/IIDP management includes also the process of spreading new solutions or novelties among potential users. Inventions become innovations when perceived as useful and actually used by consumers. The provided information must therefore persuade potential consumers that the potential benefit will be real for them. Rogers (2003) studied on the case of agriculture the whole process of diffusion of novelties from the research laboratories or companies to their potential and end users – farmers. There are several organizations US wide on which a similar case study could be made. A society is so convinced of the greater benefit for everyone, that governmental agencies are acting as promoters of inventions – in the areas of public health, safety, education, agriculture…

Rogers' theory on diffusion of novelties tackles difficulties when trying to implement the new solutions among people as well as methods to support diffusion. Diffusion is at the same time:

1. Communication process among people who know a novelty well (inventor, producer) and potential users;
2. Exchange of information and preparation process for decision making;
3. Including uncertainties and risks,
4. Including a process of changing the society.

Table 7. Expectable suppliers and customers per elaboration levels of novelties

Elaboration level of the novelty	Expectable suppliers	Expectable customers
Suggestion (a recorded promising invention)	Inventors and research organizations with a poor feel and knowledge for business, technical development, production, marketing etc.	Entrepreneurs ready for critical risk and law remuneration for the inventor or research organization owning suggestion
Potential innovation (a usable promising and elaborated suggestion)	Inventors and research organization with feel and knowledge for engineering, but less so for production, marketing etc.	Entrepreneurs ready for production and marketing risk, less so for R&D and other early phases risks
Innovation (a proven beneficial novelty accepted by users)	R&D and production/service organizations wishing a rent and enlargement of their market	Less entrepreneurial managers ready less for the production and marketing than for obsolescence and dependence risks

Table 8. Matrix of essential attributes of diffusion process (A case; Germ, 2003; Leder, 2004)

Viewpoints to be considered		Phases of users' decision making about a novelty				
		1 Awareness	2 Persuasion	3 Decision	4 Application	5 Reconfirmation
Novelty customers (potential)	Customers – innovators					
	Early customers					
	Early majority					
	Late majority					
	Laggards					
Opinion leaders						
Attributes of novelty	Relative advantage					
	Compatibility					
	Complexity					
	Testability					
	Visibility					
Communica-tion channels	Public					
	Interpersonal					
Nature of the social system of customers						
Decision type about novelty	Optional					
	Group					
	Authority					
Consequenc-es of novelty	Desired Undesired					
	Indirect Direct					
	Anticipated Unanticipated					

Legend: the darker the field, the bigger the need for change agents' impact

Novelty (Table 4) is any new idea, service, process, solution or method that the possible user considers something new and worth considering as useful. Some novelties are more easily accepted by the possible users when:

1. Users can see the possible advantages.
2. Novelty can be applied together with the established methods (similar technology, same equipment can be used).
3. Novelty appears less complicated and complex, which makes it more likely to be accepted.

4. There is a verification stage. The potential user can study the novelty - samples, testers, model plants.
5. Results of the novelty are easily seen, measured, being already installed somewhere.

Decision about the novelty can be of three basic types and their combinations: 1. individual decision, 2. group decision, and 3. governmental decision. Every decision-making process includes dealing with uncertainties and risks and includes several stages. First we attain the awareness about the novelty. This is a process of gathering data and information about the novelty. It is a social system of spreading the news about something new, what kind of problems it solves or is designed for and how it works or why it can work.

After the phases exposed in Table 7 have brought inventions / suggestions / potential innovations / innovations to market, more benefit can be provided for both the suppliers and customers of the novelty at stake, if the diffusion of novelties is taken care of (Rogers, 2003). We are providing a case of it in Table 8.

ENTERPRISE INFORMATION SYSTEM RELATED TO IIDP

The traditional enterprise information system related to the IIDP has been covering much more the invention-creating phase than the later two phases of innovation making in market (outside or inside the authors' organizations) and diffusion of innovation. In addition, as one can see in the Oslo Manual it covers mostly the technological part of the IIDP rather than all other contents summarized in Table 4 or phases summarized in Table 3 and related to market types in Table 7, not to speak of all phases and demands to be dealt with in the diffusion process as summarized in Table 8 or all preconditions of making of an innovation summarized in Table 2, or even the synergies of all of them. Thus, application of the law of requisite holism (Table 1) is a must, and it includes a less one-sided view of all information that are necessary for an IIDP to yield success more frequently than so far. As we have mentioned earlier, DST offers a very helpful basis for it.

HOW TO USE DST FOR REQUISITELY HOLISTIC CREATION OF INFORMATION BASES FOR IIDP

Let us brief and extend the previously mentioned attributes of DST-type behavior (Tables 1 – 8) by applying them for creation of requisite information bases for the IIDP management (Potocan, Mulej,

2006; Mulej, Potocan, 2007; Potocan, 2008). We will make short comments per all six components and their relations in DST: laws of

1. Entropy;
2. Requisite holism;
3. Succession and interdependence;
4. Guidelines for goals definitions;
5. Guidelines for goals realization; and
6. USOMID as the applied methodology to use all five of them in synergy with no word of theory among practitioners.

Ad 1: Alienation (of decision makers from reality) by one-sided decision-making of management causes entropy (as the permanent natural tendency of everything to change/disappear) of society to grow. Requisite holism and wholeness of information is needed against alienation and entropy realization.

Ad 2: Requisite holism must therefore replace the fictitious one, which is e.g. limited to stockholders rather than all stakeholders. Requisite holism and wholeness of information supports the requisite holism of human action better than the lack of requisite holism and wholeness of information does.

Ad 3: To introduce this necessary innovative change, one must start from the influential persons, thus from subjective starting points of decision-makers. But one must also consider their interdependence with their circumstances in business and society, and all the process from defining the starting points to the very end – the result, e.g. the requisite holism and wholeness of information and decision, and diminished alienation and danger of entropy.

Ad 4: The ten guidelines concerning making the starting points may be briefed as follows:

- Both the contemporary human capacity of global influences and the interdependence require humans to innovate their culture toward more holism/wholeness of the

Bertalanffian type, including requisite holism and wholeness of information. This is what we tend to help people attain by this contribution.

- Systemic/holistic thinking/behavior must replace one-sidedness in the role of the methodology of human behavior, especially thinking, decision-making, and action.
- If the problem is alienation by one-sidedness, and (requisite) holism/wholeness is the objective, then more of the requisite holism and wholeness of information can be a task (among many more).
- Application of the (dialectical) systems theory can belong to the necessary procedures for more requisite holism and wholeness of information.
- Double-checking, whether this is enough or not, says that no single theory is enough, but practice of system thinking, related legal and political institutions, and prevailing culture must support requisitely holistic behavior, including requisite holism and wholeness of information.
- Hence, the dialectical systems thinking, which stresses interdependence and creative co-operation of mutually different viewpoint-holders, such as the interested parties in business and society, is needed as a human attribute. It is supported by requisite holism and wholeness of information.
- Teamwork-like co-operation of stakeholders enables requisite holism and wholeness of information and behavior, especially decision-making, to diminish alienation. It is supported by requisite holism and wholeness of information.
- Innovation of the subjective starting points of co-operating entities toward ethics of interdependence and knowledge of co-operation make their teamwork easier. It is supported by requisite holism and wholeness of information.
- For it, both knowledge and values/culture/

ethic/norms need innovation because they are interdependent and mutually supportive, either toward creative co-operation and requisite holism and wholeness of information and behavior, especially decision-making, or against them.

- Innovation of human subjective starting points toward more holism is rarely easy, if the experience of the tackled humans lets them prefer the old ones and allows the old ones to keep impacting the current behavior, although circumstances and conditions have changed. In such a case it would be difficult to define up-to-date starting points and resulting salient objectives. - The likely alternative is poor success due to lagging behind competitors due to a lack of requisite holism and wholeness of information and behavior, especially decision-making.

Ad 5: The ten guidelines concerning realizing the starting points may be briefed as follows:

- After the objectives of e.g. requisitely holistic information and decision-making have been defined, tasks and procedures for narrower specialists have their turn. Still, success may be poor, if specialists do not work hard enough on their own requisite holism. Requisite holism and wholeness of information may help them keep the requisite holism and wholeness in mind.
- Holism, including the one concerning/by requisitely requisite holism and wholeness of information and behavior, especially decision-making, is very rarely attained with a lack of co-operation, and hence specialists must be open to each other, because they differ from each other. Requisite holism and wholeness of information may help them be so.
- Many specialists lack training in openness and must change / innovate their knowledge and values in this respect. Requisite

holism and wholeness of information about each other may help them be so and come closer to the 3-T paradigm (Florida, 2005): tolerance for differences attracts talents and makes investment in technology make sense.

- Openness is closer to specialists, as long as they may stay inside their own specialty, but inter-disciplinary approach links several of them into synergies and is equally or even more necessary for requisite holism and wholeness. No specialist is neither unnecessary nor the only necessary one.

- Because of the unavoidably narrow specialization of all humans, one can never know and master totally everything; rather, a hard-to-define level of probability/risk must be expected. Deterministic information is impossible: it ought to be total, which reaches beyond human capacity due to complexity of nature, including humans.

- If specialists use the modern dialectics rather than the one-sided medieval metaphysics, all the above five demands that concern specialists, can be met more easily and reliably: ethics and practice of interdependence support co-operation and changing, including innovation of human subjective starting points. Requisite holism and wholeness of information may help them reach so far.

- Though, co-operation is easier to attain, if jobs of specialists are precisely delimited, like in systems and models typology. Requisite holism and wholeness of information may help them to have clear boundaries.

- Once every specialist does his or her own job, one must from time to time generalize findings / results; this phase includes a simplification, some details being omitted. It is important that this generalization is realistic, e.g. for a salient judgment about the

level of requisite holism and wholeness of information and behavior, especially decision-making attained so far.

- To make the judgment realistic, one should go for requisite holism by using the dialectical system, rather than a total or fictitious / one-sided one. Requisite holism and wholeness of information may help them humans do so.

- Judgment results from analysis and from synthesis following it. But there is also another synthesis with a crucial impact: synthesis of the subjective starting points before and as the basis of analysis. This synthesis influences the level of holism of specialists crucially, including in the topic of requisite holism and wholeness of information and behavior, especially decision-making.

The mentioned facts and cognitions present a base for (philosophical) discussion about definition of holism and holistic thinking, of information, innovation of business information management, and creation of more or even requisitely holistic (business) information base for the IIDP management.

FUTURE TRENDS

Innovative business can no longer be avoided. Even more, the crisis that is called a financial crisis superficially in 2008 can hardly be solved with means that have caused it. Innovation will even more than so far have to be in focus. But ideas cannot become innovation as results attaining requisite wholeness, unless the requisite holism of IIDP management and execution is attained. So far it has not been. This is the essence of the environmental, financial, climate change and all other crises of the current times. They are far from easy to master and overcome, and humans will have to learn to live with them and resolve their problems gradually. (Metcalf, in Božičnik, Ećimović, Mulej, 2008). Requisite holism and wholeness of information may help them humans do so.

SOME CONCLUSIONS

Application of the Mulej/Kajzer law of requisite holism (Table 1) lets us perceive complexity of the IIDP in terms of preconditions for innovation, as a new proven users' benefit from a new idea, to be created, in terms of the many phases of the IIDP, in terms of its diverse markets/users, as well as in terms of its beneficial and potentially detrimental consequences. Innovation management includes the diffusion process. Many different people are involved. It includes efforts, financial means and risk. It takes time to make an innovation and it is at the same time also a process of changing the society. The Dialectical Systems Theory helps humans create and manage their behavior in this unavoidable direction. Requisite holism and wholeness of information may help them humans do so. Criterion of requisite holism and wholeness of information is briefly expressed in information requirement of every activity and the entire IIDP.

REFERENCES

Avsec, D. (1986). *Finančne oblike družbenega pospeševanja (so)delovanja mnogih v socialistični samoupravni družbi.* Maribor, Slovenija. Univerza v Mariboru, Ekonomsko-poslovna fakulteta, Bertalanffy, v. L. (1979) *General systems theory. Foundations, development, application.* New York: Braziller.

Božičnik, S., Ećimović, T., Mulej, M., et al. (2008). *Sustainable future, requisite holism, and social responsibility (against the current abuse of free market society).* Ansted University, British Virgin Islands, and Penang, in cooperation with SEM Institute for Climate Change, Korte, and IRDO Institute for development of Social Responsibility, Maribor.

Creech, B. (1994). *The five pillars of TQM. How to make total quality work for you.* Dutton, NY: Truman Taley Books.

De Bono, E. (2005). *Šest klobukov razmišljanja.* Ljubljana, Slovenija. New Moment, 28 (all journal).

Drucker, P. (1985). The discipline of innovation. *Harvard Business Review,* May-June.

Germ Galič, B. (2003). *Dialektični sistem kazalnikov inoviranja in kakovosti poslovanja.* Maribor, Slovenija. University of Maribor, Faculty of Economics and Business.

Leder, B. (2004). *Inoviranje trženja turizma na slovenskem podeželju.* Maribor, Slovenija. University of Maribor, Faculty of Economics and Business.

Likar, B. (1998). *Inoviranje.* Koper, Slovenija. Visoka šola za management, Koper.

Mulej., et al. (Eds.). of PODIM conferences since 1978; e.g.: Rebernik, M., Mulej, M., Rus, M., Krošlin, T. (2007c). *Nurturing champions of innovation and entrepreneurship: Proceedings of the 27th Conference on Entrepreneurship and Innovation PODIM,* Maribor, Slovenija. Faculty of Economics and Business, Institute for Entrepreneurship and Small Business Management.

Mulej, M. (1982). Dialektično-sistemsko programiranje delovnih procesov – metodologija USOMID. Maribor, Slovenija. *Naše gospodarstvo, 28*(3), 206-209.

Mulej, M. (2007a). Systems theory: A worldview and/or a methodology aimed at requisite holism/realism of humans' thinking, decisions and action. *Systems Research and Behavioral Science, 24*(3), 347–357. doi:10.1002/sres.810

Mulej, M., et al. (1986). *Usposabljanje za ustvarjalnost. USOMID.* (Training for Creativity. USOMID Methodology. In Slovene). 4th revised and reworked edition. Ekonomski center, Maribor. Slovenija.

Mulej, M., Čančer, V., Hrast, A., Jurše, K., Kajzer, S., Knez-Riedl, J., et al. *(2007d).* The law of requisite holism and ethics of interdependence: Basics of the dialectical systems thinking (applied to innovation in catching-up countries). *On GESI Website, Buenos Aires.*

Mulej, M., Devetak, G., Drozg, F., Ferš, M., Hudnik, M., Kajzer, Š., et al. (1987). *Inovativno poslovanje.* Ljubljana, Slovenija. Gospodarski vestnik.

Mulej, M., Hyvaerinen, L., Jurše, K., Rafolt, B., Rebernik, M., Sedevčič, M., & Uršič, D. (1994). *Inovacijski management, I. del: Inoviranje managementa.* Maribor, Slovenija. University of Maribor, Faculty of Economics and Business.

Mulej, M., & Kajzer, S. (1998). Ethics of interdependence and the law of requisite holism. In M. Rebernik & M. Mulej (Eds.), *STIQE ,98. Proceedings of the 4th International Conference on Linking Systems Thinking, Innovation, Quality, Entrepreneurship and Environment.* Maribor, Slovenija. University of Maribor, Faculty of Economics and Business, Institute for Entrepreneurship and Small Business Management, and Slovenian Society for Systems Research.

Mulej, M., Kajzer, Š., Treven, S., & Jurše, K. (1997). Sodobno gospodarstvo med odpori do inovacij in življenjem od njih. *Naše gospodarstvo, 43*(3-4), 339-349.

Mulej, M., Likar, B., & Potočan, V. (2005). Increasing the capacity of companies to absorb inventions from research organizations and encouraging people to innovate. *Cybernetics and Systems, 36,* 491–512. doi:10.1080/01969720590944276

Mulej, M., & Mulej, N. (2006). Innovation and/by systemic thinking by synergy of methodologies "Six thinking hats" and "USOMID". In R. Trappl (Ed.), *Cybernetics and systems 2006: Proceedings of the Eighteenth European Meeting on Cybernetics and Systems Research* (pp. 416-421). Vienna, Austria: Austrian Society for Cybernetic Studies.

Mulej, M., & Potocan, V. (2007). Requisite holism - precondition of reliable business information. *Kybernetes, 36*(3/4), 319–332. doi:10.1108/03684920710746986

Mulej, M., Potočan, V., Rosi, B., Ženko, Z., Jurše, K., & Udovičič, K. (2006). Role models: Do what you preach on innovation, government/public sector. In *Advancing business and management in knowledge-based society: [proceedings of] the 7th International Conference of the Faculty of Management* (pp. 1499-1508). Koper, MIC'06, Portorož, University of Primorska.

Mulej, M., & Ženko, Z. (2004). *Introduction to systems thinking with application to invention and innovation management.* Maribor, Slovenija: Management Forum.

Mulej. M. (2007b). *Inoviranje navad države in manjših podjetij.* Koper, Slovenija. Univerza na Primorskem, Fakulteta za management.

Osborne, A. F. (1953). *Applied imagination.* New York: Scribners.

Pečjak, V. (2001). *Poti do novih idej. (Ways to create new ideas).* Ljubljana, Slovenija. New Moment.

Potocan, V. (2008). Organizational knowledge and education on information technology. In E. Kioulafas (Ed.), *Proceedings of the 4th International Conference on Institutional Evaluation Techniques in Education, Samos Island, Greece, 27-29 June 2008* (pp. 63-71). Athens: National and Kapodistrian University of Athens

Potocan, V., & Mulej, M. (2006). Reliability of information: Case of business information. In B. Aurer, & M. Baca (Eds.) *Proceedings of the 17th International Conference on Information and Intelligent Systems, September 20-22, 2006, Varazdin, Croatia* (pp. 113-120). Varaždin: Faculty of Organisation and Informatics, FOI.

Potočan, V., & Mulej, M. (Eds.). (2007). *Transition into an innovative enterprise*. Maribor, Slovenija: University of Maribor, Faculty of Economics and Business.

Rebernik, M. (1990). *Ekonomika inovativnega podjetja*. Ljubljana, Slovenija. Gospodarski vestnik.

Rogers, E. (2003). *Diffusion of Innovation* (5th ed.). New York: The Free Press.

SZK. (2007). *16. konferenca Slovenskega združenja za kakovost, Kakovost, inovativnost in odgovornost. Zbornik.* Ljubljana, Slovenija. Slovensko združenje za kakovost.

The Economist. (2007, October 13). Something new under the sun. A special report on innovation. *The Economist.*

Uršič, D. (1993). *Inoviranje podjetja kot poslovno-organizacijskega sistema.* Maribor, Slovenija. Univerza v Mariboru, Ekonomsko-poslovna fakulteta.

ENDNOTES

[1] Contribution is based on research program "From the Institutional to the Real Transition to an Innovative Enterprise", which enjoys support of the Public Agency for Research, Republic of Slovenia, in 2004-2007.

[2] Contribution is based on research program "From the Institutional to the Real Transition to an Innovative Enterprise", which enjoys support of the Public Agency for Research, Republic of Slovenia, in 2004-2007.

Chapter 21
Exploring Enterprise Information Systems

Malihe Tabatabaie
University of York, UK

Richard Paige
University of York, UK

Chris Kimble
Euromed Marseille École de Management, France

ABSTRACT

The concept of an Enterprise Information System (EIS) has arisen from the need to deal with the increasingly volatile requirements of modern large-scale organisations. An EIS is a platform capable of supporting and integrating a wide range of activities across an organisation. In principle, the concept is useful and applicable to any large and SMEs, international or national business organisation. However, the range of applications for EIS is growing and they are now being used to support e-government, health care, and non-profit / non-governmental organisations. This chapter reviews research and development efforts related to EIS, and as a result attempts to precisely define the boundaries for the concept of EIS, i.e., identifying what is and what is not an EIS. Based on this domain analysis, a proposal for using goal-oriented modelling techniques for building EIS is constructed; the proposal is made more concrete through illustration via an example.

INTRODUCTION

This chapter focuses on a grand challenge for organisations: dealing with their evolving requirements and goals, and the impact of these changes on their Information Technology (IT). In particular, we are interested in large-scale organisations such as multi-national companies, or public-sector organisations, which are sometimes called *enterprises* in the literature.

Organisations use IT in many different ways: to facilitate communication, to support commercial transactions, to advertise, etc. In order to understand the effect of organisational and enterprise changes on use of IT, we start by defining the nature of an organisation. The current literature defines that an organisation is thus about a group of elements (human, automated system, structure, policy etc) that

DOI: 10.4018/978-1-60566-856-7.ch021

are arranged in a specific manner to accomplish a particular purpose (Buck, 2000; Laudon & Laudon, 2007; Terry, 1975). This definition applies to small, medium, and large-scale organisations.

As we said earlier, a large-scale organisation can sometimes be designated by the word *enterprise*. However, we find it helpful to be more precise in defining enterprise; in our view, an enterprise is a large-scale organisation that is involved in, and must orchestrate, more than one independent business processes. We come to this definition by observing that many organisations, such as small IT houses, engage in a single business process. Identically some large organisations, such as online retailers, have a single business process. Organisations that have many different business processes, that must be coordinated in some way, such as Mitsubishi, have different requirements and different characteristics. Such organisations are often very large scale (e.g., public health organisations) and multi-national. In our view, the need to coordinate different business processes is a key characteristic in distinguishing an enterprise from another organisation.

This paper investigates the validity of an assumption regarding the root of complexity of IT systems in complex organisations, where the IT systems support business processes directly. The assumption is that complexity is due to the following factors:

- Increasing size of IT systems and the organisation itself;
- The interactions between different IT systems;
- The involvement of many different organisations in the constructions and use of these IT systems; and,
- The increasing rate of organisational and social change.

By investigating the validity of this assumption, and the importance of these factors, this chapter aims to contribute a better understanding of Enter-

prise Information Systems (EIS), their dimensions, their boundaries, and the challenges that arise in their construction and development.

As part of this investigation, and as a result of the analysis of the literature that commences in the next section, we propose one key challenge for understanding and building EIS:

- *Understanding diverse and volatile stakeholder requirements.*

To aid in understanding these constructs, we propose the use of goal-oriented modelling techniques; this is discussed in the last section of this chapter.

The rest of the chapter is organised as follow: The *background* section outlines the challenges in large-scale organisations as a motivation for discussing the systems that can address these challenges. A specific instance of large-scale organisations is an enterprise; hence, section 2 also discusses the requirements of IT systems for enterprises. One of the main difficulties in this area is the imprecise definition for EIS, and how an EIS differs from a general purpose IT system. Hence, we provide a working definition for EIS in this section.

The *Enterprise Information System* section describes EIS in more detail by discussing state-of-the-art definitions and effective elements, such as business and organisation, based on a literature review. The *future trend* section describes goal-oriented modelling techniques as a promising approach for attacking one of the main challenges of building an EIS by making the system more clear for its stakeholders. Section 4 also provides an example to clarify this idea.

BACKGROUND

A brief review of the history of enterprises and software systems helped us to construct a working definition for EIS. This working definition is our basis for presenting an argument about what is and what is not an EIS, and for refining our understanding of the objectives for this type of systems. This section therefore discusses some examples of EIS to shape the argument.

Challenges of Large Scale Software System

Since the 1950s organisations have been developing computer-based information systems to support their business processes. Through improvements to IT, computer based systems have become more complex and yet more reliable; therefore increasing functional requirements have been placed upon these systems (Edwards, Ward, & Bytheway, 1993). However, building this kind of system has many challenges, including fundamental challenges regarding the construction of such systems, and the challenges of evolving systems to accommodate new requirements. Understanding the challenges of building such IT systems is essential for planning, designing, and development in order to provide as early as possible risk understanding, as well as understanding of the potential means for mitigation.

The challenges of understanding and building large-scale software systems can be observed in both the public and private sectors. In the public sector, understanding the challenges, and reflecting based on these challenges during the development process, is important because failure (whether financial or otherwise) can result in significant damage to the reputation of the government.

The National Audit Office/Office of Government Commerce lists the common causes of the project failure as follow (Projects, 2004):

1. Lack of clear connections between the project and the organisation's key priorities, including agreed measures of success
2. Lack of clear senior management and Ministerial ownership

3. Lack of effective engagement with stakeholders
4. Lack of skills and proven approach to project management
5. Lack of understanding of and contact with the supply industry at senior levels in the organisation
6. Evaluation of proposals driven by initial price rather than long term value for money (especially securing delivery of business benefits)
7. Too little attention to breaking development and implementation into manageable steps
8. Inadequate resources and skills to deliver the total portfolio

The first item in this list refers to the conceptual gap between project priorities and those of organisations; later in this chapter, more discussions address this challenge. In addition to these causes, hidden challenges threaten the IT projects; in particular the large-scale ones. For example, stakeholders should understand the conditions and limitations of the system. Having unreliable expectations from the system can move the domain of the project out of its limits and cause failure.

Another important and hidden challenge is the lack of visualisation in the software systems. Software is not visible and tangible for the stakeholders; therefore, stakeholders cannot picture the functionality of the software before it actually built, which can cause unrealistic expectations and other undefined problems. For example, in the case of constructing a building, stakeholders can visualise the building by looking at its mock-up; in the case of software there is no such a clear and easy to understand mock-up.

Flexibility and supporting changes are other challenges that software systems should deal with. It is important to note that software systems can improve the speed of the processes in organisations and deal with the complex and well-defined processes. However, they are not intelligent enough to improve the business model; hence, software systems are not the solution for the ill-defined business model. This challenge can be seen mainly in large-scale software systems that deal with businesses in organisations, such as EIS. The term Enterprise Information System is a common term in today's industry, which suffers from misinterpretation and an imprecise definition. The rest of this chapter discuss this type of systems in more detail.

Large Scale Software System: Enterprise Information System

A specific kind of large scale IT system is those that support enterprises. We call these software systems, EIS. The business aspect of organisations motivates engineers to develop systems that satisfy real requirements of organisations, particularly requirements associated with business processes. As a result, technologies such as Service Oriented Architecture (SOA) are currently popular in design and implementation of systems for businesses. However, the term business often implies a process that focuses on delivering financial value; but in practice, large-scale processes, and their associated IT systems, i.e. EIS, can support delivery of different kinds of outcome, which are not always directly linked to financial value. In fact, today's businesses include both financial organisations as well as public organisations, which deliver services to the public. The success or value of these types of services is not always evaluated by the financial results they deliver.

To commence our main discussion on EIS, we first discuss enterprises; in our view, an EIS supports business processes of an enterprise. It is important to have an understanding of an enterprise to understand what an EIS is.

What Is an Enterprise?

The literature is not rich on the history of enterprises; however, Fruin (1992) is one of the researchers that explained the history of enterprises briefly and with an eye on the Japanese revolution in industry and business. According to this book:

The enterprise system appeared around the turn of the twentieth century when the factory system was effectively joined with a managerial hierarchy in production and distribution. It is the emerging coordination of previously independent organizations for production, management, and distribution-shop-floor, front office, and sales office- that generates the organizational innovation known as the Japanese enterprise system. (Fruin, 1992, p. 89).

According to Fruin (1992), the notion of an enterprise system was established after the First World War, when new industries came to the market and many industries combined and amalgamated. Three types of enterprises were identified: National, Urban and Rural; which all have some common elements such as inter-firm relations, Marketing, Mode of Competition, Finance, Ownership, Management, Administrative Coordination, Government Relations.

Mitsubishi is an example of an enterprise dating back to 1926; it integrates distinct yet affiliated companies, particularly Mitsubishi Heavy Industry, Mitsubishi Warehousing, Mitsubishi trading, Mitsubishi Mining, Mitsubishi Bank, Mitsubishi Electric, Mitsubishi Trust, Mitsubishi property, Mitsubishi steel, Mitsubishi Oil, Nippon Industrial Chemicals, and Mitsubishi Insurance (Fruin, 1992). There are many other examples of enterprises including Boeing, General Electric, Kodak, IBM, Norwich Union, Samsung, and Philips. From a consumer or client's point of view, these enterprises are often perceived as involving only one single organisation (e.g., Mitsubishi's car division). Another example in this area is General Electric, which has independent divisions focusing on healthcare, aviation, oil and gas, energy, electrical distribution, security, and many others (GeneralElectric, 2008).

History shows that enterprises have existed from the turn of the twentieth century; nevertheless, the concept still suffers from an unclear definition.

Conclusion

Today's large-scale IT systems increasingly provide support for the business processes of organisations. The aim of using information systems is to increase the automation of the processes within organisations. Enterprises integrate organisations, departments, and even entire businesses to achieve shared goals. Processes within enterprises can benefit from IT infrastructure; in this section, we have argued for calling such IT infrastructure an EIS.

Working Definition

From the discussion on the history of enterprises and challenges of large scale software systems, we see that EIS are computer-based systems that satisfy the requirements of enterprises. EIS are designed and developed for enterprises rather than a single business unit or department. They can deal with the problems of a large organisation (which includes different SMEs or different partners), and they can deal with the problems of a medium or small enterprise (which is an organisation that includes different departments).

This working definition will be refined in later sections. After providing a brief background for EIS, we will discuss the definition in more detail.

ENTERPRISE INFORMATION SYSTEMS

Introduction

Based on the working definition developed in the last section, in this section we focus on refining the definition to include additional detail, particularly in the organisational and business context. As a result, this section proposes a concrete definition for EIS. To help explain the definition further, and partly to validate it, we relate it to well-known examples of organisations.

Challenges

The notion of enterprise is a widely used term for instance in the case of Mitsubishi. However, a precise definition of what constitutes an enterprise – and hence, what precisely constitutes an EIS – is still missing. One of the main difficulties in defining what is an EIS is in distinguishing it from any other large-scale software system. For example, perceived challenges in designing and developing an EIS will arise in the form of having to meet fixed costs of development, in dealing with volatile requirements, and in managing the complexity of the EIS. However, these are also challenges all kinds of large-scale software systems. Therefore, we do not aim to enumerate all of the design and development challenges of EIS; instead, this section will address one of the essential challenges, which is unclear definition for EIS; hence, we aim to propose a definition for this term.

To define EIS, this study reviewed the current definitions found in the literature; the next section will cover some of them.

State of the Art Definition

Organisations continue to find that they need systems that span their entire organisation and tie various functionalities together. As a result, an understanding of enterprise systems is critical to succeed in today's competitive and ever changing world (Jessup & Valacich, 2006).

A good definition for EIS introduced it as a software system with the specific ability to integrate other software systems of an organisation.

Enterprise systems integrate the key business processes of a firm into a single software system so that information can flow seamlessly through the organization, improve coordination, efficiency, and decision making. Enterprise software is based on a suite of integrated software modules and a common central database. The database collects data from and feeds the data into numerous applications that can support nearly all of an organization's internal business activities. When new information is entered by one process, the information is made available immediately to other business processes. Organization, which implements enterprise software, would have to adopt the business processes embedded in the software and, if necessary, change their business processes to conform to those in the software. Enterprise systems support organizational centralization by enforcing uniform data standards and business processes throughout the company and a single unified technology platform. (Laudon & Laudon, 2007, p. 382)

This definition seems very specific on what is an EIS; however, there are points that are ignored by this definition. For example, the argument that mentioned when new information is entered by one process, the information is made available immediately to all other business processes. However, it can be argued that the information should be available to the other processes depending on their access domain. By this, we mean the level of access to the information should be different from process to process. It is not reasonable to expose information to the processes, which do not require it. Therefore, based on the access level of processes, only the suitable and updated information should be visible. This security policy does not have any contrast with the idea of enterprise processes, which their goal is to let the information flow seamlessly.

Moreover, (Strong & Volkoff, 2004, p. 22) defines an ES as a system which its task is to support and *"integrate a full range of business processes, uniting functional islands and making their data visible across the organization in real time"*. This definition adds to the previous definition, the fact that the data and information entailed by the system should be understandable by all its business processes.

Another definition for enterprise systems is based on legacy systems; a legacy system is an existing computer system or application program, which continues to be used because the company does not want to replace or redesign it (Robertson, 1997). Most established companies, who have been using a system for long time, are in this group. Legacy systems mainly suffer from deficiency of documentation, slow hardware and difficulties in improvement, maintenance and expansion. However, there is evidence that overtime EIS replaces the stand alone applications and the functionality of legacy systems (Strong & Volkoff, 2004). In contrast to enterprise systems, legacy systems are not designed to communicate with other applications beyond departmental boundaries (Jessup & Valacich, 2006) even if middleware offers a potential solution to adapt the novel parts with the legacy system. Nevertheless, regarding the price of developing a middleware, the following question comes to mind: can middleware alone solve the problem of integrating new subsystems with a legacy system?

In short, the common idea in the existing definitions illustrates that an EIS is about various businesses, business processes, organisations, information systems, and information that circulates across the enterprise. In other words, EIS is about the businesses model in the organisation. Therefore, the two main elements of EIS are organisation and business. The two following sections cover these points.

Organisation

The EIS definitions that we extracted from the literature linked the EIS to organisations (Laudon & Laudon, 2007; Strong & Volkoff, 2004) or

Table 1. Organisations' categories

Type of Organisation	Decision Makers	Value for Money	Owner	Goal(s)	Example
Public	Elected members	Yes	Public	Supply Services to or for the Public	UK central Government
Private	Share holders	No	Share holders	Satisfy customers/ Satisfy staff/ Satisfy owners	Mitsubishi
Not for Profit	Elected Manager	Yes	Members/ Customers	Provide some services for the society or members	NCH (Children Charity)

large companies (Jessup & Valacich, 2006) and we assume that in both cases the definitions refer to the same concept: organisation. Based on this assumption, it is vital to review the different types of organisations that can influence the different types of EIS. Therefore, this section discusses categorise of organisations based on their goals. Elizabeth Buck categorises organisations in three groups (Buck, 2000):

- Public Organisations
- Private Organisations
- Not for Profit Organisations

The *public organisations* include central or local government, where elected members (e.g., minister) will decide on the goals of organisations, and may influence how goals are achieved. The aim of this type of organisation is to supply services to or for the public, considering a 'value for money' rule. Examples of this type of organisation can be health service, prison, police, social security, environmental protection, the armed forces, etc.

Individuals or other private organisations own *private sectors* organisations. This group of organisations can have the following goals:

- Satisfy their customer
- Satisfy their staff
- Satisfy their owners

All the above goals focus on increasing the market demands for products or services.

Examples of *not for the profit* organisations could be charities, mutual societies, etc, which provide some services for the society. The customers are also the member of the mutual society; therefore, they are the owner of the business. The value for money rule exists in this group too. The usual way to evaluate the success of this group of organisations is to measure how well they achieve their goals considering the available resources. Table 1 illustrates some of the characteristics of organisations that were described; it also summarises the different type of organisations.

By understanding the categories of organisations, we can focus on understanding their goals. By knowing the goals of organisations we can design and develop an EIS that satisfy the defined requirements and goals; but there are other questions in this area: what are the EIS' goals? Are the goals of EIS similar to the goals of organisations? It seems that EIS' goals could be a sub set of the organisations' goals. When the EIS' goals get closer to the goals of organisations it could become a better EIS. The final and optimistic goal for an EIS is to improve the goals of the organisation it services. However, defining the goals of an EIS is the path for analysing and developing the organisation's business model and thus the next section will explore the role of business in the definition of EIS.

Figure 1. Business model [based on (Kaisler, Armoiur, & Valivullah, 2005)]

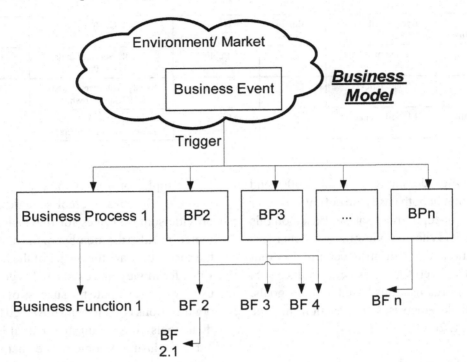

Business

Another main factor that influences the architecture and functionality of an EIS is the business model (Figure 1). Supporting the strong relationship between business processes is the aim of ES. In fact, the ability to define various business processes in enterprise systems is the element that distinguishes them from normal systems for a company or a department; for example BMW involves in a diversity of businesses to produce cars or engines for other car brands (e.g. Rolls-Royce), in addition to building bicycles and boats. A normal system in a company contains components and subsystems that belong to one specific business and satisfy its requirements. A normal company may need to contact other companies to continue its business but involving partners or suppliers is not their main concern. In contrast to normal company where the focus is on one particular business, an enterprise focuses on a collection of business processes which could be relevant to each other or not but all of them are under the arch of the main principals of the enterprise. Indeed, making profit is not one of the essences of business model. There are non-profit governmental or non-governmental organisations such as healthcare organisations that can have their own business model which deals with the process of treating patients.

The presentation of Enterprise System in this chapter is not about detailed implementation of business functions; its focus is mainly about a very top-level view on the whole business model of an organisation as defined by Clifton (2000):

business involves a complex mix of people, policy and technology, and exist within the constraints of economics and society (Clifton, Ince, & Sutcliffe, 2000, p. 1).

Figure 1 illustrates the general structure of a business model where the business model includes business processes and business functions. Business processes are "*a set of logically related tasks performed to achieve a defined business outcome*" (Davenport & Short, 1990, p. 100). For example, in the case of BMW, the business processes is putting new orders for part suppliers. When there is a new demand for specific car (e.g. model Z5), this new market request creates a business event that triggers a set of business processes such as increasing the amount of resources for producing the Z5 (e.g. BP2 in Figure 1), and putting new orders for parts suppliers. Each of these business processes is subdivided into different business functions (e.g. BF2 and BF3 in Figure 1). Examples include the functions required for inputting new orders such as checking the parts suppliers' ability for new demands, organising the time that is needed for each part to arrive to assembly line, etc.

According to (Kaisler, Armoiur, & Valivullah, 2005, p. 2) "*business processes must be modelled and aligned across the function, data and information systems that implement the processes*". Therefore, the term business function in our research refers to the functionality that is required for implementing a business process. Figure 1 is a simple explanation for business process model. Each of these business functions can trigger a business process too. Moreover, the business processes can breakdown to other business processes, which is not shown in this diagram to keep it simple to understand. The aim of this diagram is mainly to explain business processes and functions in a general business model.

Understanding business models is helpful for developing EIS because their role is to integrate a full range of business processes (Strong & Volkoff, 2004). Before defining the concept of EIS, Legacy systems were the type of systems that were developed to handle the requirements of organisations (Robertson, 1997). However, legacy systems are not designed to communicate with other applications beyond departmental boundar-

ies (Jessup & Valacich, 2006); hence the concept of EIS has grown to fill this gap.

In short, the common idea in existing definitions illustrates that an EIS amalgamates concerns from various businesses, business processes, organisations, information systems, and information that circulate across an enterprise. In other words, it is about the business models of the organisation. However, a definition for EIS that just emphasises the financial profit side of businesses for organisations is out of date. In the next section, a definition that considers other aspect of organisations, the domain and objectives of EIS is proposed.

Enterprise Information System Definition

This section proposes a definition for EIS, which is the result of our analysis of the state-of-the-art definitions and of industrial case studies. The definition that considers business and organisational aspects of EIS is as follow:

An Enterprise Information System is a software system that integrates the business processes of organisation(s) to improve their functioning.

Integration of business processes plays an important role in this definition. Integration could be accomplished by providing standards for data and business processes. These standards will be applied to various part of the system such as a database or clusters of databases. As the result of such integration, information may flow seamlessly.

Another point in this definition is the software characteristics of EIS. At this stage, we consider EIS as a type of Information System; therefore, this software system includes both humans and hardware.

The next term, used in the definition is organisation. Different types of organisations are discussed earlier in this chapter. Organisations may include an organisation with its partners, or a group of organisations. Table 2 refines the above definition

Table 2. EIS boundaries, objectives and challenges

Objective	Integrity of the organisation and collaborators
	Seamless Information flow
	Suitable access to data and information for various stakeholders
	Matching the software system structure with organisation structure
Goal	Improving coordination, efficiency, and decision-making of business process in an organisation
Domain	Covers the internal and external business activities of organisation
Challenge	Security challenges that should be considered carefully for organisations' processes. Otherwise, mixing the required information of one business process with another one can cause problem for the organisation
	Improve flexibility in organisation processes

and describes what we propose as the objectives, goals, domain, and challenges of EIS.

In addition, Figure 2 describes the definition of EIS graphically. Note that BP in this figure are business processes. As it can be seen in this figure, each organisation contains various business processes. Moreover, in Figure 2, the database could be a cluster of databases; however, it is highly likely that there would be a single interface to exchange data with the database without having a concern about where the data is and what are the various resources. As can be seen in this figure, the bigger rectangle describes the boundaries of EIS, which is flexible.

The two following sections aim at continuing the discussion about EIS by presenting some examples in this area. The results of reviewing these examples lead to a better clarification of what is an EIS and what is not.

Examples of Enterprise Information System

The review of the industrial cases of what might be considered as an EIS moves our discussion toward the example of Mitsubishi. As was mentioned earlier, Mitsubishi with more than 400 companies all around the word is an example of enterprises (Mitsubishi, 2007). Thirty top-level managers manage all the individual Mitsubishi's companies. This does not mean that each company

does not have enough freedom to make their own decisions; it means that this group of thirty managers will make some of the top-level decisions and they provide the high-level standards that all these companies should consider. In this case, if there is a computer based system that links various parts of the Mitsubishi organisation (including high-level managers) together and makes information flow seamlessly between them, then we view this system as an EIS. Developing such a system is a large and complex problem; hence, there is a need for powerful, reusable solutions to develop this type of system in a manner that can benefit all of the enterprise.

Another example in this area is the infrastructure being developed to support the National Health Service (NHS) in the United Kingdom where the information systems being developed to support management of patients' records and prescriptions can be considered as an EIS, because such IT infrastructure aims to connect independent departments within and outside of the NHS. While we are looking at the NHS, which is a public sector organisation, we can raise e-Government as another example of public sector organisation that may be supported by and hence benefit from, EIS infrastructure because it connects various governmental organisations or departments together to let information flow seamlessly between them.

Figure 2. An enterprise information system

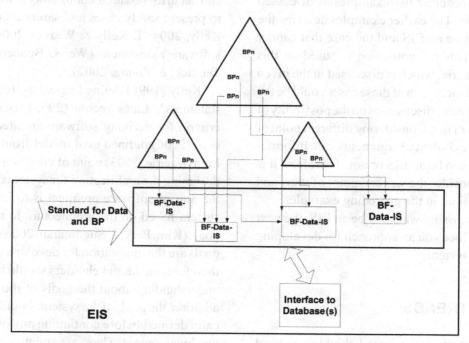

What Cannot Be an Enterprise Information System

As we were discussing the public, private, and governmental examples for an EIS, the next step is introducing some examples of Information Systems that are not EIS according to our definition.

eBay is one of the well known international Information Systems that focuses in the auction industry. This online market which involves around 147 million people (Gopalkrishnan & Gupta, 2007) provides a platform for individuals or companies to trade their products or services; but it does not connect the business processes of organisations together. Therefore, according to our definition, an EIS connects different business processes of organisations or departments of organisation together to make the information flow seamlessly and thus it seems that based on this characteristic of EIS, eBay is not an EIS. The information system is the element that processes

data and put them online, there is no evidence of connection between business processes because it is not a requirement in this Information System. The same argument can be followed in the case of Amazon, therefore even though it is large-scale and international online shop but it is not an EIS.

Conclusion

In short, this section described EIS in more detail by providing the definition for EIS. Defining any kind of system is essential for defining its domain and objectives. Without this basic information, the researches on the similar area will not be consistent. However, there is no claim that the given definition is the only definition for EIS. This definition is based on our studies, observations, interviews, and comparisons on the current theoretical and practical definitions and case studies. Part of this ongoing work is presented in this chapter.

To make the results of our study on the definition of EIS more clear, two examples are discussed in this section. The earlier examples describe the case that can be an EIS and the case that cannot be an EIS. This categorisation is based on this chapter's criteria, which is discussed in the given definition. Hence, each of these cases could be the objective for more discussions on the possibility of being an EIS or not. Considering different point of views and the context of arguments, one Information System can be an EIS or not. Therefore, it is crucial to consider the writers' point of view and given definition, in the preceding examples.

After discussing what can be an EIS, the next section will focus on an approach for developing this type of system.

FUTURE TRENDS

Goal-based and goal-oriented thinking is used to plan for the future or to solve problems (Kim, Park, & Sugumaran, 2006). The concept of using goal-oriented techniques has been proposed as one possible way to manage some of the difficulties associated with developing large-scale complex systems (Kavakli, Loucopoulos, & Filippidou, 1996), particularly the challenge of clearly identifying and specifying requirements. As we discussed in the previous section, an EIS is an instance of large-scale complex system. This section promotes the idea of using goal-oriented modelling techniques for developing EIS by briefly discussing them and their roles in defining EIS system requirements. We will summarise our discussion on goal-oriented techniques by presenting an example of goal graph.

Goal Oriented Techniques

Goal oriented techniques have been widely discussed in the requirement engineering domain (T. P. Kelly, McDermid, Murdoch, & Wilson, 1998; Axel van Lamsweerde, 2001; A. V. Lamsweerde, 2004). Goals are also used in the safety and security research community – for example, to present safety cases and safety arguments (T. Kelly, 2004; T. Kelly & Weaver, 2004) - and in software assessment (Weiss, Bennett, Payseur, Tendick, & Zhang, 2002).

Kelly (1998) defined a goal as 'requirements statement', Lamsweerde (2003) used goals as criteria for deriving software architecture. Kim et al (2006) defined goal model from (Axel van Lamsweerde, 2003) point of view as a criteria for designing the architecture for systems; therefore, the aim of software architect is to implement a system based on the architecture to accomplish goals (Kim, Park, & Sugumaran, 2006). Logically goals are the motivation for developing a system; therefore, all the stakeholders should have a clear understanding about the goals of the system. In addition, the goals of the system should be realistically defined before continuing any other step of the development. There are attempts to show the goals in graphical notations such as GSN (Timothy Patrick Kelly, 1998), Kaos (Axel van Lamsweerde, 2001), and (Kim, Park, & Sugumaran, 2006). Moreover, Kaos defines the formal textual notation to describe the goals in addition to informal text. This attempt is respectful because it considers the larger group of audience to understand and benefit from the goal model.

Different stakeholders require different forms of presentation for their goals. For example, the high-level manager may not require seeing a formal explanation of the goals because they may not understand it; however, they can better understand an informal explanation in a simple diagram. On the other hand, there is a good possibility that a programmer's team, requires the formal explanation for the goals in detail to understand and implement the system in the correct and expected way. It is important to bear in mind that goal diagrams are aimed at making the system more clear to different stakeholders, therefore goal-oriented ideas should prevent adding more confusions for different stakeholders. Any approach that makes the goals of the system more clear for stakeholders should be considered; it can be different goal models for different stakeholders.

The next section explains an approach for designing a goal model. This approach is very high level without explaining the details. The aim is to introduce a possible approach for developing a goal model to readers. This approach benefits from the information in similar studies in this area such as (Timothy Patrick Kelly, 1998; Kim, Park, & Sugumaran, 2006; Axel van Lamsweerde, 2001).

Designing a Goal Model

One of the main reasons for developing unsuccessful software systems is unrealistic planning and design. Hence, the aim of goal-oriented approaches, as discussed in the previous section, is to provide an environment such that different stakeholders can understand the goals at different levels of abstraction and decomposition. One way to accomplish this is to use a graphical modelling language, such as GSN; another way is by documenting the requirements and design precisely and accurately using a textual format. It is also possible to present the prototype of the system and discuss it with various stakeholders. All these approaches and other similar ones could be beneficial for different type of systems. The approach that is discussed in this section is a simple approach for developing a goal model. The aim is to develop a goal model that can present the system's high-level goals clearly. Furthermore, it does not involve the details of the goals or their descriptions; this can help to provide an understandable top down model for high-level goals of the system for non-technical decision makers.

The basics of this approach for designing a goal model is to create a list of goals, a list of actions, and a list of occurred problems. Goals were defined earlier; actions according to (Kim, Park, & Sugumaran, 2006, p. 543) *"are the atomic unit for representing software behaviour, which can be observed at runtime and has a start and*

end point of execution". This paper also argues that most methods in the class diagram can be action, but because the runtime of actions should be observable, the size of the action should be restricted in a manner that makes it possible to be observed in the software model.

The issues in this case are the challenges and difficulties that occur when developers consider the implementation and the execution of a system. These challenges can be a technical difficulties, or goal conflicts, etc.

After producing the goals, actions, and problems lists, the relation between these elements should be created. The notation here is similar to the notation in (Kim, Park, & Sugumaran, 2006), which is as follows:

$$(G_z, A_n) \rightarrow P_x$$

A represents an action, G represents a Goal, and z and n are the symbolized identification of random variables that present the ID of the goal, for instance, it can be G 1.1.2, which means goal with ID 1.1.2. An example of action could be 1.1.2/1, which presents the required action that can be done to achieve this goal.

The next notation illustrates the relationship between a goal, action, and problem. Following is an example of this notation:

$$P_x \rightarrow (G_z, A_n)$$

The above notation means, the Action with ID n which is required for satisfying Goal with ID z can cause the problem with ID x. This notation describes the case where action that belongs to a goal causes a problem or problems. The next notation describes the case that a problem can be solved using a specific action:

$$P_x \rightarrow (G_z, A_n)$$

The above notation means to solve the problem P with ID x, the Goal G with ID z is required,

427

and to satisfy this goal Action with ID n should be done.

In the case that the developer team does not know the required action yet, action n (An) can be replaced with '?'. Before starting to implement the system, all the question marks (?) should be filled with actions as solutions to satisfy goals. Nevertheless, in the case that as the result of limitations in the technology, resources, etc. one or more question mark (?) cannot be replaced by solution, there could be a bottom-up check to see if the system is still worth implementing; considering the unsolved problem(s), the functionality of the system should not rely on the non available solutions.

However as it was discussed before, a goal model should have different levels of abstractions for different users. Hence, designers should avoid destroying the purpose of the goal model, which is to make the systems goals clear for stakeholders by mixing and presenting all the information to the ones who does not require it. The next section will provides an example of goal model for stroke care.

Example

The aim of the case study is to design the goal model for a system that collects the data of treatment for a specific serious condition. The data can be collected from different sources such as doctors, researchers, nurses, emergency staff, etc. Moreover, each of these stakeholders can have a different way of communicating with the database, for instance, laptop, paper, phone, etc. The role of this system is to collect the data from various sources, analyse them and provide some data as an output for different purposes. Based on the case study in (Bobrow.D.G, 2002) we can call this system a knowledge sharing system.

Figure 3 illustrates the described system. In this figure the boundaries of the described system is shown as a box surrounding it. The big arrow in the left hand side of the box illustrates the fact that this system is one of the information systems in the defined enterprise. The enterprise in this figure is shown using a pyramid, which is mainly a symbol of organisation.

To make this figure simple and clear we did not include the option that this EIS can be shared and used with other enterprises around the globe. Note that by having a design for EIS, we try to have a big picture of enterprise that includes the possible changes and extension in the future. The EIS does not have a local design that cannot be used when changes occur. The current solution for extending a system or merging systems is mainly developing middleware, which enterprise architect should avoid relying just on middleware. Considering that in some cases middleware can be so expensive that the organisation's decision makers may decide to use manual paper based system instead.

After drawing an overall view of the requested system, the goal of the system should be defined. Each goal should have its own action, which acts as a solution for the system and the possible problems. Figure 4 illustrates the goal diagram for this system. This diagram is very high-level, which targeted non-technical decision makers. This diagram is the starting point for creating a complete goal model for this system. As can be seen in this diagram, goals have their unit identity, which in this case is shown by numbers. These numbers makes the traceability of goals possible within this model. In addition, it is possible to implement it in tools for drawing diagrams. This is a AND-OR graph and it means the parent goal with OR child can be satisfied when at least one of the child goal reach to the solution. It is similar to AND-OR in logic mathematic. Furthermore, goal graph is a weight graph; hence, the goals in the same level can be prioritised over other goals.

Prioritizing goals is helpful in different context. For example, in allocating resources or in some cases, when satisfying a lower priority goal is depend on satisfying the higher priority goal. In general, Figure 4 shows the basic requirements for

Figure 3. Example of knowledge sharing system

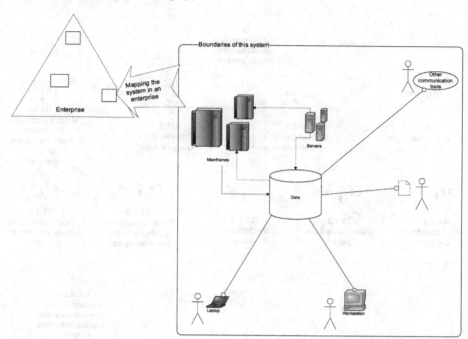

the goal graph. We emphasise that the aim of this graph is to provide the high-level clear image of the system's goals and present it to the stakeholders to be used for brainstorming for example.

Conclusion

In conclusion, this section proposed the future work for the study on how to develop EIS. The fact that developing required components for EIS can be similar to other large-scale complex system makes this field of work valuable; because finding better solutions for different challenges of Information Systems provides a platform for developing various kinds of suitable systems. This effort and study on EIS provides an easier and safer life for individuals and organisations that benefit from this type of IT products. It influences the government's performance, it provides better innovative platform for industries. All these reasons bestow enough motivations for us to continue improving this study.

CONCLUSION

By looking at various ways that the word 'enterprise' is used, it becomes clear that there is an ambiguity in this term. Yet this term and others such as 'Enterprise Architecture', 'Enterprise Information System', etc. are increasingly used. This fact encourages us to look at these terms and clarify them for future use in our research and other relevant ones. The simple definition for enterprise is an entity engaged in economic activities. This definition does not cover requirements for defining an EIS. The argument in this chapter illustrates that an EIS covering the requirements of any entity engaged in economy activity is simply an IS and they can hardly be categorized as a separate group with the name of EIS. The fact that the number of people employed by an organisation can increase the complexity of the software system in some cases is hardly the leading factor in developing an EIS. The basic requirement for research on how to improve the development of EIS is to achieve more knowledge on what an EIS is.

Figure 4. Goal graph

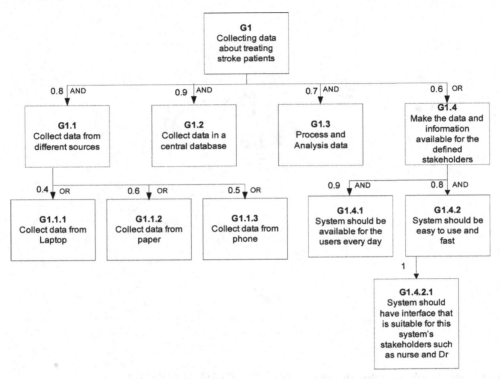

Consequently, the main objective of this chapter was to explore the boundaries of EIS; this was achieved by developing a definition for EIS. This definition captured what we believe are the important characteristics that should be considered while we attempt to build an EIS; characteristics such as organisations, their goals, business processes, and the business model. None of these characteristics is based on the size of the organisation; therefore, it can cover different sizes of enterprises, small, medium, or large. Accordingly, this chapter did not use a specific term such as SME, Small and Medium Enterprises, to define EIS.

Any discussion of EIS encompasses a number of facets, including general IT system development, requirements, organisational theory, and distributed systems technology. Our aim is to more precisely define what an EIS is, and what it is not, to assist in providing better methodologies and techniques for building such increasingly important software systems. We believe that it is clear that the volatile requirements of modern organisations require special business processes, and these business processes cannot be fully achieved without IT systems and in some cases without an EIS. A high-quality EIS can provide a connection between the different, independent business processes in an enterprise.

As discussed, we argue that goal-oriented modelling techniques are important for helping to understand what is required for a business or organisation, and for understanding what an EIS should provide. Thus, we argue that a first step for developing a system for an enterprise is to find and justify the enterprise's goals. When all the stakeholders have a clear idea about the goals of the enterprise, their expectations will be realistic in principle; the desired system's boundary should be more precisely defined, and in principle building the system should be possible. We do not claim that following this approach will provide a full guarantee for developing a suitable EIS: such systems are always challenging to build, and goal-oriented techniques only tackle an important part of a large problem. Additional research and experiments are needed to identify what further techniques are needed to supplement goal-oriented modelling for designing, implementing, deploying, and maintaining Enterprise Information Systems.

ACKNOWLEDGMENT

We would like to thank Dr. Fiona Polack for her valuable suggestions.

REFERENCES

Bobrow.D.G, W. J. (2002). Community knowledge sharing in practice: The Eureka story. *Society for organizational learning and Massachusetts Institute of Technology, 4,* 47-59.

Buck, E. (2000). Different Types of organisation. *NEBS Management/QMD Ltd.* Retrieved September 1, 2008 from http://www.teamsthatwork.co.uk/Organise%20&%20improve%20team%20work%201.pdf

Clifton, H., Ince, D. C., & Sutcliffe, A. G. (2000). *Business information systems* (6th ed.). Essex, England: Pearson Education Limited.

Davenport, T. H., & Short, J. E. (1990). The New industrial engineering, information technology and business redesign. In M. Lewis & N. Slack (Eds.), *Operations management: Critical perspectives on business and management* (pp. 97-123). London and New York: Routledge.

Edwards, C., Ward, J., & Bytheway, A. (1993). *The essence of information systems* (2nd ed.). London: Prentice Hall.

Fruin, M. W. (1992). *The Japanese enterprise system.* New York: Oxford University Press.

GeneralElectric. (2008). Product and services. Retrieved September 1, 2008 from http://www.ge.com/products_services/index.html

Gopalkrishnan, J., & Gupta, V. K. (2007). eBay: "The world's largest online marketplace" - A Case Study. *Conference on Global Competition and Competitiveness of Indian Corporate* (pp. 543-549).

Jessup, L., & Valacich, J. (2006). *Information systems today, why is matters* (2nd ed.). NJ: Pearson Education, Inc.

Kaisler, S., Armoiur, F., & Valivullah, M. (2005). *Enterprise architecting: Critical problems.* Paper presented at the 38th Annual Hawaii International Conference on System Sciences, Island of Hawaii, HI.

Kavakli, E. V., Loucopoulos, P., & Filippidou, D. (1996). *Using scenarios to systematically support goal-directed elaboration for information system requirements.* Paper presented at the IEEE Symposium and Workshop on Engineering of Computer Based Systems(ECBS '96), Friedrichshafen, Germany.

Kelly, T. (2004). *A Systematic approach to safety case management.* Paper presented at the SAE 2004 World Congress, Detroit, MI.

Kelly, T., & Weaver, R. A. (2004). *The goal structuring notation - A safety argument notation.* Paper presented at the 2004 International Conference on Dependable Systems and Networks (DSN 2004), Florence, Italy.

Kelly, T. P. (1998). *Arguing Safety- A systematic approach to managing safety cases.* University of York, York.

Kelly, T. P., McDermid, J., Murdoch, J., & Wilson, S. (1998). The goal structuring notation: A means for capturing requirements, rationale and evidence. In A. J. Vickers & L. S. Brooks (Eds.), *Requirements engineering at the University of York*: University of York.

Kim, J. S., Park, S., & Sugumaran, V. (2006). Contextual problem detection and management during software execution. *Industrial Management & Data Systems*, *106*, 540–561. doi:10.1108/02635570610661615

Lamsweerde, A. v. (2001). *Goal-oriented requirements engineering: A guided tour.* Paper presented at the 5th IEEE International Symposium on Requirements Engineering (RE'01), Toronto, Canada.

Lamsweerde, A. v. (2003). *From system goals to software architecture. Formal methods for software architectures* (. *LNCS, 2804,* 25–43.

Lamsweerde, A. V. (2004). *Goal-oriented requirements engineering: A roundtrip from research to practice.* Paper presented at the 12th IEEE Joint International Requirements Engineering Conference(RE'04,), Kyoto, Japan.

Laudon, J. P., & Laudon, K. C. (2007). *Management information systems: Managing the digital firm* (10th ed.). Prentice Hall.

Mitsubishi. (2007). *About Mitsubishi*. Retrieved September 1 2008, from http://www.mitsubishi.com/e/group/about.html

Projects, T. C. C. I. (2004). The challenges of complex IT projects. Retrieved September 1, 2008, from http://www.bcs.org/server_process.php?show=conWebDoc.1167

Robertson, P. (1997). Integrating legacy systems with modern corporate applications. *Communications of the ACM, 40*(5), 39–46. doi:10.1145/253769.253785

Strong, D. M., & Volkoff, O. (2004). A roadmap for Enterprise system implementation. *IEEE Computer Society, 37,* 22–29.

Terry, P. (1975). Organisation behaviour. *Industrial & Commercial Training, 7*(11), 462–466. doi:10.1108/eb003504

Weiss, D. M., Bennett, D., Payseur, J. Y., Tendick, P., & Zhang, P. (2002). *Goal-oriented software assessment.* Paper presented at the 24th International Conference on Software Engineering (ICSE '02), Orlando, FL.

Section 4
Critical Success Factors and Case Studies

Chapter 22
Enterprise Information Systems:
Two Case Studies

Hui-Lien Tung
Paine College, USA

Tina Marshall-Bradley
Paine College, USA

Joseph Wood
US Army

Donald A. Sofge
Naval Research Laboratory, USA

James Grayson
Augusta State University, USA

Margo Bergman
Michael E. DeBakey VA Medical Center, USA

W.F. Lawless
Paine College, USA

ABSTRACT

Enterprise Information Systems (EIS) provide a platform that enables small organizations and distant collections of organizations to better integrate and coordinate their operations. We provide a theory of organizations and review two case studies beginning to use EIS-type architectures that form common information infrastructures to be more responsive, flexible and agile first for a system of medical organizations and second for a small college. The system of organizations is a distributed collection of military medical department research centers (MDRC) whose mission is to train physicians how to conduct and publish research; and the small college is providing a liberal arts education (Future College). Both MDRC and Future College (pseudonyms) are reorganizing their operations. We review theory for our approach, the two case studies, field evidence, computational models, and future prospects.

DOI: 10.4018/978-1-60566-856-7.ch022

INTRODUCTION

Enterprise Information Systems (EIS) attempt to reduce the fragmentation and uncertainty in the information gathered from an organization on its internal and external interactions among agents, where agents are individuals, machines, or other organizations. Many social psychological forces oppose standardization. At a fundamental level, whether for individual agents, groups or organizations, bistable perceptions require uncertainty in the interaction. As one agent or collective acts while its partner(s) observe, uncertainty exists for both action and observation behaviors. An interaction occurs when these two behaviors are interdependent during an interaction, entangling the two agents or collections of agents together. Entanglement produces two effects: the conservation of information (COI) and mutual or bistable changes.

Interactions between action and observation under uncertainty introduce illusions into connections between worldviews and reality (Kuhn, 1970), making management and research both struggle to understand the information derived from the interactions in an enterprise. We attribute these struggles to managers and scientists embedded in the social fabric (Axsom & Lawless, 1992), the lack of a measurement theory of interdependence, and the difficulty of testing interdependence in the laboratory. In addition to our two case studies, we include field research with observations of citizen organizations advising the Department of Energy (DOE) on its environmental cleanup; laboratory simulations of DOE field results; stock market data; and computational modeling (coupled differential equations, control theory, AI, Gaussian distributions, uncertainty models, Fourier transform pairs, continuous and discrete wavelets). Results from our laboratory experiments and stock market data agree with our theory (e.g., Lawless et al., 2008a), but many questions remain. Our objective is to incorporate computational interdependent uncertainty into providing information that can be used autonomously and online with EIS metrics to better manage organizations entangled internally with their personnel and externally with other organizations.

Four Objectives for the Two Case Studies

In general, in the following four objectives for the EIS system used in the two Case Studies, we address document and content management, website management and maintenance, customer relationship management, financial costs, internal and external communication processes, and training. However, both of our case studies are just beginning to implement their EIS systems; thus, objectives 2-4 are more for future rather than immediate objectives.

- As our primary focus, we introduce and discuss the challenges and problems associated with the differing social, organizational and technological perspectives. This includes the implications for the organization and its members for the new technologies. We discuss the social aspects by focusing on the resistance to change and the levels of trust and confidence in the new system.
- We discuss the importance of an EIS to small and medium enterprises and the technology functionality used to integrate information and administer the enterprises by generating more reliable and relevant operational information. This first objective entails the design, execution and impact of a new system in both case studies, with a particular focus on the impact of the EIS system on the functional areas of the organization (new units that are included; changes in employment numbers, employee reassignments, etc.).
- We present the practical solutions used in the two case studies to produce tailor-made

EIS systems. This includes the problems that arise and how those problems are being solved. This objective addresses collaboration and command decisions. In both case studies, we look at collaboration at a distance and its relevance to networked and virtual organizations (NVOs; see Lawless et al., 2008b).

- We discuss integrated solutions, including the enterprise architecture design, modeling and integration. The focus here is on how well the new system integrates with legacy information systems. In addition, we review how well integration occurred. The end result is expected to improve operational performance. What metrics are key performance indicators and the parameters that were used to gauge improvements in organizational productivity are reviewed and discussed. Critical success factors are included and discussed.

BACKGROUND

In this section, we define and review key terms. At the end of our paper, we briefly summarize the key terms.

Enterprise Information System (EIS). An EIS is a centralized service for standardizing data in an organization or system (Moore et al., 2005). It reduces information fragmentation by replacing independent formats with a standardized template or structure for data that reduces variability across the internal borders of an organization. The template replaces programming. An EIS increases data sharing in an organization and makes data mining and computational organizational models possible, generating trends from using business intelligence mined from the organizational data. In turn, models make available web-based enterprise control (decision-making) for the organization that entails planning, execution, resource management, and timing of events (coordination). The model drives an EIS, making data prediction and control

of data flow possible (Lewis et al., 2001). Artificial Intelligence (AI) and agent-based modeling (ABM) are used to implement the controls with an EIS. Models also facilitate the reengineering of organizations. However, not fully considered now but planned for the future, an EIS creates various issues that an organization must address regarding security (briefly considered at this time; see UTM in Footnote 4), data transport, and transactions.

Conservation of Information (COI). The conservation of information (COI) is derived from signal detection theory (SDT). It is based on duration-bandwidth tradeoffs. We have extended the ideas behind COI to organizational performance and to mergers and acquisitions (M&A) (Lawless et al., 2007). Briefly, the shorter the duration of a signal, the wider becomes its bandwidth and vice versa. Applied to organizations, an organization's focus (e.g., situational awareness) can be directed on a broad business model, thereby reducing its ability to execute and vice versa.

Uncertainty. Uncertainty for organizations leads to predictions of counterintuitive effects that can be exploited with an online EIS system to formulate a set of metrics for applying the conservation of information (COI) to organizational performance. In preparation for the possibility of machine-based real-time metrics afforded by today's technology, the results from our field, laboratory and case studies demonstrate a successful theory and its wide application in the field of COI for organizations.

Bistability. Bistability is best illustrated with an illusion. It occurs when one data set can produce two mutually exclusive interpretations. While the entire data set is processed cognitively by an individual, both interpretations of a bistable illusion cannot be held in awareness simultaneously (Cacioppo et al., 1996). According to Bohr (1955), multiple interpretations support the existence of different cultures. Bohr makes it conceivable that the same data has different interpretations in different organizations, either promoting two different cultures or being impacted by them. Given the importance of feedback to social dynamics (Lawless et al., 2007), the possibility of rapid shifts between each bistable interpretation increases uncertainty in a non-observed interpretation which not only can create social problems between different groups, but also support the existence of uncertainty for COI, characterized as tradeoffs between incommensurable views. We propose that measurements with metrics of bistable phenomena collapse interdependence, decreasing uncertainty in observed aspects of a bistable phenomenon while increasing uncertainty in non-observed aspects.

Conservation of Information for Organizations. COI acts as a tradeoff in attention directed at reducing the uncertainty in one factor, such as a worldview or business model, with the result that the uncertainty in a second, interdependent factor is inversely increased, such as the execution of a business model. The more focused a collective of individuals are on acting out a series of steps, the less observant they become of their actions. Applied to organizations, action-observation uncertainty couples form a causal path for different cultures based on multiple interpretations of the same business model or worldview (e.g., religion, liberalism, conservatism). An EIS is designed to reduce multiple interpretations. COI for organizations links uncertainty between planning and execution as well as between resource availability and duration for plan execution (Lawless et al., 2007).

Organizations. Organizations perform a function which cannot be done by an individual alone by assigning interdependent roles to a set of independent individuals, which requires information coordination, channeling and blocking to form its members into a working collective, but which consequently amplifies the capabilities of an individual (Ambrose, 2001). An organization is functional when its operational costs are less than the benefits it accrues and provides to its members. It is likely constructed around a geo-

graphical centroid (Δx_{COG}, defined below) about which its business attributes are centered, planned and modeled (Sukthankar, 2008). But multiple theories of organizations exist (Weick & Quinn, 1999). Pfeffer and Fong (2005) concluded that one of the problems is the lack of a foundational theory for organizations; they proposed the need to incorporate illusions into basic organizational theory. Although "illusions" could be metaphorical, imaginary factors are instrumental in engineering to model oscillations. We propose that illusions injected into discussions interact with real world feedback to generate discussion oscillations until interdependence collapses (metrics about profitability, operational success or failure).

Technology. Technology, such as an EIS, affects the effectiveness and size of organizations. The size of an organization has a limit that is raised by technology (Mattick & Gagen, 2005); i.e., as size increases, competitiveness decreases, but that effect is countered by new technology (e.g., "back office" integration from EIS software). Technology helps to manage tradeoffs in performance, but they still remain (Csete & Doyle, 2002). Mergers often occur to acquire the technology of a firm owning an R&D breakthrough technology to maintain market leadership or to survive. Technology limits a business model. But technology integration can change a business model, which it did for J.P. Morgan Chase, to better manage costs and productivity and to better compete, as in our field research with training physicians in conducting and publishing research for the U.S. Army. Technology can produce market shocks (Andrade et al., 2001) if new companies unexpectedly take the leadership to control a market.

MAIN FOCUS OF THE CHAPTER

An EIS rationalizes observational data by placing it into a common format. But this obscures a fundamental problem with observations. In general, most of social science is predicated on the assumption that observations of behavior, especially the self-observations made in response to data from questionnaires, provide rational, perfect or near perfect information about a target behavior, thereby leaving no room for an uncertainty principle. However, striking problems exist with asking agents about the causes of their behavior (self-reports, surveys, structured interviews, case studies). Baumeister et al. (2005) found that a 30-year meta-analysis of survey data on self-esteem correlated poorly with academic and work performance, casting doubt on one of the most studied phenomena in psychology and also on the ability of self-reports to capture targeted phenomena. Similarly, in an attempt to prove the value of air combat maneuvering for Air Force educators, Lawless and his colleagues (2000) found no association between air combat outcomes (wins-losses) and examination scores on air-combat knowledge. And at the end of his distinguished career in testing game matrices, Kelley (1992) found no association between the preferences as measured by surveys before games were played and the choices actually made during games.

To summarize, EIS metrics interfere with the social process; measurement collapses interdependence, producing static information. Being mindful of this problem, for our EIS-based metrics, we plan to use COI to predict the information about organizational outcomes.

We plan to study organizations with computational models. However, Bankes (2002) and Conzelmann and his colleagues (2004) have both concluded that current computational models of organizations are not predictive, principally with Agent-Based Models (ABMs). We plan two correctives: first, to test models using social configurations addressed by our COI organizational model to reproduce the results that we have predicted and found in the field and laboratory; and second, to build bistable organizations constituted with bistable artificial agents.

Organizational Theory and COI

No theory of organizations is widely accepted today (Pfeffer & Fong, 2005). From Kohli and Hoadley (2006), "few studies have addressed the effectiveness of … ERP … due … to the lack of … organizational measures" (p. 40). In this section, we provide a brief discussion of the problems with traditional organizational theory and, focusing on fundamentals, a classical (conservation of information) alternative model that accounts for traditional theory and field evidence.

Organizational Theory and COI. In contrast to traditional social science, we have attempted to combine individuals with organizations and systems, statics with dynamics, and empirical approaches with theory. In the metric of organizational performance, we incorporate dynamics in our model with the effects of feedback on oscillations within an organization. We incorporate organizations in our model by introducing control as organizations seek to improve in performing or revising their mission (Mattick & Gagen, 2005).

To implement control theory (Csete & Doyle, 2002), we need to quantify an organizational or system's level model. In line with COI, an organization controls at least four aspects of the decision-making process. First, by helping to set or choose its reference or threshold set-points (e.g., culture, decision processes, expectations, planning; and in Case Study 1, mission and vision). Second, by damping unexpected disturbances. Third, by filtering and transforming incoming information about system internal states, inputs, and responses to form patterns and decisions. Finally, by taking actions then collecting feedback to revise decisions. However, Conant and Ashby (1970) concluded that feedback to minimize errors is not an optimal solution for control, that the optimum solution avoided errors (e.g, with a plan that produces the most efficient operation possible).

Mathematics

We have proposed the following mathematical COI relationships (Lawless & Sofge, 2008c).

Geospatial interdependence. Multitasking degrades performance at the individual level (Wickens, 1992). In contrast, the function of a group or organization is to multitask (Ambrose, 2001), implying the existence of interdependence in business models (Jervis, 1997), chains of command, and centers of gravity (COG) (Arnold, 2006). Multitasking requires a coordination between one activity interdependent with several interlinked activities or events, an interdependence between the uncertainty in localizing an event, Δx_{COG}, amid the spatial frequencies for a chain of events, Δk, where $k = 1/\lambda$ and λ is the uncertainty in the distance between spatially observed or geographically controlled interdependent events. For the conservation of information (COI),

$$\Delta x_{COG} \Delta k \geq c. \tag{1}$$

In support of Equation (1), based on suicide bombings in Jerusalem, the pattern for where IEDs will be planted "is always a tradeoff between model accuracy and area reduction that we can describe for any given model" (Willis, 2007, p. 2). Social interdependencies form geospatial wave patterns for the transmission of information, like traffic congestion waves occurring at a critical density when traffic is sufficiently interdependent to transmit waves (Helbing, 2001). Other examples are Wal-Mart's distribution system approaching the holidays; air-traffic patterns at major airports during busy cycles, such as Atlanta or Chicago; and the launch of military operations against Baghdad identified by General Tommy Franks as the COG during Operation Iraqi Freedom (OIF) (Arnold, 2006, p. 13).

Our research has indicated that risk perceptions (illusions), as opposed to risk determinations (science), interfere with achieving practical organizational decisions (Lawless et al., 2008a).

We have found that illusions increase in number and virulence under enforced cooperative decision-making, but that they can be reduced or better managed under a competition for the best among a series of ideas (e.g., see Holmes, 1919). We have revised Equation (1) into Equation (2) to model and study illusions in groups and organizational decision-making. The research of Adelson (2000) suggests the existence of a social cognitive "screen" upon which interference between the entangled ideas of a group plays out. In the future, this model would allow us to calculate the entropy of a plan, agreement, decisions and their execution (Lawless et al., 2007).

We have revised Equation (1) to model cognitive uncertainty in organizational plans or business models (ΔBM_{COG}) and the conjugate uncertainty in the execution or enaction of these plans or models, Δv (see Lawless et al., 2007 for the derivation):

$$\Delta BM_{COG} \Delta v \geq c. \tag{2}$$

Energy-Time interdependence. Based on COI, Equation (1) can be reconfigured as an energy, ΔE, time, Δt, relationship:

$$\Delta E \Delta t \geq c. \tag{3}$$

We have used the model presented in Equations 1-3 to study human organizations making decisions under uncertainty by addressing complex situations like the environmental cleanup of its nuclear facilities undertaken by the Department of Energy, or mergers and acquisitions. The primary characteristic of this interdependence is reflected in tradeoffs between coordinating social objects communicating to solve problems while in states of uncertainty (Lawless et al., 2007). In Case Study 1, we apply Organization COI to a system of seven MDRCs (Medical Department Research Training Center). Our goal is to help those MDRCs with an EIS to become more productive in meeting their assigned mission. This means that the MDRC system would shift from a fragmented to a more ordered group of organizations, thereby increasing productivity. In our model, to exploit the power of the EIS, we propose to use a rate equation to measure in real-time with machines the system performance, thus offering management insight as to the factors to change in a tradeoff that enhances organizational performance.

Evidence: Field

Department of Energy Citizen Advisory Boards. In our search for a classical organizational uncertainty principle, we have found in the field and confirmed in the laboratory a planning cognitive-execution tradeoff between consensus-seeking and majority rule decision-making as citizen groups made decisions over complex issues like nuclear waste management (Lawless et al., 2008a). Two forms of consensus were found to exist: Worldview consensus and action consensus. The former is more likely to be derived from cooperative processes and the latter from competitive processes (Wood et al., 2008). In the first field study, we looked at the decisions of all nine of the Department of Energy's Citizen Advisory Boards as they responded to DOE's formal request to support DOE's plans to speed the shipments of transuranic wastes to its WIPP repository in New Mexico as part of its mission to accelerate the cleanup of DOE facilities across the U.S. These nine DOE Boards were geographically separated and located at the DOE sites where the transuranic wastes were being removed and shipped to WIPP. DOE's plans were detailed in concrete recommendations and explained to the various Boards by DOE engineers. As predicted, most of DOE's majority-rule boards endorsed these recommendations, while most of its consensus-ruled boards rejected them. In addition, the time spent in deciding for majority-ruled boards was significantly less than the time taken by the consensus-ruled boards.

In a follow-on field study of consensus decisions by the Hanford Board in Washington State and majority rule decisions at the Savannah River Site Board in South Carolina, Boards located at the two DOE sites with the largest cleanup budgets, we found that consensus rule decisions produced "gridlock" when the single worldview of the Board conflicted with DOE's vision, increasing social volatility (Lawless et al., 2008a). We have found that gridlock is more likely under cooperative decision making because of the inability to accept challenges to illusions (Lawless et al., 2008b). In contrast, we have found that the cognitive disambiguation from competition improves social welfare with practical decisions that feedback amplifies or accelerates.

Evidence: Laboratory

Preliminary data from a laboratory experiment nearing completion with college students making recommendations to improve their college experiences appears to have replicated parts of the DOE CAB study. In this study, we asked college students in 3-person groups ($N = 53$ groups) at a Historically Black College and a nearby University to proposed open-ended recommendations to improve operations affecting them at their schools (e.g., with cafeteria food, library, student government, etc.). Students were randomly assigned to three-person groups who made recommendations either under consensus (CR) or majority rules (MR). Time for both types of groups was held constant. Tentatively, we predicted and found that while CR produces significantly more discussions (oscillations), indicating less time available to craft recommendations, MR produces significantly more total recommendations (our analyses are ongoing).

Case Study 1

Evidence: Military Medical Department Research Training Centers (MDRCs)

Overview. Military Department Research Center (MDRC): Basic publication citation data had been gathered annually as part of the administration of research practices, but no coherent link had been established between research products (publications, conferences, workshops) and the organization's mission and vision for revising its mission. Nor could the MDRCs establish whether each site was contributing to the mission, by which units at a site, or which personnel or which strategy was effective. MDRC data was simply aggregated at the end of the year and dumped into annual reports without evaluation. The first step has been to collaborate among the decentralized commands spread across the U.S. as part of a process to decide on an eIRB system. This system will provide an opportunity for a trial MDRC to integrate itself and to set a pattern to integrate all of the seven MDRCs across the U.S. Organizational metrics have been completed for one organization and extrapolated to the others. The evidence tentatively indicates the potential for significant savings. It may also mean a savings in administrative costs. As already demonstrated at the highest levels of management, one significant advantage to the new EIS-type system is the ability to participate electronically in meetings to make decisions impacting MDRC or system of MDRCs from any location across the U.S.

Background of MDRCs. Guided by our theoretical and field results in applying the organizational uncertainty principle, we have been assisting a system of seven military MDRCs (Wood et al., 2008) to become more productive; e.g., produce more research with greater scientific impact; improve patient care; and reduce the costs of care. Specifically, when we began this case study, we found little knowledge existed at the organizational level that directly linked each research product (publications, presentations, workshops) with MDRCs assigned mission. Instead, every MDRC had to collect its own site's basic citations for each publication; not all publications were captured in the various databases; nor were all conferences attended captured.

Based on feedback from metrics of organizational performance linked to eIRBSs, adminis-

trators have the ability to execute their mission effectively and efficiently; e.g., with Lean Six Sigma processes. But efficiency alone reduces adaptability to uncertain future missions (Smith & Tushman, 2005). Thus, concomitantly, a group internal to each MDRC and a national group of elite professionals from all MDRC units could gather annually to transform the mission, goals, and rules guided by the same feedback and metrics. As these two systems compete in a bistable relationship to control the Mission, the two systems operate in tension (interdependence), producing a natural evolution of the system.

Evidence: Case Study 1. Application of the Theoretical Model. The military has just purchased a secure web-based system for one MDRC for the submission of IRB research protocols by its investigators (viz., human and animal research Institutional Review Boards). The other MDRCs are included in the hope that the benefits of the new eIRB will secure funding for the other sites. The eIRB includes routing of submissions to IRB members; receipt of comments from IRB reviewers; transmission of modification requests to investigators; development of IRB meeting minutes; tracking of protocol status; automatic notification of investigators of continuing review deadlines; and tracking metrics. The technology provides a platform for collaboration across the organization between Principal Investigators and team members when drafting protocol proposals. It provides feedback among IRB reviewers, the PI and study team, and Administrators. It tracks Adverse Events (medical and drugs); provides guided electronic input and assistance and error checking and reporting to PIs and Administrators; but more importantly, it is a platform for integrated management and reporting.

In installing the eIRB, MDRC will be better positioned to leverage business intelligence (BI) tools that automatically pull together data for metrics with machines from this new electronic system and from other disparate database systems already in place (e.g., electronic medical records).

However, only until MDRC has EIS-type standardized database systems across all aspects of biomedical research and medical care delivery and the BI tools to link these often incongruent systems together will it be able to generate real time data for EIS-based machines to study, define and improve MDRC processes. Once in place, MDRC can make decisions in real-time rather than with data many months old thereby closing the gap between the mission and the vision and pushing the organization faster towards innovation.

Current Status. The contract has been awarded to a firm to build the eIRB and MDRC is operating on a short timeline with a plan to go live by December. First, it will have a virtual meeting with some of the key people from each site who are involved in the implementation process (primarily protocol coordinators). Second, three key staff members will telecommunicate to finalize the draft of the cover sheet (template; see Table 1). The cover sheet is how staff will capture the vital data for the generation of MDRC annual reports; there will be one for the protocol and one for publications. This will be approximately an 80-90% solution for this first iteration of the eIRB system. The attached is an earlier draft; MDRC spent almost 3 h doing revisions and the latest version will be approved soon by the firm providing the eIRB. Using this approach (cover sheets), each of the seven sites will continue to use their existing protocol templates and business processes. However, the cover sheet will be filled out by all MDRC investigators thereby standardizing the data set. In the future, all MDRCs plan to use the same protocol templates and processes but in the meantime, they can have an operational system AND have the dataset they need. It is anticipated that it will take a while to get everyone at all MDRCs to reach consensus on templates and business processes. In addition, upper military administrators (governance group) are to be briefed on the project before it becomes operational.

In order to get previously approved protocols onto the system, MDRC will ask all investigators who have existing protocols to log in their previously approved protocols onto the system, fill out the cover sheet data elements and upload all their documents into the system. Otherwise, if the MDRCs wait until their annual reviews are due, not all protocols will be in the system and be able to generate their annual report for next year.

Assessment of Case Study One. We began Case Study 1 by contrasting the organizational performance of MDRC against the specifics listed in its assigned mission: improving patient care in the field; reducing the costs of care; and increasing the impact of research products. We found no clear link between research products and the mission; no measure of publication impacts; and no direct way to measure organizational productivity against its peers (reduced or negligible states of interdependence). In general, the organizations in the MDRC network were fragmented, with each pursuing its own path to mission success. No overarching measure of system performance existed for the MDRCs that the separate organizations could follow to guide their collective behavior. As a consequence, long-term work practices and cultural differences predominated. Subsequently, the move to adopt a web-based eIRB has set the stage to turn around the lack of organizational and system-wide knowledge. With the adoption of the Cover Sheet (template), MDRC is preparing for real-time organizational and system-wide based metrics from its EIS, improvements and future transformations.

Case Study 2

Evidence: Application of Theoretical Model to a College

Overview. Future College. Multiple, non-integrated information systems existed to administer the college and its outlying branch. The goal was to install a "main" EIS system that integrates information flow across the organizational units. An EIS provides the opportunity for more joint

Table 1. Draft research project cover sheet acts to feed into the enterprise information system to collect data from across the entire MDRC enterprises.

#	Item	Instructions/ Question	Response Type	Possible Values	Notes
1	PI Information				Primary PI Only
1.1	PI Name and Degrees	n/a	n/a	n/a	Automatically populated
1.2	PI Identifier		Plain Text		Unique identifier for indexing.
1.3	PI Status and Service	Please select the Status and Service of the Principal Investigator.	Radio Buttons	* Military – Army * Military – Navy * Military – Air Force * Military – Other DOD * Civilian – Army * Civilian – Navy * Civilian – Air Force * Civilian – Other DOD * Civilian – Other Gov. (non-DOD) * Civilian – Non-Gov.	If Mil go to 1.4 Else skip to 1.6
1.4	PI Rank	Please select the Rank of the Principal Investigator.	Dropdown List	* Rank list	Appropriate Ranks for all Services.
1.5	PI Branch	Please select the Branch of the Principal Investigator.	Radio Buttons	* Medical Corps * Nurse Corps * Dental Corps * Medical Specialty Corps * Other	
1.6	PI Staff Status	Please select the Staff Status of the Principal Investigator.	Radio Buttons	* Staff * Medical Student * Intern * Resident * Fellow	
1.6	PI MTF	Please select the MTF of the Principal Investigator.	Radio Buttons	* Medical Treatment Facility list	
1.7	PI Department	Please select the Department and Service of the Principal Investigator.	Radio Buttons	* Dept/Service list. e.g., Dept of Medicine/ Cardiology… etc…	
2	Associate Investigator Information				Information collected for each additional Investigator.
2.1	AI Name and Degrees	Please provide the name of the Associate Investigator.	Plain Text		
2.2	AI Identifier		Plain Text		Unique identifier for indexing.
2.3	AI Status and Service	Please select the Status and Service of the Associate Investigator.	Radio Buttons	* Military – Army * Military – Navy * Military – Air Force * Military – Other DOD * Civilian – Army * Civilian – Navy * Civilian – Air Force * Civilian – Other DOD * Civilian – Other Govnt (non-DOD) * Civilian – Non-Govnt	If Mil go to 2.4 Else skip to 3.1

continued on following page

Table 1. continued

#	Item	Instructions/ Question	Response Type	Possible Values	Notes
2.5	AI Branch	Please select the Branch of the Associate Investigator.	Radio Buttons	* Medical Corps * Nurse Corps * Dental Corps * Medical Specialty Corps * Other	
3	Project Information				
3.1	Protocol Title	n/a	n/a	n/a	Automatically populated
3.2	Protocol Abstract	Please provide an abstract that describes this protocol.	Rich Text	n/a	
3.3	Research Category	Please select the appropriate category for this project.	Radio Buttons	* Human * Lab Based * Animal * Other	"Other" is necessary?
3.4	Research Type	Please select the appropriate Research Type for this project.	Radio Buttons	* Behavior Research * Drug Research * Device or Surgical Procedure Rsrch * Database or Records Only Rsrch * Other	"Other" is necessary?
3.5	Vulnerable Populations	Please indicate all vulnerable populations that may be research subjects for this project.	Checkbox List	* Children * Prisoners * Pregnant Women * etc…	Can select multiple.
3.6	Multi-Site Status	Please indicate the multi-site status for this research site.	Radio Buttons	* This study is a multi-site study and this site is the lead site. * This study is a multi-site study but this site is not the lead site. * This study is not a multi-site study.	If a multi-site study, proceed to 3.7.
3.7	IRB of Record	Please indicate the IRB of Record for this project.	Plain Text		
4	Funding Information				
4.1	Total Funding Amount	Please enter the total funding amount for this project.	Plain Text	n/a	
4.2	Primary Funding Source	Please indicate the primary funding source.	Radio Buttons	* Intramural * Extramural – DoD * Extramural – Government * Extramural – Non-Government	
4.3	Foundations	Are any of the following foundations managing any part of this funding?	Checkbox List	* Geneva * Jackson * Samueli * True	Can select multiple.

partnerships between the Future College and other organizations (e.g., currently, it is managing and administering federal and private grants and research projects with other universities, but it could mean additional joint operations with widely distributed partners, including overseas). An assessment has been completed that indicates the difficulty in gaining organizational-wide access to records and databases. The EIS also provides a means to establish better internal communications.

Incipient steps have been taken to formulate metrics for operational performance, including for IT and Business departments. The initial plan is to use the EIS system to find and reduce organizational inefficiencies unit by unit. This may mean fewer or reassigned employees. The impact of these effects will be studied in the future.

Future College: Background

Future College is an organization whose primary function is higher education. Although all institutions of higher education are tasked with the production of new knowledge within fields where they offer degrees, this organization's primary purpose is to train the next generation of citizens, primarily inner-city minorities, with a liberal arts curriculum. Its Vision statement technology is highlighted in a way that "it provides information technologies that link its students' total academic and social experiences to the global world".[1]

Future College employs a faculty and staff of approximately 200 individuals with the majority of individuals servicing as instructional personnel providing instruction for a student body of less than 1,000 students studying at the undergraduate level. Besides instructional staff there are administrative staff members, staff who provide support services to students, a unit that manages the fiscal enterprise of the organization and a unit responsible for external partnerships and fund raising. All areas of the institution rely heavily on the efficient function of all of its other areas. As with many small organizations, Future College relies on informal communications. When it is necessary to make changes, this lack of structure and efficient policies and procedures limit the organization's ability to respond appropriately (Tung et al., 2008).

Future College: EIS Before 2008

The overall condition of the Future College MIS was extremely poor and in need of immediate attention: the core switch[2] usage had exceeded its operational lifetime, the internet connection was not steady and the bandwidth was not adequate to satisfy present and future needs.[3] There was no formal EIS in place. Every unit chose its own preferred software applications to conduct tasks, making it difficult to communicate with other units. Data sharing was done by paper or it was nonexistent. Business process and procedures were not defined. Faculty and students often found it hard to finish a task that involved more than one business unit. For example, to register students, the advisor had to use its legacy MIS software program (Jenzabar™) to remove student holds in order to permit students to register for classes and then use a different program, CampusWeb, to check course availability, pick courses, and obtain a student's schedule. Students then took the paperwork to the Business office to pay and brought the receipt to the Registrar's office to "officially" register. The legacy software was required but often unavailable during pre-registration which forced students into multiple trips to their advisor's and the Registrar's offices. To advisors, the legacy software was only being used in this one function although it offered many others. The database was not updated, making the student record module non-functional.

Although Future College had already performed an IT analysis twice prior to 2008 by two different companies, no follow up or changes resulted from either evaluation report. The MIS Director retired in August 2007 leaving IT college-wide support provided by two staff members, one who dealt with hardware issues and the other with software and network issues. Network design and setup was outsourced due to insufficient expertise and the lack of human resources (personnel). MIS personnel spent the majority of their time reacting to crises and failures rather than accomplishing required maintenance, upkeep and management of the equipment and software for which they were responsible. In all aspects, this negatively impacted the storage of data, data quality, and systems availability for the student body, faculty and staff of Future College.

Managed Information Systems (MIS) is another crucial unit that needed Business Process Reengineering (BPR). Without proper processes and procedures various units at Future College experienced challenges to their productivity. A system of requesting support had not been established. Priority should have been given to issues that impacted the whole network. However, the extent to which users were supported was related to their location in the organizational hierarchy with senior management serviced before others. This caused dissatisfaction about IT services from faculty and staff members. A Help Desk software system was installed but it was not utilized because of technological problems and the lack of human resources. This became an example of financial waste.

Future College: MIS Current State

The lack of a coherent MIS Strategic Plan and EIS had negatively affected the organization's performance collectively and individually. The faculty and staff were generally frustrated with old computers (or no office computer to use), lack of peripherals, and network performance. Technology that should be aiding job performance was not available. Internet access and speed were not satisfactory. Additionally, they encountered the limitations of MIS staff and hardware which prevented the implementation and use of cutting edge technologies as described in Future College's Vision statement. Students often found it impossible to accomplish required work on the campus computers available to them. The extremely slow access to the Internet prevented them from getting their work done to the point of negatively impacting grades.

Future College's new administration, which took office in January 2008, had identified a number of issues with the college's Information Systems (IS) equipment, applications and inter-

faces. It also realized the need to evaluate the current information technology infrastructure and the need for change. It had determined that these issues were having a negative impact upon the college's ability to administer to its student body, to track and report on critical data, and to fulfill its vision and mission. Among the issues unresolved were the reduction of Future College's MIS staff efficiency and the hindering of Future College's efforts to successfully complete external fundraising activities. The lack of a technology infrastructure was impacting student retention, student, faculty and staff morale, and hindering the development of an effective learning environment.

The Future College administration has undertaken the initiative to conduct a thorough analysis of its MIS to determine possible courses of action, and to aid in the establishment of a campus-wide MIS Strategic Plan. After the preliminary investigation, the first need identified was to overhaul and redesign its website. The previous version did not clearly represent the organization due to its "commercial" rather than academic feel. Then an IT inventory survey was conducted to find out what systems were available, system utilization by business units, the merit of these choices and the costs associated with each system. To find an enterprise-wide solution, Future College hired an IT consultant in June 2008 to evaluate the current infrastructure and suggest the best solution. Future College requested that the consultant provide guidance on skills sets that would be required to implement the plan.

A new MIS director was hired in August 2008. The director started implementing the plan as soon as he arrived on campus, beginning with the diagnosis of technology issues. A careful analysis of the core switch discovered that the hardware was three years past its life cycle. In September of 2008 and after soliciting and receiving a series of proposals, personnel in the MIS department recommended that the core switch be replaced. The recommendation stated that the benefit to Future College students, faculty and staff were manifold.

These benefits would include stable Future College network communications, enhanced access to the Internet from all on campus locations, and the ability for MIS to monitor the system. With MIS monitoring the system, it would be able to better troubleshoot and correct network issues, lowering support costs by eliminating off-site support. In addition, the new UTM[4] system would provide added security and monitoring features helps to ensure the availability of the network for established functions. In addition, the migration from one system to another has the potential to save Future College $265,400 over the next five years as other outdated equipment is replaced and yearly maintenance fees eliminated for manufacturer support and warranties.

Along with addressing other hardware and software issues at Future College, the director of MIS felt the need to change the culture of the campus. His proposal was accepted by the senior administration of Future College to change the name of the Department responsible for MIS software to the Department of Information Technology Services (ITS). This change was in line with information that for the past fifteen years there had emerged a wide, rich, and mission-critical array of student and institutional services directly linked to core campus information. This is known as enterprise resource planning (ERP) in light of the revised coordination that needs to happen to free up and redirect limited resources within an organization. These new functions and services such as alumni information and services, learning management systems, electronic assessments, e-services (i.e., online registration, fee payment, electronic giving), and portals, are all firmly dependent not only on the web but also on real-time interaction with elements of the "old" MIS, particularly student records and institutional finances (Green, 2007). Moreover, unlike the "old" MIS, in many ways a protected silo inaccessible to students and faculty, the proposed ITS will provide all of the customary services with a new sense of discipline and management with the computing environment.[5]

Future College: ITS Path Forward

Future College's current MIS status is like organizations in the 1970s that created "islands of automation" (McKenney & McFarlan, 1982). Multiple systems contained the same data elements in different forms. The data in different systems often did not agree because of high error rates from duplicate data entries and different system update schedules. Sometimes, records were missing. Decision makers did not get the whole picture of the organization. The total organizational costs of maintaining this loose patchwork of redundant and overlapping systems grew, eclipsing the funds available for building new ones (Lientz & Swanson, 1980).

Throughout the 1980s and 1990s, software entrepreneurs were developing integrated software packages where multiple functional applications shared a common database. These packages became known as enterprise resource planning (ERP) systems (Markus & Tanis, 2000). Future College had legacy software (Jenzabar™) which had been in place but had not been used to its full potential due to the lack of training and the lack of a college-wide understanding of the purpose of the system. It was only being used as a "pre-registration" tool for advisors to give students permission to register. The organization is now working to establish a culture of understanding of the connectivity of the functions of offices. Currently all vital units are being trained and retrained on their updated EIS functions. However, there is a need to promote the use of the system to the whole organization by offering information and training sessions on EIS to all personnel.

To integrate all systems and to best utilize enterprise resources, an EIS is being instituted in Future College. EIS provides a single system central to the organization to ensure that information can be shared across all functional and managerial levels. It can eliminate the problem of information fragmentation caused by multiple information systems in an organization like Future

College. An EIS has several characteristics, each with important implications for the organizations that adopt them: integration, long-term relationship with vendor and best practices. There are other high education institutions, e.g., (University of North Texas, Mississippi State University) using EIS as their primary administrative information system with a portal for easy access.

While the initial overview of Future College may seem far from optimal, the current status of technology services at Future College only required a few basic changes to realize significant improvement. Future College's short-term goal, as of now, is to focus on "fixing" its IT infrastructure. The impact has been immediate: the network traffic has flowed better after the completion of the Core Switch replacement in September 2008. Faculty members have already reported being able to use resources found on the Internet as a part of their instruction that they have not been able to use previously. Students saw the immediate impact of the change and the responsiveness of the ITS staff to their needs as a reason to feel better about their collegiate experience. After the completion of the core switch replacement and initial network assessment, a phased replacement of the desktops has started to increase productivity throughout the college. In that the priority was to put students first, the various computer labs at Future College have received the highest priority.

For the long-term, an EIS should provide a technology platform that enables Future College to integrate and coordinate its business processes and fulfill its mission. Also an ITS Strategic Plan is to be developed and used to guide future IT development. A technology oversight committee consisting of the ITS Director and representatives from faculty, staff and the student body is being formed to oversee the process. At the same time, technology management policies, procedures, processes and change control, with adequate means of compliance enforcement are to be established to guarantee work control and alignment with BPR efforts that corresponds to Future College's

overall strategic plan. At this time, its "Future College Net" has not become fully implemented; but once operational, its students can use Future College Net for all registration needs. The system has been designed so that students would be able to select their courses on Future College Net, check their financial aid and accept it and then pay any balance on their account. There remains the need for personnel training, and an implementation plan for the entire system before Future College Net will become fully operational.

Assessment of Case Study Two. With a new administration, this organization has realized the need to evaluate its IT infrastructure and the need for changes to fulfill its mission and vision. After preliminary investigation, the first need identified was to overhaul and redesign the website. The previous version did not represent the academic organization due to its commercial feel. Then an IT inventory survey was conducted to find out what systems were available, which systems were being utilized by which unit (or not at all), the merit of these choices, and the costs associated with each system. To find an enterprise-wide EIS solution, the institution began with an IT consultant to evaluate the current infrastructure (conceptual model), and offer the best solution.

FUTURE TRENDS

In this section, we review Future Trends and works in progress with our models (presently restricted to agent-based models and Monte Carlo models).

The most important future trend is the use of agent-based models (ABMs) to model social and organizational effects to measure their effectiveness with the EIS. Agent-Based systems have been endowed with auction based mechanisms for distributing their resources (Gibson and Troxell, 2007). In this scenario, the various entities would "bid" for the information they require, ensuring that the entity that valued the information the most would receive it in the timeliest manner for their decision making. Double auctions have been used for similar analyses with genetic algorithms (Choi et al., 2008).

Natural Computation. Natural computation models will permit us to test field data and model the organizations that produce this data, especially the MDRC system in Case Study 1 and later the college in Case Study 2. We propose to test the data and organizational models with artificial agents evolved using biologically inspired natural selection (De Jong, 2008) and social methods of decision-making (e.g. "voting" mechanisms, ensembles). Based on our field research, we predict longer decision times and more oscillations under consensus rule (CR) than majority rule (MR). That is, we expect CR to model serial sequential individual decision processes. Surowiecki (2004) presented evidence and case studies of why agent ensembles often outperform individual experts. Earlier, Opitz and Maclin (1999) empirically showed that ensembles often outperform individuals, with theoretical support provided by Brown and colleagues (2005) and Tang (2006).

Works in Progress: ABM Computational Modeling

ABMs assign different rules of behavior to software agents and allow them to interact and solve for the optimal path. Here we create two sets of agents, those that use an electronic IRB (i.e., eIRB) submission process and those that operate under the more traditional non-electronic IRB submission process. The model is as follows:

$$1/\omega * E = p * 1/k \qquad (4)$$

Here $1/\omega$ stands for time in the model. We set this as a constant of 100 days, assuming this to be a reasonable length of time to initiate and complete a submission to an IRB. E is the resources required for the different processes. The resources (or energy) in the model will be dependent on the inputs from the business model (in this case eIRB

vs non eIRB) which is modeled in the equation by $1/k$. Here E takes a reduced Cobb-Douglass (1928) form. The Cobb-Douglass production model is a standard economic model of production that typically takes two inputs. Often we hold one of the inputs constant and vary the other, giving the reduced form of $(1/k)^\alpha$. In addition, p is the speed of execution of the plans of the organization. This is the variable of interest in the model, where we are concerned with whether a different IRB process will result in reduced organizational uncertainty. Also, $1/k$ is the Business model. We model here both the eIRB and the non- eIRB processes to compare the two. Then $1/k$ takes the functional form:

$$1/k = A_1 * A_2 * A_3 * .... A_n \qquad (5)$$

In this model we use five attributes (A_1 to A_5) taken from theory above: routing of submissions to IRB members, receipts of comments from IRB reviewers, transmission of modification requests to investigators, tracking of protocol status, and tracking metrics. All attributes are expressed in terms of days to process each of these steps. As the first attempt, the attributes are randomly drawn from a Poisson distribution (making the model non-interdependent).

With each random association of attributes, we compute the resources required for the different combinations and solve for the associated time to execute plans. The results are as follows in Figure 1.

We can see from Table 2 that the mean resources and time to execute plans in the eIRB model is much less than in the non-eIRB model. This implies that the eIRB will significantly improve the ability of the MDRC to execute their mission. In the future, we plan to consider an attempt to model interdependence.

Figure 1. eIRB results

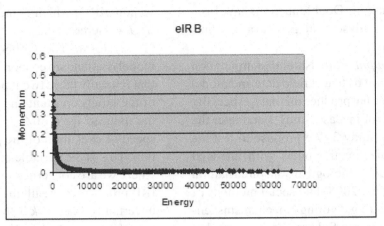

Works in Progress: Monte Carlo Simulations

Monte Carlo Simulations. Monte Carlo simulation is a technique that allows the simultaneous iteration of many uncertain variables to understand the impact of input uncertainties on one or more outcome variables. Developed during the 1940s as part of the Manhattan Project, and named after the famous casino in Monaco, Monte Carlo techniques are used today in fields ranging from manufacturing to finance, engineering and life sciences.

The basic concept in Monte Carlo simulation is that each uncertain variable, which we call a

Table 2. eIRB r esults

Mean Resources	13111.2
Standard Deviation Resources	11819.6
Mean Time to Execute Plans	0.0235226
Standard Deviation Time to Execute Plans	0.0427595

Table 3. Non-eIRB results

Mean Resources	659523
Standard Deviation Resources	821524
Mean Time to Execute Plans	0.56595
Standard Deviation Time to Execute Plans	0.550244

random variable, is simulated by a probability distribution (non-interdependence). For each trial of a simulation, each random variable is sampled from its corresponding probability distribution and the sampled value is used to compute the output variable(s) for the model. Many such trials are conducted and a value is collected for each outcome variable for each simulation trial. At the conclusion of all trials a distribution of outcomes can be constructed to better understand the distribution of uncertainties for an outcome given the uncertainties in the input variables.

Rate equation. Lawless and his colleagues (2007) devised a mathematical model of social interaction rates (this approach will allow future tests of this model constructed with machine learning using recombination operators; De Jong, 2008). We propose to adapt this model to guide our future research on organizations, e.g., training MDRC physicians with the experimental method or educating students unprepared for college courses with enhancement classes. In the latter case, the model becomes,

$$\Gamma = N_1 N_2 v_{12} \sigma_{12} \exp(-\Delta A/<A>), \qquad (7)$$

where Γ is the physician-as-student publication rate; N_1 represents those in the physician population who have not yet learned how to publish

Figure 2. Non-eIRB results

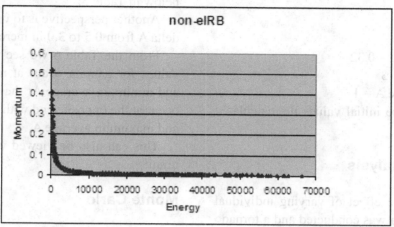

scientific papers; N_2 represents the population of those who have learned (viz., mentors); v_{12} represents the velocity of knowledge passed between them, with the minimum effect occurring under censorship; σ_{12} represents how well the two groups match their beliefs, with the maximum effect occurring under social agreement (interdependence, reflecting social resonance); and $exp\ (-\Delta A/<A>)$ represents the probability of graduation or knowledge exchanges, where ΔA represents the energy or effort required for the knowledge to be acquired, and $<A>$ represents the average amount of effort being expended by the targeted MDRC, its mentors and support staff, and its physician students. Before we address the implications of equation (7), let's rearrange it. If χ represents the knowledge required before a student can be declared to be published, then $\Gamma = \partial\chi/\partial t \approx \Delta\chi/\Delta t$, and

$$\Delta\chi = \Delta t\ N_1\ N_2\ v_{12}\ \sigma_{12}\ exp\ (-\Delta A/<A>). \qquad (8)$$

From equation (8), given an average time to learn experimental and publication methods at an MDRC, various opportunities exist as tradeoffs for an MDRC as an organization to improve the probability that its physician students will publish ($\Delta\chi$) a paper (article, book chapter, etc.). Increasing the numbers of those who actively support the student increases the occurrence of mentor-support

group (N_1) to student (N_2) speech acts. Increasing the velocity (v_{12}) of knowledge passed between the two groups improves the acquisition of knowledge. Increasing the match (σ_{12}) between mentor-support groups and physician student groups can dramatically increase the knowledge gained (e.g., study groups; student focus groups; mentor-student focus groups; *enhancement* groups). But also the probability of publishing can be increased by reducing the barriers that students face ($-\Delta A$; e.g., either lowering requirements, choosing better qualified entrants, or enhancing the skills of weaker entrants). Finally, by increasing the overall average effort or excitement by an MDRC directed toward learning and publishing ($<A>$), an MDRC can strongly improve the odds that its students will become published. Inversely, changing these factors can also decrease or adversely increase the time required for graduation.

Applying Sensitivity Analysis and Monte Carlo Simulation Methods to EIS model

Model

A model was developed in Microsoft EXCEL to compute gamma, Γ. The following values were used as a base case:

N_1 = N1 = 240
N_2 = N2 = 12
v_{12} = V12 = 2
σ_{12} = Sigma 12 = 0.32
ΔA = delta A = 3
$<A>$ = average A = 1

Based on these initial values the calculated gamma is 91.8.

Sensitivity Analysis

To understand the effect of varying individual factors on gamma was conducted and a tornado chart (Figure 3) was created using the EXCEL add-in Crystal Ball TM by varying factors from -10% to +10% of nominal values to see the effect on gamma.

We see from the tornado diagram that the factors with the most impact on gamma are delta A and average A. For all other factors, individuals have about the same level of impact on gamma. Specific values used in the analysis are shown

Table 4. Spreadsheet model

N1	number students	240
N2	number faculty	12
v12	velocity of information	2
sigma 12	resonance	.32
delta a	energy required	3
avg a	avg energy available	1
gamma		91.77

below in Table 5:

Another perspective is to vary average A and delta A from 0.5 to 3.0 in increments of 0.5.

From the Table 6 we see that the "lowest" values for gamma occur at maximum delta A and minimum average A; the "highest" gamma occur at the opposite end with minimum delta A and maximum average A.

This can also be viewed with a scatter diagram:

Monte Carlo

To study the effect of these factors varying together (randomly) we model the most significant factors

Figure 3. Tornado chart

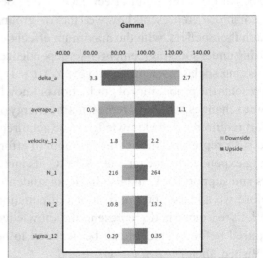

Table 5. Results for Gamma

	Gamma			*Input*		
Variable	Downside	Upside	Range	Downside	Upside	Base Case
delta_a	123.87	67.98	55.89	2.7	3.3	3
average_a	65.75	120.54	54.79	0.9	1.1	1
velocity_12	82.59	100.94	18.35	1.8	2.2	2
N_1	82.59	100.94	18.35	216	264	240
N_2	82.59	100.94	18.35	10.8	13.2	12
sigma_12	82.59	100.94	18.35	0.29	0.35	0.32

Table 6. Data table

		Delta A					
	91.76752442	0.5	1.0	1.5	2.0	2.5	3.0
Average A	0.5	678.0754	249.45	91.76752	33.75939	12.41938	4.568836
	1.0	1117.957	678.0754	411.2735	249.45	151.2991	91.76752
	1.5	1320.711	946.3304	678.0754	485.8622	348.1355	249.45
	2.0	1435.486	1117.957	870.666	678.0754	528.0856	411.2735
	2.5	1509.085	1235.534	1011.57	828.2031	678.0754	555.1612
	3.0	1560.235	1320.711	1117.957	946.3304	801.0514	678.0754

(Winston & Albright, 2008). We modeled these as normal distributions with delta A normal (3,0.3) and average A normal (1,.1) (read: the mean is "1" with a standard deviation of "0.1").

Running 10,000 trials with these two variables each being sampled from their respective normal distributions using the EXCEL add-in Crystal Ball TM we obtain a gamma result in the forecast chart above with a mean of 97.36. Additionally we note that gamma could vary substantially from less than 8 to more than 358 as seen in the statistics shown below:

Advice to MDRC Management From the Monte Carlo Model. The output (gamma) is most sensi-

tive to variations in the nominal for factors delta A and average A. Of these the most influential (from observing the data table for a range of each factor from 0.5 to 3.0) is delta A. Gamma improves by lowering delta A (reducing the publishing standards for the physician students) or by raising average A (increasing the motivation of the students, raising their quality, or placing them in "high-energy" mentoring groups). Assuming a starting delta A of 3.0, with an average A of 1.0, decreasing delta A to the minimum range evaluated of 0.5 results in an improvement of about 1100%; however, from a starting delta A of 3.0 with an average A of 1.0, improving average A

Figure 4. Gamma sensitivity analysis

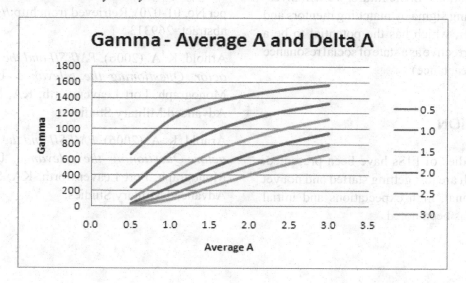

Figure 5. Monte Carlo results.

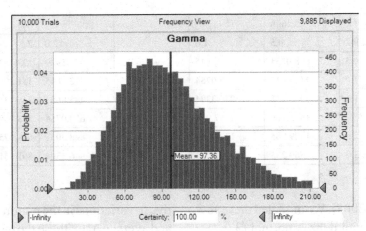

to the maximum range evaluated of 3.0 results in an improvement of about 637%.

Ideally we would like to improve both delta A (decreased physician requirements) and improve average A (increased quality of the students or mentorship) to obtain a best value for gamma; however, within the context of this problem if management could only do one thing it would be to improve systems so that it is "easier" (less energy required) to produce an output as opposed to increasing the average energy available. But while the easiest approach, it also means lower quality publications. In the future, we will investigate increasing sigma by matching mentors and students better, which has the potential to be a significant corrective as a state of social resonance occurs (low reactance).

CONCLUSION

Two case studies of EISs have been presented. Although both are just getting started and not yet fully operational, high expectations and initial satisfaction has been noted.

REFERENCES

Adelson, E. H. (2000). Lightness perceptions and lightness illusions. In M. Gazzaniga (Ed.), *The new cognitive sciences*(2nd ed.). Cambridge, MA: MIT Press.

Ambrose, S. H. (2001). Paleolithic technology and human evolution. *Science, 291*, 1748–1753. doi:10.1126/science.1059487

Andrade, G. M.-M., Mitchell, M. L., & Stafford, E. (2001). *New evidence and perspectives on mergers* (Harvard Business School Working Paper No. 01-070). Retrieved from http://ssrn.com/abstract=269313

Arnold, K. A. (2006). *PMESII and the non-state actor. Questioning the relevance*. US Army Monograph, Fort Leavenworth, KA, School of Advanced Military Studies.

Arnold, K. A. (2006). *PMESII and the non-state actor. Questioning the relevance*. US Army Monograph, Fort Leavenworth, KA, School of Advanced Military Studies.

Axsom, D., & Lawless, W. F. (1992). Subsequent behavior can erase evidence of dissonance-induced attitude change. *Journal of Experimental Social Psychology, 28*, 387–400. doi:10.1016/0022-1031(92)90052-L

Baumeister, R. F., Campbell, J.D., Krueger, J.I., & Vohs, K.D. (2005, January). Exploding the self-esteem myth. *Scientific American.*

Brown, G., Wyatt, J., Harris, R., & Yao, X. (2005). Diversity creation methods: A survey and categorization. *Journal of Information Fusion, 6*, 5–20. doi:10.1016/j.inffus.2004.04.004

Cacioppo, J. T., Berntson, G. G., & Crites, S. L., Jr., (Eds.). (1996). Social neuroscience: Principles, psychophysiology, arousal and response. *Social psychology handbook of basic principles*. New York, Guilford.

Choi, J., Ahn, H., & Han, I. (2008). Utility-based double auction mechanism using genetic algorithms. *Expert Systems with Applications: An International Journal, 34*(1), 150–158. doi:10.1016/j.eswa.2006.08.024

Cobb, C. W., & Douglas, P. H. (1928). A theory of production. *The American Economic Review, 18*(Supplement), 139–165.

Conant, R. C., & Ashby, W. R. (1970). Every good regulator of a system must be a model of that system. *International Journal of Systems Science, 1*(2), 899–97. doi:10.1080/00207727008920220

Csete, M. E., & Doyle, J. C. (2002). Reverse engineering of biological complexity. *Science, 295*, 1664–1669. doi:10.1126/science.1069981

De Jong, K. A. (2008, February). Evolving intelligent agents: A 50 year quest. *Computational Intelligence Magazine, 3*(1), 12–17. doi:10.1109/MCI.2007.913370

Green, K. C. (2007). *The 2007 Campus Computing Survey*. Campus Computing Project, Retrieved October 8, 2008 from http://www.campuscomputing.net/survey-summary/2007-campus-computing-survey

Jervis, R. (1997). *Systems effects: Complexity in political and social lifer*. Princeton, NJ: Princeton University Press.

Kelley, H. H. (1992). Lewin, situations, and interdependence. *The Journal of Social Issues, 47*, 211–233.

Kohli, R., & Hoadley, E. (2996). Towards developing a framework for measuring organizational impact of IT-enabled BPR: case studies of three firms. *ACM SIGMIS Database, 37*(1), 40-58.

Kuhn, T. (1970). *The structure of scientific revolutions*. Chicago: University of Chicago Press.

Lawless, W. F., Bergman, M., Louçã, J., Kriegel, N. N., & Feltovich, N. (2007). A quantum metric of organizational performance: Terrorism and counterterrorism. *Computational & Mathematical Organization Theory, 13*, 241–281. doi:10.1007/s10588-006-9005-4

Lawless, W. F., Castelao, T., & Ballas, J. A. (2000). Virtual knowledge: Bistable reality and solution of ill-defined problems. *IEEE Systems, Man, & . Cybernetics, 30*(1), 119–124.

Lawless, W. F., Howard, C. R., & Kriegel, N. N. (2008c). A quantum real-time metric for NVOs. In G. D. Putnik & M.M. Cunha (Eds.), *Encyclopedia of Networked and Virtual Organizations*. Hershey, PA: Information Science Reference.

Lawless, W. F., & Sofge, D. (2008b). Conservation of information (COI). A concept paper on virtual organizations and communities. *NSF Computational Workshop: Building CIML Virtual Organizations*. October 24, 2008, Fairfax, VA.

Lawless, W. F., Whitton, J., & Poppeliers, C. (2008a). Case studies from the UK and US of stakeholder decision-making on radioactive waste management. *Practice Periodical of Hazardous, Toxic, and Radioactive Waste Management, 12*(2), 70–78. doi:10.1061/(ASCE)1090-025X(2008)12:2(70)

Lewis, G.A., Cornella-Dorda, S., Place, P., Plakosh, D., & Secord, R.C. (2001). *An Enterprise Information System Architecture guide* (CMU/SEI 2001-TR-018).

Lientz, B. P., & Swanson, E. B. (1980). *Software maintenance management.* Boston, MA: Addison-Wesley Longman Publishing.

Markus, M. L., & Tanis, C. (2000). The enterprise system experience—From adoption to success. In R. W. Zmud & M. F. Price (Eds.), *Framing the domains of IT management: Projecting the future through the past* (pp. 173-207). Pinnaflex Educational Resources.

Mattick, J. S., & Gagen, M. J. (2005). Accelerating networks. *Science, 307,* 856–858. doi:10.1126/science.1103737

McKenney, J. L., & McFarlane, F. W. (1982). The information archipelago - maps and bridges. *Harvard Business Review, 60*(5), 109–119.

Moore, W., Allen, C., Bracht, R., Koch, D., & Marrazzo, D. (2005). *Managing information access to an Enterprise Information System using J2EE and Services Oriented Architecture* (IBM SB246371-00). Retrieved October 11, 2008 from www.redbooks.ibm.com/abstracts/SG246371.html

Pfeifer, R., Lungarella, M., & Lida, F. (2007). Review: Self-organization, embodiment, and biologically inspired robots. *Science, 318,* 1088–1093. doi:10.1126/science.1145803

Smith, W. K., & Tushman, M. L. (2005). Managing strategic contradictions: A top management model for managing innovation streams. *Organization Science, 16*(5), 522–536. doi:10.1287/orsc.1050.0134

Sukthankar, G. (2008, June 10). *Robust and eficient plan recognition for dynamic multi-agent teams.* Presentation to the Information Technology Division, Nav Res Lab, DC.

Tang, E. K., Suganthan, P. N., & Yao, X. (2006). An analysis of diversity measures. *Machine Learning, 65,* 247–271. doi:10.1007/s10994-006-9449-2

Tung, H.-L., Bergman, M., Wood, J., & Lawless, W. F. (2008). Metrics of organizational performance that are independent of cultural effects. *International Journal of Management Theory and Practices, 9*(1), 69–84.

Weick, K. E., & Quinn, R. E. (1999). Organizational change and development. *Annual Review of Psychology, 50,* 361–386. doi:10.1146/annurev.psych.50.1.361

Wickens, C. D. (1992). *Engineering psychology and human performance* (2nd ed). Columbus, OH: Merrill Publishing.

Willis, R. P. (2007). *The counterinsurgency pattern assessment (CIPA) Program 2007.* Naval Research Laboratory.

Winston, W. L., & Albright, S. C. (2008). *Practical management science* (3rd ed.). South-Western College Publishing.

Wood, J., Tung, H.-L., Grayson, J., Poppeliers, C., & Lawless, W. F. (2008). A classical uncertainty principle for organizations. In M. Khosrow-Pour (Ed.), *Encyclopedia of Information Science & Technology* (2nd ed.). Hershey, PA, IGI Global.

KEY TERMS AND DEFINITIONS

Enterprise Information System: A centralized service to standardize data for an organization or system. It reduces database fragmentation by replacing independent formats with a standardized template or structure for data entry instead of *ad hoc* programming. An EIS reduces data variability across the business units of an organization. It increases data sharing in an organization with organization-wide data mining and computational organizational models made possible to generate trends from using business intelligence on the organizations data.

Conservation of Information (COI): The conservation of information (COI) is derived from signal detection theory (SDT). It is based on duration-bandwidth tradeoffs. We have extended the ideas behind COI to organizational performance and to mergers and acquisitions (M&A). Briefly, the shorter the duration of a signal, the wider becomes its bandwidth and vice versa. Applied to organizations, an organization's focus (e.g., situational awareness) can be directed on a broad business model, but reducing its ability to execute and vice versa

Uncertainty: Uncertainty for organizations leads to predictions of counterintuitive effects that can be exploited with an online EIS system to formulate a set of metrics for applying conservation of information (COI) to organizational performance. It exists fundamentally for all actions and observations made by an organization or its members.

Bistability: While an entire data set is processed cognitively by an individual: both interpretations of a bistable illusion cannot be held in awareness simultaneously. Multiple interpretations support the existence of different cultures. Bohr makes it conceivable that the same data has different interpretations in different organizations, either promoting two different cultures or being impacted by them

Conservation of Information for Organizations: COI acts as a tradeoff in attention directed at reducing the uncertainty in one factor, such as a worldview or business model, with the result that the uncertainty in a second, interdependent factor is inversely increased, such as the execution of a business model. The more focused a collective of individuals are on acting out a series of steps, the less observant they become of their actions

Organizations: Organizations perform a function which cannot be done by an individual alone by assigning interdependent roles to a set of independent individuals, which requires information coordination, channeling and blocking to form them into a working collective, but which consequently amplifies the capabilities of an individual. An organization is functional when its operational costs are less than the benefits it accrues and provides to its members. It is likely constructed around a geographical centroid (x) about which its business attributes are centered, planned and modeled

Technology: Technology, such as EIS, is important to organizations. Technology limits the efficiency, effectiveness and size of an organization

ENDNOTES

[1] Future College's Mission Statement, Vision Statement, and Strategic Plan.

[2] There are two mainframe computer switches: Director and Core. A director switch is a large port count, high bandwidth fabric switch to provide the highest availability and performance. While they offer high port counts, core switches lack many of the capabilities for director switches such as highest availability, un-compromised performance, and mainframe support. A core switch is a 16-switch mesh. Although easier to develop, a core switch is plagued with the block-

ing and latency issues inherent to a mesh design (www.enterprisestorageforum.com/hardware/features/article.php/1382291)

3   Future College internal IT analysis report, 2008.

4   Unified Threat Management, where threats are to organizational and member security.

5   Internal Future College document presented to the Administrative Council of Future College.

Chapter 23
Modern ICT Technologies In Business Administration:
The Case Of The DERN Project for a Digital Enterprise Research Network

Adamantios Koumpis
ALTEC S.A., Greece

Vasiliki Moumtzi
ALTEC S.A., Greece

ABSTRACT

In this chapter, we present the DERN project and discuss a set of complementary methodologies that have been used to promote intra-enterprise training in the area of modern business administration technologies and corporate capacity building.

INTRODUCTION

The issue of enterprise learning might be regarded as marginally relevant to the core topic of this book, namely this of Enterprise Information Systems in SMEs. Based on our experience, several success and quite many failure stories, we derived enough knowledge on the role of corporate learning in general and the importance of introducing scalable learning processes that extend the already existing business processes of the enterprise. Especially for SMEs that have traditionally limited access not only to financial, human and technology but also to intellectual capital resources, this issue takes a higher priority as it may act as a disabling factor for their growth and sustained development.

We draw our experiences from the DERN (Digital Enterprise Research Network) project that has aimed at building a research network among some of the most important academic, research and technological Bodies and Enterprises of Greece.

Background on the DERN Project

The central gravity of the DERN project has been set on the use of modern ICT technologies in **business administration**. From our perspective as an industrial partner, the main interest was in the different ways that can be employed in order to help corporate employees build new capacities or improve and extend existing ones.

DOI: 10.4018/978-1-60566-856-7.ch023

Table 1. Different categories of employee specialisation

1. Specialist	2. Generalist	3. Versatilist
• Deep skills	• Broad scope	• Deep skills
• Narrow scope	• Shallow skills	• Wide scope of roles
• Peer-recognised	• Quick response	• Broad experience
• Unknown outside domain	• Others lack confidence	• Recognized in otherdomains

The project has been cofinanced by the General Secretariat of Research and Technology of Greece and was coordinated by the Department for **Business Administration** of the University of Macedonia. In the project there was an equal representation from the academia (Institute of Communication and Computer Systems, National Technical University of Athens - Information Management Unit, and the Athens University of Economics and Business - ELTRUN/OIS), and the industry with two major actors from the Greek ICT market, namely FORTHnet S.A. and ALTEC S.A. it is worth to mention that both ALTEC and FORTHnet operate a huge (at least for the Greek market reality) installed base of corporate customers all of which (at least at some more than 95% proportion) are SMEs. More information can be retrieved from the official site of the project http://islab.uom.gr/dern/.

It is difficult for an SME to recruit experts – usually cost matters are regarded as a barrier but the tougher reality relates to the rather naïve issue of which expert they should actually recruit? An expert for sales? Or for marketing? Or for supply chain management? Or for knowledge management? Or for human resources? Or for new product development? An LGE, again, can afford to recruit several experts from different domains to address needs of different departments, or, though less frequently, several experts from the same domain in order to create excellence in a selected field. But an SME is unable to compete with this unfavorable reality. This means that the only way for an SME to capture the fruits of an expert's knowledge and expertise is by means of forming human networks for research and de-

velopment as well as training with organizations that are expected to exhibit a high concentration of experts. And as such are to be regarded both universities and research centres. In this respect the DERN network provides a role model organization for demonstrating how the acquisition of expert knowledge can take place within SMEs. In Table 1 below we present an attempt to classify levels and depth of knowledge according to three generally accepted knowledge worker categories (Gartner, 2005). It is easy to see that an SME usually needs to rely on workforce that belongs mainly to category 2 (generalist), while limiting the amount of category 1 employees to a minimum (related usually to their core business or core process). Category 3 is welcome not only for SMEs but also for LGEs – but according to our experience it is like work-in-progress and, from our perspective, the goal of any intra-enterprise learning initiative. You *cannot* teach people to become *specialists* if they are not. You *should not* teach people to become *generalists*. But definitely you *ought* to help people learn how to become *versatilists*.

The main idea in DERN is that educational bodies and productive enterprises cooperate for the formation of a human network of research and technological training. The academic bodies are the backbone of the Network. The productive enterprises are important factors of the national economy.

In the frame of this human network formation, five educational Training Programs will be held (one by each partner). The trainees may be University graduates, researchers, post-graduate students, scientists, business executives. Each program will include both theoretic and practical training. The total duration of each program varies from 80 to 120 hours.

The increasing need of the existing human resources' re-training on ICT is a phenomenon rather strong in the antagonistic environment of private business as well as public bodies. Scientists are obliged to train themselves to new evolutions so that their **knowledge** doesn't loose its value. Business executives must update their **knowledge** and skills so that they can bring an antagonistic advantage to their businesses. Lack of information on new technologies can lead both scientists and business executives to being set aside. New technologies have recently entered Public Administrations in order to improve internal procedures and public services (e-Government) as well as increase the peoples' participation (e-Participation).

The project aims at creating a network of development and **knowledge** exchange on the use of ICT, the production of **knowledge** and the application of innovations on **business administration**. The projects' benefits are about the Greek economy in general, since ICT are the core of the "New Economy" that is evolving on a worldwide scale and at which **knowledge** is the most important business source that is capable of leading into innovations.

More specifically, the objectives achieved through the Network are:

- Timely training of researchers and business executives on modern ICT on **Business Administration** through five different programs.
- Post-graduate students training on research and enterprise technology through theoretic and practical exercise.
- Transfer of know-how among the Network's members by meetings and workshops.

- Dissemination of research and technological **knowledge** through 2 events during which relevant material will be handed out (flyers, posters)
- Isolation reduction of research groups in the Greek regions (the Network consists of Bodies located in the three major regions of Greece).
- Update on issues of international scientific and technological developments by bringing two special scientists from abroad to teach.
- Support of the Greek economy's competitiveness by participation of private business executives at the training programs.
- Development of a permanent mechanism for the cooperation of the Network's members on scientific matters. This will be achieved through mutual publications and research cooperation.

Finally, the main deliverables of the project relate with a set of training programs carried by all partners as follows:

1. "The use of ICT in Organisations: past and future" (Information Systems Laboratory/ University of Macedonia).
2. "Administration in the Business of **Knowledge**. Semantic Technologies". (IMU-ICCS)
3. "Modern business **practices** and ICT" (ELTRUN)
4. "Mobile Internet technologies and innovative business models in Education and Tourism (FORTHNET)
5. "Value chains organization and management with the use of ERP" (ALTEC)

In the following we elaborate on the methodologies and the approach taken for the last module, namely this of ALTEC.

Value Chains Organization and Management with the Use of ERP

What has become obvious to us as a result of our exposure to several new technologies and / or organizational **practices** adoption pitfalls, is that enterprises are not facing a lack on enabling technologies but on paradigms to successfully deploy them within their working environment and as part of their routine tasks and existing / operational business process grid. In this context, we turned to **capacity building**, in order to provide the means for public organizations to develop a set of relevant capacities that will help them adopt such new **practices** and technologies.

The Need to Invest in Intangibles

An important challenge in establishing lasting changes of culture and values in an organisation involves ensuring that organized learning processes are anchored within the organisation. Traditional courses and training are considered efficient, but it often seems as if the long-term effect is missing. Furthermore, traditional courses are often used by organisations to train their employees so they can perform better, but in the same ways as they always have done.

There are several positive aspects to both tactics, but if the goal of the learning is to gain new **knowledge** and to establish changes in behaviour as well as further learning in the organisation, it is important to use a strategy based on pedagogical theories and methods that take individual as well as organizational learning into consideration. There is a saying: 'Those that have hammers, will see only nails'. In the greater scheme of things, corporate decision-making includes more than scientific approaches and methods.

Our own experience working with decision-making processes dates back to the beginning of 1990. We have been closely involved with a wide range of different organisations in the research, the business software and the IT industry in general,

and different types and levels of decision-making styles and cultures. In all these settings, we have been exposed to different **learning strategies** based on problem-based and project-organised approaches, and our experience is that they provided quite another learning outcome. We consider this Situation-Room learning approach an effective and motivating way to organise the kind of learning situations needed when working with changes in behaviour, strategies, and innovative processes in companies and organizations, as it is for the case of product development.

Authors like (Nonaka, 1991; Nonaka and Takeuchi, 1995), (Leonard-Barton, 1995), (Sveiby, 1997), (Sveiby and Lloyd, 1988), and many more, claim that **knowledge** is the most important resource. "In an economy where the only certainty is uncertainty, the sure source of lasting competitive advantage is **knowledge**" (Nonaka, 1995). However, this does not mean that the **knowledge**-based view is a synonym for the resource-based view. The most important and fundamental difference is that the resource-based view only implicitly refers to **knowledge**, whereas the **knowledge**-based view gives extensive elaboration on the nature and definition of **knowledge** and the way it should be managed (Thompson Klein, 1996). **Knowledge** management literature can be seen as a further specification or extension (Bontis, 2002) of the resource-based view into a '**knowledge**-based theory of the firm'.

In parallel a closely related and more holistic perspective on the value creating resources of the organisation emerged. This intangible-based view of the firm is based on the work of authors like (Sveiby, 1997), (Stewart, 1997) and (Edvinsson, 1997). This so-called Intellectual Capital movement uses **knowledge** and intellectual capital interchangeably. Although closely related, the meaning of **knowledge** in this movement fundamentally differs from the definition of **knowledge** in the **knowledge**-based view of the firm. Intellectual capital, intellectual assets, **intangible assets**, intangibles, **knowledge** assets, **knowledge** capital or whatever term is used within this movement, refers to the traditional hidden sources of value creation (of which **knowledge** is just one). Hidden in the sense that existing management techniques do not have the methods or instruments to reveal them.

This intangible-based view of the firm inspired the intellectual capital movement to further elaborate on the nature of intangible resources and the way they should be measured and managed. This view serves as a starting point for application within the corporate environment.

(Weick, 1995) presents a detailed theory of sensemaking in organizational contexts, particularly those characterized by novelty or other forms of description. He suggests that individual and group activities are inextricably intertwined. Weick's work is compatible with constructivist perspectives of **knowledge**, in that situations become 'real' only through the interpretive processes of sensemaking which reveal how different parties construe the situation. (Choo, 1999) summarizes three-step processes that are central to sensemaking: *Enactment:* the process by which individuals in an organization actively create the environment which they face; *Selection:* the process by which people in an organization generate an enacted environment that provides a cause-and-effect explanation of what is taking place; *Retention:* enacted or meaningful environments are stored for future retrieval upon occurrence of new equivocal situations.

According to Weick, people engage in sensemaking in two main ways. Belief driven sensemaking takes place through arguing (creating meaning by comparing dissimilar ideas) or expecting/confirming (creating meaning by connecting similar ideas). Action-driven sensemaking involves people committing (engaging in highly visible actions to which they have commitment) or manipulating (acting to create an environment that people can comprehend).

Weick addresses the social dimensions of **knowledge** sharing by drawing on Wiley's work

(Wiley, 1988) which suggests that there are three levels of sensemaking above that of the individual: *Intersubjective:* synthesis of self from I to We; *Generic subjective:* interaction to create meaning at the group or organizational level; *Extrasubjective:* meaning attains the strength of culture – 'pure meanings'.

Bringing these concepts together, therefore, Weick sees organizational sensemaking as the drive to develop generic subjectivity through arguing, expecting, committing and manipulating. These social dimensions converge with Nonaka and Takeuchi's (Nonaka, 1995) view on the role of socialization in transforming tacit to explicit **knowledge**. Companies provide many different types of services to their employees and stakeholders; the interactions between the abstract entity of a corporation and its people are mostly process-based and can be categorised as follows (Lenk, 1999): structured procedures or routines, semi-structured decision processes and negotiation-based case-solving.

(Capurro, 2004) furthermore states that what can be managed is information or explicit **knowledge** and that implicit **knowledge** can only be "enabled". In this context, explicit means that it can be clearly observed and expressed (and also digitalised), as opposed to implicit **knowledge** that can not be directly formulated (skills, experiences, insight, intuition, judgement, etc.) When **knowledge** is explicit, it can be represented as declarative or procedural **knowledge**. We are aware that in the domain of cognitive sciences, the distinction between procedural and declarative models is related to the brain memory system - see for example (Ullman, 2001), but here we used these terms here in a limited sense, as defined in computer science: *Declarative **knowledge** components* represent facts and events in terms of concepts and relations; *Procedural **knowledge** components* describe actions to be taken in order to solve a problem step by step.

For cases where **knowledge** is implicit and cannot be formalized, we introduced the concept of distribution: **knowledge** can be individual or collective, and in both cases components identify who has this **knowledge** or where it can be found. Finally we added a set of metadata (know-where, know-when, know-who, etc.) that describe these **knowledge**-components and that make it possible to manage them.

The Training Program

In ALTEC we have designed our training program structured in 9 subunits which are listed below with a brief description of the included thematic fields covered.

Training Unit 1: Fundamental principles of interdisciplinary approaches and the Theory U model in the field of corporate organization

- Basic principles of cross-disciplinary research methods
- Bibliography and modern interdisciplinary adoption patterns
- The Scandinavian model for Participatory Design and the Experience Application Research model
- Weaknesses and shortcomings in the above models
- The Theory U model
- Practical applications in the corporate working environment
- Success and failure stories

Training Unit 2: Corporate value chains management technologies with use of Enterprise Resource Planning systems (ERP)

- Distributed resource planning systems
- Selection of representative enterprise resource planning systems
- Corporate value chains: what are they, how they operate and how much woth they are (: assessment, valuation and residual value for the company)
- Introduction techniques and organization

patterns for value chain management in the modern enterprise environment
- Costing and pricing of services for design and development of corporate value chains: the case of private sector companies
- Costing and pricing of services for design and development of corporate value chains: the case of public sector organisations

Training Unit 3: Tools and practical applications for enterprise-wide value chains with the use of ERP systems

- Workflow management applications
- Service flow management applications
- ISO management systems
- Web information system management tools
- Business integration and interoperability of information systems and processes
- Human resource integration aspects and the corporate culture

Training Unit 4: Case study 1: **Knowledge** management for the fostering of business development activities

- Presentation of sectorial information from the international bibliography
- Critical parameters analysis
- Linkage with training material presented in units 1-3
- Case study examination
- Development of good practice guides for the implementation of similar applications in a company / organisation

Training Unit 5: Case study 2: Process change management for the improvement of corporate culture

- Presentation of sectorial information from the international bibliography
- Critical parameters analysis

- Linkage with training material presented in units 1-3
- Case study examination
- Development of good practice guides for the implementation of similar applications in a company / organization

Training Unit 6: Case study 3: Design and lifecycle management for new services and products

- Presentation of sectorial information from the international bibliography
- Critical parameters analysis
- Linkage with training material presented in units 1-3
- Case study examination
- Development of good practice guides for the implementation of similar applications in a company / organisation

Training Unit 7: Case study 4: implementation of joint actions with the corporate value chains

- Presentation of sectorial information from the international bibliography
- Critical parameters analysis
- Linkage with training material presented in units 1-3
- Case study examination
- Development of good practice guides for the implementation of similar applications in a company / organisation

Training Unit 8: Specialised tools for project management of corporate value chains

- Project management techniques in value chains
- Monitoring and reporting tools
- Benchmarking applications in value chains
- Creation of your own value chain management toolkit

Training Unit 9: Exploitation techniques for the corporate working environment

The Capacity Building Platform

According to wikipedia (http://en.wikipedia.org/wiki/ Capacity_building) **Capacity Building** involves more than just training and includes the following:

- Human resource development, the process of equipping individuals with the understanding, skills and access to information, **knowledge** and training that enables them to perform effectively.
- Organizational development, the elaboration of management structures, processes and procedures, not only within organizations but also the management of relationships between the different organizations and sectors (public, private and community).
- Institutional and legal framework development, making legal and regulatory changes to enable organizations, institutions and agencies at all levels and in all sectors to enhance their capacities

All the above fit perfectly when we think of creating a **capacity building** platform to support corporate training activities, because:

- Employees need to acquire the skills and **knowledge** required for deploying, maintaining and using any type of new ICT solution or organisational practice.
- Corporate processes need to be adapted for use in any new ICT environment such as those posed by the introduction of a new ERP system. This does not simply involve a direct transformation of existing processes to electronic ones. An adaptation of existing processes is required, in order to exploit the advantages that the IT can offer over the traditional methods.

Figure 1. Main page of ALTEC's capacity building portal

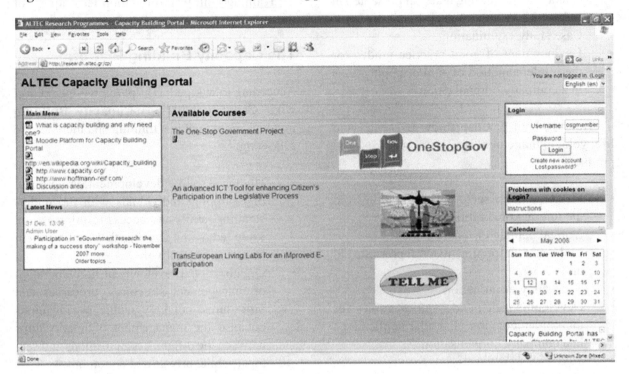

- And finally, the legal aspect is obviously of great importance in the corporate application area, and all aspects related to the adoption of a new ERP solution (validity of e-processes, privacy and data protection issues, etc) must take into account this factor especially when we consider the case of Value Chains that go beyond the boundaries of a Supply Chain, thus involving exchange of **knowledge** and other forms of structured know how amongst the value chain partners.

The idea behind the developed Portal is that although an(y) ERP implementation project will result in a ready-for-use system, companies and organizations will need to develop a set of relevant capacities in order to be able to adopt our solution.

Achieving active use of the created portal, will take us a step further. It shall give both ALTEC as ERP platform provider and the companies (i.e. the customers) a realistic experience on using the **capacity building** platform for preparing the adoption of the ALTEC ATLANTIS ERP platform, and could highly leverage the uptake of successful **practices** by the ERP users.

Our vision is to understand how to capitalise on the interactions between ERP users and developers as part of a value chain that creates new intellectual capital for new enterprise-wide application types and services by exploring problem-solving principles in computer science and other disciplines. This necessitates the existence and fostering of closer links between the sides of the users and the developers, both of which need to share a space for expressing as well as exploring their own modes of thought and help improve their problem-solving paradigm.

Better understanding and communication with the future users of an ERP system requires the software creation to be placed at the level of abstraction

Figure 2. Impact and influence patterns amongst people, processes, practices and policies

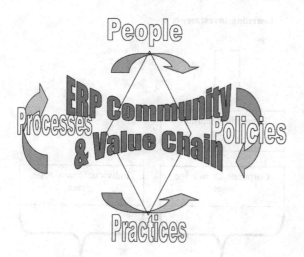

the users can understand. Better communication between IT- and application field-specialists will lead to avoidance of misunderstanding, loss of time and resources and in the effect to systems that better address the needs of the end users. This refers to the creation of *policies*, *processes* and *practices* that will enrich the *people* in both communities of users and developers to coexist smoothly and gain from their interactions.

The Research Agenda

Our research agenda includes the following topics:

- *Corporate Intellectual Capital vs Individual (worker) knowledge assets:* How can the company document as (licensed or leased) assets the **knowledge** assets of its workers? How can synergetic ways be developed that shall guide (not only at the transactional / trade level but also at the cultural one) the interactions between what the two parts offer to each other? And how can amortization of learning investments and **knowledge** assets be organised within

the real-word market environment as part of corporate implementation of the relevant International Accounting Standards?

- *Corporate Human Resources, E.R.P. and accounting systems vs Corporate Intangible Assets Accounting:* Corporate accounting of intangibles has been mainly treated as a set of activities related more (or solely) with patents, copyrights, trademarks and licensing agreements and not about the people and the **knowledge** they carry which they can document into patents, protect with a copyright or express as a tradable entity or brand identity by means of a trademark. Our research aspires to provide an integrated approach (methodology + accompanying **practices** + application platform) to account for learning and **knowledge** assets.

- *Interaction and interface of the Learning Assets Management system with the users and positioning within the corporate business process grid and culture.* Though this part of the research does not involve technology risks from its implementation perspective, it is at a central position for the success of the research and the exploitation potential of the research outcomes. Of interest are here the approaches taken for documenting a learning asset, for configuring a learning portfolio for an individual or for a corporate business unit, etc.

- *Bridging the gaps amongst the different edges of the research topics star visualisation.* This last item of our research agenda is going beyond the medium-term nature of the research project. More specifically, it aims to put the foundations for new research in the areas that are depicted at each of the five separate star's edges in the figure below. In the context of the research, we provide as output a showcase demonstrator (i.e. fully functional for demonstration purposes but not capable for operational use) for a futuristic Learning Assets Management system.

The Research Methodology

In the research, we came across a set of different methods that have been examined with respect to their appropriateness and adequacy to the research field. This short overview is not exhaustive, but serves as a starting point for conduct of the research. It should be mentioned that in this first section we only limit ourselves to the objective presentation of methods examined and not taking a position with respect to them.

We briefly elaborate on the methods we selected specifically to involve the user in the development of software, specifically requirement analysis that involves systems with a user interface. Each method is briefly described.

- *User-centred design* (Gulliksen et al, 2001). Not only are users involved, but also in their own context. Emphasis is on iterative short cycles and prototypes. User-centred design is multidisciplinary.
- *Participatory design* (Kuhn and Muller, 1993). The goal is to work directly with users in designing computer systems that are a part of human work. Participatory design is rooted in Scandinavian countries with strong labour unions and democracy in the workplace. It has then moved on to other parts of the world. Muller et al (1993) give an overview of participatory design **practices** and thereby answer questions such as: who participates with whom and in what? Where do they participate in the development lifecycle? What are the appropriate sizes of groups? The users participate in the design and are not merely a subject of research.
- *Co-creation* (Garrett, 2003). Designers and users are partners in design, and users

Figure 3. Learning assets management system diagram

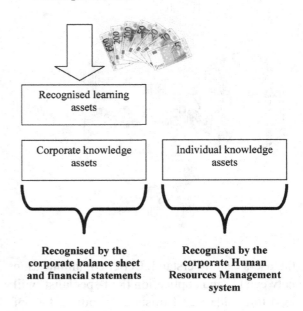

Figure 4. Research topics star

participate actively in the design, not only as evaluators, but also as designers. End-user programming, where users write their own programmes may be classified under this method.

- *Contextual design* (Beyer and Holtzblatt, 1998) have different parts: contextual inquiry; work modelling; consolidation of work models through affinity diagrams; work redesign; user environment design; mock-up and test with customers; and putting the new design into practice.
- *Activity theory* (Bertelsen and Bødker, 2003): What sets activity theory apart is that it takes into considerations the capabilities of the individual groups instead of addressing the generic user. It concerns itself also with collaboration of humans instead of focusing only on one user's work. There is also strong focus on artefacts and their role in work activities.
- *Scenario based development of human-computer interaction* (Rosson and Carroll, 2002). Scenarios are used throughout the software development, first in requirements analysis and then through design, documentation and evaluation. Scenarios describe a sequence of interactions between a user and a computer, its contexts, and users' mental activities such as goals, plans and reactions. Trade-offs is a fundamental aspect, as well as prototypes.

The Envisaged Solution

One criticism that the authors have received was that what we shall in the following paragraphs describe as our proposed 'envisaged solution' is actually dated 'from stats published more than a decade ago' and is 'focused on larger corporations rather than SMEs'. How can it be that both the aforementioned (rather unfairly harsh) criticism and our position coexist? Though at first level this might seem like a paradoxical situation, it is actually not! More specifically, solutions that would be regarded in the past as non-appropriate for a small or medium-sized enterprise are now a must for them. And while in the past only an LGE (large or giant enterprise) might afford to operate

such a solution for all three reasons (money, people and technology), nowadays it is only a matter of will to adopt such a system.

More specifically we propose a system that provides the corporate Management with a continuous access to the formation of learning assets and the ability to transform them into corporate **knowledge** assets, which – with the use of International Accounting Standards – can become an extension of existing ERP, HRM and LMS systems.

Since 1980, the average ratio of market capitalization to book value for companies has swelled from just over 1 to more than 5 - even after the recent fall in stock prices. In this respect, differences in market and book value are rough estimates of the value of intangibles. But, on average, **intangible assets** now represent about 80 percent of the market value of public companies (Ernst & Young, 1997). One possible explanation for the growth, is that irrational exuberance has inflated corporate stock prices far beyond the value of the assets that the shares have claim to. The more likely explanation, however, is that financial statements prepared according to the particular accounting **practices** that exist, fail to reflect the true value of a company's assets and operating performance. It is exactly at this point where the unique contribution of our research can fill the **knowledge** and asset gaps (Gelinas, 2002).

A growing number of academics, consultants, and regulators see the absence of most **intangible assets** from the books as a major deficiency in the existing accounting 'regime'. They argue that those assets increasingly drive the value of corporations, and yet currently receive next to no recognition in financial disclosures. In an increasingly competitive, **knowledge**-based economy, **intangible assets**, such as brand awareness, innovation, and employee productivity, have become the key determinants of corporate success (Edvinsson, 1997). Given that the investments companies make to build those **intangible assets** – such things as corporate infrastructures for **Knowledge** Management, employee training, and R&D – have real costs and real impacts, the fact that they are 'flushed' through the balance sheets means the books increasingly become a poor reflection of the true value of companies' businesses.

Corporate executives, however, see more to lose than gain from increased transparency (Andriessen, 2004). **Intangible assets** essentially represent the secrets of a business enterprise - the key resources and factors that enable it to compete effectively in the marketplace. If the company shares those secrets with investors (and with competitors), it could hasten the erosion of the value of those very intangibles. Furthermore, the added transparency could open up a whole new avenue of attack for plaintiff's lawyers. If corporate disclosures of intangible values prove wrong - and it is easy to be wrong about intangible values - shareholders will have plenty of ammunition for lawsuits.

R&D work to date has mainly focused on analyzing the impact of information exchange on information "supply-chain dynamics". One interesting outcome of our preliminary study of the area under consideration in the intended research was a characterization of situations where individual corporate information suppliers must share information to remain competitive (Kunte, 2002).

The major problems of managing heterogeneous corporate information sources in organisations in which a solution like the one we envisage is implemented, can be summarised as (Leonard-Barton, 2002):

- *Insufficient modelling and understanding* of the source data located in various sites across the organisation, due to lack of a common terminology and documentation, differing implementations of reporting infrastructures, and source data not being placed in the context of the dynamic aspects of the organisation.

- *Difficulty in organising ad hoc processing of such information*, making users (corporate management, shareholders, internal and external auditors, etc.) dependent for their information needs on e.g., information resource management departments with the usual shortcomings of this approach (relatively limited reliability of the provided information, need for authentication, etc.).

- *Lack of facilities for maintaining these resources*, thus making more difficult the task of keeping the various systems in step with the ever increasing rate of change in modern business organisations.

These problems are particulary difficult in small and medium sized enterprises, which have variable access to distinct and heterogeneous information suppliers. However, we understand this marketplace well and are well placed to address it in a complementary partnership.

The bigger barrier to sharing information about intangibles, however, is the lack of workable reporting standards (IFAC, 1998). The internal metrics currently used to evaluate **intangible assets** and capabilities fall far short of fitting the overall accounting **practices** and frameworks currently under use (Bontis, 2002). Part of the problem derives from confusion in distinguishing between the investments made to develop **intangible assets** and the value resulting from those investments. The same difficulties apply to accounting for internally developed intangibles. In fact, attempting to isolate and directly value the **intangible assets** of companies may be counterproductive; the value of an intangible asset comes from its interplay with other assets - both physical and intangible - and attempting to value it on a stand-alone basis is pointless.

The Expected End Products

The major end product is a Learning Assets Management system (LAM) interoperable with best breed of the following:

- Human Resources Management systems like HRnet by HRnet Software Systems and Employee Performance & Talent Management Suite by Halogen Software
- ERP systems and accounting engines (both free / open source and proprietary such

as ERP5, GNU Enterprise, WebERP and PeopleSoft from Oracle, mySAP from SAP and ATLANTIS from ALTEC)
- Learning Management Systems (both Open Source as moodle and ATutor and commercial as Saba Software and SAP Enterprise Learning).

In addition to this, we deliver a fully functional methodology for organising the codification and recording of learning assets in the financial, accounting and bookkeeping operations of the

Figure 5. LAM (learning assets management) system

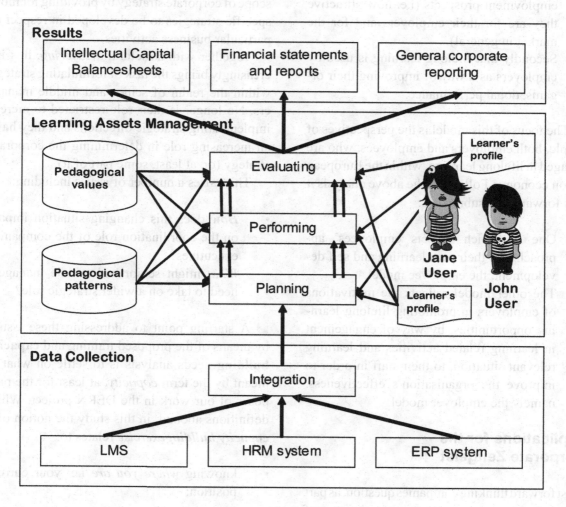

companies in compliance with the participating countries legislative frameworks and the International Accounting Standards (IAS).

Third end product of is a showcase demonstrator (i.e. fully functional for demonstration purposes but not capable for operational use) for a futuristic Learning Assets Management system.

Fourth end product is a model for integrating pedagogical and organisational approaches by means of a lifelong learning module as part of the operating corporate organisational development. This model builds on two drivers:

- Firstly, that lifelong learning is used by employees to improve their current, or future, employment prospects (i.e. how attractive they are for their employers and for the market in general).
- Secondly that lifelong learning is used by employers as a way of improving their organisational performance.

The focus of this model is the perspectives of people, both employers and employees, who are engaged in lifelong learning, within the European Union economy. Following the above analysis it puts forward two submodels:

- One of which reflects employees' approaches to their own learning and self development, the employee model.
- The other model reflects the motivations of employers in promoting lifelong learning opportunities, by way of engagement in learning related activities and learning relevant situation, to their staff in order to improve the organisation's effectiveness, namely the employer model.

Implications for the Corporate Zeitgeist

Most forward thinking companies question, as part of their strategic processes, the appropriateness of

their structures in achieving business outcomes. Indeed, even successful structural platforms need to be challenged if companies are to continue to succeed into the future. In order to increase corporate responsiveness and flexibility in a rapidly changing world, many companies have broken down the traditional, hierarchical bureaucracies that served them well in the past in favour of a number of smaller structures often clustered around different business activities. A feature of such restructures has been the doing away with levels of management coupled, in many instances, with the introduction of a form of 'self-directed' team work.

Restructuring along these lines broadens the scope of corporate strategy by providing for more specific strategies to be developed in respect of particular business activities.

Together with structural *delayering*, this increasingly brings the task of formulating strategy within the realm of senior and middle managers. No longer is their role restricted to merely implementing strategic directions and they have an increasing role in determining the corporate strategy (or, at least, some part of it).

This raises a number of issues including:

- *How* does this changing situation impact on the coordination role of the companies executives?
- *What* might senior and middle managers need to take on a wider strategic role?

A starting point to addressing these issues by means of the proposed training and **capacity building** needs analysis is to settle on what is meant by the term *capacity*, at least for the purposes of our work in the DERN project. While definitions abound, in this study the notion of a *capacity building exercise* relates to:

- knowing *where you are* i.e. your current position;

- knowing *where you want to go* i.e. your target position; and
- knowing *how you are going to get there* i.e. the means to support the transition from your current to the target position, as well as the cost matters which you shall need to take into account in order to achieve this), and having the capability to respond to change on the way.

The conducted analysis and the business application scenarios indicate that 'prototyping' of an experiential **capacity building** session within a corporate setting can contribute to the increase of the corporate intellectual capital in at least three key ways:

- By helping to develop understanding about the essence or essential factors of a corporate decision-making experience, as it simulates important aspects of the whole or parts of the relationships between people, events and contexts, as they unfold over time.
- In exploration, shaping and evaluation of ideas and attitudes: **capacity building** can provide inspiration, confirmation or rejection of ideas based upon the quality of experience they engender. It produces answers and feedback to decision-makers' questions about proposed solutions in terms of 'what would it feel like if...?'
- In communication of issues and ideas: by enabling others to engage directly in a proposed new training situation, it provides common ground for establishing a shared point of view. Such a point is to be regarded as a collective asset – not property of an individual but of the team that has contributed to its creation.

From this perspective, it follows that the aim of our work was not about the creation of a formalized toolkit or set of training techniques, but is about developing an attitude and corporate culture to solve problems and respond to challenges of the business environment.

CONCLUSION

Companies are investing in their people, by means of motivating the latter to participate in training programs or re-education projects, as part of their other core business activities. Independently on the motivation (in many cases it is simply because expenses for such activities are subsidised by the national authorities), companies are aware that they have to invest in their human resources to improve their business cycles and increase their capacities (Sveiby, 1997) and (Edvinsson, 2002). However, they are not able to exhibit the existence of a traceable process for managing their investments for learning (Simmons, 2006).

Individual workers, are aware that in order to ensure that the value (and the utility) that they carry for their company is not fixed but continuously under negotiation. Therefore, in order to remain attractive they have to invest in themselves and increase their learning and **knowledge** capital, so that they are able to keep on selling their services to their employer or seek for a new one that can better reward them for their value (and utility). An important reason for lagging behind in this area of soft infrastructures has been the fact that till today the workflows of learning and **knowledge** management related projects have been kept apart from the corporate heart which is the corporate accounting system (Stewart, 1997).

The major problems of managing heterogeneous corporate information sources in organisations in which our approach is implemented, can be summarised as:

- *Insufficient modelling and understanding* of the source data located in various sites across the organisation, due to lack of a common terminology and documentation, differing implementations of reporting infrastructures, and source data not being placed in the context of the dynamic aspects of the organisation.

- *Difficulty in organising ad hoc processing of such information*, making users (corporate management, shareholders, internal and external auditors, etc.) dependent for their information needs on e.g., information resource management departments with the usual shortcomings of this approach (relatively limited reliability of the provided information, need for authentication, etc.).
- *Lack of facilities for maintaining these resources*, thus making more difficult the task of keeping the various systems in step with the ever increasing rate of change in modern business organisations.

The major end product of our research is a Learning Assets Management system (LAM) interoperable with best breed of the following: (a) human resources management systems and Employee Performance & Talent Management Suite (b) ERP systems and accounting engines and (c) learning management systems.

REFERENCES

Andriessen, D. (2004) *Making sense of intellectual capital: Designing a method for the valuation of Intangibles*. Butterworth – Heinemann

Bertelsen, O. W., & Bødker, S. (2003). Activity theory. In J. M. Carroll (Ed.), *HCI models, theories and frameworks*. Elsevier Science.

Beyer, H., & Holtzblatt, K. (1998) *Contextual design*. Morgan Kaufman

Bontis, N. (2002) Managing organizational knowledge by diagnosing intellectual capital. Framing and advancing the state of the field. In N. Bontis & C.W. Choo (Eds.), *The strategic management of intellectual capital and organizational knowledge* (pp. 621-642). Oxford, New York: Oxford University Press.

Capurro, R. (2004). Skeptical knowledge management. In H.-C. Hobohm (Ed.) *Knowledge Management: Libraries and librarians taking up the challenge* (IFLA Publication, 108, pp. 47-57). Munich: Saur.

Choo, C. W. (1999) *The knowing organization: How organizations use information to construct meaning, create knowledge, and make decisions*. Oxford: Oxford University Press.

Edvinsson, L. (2002) *Corporate longitude: What you need to know to navigate the knowledge economy*. Financial Times Prentice Hall.

Edvinsson, L., & Malone, M. S. (1997). 'Intellectual capital', *The proven way to establish your company's real value by measuring its hidden brainpower*. London: HarperBusiness.

Ernst and Young. (1997). *Measures that matter.* Ernst and Young LLP.

Garrett, J. J. (2003). *The elements of user experience: User-centered design for the web*. New Riders Publishing Gartner Group (2005). *Gartner's top predictions for 2006 and beyond*. Gartner Research.

Gelinas, U., Oram, A., & Wiggins, W. (2002). *Accounting information systems*. New York: South-Western Publishing Co.

Gulliksen, J., Göransson, B., & Lif, M. (2001). A user-centred approach to object-oriented user interface design. In M. Van Harmelen (Ed.), *Object modelling and user interface design*. Addison-Wesley.

IFAC International Federation of Accountants. (1998). *The measurement and management of intellectual capital*. International Federation of Accountants.

Kuhn, S., & Muller, M. (Eds.). (1993). Special Issue on Participatory Design. *Communications of the ACM, 36*(4).

Kunte, A., Hamilton, K., Dixon, J., & Clemens, M. (2002). Estimating national wealth: Methodology and results. *Environmental Economics Series, 57*, 110–129.

Lenk, K., & Traunmueller, R. (1999). Perspektiven einer radikalen Neugestaltung der oeffentlichen Verwaltung mit Informationstechnik. In *Oeffentliche Verwaltung und Informationstechnik. Schriftenreihe Verwaltungsinformatik*. Heidelberg: Decker's Verlag.

Leonard-Barton, D. (1995). *Wellsprings of knowledge, building and sustaining the sources of innovation*. Boston, MA: Harvard Business School Press.

Leonard-Barton, D., & Kraus, W. (2001). Implementing new technology. *Harvard Business Review, 12*(2), 102–110.

Muller, M. J., Wildman, D. M., & White, E. A. (1993). Taxonomy of PD Practices: A brief practitioner's guide. *Communications of the ACM, 36*(6).

Nonaka, I. (1991). The knowledge creating company. *Harvard Business Review, 69*(6), 96–104.

Nonaka, I., & Takeuchi, H. (1995). *The knowledge creating company*. Oxford: Oxford University Press.

Rosson, M. B., & Carroll, J. (2002). *Usability engineering: Scenario-based development of human-computer interaction*. Morgan Kaufmann.

Simmons, J. (2006). E-learning and earning: The impact of lifelong e-learning on organisational development. *The European Journal of Open and Distance Learning (EURODL), November*.

Stewart, T. A. (1997). *Intellectual capital: The new wealth of organizations*. New York: Doubleday.

Sveiby, K. E. (1997). *The new organizational wealth. Managing and measuring knowledge-based assets*. San Francisco: Berret-Koehler Publishers Inc.

Sveiby, K. E., & Lloyd, T. (1988). *Managing knowhow. Increase profits by harnessing the creativity in your company*. London: Bloomsbury.

Thompson, K. J. (1996). *Crossing boundaries: Knowledge, disciplinarities, and interdisciplinarities*. Charlottesville VA: University Press of Virginia.

Ullman, M. T. (2001). A neurocognitive perspective on language: The declarative/procedural model. *Nature Reviews. Neuroscience, 2*(10), 717–726. doi:10.1038/35094573

Weick, K. E. (1995). *Sensemaking in organizations*, Thousand Oaks, CA: Sage Publications.

Wiley, N. (1988). The micro-macro problem in social theory. *Sociological Theory, 6*, 254–261. doi:10.2307/202119

Chapter 24
Motivations and Trends for IT/ IS Adoption:
Insights from Portuguese Companies

João Varajão
Centro Algoritmi and University of Trás-os-Montes e Alto Douro, Portugal

Antonio Trigo
Escola Superior de Tecnologia e Gestão de Oliveira do Hospital, Portugal

João Barroso
Instituto Superior de Engenharia do Porto, Portugal

ABSTRACT

Over the past few decades, information systems and technologies have taken on a wide variety of roles within organizations, ranging from operational support to the strategic support of the company. Therefore, there have been significant changes in the motives for their adoption that are vital to understand to guarantee that investment is properly managed. With the purpose of identifying and characterizing the motivations currently behind the adoption of information technologies in large Portuguese companies, which systems the companies have been implementing, in which systems they intend to invest in short-term, and what is the current role of information technology within the organization, we carried out a study with the participation of several chief information officers. The findings of this study reveal that the reasons for adoption and the role that information systems and technologies play is evolving in Portuguese companies and that the adoption of certain types of systems like Enterprise Resource Planning systems is now consolidated, whereas the adoption of other systems like Business Intelligence systems should increase significantly in the near future.

INTRODUCTION

Over the past few decades, Information Technologies and Information Systems (IT/IS) have known very different roles within organizations: much has changed from the time when computation surged, where IT/IS were used merely for operational support, to the most recent role of being the driver of an organization's competitiveness.

Initially, its use was practically restricted to the operational level, in the scope of the systems for processing transactions. But, over time, with the development of new features and potentialities, companies began finding other applications at the most diverse levels and today IT/IS play an absolutely central and crucial role in organizations.

Companies currently use multiple solutions of IT/IS to support their activities at all management levels and few of them try to conduct their businesses without exploiting the advantages of IT/IS solutions (Trigo, Varajão, Figueiredo, & Barroso, 2007). Among the systems adopted by companies we can find Enterprise Resource Planning (ERP) systems, Customer Relationship Management (CRM) systems, Business Intelligence (BI) systems, and many others. Such systems assure a wide spectrum of activities, ranging from operational support to the strategic support of the company.

Although the scope of application of the information technologies was confined to the operational level, the motives for its adoption were, in a certain way, clear and had to do, generically, with task automation to increase work productivity and reduce costs. As the scope of its use began covering, first the tactical level and, later, the strategic level of enterprises, the set of motivations was extended; therefore, the motivations for the adoption of IT/IS have also evolved significantly to include, for example, improving the time to market, the establishment of strategic partnerships, or the exploration of new markets.

The great diversity of IT/IS applications implies a great diversity of motivations for their adoption. For instance, the inherent set of motives for the adoption of a CRM system will probably be different from the set of motives for investing in a new version of an operational system. On the other hand, the motives for adopting a specific system of BI could be the same as those leading to the acquisition of a particular expert system.

Nevertheless, there is a set of generally inherent motivations to IT/IS adoption that is important to identify and understand to conduct investments, and serve as a guide to maximizing the degree of satisfaction with IT/IS investment initiatives, given the generally significant sums involved in these investments.

With the purpose of identifying and characterizing the motivations for IT/IS adoption, which systems the Portuguese companies have been implementing, in which systems they intend to invest in the short-term, and what is the current role of information technology within the organization, we developed a survey with the participation of several chief information officers of Portuguese companies.

The general methodology involved a questionnaire that was sent to 500 Chief Information Officers (CIOs) of Portuguese companies. The questionnaire was sent to the subjects in February 2008. Three months later, after three rounds, the data collection process was concluded, with a response rate of 12.9%.

In this article, we present the results obtained from the study conducted: current motivations for IT/IS adoption; current implemented systems; current role of IT/IS; and trends for IT/IS adoption.

Next, after a literature review, we present the scope, research process, analysis, and discussion of the results obtained.

BACKGROUND

A common approach to examining the types of IT/IS solutions used within organizations is to categorize them by the roles they play at various management levels within the organizational structure (Belle, Eccles, & Nash, 2003; Laudon & Laudon, 2005), according to Robert Anthony's pyramid (1965) of operational control, managerial control, and strategic planning.

At the lowest level of the organizational hierarchy, we find the transaction processing systems (TPS) that support the day-to-day activities of the business. These applications are normally the first to be computerized and are characterized by large numbers of transactions updating the corporate database. Clerical staff performing routine daily business activities, such as invoicing or issuing of stock, and following well-defined business procedures mainly uses these systems. Low-level managers and supervisors responsible for monitoring the transactions that are occurring and dealing with any problems that may arise occupy the next level in the organizational hierarchy. Management Information Systems (MIS) use the data collected by the TPS to assist the operations and line managers with the control of the business process activities, usually by means of standard, regular reports. Tactical management occupies the next level in the organizational hierarchy. These managers are responsible for ensuring that plans and targets set by senior management are achieved. They decide on budgets, set targets, identify trends, and develop short-term plans for the business. To achieve this, tactical managers need to have more interactive applications that actually assist them with the decision making process of middle management. These applications are called Decision Support Systems (DSS) and allow managers to request the relevant data, select and apply the appropriate decision model, and generate the output report in the format required. At the top of the pyramid, strategic management is responsible for defining the long-term goals of the company, and how it intends to position itself within its particular industry. They require an information system that will enable them to identify problems that may threaten their organization's competitive position or opportunities and

trends that may enhance it. Executive Information Systems (EIS) assist top-level executives with their daily information needs for top management control, as well as their strategic decision making (Belle et al., 2003; Laudon & Laudon, 2005).

Knowledge management (KM) embraces all the management levels, since it aims to capture organizational learning and core competencies of the organization from day-to-day operations (Cuffe, 2005). KM is used to achieve better performance due to effective knowledge sharing and organizational learning (Okkonen, Pirttimäki, Lönnqvist, & Hannula, 2002) and tries to prevent the waste of resources by seeking the best practices (Wah, 2000). KM objectives are: to capture, store, retrieve and distribute tangible knowledge assets; to gather, organize and disseminate intangible knowledge; and finally, to create an interactive learning environment where people transfer, and share, their knowledge, and apply it in order to accumulate new knowledge (Wah, 2000). Knowledge Management Systems store information in a repository which is updated during an organization's life cycle and can assist them in reducing their research and development, maintain internal best-practices repositories, and reduce the loss of expertise when key individuals depart (Cuffe, 2005). KM is also used to support the strategy process. For example, analyzing employees' competencies can identify organization's core competencies. Sometimes the strategy is formulated around the core competencies. On the other hand, KM activities can be used to implement strategic objectives, such as the decrease in costs by more effective knowledge sharing, or the gain in new know-how among the employees of the organization (Okkonen et al., 2002).

There is yet another group of IT/IS solutions used by all the management levels, the group of IT/IS solutions that provide an interface to external entities, which include all customers, business partners, and third parties. While the majority of IT/IS solutions in the past focused on applications within the boundaries of the enterprise, the focus is gradually shifting outwards, with many managers participating in new IT projects to take advantage of Internet capabilities (Cuffe, 2005), as is the case of Business-to-Business (B2B), Business-to-Consumer (B2C), Customer-to-Business (C2B), SCM, CRM, and so forth. Electronic commerce is an emerging business model that streamlines the operations of a business and results in efficiency and profitability (Li, Tseng, & Lu, 2007).

IT/IS role in organizations is materialized by the use of diverse IT/IS solutions, such as Enterprise Resource Planning systems; Customer Relationship Management systems; Supply Chain Management Systems; Business Intelligence; Collaboration and Groupware; and Workflow Management Systems.

Enterprise Resource Planning (ERP) systems are commercial software packages, often transversal to all the management levels of the enterprise, that aim to fulfill all the information system requirements of a business (Belle et al., 2003) and to integrate all the information flowing through a company—financial and accounting information, human resource information, supply chain information, customer information, and so forth (Davenport, 1998).

To be considered an ERP system, a software package must simultaneously possess at least the three following characteristics (Lequeux, 1999): the effective management of various company activities; the existence of a common database; and the capability to react quickly to operating rules.

ERP systems evolved from the idea of Material Requirement Planning (MRP) and Manufacturing Resource Planning (MRP II) systems towards the end of the 1980s. ERP came into picture only in 1993 (Gupta, Priyadarshini, Massoud, & Agrawal, 2004) and was first phrased by the Gartner Group of Stamford, Connecticut (Stevens, 2003).

The ERP functional capabilities expanded from legacy systems incorporating only basic modules for core business functions to sophisticated systems with numerous add-ons for analyti-

cal and e-business applications, appearing with the power of enterprise-wide inter-functional coordination and integration. ERP technology has moved from mainframe-based batched operations to the client-server architecture and Internet enabled real-time operations.

An ERP system is primarily responsible for managing the transactional processing operations of the business in its various areas (e.g., accounting, finance, human resources, marketing, manufacturing, logistics, sales, procurement, etc.) usually supported by a software module (or modules) designed to integrate with the other modules. These packaged modules then need to be configured, and sometimes customized to meet the specific demands of the company implementing the ERP. Since ERP systems consist of different modules, companies only need to purchase the modules they need (Pairat & Jungthirapanich, 2005). Due to the integrated nature of ERP, its modules overcome many of the drawbacks of legacy systems and enable online integration not only within the same function but also within and across the other functions of the business. As a result, ERP systems are considered good candidates for forming a technology platform to support the integration of other intra- and inter-organizational applications like SCM, CRM, and e-commerce.

One of the most visible benefits of ERP systems is the replacement of legacy systems with standardized, cross-functional transaction automation, resulting in reduced cycle times, improved throughput, customer response times, and delivery speeds (Cotteleer & Bendoly, 2006; McAfee, 2002). All enterprise data is collected once during the initial transaction, stored centrally, and updated in real time. This ensures that all levels of planning are based on the same data and that the resulting plans realistically reflect the prevailing operating conditions of the firm (Hendricks, Singhal, & Stratman, 2007). Taken together, the standardized firm-wide transactions and centrally stored enterprise data greatly facilitate the governance of the firm (Scott & Vessey, 2000). ERP reports provide managers with a clear view of the relative performance of the various parts of the enterprise, which can be used to identify needed improvements and take advantage of market opportunities (Hendricks et al., 2007). These visible benefits are related to the motivations of an organization seeking to adopt an ERP system. For Oliver and Romm (2000), three categories of factors determine an organization's initial search for an ERP solution: the need to improve the performance of current operations; the need to integrate data and systems; and the need to prevent a competitive disadvantage or a business risk from becoming critical. Ross and Vitale (2000) identify six reasons generally cited by enterprises, classifying them into three categories (infrastructure, capacity, and performance) and underscore their overlapping character; the new common systems platform (infrastructure) makes it possible to acquire new capabilities (process improvement, data visibility), which in turn are supposed to allow improvements in organizational performances (cost reduction, strategic decision making, customer responsiveness). Parr (2000) takes up the same motives, but gives the categories different names: technological (common platform, obsolescence of legacy systems), operational (process improvement, data visibility, operating cost reductions), and strategic (multi-site standardization, customer responsiveness, decision-making improvement, need for efficiencies and integration, business restructuring).

Customer Relationship Management (CRM) means different things to different people. For some, CRM is a term used to describe a set of IT/IS solutions that automate customer-facing processes in marketing, sales, and service functions of the business. For others, it is about an organizational desire to be more customer-focused and includes consideration of people and processes, not only technology. For another group, CRM focuses on the analysis and exploitation of customer data (Iriana & Buttle, 2006).

One key to managing customer relationships is by providing the same information to everyone within the company so that every product or service need of the customer is met. It provides to individuals within organizations a "Single Customer View." Whether working with a customer from a customer service level, technical support level, or even from a back-office marketing standpoint, all individuals will have a single point of view in understanding the customer. Therefore, with CRM, everyone within the enterprise will be wholly focused on a customer's needs, whether it is for sales or service.

The essence of CRM is to change organizations from a products-centric to customer-centric philosophy. Therefore, one of the most important processes of CRM is extracting valid, previously unknown, and comprehensible information from a large database and using it for profit. CRM employs many technologies and decision-science applications like data mining and data warehousing to perform effectively. Customer relationship management has rapidly become one of the leading competitive business strategies in the new millennium (Kim, 2003).

CRM technologies can be segregated into three broad, yet distinctive, categories (Karimi, Somers, & Gupta, 2001; META Group, 2001): Operational, Collaborative, and Analytical, as described below. Operational CRM includes business processes and technologies that can help improve the efficiency and accuracy of day-to-day customer-facing operations. Operational CRM includes sales automation, marketing automation, and service automation.

Collaborative CRM is concerned with the components and processes that allow an enterprise to interact and collaborate with its customers. These include voice technologies, Web storefronts, e-mail, conferencing, and face-to-face interactions. Collaborative CRM technologies are all about communicating and sharing information within the company, with business partners and suppliers, and with customers. Analytical CRM is that portion of the CRM ecosystem that provides analysis of customer data and behavioral patterns to improve business decisions. This includes the underlying data warehouse architecture, customer profiling/segmentation systems, reporting, and analysis. Analytic CRM tools provide companies with the means to manage their customer-facing processes and help them acquire, grow, and retain customers. Analytic CRM technologies include Data Warehouse Building and Management tools for consolidating and cleansing customer data from disparate systems located throughout a company. Data Mining software performs exploratory data analysis and modeling to discover the hidden patterns and associations needed to make predictions about customer behavior. Online Analytical Processing (OLAP) solutions perform dynamic analyses of the effect the company's actions are having on select customers over time (META Group, 2001).

More recently, Buttle (2004) has also referred to the strategic, operational, analytical CRM triptych. He defines each as follows: Strategic CRM is a top-down perspective on CRM, which views CRM as a customer-centric business strategy that aims at winning and keeping profitable customers; operational CRM is a perspective on CRM that focuses on major automation projects within the front-office functions of sales, marketing, and service; analytical CRM is a bottom-up perspective, which focuses on the intelligent mining of customer data for strategic or tactical purposes.

The CRM philosophy places the customer rather than the product or process at the centre of the organization in the belief that the development of a close relationship with the customer will enable the organization to determine, fulfill, and even predict the needs of the customer (Beckett-Camarata, Camarata, & Barker, 1998). Successful CRM initiatives enable organizations to retain existing customers, increase customer loyalty, acquire new customers, and improve the relationship with existing customers (Ryals & Knox, 2001). The main motivations for the adoption of CRM systems are (Elliott, 1997; Kalakota & Robinson, 2000; Ryals & Knox, 2001): help to identify the most profitable customers; creation of value for the customer; customization of products and services; receiving customer feedback that leads to new and improved products or services; help to avoid wasting marketing money on ineffective marketing programs; enable companies to reduce sales inventory costs through better forecasting; development of a stronger customer base and increased customer loyalty and profitability; faster response to customer inquiries; and obtaining information that can be shared with business partners.

The supply chain encompasses all activities associated with the flow and transformation of goods from the raw materials stage, through to the end user, as well as the associated information flows. Supply Chain Management (SCM) is the integration of these activities through improved supply chain relationships, to achieve a sustainable competitive advantage (Nichols & Handfield, 1999). In essence, SCM integrates supply and demand management within and across companies, allowing the collaboration and cooperation of firms across the entire supply chain as a whole to improve operational efficiency and market competitiveness, via the coordination of all forms of activities, information, and materials from the initial source to the end-user (Stadtler, 2000).

SCM software applications provide real-time analytical systems that manage the flow of product and information throughout the supply chain network. They are designed to enhance SCM operations - supplier sourcing, production planning, inventory planning, transportation planning, demand planning, and so on. At present, the SCM solutions are fragmented along these functional applications into specific spaces - for example, advanced planning and scheduling for the manufacturing plant, demand planning for the sales group, and transportation planning for the distribution center (Wu, 2000).

The primary benefits of SCM systems are better operational and business planning. SCM systems use finite capacity planning algorithms that do not require iterative adjustments to the master schedule, and real-time planning capabilities that allow firms to react quickly to supply and demand changes. Increased revenue, increased productivity, operational cost savings, lower inventory, and reduced order-to-fulfillment cycle time are some of the benefits from SCM system implementations (Hendricks et al., 2007).

Business intelligence (BI) is a generic term for applications, platforms, tools and technologies that support the process of exploitation of data and business analysis of their correlations and trends. BI applications provide businesses with the means to collect and prepare data to facilitate the generation of reports, analysis and decision. The purpose of BI systems is to support better business decision-making (Power, 2007).

Business intelligence technology has coalesced in the last decade around the use of data warehousing and on-line analytical processing (OLAP). Data warehousing is a systematic approach to collecting relevant business data into a single repository, where it is organized and validated so that it can be analyzed and presented in a form that is useful for business decision making. The various sources for the relevant business data are referred to as the operational data stores (ODS). The data is extracted, transformed, and loaded (ETL) from the ODS systems into a data mart. An important part of this process is data cleansing in which variation on schemas and data values from disparate ODS systems are resolved. In the data mart, the data is modeled as an OLAP cube (multidimensional model), which supports flexible drill-down and roll-up analyses (Cody, Kreulen, Krishna, & Spangler, 2002).

Recent developments in BI include business performance measurement, business activity monitoring, and the expansion of BI from being a staff tool to being used by people throughout the organization (BI for the masses). In the long-term, BI techniques and findings will be embedded into business processes (Negash & Gray, 2008).

Some of the benefits of having a BI system include the ability to access data in a common format from multiple sources, a way to measure goals and analyze cross-departmental data, to see who your organizations good and bad customers are, and to track customer behavior in order to improve services and relationships. These systems can also help to track specific product sales and distributors to improve supply and production, as well as track external trends to improve processes, track market trends to improve an organization's competitiveness, and fine-tune pricing and marketing policies.

Groupware, also referred to as collaborative software, is a general term for a repertoire of Information Communication and Technology (ICT) applications that support cooperative work between and among groups of people, even though they may not actually be together (Pumareja & Sikkel, 2006) in time or space (Coleman, 1997). Groupware systems are used to support and carry out the social domains of work, that is, the aspect of one's job in which interpersonal interaction and cooperative processes take place (Pumareja & Sikkel, 2006). According to Andriessen (2003), groupware systems can be distinguished from other ICT applications by having functions that serve the following human interaction processes: communication; cooperation; coordination; information sharing and learning; and social interaction.

According to Coleman (1997), the primary motivations for the adoption of groupware systems are: better cost control; increased productivity; better customer service; support for Total Quality Management; fewer meetings; automating routine processes; extending the organization to include both the customer and the supplier; integration of geographically disparate teams; increased competitiveness through faster time to market; better coordination globally; providing a new service that differentiates the organization; and leveraging professional expertise.

Workflow can be described simply as the movement of documents and tasks through a business process. Workflow can be a sequential progression of work activities or a complex set of processes each taking place concurrently, eventually impacting each other according to a set of rules, routes, and roles (Center for Technology in Government [CTG], 1997). Workflow Management Systems allow organizations to define and control the various activities associated with a business process and also the opportunity to measure and analyze the execution of the process so that continuous improvements can be made. Most workflow management systems also integrate with other systems used by the organization like document management systems, databases, e-mail, office automation products, Geographic Information Systems, production applications, and so forth. (CTG, 1997). This integration provides structure to a process, which employs a number of otherwise independent systems (Milutinović & Patricelli, 2002). Some typical features associated with these systems are a process definition tool; the simulation, prototyping, and piloting of a workflow; task initiation and control; document routing; invocation of applications to view and manipulate data; work lists; task automation; event notification; process monitoring; access to information over the Web; tracking and logging of activities; and administration and security (Milutinović & Patricelli, 2002).

Many benefits can be accrued if the workflow management system is implemented as part of a broader business solution, such as less intervention to manage business processes; improved communication between employees, provided by notifications and document sharing; improved understanding of the process itself, which can lead to increased collaboration among team members and/or across teams and business units; separation of IT from workflow management, putting the business process immediately and directly under the control of the people using the system; building corporate knowledge; and improved security and reliability (CTG, 1997). A workflow management system also eases the costs of developing new enterprise applications and reduces the maintenance of standard enterprise software. From an IT point of view, two important reasons for enterprises to adopt a workflow management system are ease of software development and reduction of risk for overall system development (James, Joonsoo, Qinyi, Ling, Calton, & William, 2007).

From the above literature revision, we note that there are different motivations that lead to adoption of the diverse IT/IS solutions, such as to reduce operational costs, to differentiate products or services in relation to the competitors, to improve the quality of products or services, to launch new products or services before competition, to improve business operations or processes, to diversify the line of products or services, to identify and to occupy new markets, to improve customer service, to reduce staff costs, to establish strategic partnerships, to increase the productivity of the employees, to improve the communication between the employees, and so forth.

RESEARCH FOCUS, DESIGN, AND METHOD

A survey was conducted to investigate several aspects of the IT/IS situation in large Portuguese companies. Specifically for this study, the survey aimed to determine which IT/IS solutions are adopted, the reasons for their adoption, the role played by IT/IS within the company, and which trends influence the adoption of IT/IS.

The general methodology involved a questionnaire that was sent to 500 Chief Information Officers (CIOs) of large Portuguese companies categorized according to their gross revenue. CIOs are responsible for managing the IT department. Therefore, they should have rich information regarding all aspects concerning IT/IS in their organization.

The questionnaire was sent to the subjects in February 2008. Three months later, after three rounds, 59 usable questionnaires were received and the data collection process was concluded. The data analysis and presentation of results occurred over the following 11 weeks.

Subjects

The survey, undertaken from February to May 2008, focused on Portugal's 1000 large companies. The subjects in this study consisted of CIOs of the largest Portuguese companies by gross revenue classified by Portugal's Instituto Nacional de Estatistica (INE, 2007b).

This particular audience was preferred because large organizations are generally leaders in technology use and application (Li, McLeod, & Rogers, 2001; Liu & Arnett, 2000; McLeod, 1995), and need to have a well-structured IT department to manage the overall information system architecture. Therefore, the use of this target group seemed most appropriate.

Questionnaire

A survey instrument was formulated (see Appendix A for selected portions) to obtain feedback from large companies in Portugal, assessing their IT/IS reality.

The structure of the questionnaire, partly based on earlier surveys (CIOMAG, 2006, 2007; Varajão, Trigo, Figueiredo, & Barroso, 2007), addressed several key aspects of IT departments with nominal scale, Likert scale, ordinal scale and ratio scale. The questionnaire was divided into several sections, each one with well defined objectives.

The proposed questionnaire was pre-tested with a small sample of CIOs and used in a previous survey (Varajão, Trigo, Figueiredo, & Barroso, 2007) to validate its content and readability

and to improve some aspects of the questions. The necessary changes were made to the final questionnaire, which was edited in an online survey tool. A briefing letter was subsequently sent to the CIOs regarding the scope and goals of the study, including a link to an Internet home page which allowed the completion of the questionnaire online. Subjects were asked to answer the questionnaire online. In the first and second rounds, the letter was sent by email and, in the third round, by post.

Data Representativeness

The survey was mailed to the CIOs of a sample group of 500 companies from the 1000 biggest Portuguese companies by gross revenue. To obtain a representative sample, we chose to use a casual sample method, the stratified sample method, by opting for a random sample of 50% of the companies in each group of 100 companies, selected according to their position in the INE list of the 1000 largest national companies (2007b).

In the first and second rounds, the number of undelivered and returned questionnaires (by email) was 111, quite a significant number perhaps due to the email policies of the companies. In the third round, the invitation letter was sent by post and then the number of undelivered and returned questionnaires was 44.

A total of 456 questionnaires were mailed. In the three rounds, a total of 68 responses were received. Of these, 9 were rejected because many items were left blank, yielding a final usable 59 responses and a response rate of 12.9%.

This response rate did not come as a surprise as it is comparable with the response rates of other studies conducted in the past few years (Enns, Huff, & Golden, 2001; Li et al., 2001; Lin & Pervan, 2003; Liu & Arnett, 2000; Sohal & Ng, 1998). This may be because some subjects are unwilling to respond to unsolicited surveys (Li et al., 2001), or simply had insufficient time (Lin & Pervan, 2003), and many more companies set a policy of rejecting survey questionnaires (Li et al., 2001; Lin & Pervan, 2003).

Tables 1 and 2 show the characteristics of the respondents. The companies of the responding CIOs represent a broad range of companies in terms of their characteristics, which indicates that the results can be used to explain the Portuguese IT/IS adoption in large companies. It is important to note that, although large organizations generally provide leadership in using information technology, differences do exist between small and large businesses (Liu & Arnett, 2000). Therefore, careful use of the results should be made, especially regarding their applicability to small businesses.

The majority of CIOs that answer the survey were male (86.4%), with a Bachelor's degree (62.7%), in their forties. They have an average tenure within their organization of 10 years and an average tenure in their current position of 7.9 years.

DATA ANALYSIS AND RESULTS

Currently, IT/IS have a large variety of applications within businesses and play a fundamental role both at the internal level and at linking companies with their external environment.

It has become increasingly self-evident that companies cannot be competitive or profitable without them (Varajão, 2006).

When the scope of IT/IS applications was solely limited to an operational level, the motives behind their selection were reasonably clear and concerned mostly the automation of work with the aim of increasing productivity and implicit cost reduction (Varajão, Ribeiro, Figueiredo, & Barroso, 2007).

As the scope of IT/IS use broadened to company tactics, at first, and strategy later, the range of motivations behind IT/IS adoption also widened, including, for instance, the improvement of the

Table 1. Characteristics of respondents' companies

Characteristics	Respondents	%
Total number of employees		
<200	10	16.9
201-500	21	35.6
501-2000	21	35.6
>2000	7	11.9
Annual sales (million Euros)		
Less than 10	2	3.4
10 to below 50	14	23.7
50 to below 250	33	55.9
Greater than 250	6	10.2
No answer	4	6.8
International presence (number of countries)		
1	20	33.9
2	10	17
3-4	9	15.2
5-20	7	11.9
>20	9	15.2
No answer	4	6.8

Table 2. Activity sectors of participating companies [a]

Sector of activity	N.º	%
Agriculture, animal husbandry, hunting, forest management and fishing	5	8.5
Extractive industries	5	8.5
Manufacturing industries	16	27.1
Electricity, gas, steam, hot and cold water and cold air	3	5.1
Wholesale and retail trade	6	10.2
Transport and storage	8	13.5
Other activities and services	9	15.2
Others	7	11.9

a) Based on the Portuguese economic activity codes (INE, 2007a).

time to market, the establishment of strategic partnerships, or the exploration of new markets.

The great diversity of IT/IS applications entails a great diversity of motivations for their adoption. Nevertheless, there is a group of generally inherent motivations for IT/IS adoption that must be identified and grasped to maximize satisfaction levels with investment initiatives in IT/IS (Varajão, Ribeiro, et al., 2007).

In the questionnaire for data collection used for this study, we asked the participants to state, in order of importance, the main motivations regarding the adoption of IT/IS in their companies, via an ordinal scale. Twelve motivations were identified in the questionnaire, which the participants were asked to grade from 1 to 12 (in case they were considered important in the specific context of their company).

The prevailing motivations for IT/IS adoption by major Portuguese firms are identified by order of importance (average) in Figure 1.

The motivation identified as being the current primary reason for IT/IS adoption in Portuguese companies, highlighted at the top of the list with a weighted average of 9.77 (out of a maximum of 12), was "To improve the quality of products or services."

It is significant that, in contrast to the results obtained by previous studies conducted in Portugal (Varajão, Ribeiro, et al., 2007), in which the highest ranking motivations were directly linked to operational aspects of the company,

Figure 1. Motivations for IT/IS adoption by large Portuguese companies

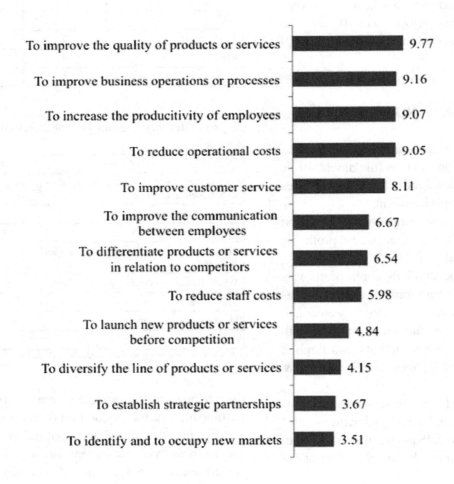

Figure 2. Current role of IT/IS in large Portuguese companies

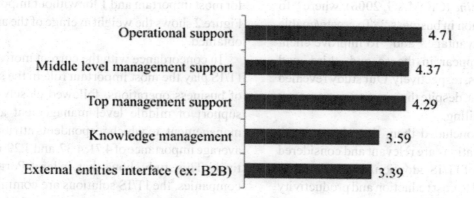

such as productivity or operational cost reduction, our study reveals a strategic motivation in the top position.

In the following three positions, with very similar averages, we have the motivation "To improve business operations or processes," with an average of 9.16, the motivation "To Increase the productivity increase of the employees," with an average of 9.07, and the motivation "To reduce operational costs," with an average of 9.05.

It is worth highlighting that these motives have been frequently identified in the past and that they continue to be of vital importance in the present, as studies have revealed in other countries. In a recent study conducted in the United States by *CIO Magazine* (CIOMAG, 2006) the most widely expected impact of IT/IS in the company, as identified by respondents, was precisely the reduction of costs due to increased productivity and efficiency. Another study conducted in Portugal in 2006 (Varajão, Ribeiro, et al., 2007) also presented "To increase the productivity of the employees" and "To reduce operational costs" as the two prevailing motivations.

The motivation "To improve customer service" appears in the fifth highest ranked position, with an average of 8.11. It is worth noting that, as will be

later stated in this article, this motive is probably linked to the prospective growth in the adoption of CRM systems.

Next on the list are the motivations "To improve the communication between the employees," "To diversify the line of products or services," and "To reduce staff costs," with an average of 6.67, 6.54, and 5.98, respectively.

At the bottom of the list, are the diverse strategic motivations: "To launch new products or services before competition," "To diversify the line of products or services," "To establish strategic partnerships," and "To identify and to occupy new markets," all of which with a weighted average below 5. On a strategic level, the main motives appear, therefore, in the lower half of the table.

Our study revealed that on the whole, the motivations identified as being the most important continue to be intimately related to operational aspects, similar to those revealed by other studies in recent years (Varajão, Ribeiro, et al., 2007). For example, these type of motivations can be found in the second, third, and fourth positions, respectively "To improve business operations or processes," "To increase the productivity of the employees," and "To reduce operational costs." In contrast to other studies in which motivations related to the strategic aspects are clearly emphasized as in, for example, in a study conducted by the *CIO Magazine* (CIOMAG, 2006), where "To enable innovation in business," "To create/enable competitive advantage," and "To improve client satisfaction" appear in the second, third, and fourth positions, respectively. Our study revealed that these issues, despite their importance, are not the most prevailing.

It can be concluded then, that although the strategic motivations are relevant and considered in the process of IT/IS adoption, the motivations directly related to cost reduction and productivity increase are the biggest drivers of investment. Nevertheless, it is important to highlight that for the first time a strategic motivation ("To improve the quality of products or services") appears prominently in the top position, which indicates a departure from our findings in previous studies (Varajão, Ribeiro, et al., 2007).

The results obtained concerning motivations are consistent with the role currently played by IT/IS in large Portuguese companies. In the survey we asked the actual role of the IT/IS in the company, based on a Likert scale where 5 stands for most important and 1 for without importance. Figure 2 shows the weight average of the answers obtained.

In concordance with the current motivations, IT/IS play the most important role in the support of business operations, followed closely by the support of middle level management and top management, to which respondents attributed an average importance of 4.71, 4.37, and 4.29, respectively. This study shows that, in large Portuguese companies, the IT/IS solutions are committed to supporting the business operations and the middle and top management levels, leaving to a second plan the knowledge management and the interface with external entities. It must be highlighted that the identified role for IT/IS concerning the three levels of management is currently very similar (with a difference lower than 0.5 in terms of the average importance), revealing that the use of technologies is no longer mainly related to operations, but, on the contrary it is dispersed

Figure 3. Implemented systems by large Portuguese companies

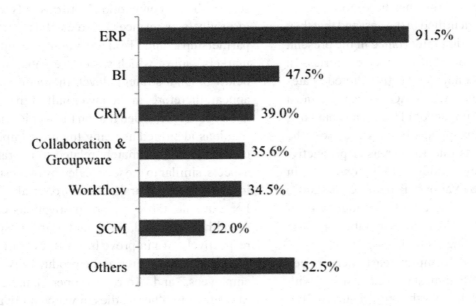

Figure 4. Current implemented systems vs. Expected implemented systems

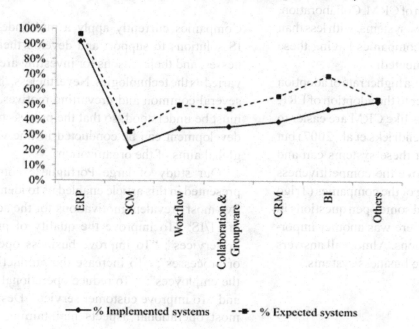

throughout the diverse levels of management. One of the questions we addressed in this study was which IT/IS systems are currently implemented in large Portuguese companies. Although the idea that large companies are leaders in the adoption of IT/IS solutions and use them for the support of all management levels is usually generalized, this is not always the case and it is of great relevance to identify which systems are currently implemented and which systems the companies intend to develop in the near future. As revealed by previous studies (Trigo et al., 2007), we expected to find a high adoption of Enterprise Resource Planning systems, since its adoption is ubiquitous in large companies (Hossain, Patrick, & Rashid, 2002; Norris, Hurley, Hartley, Dunleavy, & Balls, 2000; Rashid, Hossain, & Patrick, 2002). On the other hand, we had high expectations concerning the adoption of systems like CRM since these kinds of systems in previous studies appeared with a relatively low adoption rate.

To perform this study, we started by investigating which systems the companies are more concerned with in a general manner, and, based on previous studies made in North America (CIOMAG, 2002, 2006; Kumar, Maheshwari, & Kumar, 2002) and Europe (Karakostas, Kardaras, & Papathanassiou, 2005; van Everdingen, van Hillegersberg, & Waarts, 2000), we identified the following systems: Enterprise Resource Planning (ERP), Customer Relationship Management (CRM), Supply Chain Management (SCM), Business Intelligence (BI), Collaboration and Groupware, and Workflow management. This study showed, as presented in Figure 1, that the majority of the companies have already implemented ERP systems, with a current adoption rate superior to that verified two years ago (Trigo et al., 2007). This is to be expected considering that ERPs have been around for a long time, since the 1980s, and they are considered the standard backbone of companies' business support (Simchy-Levy, Kaminsky, & Simchy-Levy, 2003).

This study reveals that there continues to be a surprisingly low adoption of CRM, Collaboration, Groupware, and Workflow systems, with less than 40% of the respondent companies having these kinds of systems implemented.

For CRM, for instance, a higher rate of adoption would be expected, closer to the adoption of ERP, not only because systems like CRM are easier to implement than ERP (Hendricks et al., 2007) but also due to the fact that these systems can and should be used to improve the competitiveness and strategic positioning of the companies (Trigo et al., 2007). We included some open questions in the survey to verify if there was another important group of IT/IS solutions. Almost all answers obtained refer to specific business systems.

FUTURE TRENDS

With this study we also intend to identify the future intentions of companies concerning the implementation of new IT/IS solutions.

In Figure 4 it is possible to observe the systems that companies have currently implemented and the systems they will have in the near future.

Practically all the companies have current IS development projects. By 2010 a slight growth in the implementation of ERP, SCM, and other business specific systems is expected. A slight growth in ERP is perfectly understandable given the high number of companies (91.5%) that already have this type of system in place.

Within those systems where one expects the most significant growth, appear BI and CRM systems. It is worth noting that these systems are closely related to two of the motivations that appeared in the top five positions in the list of previously identified motivations for the adoption of IT/IS: "To improve the quality of products or services" and "To improve customer service."

CONCLUSION

Companies currently apply a multitude of IT/IS solutions to support and develop their businesses, and their reasons for investing are just as varied as the technologies. Nevertheless, there are several common and prevailing motives, which must be understood, so that the process of IT/IS development can be conducted in line with the global aims of the organization.

Our study of large Portuguese companies presented in this article enabled us to identify the five most prevalent motivations for the adoption of IT/IS: "To improve the quality of products or services"; "To improve business operations or processes"; "To increase the productivity of the employees"; " To reduce operational costs"; and "To improve customer service." Despite the most operational aspects maintaining a very important role as motivators for the adoption of IT/IS (CIOMAG, 2006; Varajão, Trigo, et al., 2007), our study revealed that a strategic motive tops the list.

Beyond the importance of IT/IS operational role, IT/IS support of a tactical and strategic nature is currently of great importance.

The IT/IS solutions available to companies are multiple and diverse. Within the systems that companies commonly adopt we can find ERP, BI, CRM, Workflow, Collaboration and Groupware, SCM systems, and others.

In large Portuguese companies the systems mainly adopted and well consolidated are ERP as is already the case in other Europeans countries (van Everdingen et al., 2000). The adoption of certain types of system, such as CRM systems, essential for enhancing a company's competitiveness, is still below the expected adoption levels.

Nevertheless, the adoption of other systems like CRM, Collaboration and Groupware, and Workflow, which less than 40% of the companies currently have, will accelerate in the short-term, rising in some cases above the rate of 50% adoption. In the case of BI systems, more significant growth than all the other systems is also expected.

REFERENCES

Andriessen, J. H. E. (2003). *Working with groupware: Understanding and evaluating collaboration technology.* London: Springer.

Anthony, R. N. (1965). *Planning and control systems: A framework for analysis.* Boston: Harvard University Press.

Beckett-Camarata, E. J., Camarata, M. R., & Barker, R. T. (1998). Integrating internal and external customer relationships through relationship management: A strategic response to a changing global environment. *Journal of Business Research, 41*(1), 71–81. doi:10.1016/S0148-2963(97)00013-1

Belle, J.-P. V., Eccles, M., & Nash, J. (2003). *Discovering information systems.* Cape Town: South African Universities Press.

Buttle, F. (2004). *Customer relationship management: Concepts and tools.* Oxford, UK: Butterworth-Heinemann.

Center for Technology in Government. (1997). *An introduction to workflow management systems.* Albany, NY: Center for Technology in Government, University at Albany.

CIOMAG. (2002). CRM: Are companies buying it? *CIO Magazine.*

CIOMAG. (2006). The STATE of the CIO '06. *CIO Magazine.*

CIOMAG. (2007). The STATE of the CIO '07. *CIO Magazine.*

Cody, W. F., Kreulen, J. T., Krishna, V., & Spangler, W. S. (2002). The integration of business intelligence and knowledge management. *IBM Systems Journal, 41*(4), 697–714.

Coleman, D. (1997). *Groupware: Collaborative strategies for corporate LANs and Intranets.* Upper Saddle River, NJ: Prentice Hall.

Cotteleer, M. J., & Bendoly, E. (2006). Order lead-time improvement following enterprise information technology implementation: An empirical study. *MIS Quarterly, 30*(3), 643–660.

Cuffe, S. S. (2005). Emerging management support systems models for global managers in the new economy. *Journal of Knowledge Management Practice, 6.*

Davenport, T. H. (1998). Putting the enterprise into the enterprise system. *Harvard Business Review, 76*(4), 121–131.

Elliott, C. (1997). Everything wired must CONVERGE. *The Journal of Business Strategy, 18*(6), 31–34. doi:10.1108/eb039894

Enns, H. G., Huff, S. L., & Golden, B. R. (2001). How CIOs obtain peer commitment to strategic IS proposals: Barriers and facilitators. *The Journal of Strategic Information Systems, 10*(1), 3–14. doi:10.1016/S0963-8687(01)00041-5

Gupta, O., Priyadarshini, K., Massoud, S., & Agrawal, S. K. (2004). Enterprise resource planning: A case of a blood bank. *Industrial Management & Data Systems, 104*(7), 589–603. doi:10.1108/02635570410550250

Hendricks, K. B., Singhal, V. R., & Stratman, J. K. (2007). The impact of enterprise systems on corporate performance: A study of ERP, SCM, and CRM system implementations. *Journal of Operations Management, 25*(1), 65–82. doi:10.1016/j.jom.2006.02.002

Hossain, L., Patrick, J. D., & Rashid, M. A. (2002). *Enterprise resource planning: Global opportunities and challenges.* Hershey, PA: Idea Group Publishing.

Instituto Nacional de Estatística. (2007a). *Classificação Portuguesa das Actividades Económicas, Revisão 3* (Vol. 322). Lisbon, Portugal: Author.

Instituto Nacional de Estatística. (2007b). *Lista das 1000 maiores empresas portuguesas. Ficheiro de Unidades Estatísticas - FUE - Base Belém*. Lisbon, Portugal: Author.

Iriana, R., & Buttle, F. (2006). Strategic, operational, and analytical customer relationship management. *Journal of Relationship Marketing, 5*(4), 23–42. doi:10.1300/J366v05n04_03

James, C., Joonsoo, B., Qinyi, W., Ling, L., Calton, P., & William, B. R. (2007). Workflow management for enterprise transformation. *Inf. Knowl. Syst. Manag., 6*(1,2), 61-80.

Kalakota, R., & Robinson, M. (2000). Customer relationship management: Integrating processes to build relationships. In R. Kalakota & M. Robinson (Eds.), *E-Business 2.0: Roadmap for Success* (pp. 109-134). New York: Addison Wesley.

Karakostas, B., Kardaras, D., & Papathanassiou, E. (2005). The state of CRM adoption by the financial services in the UK: An empirical investigation. *Information & Management, 42*(6), 853–863. doi:10.1016/j.im.2004.08.006

Karimi, J., Somers, T. M., & Gupta, Y. P. (2001). Impact of information technology management practices on customer service. *Journal of Management Information Systems, 17*(4), 125–158.

Kim, J., Suh, E., & Hwang, H. (2003). A model for evaluating the effectiveness of CRM using the balanced scorecard. *Journal of Interactive Marketing, 17*(2), 5–19. doi:10.1002/dir.10051

Kumar, V., Maheshwari, B., & Kumar, U. (2002). Enterprise resource planning systems adoption process: A survey of Canadian organizations. *International Journal of Production Research, 40*(3), 509–523. doi:10.1080/00207540110092414

Laudon, K. C., & Laudon, J. P. (2005). *Management information systems: Managing the digital firm* (9th ed.). Upper Saddle River, NJ: Prentice Hall.

Lequeux, J.-L. (1999). *Manager avec les ERP: Progiciels de gestion intégrés et Internet*. Paris: Éditions d'Organisation.

Li, E., Tseng, P. T. Y., & Lu, E. (2007, September 21-25). *Measuring the strength of partner relationship in B2B EC: An exploratory research*. Paper presented at the International Conference on Wireless Communications, Networking and Mobile Computing (WiCom 2007), Shanghai, China.

Li, E. Y., McLeod, R., & Rogers, J. C. (2001). Marketing information systems in Fortune 500 companies: A longitudinal analysis of 1980, 1990, and 2000. *Information & Management, 38*(5), 307–322. doi:10.1016/S0378-7206(00)00073-2

Lin, C., & Pervan, G. (2003). The practice of IS/IT benefits management in large Australian organizations. *Information & Management, 41*(1), 13–24. doi:10.1016/S0378-7206(03)00002-8

Liu, C., & Arnett, K. P. (2000). Exploring the factors associated with Web site success in the context of electronic commerce. *Information & Management, 38*(1), 23–33. doi:10.1016/S0378-7206(00)00049-5

McAfee, A. (2002). The impact of enterprise information technology adoption on operational performance: An empirical investigation. *Production and Operations Management, 11*(1), 33–53.

McLeod, R. (1995). Systems theory and information resources management: Integrating key concepts. *Information Resources Management Journal, 18*(2), 5–14.

META Group. (2001). *Integration: Critical Issues for Implementation of CRM Solutions*. Stamford, CT: Author.

Milutinović, V., & Patricelli, F. (2002). *E-business and e-challenges: Emerging communication.* Amsterdam, the Netherlands: IOS Press.

Negash, S., & Gray, P. (2008). Business intelligence. In F. Burstein & C. W. Holsapple (Eds.), *Handbook on Decision Support Systems 2* (pp. 175-193). Berlin, Germany: Springer.

Nichols, E. L., & Handfield, R. B. (1999). *Introduction to Supply Chain Management*: Upper Saddle River, NJ: Prentice Hall.

Norris, G., Hurley, J. R., Hartley, K. M., Dunleavy, J. R., & Balls, J. D. (2000). *E-business and ERP—transforming the enterprise.* New York: John Wiley & Sons.

Okkonen, J., Pirttimäki, V., Lönnqvist, A., & Hannula, M. (2002, May 9-11). *Triangle of performance measurement, knowledge management and business intelligence.* Paper presented at the 2nd Annual Conference on Innovative Research in Management (EURAM), Stockholm, Sweden.

Oliver, D., & Romm, C. (2000). *ERP systems: The route to adoption.* Paper presented at the 6th Americas Conference on Information Systems Association for Information Systems (AMCIS), Long Beach, California.

Pairat, R., & Jungthirapanich, C. (2005, September 11-13). *A chronological review of ERP research: An analysis of ERP inception, evolution, and direction.* Paper presented at the International Engineering Management Conference (IEMC), St. John's, Newfoundland, Canada.

Parr, A. N. (2000, January 4-7). *A taxonomy of ERP implementation approaches.* Paper presented at the 33rd Hawaii International Conference on System Sciences, Maui, Hawaii.

Power, D. J. (2007). *A brief history of decision support systems*: Retrieved 2008, from http://dssresources.com/history/dsshistory.html

Pumareja, D. T., & Sikkel, K. (2006). Getting used with groupware: A first class experience. *Journal of Human-Centred Systems, 20*(2), 189–201.

Rashid, M. A., Hossain, L., & Patrick, J. D. (Eds.). (2002). *Enterprise resource planning: Global opportunities and challenges.* Idea Group Publishing.

Ross, J. W., & Vitale, M. R. (2000). The ERP revolution: Surviving versus thriving. *Information Systems Frontiers, 2*(2), 233–241. doi:10.1023/A:1026500224101

Ryals, L., & Knox, S. (2001). Cross-functional issues in the implementation of relationship marketing through customer relationship management. *European Management Journal, 19*(5), 534–542. doi:10.1016/S0263-2373(01)00067-6

Scott, J. E., & Vessey, I. (2000). Implementing enterprise resource planning systems: The role of learning from failure. *Information Systems Frontiers, 2*(2), 213–232. doi:10.1023/A:1026504325010

Simchy-Levy, D., Kaminsky, P., & Simchy-Levy, E. (2003). *Designing & managing the supply chain—concepts, strategies & case studies.* New York: McGraw-Hill.

Sohal, A. S., & Ng, L. (1998). The role and impact of information technology in Australian business. *Journal of Information Technology, 13*(3), 201–217. doi:10.1080/026839698344846

Stadtler, H. (2000). Supply chain management—an overview. In C. Kilger (Ed.), *Supply chain management and advanced planning: Concepts, models, software and case studies* (pp. 7-27). Berlin, Germany: Springer-Verlag.

Stevens, C. P. (2003). Enterprise resource planning: A trio of resources. *Information Systems Management, 20*(3), 61–67. doi:10.1201/1078/43205.20.3.20030601/43074.7

Trigo, A., Varajão, J., Figueiredo, N., & Barroso, J. (2007, June 23-26). *Information systems and technology adoption by the Portuguese large companies.* Paper presented at the European and Mediterranean Conference on Information Systems (EMCIS), Valence, Spain.

van Everdingen, Y., van Hillegersberg, J., & Waarts, E. (2000). Enterprise resource planning: ERP adoption by European midsize companies. *Communications of the ACM, 43*(4), 27–31. doi:10.1145/332051.332064

Varajão, J. (2006, January-March). Gestão da função de sistemas de informação. *Dirigir - Revista para chefias e quadros, IEFP,* 3-9.

Varajão, J., Ribeiro, A. T., Figueiredo, N., & Barroso, J. (2007, July 12-15). *Motivações inerentes à adopção de Tecnologias e Sistemas de Informação nas grandes empresas portuguesas.* Paper presented at the 6ª Conferência Ibero-Americana em Sistemas, Cibernética e Informática (CISCI), Orlando, Florida.

Varajão, J., Trigo, A., Figueiredo, N., & Barroso, J. (2007). TI nas empresas nacionais. *Revista CXO, 2,* 19–23.

Wah, L. (2000). Behind the buzz: The substance of knowledge management. In J. Cortada & J. A. Woods (Eds.), *The Knowledge Management Yearbook 2000-2001* (pp. 307-317). Boston: Butterworth-Heineman.

Wu, J., Ulieru, M., Cobzaru, M., & Norrie, D. (2000, November 12-15). Supply chain management systems: State of the art and vision. In *Proceedings of the 2000 IEEE International Conference on Management of Innovation and Technology (ICMIT 2000),* Singapore (Vol. 2, pp. 759-764). IEEE.

APPENDIX A

Implemented systems in company. Please choose *all* that apply:

☐ ERP (Enterprise Resource Planning)
☐ CRM (Customer Relationship Management)
☐ SCM (Supply Chain Management)
☐ BI (Business Intelligence)
☐ Collaboration & Groupware
☐ Workflow
☐ Business specific
☐ Other: _____

What is the actual role of IT/IS solutions (where 1 is without importance and 5 the very important)? Please choose the appropriate response for each item:

	1	2	3	4	5
Operational support	○	○	○	○	○
Middle level management support	○	○	○	○	○
Top management support	○	○	○	○	○
Knowledge management	○	○	○	○	○
External entities interface (ex: B2B)	○	○	○	○	○

Systems in developing stage or planned for the near future? Please choose all that apply:

☐ ERP (Enterprise Resource Planning)
☐ CRM (Customer Relationship Management)
☐ SCM (Supply Chain Management)
☐ BI (Business Intelligence)
☐ Collaboration & Groupware
☐ Workflow
☐ Other: _____

What are the main motivations behind IT/IS adoption? Please number each box in order of preference from 1 to 12:

☐ To reduce operational costs
☐ To differentiate products or services in relation to the competitors
☐ To improve the quality of products or services
☐ To launch new products or services before competition
☐ To improve business operations or processes
☐ To diversify the line of products or services
☐ To identify and to occupy new markets
☐ To improve customer service
☐ To reduce staff costs
☐ To establish strategic partnerships
☐ To increase the productivity of the employees
☐ To improve the communication between the employees

Chapter 25
Semantic Web Based Integration of Knowledge Resources for Expertise Finding

Valentina Janev
The Mihajlo Pupin Institute, Serbia

Jovan Duduković
The Mihajlo Pupin Institute, Serbia

Sanja Vraneš
The Mihajlo Pupin Institute, Serbia

ABSTRACT

This article discusses the challenges of expertise data integration and expert finding in modern organizations using an illustrative case study of a concrete research-intensive establishment, the Mihajlo Pupin Institute (MPI). It presents how the latest semantic technologies (Ontologies, Web services, Semantic Wiki) could be used on the top of the commercial ERP (Enterprise Resource Planning) software (SAP®) and the open-source ECM (Enterprise Content Management) software (Alfresco) to ensure meaningful search and retrieval of expertise for in-house users, as well as the integration into the Semantic Web community space. This article points out the necessary adjustments in enterprise knowledge management infrastructure in the light of uprising initiatives for standardization of the Semantic Web data.

INTRODUCTION

Knowledge resources of an organization, apart from knowledge artifacts and standardized business processes, include as the most precious asset, their creative human resources and their explicit and tacit knowledge and experience (Nonaka & Takeuchi, 1995; Suh, Derich Sohn, & Kwak, 2004; Rodrígues, Castellanos, & Ranguelov, 2004). In order to facilitate reusability of human knowledge and experience, knowledge artifacts should be easily accessible, while human resource data have to be up-to-date, explicit, and transparent. This is possible by a wise organization and efficient management of knowledge artifacts and human resource (HR) data.

Most of the actual knowledge management systems in the HR sector practice either the information integration approach or content management approach. The information integration–based solutions mainly focus on the integration of distributed legacy databases, typically in the form of a data warehouse where the fact data (i.e., employee data) is arranged in order to answer the analytical queries efficiently. Personal profiles here usually rely on the self declared expertise. Employees keep track of their areas of expertise manually by maintaining a list of keywords or phrases and this list of key qualifications is being defined in the HR sector. This approach is error prone since users are typically subjective, biased, and reluctant to update the file regularly. Also, manually created lists cannot be an exhaustive description of the person's expertise areas. The content based approaches (Sim, Crowder, & Wills, 2006) to expertise extraction, profiling, and finding focus on the automatic identification of expertise entities in the semi-structured and unstructured documents containing the expertise information as well as on the annotation of identified expertise entities with a semantic mark-up. The input documents are: (1) curricula vitae and resume that have been published in formats like text, PDF, DOC, and HTML; (2) publications and other legacy documents (Balog, Azzopardi, & de Rijke, 2006; Balog & de Rijke, 2008); (3) e-mails, blog sites (Agarwal, Liu, & Tang 2008), and other Web collaboration related context. Expertise extraction and profiling is based on the linguistic analysis, statistical and machine learning classification methods, as well as on the inductive logic programming techniques to discover rules for extracting fields from documents (Fang & Zhai, 2007; Petkova & Bruce Croft, 2006; Jung, Lee, Kang, Lee, & Sung, 2007).

In the meantime, parallel to this techno-centric approach, organizations started to practice other forms of knowledge management that rely on the social tools that enable people to share information face-to-face tools like communities of practice (CoP) and peer assists. This approach aims to provide collaboration and inter-personal knowledge sharing. The social tools include groupware and collaboration solutions, portals, and e-learning tools, among others.

In recent years, with the evolution of the Web toward the Semantic Web (SW), new social computing technologies such as Wiki, blogs, and folksonomies have appeared that enable workers to socialize or interact with each other throughout the World Wide Web and thus form the Social Web. The emerging Semantic Web technologies dictate new trends in the design and implementation of expert finding systems (Aleman-Meza, 2007; Demartini, 2007; Hogan & Harth, 2007; Li, Boley, Bhavsar, & Mei, 2006; Pavlov & Ichise, 2007). In addition, there is a tendency (Bojars, Breslin, Peristeras, Tummarello, & Decker, 2008) toward publishing personal and HR data in a structured way using emerging SW standards such as FOAF[1], DOAP[2], DOAC[3], SIOC[4], and so forth. Herewith, the following research questions arise:

- What are the state-of-the-art technologies that support the KM needs of an organization especially in the field of the expertise analysis and reusability of internal and external knowledge?

- How does the KM infrastructure of an organization change and look like in the light of the uprising initiatives for the standardization of Semantic Web data ?

In this article, we will discuss these research questions using the illustrative case study of the Mihajlo Pupin Institute (MPI), the biggest research and development (R&D) institution in high-tech sector in South-East Europe. We will present a Semantic Web based approach to knowledge integration where the latest semantic technologies (Ontologies, Semantic Wiki) are used on the top of the commercial ERP (Enterprise Resource Planning) software (SAP®) and open-source ECM (Enterprise Content Management) software (Alfresco). The paper is organized as follows.

First, in Section 2, expertise finding challenges in modern organizations are discussed, requirements for the expert finder solution are derived, and the MPI knowledge infrastructure for expertise profiling, search, and retrieval is introduced. Next, Sections 3 and 4 discuss the establishment of two knowledge repositories (the *MPI HR knowledge pool* and the *MPI expertise document base*), as well as present results of their exploitation in MPI daily activities. Section 5 and 6 show the ways of using the existing ontology models (FOAF, DOAC, DC) for capturing expert profiles in the MPI ontological base, and exposing the expertise information on Semantic Web, as well as present some initial results of semantic expertise search and retrieval. Finally, Section 7 discusses the synergy of SAP HCM, Alfresco ECM and semantic technologies as well as some open issues and future plans.

PROBLEM FORMULATION

The business process of a modern organization in the hi-tech sector (information and communication technologies, ICT), is a very complex one and is driven, on one hand, by market "pool" factors, and relations with industry (both public and private sector), and, on the other hand, by science "push" factors, societal needs, and expectations (public sector). Since MPI performs applied research in ICT sector, with the outcomes directly applicable in industry, it takes advantage of it and successfully performs technology transfer from academia to industry. As a result, more than 90% of its turnover comes from the market and only 10% is accounted to research funds, coming predominantly from the Serbian Ministry of Science and European Commission. MPI is organized as a holding company (see Figure 1) with one mother company, dealing with research and innovation (illustrated as a box in the center), and seven daughter companies that operate as independent departments of the parent holding company, dealing mainly with the implementation of research results and technology transfer toward industry (illustrated as boxes that surround the central box). Each daughter company is partly independent and responsible for its policy (both technical and financial), and partly integrated into a unified system (general vision, mission, policy, strategy, integral planning and resource management, marketing strategy, etc.). This dual nature of MPI business activities requires a flexible organizational structure where human resources are shared among companies and complex multidisciplinary projects are undertaken by ad-hoc assembling of a project team that is the most suitable for the problem at hand. Most often, an employee is involved both in research (at the mother company) and in implementation of the research results and technology transfer toward industry (at the daughter company). However, to reuse the employee's experience, an employee could be lent or borrowed by the third company. Finding the expertise (either a person and/or accompanied knowledge items) in such a dynamic, fluid, and rather complex organizational structure that is supported by the extended information system is a challenging issue.

Figure 1. The MPI organizational structure

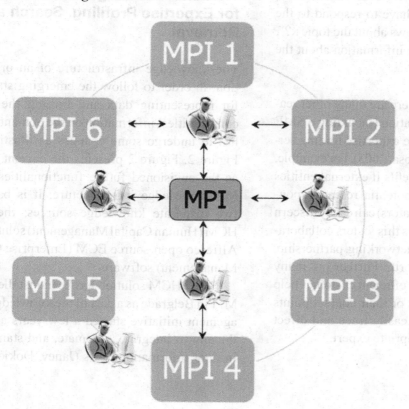

The Expertise Finding Problem Defined

The key challenge in expertise profiling and, later on, expertise finding is to infer the association between a person (i.e., a candidate expert) and an expertise area (i.e., a topic) from the supporting knowledge items (i.e., key qualifications list, expertise description, other supporting document collection). Modern environments, especially in ICT sector, need two types of services:

- services that will enable finding experts indoors easily, as well as deploying the right people with the right skills at the right positions. This includes cases such as seeking a consultant, employee or contractor; seeking a collaborator, team member, community, or committee member, or a journal or conference reviewer; seeking a speaker, presenter, researcher, promoter, and so forth. Electronic services have to give answers to the questions: "how much (well) does y know about the topic x?", "What else does y know?", "How does y compare with others his knowledge of x?"

- services that will enable identification of experts that work in a specific research area as well as effectively identifying and retrieving reusable knowledge items. The scenarios for seeking for the expert and expertise are: retrieving expert knowledge from the document management system using the keywords search engine, looking for an expert as a supplier of non-documented information, looking for an expert to leverage the others' expertise and minimize the effort and time required to find some piece of information, and so forth. In this case, electronic services have to respond to the questions: "who knows about the topic x?", "where to find more information about the topic x?"

In addition to these, there are many other reasons that urge an organization (including a SME organization) to introduce expertise finding services (Yimam-Seid & Kobsa, 2003). For example, the organization also benefits if external entities (industry, the public, and potential research sponsors and research collaborators) can easily discern the expertise of its staff, as this fosters collaboration, crossorganizational networking, partnership, a better image, and so forth. Further on, many organizations can deliver efficient customer help services if the customers or their contact points in the organization, can easily trace and direct their queries to the appropriate expert.

The MPI Knowledge Infrastructure for Expertise Profiling, Search and Retrieval

The knowledge infrastructure of an organization, in order to follow the emerging standards for representing data and linking the online communities' information on the Semantic Web, has to undergo some changes as illustrated in Figure 2. Figure 2 presents the current as well as the envisioned future functionalities of the MPI knowledge infrastructure. It is based on two disparate knowledge sources: the SAP® HCM (Human Capital Management) solution and Alfresco open-source ECM (Enterprise Content Management) software.

SAP® HCM solution has been installed at the MPI in Belgrade as a part of the knowledge management initiative started a few years ago with the aim to integrate, automate, and standardize in-door information flows (Janev, Đokić, Minić

Figure 2. The MPI knowledge architecture

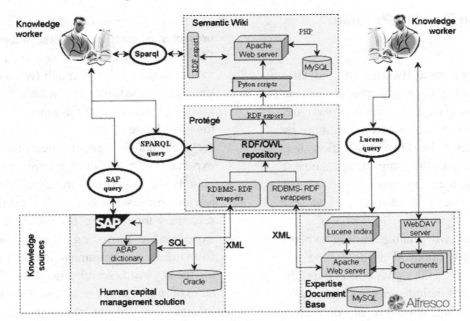

& Vraneš, 2008; Janev & Vraneš, 2005; Janev & Vraneš, 2006). The standard SAP® HCM functionalities ensure standardized integration and automation of HR activities, record the whole life-cycle of an employee from his or her recruitment, training, development, deployment to retirement, as well as provide a wide range of reporting options. However, as a standard SAP HCM solution does not cover the specific aspects of R&D business process, additional functionalities were built on the standard SAP system to keep an extensive record of the employee professional and scientific life including scientific and professional skills and expertise, certificates obtained, information about engagements in concrete projects with details about their roles and competences, scientific achievements (patents, technical solutions, scientific papers and books), other achievements and awards, and so forth.

As a result of the bottom-up identification and integration of knowledge items, a document base was established that stores the results of the research process in a systematic way. For this purpose, the Alfresco ECM was used. Alfresco ECM is built around a content repository that is a set of services used to import, classify, store, search, access, and control content. In addition, Alfresco integrates WebDAV server and Apache Lucene[5] full text indexing and searching service. Using Lucene, one can explore the document contents as well as the automatically extracted and user defined metadata. The new social software functionalities (e-mail, forum, and blog support) enable capturing the additional valuable information about the users' expertise.

SAP® HCM knowledge pool and Alfresco ECM will be used as knowledge sources in order to establish the ontological knowledge base aimed for semantic expertise finding and retrieval. The MPI knowledge infrastructure envisions the establishment of an ontological knowledge base using common ontologies like FOAF, SIOC, DOAC, Dublin Core, and others. On top of this knowledge base, the Semantic WIKI Portal will be mounted and that will facilitate, in a way, the integration of MPI with the broader Semantic Web community.

THE MPI HR KNOWLEDGE POOL

Taking into consideration that a prerequisite of successful knowledge retrieval is the availability and quality of data sources, in March 2007 a project was initiated with the aim to replace the old ERP system with a new SAP® ERP delivered by S&T, SAP partner (S&T, 2007). Choosing SAP ERP system to integrate and automate in-house information flows, MPI joined 21 universities in Austria and many other universities in Europe and elsewhere (e.g., University of Westminster, University of Leeds, University of Toronto) and others that use SAP® software for HCM (SAP, 2007). The SAP® ERP replaced the obsolete, 15-year-old, home-made ERP system and, in addition, integrated information from numerous data repositories: scientific projects and publications database, registry of technical documentation, and registry of research results and commercial products. As highly educated and skilled employees with their business activities and results are the most crucial assets of the company, special attention in the design and implementation of the ERP system was paid to the integration of HR data and establishment of a knowledge repository where up-to-date information about the researchers' professional skills, experience, and expertise is kept.

After a thorough analysis of the MPI HR requirements in SAP blueprint design phase, it was concluded that considerable modifications have to be made to the standard SAP HCM solution in order to meet the MPI requirements and the adopted ISO 9001 Quality Assurance standards (MPI, 2004). Modifications concern, first, the specifics of the flexible MPI organizational structure, and second, the specifics of human resource data in the research sector. In order to cover the specific organizational aspects of the MPI and the need to organize and keep an extensive record of employee professional and scientific life, SAP HCM solution was configured and changed as follows:

- From a financial point of view, the MPI is organized as one controlling area with nine companies,
- On a global level, an employee is identified with one ID number,
- A person has as many files as there are companies he is / was hired by. In one company, a person has a unique file number as an employee and a unique file number as an external expert/collaborator. Therefore, a person's history of employment is different for each company, while her/his personal data is unique.
- The SAP employee master data was supplemented by data specific for scientific research environments and the scientific data was organized and classified in accordance with the Serbian Ministry of Science standards (Serbian National Scientific Council, 2008), which themselves reflect SCI, ISI, and IEEE standards. Each employee is assigned a profession code in accordance with the Serbian system of classification of professions.

The new SAP HCM solution was put into production in January 2008. It keeps information on 450 current MPI employees and the complete employment history of 900 former MPI employees from 1960 until now. Currently, it is used by the HR department staff on an everyday basis and occasionally it is used by additional users, mainly project managers, for reporting purposes. We could distinguish different types of exploitation of the HR knowledge pool as follows.

- Reporting on a global level: Key users from the HR department have full access to the MPI human resources data. HR department reports to the MPI management, the Ministry of Science and Statistical Office of the Republic of Serbia.
- Reporting on a company level: On a company level, the person responsible for the HR reporting has full read access only to the data of employees from the actual company and restrictive access to reporting functionalities on a global level.
- Analysis of the qualification structure and search for expertise: The HR analyst has an overview of the qualification structure of the researchers in the whole MPI. As part of his/her job, he or she is often searching for expertise in a specific domain. An example

Figure 3. Searching for experts in SAP HCM knowledge pool

of querying the SAP HCM knowledge pool is given in Figure 3. The left side window shows the interface for entering the query. The query aims to retrieve "all employees older than X years with key qualification in signal processing field and involved in signal processing projects." In the right side window, we can see the results of query.

THE MPI EXPERTISE DOCUMENT BASE

The MPI Expertise document base pursues to integrate all relevant documents that are created in the MPI business process in a systematic way. When introducing a corporate document base, as information system design practice prompts, one has to: (1) choose the right DMS solution, (2) define the range of the content types, for example, publications, project documentation, product documentation, and so forth that will be stored, (3) define the folder structure, (4) define the custom metadata model and the necessary metadata extraction algorithms, (5) define the classification vocabulary and topic classification models, (6) define user groups and access policies, and so forth.

In order to choose the most suitable collaboration and content management system that will provide an information storage, sharing and exchange infrastructure, we consulted CMS Matrix[6]. Using the CMS Matrix rates, we compared four open source Java based systems: OpenCMS[7], Apache Lenya[8], Magnolia[9], and Alfresco[10], and have selected Alfresco ECM due to the following reasons:

- Alfresco is one of the leading open source enterprise content management systems developed by ECM professionals (former employees of *Documentum*, the leading commercial DMS).

- Alfresco integrates Apache Lucene search engine which is the leading open source full-text search engine. Alfresco has extended Lucene to not only understand the text within a content object, but also its metadata and categories, and allows several repositories to be searched simultaneously.

- Alfresco supports many of the latest information technology standards including the JSR-170 file access API, the JSF tag based interface, the Spring framework, JSR-168 portlets and WebDAV file transfers.

- Apart from the content management functions, Alfresco supports groupware and collaboration software and thus offers additional channels (forums, blogs) for expertise exchange.

Alfresco EMS was customized for keeping different document types, for example, the *Researcher file*, Publications, Patents, Products, Projects, PhD and MSc theses, and others. Each type is described with user-defined metadata that is currently entered in a semi-automatic way. The left side of the Alfresco screenshot presents the structure of the MPI Expertise document base, that is, the structure of the *Researcher files* space.

Further on, the category and classification vocabularies related to the MPI research activities were defined and also aligned with the standards of the Serbian Ministry of Science. Regarding the ICT field, we are considering the adoption of the Association for Computing Machinery (ACM) classification system (ACM, 2008), as shown in Figure 4 (right side). The ACM Computing Classification System Topic hierarchy is used in IEEE Computer Society Manuscript Central System[11], *J.UCS (Journal of Universal Computer Science)*[12], and so forth.

On upload, Alfresco supports the automatic extraction of some common metadata such as name, title, description, creator, content type (Figure 5). It also supports accompanying the Dublin Core metadata that have to be, together

Figure 4. The expertise document base

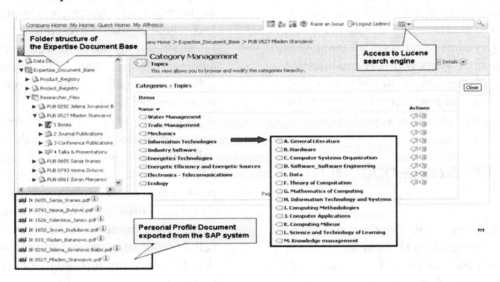

Figure 5. Document user-defined metadata

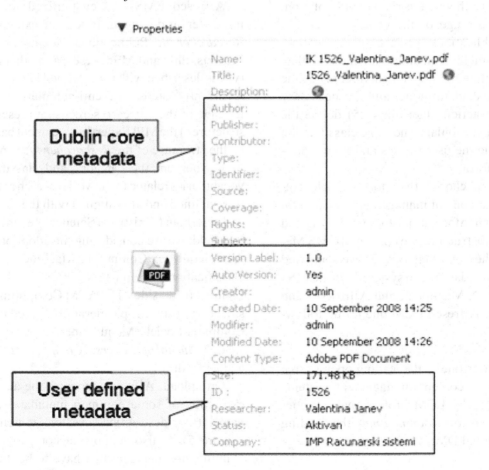

Figure 6. Searching the expertise document base with Lucene full text indexing and searching service

with user defined metadata, entered manually. The Dublin Core standard includes a standard set of meta-tags that are used to track objects in a library collection, making the collections objects searchable in a standard manner. In practice, the standard tags are typically modified or customized for internal use. In our case, a *Researcher file* document is described with basic information that identifies the researcher: ID number, personal data, current status in the company, and the organizational unit.

Figure 6, capturing the Alfresco screenshot, depicts the user interface for the advanced search upon the Expertise document base. Lucene full text indexing and searching service offers a wide range of searching options, for example, to constrain the search to a specific space, to constrain the search to a knowledge item with a specific category assigned, to constrain the search to a knowledge item with a specific type, and so forth. In the right bottom corner of Figure 6, we see that MPI Alfresco ECM is customized for searching user-defined metadata.

THE MPI ONTOLOGICAL BASE

Semantic Web technologies (i.e., ontologies and web services) offer new possibilities for employees' expertise data integration. Roughly, ontologies correspond to generalized database schemes made up of concepts, and the relations between them, that are relevant for a specific domain of knowledge. However, an ontology not only provides a database scheme for storing metadata but facilitates semantic content annotation, that is, assigning semantics to a set of knowledge sources (documents), and definition of rules that are both tractable by machines and understandable for humans. Therefore, ontologies are now often used for building integrating inter- and intra-organization business services and to make the search and retrieval both efficient and meaningful.

Instead of proposing a new ontology for tackling the challenges of semantic expertise finding in ICT field we rather suggest a framework of existing vocabularies, which shall be fruitfully

Figure 7. FOAF + DOAC ontology

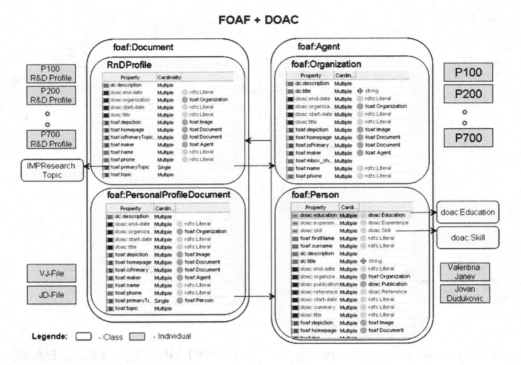

combined. Ontologies relevant for building an expertise finding system are as follows.

- The FOAF is a vocabulary for expressing personal profile and social networking information. It defines machine readable information/metadata for people, groups, organizations, and other related concepts.
- DOAC is a vocabulary for describing professional capabilities of workers gleaned for example from CVs or resumes. DOAC has been designed to be compatible with the European CV (known as Europass).
- DOAP is a vocabulary for describing software projects, in particular open source.
- SIOC ontology for expressing information contained within online community sites (weblogs, message boards, Wikis, etc.).

Ontologies are written using the computer languages RDF and OWL. RDF is a general-purpose language for representing information on the Web.

It defines a framework in which independent communities can develop vocabularies that suit their specific needs and share vocabularies with other communities. In order to share vocabularies, the meaning of terms must be specified in detail. The descriptions of these vocabulary sets are called RDF Schemas. A schema defines the meaning, characteristics, and relationships of a set of properties, and this may include constraints on potential values and the inheritance of properties from other schemas. The RDF language allows each document containing metadata to clarify which vocabulary is being used by assigning each vocabulary a Web address. RDF Schema uses Uniform Resource Identifier (URI) references for naming. URI reference is a string that represents a URI, that is, name or address of an abstract or physical resource on the Web.

OWL facilitates greater machine interpretability of Web content than that supported by RDF and RDF Schema by providing an additional vocabulary along with formal semantics.

In Figure 7, we present an example of combining concepts from FOAF and DOAC vocabularies for describing the knowledge captured in the *MPI HR knowledge pool* and the *MPI expertise document base*. The main "components" of combined ontology are: *foaf:Person, foaf:Organisation, foaf:Document, foaf:PersonalProfileDocument, foaf:Project, doac:Education, doac:Skill, doac:Experience,* and so forth. The links and relations between the components are defined with properties like *foaf:interest, foaf:made/maker, foaf:topic, foaf:primaryTopic, foaf:homepage,* and so forth.

To profile the MPI activities with the topics relevant for MPI ICT fields we initiated the MPI Business Topic Hierarchy with the following topics: *Information and Computer Science, Automation and Control, Sensors and Measurements, Telecommunications, Traffic Management,* and *Robotics.* The subtopics of the topic *Information and Computer Science* are as follows: *Business Information Systems, Communications, Databases, Document Management, DSS and Artificial Intelligence, Groupware and Collaboration, Semantic Web, System Architectures,* and so forth.

In Figure 8, we present an example of using SPARQL Query Language for RDF for querying the ontology repository. Our investigation of semantic technologies (Janev, 2008; Polleres, Scharffe, & Schindlauer, 2007) has shown that it has been accepted as a standard query language for the Semantic Web. Using the personal profile documents of the employees, we can retrieve the

expertise areas that an organizational unit could offer to its clients.

The results of querying the ontological knowledge base using the SPARQL query language are obtained using Protégé 3.4 open-source Ontology Editor and Knowledge Acquisition.

THE SEMANTIC WIKI PORTAL

It is a major trend to enhance the Web technologies that already widely used in the Web with the explicit semantics. The examples of this are Semantic Wikis (Schaffert, Bry, Baumeister, & Kiesel, 2008) that enhance the Wikis, the most popular tools for collaborative collecting and sharing of information on the Web, with explicit machine readable information, that is, semantic annotations. Semantic Wikis use RDF/OWL language for internal representation of the annotations and thus simplify the exchange of data with other applications. The annotations in the Semantic Mediawiki are page centric, which means that the information in the annotations refers to the abstract concept represented by the given Wiki page. Thus, unlike RDF statements (subject-predicate-object) the annotations have only a predicate and object, as the subject is implicitly given by the location of the annotation (i.e., by the page they are entered). The Semantic Mediawiki provides a semantic knowledge base around the Wiki pages, its own reasoning services for the knowledge base, which mostly deal with

Figure 8. SPARQL sample query against the ontological knowledge base

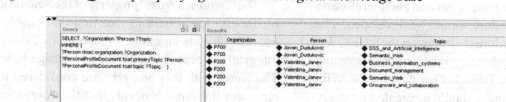

Figure 9. Semantic Web portal architecture

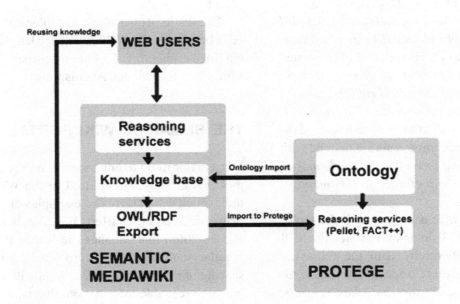

query answering, and the OWL/RDF export for reusing the knowledge present in the Wiki.

Figure 9 presents the MPI Semantic Mediawiki portal that is support by the MPI ontological knowledge base maintained with Protégé. The two systems are loosely coupled via import/export functionalities. By import, we mean converting the MPI ontological knowledge base into a Semantic Mediawiki knowledge base, while export serves for checking the consistency of the Semantic Mediawiki knowledge base.

The portal ontology built in the Protégé or coming from some other OWL knowledge base can be imported to Semantic Mediawiki. As of version 1.2 of the Semantic Mediawiki there is no functionality to import ontologies in the Wiki knowledge base in general and therefore an automated procedure should be developed. The automated procedure shall convert the RDF/OWL entities into the Mediawiki components, using the mappings in Table 1. One page in the Wiki Category namespace should be created for every Class (e.g., *foaf:Person*), for every Property (e.g., *foaf:firstName*) we must create a Wiki page in the

Property namespace, and for every individual a normal Wiki page should be made. For the class instantiations of individuals from the ontology, Category annotations are created in the Wiki, and for properties of the individuals the Property annotations should be made. This completes the mappings, but although the ontological elements are present in the Semantic Wiki knowledge base, their meanings are now local to the Wiki. For example, we would like to say explicitly that the *Category:Person* in our MPI Semantic Mediawiki has a the same meaning as *foaf:Person* concept. Fortunately, the SemanticMedia Wiki has two mechanisms for doing so, the "*imported from*," and the "*Equivalent URI*" properties (see Figure 10).

The "*imported from*" property of the Semantic Mediawiki has a built-in meaning that enables users to provide an explicit meaning to the ontological concepts in the Wiki knowledge base. The pages with this property are considered to represent the same concepts that the "*imported from*" annotation says. For example, in the MPI portal the *Category:Person* contains the following

Table 1. Description Logic entities to Semantic MediaWiki entities mapping

	OWL DL	Semantic Mediawiki	Example
T BOX	Class	Page in Category namespace	www.web4web.org/portal/Category:Project
	Property	Page in Property namespace	www.web4web.org/portal/Property:homepage
A BOX	Individual	Page in Main namespace	www.web4web.org/portal/Web4WeB
	Class membership	Category annotation on normal page	[[Category:Project]] (annotation on Wiki page)
	Relations	Property annotation on the subject page	[[Homepage:http://www.web4web.org]] (annotation on Wki page)

Figure 10. A Category and an Individual page in Semantic Mediawiki

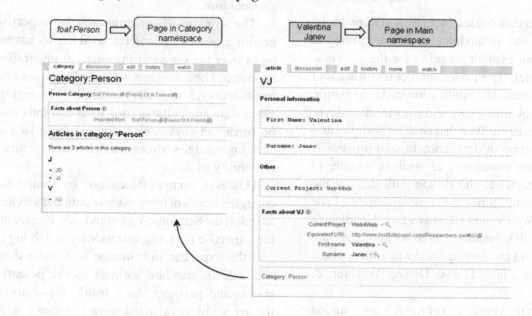

annotation *[[imported from::foaf:Person]]* that says that instead of having a local meaning to the Wiki the *Person* class represents the *foaf:Person* class. This information is used by all exports of the knowledge contained in the Wiki. In order to enable the use of FOAF ontology with the "*imported from*" property the Wiki administrator must create a page in the Wiki that defines the usage of FOAF ontology in the Wiki. For every ontology that is to be used in the Wiki a new special page must be created, and mappings for all ontological elements that can be used with the "*imported from*" property must be defined. The advantage of this approach is that Wiki annotations do not use full URIs of the ontological concepts but shortened

versions. In the previous example instead of using full URL: http://xmlns.com/foaf/0.1/# of the ontology the shorthand *foaf:Person* is used. The other mechanism for giving explicit semantics to local ontological elements of the Wiki is "*equivalent URI*" property. This property is suitable for individuals. The "*equivalent URI*" is a special property in Semantic MediaWiki with a built-in meaning; it marks a page in the Wiki as having a well-known meaning beyond this Wiki. The meaning is defined by the external URI. In RDF Export the "Equivalent URI" special property exports as "*owl:sameAs*." This OWL property indicates that the article in the Wiki and the external URI actually refer to the same "identity."

For creating an automated script for importing the ontological elements from OWL/RDF to the Wiki we used Python programming language[13], with a great help from two external libraries, Pywikibot, and RDFlib.

THE IMPACT OF SEMANTIC TECHNOLOGIES ON INFORMATION SYSTEMS

Semantic technologies include software tools, standards, and methodologies that are aimed at providing an explicit meaning for the information separately from data and content files, and separately from the application code. Semantic Web technologies provide an abstraction layer above the existing Web that enables bridging and interconnection of data, content, and processes. This enables machines, as well as people, to understand, share, and reason with them at the execution time. Since the announcement of the Semantic Web vision (Berners-Lee, Hendler, & Lassila, 2001), Semantic Web technologies are maturing and are finding their way into applications (Auer, 2008; Doms, Dietze, Wachter, & Schroeder, 2008).

To meet the challenges of today's information economy and be competitive in global market, enterprises are constantly adapting their business processes and adjusting their information systems. In the context of expertise profiling and searching problem, we have presented three different approaches to data and knowledge integration: the information integration–based approach, the content based approach, and the innovative Semantic Web based approach.

The information integration approach illustrated by the MPI Human resources knowledge pool is a classical approach of integrating data in the form of a central relational database (RDBMS). To be useful, this database should be constantly updated, or it becomes obsolete. An advantage of this approach is that the employees' expertise, as well as the results of their work, are explicitly recorded, thus enabling searching without involving sophisticated information extraction or data and text mining algorithms, as is the case in the content based approach. Supporting aggregation, the relational databases are well suited for the reporting purposes and conducting analysis on the expertise potential of a group or an organizational unit.

The content-based approach to expertise profiling, searching, and retrieval has its advantages over the classical information integration approach. The contemporary knowledge management solutions, such as Alfresco ECM integrate groupware and collaboration tools and thus support different ways for recording expertise. Hence, such knowledge sources are richer and facilitate reusability as well.

However, companies cannot go around the emerging trends of integration of data and services based on the Semantic Web standards. Regarding the expertise data, organizations are striving to pull the expertise information and make them available in standard formats to the potential clients and partners. As a result, the state-of-the-art knowledge management systems (Cai, Wang, Jiao, Akiyoshi, & Komoda, 2008; Benbya, 2008) are based on open standards (JEE, XML, XSLT), as well as on semantic technologies like RDF/RDFS, OWL, SPARQL, and others recommended by W3C[14]. However, some open issues have to be overcome to get the full potential from the semantic retrieval approach, such as the lack of synchronization and interoperability between the OWL/RDF-based knowledge bases and the traditional persistence mechanisms, the lack of inference and reasoning standards that are crucial for realization of the Semantic Web vision, as well as the lack of semantic privacy protection standards.

CONCLUSION

The modern organizations feature a flexible organizational structure where human resources are shared by different processes and projects. Also, in the present competitive environment, companies have to follow the information technology trends, for example, the Semantic Web initiatives like SIOC and FOAF. Finding expertise (either a person or/and accompanied knowledge items) in such a dynamic, fluid, and often complex organizational structure, that is supported by an extended information system, is a challenging issue.

This article analyzes state-of-the-art approaches and technologies for expertise integration, profiling, searching and retrieval. In the case of the MPI, we pointed out the way of responding to these challenges, as well as the changes that the enterprise knowledge management infrastructure underwent in the light of the uprising initiatives for standardization of the Semantic Web data. Hereby, we proposed an approach to development and implementation of an integrated knowledge management platform for R&D organizations and illustrated its usage in practice. Following the approach, the MPI business processes in HR sector have been integrated and automated in accordance with the adopted ISO 9001 Quality Assurance standard. Scientific data has been organized and classified in accordance with the Serbian Ministry of Science standards, which themselves reflect SCI, ISI, and IEEE standards.

In conclusion, we can state that modern organizations can derive significant added value from embracing knowledge management principles to promote a smooth flow, sharing, and reuse of both internal and external knowledge and information. However, since R&D organizations' innovation charter demands a focus different from that of other types of organizations, specifically, to nurture open access to human resources' extensive knowledge and experience, both explicit and tacit, significant adjustment of standard KM solutions and practices are necessary to suit their needs.

One successful example of such an adjustment has been presented in this article.

ACKNOWLEDGMENT

This work has been partly supported by the EU Sixth Framework Programme (Web4Web - Web technologies for West Balkan countries, Pr. No.: INCO-CT-2007-043619) and partly by the Ministry of Science and Technological Development of Republic of Serbia (Pr. No.: TR-13004).

REFERENCES

ACM. (2008). *The ACM computing classification system*. Retrieved August 5, 2008, from, http://oldwww.acm.org/class/

Agarwal, N., Liu, H., & Tang, L. (2008). Identifying the influential bloggers in a community. In *Proceedings of the First ACM International Conference on Web Search and Data Mining (WSDM 2008)*, Stanford, CA (pp. 207-218). ACM Publishing.

Aleman-Meza, B., Bojars, U., Boley, H., Breslin, J., Mochol, M., Nixon, L. J. B., et al. (2007, June 3-7). Combining RDF vocabularies for expert finding. In E. Franconi, M. Kifer, & W. May (Eds.) *The Semantic Web: Research and applications: 4th European Semantic Web Conference (ESWC2007)*, Innsbruck, Austria (LNCS 4519, pp. 235-250).

Auer, S. (2008). Methods and applications of the social Semantic Web. In S. Vraneš (Ed.), *Semantic Web and/or Web 2.0: Competitive or complementary?* (pp. 100-128). Belgrade, Serbia: Academic Mind.

Balog, K., Azzopardi, L., & de Rijke, M. (2006). Formal models for expert finding in enterprise corpora. In S. Dumais, E. N. Efthimiadis, D. Hawking, & K. Järvelin (Eds.), *Proceedings of the 29th Annual International ACM SIGIR Conference on Research & Development on Information Retrieval* (pp. 43-50). ACM.

Balog, K., & de Rijke, M. (2008, March 30-April 3). Associating people and documents. In C. Macdonald, I.Ounis, & V. Plachouras (Eds.), *Advances in Information Retrieval: 30th European Conference on Information Retrieval (ECIR 2008)* Glasgow, Scotland (LNCS 4956, pp. 296-308).

Benbya, H. (2008). *Knowledge management systems implementation: Lessons from the Silicon Valley.* Oxford, UK: Chandos Publishing.

Berners-Lee, T., Hendler, J., & Lassila, O. (2001, May). The Semantic Web. *Scientific American.* Retrieved January 15, 2007, from http://www.sciam.com/article.cfm?id=the-semantic-web

Bojars, U., Breslin, J., Peristeras, V., Tummarello, G., & Decker, S. (2008). Interlinking the social Web with semantics. *IEEE Intelligent Systems, 23*(3), 29–40. doi:10.1109/MIS.2008.50

Cai, L., Wang, Z., Jiao, Y., Akiyoshi, M., & Komoda, N. (2008). Prototype of knowledge management system in Chinese offshore software development company. *WSEAS Transactions on Information Science & Applications, 3*(5), 252–257.

Demartini, G. (2007, November 12). Finding experts using Wikipedia. In *Proceedings of the 2nd International ISWC+ASWC Workshop on Finding Experts on the Web with Semantics,* Busan, South Korea (pp. 33-41). CEUR Workshop Proceedings.

Doms, A., Dietze, H., Wachter, T., & Schroeder, M. (2008). Literature search with ontologies, a tutorial. In S. Vraneš (Ed.), *Semantic Web and/or Web 2.0: Competitive or complementary?* (pp. 81-100). Belgrade, Serbia: Academic Mind.

Fang, H., & Zhai, C. X. (2007, April 2-5). Probabilistic models for expert finding. In *Advances in Information Retrieval: Proceedings of the 29th European Conference on Information Retrieval (ECIR 2007)* Rome, Italy (LNCS 4425, pp. 418-430).

Hogan, A., & Harth, A. (2007). *The ExpertFinder Corpus 2007 for the benchmarking and development of ExpertFinding systems.* Paper presented at the 1st International ExpertFinder Workshop, Berlin, Germany. Retrieved August 5, 2008, from, http://lsdis.cs.uga.edu/~aleman/efw2007/program/

Janev, V. (2008). A comparison and critical assessment of cutting edge Semantic Web products and technologies. In S. Vraneš (Ed.), *Semantic Web and/or Web 2.0: Competitive or complementary?* (pp. 148-165). Belgrade, Serbia: Academic Mind.

Janev, V., Đokić, A., Minić, M., & Vraneš, S. (2008). Knowledge management in the HR sector of R&D organizations. In L. Vladareanu, V. Chiroiu, P. Bratu, & I. Magheti (Eds.), *Proceedings of the 9th WSEAS International Conference on Automation and Information (ICAI'08),* Bucharest, Romania (pp. 315-321). Stevens Point, WI: World Scientific and Engineering Academy and Society.

Janev, V., & Vraneš, S. (2005). Comparative analysis of commercial knowledge management solutions and their role in enterprises. *Journal of Information and Knowledge management, 10*(4), 71-81.

Janev, V., & Vraneš, S. (2006). Integration of knowledge resources at R&D organizations: The case of Mihajlo Pupin Institute. In M. C. Cunha, B. C. Cortes, & G. Putnik (Eds.), *Adaptive technologies and business integration: Social, Managerial and Organizational dimensions* (pp. 263-280). Hershey, PA: IDEA Group Inc.

Jung, H., Lee, M., Kang, I.-S., Lee, S.-W., & Sung, W.-K. (2007, November). Finding topic-centric identified experts based on full text analysis. In A. V. Zhdanova, L. J. B. Nixon, M. Mochol, & J. G. Breslin (Eds.), *Finding Experts on the Web with Semantics 2007, Proceedings of the 2nd Intl. ISWC+ASWC ExpertFinder Workshop (FEWS'07),* Busan, Korea. Retrieved August 5, 2008, from CEUR-WS.org/Vol-290

Li, J., Boley, H., Bhavsar, V. C., & Mei, J. (2006). Expert finding for eCollaboration using FOAF with RuleML rules. In L. Logrippo, H. Mili, & A. Salah (Eds.), *Proceedings of the 2006 Montreal Conference on eTechnologies* (pp. 53-65). Québec, Canada.

MPI. (2004). *Quality control system documentation.* (Confidential). Belgrade, Serbia: Author.

Nonaka, I., & Takeuchi, H. (1995). *The knowledge creating company.* New York: Oxford University Press.

Pavlov, M., & Ichise, R. (2007, November). Finding experts by link prediction in co-authorship metworks. In A. V. Zhdanova, L. J. B. Nixon, M. Mochol, & J. G. Breslin (Eds.), *Finding Experts on the Web with Semantics 2007, Proceedings of the 2nd Intl. ISWC+ASWC ExpertFinder Workshop (FEWS'07),* Busan, Korea. Retrieved August 5, 2008, from CEUR-WS.org/Vol-290

Petkova, D., & Bruce Croft, W. (2006). Hierarchical language models for expert finding in enterprise corpora. In *Proceedings of the 18th IEEE International Conference on Tools with Artificial Intelligence* (pp. 599 – 608). IEEE Computer Society.

Polleres, A., Scharffe, F., & Schindlauer, R. (2007). SPARQL++ for mapping between RDF vocabularies. In R. Meersman & Z. Tari (Eds.), *On the Move to Meaningful Internet Systems 2007: CoopIS, DOA, ODBASE, GADA, and IS,* Vilamoura, Portugal (LNCS 4803, pp. 878-896).

Rodrígues, J. L., Castellanos, A. R., & Ranguelov, S. Y. (2004). Knowledge management analysis of the research & development & transference process at HEROs: A public university case. In K. Tochtermann & H. Maurer (Eds.), *Proceedings of the International conference on knowledge management (I-KNOW'04)* (pp. 61-67). Graz, Austria: J.UCS, Know-Center.

SAP. (2007). *SAP for higher education & research.* Retrieved January 15, 2007, from http://www.sap.com/industries/highered/

Schaffert, S., Bry, F., Baumeister, J., & Kiesel, M. (2008). Semantic Wikis. *IEEE Software, 25*(4), 8–11. doi:10.1109/MS.2008.95

Serbian National Scientific Council. (2008, April 14). Act standard for valuating and quantity presenting of the scientific results of the researcher. *Službeni glasnik Republike Srbije 16*(38).

Sim, Y. W., Crowder, R. M., & Wills, G. B. (2006, May 9-11). *Expert finding by capturing organizational knowledge from legacy documents.* Paper presented at the IEEE International Conference on Computer & Communication Engineering (ICCCE '06), Kuala Lumpur, Malaysia.

S&T. (2007). *S&T—IT solutions and services.* Retrieved January 22, 2008, from http://www.snt.co.yu/

Suh, W., Derich Sohn, J. H., & Kwak, J. Y. (2004). Knowledge management as enabling R&D innovation in high tech industry: The case of SAIT. *Journal of Knowledge Management, 8*(6), 5–15. doi:10.1108/13673270410567594

Yimam-Seid, D., & Kobsa, A. (2003). Expert finding systems for organizations: Problem and domain analysis and the demoir approach. *Journal of Organizational Computing and Electronic Commerce, 13*(1), 1–24. doi:10.1207/S15327744JOCE1301_1

ENDNOTES

[1]   http://www.foaf-project.org/.

[2]   http://trac.usefulinc.com/doap.

[3]   http://ramonantonio.net/doac/.

[4]   http://sioc-project.org/.

[5]   http://lucene.apache.org/.

[6]   www.cmsmatrix.org.

[7]   http://www.opencms.org/en/.

[8]   http://lenya.apache.org/.

[9]   http://www.magnolia.info.

[10] http://www.alfresco.com.

[11] http://mc.manuscriptcentral.com/ieee.

[12] http://www.jucs.org/.

[13] http://www.python.org/.

[14] The World Wide Web Consortium, Semantic Web Activity, http://www.w3.org/2001/sw/.

This work was previously published in The International Journal of Enterprise Information Systems 5(4), edited by A. Gunasekaran, copyright 2009 by IGI Publishing (an imprint of IGI Global).

Compilation of References

Abadi, M. (2005). *Issues and challenges in communication within design teams in the construction industry*. PhD Thesis, Faculty of Engineering and Physical Sciences, School of Mechanical, Aerospace and Civil Engineering, the University of Manchester.

Abdullah, R., Tiun, S., & Kong, T. E. (2001). Automatic topic identification using ontology hierarchy. In *Proceedings, Computational Linguistic and Intelligent Text Processing, Second International Conference CICLing*, Mexico City, Mexico (pp. 444-453). Berlin, Germany: Springer.

Abels, S., Haak, L., & Hahn, A. (2005). Identification of common methods used for ontology integration tasks. Interoperability of heterogeneous information systems. In *Proceedings of the first international workshop on Interoperability of heterogeneous information systems*, Bremen, Germany (pp. 75-78). New York: ACM.

Abouelhoda, M. I., & Kurtz, S. (2005). Replacing suffix trees with enhanced suffix arrays. *Journal of Discrete Algorithms, 2*, 53–86. doi:10.1016/S1570-8667(03)00065-0

Achterkamp, M. C., & Vos, F. J. F. (2006). A Framework for making sense of sustainable innovation through stakeholder involvement. *International Journal of Environmental Technology and Management, 6*(6), 525–538. doi:10.1504/IJETM.2006.011895

Ackoff, R. L. (1999). *Re-creating the corporation*. New York: Oxford University Press.

Adams, D. (2002). *The salmon of doubt: Hitchhiking the galaxy one last time*. London: William Heinemann.

Adelson, E. H. (2000). Lightness perceptions and lightness illusions. In M. Gazzaniga (Ed.), *The new cognitive sciences* (2nd ed.). Cambridge, MA: MIT Press.

Afuah, A. (2003). *Business models: A strategic management approach*. New York: McGraw-Hill/Irwin.

Afuah, A., & Tucci, C. L. (2002). *Internet business models and strategies: Text and cases*. New York: McGraw-Hill/Irwin.

Agarwal, N., Liu, H., & Tang, L. (2008). Identifying the influential bloggers in a community. In *Proceedings of the First ACM International Conference on Web Search and Data Mining* (*WSDM 2008*), Stanford, CA (pp. 207-218). ACM Publishing.

Agyapong-Kodua, K., Ajaefobi, J.O., & Weston, R.H. (2009). Modelling dynamic value streams to support process design and evaluation. *Int. J. of Computer Integrated Manufacturing*.

Aho, A. V., Sethi, R., & Ullman, J. D. (1998). *Compiladores: Principios, técnicas y herramientas*, Mexico: Addison Wesley Longman.

Ajaefobi, J. O., Wahid, B., & Weston, R. H. (2008). *Proc. of the ICAM*, Western Michigan University, USA.

Alavi, M. (1997). *KPMG Peat Marwick U.S.: One giant brain* (Report Nr. 9-397-108). Boston: Harvard Business School.

Alberts, D. S. H., & Richard, E. (2003). Power to the edge: Command...control...in the information age. In C. f. A. C. & Technology (Eds.), *Information age transformation series*. Center for Advanced Concepts and Technology.

Aleman-Meza, B., Bojars, U., Boley, H., Breslin, J., Mochol, M., Nixon, L. J. B., et al. (2007, June 3-7). Combining RDF vocabularies for expert finding. In E. Franconi, M. Kifer, & W. May (Eds.) *The Semantic Web: Research and applications: 4th European Semantic Web*

Conference (ESWC2007), Innsbruck, Austria (LNCS 4519, pp. 235-250).

Alison, B., O'Sullivia, O.A., Rice, J., Rothwell, A., & Sanders, C. (2001). *Research skills for students.*

Allen, D. (2002). *Getting things done: The art of stress-free productivity.* New York: Penguin.

Allen, P. (2001). *Realizing e-business with components.* Reading, MA: Addison-Wesley.

Ambrose, S. H. (2001). Paleolithic technology and human evolution. *Science, 291,* 1748–1753. doi:10.1126/science.1059487

Amdahl, G. M., Blaauw, G., & Brooks, F. (1964). Architecture of the IBM system/360. *IBM Journal of Research and Development, 8*(2), 21–36.

AMICE (Ed.). (1993). *Open system architecture for CIM, ESPRIT Consortium* (2nd ed.). New York: Springer-Verlag.

Amin, S. (1990). *Maldevelopment: Anatomy of a global failure.* London: Zed Book.

Andenas, M. (2008). Who is going to supervise Europe's financial markets. In M. Adenas & Y. Avgerinos (Eds.), *Financial markets in Europe: Towards a single regulator.* London: Kluwer Law International.

Andersen, A., & APQC (American Productivity and Quality Center). (1996). *The KM assessment tools: External benchmarking version. Winter.*

Andrade, G. M.-M., Mitchell, M. L., & Stafford, E. (2001). *New evidence and perspectives on mergers* (Harvard Business School Working Paper No. 01-070). Retrieved from http://ssrn.com/abstract=269313

André Vasconcelos, A. C., Sinogas, P., Mendes, R., & Tribolet, J. (1999). *Arquitectura de sistemas de informação: A ferramenta de alinhamento negócio / sistemas de informação?* Lisboa, Portugal: Fundação Portuguesa de Ciência e Tecnologia, programa POSI, FEDER.

Andriessen, D. (2004) *Making sense of intellectual capital: Designing a method for the valuation of Intangibles.* Butterworth – Heinemann

Andriessen, J. H. E. (2003). *Working with groupware: Understanding and evaluating collaboration technology.* London: Springer.

Andro, M. D. A. Team. (2008, April 21). *AndroMDA.* Retrieved November 24, 2008, from http://www.andromda.org/

Anna H. Perrault, V. L. G. (2000). Think global, act local: The challenges of taking the website global*. *INSPEL, 34.*

Ansoff, H. I. (1965). *Corporate strategy.* New York: McGraw-Hill.

Anthony, R. N. (1965). *Planning and control systems: A framework for analysis.* Boston: Harvard University Press.

Arakji, R. Y., & Lang, K.-R. (2007). Digital consumer networks and producer-consumer collaboration: Innovation and product development in the digital entertainment industry. In *Proceedings of the 40th Annual Hawaii International Conference on System Sciences (HICSS'07).*

Arlow, J., & Neustadt, I. (2005). *Uml 2.0 and the unified process.* Reading, MA: Addison Wesley.

Arnold, K. A. (2006). *PMESII and the non-state actor. Questioning the relevance.* US Army Monograph, Fort Leavenworth, KA, School of Advanced Military Studies.

Ashfort, B. E. (2001). *Role transition in organisational life: An identity-based perspective.* Mahwah, NJ: Lawrence Erlbaum Associates.

Ashworth, R., Boyne, G., & Delbridge, R. (2007). Escape from the iron cage? Organizational change and isomorphic pressures in the public sector. *Journal of Public Administration Research and Theory,* April.

Aslesen, S. (2005). *EU-utvidelsen – mulige tilpasningsstrategier i norske skipsverft.* Fafo-notat 2005:07.

Aslesen, S., & Bertelsen, S. (2008). Last planner in a social perspective – a shipbuilding case. P. Tzortzopoulos & M. Kagioglou (Eds.), *IGLC 16 Proceedings 16th Annual Conference of the International Group for Lean Construction, Manchester, United Kingdom.*

Astels, D. (2003). *Test driven development: A practical guide.* Upper Saddle River, NJ: Prentice Hall.

Auer, S. (2008). Methods and applications of the social Semantic Web. In S. Vraneš (Ed.), *Semantic Web and/or*

Web 2.0: Competitive or complementary? (pp. 100-128). Belgrade, Serbia: Academic Mind.

Ávila, P., Putnik, G. D., & Cunha, M. M. (2002). Brokerage function in agile/virtual enterprise integration - a literature review. In L. M. Camarinha-Matos (Ed.), *Collaborative business ecosystems and virtual enterprises* (pp. 65-72). Boston: Kluwer Academic Publishers.

Ávila, P., Putnik, G. D., & Cunha, M. M. (2005). Broker performance for agile/virtual enterprise integration. In G. D. Putnik & M. M. Cunha (Eds.), *Virtual enterprise integration: Technological and organizational perspectives* (pp. 166-185). Hershey, PA: Idea Group Publishing.

Avsec, D. (1986). *Finančne oblike družbenega pospeševanja (so)delovanja mnogih v socialistični samoupravni družbi.* Maribor, Slovenija. Univerza v Mariboru, Ekonomsko-poslovna fakulteta, Bertalanffy, v. L. (1979) *General systems theory. Foundations, development, application.* New York: Braziller.

Axsom, D., & Lawless, W. F. (1992). Subsequent behavior can erase evidence of dissonance-induced attitude change. *Journal of Experimental Social Psychology, 28,* 387–400. doi:10.1016/0022-1031(92)90052-L

Ballard, H. G. (2000). *The last planner system of production control.* Doctoral thesis submitted to the faculty of Engineering, University of Birmingham, United Kingdom.

Balog, K., & de Rijke, M. (2008, March 30-April 3). Associating people and documents. In C. Macdonald, I. Ounis, & V. Plachouras (Eds.), *Advances in Information Retrieval: 30th European Conference on Information Retrieval (ECIR 2008)* Glasgow, Scotland (LNCS 4956, pp. 296-308).

Balog, K., Azzopardi, L., & de Rijke, M. (2006). Formal models for expert finding in enterprise corpora. In S. Dumais, E. N. Efthimiadis, D. Hawking, & K. Järvelin (Eds.), *Proceedings of the 29th Annual International ACM SIGIR Conference on Research & Development on Information Retrieval* (pp. 43-50). ACM.

Balzert, H. (1982). *Die entwicklung von software systemen.* Reihe Informatik/34, BI Wis- senschaftsverlag.

Balzert, H. (1989). *CASE - systeme und werkzeuge.* B-I Wissenschaftsverlag.

Barber, K. D., Dewhurst, F. W., Burns, R. L. D. H., & Rogers, J. B. B. (2003). Business–process modelling and simulation for manufacturing management: A practical way forward . *Business Process Management Journal, 9*(4). doi:10.1108/14637150310484544

Barber, M. I., & Weston, R. H. (1998). Scoping study on business process reengineering: Towards successful IT application . *International Journal of Production Research, 36,* 574–601.

Barbour, I. (1993). *Ethics in age of technology.* San Francisco: Harper.

Bardhan, A. (2008). *Of subprimes and subsidies: The political economy of the financial crisis.* Retrieved October 20, 2008, from http://ssrn.com/abstract=1270196

Bargiel, B. (2008). *iGTD2 online portal.* Retrieved November 26, 2008, from http://www.igtd.pl/iGTD/iGTD2/

Bass, G. J. (2008). *Freedom's battle: The origin of humanitarian interventions.* New York: Knopf.

Baumeister, R. F., Campbell, J.D., Krueger, J.I., & Vohs, K.D. (2005, January). Exploding the self-esteem myth. *Scientific American.*

Bebchuk, L. A. (2008). *A plan for addressing the financial crisis* (Harvard Law and Economics Discussion Paper No. 620).

Beck, K. (2003). *Extreme programming.* Reading, MA: Addison-Wesley Longman.

Beck, K., & Andres, C. (2004). *Extreme programming explained: Embrace change.* Boston, MA: Addison-Wesley.

Beck, K., et al. (2002). *Manifesto for agile software development.* Retrieved from http://agilemanifesto.org/

Beckett-Camarata, E. J., Camarata, M. R., & Barker, R. T. (1998). Integrating internal and external customer relationships through relationship management: A strategic response to a changing global environment. *Journal of Business Research, 41*(1), 71–81. doi:10.1016/S0148-2963(97)00013-1

Beer, S. (1981). *The brain of firm.* Chichester, UK: John Wiley & Sons.

Beeson, I., & Green, S. (2003, April 9-11). Using a language action framework to extend organizational process modelling. Paper presented at the UK Academy for Information Systems Conference, University of Warwick.

Bellagio, D. E., & Milligan, T. J. (2005). *Software configuration management strategies and IBM rational ClearCase: A practical introduction.* Armonk, NY: IBM Press.

Belle, J.-P. V., Eccles, M., & Nash, J. (2003). *Discovering information systems.* Cape Town: South African Universities Press.

Benbya, H. (2008). *Knowledge management systems implementation: Lessons from the Silicon Valley.* Oxford, UK: Chandos Publishing.

Berander, P., & Andrews, A. (2005). Requirements prioritization. In *Engineering and managing software requirements* (pp. 69-94).

Berio, G., & Vernadat, F. B. (1999). New developments in enterprise modelling using CIMOSA. *Computers in Industry, 40*(2), 99–114. doi:10.1016/S0166-3615(99)00017-2

Bernard, S. A. (2005). *An introduction to enterprise architecture.* Bloomington, IN: AuthorHouse.

Berners-Lee, T., Hendler, J., & Lassila, O. (2001, May). The Semantic Web. *Scientific American.* Retrieved January 15, 2007, from http://www.sciam.com/article.cfm?id=the-semantic-web

Bernus, P. (2003). Enterprise models for enterprise architecture and ISO9000:2000. *Annual Reviews in Control, 27*, 211–220. doi:10.1016/j.arcontrol.2003.09.004

Bernus, P. (2003). *Handbook on enterprise architecture.* New York: Springer.

Bertalanfyy, L. v. (1951). General system theory - a new approach to unity of science (Symposium). *Human Biology, 23*, 303–361.

Bertelsen, O. W., & Bødker, S. (2003). Activity theory. In J. M. Carroll (Ed.), *HCI models, theories and frameworks.* Elsevier Science.

Beyer, H., & Holtzblatt, K. (1998) *Contextual design.* Morgan Kaufman

Bhagwati, N. (2004). *In defence of globalisation.* New York: Oxford University Press.

Bille, P. (2005). A survey on tree edit distance and related problems. *Theoretical Computer Science, 337*(1-3), 217–239. doi:10.1016/j.tcs.2004.12.030

Blaauw, G. (1972). Computer architecture. *El. Rechenanl, 14*(4), 154.

Blethyn, S. G., & Parker, C. S. (1990). *Designing information systems.* Butterworth-Heinemann.

BMVg (Ed.). (1997). *V-Modell - entwicklungsstandard für IT-systeme des bundes (EStddIT) Stand Oct. 1997* (Tech. Rep.). Germany: BMVg.

Bobrow.D.G, W. J. (2002). Community knowledge sharing in practice: The Eureka story. *Society for organizational learning and Massachusetts Institute of Technology, 4*, 47-59.

Boddy, D. (2004). Responding to competing narratives: Lessons for project managers. *International Journal of Project Management, 22*(3), 225–234. doi:10.1016/j.ijproman.2003.07.001

Boehm, B. (1976). Software engineering. *IEEE Transactions on Computers, C-25*(12), 1226–1241. doi:10.1109/TC.1976.1674590

Boehm, B. (1986). A spiral model of software development and enhancement. *ACM SIGS- OFT - Software Engineering Notes, 11*(4), 22-42.

Boehm, B., Grünbacher, P., & Briggs, B. (2001). Developing groupware for requirements negotiation: Lessons learned. *IEEE Software, 18*(3), 46–55. doi:10.1109/52.922725

Bojars, U., Breslin, J., Peristeras, V., Tummarello, G., & Decker, S. (2008). Interlinking the social Web with semantics. *IEEE Intelligent Systems, 23*(3), 29–40. doi:10.1109/MIS.2008.50

Bontis, N. (2002) Managing organizational knowledge by diagnosing intellectual capital. Framing and advancing the state of the field. In N. Bontis & C.W. Choo (Eds.), *The strategic management of intellectual capital and organizational knowledge* (pp. 621-642). Oxford, New York: Oxford University Press.

Booch, G., Jacobson, I., & Rumbaugh, (2004). *El proceso unificado de desarrollo de software*. Reading, MA: Addison Wesley.

Booch, G., Jacobson, I., & Rumbaugh, J. (2000). *OMG unified modeling language specification*. Retrieved November 24, 2008, from http://www.omg.org/docs/formal/00-03-01.pdf

Booch, G., Rumbaugh, J., & Jacobson, I. (2005). *The unified modeling language user guide*. Reading, MA: Addison-Wesley.

Booker, P. J. (1963). *A history of engineering drawing*. London: Chatto & Windus.

Boonstra, A. (2003). Structure and analysis of IS decision making processes. *European Journal of Information Systems*, *12*(3), 195–209. doi:10.1057/palgrave.ejis.3000461

Boonstra, A. (2006). Interpreting an ERP implementation from a stakeholder perspective. *International Journal of Project Management*, *24*(1), 38–52. doi:10.1016/j.ijproman.2005.06.003

Boucock, C. (2000). *In the grip of freedom: Law and modernity in Max Weber*. University of Toronto.

Bouldin, B. (1989). *Agents of change - managing the introduction of automated tools*. Your- don Press.

Božičnik, S., Ećimović, T., Mulej, M., et al. (2008). *Sustainable future, requisite holism, and social responsibility (against the current abuse of free market society)*. Ansted University, British Virgin Islands, and Penang, in cooperation with SEM Institute for Climate Change, Korte, and IRDO Institute for development of Social Responsibility, Maribor.

Bradbury, D. (2007). Web 2.0 - beyond the buzz words. *Computer Weekly*.

Brandenburger, A. M., & Nalebuff, B. J. (1996). *Coopetition*. New York: Currency Doubleday.

Bravocco, R. R., & Yadav, S. B. (1985). Requirements definitions architecture – an overview. *Computers in Industry*, *6*, 237–251. doi:10.1016/0166-3615(85)90046-6

Brehm, N., & Haak, L. (2008). Ontologies supporting VLBAs: Semantic integration in the context of FERP.

In *Proceedings of the 3rd International Conference on Information and Communication Technologies: From Theory To Applications, ICTTA 2008*, (pp. 1-5).

Brown, G., Wyatt, J., Harris, R., & Yao, X. (2005). Diversity creation methods: A survey and categorization. *Journal of Information Fusion*, *6*, 5–20. doi:10.1016/j.inffus.2004.04.004

Browne, J., & Zhang, J. (1999). Extended and virtual enterprises: Similarities and differences. *International Journal of Agile Management Systems*, *1*(1), 30–36. doi:10.1108/14654659910266691

Brownell, H., Pincus, D., Blum, A., Rehak, A., & Winner, E. (1997). The effects of right hemisphere brain damage on patients. *Brain and Language*, *57*, 60–79. doi:10.1006/brln.1997.1834

Brusoni, S., & Tronchetti-Provera, S. (2005). The limits to specialization: Problem solving and coordination in 'modular networks'. *Organization Studies*, *26*(12), 1885–1907. doi:10.1177/0170840605059161

Bryson, J. M. (2004). What to do when stakeholders matter. Stakeholder identification and analysis techniques. *Public Management Review*, *6*(1), 21–53. doi:10.1080/14719030410001675722

Buck, E. (2000). Different Types of organisation. *NEBS Management/QMD Ltd*. Retrieved September 1, 2008 from http://www.teamsthatwork.co.uk/Organise%20&%20improve%20team%20work%201.pdf

Buckley, W. (1967). *Sociology and modern systems theory*. Englewood Cliffs, NJ: Prentice Hall.

Bueno, E. (1987). *Dirección estratégica de la empresa: Metodología, técnicas y casos*. Madrid, Spain: Pirámide.

Bundesamt f. Informatik. (1995). *Hermes - führung und abwicklung von informatikprojek- ten* (Tech. Rep.). Bern, Switzerland: Bundesamt f. Informatik, Schweizerische Bundesverwaltung.

Burkhardt, S., Kärkkäinen, J., & Sanders, P. (2006). Linear work suffix array construction. [JACM]. *Journal of the ACM*, *53*(6), 918–936. doi:10.1145/1217856.1217858

Buttle, F. (2004). *Customer relationship management: Concepts and tools*. Oxford, UK: Butterworth-Heinemann.

Cacioppo, J. T., Berntson, G. G., & Crites, S. L., Jr., (Eds.). (1996). Social neuroscience: Principles, psychophysiology, arousal and response. *Social psychology handbook of basic principles*. New York, Guilford.

Cahn, E., & Rowe, J. (1992). *Time dollars*. Emmaus, PA: Rodale Press.

Cai, L., Wang, Z., Jiao, Y., Akiyoshi, M., & Komoda, N. (2008). Prototype of knowledge management system in Chinese offshore software development company. *WSEAS Transactions on Information Science & Applications*, *3*(5), 252–257.

Camarinha-Matos, L. M., & Afsarmanesh, H. (2004). The emerging discipline of collaborative networks. In L. M. Camarinha-Matos (Ed.), *Virtual enterprises and collaborative networks* (pp. 3-16). Boston: Kluwer Academic Publishers.

Capurro, R. (2004). Skeptical knowledge management. In H.-C. Hobohm (Ed.) *Knowledge Management: Libraries and librarians taking up the challenge* (IFLA Publication, 108, pp. 47-57). Munich: Saur.

Carbone, J. A. (2004). *IT architecture toolkit*. Upper Saddle River: Prentice Hall PTR.

Cardoso, H., & Oliveira, E. (2004, October 20-24). Virtual enterprise normative framework within electronic institutions. In M.-P. Gleizes, A. Omicini, & F. Zambonelli (Eds.), *Engineering Societies in the Agents World V: 5th International Workshop*, Toulouse, France (LNCS 3451, pp. 14-32).

Cardoso, H., & Oliveira, E. (2008). Electronic institutions for B2B: Dynamic normative environments. *Artificial Intelligence and Law*, *16*(1), 107–128. doi:10.1007/s10506-007-9044-2

Caro Herrero, J. L. (2003). *Metodología de modelado de procesos cooperativos en ingeniería de software*. Unpublished master's thesis, University of Málaga, Spain.

Caro, J. L., Guevara, A., & Aguayo, A. (2003). Workflow: A solution for the cooperative development of an information system. *Business Process Management*, *9*(2), 208–220. doi:10.1108/14637150310468407

Caro, J. L., Guevara, A., Aguayo, A., & Leiva, J. L. (2004). *Communication based workflow loop formalization using temporal logic of actions (TLA)*. Paper presented at the 6th International Conference on Enterprise Information Systems, ICEIS 2004, Porto, Portugal.

Carrillo, A., Falgueras, J., & Guevara, A. (2006). *GDIT: Tool for the design, specification and generation of goals driven user interfaces*. Paper presented at the 8th International Conference on Enterprise Information Systems ICEIS, 2006, Paphos, Cyprus.

Casti, J. L. (1991). *Searching for certainty: What scientists can know about the future*. New York: Morrow.

Cavaye, A. L. M. (1995). User participation in system development revisited. *Information & Management*, *28*(5), 311–326. doi:10.1016/0378-7206(94)00053-L

Cederqvist, P. (2002). *Version management with CVS*. Network Theory Ltd.

Center for Technology in Government. (1997). *An introduction to workflow management systems*. Albany, NY: Center for Technology in Government, University at Albany.

Chambers, R. (1995). Poverty and livelihoods. *Environment and Urbanization*, *7*(1), 173–204.

Champy, J., & Hammer, M. (1994). *Reengineering*. Ed. Norma.

Chan, C. K., & Lee, H. W. J. (2005). *Successful strategies in supply chain management*. Hershey, PA: IDEA Group Inc.

Charbonneau, S. (2006). *Droit communautaire de l'environnement*. Paris: L'Harmattan.

Chatha, K. A., Ajaefobi, J. O., & Weston, R. H. (2007). Enriched multi-process modelling in support of the life cycle engineering of business processes. *International Journal of Production Research*, *45*(1), 103–141.

Cheesman, J., & Daniels, J. (2001). *UML components*. Reading, MA: Addison Wesley.

Chestnut, H. (1967). *Systems engineering methods*. New York: Wiley.

Choi, J., Ahn, H., & Han, I. (2008). Utility-based double auction mechanism using genetic algorithms. *Expert Systems with Applications: An International Journal*, *34*(1), 150–158. doi:10.1016/j.eswa.2006.08.024

Choo, C. W. (1999) *The knowing organization: How organizations use information to construct meaning, create knowledge, and make decisions.* Oxford: Oxford University Press.

Chrissis, M. B., Konrad, M., & Shrum, S. (2006). *CMMI: Guidelines for process integration and product improvement.* Boston, MA: Addison-Wesley.

Christensen, L. C., Johansen, B. W., Midjo, N., Ornarheim, J., Syvertsen, T. G., & Totland, T. (1995). Enterprise modelling-practices and perspectives. In *Proc. of the ASME 9th Engineering Database Symposium,* Boston, US.

Christiaanse, E., & Markus, M. L. (2003, January 6-9). Participation in collaboration electronic marketplaces. In *Proceedings of the 36th Hawaii International Conference of Systems Sciences (HICSS 03)* (Vol. 7, pp. 178-185).

Chroust, G. (1992). *Modelle der software-entwicklung - aufbau und interpretation von vorgehensmodellen.* Oldenbourg Verlag. 31

Chroust, G. (1994). Partial process models. In M. M. Tanik, W. Rossak, & D. E. Cooke (Eds.), *Software Systems in Engineering, The American Soc. of Mechanical Engineers Engineers,* New Orleans, LA (pp. 197-202).

Chroust, G. (2000). Software process models: Structure and challenges. In Y. Feng, D. Notkin, & M. C. Gaudel (Eds.), *Software: Theory and Practice - Proceedings, IFIP Congress 2000,* Beijing, China (pp. 279-286). Amsterdam: Kluwer.

Chroust, G. (2006). Motivation in component-based software development. In C. Ghaoui (Ed.), *Encyclopedia of human computer interaction* (pp. 414-421). Hershey, PA: Idea Group Reference.

Chroust, G. (2007). Psychologische widerstände bei der einführung computer-gestützter vorgehensmodelle. In *Proceedings of the Workshop der Fachgruppe WI-VM 2007 der GI.* Garching b. München, Germany.

Chroust, G. (2007). Software like a courteous butler - issues of localization under cultural diversity. In *Proceedings of the ISSS 2007. The 51th Annual meeting and Conference for the System Sciences.* Tokyo, Japan: Curran Associates, Inc.

Chroust, G. (2008a). Localization, culture and global communication. In G. D. Putnik & M. M. Cunha (Eds.), *Encyclopedia of networked and virtual organizations* (pp. 829-832). Hershey, PA: Information Science Reference.

Chroust, G. (2008b). Psychologische widerstände bei der einführung computer-gestützter vorgehensmodelle. In R. Höhn, R. Petrasch, & O. Linssen (Eds.), *Proceedings of the Vorgehensmodelle und der product life-cycle - projekt und betrieb von IT-lösungen (15. Workshop der FG WI-VM der GI* (pp. 258-259). Aachen, Germany: Shaker Verlag.

Chroust, G., Gschwandtner, O., & Mutschmann-Sanchez, D. (1988). Das entwicklungssy- stem ADPS der IBM. In T. Gutzwiller & H. Österle (Eds.), *Anleitung zu einer praxisorientier- ten Software-Entwicklungsumgebung, Band 2 AIT Verlag München* (pp. 123-148).

Chroust, G., Kuhrmann, M., & Schoitsch, E. (2010). Modeling software development processes. In M. M. Cruz-Cunha (Ed.), *Social, managerial and organizational dimensions of enterprise information systems.* Hershey, PA: Business Science Reference.

CIO, I. (2006). *Field report: Security in the world of Web 2.0.* Cio Insight.

CIOMAG. (2002). CRM: Are companies buying it? *CIO Magazine.*

CIOMAG. (2006). The STATE of the CIO '06. *CIO Magazine.*

Claessens, S., Kose, M. A., & Terrones, M. (2008). *What happens during recessions, crunches and busts?* IMF Working Paper.

Clements, P., & Northrop, L. (2002). *Software product lines - practices and patterns.* Reading, MA: Addison Wesley.

Clemons, E. K. (1993). *Information technology and the changing boundary of the firm: Implications for Restructuring* (Research Report). Wharton School.

Clemson, B. (1984). *Cybernetics: A new management tool.* Tumbridge Wells, UK: Abacus Howe.

Clifton, H., Ince, D. C., & Sutcliffe, A. G. (2000). *Business information systems* (6th ed.). Essex, England: Pearson Education Limited.

Coase, R.H. (1937). The Nature of the Firm. *Economica*, 4(N.S.):386-405.

Cobb, C. W., & Douglas, P. H. (1928). A theory of production. *The American Economic Review*, *18*(Supplement), 139–165.

Cockburn, A. (2001). *Agile software development*. Boston, MA: Addison-Wesley.

Cody, W. F., Kreulen, J. T., Krishna, V., & Spangler, W. S. (2002). The integration of business intelligence and knowledge management. *IBM Systems Journal*, *41*(4), 697–714.

Coleman, D. (1997). *Groupware: Collaborative strategies for corporate LANs and Intranets*. Upper Saddle River, NJ: Prentice Hall.

Collins, R. W. (2002). Software localization for Internet software: Issues and methods. *IEEE Software*, *19*(2), 74–80. doi:10.1109/52.991367

Coman, N., & Diaconu, P. (2006). The impact of globalization on accounting research. In *Proceedings of the International Conference on Business Excellence, ICBE – 2006*, Brasov, Romania.

Conant, R. C., & Ashby, W. R. (1970). Every good regulator of a system must be a model of that system. *International Journal of Systems Science*, *1*(2), 899–97. doi:10.1080/00207727008920220

Corporation, I. B. M. (2008). *Telelogic doors*. Retrieved November 24, 2008, from http://www.telelogic.com/products/doors/index.cfm

Costagliola, G., Deufemia, V., Ferrucci, F., & Gravino, C. (2006). Constructing meta-CASE workbenches by exploiting visual language generators. *IEEE Transactions on Software Engineering*, *32*(3), 156–175. doi:10.1109/TSE.2006.23

Cotteleer, M. J., & Bendoly, E. (2006). Order lead-time improvement following enterprise information technology implementation: An empirical study. *MIS Quarterly*, *30*(3), 643–660.

Covisint. (2009a). Covisint-services–portal & collaboration services. Retrieved January 2009, from http://www.covisint.com

Covisint. (2009b). *Collaboration portals, Web messaging and security delivered as a service–covisint.com*. Retrieved January 2009, from http://www.covisint.com/services/portal/

Crane, D., Kawashima, N., & Kawasaki, K. (2002). *Global culture: Media, arts, policy and globalisation*. London: Rutledge.

Creech, B. (1994). *The five pillars of TQM. How to make total quality work for you*. Dutton, NY: Truman Taley Books.

Crnkovic, I., Larsson, S., & Stafford, J. (2002). Component-based software engineering: Building systems from components. *Software Engineering Notes*, *27*(3), 47–50. doi:10.1145/638574.638587

Csete, M. E., & Doyle, J. C. (2002). Reverse engineering of biological complexity. *Science*, *295*, 1664–1669. doi:10.1126/science.1069981

Cuenca, L., Ortiz, A., & Vernadat, F. (2006). From UML or DFD models to CIMOSA partial models and enterprise components. *International Journal of Computer Integrated Manufacturing*, *19*(3), 248–263. doi:10.1080/03081070500065841

Cuffe, S. S. (2005). Emerging management support systems models for global managers in the new economy. *Journal of Knowledge Management Practice, 6*.

Cummings, J. L., & Doh, J. P. (2000). Identifying who matters: Mapping key players in multiple environments. *California Management Review*, *42*(2), 83–105.

Cummings, T. G., & Worley, C. G. (2005). *Organization development and change*. Mason, OH: Thomson.

Cunha, M. M., & Putnik, G. D. (2005). Business alignment requirements and dynamic organizations. In G. D. Putnik & M. M. Cunha (Eds.), *Virtual enterprise integration: Technological and organizational perspectives* (pp. 78-101). Hershey, PA: Idea Group Publishing.

Cunha, M. M., & Putnik, G. D. (2006a). On the dynamics of agile/virtual enterprise reconfiguration. *International Journal of Networking and Virtual Organisations*, *3*(1), 102–123. doi:10.1504/IJNVO.2006.008787

Cunha, M. M., & Putnik, G. D. (2006b). Identification of the domain of opportunities for a market of resources for virtual enterprise integration. *International Journal of Production Research, 44*(12), 2277–2298. doi:10.1080/00207540500409947

Cunha, M. M., & Putnik, G. D. (2006c). *Agile/virtual enterprise: Implementation and management support.* Hershey, PA: Idea Group Publishing.

Cunha, M. M., & Putnik, G. D. (2008). Market of Resources–a cost and effort model. In G. D. Putnik & M. M. Cunha (Eds.), *Encyclopedia of networked and virtual organizations* (pp. 891-888). Hershey, PA: IGI Reference.

Cunha, M. M., Putnik, G. D., & Ávila, P. (2000). Towards focused markets of resources for agile/virtual enterprise integration. In L. M. Camarinha-Matos, H. Afsarmanesh, & H. Erbe (Eds.), *Advances in networked enterprises: Virtual organisations, balanced automation, and systems integration* (pp. 15-24). Berlin, Germany: Kluwer Academic Publishers.

Cunha, M. M., Putnik, G. D., & Ávila, P. S. (2008). Market of resources for virtual enterprise integration. In G. D. Putnik & M. M. Cunha (Eds.), *Encyclopedia of networked and virtual organizations* (pp. 918-925). Hershey, PA: IGI Reference.

Cunha, M. M., Putnik, G. D., & Gunasekaran, A. (2003). Market of resources as an environment for agile/virtual enterprise dynamic integration and for business alignment. In O. Khalil & A. Gunasekaran (Eds.), *Knowledge and information technology management in the 21st century organisations: Human and Social Perspectives* (pp. 169-190). Hershey, PA: Idea Group Publishing.

Currid, Ch. (1995). *Strategies for reengineering your organization.* Roseville, CA: Prima Lifestyles.

D'Souza, D. (1998). Interface specification, refinement, and design with uml/catalysis. *Jour- nal of Object-Oriented Programming, 11,* 12-18.

Dahlstedt, Å., & Persson, A. (2005). Requirements interdependencies: State of the art and future challenges. In *Engineering and managing software requirements* (pp. 95-116).

Dai, Q., & Kauffman, R. (2001). *Business models for Internet-based e-procurement systems and B2B electronic markets: An exploratory assessment.* Paper presented at the 34th Hawaii International Conference on Systems Science, Maui, HI.

Dankbaar, B. (2007). Global sourcing and Innovation: The consequences of losing both organizational and geographical proximity. *European Planning Studies, 15*(2), 271–288. doi:10.1080/09654310601078812

Danube. (2008). *ScrumWorks Pro.* Retrieved November 26, 2008, from http://www.danube.com/scrumworks

Davenport, T. H. (1993). *Process innovation: Reengineering work through information technology.* Boston, MA: Harvard Business Press.

Davenport, T. H. (1998). Putting the enterprise into the enterprise system. *Harvard Business Review, 76*(4), 121–131.

Davenport, T. H., & Prusak, L. (1998). *Working knowledge: How organizations manage what they know.* Cambridge, MA: Harvard Business School Press.

Davenport, T. H., & Short, J. E. (1990). The New industrial engineering, information technology and business redesign. In M. Lewis & N. Slack (Eds.), *Operations management: Critical perspectives on business and management* (pp. 97-123). London and New York: Routledge.

Davidow, W. H., & Malone, M. S. (1992). *The virtual corporation-structuring and revitalising the corporation for the 21st century.* New York: HarperCollins.

Davis, L. E. (1982). Organisational design. In G. Salvendy (Ed.), *Handbook of industrial engineering* (pp. 2.1.1-2.1.29). New York: Wiley & Sons.

De Bono, E. (2005). *Šest klobukov razmišljanja.* Ljubljana, Slovenija. New Moment, 28 (all journal).

De Jong, K. A. (2008, February). Evolving intelligent agents: A 50 year quest. *Computational Intelligence Magazine, 3*(1), 12–17. doi:10.1109/MCI.2007.913370

Demartini, G. (2007, November 12). Finding experts using Wikipedia. In *Proceedings of the 2nd International ISWC+ASWC Workshop on Finding Experts on the Web with Semantics,* Busan, South Korea (pp. 33-41). CEUR Workshop Proceedings.

Dementiev, R. (2006). *Algorithm engineering for large data sets.* Unpublished doctoral dissertation, University of Saarland, Saarbrücken.

deRemer, F., & Kron, H. (1976). Programming-in-the-large versus programming-in-the- small. *IEEE Transactions on Software Engineering*, *2*(2), 80–86. doi:10.1109/TSE.1976.233534

de-Shalit, A. (1998). *Why posterity matters*. London: Rutledge.

Dewett, T., & Jones, G. (2001). The role of information technology in the organization: a review model and assessment. *Journal of Management*, *27*(3), 313–345. doi:10.1016/S0149-2063(01)00094-0

Di Lucca, G., Fasolino, R., Pace, P., Tramontana, P., & De Carlini, U. (2002). *WARE: A tool for the reverse engineering of Web applications*. Paper presented at the *6th* European Conference on Software Maintenance and Reengineering, IEEE Computer Society, Budapest, Hungary.

Diaconu, P., Sr. (2007). *Impact of globalization on international accounting harmonization*. Retrieved October 17, 2008, from http://papers.ssrn.com/sol3/papers.cfm?abstract_id=958478

Diamond, J. (2005). *Collapse: How societies choose to fail or succeed*. New York: Viking.

Dietz, J. L. G. (2003). The atoms, molecules and fibers of organizations. Data & Knowledge Engineering, *47*(3), 301–325. doi:10.1016/S0169-023X(03)00062-4

Dietz, J. L. G. (2006). The deep structure of business processes. Communications of the ACM, *49*(5), 59–64. doi:10.1145/1125944.1125976

Dogac, A. (1998, March). *A survey of the current state-of-the-art in electronic commerce and research issues in enabling technologies*. Paper presented at the Euro-Med Net 98 Conference, Electronic Commerce Track, Nicosia, Cyprus.

Doherty, N. F., King, M., & Al-Mushayt, O. (2003). The impact of inadequacies in the treatment of organisational issues on information systems development projects. *Information & Management*, *41*(1), 49–62. doi:10.1016/S0378-7206(03)00026-0

Doms, A., Dietze, H., Wachter, T., & Schroeder, M. (2008). Literature search with ontologies, a tutorial. In S. Vraneš (Ed.), *Semantic Web and/or Web 2.0: Competi-tive or complementary?* (pp. 81-100). Belgrade, Serbia: Academic Mind.

Don Tapscott, A. W. (Ed.). (2006). *Wikinomics*. New York: Portfolio.

Doumeingts, G., Vallespir, B., & Marcotte, F. (1995). A proposal for integrated modelling of manufacturing system: Application to the re-engineering of an assembly shop. *Control Engineering Practice*, *3*(1), 59–67. doi:10.1016/0967-0661(94)00065-O

Downs, E., Clare, P., & Coe, I. (1988). Structured systems analysis and design method. *Prentice Hall, Englewood Cliffs*.

Dröschel, W., & Wiemers, M. (1999). *Das V-Modell 97. Der standard für die entwicklung von IT-systemen mit anleitung für den praxiseinsatz*. München, Germany: Oldenbourg.

Dröschel, W., & Wiemers, M. (1999). *Das V-Modell 97*. Oldenburg.

Drucker, P. (1985). The discipline of innovation. *Harvard Business Review*, May-June.

Drucker, P. F. (2001). The coming of the new organization. *Harvard Business review on Knowledge Management*, 1-19.

Drucker, P.F. (1990). The emerging theory of manufacturing. *Harvard Business Review, May-June*(3), 94-104.

Duarte, C. S. R., & Lima, R. M. (2008, 2008.09.02-2008.09.04). *Proposta de Melhoria do Processo de Gestão de Células de Fabrico de Coberturas para Assentos Dedicados à Indústria Automóvel [portuguese]*. Paper presented at the 5º Congresso Luso-Moçambicano de Engenharia (CLME'2008), Maputo - Moçambique.

Dumas, M., van der Aalst, W. M. P., & ter Hofstede, A. H. M. (2005). Process-aware information systems: Bridging people and software through process technology. New York: John Wiley & Sons.

Easterly, W. (2001). *The elusive quest for growth: Economists' adventures and misadventures*. Cambridge, MA: MIT Press.

Eclipse Foundation. (2007). *Das eclipse process framework (EPF) online portal*. Retrieved

Eclipse Foundation. (2008, August 13). *Eclipse process framework*. Retrieved November 24, 2008, from http://www.eclipse.org/epf/

Edmondson, A., & Moingeon, B. (1998). From organizational learning to the learning organization. *Management Learning, 29*(1), 5–20. doi:10.1177/1350507698291001

Edvinsson, L. (2002) *Corporate longitude: What you need to know to navigate the knowledge economy*. Financial Times Prentice Hall.

Edvinsson, L., & Malone, M. S. (1997). *'Intellectual capital', The proven way to establish your company's real value by measuring its hidden brainpower*. London: HarperBusiness.

Edwards, C., Ward, J., & Bytheway, A. (1993). *The essence of information systems* (2nd ed.). London: Prentice Hall.

Eldredge, N. (2002). *Life on earth: An encyclopaedia of biodiversity, ecology and evolution*. Santa Barbara, CA: ABC-CLIO, Inc.

Elemica. (2005). *Elemica overview*. Retrieved April 2005, from http://www.elemica.com

Elemica. (2008). *Top chemical company selects Elemica's business process network to automate global procurement*. Retrived January 2009, from http://www.elemica.com/News-Events/Press-Releases-and-News/page.aspx?cid=153

Elliott, C. (1997). Everything wired must CONVERGE. *The Journal of Business Strategy, 18*(6), 31–34. doi:10.1108/eb039894

Ellis, C. D. (2008). *The partnership: The making of Goldman Sachs*. New York: Penguin Press.

eMarketServices. (2008). *Directory of electronic marketplaces*. Retrieved March 2005, from http://www.emarketservices.com/start/eMarket-Directory/index.html

Emmitt, S., & Gorse, C. (2006). *Communication in construction teams*. London and New York: Spon Research, Taylor & Francis.

Enns, H. G., Huff, S. L., & Golden, B. R. (2001). How CIOs obtain peer commitment to strategic IS proposals: Barriers and facilitators. *The Journal of Strategic Information Systems, 10*(1), 3–14. doi:10.1016/S0963-8687(01)00041-5

Erl, Th. (2004). *Service-oriented architecture*. Upper Saddle River, NJ: Pearson Professional Edition.

Ernst and Young. (1997). *Measures that matter*. Ernst and Young LLP.

ESA. (1991). *ESA software engineering standards* (ESA-PSS-05-0 issue 2). Paris: European Space Agency.

European Commission-Information Society Directorate-General. (2005). *Report of the SEEMseed workshop held at the European Commission in Brussels on May 30, 2005*. Retrieved from http://www.seemseed.org/default.aspx

Evans, J. R., & Lindsay, W. M. (1993). *The management and control of quality* (2nd ed.). Minneapolis, MN: West Publishing Coy.

Falgueras, J., Guevara, A., Aguayo, A., Gálvez, S., & Gómez, I. (1997). *El interfaz de usuario en el diseño participativo de sistemas de información*. Cádiz, Spain: III Jornadas de Informática.

Fang, H., & Zhai, C. X. (2007, April 2-5). Probabilistic models for expert finding. In *Advances in Information Retrieval: Proceedings of the 29th European Conference on Information Retrieval (ECIR 2007)* Rome, Italy (LNCS 4425, pp. 418-430).

Fayad, M. E., & Johnson, R. E. (1999). *Domain-specific application frameworks: Frameworks experience by industry*. New York: John Wiley & Sons.

Fed, S. Strategy Unit for Inf. Tech. (2004). *Hermes - management and execution of projects in information and communication technologies (ICT) - foundations* (Doc. No. 609.204.e). Retrieved from http://www.hermes.admin.ch/ict_project_management/manuals-utilities

Feiler, P., & Humphrey, W. (1993). Software process development and enactment: Concepts and definitions. In *Proceedings of the 2nd Int'l Conf. on Software Process*, CA (pp. 28-40). Retrieved from http://www.eclipse.org/epf/

Firesmith, D., & Henderson-Sellers, B. (2001). *The OPEN process framework: An introduction*. Boston, MA: Addison-Wesley Professional.

Flores, M., & Molina, A. (2000). Virtual industry clusters: Foundation to create virtual enterprises. In L. M. Camarinha-Matos, H. Afsarmanesh, & H. Erbe (Eds.), *Advanced Network Enterprises, Virtual Organizations, Balanced Automation, and Systems integration* (pp. 111-120). Deventer, the Netherlands: Kluwer B.V.

Flynn, S. (2007). *The edge of disaster: Rebuilding a resilient nation.* New York: Random House.

Forrester, R. (2006). *Preparing For the new IT ecosystem — building the foundation.* Forrester Research.

Foss, N. J. (2001). Misesian ownership and Coasian authority in Hayekian settings: The case of the knowledge economy. *The Quarterly Journal of Austrian Economics, 4*(4), 3–24.

Fowler, A., & Walsh, M. (1999). Conflicting perceptions of success in an information systems project. *International Journal of Project Management, 17*(1), 1–10. doi:10.1016/S0263-7863(97)00063-X

Fowler, M. (2002). *Patterns of enterprise application architecture.* Boston: Addison-Wesley Professional.

Fox, M. S., & Gruninger, M. (1998). Enterprise modelling. *AI Magazine,* 109–112.

Freeland, C. (2000). *Sale of the century: The inside story of the second Russian revolution.* London: Little, Brown & Co.

Freeman, R. E. (1984). *Strategic management, a stakeholder approach.* Boston: Pitman.

Friedman, T. L. (2005). *The world is flat: A brief history of the twenty-first century.* New York: Farrar Straus and Giroux.

Friedrich, J., Hammerschall, U., Kuhrmann, M., & Sihling, M. (2008). *Das V-Modell XT.* Berlin, Germany: Springer.

Fruin, M. W. (1992). *The Japanese enterprise system.* New York: Oxford University Press.

Fulk, J. (1993). Social construction of communication technology. *Academy of Management Journal, 36,* 921–950. doi:10.2307/256641

Gálvez. S. (2000), *Participación del usuario en el diseño cooperativo de bases de datos. Metodología y Herramientas.* Master's thesis, University of Málaga, Spain.

Garg, P., & Jazayeri, M. (Eds.). (1996). *Process-centered software engineering environ- ments.* Washington, DC: IEEE Computer Soc Press.

Garrett, J. J. (2003). *The elements of user experience: User-centered design for the web.* New Riders Publishing Gartner Group (2005). *Gartner's top predictions for 2006 and beyond.* Gartner Research.

Garrido, J. L. (2003). *AMENITIES: Una metodología para el desarrollo de sistemas cooperativos basada en modelos de comportamiento y tareas.* Unpublished master's thesis, University of Granada, Spain.

Gea, M., Gutiérrez, F. L., Garrido, J. L., & Cañas, J. J. (2003). *Teorías y modelos conceptuales para un diseño basado en grupos.* Paper presented at the IV Congreso Internacional de Interacción Persona-Ordenador, Vigo, Spain.

Gelinas, U., Oram, A., & Wiggins, W. (2002). *Accounting information systems.* New York: South-Western Publishing Co.

General Electric. (2008). Product and services. Retrieved September 1, 2008 from http://www.ge.com/products_services/index.html

Germ Galič, B. (2003). *Dialektični sistem kazalnikov inoviranja in kakovosti poslovanja.* Maribor, Slovenija. University of Maribor, Faculty of Economics and Business.

Gibson, K. (2000). The moral basis of stakeholder theory. *Journal of Business Ethics, 26*(3), 245–257. doi:10.1023/A:1006110106408

Gilb, T., & Graham, D. (1993). *Software inspection.* Reading, MA: Addison-Wesley.

Glass, R. (2001). Frequently forgotten fundamental facts about software engineering. *IEEE Software, 18*(3), 112–110. doi:10.1109/MS.2001.922739

GlobalSources. (2009). *Global sources overview.* Retrieved July 25, 2009, from http://www.corporate.globalsources.com/PROFILE/BGROUND2.HTM

Goldkuhl, G., & Lind, M. (2004). The generics of business interaction - emphasizing dynamic features through the BAT model. In M. Aakhus & M. Lind (Eds.), Proceedings of the 9th Conference on the Language-Action Perspective on Communication Modelling (LAP 2004) (pp. 1-26). New Brunswick, NJ: Rutgers University.

Goldman, S. L., Nagel, R. N., & Preiss, K. (1995). *Agile competitors and virtual organisation*. New York: Van Nostrand Reinhold.

Goldsmith, E., & Piélat, T. (2002). *Le Tao de l écologie*. Monaco, Principality of Monaco: Edition du Rocher.

Gonzalez, R., & Dahanayake, A. (2007). Responsibility in user participation in information system development. In M. Khosrow-Pour (Ed.), *Managing Worldwide Operations and Communications with Information Technology* (pp. 849-851). Hershey, PA: IGI Publications. Håckanson, H. (1989). *Corporate technological behaviour: Co-operation and networks*. London: Routledge.

Goode, H. H., & Machol, R. E. (1957). *System engineering: An introduction to the design of large-scale systems*. New York: McGraw-Hill.

Goodman, R. A., & Goodman, L. P. (1976). Some management issues in temporary systems: a study of professional development and manpower – the theatre case. *Administrative Science Quarterly, 21*, 494–501. doi:10.2307/2391857

Gopalkrishnan, J., & Gupta, V. K. (2007). eBay: "The world's largest online marketplace" - A Case Study. *Conference on Global Competition and Competitiveness of Indian Corporate* (pp. 543-549).

Grabher, G. (2002). Cool projects, boring institutions: Temporary collaboration in social context. *Regional Studies, 36*(3), 206–214.

Grabski, B. Günther, S., Herden, S., Krüger, L., Rautenstrauch, C., & Zwanziger, A. (2007). *Very large business applications*. Berlin, Germany: Springer.

Granollers. (2004). *MPIu+a. Una metodología que integra la ingeniería del software, la interacción persona-ordenador y la accesibilidad en el contexto de equipos de desarrollo multidisciplinares*. Unpublished master's thesis, University of Lleida, Spain.

Gransier, T., & Werner, S. (1995). Validation of CIMOSA. *Computers in Industry, 27*, 95–100. doi:10.1016/0166-3615(95)00048-0

Great Britain Office of Government Commerce. (2007). *Think PRINCE2 (managing suc- cessful projects)* (Tech. Rep.). Great Britain Office of Government Commerce, Sta- tionery Office Books.

Green, K. C. (2007). *The 2007 Campus Computing Survey*. Campus Computing Project, Retrieved October 8, 2008 from http://www.campuscomputing.net/survey-summary/2007-campus-computing-survey

Grolimund, D. (2007). *Wuala - a distributed file system*. Caleido AG, ETH Zuerich. Online Publication in Google Research, Google TechTalks.

Grünbacher, P., Egyed, A., & Medvidovic, N. (2001). Reconciling software requirements and architectures: The CBSP approach. In *Proceedings of the 5th IEEE International Symposium on Requirements Engineering (RE01)*, Toronto, Canada.

Guevara, A., Aguayo, A., Falgueras, J., & Triguero, F. (1995). *Metodología métrica y utilización de técnicas cooperativas (CSCW) en el desarrollo de sistemas de información*. Paper presented at the IV Jornadas sobre Tecnologías de la Información para la Modernización de las Administraciones Públicas. TECNIMAP'95, Palma de Mallorca, Spain.

Guevara, A., Aguayo, A., Triguero, F., & Falgueras, J. (1995). User participation in information systems development techniques and tools. *ACM SIGOIS Bulletin, 16*(1), 68–78. doi:10.1145/209891.209908

Gulliksen, J., Göransson, B., & Lif, M. (2001). A user-centred approach to object-oriented user interface design. In M. Van Harmelen (Ed.), *Object modelling and user interface design*. Addison-Wesley.

Gupta, O., Priyadarshini, K., Massoud, S., & Agrawal, S. K. (2004). Enterprise resource planning: A case of a blood bank. *Industrial Management & Data Systems, 104*(7), 589–603. doi:10.1108/02635570410550250

Haase, V. (1994). Bootstrap: Fine-tuning process assessment. *IEEE Software, 11*(4), 25–35. doi:10.1109/52.300080

Hammer, M., & Champy, J. (1993). *Reengineering the corporation*. New York: HarperBusiness.

Hammond, J. (2007). Developing enterprise Web 2.0 applications. Forrester Research.

Hands, J., Bessonov, M., Blinov, M., Patel, A., & Smith, R. (2000). An inclusive and extensible architecture for electronic brokerage. *Decision Support Systems, 29*, 305–321. doi:10.1016/S0167-9236(00)00080-4

Handy, C. (1993). *Understanding organisations* (4th ed.). New York: Harmondsworth, Penguin.

Hanson, M. T. (1999). The search-transfer problem: The role of weak ties in sharing knowledge across organizational subunits. *Administrative Science Quarterly, 44*, 82–111. doi:10.2307/2667032

Harrison, D. K., & Petty, D. J. (2002). *Systems for planning and control in manufacturing*. Newness, Oxford.

Harrison, R., West, A. A., Weston, R. H., & Monfared, R. P. (2001). Distributed engineering of manufacturing machines. In *Proc. of the Instn. of Mech. Engrs., Vol. 215, Part B Journal of Engineering Manufacture* (pp. 217-231).

Hauptman, O., & Hirji, K. K. (1996). The influence of process concurrency on project outcomes in product development: An empirical study of cross-functional teams. *IEEE Transactions on Engineering Management, 43*(2), 153–164. doi:10.1109/17.509981

Hausen, H. M. M. (1982). Software engineering environments: State of the art, problems and perspectives. In . *Proceedings of the Compsac, 82*, 326–335.

Heizer, J., & Render, B. (2004). *Operations management* (7th ed.). Upper Saddle River, NJ: Prentice Hall.

Hendricks, K. B., Singhal, V. R., & Stratman, J. K. (2007). The impact of enterprise systems on corporate performance: A study of ERP, SCM, and CRM system implementations. *Journal of Operations Management, 25*(1), 65–82. doi:10.1016/j.jom.2006.02.002

Herbsleb, J. D., & Goldenson, D. (1996). A systematic survey of CMM experience and results. In *Proceedings of the 18th Int. Conf on Software Engineering* (pp. 323-330).

Hillary, R. (2000). *Small and medium sized enterprises and the environment business imperatives*. Sheffield, UK: Greenleaf Pub.

Hirschheim, R., & Klein, K. (1989). Four paradigms of information system development. *Communications of the ACM, 32*(10), 1199–1217. doi:10.1145/67933.67937

Hitch, Ch. (1955). An application of system analysis. In St. L. Opter (Ed.), *System analysis*. Middlesex, England.

Hitchings, H. (2008). *The secret life of words: How English became English*. London: John Murray.

Hogan, A., & Harth, A. (2007). *The ExpertFinder Corpus 2007 for the benchmarking and development of Expert-Finding systems*. Paper presented at the 1st International ExpertFinder Workshop, Berlin, Germany. Retrieved August 5, 2008, from, http://lsdis.cs.uga.edu/~aleman/efw2007/program/

Hollingsworth, J. K., & Williams, C. C. (2005). Automatic mining of source code repositories to improve bug finding techniques. *IEEE Software Engineering, 31*(6), 466–480. doi:10.1109/TSE.2005.63

Holsapple, C., & Joshi, K. D. (2001). Knowledge management: A three-fold framework. *The Information Society, 18*(1), 47–64. doi:10.1080/01972240252818225

Hoogendijk, W. (1993). *The economic revolution: Towards a sustainable future by freeing the economy from money-making*. Utrecht, The Netherlands: International Books.

Hossain, L., Patrick, J. D., & Rashid, M. A. (2002). *Enterprise resource planning: Global opportunities and challenges*. Hershey, PA: Idea Group Publishing.

Howell, I., & Batcheler, B. (2005). Building information modeling two years later – Huge potential. Some Success and Several Limitations. *Laiserin Letter, 24*. Available at http://www.laiserin.com/features/bim/newforma_bim.pdf

Hoyer, C. (2007). *ProLiSA - an approach to the specification of product line software architecturs*. Unpublished doctoral dissertation, J. Kepler University Linz.

Hsu, S. P. C. (1995). *Strategic information systems planning: A review*. Paper presented at the Information Resources Management Association International.

Huber, G. P. (1990). A theory of the effect of advanced information technologies on organizational design, intelligence, and decision making. *Academy of Management Review, 15*(1), 47–71. doi:10.2307/258105

Huenke, H. (Ed.). (1980). *Software engineering environments, Proceedings*, Lahnstein, BRD, North Holland.

Hughes, J., & Lang, K.-R. (2006). Transmutability: Digital decontextualization, manipulation, and recontextualization as a new source of value in the production and consumption of culture products. In *Proceedings of the 39th Annual Hawaii International Conference on System Sciences (HICSS'06)*.

Humphrey, W. (1989). *Managing the software process*. Reading, MA: Addison-Wesley.

IBM Corp. (1978). DV-Verfahrenstechnik - eine methodische vorgehensweise zur entwick- lung von DV-anwendungen. *Schriftenreihe Management- und Methoden-Institut, IBM Deutschland, Form No. SR12-1657-0*.

IEC. (1998). *IEC 61508: Functional safety of electric/electronic/programmable electronic systems, part 1 - 9* (Tech. Rep.). IEC, International Electronic Commission.

IFAC International Federation of Accountants. (1998). *The measurement and management of intellectual capital*. International Federation of Accountants.

Instituto Nacional de Estatística. (2007a). *Classificação Portuguesa das Actividades Económicas, Revisão 3* (Vol. 322). Lisbon, Portugal: Author.

Instituto Nacional de Estatística. (2007b). *Lista das 1000 maiores empresas portuguesas. Ficheiro de Unidades Estatísticas - FUE - Base Belém*. Lisbon, Portugal: Author.

Iriana, R., & Buttle, F. (2006). Strategic, operational, and analytical customer relationship management. *Journal of Relationship Marketing, 5*(4), 23–42. doi:10.1300/J366v05n04_03

ISO (Ed.). (2008). *ISO 26262: Road vehicles - functional safety* (Tech Rep.). International Organization for Standardization.

ISO/IEC. (2001). *ISO/IEC 9126-1:2001 software engineering - product quality - part 1: Quality model* (Tech. Rep.). Internat. Org. for Standardization.

ISO/IEC. (2004). *ISO/IEC 15504-1:2004 information technology - process assessment - part 1: Concepts and vocabulary* (Tech. Rep. ISO/IEC JTC 1/SC 7/WG 10).

ISO/IEC. (2006). *ISO/IEC 15288:2006: Systems engineering - system life cycle processes* (Tech. Rep. ISO/IEC JTC 1/SC 7/WG 7). Internat. Org. for Standarization.

ISO/IEC. (2008). *ISO/IEC 14102 - information technology - guideline for the evaluation and selection of case tools* (Tech. Rep.). Geneva: Internat. Org. for Standarization, ISO.

Jacobson, I., Booch, G., & Rumbaugh, J. (1999). The unified process. *IEEE Software, 16*(3), 96–102.

James, C., Joonsoo, B., Qinyi, W., Ling, L., Calton, P., & William, B. R. (2007). Workflow management for enterprise transformation. *Inf. Knowl. Syst. Manag., 6*(1,2), 61-80.

Janev, V. (2008). A comparison and critical assessment of cutting edge Semantic Web products and technologies. In S. Vraneš (Ed.), *Semantic Web and/or Web 2.0: Competitive or complementary?* (pp. 148-165). Belgrade, Serbia: Academic Mind.

Janev, V., & Vraneš, S. (2005). Comparative analysis of commercial knowledge management solutions and their role in enterprises. *Journal of Information and Knowledge management, 10*(4), 71-81.

Janev, V., & Vraneš, S. (2006). Integration of knowledge resources at R&D organizations: The case of Mihajlo Pupin Institute. In M. C. Cunha, B. C. Cortes, & G. Putnik (Eds.), *Adaptive technologies and business integration: Social, Managerial and Organizational dimensions* (pp. 263-280). Hershey, PA: IDEA Group Inc.

Janev, V., Đokić, A., Minić, M., & Vraneš, S. (2008). Knowledge management in the HR sector of R&D organizations. In L. Vladareanu, V. Chiroiu, P. Bratu, & I. Magheti (Eds.), *Proceedings of the 9th WSEAS International Conference on Automation and Information (ICAI'08)*, Bucharest, Romania (pp. 315-321). Stevens Point, WI: World Scientific and Engineering Academy and Society.

Jang, K.-J. (2003). A model decomposition approach for a manufacturing enterprise in business process reengineering. *International Journal of Computer Integrated Manufacturing, 16*(3), 210–218. doi:10.1080/0951192021000039594

Jean, R.-J., Sinkovics, R. R., & Kim, D. (2008). International technology and organizational performance within international business to business relationships. *International Marketing Review, 25*(5), 563–583. doi:10.1108/02651330810904099

Jenkinson, N., Penalver, A., & Vause, N. (2008). Financial innovation: What have we learnt? *Bank of England Quarterly Bulletin, 2008*, Q3.

Jervis, R. (1997). *Systems effects: Complexity in political and social lifer.* Princeton, NJ: Princeton University Press.

Jessup, L., & Valacich, J. (2006). *Information systems today, why is matters* (2nd ed.). NJ: Pearson Education, Inc.

Johnson, G., & Scholes, K. (2001). *Exploring corporate strategy.* Hemel Hempstead, UK: Prentice Hall.

Jones, E. (2003). *The European miracle: Environments, economies and geopolitics in the history of Europe and Asia* (3rd ed.). Cambridge, MA: Cambridge University Press.

July 9, 2007, from http://www.eclipse.org/epf

Jung, H., Lee, M., Kang, I.-S., Lee, S.-W., & Sung, W.-K. (2007, November). Finding topic-centric identified experts based on full text analysis. In A. V. Zhdanova, L. J. B. Nixon, M. Mochol, & J. G. Breslin (Eds.), *Finding Experts on the Web with Semantics 2007, Proceedings of the 2nd Intl. ISWC+ASWC ExpertFinder Workshop (FEWS'07),* Busan, Korea. Retrieved August 5, 2008, from CEUR-WS.org/Vol-290

Jupiter, R. (2006). *Jupiter RSS consumption March 2005* (Research report). Jupiter Research.

Kaisler, S., Armoiur, F., & Valivullah, M. (2005). *Enterprise architecting: Critical problems.* Paper presented at the 38th Annual Hawaii International Conference on System Sciences, Island of Hawaii, HI.

Kalakota, R., & Robinson, M. (2000). Customer relationship management: Integrating processes to build relationships. In R. Kalakota & M. Robinson (Eds.), *E-Business 2.0: Roadmap for Success* (pp. 109-134). New York: Addison Wesley.

Kanter, J. (1966). Integrated management and control systems. In *The computer and executive* (pp. 45-56). Englewood Cliffs, NJ: Prentice Hall.

Karakostas, B., Kardaras, D., & Papathanassiou, E. (2005). The state of CRM adoption by the financial services in the UK: An empirical investigation. *Infor-mation & Management, 42*(6), 853–863. doi:10.1016/j.im.2004.08.006

Karimi, J., Somers, T. M., & Gupta, Y. P. (2001). Impact of information technology management practices on customer service. *Journal of Management Information Systems, 17*(4), 125–158.

Karl, T. L. (1997). *The paradox of plenty: Oil booms and petrol-states.* Berkeley, CA: University of California Press.

Kavakli, E. V., Loucopoulos, P., & Filippidou, D. (1996). *Using scenarios to systematically support goal-directed elaboration for information system requirements.* Paper presented at the IEEE Symposium and Workshop on Engineering of Computer Based Systems(ECBS '96), Friedrichshafen, Germany.

KBst - Koord. - und Beratungsstelle d. B-Reg. f. Informationstechnik. (2006). *Das neue V-Modell(R) XT - der Entwicklungsstandard für IT-Systeme des Bundes.* Retrieved from http://www.v- modell-xt.de/

Kelley, H. H. (1992). Lewin, situations, and interdependence. *The Journal of Social Issues, 47*, 211–233.

Kelly, T. (2004). *A Systematic approach to safety case management.* Paper presented at the SAE 2004 World Congress, Detroit, MI.

Kelly, T. P. (1998). *Arguing Safety- A systematic approach to managing safety cases.* University of York, York.

Kelly, T. P., McDermid, J., Murdoch, J., & Wilson, S. (1998). The goal structuring notation: A means for capturing requirements, rationale and evidence. In A. J. Vickers & L. S. Brooks (Eds.), *Requirements engineering at the University of York*: University of York.

Kelly, T., & Weaver, R. A. (2004). *The goal structuring notation - A safety argument notation.* Paper presented at the 2004 International Conference on Dependable Systems and Networks (DSN 2004), Florence, Italy.

Kempf, H. (2007). *Comment les riches détruisent la planète.* Paris: Editions du Seuil.

Kerschberg, L. (2001). Knowledge management in heterogeneous data warehouse environments. In Y. Kambayashi, W. Winiwarter, & M. Arikawa (Eds.), *Proceedings of the Third International Conference on*

Data Warehousing and Knowledge Discovery, DaWaK 2001 (LNCS 2114, pp. 1-10). Munich, Germany: Springer-Verlag.

Kerschberg, L., & Weishar, D. (2002). Conceptual models and architectures for advanced information systems. *Applied Intelligence, 13*(2), 149–164. doi:10.1023/A:1008340529122

Kherdjemil, B., Panhuys, H., & Zaoual, H. (1998). *Territoires et dynamiques économiques*. Paris: L'Harmattan.

Kim, J. S., Park, S., & Sugumaran, V. (2006). Contextual problem detection and management during software execution. *Industrial Management & Data Systems, 106*, 540–561. doi:10.1108/02635570610661615

Kim, J., Suh, E., & Hwang, H. (2003). A model for evaluating the effectiveness of CRM using the balanced scorecard. *Journal of Interactive Marketing, 17*(2), 5–19. doi:10.1002/dir.10051

Kim, S. M., & Mahoney, J. T. (2006). Mutual commitment to support exchange: relation-specific IT system as a substitute for managerial hierarchy. *Strategic Management Journal, 27*(5), 401–423. doi:10.1002/smj.527

Kim, W. Ch., & Mauborgne, R. (2005). *Blue ocean strategy*. Boston: Harvard Business School Press.

King, R. C., & Xia, W. (1999): Media appropriateness: Effects of experience on communication media choice. In K. E. Kendall (Ed.), *Emerging information technologies: Improving decisions, cooperating and communication technology* (pp. 194-218). Newbury Park, CA; Sage.

Kleppe, A., Warmer, J., & Bast, W. (2003). *Mda explained: The model driven architecture: Practice and promise*. Reading, MA: Addison-Wesley

Klir, G. J. (1985). *Architect of problem solving*. New York: Plenum Press.

Kneuper, R. (2006). *CMMI - Verbesserung von software-prozessen mit capability maturity model integration*. Auflage, dpunkt.verlag.

Kobayashi-Hillary, M. (2005). *Outsourcing to India. The offshore advantage*. Berlin, Germany: Springer.

Koch, G. (1993). Process assessment: The bootstrap approach. *Information and Software Technology, 35*(6/7), 387–402. doi:10.1016/0950-5849(93)90010-Z

Kohli, R., & Hoadley, E. (2996). Towards developing a framework for measuring organizational impact of IT-enabled BPR: case studies of three firms. *ACM SIGMIS Database, 37*(1), 40-58.

Koordinierungs- und Beratungsstelle der Bundesregierung für Informationstechnik in der Bundesverwaltung. (2008). *V-Modell XT online portal*. Retrieved November 24, 2008, from http://www.v-modell-xt.de/

Kopetz, H. (1997). *Real-time systems - design principles for distributed embedded appli- catins*. Dordrecht, The Netherlands: Kluwer Academic Publishers.

Kopp, C. (2002, Jan). *Moore's law and its implications for information warfare*. Paper presented at the The 3rd International AOC EW Conference, Zurich.

Koppensteiner, S. (2008). *Process mapping and simulation for software projects*. VDM Verlag Dr. Müller.

Korner, T. E. (2006). On the fundamental theorem of algebra. *Journal Storage, 113*(4), 347–348.

Kosanke, K. (1995). CIMOSA- overview and status. *Computers in Industry, 27*, 101–109. doi:10.1016/0166-3615(95)00016-9

Kothary, R. (1989). *Rethinking development: In search of human alternatives*. Far Hills, NJ: New Horizons Press.

Kraft, P. (1977). *Programmers and managers*. Heidelberg, Germany: Springer.

Krafzig, D., et al. (2004). *Enterprise SOA*. Upper Saddle River, NJ: Prentice Hall.

Krinke, J. (2006). Mining control flow graph from crosscutting concerns. In *Proceedings of the 13th Working Conference on Reverse Engineering (WCRE): IEEE International Astrenet Aspect Analysis (AAA) Workshop*, Benevento, Italy (pp. 334-342).

Kristensen, L. M., Christensen, S., & Jensen, K. (1998). The practitioner's guide to coloured Petri nets. *International Journal on Software Tools for Technology Transfer, 2*, 98–132. doi:10.1007/s100090050021

Kroll, P., & Kruchten, P. (2003). *The rational unified process made easy – a practicioner's guide to RUP*. Reading, MA: Addison-Wesley.

Kruchten, P. (1998). *The 'rational unified process' - an introduction*. Reading, MA: Addison Wesley.

Kuhn, S., & Muller, M. (Eds.). (1993). Special Issue on Participatory Design. *Communications of the ACM, 36*(4).

Kuhn, T. (1970). *The structure of scientific revolutions*. Chicago: University of Chicago Press.

Kuhrmann, M. (2008). *Konstruktion modularer vorgehensmodelle*. Unpublished doctoral dissertation, Technische Universität München.

Kuhrmann, M., & Hammerschall, U. (2008). *Anpassung des V-Modell XT - Leitfaden zur organisationsspezifischen Anpassung des V-Modell XT*. Projektbericht, Technische Uni- versität München.

Kuhrmann, M., & Kalus, G. (2008). Providing integrated development processes for distributed development environments. In *Proceedings of the Workshop on Supporting Distributed Team Work at Computer Supported Cooperative Work (CSCW 2008)*.

Kuhrmann, M., & Kalus, G. (2008). Providing integrated development processes for distri- buted development environments. In *Proceedings of the Workshop on Supporting Distributed Team Work at Computer Supported Cooperative Work (CSCW 2008)*, San Diego, CA.

Kuhrmann, M., & Ternité, T. (2006). Implementing the Microsoft Solutions framework for agile sw-development as concrete development-method in the V-Modell XT. *In- ternational Transactions on Systems Science and Applications, 1*, 119-126.

Kuhrmann, M., Kalus, G., & Chroust, G. (2010). Tool-support for software development pro- cesses. In M. M. Cruz-Cunha (Ed.), *Social, Managerial and Organizational Dimensions of Enterprise Information Systems*. Hershey, PA: Business Science Reference.

Kuhrmann, M., Kalus, G., & Diernhofer, N. (2008). Generating tool-based process-environments from formal process model descriptions - concepts, experiences and samples. In *Proc. of the IASTED International Conference on Software Engineering (SE 2008)*. ACTA Press.

Kumar, V., Maheshwari, B., & Kumar, U. (2002). Enterprise resource planning systems adoption process: A survey of Canadian organizations. *International Journal of Production Research, 40*(3), 509–523. doi:10.1080/00207540110092414

Kunte, A., Hamilton, K., Dixon, J., & Clemens, M. (2002). Estimating national wealth: Methodology and results. *Environmental Economics Series, 57*, 110–129.

Lakoff, G., & Johnson, M. (1980). *Metaphors we live by*. Chicago: Univ. of Chicago Press.

Lamsweerde, A. v. (2001). *Goal-oriented requirements engineering: A guided tour*. Paper presented at the 5th IEEE International Symposium on Requirements Engineering (RE'01), Toronto, Canada.

Lamsweerde, A. v. (2003). *From system goals to software architecture. Formal methods for software architectures* (. *LNCS, 2804*, 25–43.

Lamsweerde, A. V. (2004). *Goal-oriented requirements engineering: A roundtrip from research to practice*. Paper presented at the 12th IEEE Joint International Requirements Engineering Conference (RE'04,), Kyoto, Japan.

Laszlo, E. (1972). *Introduction to systems philosophy*. New York: Harper Torchbooks.

Latouche, S. (2004). *Survivre au développement: De la décolonisation de l□imaginaire économique à la construction d□une société alternative*. Paris: Mille et une Nuits.

Latouche, S. (2007). *Petit traité de la décroissance sereine*. Paris: Mille et une Nuits.

Laubacher, R., & Malone, T. W. (2003). Inventing the organizations of the 21st century. In T. W. Malone, R. Laubahcer, & M. S. S. Morton (Eds.), *Inventing the organizations of the 21st century* (pp. 3-14). Boston: MIT Press.

Laudon, J. P., & Laudon, K. C. (2007). *Management information systems: Managing the digital firm* (10th ed.). Prentice Hall.

Lawless, W. F., & Sofge, D. (2008b). Conservation of information (COI). A concept paper on virtual organizations and communities. *NSF Computational Workshop: Building CIML Virtual Organizations*. October 24, 2008, Fairfax, VA.

Lawless, W. F., Bergman, M., Louçã, J., Kriegel, N. N., & Feltovich, N. (2007). A quantum metric of organizational performance: Terrorism and counterterrorism. *Computational & Mathematical Organization Theory*, *13*, 241–281. doi:10.1007/s10588-006-9005-4

Lawless, W. F., Castelao, T., & Ballas, J. A. (2000). Virtual knowledge: Bistable reality and solution of ill-defined problems. *IEEE Systems, Man, & . Cybernetics*, *30*(1), 119–124.

Lawless, W. F., Howard, C. R., & Kriegel, N. N. (2008c). A quantum real-time metric for NVOs. In G. D. Putnik & M.M. Cunha (Eds.), *Encyclopedia of Networked and Virtual Organizations*. Hershey, PA: Information Science Reference.

Lawless, W. F., Whitton, J., & Poppeliers, C. (2008a). Case studies from the UK and US of stakeholder decision-making on radioactive waste management. *Practice Periodical of Hazardous, Toxic, and Radioactive Waste Management*, *12*(2), 70–78. doi:10.1061/(ASCE)1090-025X(2008)12:2(70)

Lecoeuche, R., Catinaud, O., & Greboval-Barry, C. (1996). Competence in human beings and knowledge-based systems. In *Proceedings of the 10th Knowledge Acquisition for Knowledge-Based Systems Workshop: Vol. 2.*, Banff, Canada (pp. 38-1:38-20).

Leder, B. (2004). *Inoviranje trženja turizma na slovenskem podeželju*. Maribor, Slovenija. University of Maribor, Faculty of Economics and Business.

Lee, G., Sacks, R., & Eastman, C. M. (2006). Specifying parametric building object behavior (BOB) for a building information modeling system. *Automation in Construction*, *15*(6), 758–776. doi:10.1016/j.autcon.2005.09.009

Leffingwell, D. W. D. (2000). *Managing software requirements – a unified approach*. Upper Saddle River, NJ: Addison-Wesley.

Lehman, M. (1980). Programs, life cycles, and laws of software evolution. In M. M. Lehman & L. A. Belady (Eds.), *Program evolution - processes of software change* (pp. 393-450). Academic Press.

Leiva, J. L., Guevara, A., & Caro, J. L. (2006). *Aplicación del Modelado workflow a la reingeniería de sistemas de información basándose en interfaces de usuario*. Paper presented at the 1ª Conferencia Ibérica de Sistemas y Tecnologías de la Información, CISTI 2006, Esposende, Portugal.

Leiva, J. L., Guevara, A., Caro, J. L., & Arenas, M. A. (2008). *A cooperative method for system development and maintenance using workflow technologies*. Paper presented at the 10th International Conference on Enterprise Information Systems, ICEIS 2008, Barcelona, Spain.

Lenk, K., & Traunmueller, R. (1999). Perspektiven einer radikalen Neugestaltung der oeffentlichen Verwaltung mit Informationstechnik. In *Oeffentliche Verwaltung und Informationstechnik. Schriftenreihe Verwaltungsinformatik*. Heidelberg: Decker's Verlag.

Leonard-Barton, D. (1995). *Wellsprings of knowledge, building and sustaining the sources of innovation*. Boston, MA: Harvard Business School Press.

Leonard-Barton, D., & Kraus, W. (2001). Implementing new technology. *Harvard Business Review*, *12*(2), 102–110.

Lequeux, J.-L. (1999). *Manager avec les ERP: Progiciels de gestion intégrés et Internet*. Paris: Éditions d'Organisation.

Levine, H. G., & Rossmoore, D. (1994). Politics and the function of power in a case study of IT implementation. *Journal of Management Information Systems*, *11*(3), 115–134.

Lévy, B. H. (2008). *Left dark times: A stand against the new barbarism*. New York: Random House.

Lewis, G.A., Cornella-Dorda, S., Place, P., Plakosh, D., & Secord, R.C. (2001). *An Enterprise Information System Architecture guide* (CMU/SEI 2001-TR-018).

Li, E. Y., McLeod, R., & Rogers, J. C. (2001). Marketing information systems in Fortune 500 companies: A longitudinal analysis of 1980, 1990, and 2000. *Information & Management*, *38*(5), 307–322. doi:10.1016/S0378-7206(00)00073-2

Li, E., Tseng, P. T. Y., & Lu, E. (2007, September 21-25). *Measuring the strength of partner relationship in B2B EC: An exploratory research*. Paper presented at the International Conference on Wireless Communications, Networking and Mobile Computing (WiCom 2007), Shanghai, China.

Li, J., Boley, H., Bhavsar, V. C., & Mei, J. (2006). Expert finding for eCollaboration using FOAF with RuleML rules. In L. Logrippo, H. Mili, & A. Salah (Eds.), *Proceedings of the 2006 Montreal Conference on eTechnologies* (pp. 53-65). Québec, Canada.

Lientz, B. P., & Swanson, E. B. (1980). *Software maintenance management*. Boston, MA: Addison-Wesley Longman Publishing.

Likar, B. (1998). *Inoviranje.* Koper, Slovenija. Visoka šola za management, Koper.

Lin, C., & Pervan, G. (2003). The practice of IS/IT benefits management in large Australian organizations. *Information & Management, 41*(1), 13–24. doi:10.1016/S0378-7206(03)00002-8

Liu, C., & Arnett, K. P. (2000). Exploring the factors associated with Web site success in the context of electronic commerce. *Information & Management, 38*(1), 23–33. doi:10.1016/S0378-7206(00)00049-5

López, B. (2007). *Modelado de la planificación estratégica a nivel de conocimiento.* Murcia, Spain: Universidad de Murcia.

Lowenstein, R. (2008, April 27). Triple-a failure. *New York Times.*

Lu, C. L., Su, Z.-Y., & Tang, C.-Y. (2001). A new measure of edit distance between labeled trees. In *Proceedings of the Computing and Combinatorics, 7th Annual International Conference, Cocoon 2001,* Guilin, China (pp. 338-348).

Lu, T., Guan, F., & Wang, F. (2008). Semantic classification and query of engineering drawings in the shipbuilding industry. *International Journal of Production Research, 46*(9), 2471–2483. doi:10.1080/00207540701737922

Ludewig, J., & Opferkuch, St. (2004). *Softwarewartung - eine taxonomie.* Softwaretechnik-Trends, Band 24 Heft 2, Gesellschaft für Informatik.

Lundin, R. A., & Söderholm, A. (1995). A theory of the temporary organization. *Scandinavian Journal of Management, 11*(4), 437–455. doi:10.1016/0956-5221(95)00036-U

Malherbe, M. (1995). *Les langages de l humanité.* Paris: Robert Laffont.

Malhotra, A., & Gosain, S. (2005). Absorptive capacity configurations in supply chains: Gearing for partner-enable market knowledge creation. *MIS Quarterly, 29*(1), 145–187.

Malhotra, Y. (Ed.). (2001). *Knowledge management and business model innovation.* Hershey, PA: Idea Group Publishing.

Mantzana, V., Themistocleous, M., Irani, Z., & Morabito, V. (2007). Identifying healthcare actors involved in the adoption of information systems. *European Journal of Information Systems, 16*(1), 91–102. doi:10.1057/palgrave.ejis.3000660

Marin, J. (1997). *Systems engineering guidebook.* Boca Raton, FL: CRC Press LLC.

Markus, M. L. (1990). Toward a "critical mass" theory of interactive media. In J. Fulk & C. Steinfeld (eds.), *Organizations and communication technology* (pp. 194-218). Newbury Park, CA: Sage.

Markus, M. L., & Mao, J. Y. (2004). Participation in development and implementation—updating and old, tired concept for today's IS contexts. *Journal of the Association for Information Systems, 5*(11-12), 514–544.

Markus, M. L., & Tanis, C. (2000). The enterprise system experience—From adoption to success. In R. W. Zmud & M. F. Price (Eds.), *Framing the domains of IT management: Projecting the future through the past* (pp. 173-207). Pinnaflex Educational Resources.

Markus, M. L., Axline, S., & Petrie, D. (2000). Learning from adopters experiences with ERP: Problems encountered and success achieved. *Journal of Information Technology, 15*(4), 245–265. doi:10.1080/02683960010008944

Martin, J. (1989). *Information engineering, book I: Introduction.* Englewood Cliffs, NJ: Prentice Hall.

Martin, J. (2005). *Organisation behaviour and management* (3rd ed.). Florence, KY: Thomson Learning.

Matos, M. (2007). *Redefinição de procedimentos de integração para planeamento da produção e redefinição de processos de gestão de produtos em fim de vida na indústria de auto-rádio [portuguese].* Universidade do Minho, Guimarães.

Mattick, J. S., & Gagen, M. J. (2005). Accelerating networks. *Science, 307,* 856–858. doi:10.1126/science.1103737

McAfee, A. (2002). The impact of enterprise information technology adoption on operational performance: An empirical investigation. *Production and Operations Management, 11*(1), 33–53.

McDermid, J. (Ed.). (1985). *Integrated project support environments.* London: P. Peregrinus Ltd.

McDonough, A. M. (1963). Information management. In *Information economics and management systems.* New York: McGraw-Hill.

McElroy, B., & Mills, C. (2003). Managing stakeholders. In R. J. Turner (Ed.), *People in project management* (pp. 99-118). Aldershot, UK: Gower.

McFarlan, F. W. (1981). Portfolio approach to information systems. *Harvard Business Review, 59,* 142–150.

McFarlan, F. W., & McKenney, J. L. (1983). The information archipelago governing the new world. *Harvard Business Review, 61,* 145–156.

McGovern, J. (2003). *The practical guide to enterprise architecture planning.* Hoboken, NJ: Wiley.

McKay, K. N., Safayeni, F. R., & Buzacott, J. A. (1995). A review of hierarchical production planning and its applicability for modern manufacturing. *Production Planning and Control, 6*(5), 384–394. doi:10.1080/09537289508930295

McKenney, J. L., & McFarlane, F. W. (1982). The information archipelago - maps and bridges. *Harvard Business Review, 60*(5), 109–119.

McLeod, R. (1995). Systems theory and information resources management: Integrating key concepts. *Information Resources Management Journal, 18*(2), 5–14.

McLoughlin, I. (1999). *Creative technological change.* London: Routledge.

Meadows, D. H. (2004). *Limit to growth: The 30 years update.* Boston: Chelsea Green.

Medina-Mora, R., Winograd, T., Flores, R., & Flores, F. (1992, November 1-4). The action workflow approach to workflow management technology. In J. Turner & R.

Kraut (Eds.), Proceedings of the 1992 ACM Conference on Computer Supported Cooperative Work (pp. 281-288). Toronto, Canada: ACM Publishing.

Mejía, R., & Molina, A. (2002, May 1-3). Virtual enterprise broker: Processes, methods and tools. In L. M. Camarinha-Matos (Ed.), *Proceedings of the IFIP Tc5/Wg5.5 Third Working Conference on infrastructures For Virtual Enterprises: Collaborative Business Ecosystems and Virtual Enterprises* (pp. 81-90). Deventer, the Netherlands: Kluwer B. V.

Mendes, C., & Castoriadis, C. (1977). *Le mythe du développement.* Paris: Seuil.

Merbeth, G. (1992). MAESTRO-II - das integrierte CASE-System von Softlab. In H. Balzert (Ed.), *CASE - Systeme und Werkzeuge 4. Auflage, B-I Wissenschaftsverlag* (pp. 215-232).

Mercurio, V., Meyers, B., Nisbet, A., & Radin, G. (1990). AD/Cycle strategy and architec- ture. *IBM Systems Journal, 29*(2), 170–188.

Merlo, C., & Girard, P. H. (2004). Information system modelling for engineering design co-ordination. *Computers in Industry, 55*(3), 317–334.

META Group. (2001). *Integration: Critical Issues for Implementation of CRM Solutions.* Stamford, CT: Author.

Meyerson, D., Weick, K. E., & Kramer, R. M. (1996). Swift trust and temporary groups. In R. M. Kramer & T. R. Tyler (Eds.), *Trust in organizations: Frontiers of theory and research,* 166-195. Thousand Oaks, CA: Sage.

MfgQuote. (2009b). *MFG.com corporate profile.* Retrieved January 2009, from http://www.mfg.com/en/about-mfg/mfg-corporate-profile.jsp

Michelini, R. C. (2008). *Knowledge entrepreneurship and sustainable growth.* New York: Nova Sci. Pub.

Michelini, R. C. (2009). The *Robot age* changeful *knowledge changeover.* New York: Nova Sci. Pub.

Michelini, R. C., & Capello, A. (1985). *Misure e strumentazione industriali: Segnali e strumenti di misura.* Turin, Italy: UTET.

Michelini, R. C., & Razzoli, R. P. (2000). *Affidabilità e sicurezza del manufatto industriale: La progettazione integrata per lo sviluppo sostenibile*. Milan, Italy: Tecniche Nuove.

Microsoft Corporation. (2007). *Team development with visual studio team foundation server*. Redmond, WA: Microsoft Press.

Microsoft. (2002). *Application architecture for .NET*.

Mikroyannidis, A. (2007). *Toward a social Semantic Web*. Washington, DC: IEEE Computer Society: Moore, G. (1965). Cramming more componentes onto integrated circuits. *Electronics, 38*(8).

Mills, J., Platts, K., & Bourne, M. (2003). Competence and resource architectures. *International Journal of Operations & Production Management, 3*(9), 977–994. doi:10.1108/01443570310491738

Milutinović, V., & Patricelli, F. (2002). *E-business and e-challenges: Emerging communication*. Amsterdam, the Netherlands: IOS Press.

Minc, A. (2008). *Une sorte de diable: Les vies de John-Maynard Keynes*. Paris: Grasset.

Ministerio de Administraciones Públicas. (2000). *Métrica versión 3*. Retrieved from http://www.csi.map.es/csi/metrica3/

Mintzberg, H. (1979). *The structuring of organizations*. Upper Saddle River, NJ: Prentice Hall.

Mintzberg, H. (1989). *Mintzberg on management: Inside our strange world of organisations*. London: MacMillan.

Mitchell, R. K., Agle, B. R., & Wood, D. J. (1997). Toward a theory of stakeholder identification and salience: Defining the principle of who and what really counts. *Academy of Management Review, 22*(4), 853–886. doi:10.2307/259247

Mitsubishi. (2007). *About Mitsubishi*. Retrieved September 1 2008, from http://www.mitsubishi.com/e/group/about.html

Molina, A., & Flores, M. (1999). A virtual enterprise in Mexico: From concepts to practice. *Journal of Intelligent & Robotic Systems, 26*, 289–302. doi:10.1023/A:1008180621733

Monfared, R. P. (2000). *A component–based approach to design and construction of change capable manufacturing cell control systems*. Unpublished doctoral dissertation, Loughborough University.

Monfared, R. P., West, A. A., Harrison, R., & Weston, R. H. (2002). An implementation of business process modelling in automotive industry. In *Proc. of the Instn. of Mech. Engineers, Vol. 216 Part B: Engineering Manufacture* (pp. 1413-1427).

Monfared, R. P., West, A. A., Harrison, R., & Weston, R. H. (2002). An implementation of the business process modelling approach in the automotive industry. *Proceedings of the Institution of Mechanical Engineers -- Part B -- Engineering Manufacture, 216*(11), 1413-1427.

Monge, P. R., & Fulk, J. (1995). *Global network organizations*. Paper presented to the International Communication Association, Albuquerque, NM, May.

Moore, W., Allen, C., Bracht, R., Koch, D., & Marrazzo, D. (2005). *Managing information access to an Enterprise Information System using J2EE and Services Oriented Architecture* (IBM SB246371-00). Retrieved October 11, 2008 from www.redbooks.ibm.com/abstracts/SG246371.html

Morton, M. S. (1995). Emerging organizational forms: Work and organization in the 21st Century. *European Management Journal, 13*(4), 339–345. doi:10.1016/0263-2373(95)00027-I

Mosto, A. (2004). *DoD architecture framework overview*. Retrieved November 2, 2008, from http://www.enterprise-architecture.info/Images/Defence%20C4ISR/DODAF.ppt

Mowshowitz, A. (1980). *Human choice and computers, 2*. Amsterdam: North-Holland.

Mowshowitz, A. (1980). On an approach to the study of social issues in computing. *Communications of the ACM, 24*(3), 146. doi:10.1145/358568.358592

MPI. (2004). *Quality control system documentation*. (Confidential). Belgrade, Serbia: Author.

Müller, H. A., Jahnke, J. H., & Smith, D. B. (2000). *Reverse engineering: A roadmap*. Paper presented at the Future of Software Engineering Track at the 22nd

International Conference on Software Engineering-ICSE 2000, Limerick, Ireland.

Müller, R., & Turner, J. R. (2007). Matching the project managers' leadership style to project type. *International Journal of Project Management*, 25(1), 21–32. doi:10.1016/j.ijproman.2006.04.003

Münch, J., & Heidrich, J. (2004). Software project control centers: Concepts and approaches. *Journal of Systems and Software*, 70.

Mulej, M. (1982). Dialektično-sistemsko programiranje delovnih procesov – metodologija USOMID. Maribor, Slovenija. *Naše gospodarstvo, 28*(3), 206-209.

Mulej, M. (2007a). Systems theory: A worldview and/or a methodology aimed at requisite holism/realism of humans' thinking, decisions and action. *Systems Research and Behavioral Science*, 24(3), 347–357. doi:10.1002/sres.810

Mulej, M., & Kajzer, S. (1998). Ethics of interdependence and the law of requisite holism. In M. Rebernik & M. Mulej (Eds.), *STIQE ,98. Proceedings of the 4th International Conference on Linking Systems Thinking, Innovation, Quality, Entrepreneurship and Environment*. Maribor, Slovenia. University of Maribor, Faculty of Economics and Business, Institute for Entrepreneurship and Small Business Management, and Slovenian Society for Systems Research.

Mulej, M., & Mulej, N. (2006). Innovation and/by systemic thinking by synergy of methodologies "Six thinking hats" and "USOMID". In R. Trappl (Ed.), *Cybernetics and systems 2006: Proceedings of the Eighteenth European Meeting on Cybernetics and Systems Research* (pp. 416-421). Vienna, Austria: Austrian Society for Cybernetic Studies.

Mulej, M., & Potocan, V. (2007). Requisite holism - precondition of reliable business information. *Kybernetes*, 36(3/4), 319–332. doi:10.1108/03684920710746986

Mulej, M., & Ženko, Z. (2004). *Introduction to systems thinking with application to invention and innovation management*. Maribor, Slovenija: Management Forum.

Mulej, M., Čančer, V., Hrast, A., Jurše, K., Kajzer, S., Knez-Riedl, J., et al. *(2007d)*. The law of requisite holism and ethics of interdependence: Basics of the dialectical

systems thinking (applied to innovation in catching-up countries). *On GESI Website, Buenos Aires.*

Mulej, M., Devetak, G., Drozg, F., Ferš, M., Hudnik, M., Kajzer, Š., et al. (1987). *Inovativno poslovanje*. Ljubljana, Slovenija. Gospodarski vestnik.

Mulej, M., et al. (1986). *Usposabljanje za ustvarjalnost. USOMID.* (Training for Creativity. USOMID Methodology. In Slovene). 4th revised and reworked edition. Ekonomski center, Maribor. Slovenija.

Mulej, M., Hyvaerinen, L., Jurše, K., Rafolt, B., Rebernik, M., Sedevčič, M., & Uršič, D. (1994). *Inovacijski management, I. del: Inoviranje managementa*. Maribor, Slovenija. University of Maribor, Faculty of Economics and Business.

Mulej, M., Kajzer, Š., Treven, S., & Jurše, K. (1997). Sodobno gospodarstvo med odpori do inovacij in življenjem od njih. *Naše gospodarstvo, 43*(3-4), 339-349.

Mulej, M., Likar, B., & Potočan, V. (2005). Increasing the capacity of companies to absorb inventions from research organizations and encouraging people to innovate. *Cybernetics and Systems*, 36, 491–512. doi:10.1080/01969720590944276

Mulej, M., Potočan, V., Rosi, B., Ženko, Z., Jurše, K., & Udovičič, K. (2006). Role models: Do what you preach on innovation, government/public sector. In *Advancing business and management in knowledge-based society: [proceedings of] the 7th International Conference of the Faculty of Management* (pp. 1499-1508). Koper, MIC'06, Portorož, University of Primorska.

Mulej. M. (2007b). *Inoviranje navad države in manjših podjetij*. Koper, Slovenija. Univerza na Primorskem, Fakulteta za management.

Mulej., et al. (Eds.). of PODIM conferences since 1978; e.g.: Rebernik, M., Mulej, M., Rus, M., Krošlin, T. (2007c). *Nurturing champions of innovation and entrepreneurship: Proceedings of the 27th Conference on Entrepreneurship and Innovation PODIM*, Maribor, Slovenija. Faculty of Economics and Business, Institute for Entrepreneurship and Small Business Management.

Muller, E. (2001). *Innovation interactions between knowledge-intensive business services and small-and-medium sized enterprises: An analysis in terms of evolution, knowledge and territories*. Berlin, Germany: Springer.

Muller, M. J., Wildman, D. M., & White, E. A. (1993). Taxonomy of PD Practices: A brief practitioner's guide. *Communications of the ACM, 36*(6).

Mullins, L. J. (2005). *Management & organisational behaviours* (7th ed.). Upper Saddle River, NJ: Prentice Hall.

Mumford, E. (2001). Action research: Helping organizations to change. In E. Trauth (Ed.), *Qualitative Research in IS: Issues and trends* (pp. 46 - 77). Hershey, PA: Idea Group Publishing.

Murata, T. (1989). Petri nets: Properties, analysis and applications. Proceedings of the IEEE, 77(4), 514–580. doi:10.1109/5.24143

Murphy, A., & Perran, S. (2007). *Beginning SharePoint 2007: Building team solutions with MOSS 2007 (programmer to programmer)*. New York: Wrox Press.

Musen, M. A. (1993). An overview of knowledge acquisition. In J. M. David, J. P. Krivine, & R. Simmons (Eds.), *Second generation of expert systems* (pp. 405-427). Berlin, Germany: Springer Verlag.

Myrdal, G. (1968). *Asian drama: An inquiry into the poverty of nations*. New York: Pantheon.

Nadler, D. A. (1993). Concepts of management of organisational change. In Mabey, et al (Eds.), *Managing Change* (2nd ed.). PCB Ltd.

Nadler, D. A., et al. (1992). *Organizational architecture*. San Francisco: Jossey-Bass.

Naess, A. (1989). *Ecology, community and lifestyle: An eco-sophy outline*. Cambridge, MA: Cambridge University Press.

Nakajo, T. K. H. (1985). The principles of foolproofing and their application in manufactu- ring. *Reports of Statistical Application Research JUSE, 32*(2), 10–29.

Nandy, A. (1987). *The intimate enemy*. Bombay, India: Oxford University Press.

Naur, P., & Randell, B. (Eds.). (1969). *Software Engineering, Proceedings of the NATO Working Conference Garmisch-Partenkirchen*. Brussels, Belgium: Scientific Affairs Division, NATO.

Ndione, E. (1994). *Réinventer le présent*. Dakar, Senegal: Enda-Graf Sahel.

Needham, J. (1969). *Within the four seas: The dialogue of east and west*. London: Allen & Unwin.

Negash, S., & Gray, P. (2008). Business intelligence. In F. Burstein & C. W. Holsapple (Eds.), *Handbook on Decision Support Systems 2* (pp. 175-193). Berlin, Germany: Springer.

Nevins, J. L., & Whitney, D. E. (1989). *Concurrent design of products and processes*. McGraw-Hill.

Newell, A. (1982). The knowledge level. *Artificial Intelligence, 18*, 87–127. doi:10.1016/0004-3702(82)90012-1

Nichols, E. L., & Handfield, R. B. (1999). *Introduction to Supply Chain Management*: Upper Saddle River, NJ: Prentice Hall.

Nicklas, D. (2005). *Ein umfassendes umgebungsmodell als integrationsstrategie für ortsbezogene daten und dienste*. Unpublished doctoral dissertation, University Stuttgart, Online Publication, Stuttgart.

Nisbett, R. E. (2003). *The geography of thought*. New York: Free Press.

Nisbett, R. E., & Ross, L. (1980). *Human inference: Strategies and shortcoming of social judgements*. Englewood Cliffs, NJ: Prentice Hall.

Nonaka, I. (1991). The knowledge creating company. *Harvard Business Review, 69*(6), 96–104.

Nonaka, I. (1994). A dynamic theory of organizational knowledge creation. *Organization Science, 5*(1), 14–37. doi:10.1287/orsc.5.1.14

Nonaka, I., & Takeuchi, H. (1995). *The knowledge creating company*. New York: Oxford University Press.

Norris, G., Hurley, J. R., Hartley, K. M., Dunleavy, J. R., & Balls, J. D. (2000). *E-business and ERP—transforming the enterprise*. New York: John Wiley & Sons.

Novell. (2008). *openSUSE*. Retrieved November 24, 2008, from http://en.opensuse.org

Noy, N. F., & Musen, M. A. (2004). Ontology versioning in an ontology management framework. *IEEE Intelligent Systems, 19*(4), 6–13. doi:10.1109/MIS.2004.33

Nunes, P. V. (2006). *Planeamento operacional baseado em efeitos (PEBE)*. Paper presented at the Sociedade em rede: competição e conflito no dominio da informação.

NUnit.org. (2008). *NUnit – home*. Retrieved November 24, 2008, from http://www.nunit.org

O'Sullivan, D. (1998). Communications technologies for the extended enterprise. *Int. Journal of Production Planning and Control, 9*(8), 742–753. doi:10.1080/095372898233515

OASIS. (2007). Web services business process execution language, V.2.0. Retrieved September 29, 2008, from http://docs.oasis-open.org/wsbpel/2.0/OS/wsbpel-v2.0-OS.html

Object Management Group. (2007). *MOF 2.0 / XMI mapping specification*. Retrieved November 24, 2008, from http://www.omg.org/technology/documents/formal/xmi.htm

Object Management Group. (2007). Unified modeling language: Superstructure, V.2.1.1. Retrieved September 29, 2008, from http://www.omg.org/docs/formal/07-02-03.pdf

Object Management Group. (2008). Business process modeling notation, V.1.1. Retrieved September 29, 2008, from http://www.bpmn.org

Object Management Group. (2008). *Software process engineering meta-model*. Retrieved November 24, 2008, from http://www.omg.org/technology/documents/formal/spem.htm

Object Management Group. (2008). *The object management group*. Retrieved November 24, 2008, from http://www.omg.org/

Office of Government Commerce. (2008). *Official ITIL website*. Retrieved November 24, 2008, from http://www.itil-officialsite.com/home/home.asp

Okkonen, J., Pirttimäki, V., Lönnqvist, A., & Hannula, M. (2002, May 9-11). *Triangle of performance measurement, knowledge management and business intelligence*. Paper presented at the 2nd Annual Conference on Innovative Research in Management (EURAM), Stockholm, Sweden.

Oktaba, H. (2005). *Modelo de procesos para la industria del software. Versión 1.3.*(NMX-059/01-NYCE-2005). Ciudad de México: Organismo nacional de normalización y evaluación de la conformidad.

Oliver, D., & Romm, C. (2000). *ERP systems: The route to adoption*. Paper presented at the 6th Americas Conference on Information Systems Association for Information Systems (AMCIS), Long Beach, California.

OMG. (2005). *Software process engineering metamodel specification* (Tech. Rep.). Retrieved from http://www.uml.org/

OMG. (2008). *Business process modeling notation, V1.1*. Retrieved June 30, 2008, from http://www.omg.org/spec/BPMN/1.1/PDF

Opferkuch, St. (2004). *Software-wartungsprozesse - ein einblick in die industrie*. Fachbericht Informatik, Nr. 11/2004, Universität Koblenz-Landau.

Orlikowski, W. J. (1992). The Duality of Technology: Rethinking the Concept of Technology in Organisations. *Organization Science, 3*(3), 398–427. doi:10.1287/orsc.3.3.398

Orlikowski, W. J. (1993). CASE tools as organizational change: Investigating incremental and radical changes in systems development. *MIS Quarterly, 17*(2), 309–340. doi:10.2307/249774

Osborne, A. F. (1953). *Applied imagination*. New York: Scribners.

Ostrom, E., & Ahn, T. K. (2005). *Foundation of social capital*. Cheltenham, UK: Edward Elgar Pub.

Ould, M. (2005). Business process management: A rigorous approach. Swindon, UK: The British Computer Society.

Oxford, UK: Oxford University Press.

Pairat, R., & Jungthirapanich, C. (2005, September 11-13). *A chronological review of ERP research: An analysis of ERP inception, evolution, and direction*. Paper presented at the International Engineering Management Conference (IEMC), St. John's, Newfoundland, Canada.

Palmer, N. (2007). *A survey of business process initiatives* [Electronic Version]. Retrieved July 1, 2008, from http://www.wfmc.org/researchreports/featured_research.htm

Panada, F. (2007). *The emerging thread*. Armonk, NY: IBM Global Services.

Panchenko, O. (2007). Concept location and program comprehension in service-oriented software. In *Proceedings of the IEEE 23rd International Conference on Software Maintenance: Doctoral Symposium, ICSM*, Paris, France (pp. 513–514).

Pandya, K. V., Karlsson, A., Sega, S., & Carrie, A. (1997). Towards the manufacturing enterprise of the future. *Int. Journal of Production. Management, 17*, 502–521.

Paniagua, E. (Ed.). (2007). *La gestión tecnológica del conocimiento*. Murcia, Spain: Universidad de Murcia, Servicio de Publicaciones.

Parr, A. N. (2000, January 4-7). *A taxonomy of ERP implementation approaches*. Paper presented at the 33rd Hawaii International Conference on System Sciences, Maui, Hawaii.

Partant, F. (1997). *La fin du développement*. Paris: F. Maspero.

Paulk, M. (2001). Extreme programming from a CMM perspective. *IEEE Software, 18*(6), 9–26. doi:10.1109/52.965798

Paulk, M., Weber, C., Curtis, B., & Chrissis, M. (Eds.). (1995). *The capability maturity model: Guidelines for improving the software process*. Reading, MA: Addison-Wesley.

Pávez, A. A. (2000). *Modelo de implantación de Gestión del Conocimiento y Tecnologías de Información para la Generación de Ventajas Competitivas*. Valparaíso, Chile: Universidad Técnica Federico Santa María.

Pavlov, M., & Ichise, R. (2007, November). Finding experts by link prediction in co-authorship metworks. In A. V. Zhdanova, L. J. B. Nixon, M. Mochol, & J. G. Breslin (Eds.), *Finding Experts on the Web with Semantics 2007, Proceedings of the 2nd Intl. ISWC+ASWC ExpertFinder Workshop (FEWS'07)*, Busan, Korea. Retrieved August 5, 2008, from CEUR-WS.org/Vol-290

Pečjak, V. (2001). *Poti do novih idej. (Ways to create new ideas)*. Ljubljana, Slovenija. New Moment.

Perks, C., & Beveridge, T. (2002). *Guide to IT architecture*. New York: Springer.

Perna, T. (1998). *Fair trade: The ethical defy to the world market*. Turin, Italy: Bollati Boringhieri.

Petkova, D., & Bruce Croft, W. (2006). Hierarchical language models for expert finding in enterprise corpora. In *Proceedings of the 18th IEEE International Conference on Tools with Artificial Intelligence* (pp. 599–608). IEEE Computer Society.

Pettigrew, A. (1973). *The politics of organizational decision making*. London: Tavistock.

Pezzey, J. (1989). *Economic analysis of sustainable growth and sustainable development*. New York: World Bank, WP 15.

Pfeffer, J., & Salancik, G. (1974). Organizational decision-making as a political process. *Administrative Science Quarterly, 19*, 135–151. doi:10.2307/2393885

Pfeifer, R., Lungarella, M., & Lida, F. (2007). Review: Self-organization, embodiment, and biologically inspired robots. *Science, 318*, 1088–1093. doi:10.1126/science.1145803

Phillips, R. (1989). State change architecture protocols for process models. In *IEEE Pro- ceedings of the Hawaii International Conference on System Sciences (HICSS-22)*, Kona, Hawaii.

Pilato, C. M., Collins-Sussman, B., & Fitzpatrick, B. W. (2004). *Version control with subversion*. Sebastopol, CA: O'Reilly Media, Inc.

Pilone, D., & Pitman, N. (2005). *UML 2.0 in a nutshell*. Sebastopol, CA: O'Reilly Media, Inc.

Pin, M. X. (2006). *China's trapped transition: The limits of developmental autocracy*. Cambridge, MA: Harvard University Press.

Pinch, T. J., & Bijker, W. E. (1997). The social construction of facts and artifacts: Or how the sociology of science and the sociology of technology might benefit each other. In W. E. Bijker, T. P. Hughes, & T. J. Pinch (Eds.), *The Social Construction of Technological Systems* (pp. 17-50), Cambridge, MA: MIT Press.

Plossl, G. (1995). *Orlicky's material requirements planning* (2nd ed.). New York: McGraw Hill.

PMI (Project Management Institute). (2000). *Guide to the project management body of knowledge, a (PMBOK® guide)*. Sylva, NC: PMI Publishing Division.

PMI (Project Management Institute). (2001). *Practice standard for work breakdown structures*. Sylva, NC: PMI Publishing Division.

Pohl, K., Böckle, G., & van der Linden, F. (2005). *Software product line engineering*. Berlin, Germany: Springer.

Polanyi, K. (1957). *The great transformation: The political and economic origin of our time*. Boston: Beacon Press.

Polanyi, K. (1977). *The livelihood of man*. New York: Academic Press.

Polleres, A., Scharffe, F., & Schindlauer, R. (2007). SPARQL++ for mapping between RDF vocabularies. In R. Meersman & Z. Tari (Eds.), *On the Move to Meaningful Internet Systems 2007: CoopIS, DOA, ODBASE, GADA, and IS,* Vilamoura, Portugal (LNCS 4803, pp. 878-896).

Pomeroy-Huff, M., Mullaney, J., Cannon, R., & Sebern, M. (2008, March 26). *The personal software process (PSP) body of knowledge*. Retrieved November 24, 2008, from http://www.sei.cmu.edu/publications/documents/05.reports/05sr003.html

Poole, M. S., & DeSanctis, G. (1990). Understanding the use of group decision support systems: The theory of adaptive structuration. In Fulk, J. and Steinfeld, C. (Eds.), *Organizations and communication technology* (173-193).

Pörsken, U. (1989). *Plastikwörter: Die sprache einer internationalen diktatur*. Stuttgart, Germany: Klett-Cotta.

Porter, M. (1990). *The competitive advantage of actions*. New York: Free Press.

Porter, M. E. (1980). *Competitive strategy: Techniques for analyzing industries and companies*. New York: Free Press.

Porter, M. E. (1996). What is strategy? *Harvard Business Review, 74*(6), 61–79.

Porter, M. E. (1998). *Competitive strategy: Techniques for analyzing industries and competitors*. New York: Free Press.

Post, G., & Kagan, A. (2000). OO-CASE tools: An evaluation of rose. *Information and Software Technology, 42*(6), 383–388. doi:10.1016/S0950-5849(99)00099-3

Potocan, V. (2008). Organizational knowledge and education on information technology. In E. Kioulafas (Ed.), *Proceedings of the 4th International Conference on Institutional Evaluation Techniques in Education, Samos Island, Greece, 27-29 June 2008* (pp. 63-71). Athens: National and Kapodistrian University of Athens

Potocan, V., & Mulej, M. (2006). Reliability of information: Case of business information. In B. Aurer, & M. Baca (Eds.) *Proceedings of the 17th International Conference on Information and Intelligent Systems, September 20-22, 2006, Varazdin, Croatia* (pp. 113-120). Varaždin: Faculty of Organisation and Informatics, FOI.

Potočan, V., & Mulej, M. (Eds.). (2007). *Transition into an innovative enterprise*. Maribor, Slovenija: University of Maribor, Faculty of Economics and Business.

Pouloudi, A., & Whitley, E. A. (1997). Stakeholder identification in inter organisational systems: Gaining insights for drug use management systems. *European Journal of Information Systems, 6*(1), 1–14. doi:10.1057/palgrave.ejis.3000252

Power, D. J. (2007). *A brief history of decision support systems*: Retrieved 2008, from http://dssresources.com/history/dsshistory.html

Prado de las Escosura, L. (2005). *Growth, inequality and poverty in Latin America: Historical evidence and controlled conjectures* (Working Paper n. 05-41). Madrid, Spain: University Carlos III. Retrieved from http://docubib.uc3m.es/WORKINGPAPERS/WH/wh054104.pdf

Projects, T. C. C. I. (2004). The challenges of complex IT projects. Retrieved September 1, 2008, from http://www.bcs.org/server_process.php?show=conWebDoc.1167

Proth, J.-M., & Xie, X. (1997). *Petri Nets: A tool for design and management of manufacturing systems*. New York: John Wiley and Sons.

Protogeros, N. (2005). *Virtual learning enterprise integration technological and organizational perspectives.* Hershey, PA: Idea Group Publishing.

Protogeros, N. (2007). *Agent and Web service technologies in virtual enterprises.* Hershey, PA: Information Science Reference.

Pumareja, D. T., & Sikkel, K. (2006). Getting used with groupware: A first class experience. *Journal of Human-Centred Systems, 20*(2), 189–201.

Putnam, R. D. (2000). *Bowling alone: The collapse and revival of American community.* New York: Simon & Shuster.

Putnam, R. D., Leonardi, R., & Nanetti, R. Y. (1993). *Making democracy work: Civic tradition in modern Italy.* Princeton, NJ: Princeton University Press.

Putnik, G. D. (2000). BM_Virtual enterprise architecture reference model. In A. Gunasekaran (Ed.), *Agile manufacturing: 21st century manufacturing strategy* (pp. 73-93). New York: Elsevier.

Putnik, G. D., Cunha, M. M., Sousa, R., & Ávila, P. (2005). Virtual enterprise integration: Challenges of a new paradigm. In G. D. Putnik & M. M. Cunha (Eds.), *Virtual enterprise integration: Technological and organizational perspectives* (pp. 2-33). Hershey, PA: Idea Group Publishing.

Putnik, G. D., Cunha, M. M., Sousa, R., & Ávila, P. (2005). Virtual enterprise integration: challenges of a new paradigm. In G. D. Putnik & M. M. Cunha (Eds.), *Virtual enterprise integration: Technological and organisational perspective.* Hershey, PA: Idea Group Publishing.

Quadrio-Curzio, A., & Fortis, M. (2005). *Research and technological innovation: The challenge for a new Europe.* London: Springer.

Quatrani, T. (1999). *Visual modeling with rational rose 2000 and UML.* Reading, MA: Addison-Wesley Professional.

Quiescenti, M., Bruccoleri, M., La Commare, U., Noto La Diega, S., & Perrone, G. (2006). Business process-oriented design of Enterprise resource planning (ERP) systems for small and medium enterprises. *International Journal of Production Research, 44*(18/19), 3797–3811. doi:10.1080/00207540600688499

Raghvinder, S., Bass, M., Mullick, N., Paulish, D. J., & Kazmeier, J. (2006). *Global software development handbook.* Boston, MA: Auerbach Publications.

Rahimifard, A., & Weston, R. (2007). The enhanced use of enterprise and simulation modelling techniques to support factory changeability. *International Journal of Computer Integrated Manufacturing, 20*(4), 307–328. doi:10.1080/09511920600793220

Rahmifard, A., & Weston, R. H. (2007). The enhanced use of enterprise and simulation modelling techniques to support factory changeability. *International Journal of Computer Integrated Manufacturing, 20*(4), 303–328.

Ramenyi, D. (1998). *Doing research in business and management: An introduction to process & method.* London: SAGE Publications.

Rankin, J. H., & Luther, R. (2006). The innovation process: adoption of information and communication technology for the construction industry. *Canadian Journal of Civil Engineering, 33,* 1538–1546. doi:10.1139/L05-128

Rashid, M. A., Hossain, L., & Patrick, J. D. (Eds.). (2002). *Enterprise resource planning: Global opportunities and challenges.* Idea Group Publishing.

Rawis, J. (1999). *A theory of justice.* Oxford, UK: Oxford University Press.

Rebernik, M. (1990). *Ekonomika inovativnega podjetja.* Ljubljana, Slovenija. Gospodarski vestnik.

Rechtin, E., & Maier, M. (1997). *The art of system architecting.* Boca Raton, FL: CRC Press LLC.

Red Hat. (2008). *Red Hat enterprise Linux 5.* Retrieved November 24, 2008, from http://www.redhat.com/rhel/

Redclift, M., & Woodgate, G. (1997). *The international handbook of environmental sociology.* Cheltenham, UK: Edward Elgar.

Reilly, T. O. (2005). *What is Web 2.0?* Sebastopol, CA: O'Reilly.

Rialp, A. (2003). *Fundamentos teóricos de la organización de empresas.* Pirámide Ediciones.

Rice, R. E., & Shook, D. E. (1990). Relationships of job categories and organizational levels to use communication channels, including electronic mail: A meta-analysis and extension. *Journal of Management Studies, 27,* 195–229. doi:10.1111/j.1467-6486.1990.tb00760.x

Richardson, R. (2007). *2007 - computer crime and security survey.* Computer Security Institute.

Riegel, K. F. (1975). *Development of dialectical operations.* Basel, Switzerland: S. Karger AG.

Rist, G. (1996). *Le développement: Histoire d une croyance occidentale.* Paris: Presse de Sciences Po.

Robertson, P. (1997). Integrating legacy systems with modern corporate applications. *Communications of the ACM, 40*(5), 39–46. doi:10.1145/253769.253785

Robertson, S., & Robertson, J. (1999). *Mastering the requirements process.* London: ACM Press.

Robillard, P., Kruchten, P., & d'Astous, P. (2002). *Software engineering process: With the UPEDU - unified process for education.* Reading, MA: Addison Wesley.

Rocha, A. P., Cardoso, H., & Oliveira, E. (2005). Contributions to an electronic institution supporting virtual enterprises' life cycle. In G. D. Putnik & M. M. Cunha (Eds.), *Virtual enterprise integration: Technological and organizational perspectives* (pp. 229-246). Hershey, PA: Idea Group Publishing.

Rodrígues, J. L., Castellanos, A. R., & Ranguelov, S. Y. (2004). Knowledge management analysis of the research & development & transference process at HEROs: A public university case. In K. Tochtermann & H. Maurer (Eds.), *Proceedings of the International conference on knowledge management (I-KNOW'04)* (pp. 61-67). Graz, Austria: J.UCS, Know-Center.

Rogers, E. (2003). *Diffusion of Innovation* (5th ed.). New York: The Free Press.

Roman Hoegg, R. M., Meckel, M., & Stanoevska-Slabeva, K. (2007). *Overview of business models for Web 2.0 communities.* Institute of Media and Communication Management.

Romero, D., Galeano, N., & Molina, A. (2007). A conceptual model for virtual breeding environments value systems. In L. Camarinha-Matos, H. Afsarmanesh, P. Novais, & C. Analide (Eds.), *Establishing the foundation of collaborative networks* (pp. 43-52). Boston: Springer.

Ross, D. T., & Schoman, K. E. (1977). Structured analysis requirements definitions. *IEEE Transactions on Software Engineering, SE-3,* 6–15. doi:10.1109/TSE.1977.229899

Ross, J. W., & Vitale, M. R. (2000). The ERP revolution: Surviving versus thriving. *Information Systems Frontiers, 2*(2), 233–241. doi:10.1023/A:1026500224101

Ross, J. W., Weill, P., & Robertson, D. (2006). *Enterprise architecture as strategy: Creating a foundation for business execution.* Boston: Harvard Business Press.

Rosson, M. B., & Carroll, J. (2002). *Usability engineering: Scenario-based development of human-computer interaction.* Morgan Kaufmann.

Rost, J. (2004). Political reasons for failed software projects. *IEEE Software, 21*(6), 104–107. doi:10.1109/MS.2004.48

Royce, J. (1976). *The world and the individual.* Gloucester, UK: Peter Smith Publisher.

Royce, W. (1970). Managing the development of large software systems. In *Proc. of the IEEE WES- CON* (pp. 1-9).

Ruhe, G. E. A., & Pfahl, D. (2002). *Quantitative WinWin – a new method for decision support in requirements negotiation.* Paper presented at the Proceedings of the 14th International Conference on Software Engineering and Knowledge Engineering (SEKE'02), Ischia, Italy.

Russell, N., ter Hofstede, A. H. M., Edmond, D., & van der Aalst, W. M. P. (2005). Workflow data patterns: Identification, representation and tool support. In L. Delcambre (Ed.), Lecture Notes in Computer Science, 3716 (pp. 353-368). Berlin, Germany: Springer.

Russell, N., van der Aalst, W. M. P., ter Hofstede, A. H. M., & Edmond, D. (2005). Workflow resource patterns: Identification, representation and tool support. In O. Pastor & J. Falcão e Cunha (Eds.), Lecture Notes in Computer Science, 3520 (pp. 216-232). Berlin, Germany: Springer.

Ryals, L., & Knox, S. (2001). Cross-functional issues in the implementation of relationship marketing through customer relationship management. *European Management Journal, 19*(5), 534–542. doi:10.1016/S0263-2373(01)00067-6

S&T. (2007). *S&T—IT solutions and services.* Retrieved January 22, 2008, from http://www.snt.co.yu/

Saarinen, T. (1996). An expanded instrument for evaluating information system success. *Information & Management, 31*(2), 103–118. doi:10.1016/S0378-7206(96)01075-0

Sachs, W. (1992). *The development dictionary.* London: Zed Book.

Sachs, W. (1999). *Planet dialectics.* London: Zed Book.

Sahlins, M. (1972). *Stone age economics.* Chicago: Aldine-Atherton.

Said, E. W. (1994). *Culture and imperialism.* New York: Vintage Books.

Sala-y-Martin, X., & Subramanian, A. (2003). *Addressing the natural resources course: An illustration from Nigeria* (NBER Working Paper n. W9804). Retrieved from http://ssrn.com/abstract=420318

Sanders, K. (2004, September). Why building information modeling isn't working... yet. *Architectual Record.* Available at http://archrecord.construction.com/features/digital/archives/0409feature-1.asp.

Sanderson, J., & Cox, A. (2008). The challenges of supply strategy selection in a project environment: evidence from UK naval shipbuilding. *Supply Chain Management: An International Journal, 13*(1), 16–25. doi:10.1108/13598540810850283

SAP. (2007). *SAP for higher education & research.* Retrieved January 15, 2007, from http://www.sap.com/industries/highered/

Schäfer, W. (Ed.). (1995). *Proceedings of the Software Process Technology - 4th European Workshop EWSPT '95 Noordwijkerhout.*

Schaffert, S., Bry, F., Baumeister, J., & Kiesel, M. (2008). Semantic Wikis. *IEEE Software, 25*(4), 8–11. doi:10.1109/MS.2008.95

Scheer, A.-W. (1999). *ARIS - business process frameworks* (3rd ed.). Berlin, Germany: Springer-Verlag.

Schekkerman, J. (2008). *Enterprise architecture good practices guide.* Victoria, Canada: Trafford Publishing.

Schlager, J. (1956). Systems engineering: Key to modern development. *IRE Transactions, EM-3,* 64–66. doi:10.1109/IRET-EM.1956.5007383

Schoitsch, E. (2008). A holistic view at dependable embedded software-intensive systems. In G. Chroust, P. Doucek, & J. Klas (Eds.), *Proceedings of the 16th Interdisciplinary Information Management Talks "Managing the Unmanageable"* (pp. 321-344). Schriftenreihe Informatik Nr. 25, Trauner Verlag Linz.

Schoitsch, E., Althammer, E., Sonneck, G., Eriksson, H., & Vinter, J. (2008). Modular cer- tification support - the DECOS concept of generic safety cases. In *Proceedings of IEEE INDIN 2008, 6th International Conference on Industrial Informatics,* Daejeon, Korea. IEEE: CFP08INI-CDR.

Schreiber, A. Th., Akkermans, J. M., Anjewierden, A. A., de Hoog, R., Shadbolt, N. R., Van de Velde, W., & Wielinga, B. J. (1999). *Engineering and managing knowledge. The CommonKADS Methodology.* Cambridge, MA: The MIT Press.

Schumacher, F. (1999). *Small is beautiful.* Washington: Hartley & Marks Publishers.

Schumpeter, J. A. (1939). *Business cycles.* New York: McGraw Hill.

Schwaber, K. (2004). *Agile project management with scrum.* Redmond, WA: Microsoft Press.

Schwaber, K., & Beedle, M. (2008). *Agile software development with scrum.* Upper Saddle River, NJ: Prentice Hall.

Scott, J. E., & Vessey, I. (2000). Implementing enterprise resource planning systems: The role of learning from failure. *Information Systems Frontiers, 2*(2), 213–232. doi:10.1023/A:1026504325010

Seabrook, J. (1993). *Victims of development.* London: Verso.

Sen, A. (2001). *Development as freedom.* New York: Oxford University Press.

Serbian National Scientific Council. (2008, April 14). Act standard for valuating and quantity presenting of the scientific results of the researcher. *Službeni glasnik Republike Srbije 16*(38).

Setrag, K. (2002). *Web services and virtual learning enterprises*. Chicago: Tect.

Shasha, D., Statman, R., & Zhang, K. (1992). On the editing distance between unordered labeled trees. *Information Processing Letters, 42*, 133–139. doi:10.1016/0020-0190(92)90136-J

Shenhar, A. J., Levy, O., & Dvir, D. (1997). Mapping the dimensions of project success. *Project Management Journal, 28*(2), 5–13.

Shiva, V. (1989). *Staying alive: Woman, ecology and development*. London: Zed Book.

Shnaidt, P. (1992). *Enterprise-wide networking*. Carmel, IN: SAMS.

Siemieniuch, C.E., Sinclair, M.A., & Vaughan, G.M.C. (1998). A method for decision support for allocation of functions and design of jobs in manufacturing based on knowledge requirements. *Int. Journal of Computer Integrated Manufacturing*.

Sifry, D. (2006). State of the blogosphere. *Technorati*.

Sim, Y. W., Crowder, R. M., & Wills, G. B. (2006, May 9-11). *Expert finding by capturing organizational knowledge from legacy documents*. Paper presented at the IEEE International Conference on Computer & Communication Engineering (ICCCE '06), Kuala Lumpur, Malaysia.

Simchy-Levy, D., Kaminsky, P., & Simchy-Levy, E. (2003). *Designing & managing the supply chain—concepts, strategies & case studies*. New York: McGraw-Hill.

Simmons, J. (2006). E-learning and earning: The impact of lifelong e-learning on organisational development. *The European Journal of Open and Distance Learning (EURODL), November*.

Skolimowski, H. (1981). *Eco-philosophy. designing new tactics for living*. Salem, NH: Marion Boyers.

Skolimowski, H. (1984). *The theater of mind*. Wheaton, IL: The Theosophical Publishing House.

Smith, W. K., & Tushman, M. L. (2005). Managing strategic contradictions: A top management model for managing innovation streams. *Organization Science, 16*(5), 522–536. doi:10.1287/orsc.1050.0134

Sohal, A. S., & Ng, L. (1998). The role and impact of information technology in Australian business. *Journal of Information Technology, 13*(3), 201–217. doi:10.1080/026839698344846

Sorenson, P. G., Findeisen, P. S., & Tremblay, J. P. (1996). Supporting viewpoints in metaview. In *Joint proceedings of the second international software architecture workshop (ISAW-2) and international workshop on multiple perspectives in software development (Viewpoints '96) on SIGSOFT '96 workshops*. San Francisco: ACM Press.

Spewak, St. H. (1993). *Enterprise architecture planning*. Hoboken, NJ: Wiley.

SPIRE Project Team. (1998). *The SPIRE handbook - better, faster, cheaper - software development in small organisations*. Dublin, Ireland: Centre of Software Engineering Ltd.

Stadtler, H. (2000). Supply chain management—an overview. In C. Kilger (Ed.), *Supply chain management and advanced planning: Concepts, models, software and case studies* (pp. 7-27). Berlin, Germany: Springer-Verlag.

Standish Group. (2008). *CHAOS*. Standish Group International Inc.

Steckel, R., & Floud, R. (1997). *Health and welfare during industrialisation*. Chicago: University of Chicago Press.

Steingart, G. (2008). *The war for wealth: Why globalisation is bleeding the west of its prosperity*. New York: McGraw-Hill.

Stephens, K. K. (2007). The successive use of information and communication technologies at work. *Communication Theory, 17*(4), 486–507. doi:10.1111/j.1468-2885.2007.00308.x

Stevens, C. P. (2003). Enterprise resource planning: A trio of resources. *Information Systems Management, 20*(3), 61–67. doi:10.1201/1078/43205.20.3.20030601/43074.7

Stewart, T. A. (1997). *Intellectual capital: The new wealth of organizations*. New York: Doubleday.

Stiglitz, J. E. (2007). *Making globalisation work*. New York: W. W. Norton.

Stiglitz, J. E., & Charlton, A. (2005). *Fair trade for all: How trade can promote development.* New York: Oxford University Press.

Stiglitz, J. E., & Greenwald, B. (2003). *Towards a new paradigm in monetary economics.* New York: Cambridge University Press.

Stragapede, A. (1999). *ECSS software process model* (Tech. Rep.). Turin, Italy: Alenia Aerospazio - Space Division.

Strong, D. M., & Volkoff, O. (2004). A roadmap for Enterprise system implementation. *IEEE Computer Society, 37*, 22–29.

Subramanian, A. (2008). *India's turn: Understanding the economic transformation.* Oxford: Oxford University Press.

Suchman, L. (1987). *Plans and situated actions: The problem of human-machine communication.* New York: Cambridge University Press.

Suh, W., Derich Sohn, J. H., & Kwak, J. Y. (2004). Knowledge management as enabling R&D innovation in high tech industry: The case of SAIT. *Journal of Knowledge Management, 8*(6), 5–15. doi:10.1108/13673270410567594

Sukthankar, G. (2008, June 10). *Robust and efficient plan recognition for dynamic multi-agent teams.* Presentation to the Information Technology Division, Nav Res Lab, DC.

SupplyOn. (2009). SupplyOn for successful supply chain management. Retrived January 31, 2009, from http://www.supplyon.com

Sussman, R. (1998). *The biological basis for human behaviour.* Englewood Cliffs, NJ: Prentice & Hall.

Sveiby, K. E. (1997). *The new organizational wealth. Managing and measuring knowledge-based assets.* San Francisco: Berret-Koehler Publishers Inc.

Sveiby, K. E. (1997). *The new organizational wealth.* San Francisco: Berrett-Koehler.

Sveiby, K. E., & Lloyd, T. (1988). *Managing knowhow. Increase profits by harnessing the creativity in your company.* London: Bloomsbury.

SZK. (2007). *16. konferenca Slovenskega združenja za kakovost, Kakovost, inovativnost in odgovornost. Zbornik.* Ljubljana, Slovenija. Slovensko združenje za kakovost.

Szulanski, G. (1996). Exploring internal stickiness: Impediments to the transfer of best practice within the firm. *Strategic Management Journal, 17*, 27–43.

Tang, E. K., Suganthan, P. N., & Yao, X. (2006). An analysis of diversity measures. *Machine Learning, 65*, 247–271. doi:10.1007/s10994-006-9449-2

Targowski, A. (1990). *The architecture and planning of enterprise-wide information management systems.* Hershey, PA: Idea Group Publishing.

Targowski, A. (1996). *Global information infrastructure.* Hershey PA: Idea Group Publishing.

Targowski, A. (2003). *Electronic enterprise: Strategy and architecture.* Hershey, PA: IRM Press.

Targowski, A. (2009a). The evolution from data to wisdom in decision-making at the level of real and virtual networks. In C. Camison *et al.* (Eds.), *Connectivity and knowledge management in virtual organizations.* Hershey, PA: Information Science Reference.

Targowski, A. (2009b). *Information technology and societal development.* Hershey, PA: Information Science Reference.

Targowski, A., & Rienzo, T. (2004). *Enterprise information infrastructure.* Kalamazoo, MI: Paradox Associates.

Tavistock Institute (1966). *Interdependence and uncertainty.* Tavistock publications.

Terrasson, F. (2002). *En finir avec la nature.* Monaco, Principality of Monaco: Edition du Rocher.

Terry, P. (1975). Organisation behaviour. *Industrial & Commercial Training, 7*(11), 462–466. doi:10.1108/eb003504

Teune, H. (1988). *Growth.* London: Sage Publication.

The Economist. (2007, October 13). Something new under the sun. A special report on innovation. *The Economist.*

Thomas, G. F., & King, C. L. (2006). Reconceptualizing e-mail overload. *Journal of Business and Technical Communication, 20*, 252–287. doi:10.1177/1050651906287253

Thompson, K. J. (1996). *Crossing boundaries: Knowledge, disciplinarities, and interdisciplinarities.* Charlottesville VA: University Press of Virginia.

Thurow, L. C. (1985). *The zero-sum solution: Building a world-class American economy.* New York: Simon & Shuster.

Tremonti, G. (2008). *La paura e la speranza: Europa crisi globale che si avvicina e la via per superarla.* Milan, Italy: Mondadori.

Trigo, A., Varajão, J., Figueiredo, N., & Barroso, J. (2007, June 23-26). *Information systems and technology adoption by the Portuguese large companies.* Paper presented at the European and Mediterranean Conference on Information Systems (EMCIS), Valence, Spain.

Tung, H.-L., Bergman, M., Wood, J., & Lawless, W. F. (2008). Metrics of organizational performance that are independent of cultural effects. *International Journal of Management Theory and Practices, 9*(1), 69–84.

Turner, J. R. (2006). Towards a theory of project management: The nature of the project. *International Journal of Project Management, 24*(2), 1–3. doi:10.1016/j.ijproman.2005.11.008

Turner, M. (2006). *Microsoft solutions framework essentials.* Redmond, WA: Microsoft Press.

Turner, M. S. (2006). *Microsoft solutions framework essentials: Building successful technology solutions.* Redmond, WA: Microsoft Press.

Tushman, M. L. (1977). Communication across organizational boundaries: special boundary roles in the innovation process. *Administrative Science Quarterly, 22*, 587–605. doi:10.2307/2392402

Tweed, R. G., & Lehman, D. (2002). Learning considered within a cultural context: Confucian and Socratic approaches. *The American Psychologist, 57*(2), 89–99.

Uchitelle, L. (2006). *The disposable America: Layoffs and their consequences.* New York: Knopf.

Ullman, M. T. (2001). A neurocognitive perspective on language: The declarative/procedural model.

Nature Reviews. Neuroscience, 2(10), 717–726. doi:10.1038/35094573

Uršič, D. (1993). *Inoviranje podjetja kot poslovno-organizacijskega sistema.* Maribor, Slovenija. Univerza v Mariboru, Ekonomsko-poslovna fakulteta.

Vachon, R. (1988). *Alternatives au développement: Approches interculturelles à la bonne vie et à la coopération internationale.* Montréal, Canada: Centre interculturel Monchanin.

Van de Velde, W. (1993). Issues in knowledge level modelling. In J.M. David, J.P. Krivine, & R. Simmons (Eds.), *Second generation expert systems* (pp. 211-231). Berlin, Germany: Springer Verlag.

Van de Ven, A. H., & Ferry, D. L. (1980). *Measuring and assessing organizations.* New York: Wiley.

Van der Aalst, W. M. P., & Hofstede, A. H. M. (2005). YAWL: Yet another workflow language. *Information Systems, 30*(4), 245–275. doi:10.1016/j.is.2004.02.002

van der Aalst, W. M. P., ter Hofstede, A. H. M., Kiepuszewski, B., & Barros, A. P. (2003). Workflow patterns. Distributed and Parallel Databases, 14, 5–51. doi:10.1023/A:1022883727209

van Everdingen, Y., van Hillegersberg, J., & Waarts, E. (2000). Enterprise resource planning: ERP adoption by European midsize companies. *Communications of the ACM, 43*(4), 27–31. doi:10.1145/332051.332064

Van Gigch, J. P. (1974). *Applied general systems theory.* New York: Harper & Row.

Varajão, J. (2006, January-March). Gestão da função de sistemas de informação. *Dirigir - Revista para chefias e quadros, IEFP,* 3-9.

Varajão, J., Ribeiro, A. T., Figueiredo, N., & Barroso, J. (2007, July 12-15). *Motivações inerentes à adopção de Tecnologias e Sistemas de Informação nas grandes empresas portuguesas.* Paper presented at the 6ª Conferência Ibero-Americana em Sistemas, Cibernética e Informática (CISCI), Orlando, Florida.

Varajão, J., Trigo, A., Figueiredo, N., & Barroso, J. (2007). TI nas empresas nacionais. *Revista CXO, 2,* 19–23.

Vernadat, F. (1996). *Enterprise modeling and integration: Principles and applications.* London: Chapman & Hall.

Vicente, J. (2007). Operações baseadas em efeitos: O paradigma da guerra do século XXI. *Jornal Defesa e Relações Internacionais.*

Villar, F. (1996). *Los indoeuropeos y los origines de europa: Language y historia.* Madrid, Spain: Editorial Gredos.

Vollmann, T. E., William, L. B., Whybark, D. C., & Jacobs, F. R. (2005). *Manufacturing planning and control for supply chain management* (5th ed.). New York: McGraw-Hill.

Vos, F. J. J., & Achterkamp, M. C. (2006). Stakeholder identification in innovation projects: Going beyond classification. *European Journal of Innovation Management, 9*(2), 161–178. doi:10.1108/14601060610663550

Wah, L. (2000). Behind the buzz: The substance of knowledge management. In J. Cortada & J. A. Woods (Eds.), *The Knowledge Management Yearbook 2000-2001* (pp. 307-317). Boston: Butterworth-Heineman.

Wainright, C. E. R., & Ridgeway, K. (1994). *The application of GRAI as a framework for manufacturing strategy process, Factory 2000-Advanced Factory Automation, Conference Publication, No. 398.* IEEE Press.

Walker, N. (2005). *Open book accounting – a best value tool.* Good practice guides – Commissioning, Change Agent Team.

Walsham, G. (1993). *Interpreting information systems in organizations.* Chichester, UK: John Wiley & Sons.

Walther, J. B., & Parks, M. R. (2002). Cues filtered out, cues filtered in: Computer-mediated communication and relationships. In M. L. Knapp and J. A. Daly (Eds.), *Handbook of interpersonal communication* (529-563). Thousand Oaks, CA: Sage.

Wang, C. X., & Benaroch, M. (2004). Supply chain coordination in B2B electronic markets. *International Journal of Production Economics, 92*(2), 113–124. doi:10.1016/j.ijpe.2003.09.016

Wang, D. J. (1979). *The history of Chinese logical thought.* Shangai, China: People's Press.

Wang, S., Shen, W., & Hao, Q. (2006). An agent-based Web service workflow model for inter-enterprise collaboration. In *Expert systems with applications.* Amsterdam: Elsevier.

Wang, Y., & King, G. (2000). *Software engineering processes.* Boca Raton, FL: CRC Press.

Ward, R. P., Fayad, M. E., & Laitinen, M. (2001). Thinking objectively: Software process improvement in the small. *Communications of the ACM, 44*(4), 105–107. doi:10.1145/367211.367291

Warnecke, H. J. (1993). *The fractal company - a revolution in corporate culture.* New York: Springer-Verlag.

Watkins, K. (2002). *Cultivating poverty: The impact of US cotton subsidies on Africa* (Oxfam Briefing paper n. 30). Retrieved from http://www.oxfam.org/en/files/pp020925_cotton.pdf

Weber, M. (1947). *The theory of social and economic organization.* New York: Oxford University Press.

Webster, M., Sugden, D. M., & Tayles, M. E. (2004). The measurement of nanufacturing virtuality. *International Journal of Operations & Production Management, 24*(7), 721–742. doi:10.1108/01443570410542019

Weick, K. E. (1995). *Sensemaking in organizations,* Thousand Oaks, CA: Sage Publications.

Weick, K. E., & Quinn, R. E. (1999). Organizational change and development. *Annual Review of Psychology, 50,* 361–386. doi:10.1146/annurev.psych.50.1.361

Weigand, H. (2006). Two decades of the language-action perspective: Introduction. Communications of the ACM, 49(5), 44–46. doi:10.1145/1125944.1125973

Weiss, D. M., Bennett, D., Payseur, J. Y., Tendick, P., & Zhang, P. (2002). *Goal-oriented software assessment.* Paper presented at the 24th International Conference on Software Engineering (ICSE '02), Orlando, FL.

Weizsäcker, E. U., Young, O. R., & Finger, M. (2005). *Limit to privatisation: How to avoid too much a good thing.* London: Earthscan Pub.

Weston, R. H. (1998). Integration infrastructure requirements for agile manufacturing systems. *Proc. of Instn of Mech. Engineers., 212*(Part B), 423-437.

Weston, R. H., Clements, P. E., Shorter, D. N., Hodgson, A. J., & West, A. A. (2001). On the explicit modelling of systems of human resources. *International Journal of Production Research, 39*(2), 185–204. doi:10.1080/00207540010001857

White, S. A., & Miers, D. (2008). *BPMN modeling and reference guide: Understanding and using BPMN.* Lighthouse, FL: Future Strategies.

Whitford, J. (2005). *The new old economy: Networks, institutions, and the organizational transformation of American manufacturing.* New York: Oxford University Press.

Whorf, B. L. (1956). *Language, thought and reality.* Cambridge, MA: MIT Press.

Wickens, C. D. (1992). *Engineering psychology and human performance* (2nd ed). Columbus, OH: Merrill Publishing.

Wiendahl, H.-H., Cieminski, G. V., & Wiendahl, H.-P. (2005). Stumbling blocks of PPC: Towards the holistic configuration of PPC systems. *Production Planning and Control, 16*(7), 634–651. doi:10.1080/09537280500249280

Wiener, N. (1948). *Cybernetics: Or the control and communication in the animal and the machine.* Cambridge, MA: MIT Press.

Wiig, K. (1993). *Knowledge management foundations: Thinking about thinking – how people and organizations create, represent and use knowledge.* Arlington, VA: Schema Press.f

Wiley, N. (1988). The micro-macro problem in social theory. *Sociological Theory, 6,* 254–261. doi:10.2307/202119

Williams, T. J. (1994). The Purdue enterprise reference architecture. *Computers in Industry, 24*(2-3), 141–158. doi:10.1016/0166-3615(94)90017-5

Williamson, O. E. (1981). The economics of organization: The transaction cost approach. *American Journal of Sociology, 87*(3), 548–577. doi:10.1086/227496

Williamson, O. E. (1985). *The economic institutions of capitalism. Firms, market, relational contracting.* New York: The Free Press.

Williamson, O., & Winter, S. (Eds.). (1991). *The nature of the firm: Origins, evolution and development.* New York: Oxford University Press.

Willis, R. P. (2007). *The counterinsurgency pattern assessment (CIPA) Program 2007.* Naval Research Laboratory.

Winchester, S. (2008). *The man who loved China: The fantastic story of the eccentric scientist who unlocked the mysteries of the middle kingdom.* New York: Harper Collins.

Winograd, T. (1987). A language/action perspective on the design of cooperative work. Human-Computer Interaction, 3, 3–30. doi:10.1207/s15327051hci0301_2

Winograd, T., & Flores, F. (1986). Understanding computers and cognition. Norwood, NJ: Ablex Publishing Corporation.

Winston, W. L., & Albright, S. C. (2008). *Practical management science* (3rd ed.). South-Western College Publishing.

Wolf, M. (2004). *Why globalisation works.* New York: Yale University Press.

Wolfe, R. A., & Putler, D. S. (2002). How tight are the ties that bind stakeholder groups? *Organization Science, 13*(1), 64–80. doi:10.1287/orsc.13.1.64.544

Womack, J. P., Jones, D. T., & Roos, D. (1990). *The machine that changed the world.* New York: Oxford Associates.

Wood, J., Tung, H.-L., Grayson, J., Poppeliers, C., & Lawless, W. F. (2008). A classical uncertainty principle for organizations. In M. Khosrow-Pour (Ed.), *Encyclopedia of Information Science & Technology* (2nd ed.). Hershey, PA, IGI Global.

Woods, S., Carriere, S. J., & Kazman, R. (1999). *A semantic foundation for architectural reengineering and interchange.* Paper presented at the International Conference on Software Maintenance-ICSM- 99, Oxford, UK.

Workflow Management Coalition. (1995). *The workflow reference model, DN:TC00-1003 (Versión 1.1).* Retrieved from http://www.wfmc.org/standards/docs/tc003v11.pdf

Workflow Management Coalition. (2007). XML process definition language, V.2.1. Retrieved September 29, 2008, from http://www.wfmc.org

Worster, D. (1988). *The end of the earth: Perspectives on modern environment history.* New York: Cambridge University Press.

WPI. (2007). *About the workflow patterns*. Retrieved July 2, 2008, from http://www.workflowpatterns.com./about/index.php

Wriston, W. B. (1997). Bits, bytes, and diplomacy. *Foreign Affairs (Council on Foreign Relations), 76*(5), 11.

Wu, I. L. (1992). *Manufacturing systems design and analysis*. London: Chapman & Hall.

Wu, J., Ulieru, M., Cobzaru, M., & Norrie, D. (2000, November 12-15). Supply chain management systems: State of the art and vision. In *Proceedings of the 2000 IEEE International Conference on Management of Innovation and Technology (ICMIT 2000)*, Singapore (Vol. 2, pp. 759-764). IEEE.

ACM. (2008). *The ACM computing classification system*. Retrieved August 5, 2008, from, http://oldwww.acm.org/class/

Xu, H. Q., Besant, C. B., & Ristic, M. (2003). System for enhancing supply chain agility through exception handling. *International Journal of Production Research, 41*(6), 1099–1114. doi:10.1080/0020754021000049826

YAWL. (2007a). YAWL editor 1.5: User manual. Retrieved July 2, 2008, from http://yawlfoundation.org/yawldocs/YAWLEditor1.5UserManual.doc

YAWL. (2007b). YAWL lexicon. Retrieved July 7, 2008, from http://www.yawlfoundation.org/resources/lexicon.html

Yimam-Seid, D., & Kobsa, A. (2003). Expert finding systems for organizations: Problem and domain analysis and the demoir approach. *Journal of Organizational Computing and Electronic Commerce, 13*(1), 1–24. doi:10.1207/S15327744JOCE1301_1

Yin, R. K. (1989). Research design issues in using the case study method to study management information systems. In J.I. Cash Jr. & P.R. Lawrence (Eds.), *The information systems research challenge: Qualitative research methods* (pp. 1-6). Boston: Harvard Business School Press. [1] Reported on cnet's news.com on Oct 24, 2007 for example; http://www.news.com/8301-13577_3-9803872-36.html (accessed January 15, 2008)f

Yogesh, M. (1998). Business process redesign: Business change of mythic proportions? *MIS Quarterly*, 121–127.

Yourdon, E. (1990). Softlab's MAESTRO. *American Programmer, 3*(3).

Yuthas, K., & Dillard, J. F. (1999). Ethical development of advanced technology: A postmodern stakeholder perspective. *Journal of Business Ethics, 19*(1), 35–49. doi:10.1023/A:1006145805087

Zachman, J. A. (1987). A framework for information systems architecture. *IBM Systems Journal, 26*(3).

Zachman, J. A. (1999). A framework for information systems architecture. *IBM Systems Journal, 38*(2/3), 454–471.

Zakaria, F. (2008). *The post-American world*. New York: W. W. Norton & Company.

Zallah, S. (2005). *Significant e-marketplaces report*. Retrieved from http://www.emarketservices.com/clubs/ems/artic/SignificanteMarkets.pdf

Zanotelli, A. (2006). *Avec ceux qui n'ont rien*. Paris: Flammarion.

Zelm, M. (2003). Towards user oriented enterprise modelling- comparison of modelling language constructs. In R. Jardim-Goncalves, et al (Eds.), *Proc. of the 10th ISPE Int. Conf. on CE: Research and applications*. Madeira Portugal: Swets & Zeitilinger.

Zelm, M., Vernadat, F. B., & Kosanke, K. (1995). The CIMOSA business modelling process. *Computers in Industry, 27*, 123–142. doi:10.1016/0166-3615(95)00018-2

Zemanek, H. (1986). Gedanken zum systementwurf. In H. Maier-Leibniz (Ed.), *Zeugen des wissens* (Vol. XX). Hase and Köhler Verlag Mainz.

Zhang, Z., Gao, M., Zhang, R., & Chang, D. (2008). Symbiotic virtual enterprise cluster ecological balance model and stability analysis. In *Proceedings of the Fourth International Conference on Natural Computation (ICNC '08)*, Jinan, China (pp.251-255). Washington, DC: IEEE Computer Society.

Zhen, M., & Weston, R. H. (2006). Simulating dynamic behaviours in complex organisations: Case study application of a well structure modelling approach. In A. Nketsa, et al (Eds.), *Proc. of the European Simulation and Modelling Conference, Modelling and Simulation (ESM'2006)*, EUROSIS-ETI, Toulouse, France (pp. 390-395).

Zvegintzov, N. (1982). What life? What cycle? In AFIPS (Ed.), *Proceedings of the National Computer Conference,* Houston, TX (pp. 562-567).

About the Contributors

Maria Manuela Cruz-Cunha is currently an Associate Professor in the School of Technology at the Polytechnic Institute of Cavado and Ave, Portugal. She holds a Dipl. Eng. in the field of Systems and Informatics Engineering, an M.Sci. in the field of Information Society and a Dr.Sci in the field of Virtual Enterprises, all from the University of Minho (Portugal). She teaches subjects related with Information Systems, Information Technologies and Organizational Models to undergraduated and post-graduated studies. She supervises several PhD projects in the domain of Virtual Enterprises and Information Systems and Technologies. She regularly publishes in international peer-reviewed journals and participates on international scientific conferences. She serves as a member of Editorial Board and Associate Editor for several International Journals and for several Scientific Committees of International Conferences. She has authored and edited several books and her work appears in more than 70 papers published in journals, book chapters and conference proceedings.

***

Jan Aalmink was born in 1967, Nordhorn, Northern Germany. His interest in computer science began in the early 80th. He received the university-entrance diploma in 1987 from Fachgymnasium Technik in Nordhorn. He studied both, informatics and mathematics at Technical University of Clausthal. After receiving degrees Dipl.-Inf. and Dipl.-Math. from Technical University of Clausthal in 1991, he entered the business IT world. After 3 years in IT Consulting Industry as a freelancer he joined SAP AG in 1994 .Prior to his recent appointment to Senior Software Engineer he was responsible for Enterprise Systems Engineering in the areas of Logistics-Controlling, Cost Containment, Financial Services, Foundation, Manufacturing and Supply Chain Management. In addition to SAP, he joined the research department VLBA - Very Large Business Applications at University of Oldenburg as an external PhD student in 2008. His research interests include Enterprise Systems Engineering and Diagnostics, Enterprise Tomography, Cloud Computing, Search Engine Technology, Algorithm Engineering and Development Efficiency.

Joseph Ajaefobi graduated with a 2:1 degree in Metallurgical & Materials Engineering in 1988 from Anambra University of Technology (ASUTECH) Enugu, Nigeria. He worked briefly at Ajaokuta Steel Complex before proceeding for theological education at Trinity College Umuahia, Nigeria, graduating with distinctions in both college diploma in theology and the University of Calabar diploma in Religious Studies in 1992. He was ordained in the Church of Nigeria (Anglican Communion) in July 1992 after which he served the Church many capacities in Nigeria . He enrolled for a PhD in Manufacturing Engineering & Management in 2000 at Loughborough University and graduated in 2004. Thereafter, he joined MSI Research Institute Loughborough University as a Research Associate. His broad research interests includes: Enterprise Modelling and Integration; Human Systems modelling, Lean Manufacturing and Value Stream Analysis.

Enrique Paniagua Arís is Bachelor in Fine Arts (1992, University of Barcelona), Postgrade Diploma in Ergonomics (1996, Polytechnic University of Catalonia), Postgrade Diploma in Audiovisual Production (1996, Polytechnic University of Catalonia), Ph.D. Degree in Science (Computer Science) (1998, Polytechnic University of Catalonia), and is currently developing his second doctoral thesis related to Architectural Space (Polytechnic University of Cartagena). Is Associate Professor of the Department of Engineering of Information and Communications (DIIC) from the University of Murcia and Coordinator of the Office of Strategic Management at the University of Murcia. The lines of investigation in which he works are: Knowledge Engineering applied to Strategic Management and Planning, Technological Knowledge Management in enterprises; Semiotics, Architectural Space and Design Methodologies; and Nonlinear Narrative Audiovisual.

Sigmund Aslesen is a researcher working at Fafo, Institute for Labour and Social Research, Norway. He is currently doing his PhD in innovation studies at the University of Oslo, Faculty of Social Sciences, Centre for Technology, Innovation and Culture TIK. Aslesen has been involved in numerous enterprise and development studies in the manufacturing industry, on topics related to production and project management, and supply chain integration

Belén López Ayuso is Computer Engineer (1998, University of Murcia) and Ph.D. Degree in Computer Science (2008, University of Murcia). He is currently Associate Professor and Director of the Department of Science Polytechnics (DCP) of the Universidad Católica San Antonio de Murcia (UCAM). The lines of investigation in which she works are: Knowledge Engineering applied to Strategic Management and Planning, Technological Knowledge Management in enterprises.

João Barroso, is a Professor at the Department of Engineering of the University of Trás-os-Montes e Alto Douro, where he teaches undergraduate and postgraduate courses on software engineering, image processing and computer vision. He has been actively involved in the definition and implementation of the Trás-os-Montes Digital project, funded by the Portuguese Government and by the European Community, and focused on the development of the information society in the North-East region of Portugal.

Margo Bergman, Ph.D. Margo is a behavioral economist currently working at the Michael E. Debakey Veteran's Administration Medical Center in Houston, TX. She is also an Instructor of Medicine, Health Services division at the Baylor College of Medicine. Her main research interests are decision making under conditions of uncertainty, with a recent emphasis on decisions involving information gained from genetic testing.

Albert Boonstra is an associate professor at the Faculty of Economics and Business at the University of Groningen, The Netherlands, where is director of the graduate programmes in Business Administration. He specializes in the organizational issues that surround the use of advanced information technologies, especially in health care environments. He has conducted extensive research and consultancy in this field, and has published in International Journal of Information Management, European Journal of Information Systems, International Journal of Project Management, Journal of Strategic Information Systems. His most recent book is Managing Information Systems, an organisational Perspective (2009, 3rd edition), with Financial Times/Prentice Hall, Harlow.

Giorgio Bruno is an Associate Professor at Politecnico di Torino, where he teaches courses on software engineering and object-oriented programming. His current interests concern the operational modeling of business processes and collaborative services, and the design of information systems and workflow systems. He has authored two books and over 120 technical papers on the above-mentioned subjects.

Jose L. Caro is a Professor of Languages and Computer Science at the University of Málaga, Spain. He is a researcher of a SICUMA (Cooperative Information Systems of Malaga University, www.sicuma. uma.es) computer science research group centred in information systems methodology and development and workflow technologies. Jose L. Caro has published various books, papers in impact journals and around 50 conference papers. Also, he works in the program committee of important conferences and he organizes international events like Turitec (www.turitec.uma.es) and he has coordinated several research projects.

Gerhard Chroust. Born 1941 in Vienna. After studies at the Technical University of Vienna (Electrical Engineering - Communications) and the University of Pennsylvania, USA (Computer Science). He received a PhD from the Technical University of Vienna. 1966 to 1991 he worked as scientist at the IBM Laboratory Vienna (Formal Definition of Programming Languages, compiler building, Software Process Models and IBM's software engineering environment ADPS). 1992 - 2007 he was tenured professor for "Systems Engineering and Automation" at the J. Kepler University Linz and Head of the Institute. Since 2007 he is Professor Emeritus with main interest in Cultural Differences and Human Aspects of Software Development, Systems Engineering, Software Process Models. and Systems Theory. He is the Secretary General of the International Federation for Systems Research (IFSR),President of the Österr. Gesellschaft für Informatik (ÖGI), Vicepresident of the Austrian Society for Cybernetic Studies (OSGK) and Board Member of the Austrian Computer Society (OCG).

Ezgi Aktar Demirtas was born on 09 August 1976. She received her Master's degree and Ph.D. in Industrial Engineering in 2001 and 2007 at Eskisehir Osmangazi University in Turkey. Since 1998 she has been working at the Department of Industrial Engineering of Eskisehir Osmangazi University. She has several national and international publications and research projects in her main research interests (http://www2.ogu.edu.tr/~eaktar/). Her main research interests are Supply Chain Management, Expert Systems, User Centered Product Design, QFD, Kansei Engineering, Statistics and Multi Variate Statistical Analysis, Multicriteria decision making, Service Systems.

Jovan Duduković, Dipl. ing., is a Junior researcher at the Mihailo Pupin Institute, Belgrade, Serbia. He has received a Dipl. Ing. degree in 2004 at the School of Electrical Engineering, University of Belgrade, Serbia. While working in scientific projects financed by the Serbian Ministry of Science and EU (FP6 and FP7) he took part in the design and implementation of several decision support systems (SARIB), design and implementation of Semantic Web Portal (Web4WeB), and implementation of enterprise applications (SUSDEV). He has experience in enterprise application software development, GIS application development, web application architecture and database development. His interests include Semantic Web, Knowledge representation and architecture of software systems.

Silvia C. Pinto Brito Fernandes is Assistant Professor at the Faculty of Economics of the University of Algarve. Her PhD is on Innovation Economics monitored by Professor Teresa Noronha of the same Faculty and Professor François Nicolas of INRA (France). Her master degree is on Technological Diffusion in Organizations monitored by Professor Monteiro Barata of ISEG (Lisbon). She is graduated on Information Technology Management at the Faculty of Science and Technology (University of Algarve). She teaches information technologies and management information systems for the Management and Economy courses at the Faculty of Economics for several years. She also teaches innovation economy and information management at master degree courses. She has several publications in national and international books and magazines and several published communications from international conferences, related with scientific subjects as: knowledge economies, technological diffusion, e-learning, e-commerce, regional innovation systems, geographic information systems, management information systems, etc.

Jorge Marx Gómez studied Computer Engineering and Industrial Engineering at the University of Applied Sciences Berlin. He was a lecturer and researcher at the University of Magdeburg (Germany) where he also obtained a PhD degree in Business Information Systems with the work Computer-based Approaches to Forecast Returns of Scrapped Products to Recycling. From 2002 till 2003 he was a visiting professor for Business Informatics at the Technical University of Clausthal, Germany. In 2004 he received his habilitation for the work Automated Environmental Reporting through Material Flow Networks at the Otto-von-Guericke-Universität Magdeburg. In 2005 he became a full professor and chair of Business Information Systems at the University of Oldenburg (Germany). His research interests include Very Large Business Applications, Business Information Systems, Federated ERP-Systems, Business Intelligence, Data Warehousing, Interoperability and Environmental Management Information Systems.

James M. Grayson, Ph.D., is a tenured Associate Professor of Management Science and Operations at the Hull College of Business Administration at Augusta State University. He received a Bachelor of Science degree from the United States Military Academy at West Point, an MBA with a Marketing emphasis from the University of North Texas, and then a Ph.D. in Management Science with an Information Systems minor also from the University of North Texas. He brings to his research considerable industry experience including about twelve years at Texas Instruments contributing in quality engineering, quality and reliability assurance management, supplier management, subcontractor management, software quality engineering management, statistical consulting, total quality management and a joint venture management (Ti - Martin Marietta). His research interests are diverse and range from unique approaches to organizational structure to applying management science methods to financial planning to operations management.

Antonio Guevara is a Professor of Languages and Computer Science at the University of Málaga, Spain. He got his Ph.D. degree in cooperative methodology. He is a professor of "Cooperative Information Systems" in Ph.D. degree in Computer Science Department. He is the director of a SICUMA (Cooperative Information Systems of Malaga University, www.sicuma.uma.es) computer science research group centred in information systems methodology and development, collaborative work and, interaction human-computer. He is the main researcher in several projects related to Information Technologies. Also, he works in the program committee of important conferences and he organizes international events like Turitec (www.turitec.uma.es).

Valentina Janev, MSc, is a Senior Researcher at the Mihailo Pupin Institute, Belgrade, Serbia. Since 1996 she has participated in design, development and implementation of many business information systems first as a Software Engineer and later as a Consultant. She is actively involved in scientific projects financed by the Serbian Ministry of Science, as well in EU FP6 and FP7 projects. Her resent interests include Semantic Web, applications of semantic technologies and W3C standards in the knowledge management field, and knowledge management architectures for R&D organizations. She is an author of more than 30 published papers, some of them in international journals and books.

Jonatan Jelen. A former executive manager with companies in Paris and New York, Jonatan Jelen is currently a business owner and avid entrepreneur. He is also Assistant Professor of Business at Parsons The New School for Design. He regularly teaches at USST in Shanghai, China, and to the Faculty of Economics of the University of Zagreb, Croatia. Jon's research interests are in Social Entrepreneurship, Leadership, Chinese Business Education, and the Nature of the Firm. Dr. Jelen earned a JD in Germany, MBAs from Ecole Supérieure de Commerce de Paris, Heriot-Watt University, Scotland, and Baruch College; LLMs from University of Pau, France, University of Paris II, Panthéon-Assas, and Fordham University School of Law, and and MPhil in Business from the City University of New York Graduate School and University Center. His first PhD is from University of Pau, France and he is s PhD candidate in Business/Computer Information Systems at Baruch College.

Georg Kalus is a research assistant at professor Broy's chair in Software & Systems Engineering at the Technische Universität München, Institut für Informatik. His research encompasses simulation of formal software development processes as well as implementation and automation of software development processes at project runtime. He has more than ten years experience as a professional software developer and has worked for software companies in many different areas, e.g. simulation of microlithography (SIGMA-C). He is an expert on the Microsoft platform and a Microsoft Certified Professional. Georg has studied computer science at the Technische Universität München and at the Istanbul Teknik Universitesi. He holds a Masters degree.

Chris Kimble is an associate professor at Euromed Marseille École de Management, France. Previously he lectured in Information Systems and Management at the University of York (UK), Information Technology at the University of Newcastle (UK) and was a researcher with the Business School and Department of Informatics at the University of Northumbria (UK). His broad research interests concern how best to manage the fit between technology and the social world. He is best known for his work on Communities of Practice and Knowledge Management but has also published articles on Information Systems and technological support for geographically distributed work.

Marko Kolakovic. After an early consulting and corporate management career in Croatia's reforming economy in the 90s, Marko Kolakovic advanced to an academic career, first at the Faculty of Law, and is now Associate Professor of Business and Economics at the University of Zagreb, Faculty of Economics, Graduate School of Economics and Business. He directs the Program in Entrepreneurship at the School, consults for various ministries of the Croatian government, and leads various projects and grants in the field of Entrerpreneurship research and practice in Croatia and neighboring Central European countries. He has published extensively in European and international journals on the topics of his expertise in entrepreneurship, and the role of networked organizations, virtualized firms, and intellectual capital in the new economy. Dr. Kolakovic obtained his BA, MSc, and PhD in Economics at the Graduate School of Economics and Business of the Faculty of Economics at the University of Zagreb.

Adamantios Koumpis heads the Research Programmes Division of ALTEC S.A., which he founded at 1996 (then as independent division of Unisoft S.A.). His previous job position was at the Institute of Computer Science, FORTH, at Heraklio, Crete, where he worked at the Rehabilitation Tele-Informatics and Human-Computer Interaction Group in several European Commission's RTD projects (RACE, ACTS and TAP). He is author of research papers, technical reports and project deliverables in the domains of Data/Information Management and Human-Computer Interaction. His research interests include quantitative decision making techniques and Information Society economics. He successfully lead many commercial and research projects both at the European and the national level in the areas of E-Commerce, public sector and business enterprise re-organisation and information logistics, concerning linking of data/information repositories with knowledge management and business engineering models.

Marco Kuhrmann born in 1978. He studied Computer Science at University of Potsdam until 2004 and got his PhD in Computer Science at Technische Universität München in 2008. He is working as research assistant to Prof. Dr. Dr. h.c. Manfred Broy at Technische Universität Munchen, Institut für Informatik – Software & Systems Engineering where he is a member of the V-Modell XT core development team. He was coaching several development and improvement projects using the V-Modell XT and trains developers, project managers and process engineers. Currently he works on process and method engineering – especially on questions related to process integration, process authoring and construction methodologies, process enactment and tool support for modular process models. The field of application of his research scales from small and medium companies up to large globally distributed acting enterprises.

William F. Lawless is a Professor of Mathematics and Psychology. He has a PhD in Social Psychology that was granted in 1992 from Virginia Tech, and a Masters Degree in Mechanical Engineering (LSU, 1977). He is a Professional Engineer with a rating in Nuclear Waste Management and he is a Senior member of IEEE. His research interests are in organizational theory, organizational performance and metrics, and in mathematical models of organizations. He has published over 33 articles and book chapters, over 100 peer-reviewed proceedings and abstracts, and over $1 million in research grants. He was a founding member of Department of Energy's Savannah River Site Citizens Advisory Board (1994-2000; 2003-2007) where he authored or coauthored over 100 sets of recommendations. He is also a past member of the European Trustnet hazardous decisions group.

Jose L. Leiva is a Professor of Languages and Computer Science at the University of Málaga, Spain. He is a researcher of a SICUMA (Cooperative Information Systems of Malaga University) computer science research group centred in information systems methodology and development. His researches are based on databases, workflow, reverse engineering and Human Computer interaction. Jose L. Leiva He is researcher in several projects related to information technologies. José L. Leiva has published various books, papers and conference papers. Also, he works in the program committee of various conferences and he has been worked with various companies at the technological park in Andalucía (PTA)

Rui M. Lima, PhD in Production and Systems Engineering, is an Assistant Professor of the Department of Production and Systems, School of Engineering of University of Minho, Portugal. His current scientific activity is centred on teaching and/or researching in Industrial and Management Engineering topics, mainly in the following areas: Production Planning and Control; Integration of Information Systems for Production; Project Management; Distributed Production Systems (DPS); Cooperative Learning in Industrial and Management Engineering. At this moment he is involved with the following research topics: Distributed Production Systems and application of software Agents for development of production systems; Integration of production management processes, namely through the development of generic models of Production Planning and Control and application of business process modelling. He is also been researching on evaluation of learning processes based on Cooperative Interdisciplinary Projects and application of project management concepts for learning improvement.

Tina Marshall-Bradley is Special Assistant to the Provost and professor of education at Paine College in Augusta, Georgia. She is the former Dean of the School of Education at Claflin University and has also worked in the Office of Teacher Education, with the Division of Teacher Quality at the South Carolina State Department of Education. She is a graduate of the College of Charleston and completed her graduate studies at Iowa State University. She has held faculty and research posts at Benedict College, the Citadel, South Carolina State University, and Norfolk State University. She engages in research related to comparative education systems, education reform and information technology in education environments.

Rinaldo C. Michelini, is retired professor at the Engineering School of the University of Genova, Italy. Main expertise is achieved in flexible automation and lifecycle design of products-services. Current research areas cover the new requirements of a service economy, complying with sustainability bylaws. He is author/co-author of over than five hundred papers/chapters/books.

Svein Erik Moen is a researcher working at Fafo, Institute for Labour and Social Research, Norway. He has a PhD in innovation studies from the University of Oslo, Faculty of Social Sciences. Currently he is involved in numerous research projects at Fafo related to topics within enterprise and development studies, both in the private and the public sector

Vasiliki (Vicky) Moumtzi is a member of the Research Programmes Division of Altec S.A. in Thessaloniki. She is a graduate Informatics and Communication Engineer from the Informatics and Communications department of Technological Educational Institute of Serres, Greece. She also worked as a researcher at the reactor of Institut fuer Festkoerperforschung Forschungszentrum Joelich at Germany and at the accelerator of ISIS Rutherford Appleton Laboratory at England for the demand of her diplomacy program AMphOrEAs(Archaeometric multiphase of ornament & element analysis), approved from the European union. This research gave her the opportunity to publish papers to international conferences and scientific magazines. She loves to work on crystallographic analysis so she keeps on this thread of research interests. In ALTEC she is responsible for the capacity building portal that she created and builds on expertise and results of a series of European e-Government projects that ALTEC has participated as technology supplier.

Matjaz Mulej. Born on Jan., 20, 1941, in Maribor, Slovenia; married, two adult children; healthy; living in Maribor, Slovenia. Retired from University of Maribor, Faculty of Economics & Business, Maribor, as Professor Emeritus of Systems and Innovation Theory. +1.400 publications in +40 countries (see: IZUM – Cobiss, 08082). Visiting professor abroad for15 semesters. Author of the Dialectical Systems Theory (see: François, 2004, International Encyclopedia ..) and Innovative Business Paradigm for catching-up countries. Member of New York Academy of Sciences (1996), European Academy of Sciences and Arts, Salzburg, European Academy of sciences and Humanities, Paris, president of IFSR (International Federation for Systems Research with 37 member associations). Many Who is Who entries. M.A. in Development Economics, Doctorates in Systems Theory and in Management.

Richard Paige is Professor of Enterprise Systems at the University of York, UK. He received his PhD in Computer Science from the University of Toronto, Canada, in 1997. He is an internationally recognised researcher for his work on Model-Driven Engineering, formal methods, software architecture and agile development. He has chaired several major international conferences in these areas, and is an editor of the Elsevier Journal of System Architecture.

Vojko Potocan, born 1962, is an Associate Professor of organization and management on the Faculty of Economics and Business, Department of Organization and Informatics, University of Maribor, Slovenia. He teaches (on the graduate level, on the undergraduate level, and on doctoral program) in FEB (Maribor, Slovenia), EF (Ljubljana, Slovenia), in FOI (Varazdin, Croatia) and in University of Applied Science (Bremen, Germany). He takes part in different foreign scientific conferences and realized a number of study visits on abroad (University of Gent, Belgium; University of Greenwich London, UK; University of Economics Vienna, Austria). He was 4 times a visiting professor abroad and gave about eight further seminars at foreign universities. He has published +350 texts (+200 in foreign languages in 28 countries), including 8 books and edited proceedings and textbooks. The fields of his research interests are Organization, and Management.

Nicolaos Protogeros is Ass. Professor of Information Systems and E-Commerce at the University of Macedonia. He received a PhD in Information Systems from the National Polytechnic Institute, France, an MSc in Remote Sensing from the University Paul Sabatier, France and a Bachelor Degree in Mathematics from Aristotle University of Thessaloniki, Greece. He has had 15 years of working experience in the private sector specializing in Information Technology and Electronic Commerce applications and over 10 years of teaching experience. Before entering the academic world, he had been the founding partner and CEO of Heletel, the first start-up company in Greece for E-Commerce which has developed some of the most innovative solutions for the business services domain. He has been the project leader for many research and development projects in the area of Web based technologies, Software Agents and Virtual Organisations. He has published papers in academic journals and he has participated in many international conferences. His current research and teaching activities are concerned with the implementation and application of SOA based ecommerce systems to support inter-organisational collaboration and Virtual Enterprises.

Aysin Rahimifard is currently a research associate in the Manufacturing System Integration (MSI) Research Institute of Loughborough University, in UK. After receiving her BSc in Industrial Engineering at Bilkent University in Turkey in 1996, she worked for the Turkish Science and Technology Council (TUBITAK) as a research and development engineer where she participated in European Eureka Projects aimed at developing IT tools to support manufacturing management and in national e-government projects. She obtained a PhD in 2004 at Loughborough University in the area of developing operations management support tools for Environmentally Conscious Manufacturing. She then joined MSI where she works with a number of large and small UK manufacturing companies on research and development projects which primarily involve organizational design and change. Her current research interests are in agile manufacturing, enterprise design and change, manufacturing management, and simulation modeling.

Roberto P. Razzoli, is researcher at the PMAR Lab of the University of Genova, Italy. His scientific activity is about CAD/CAM aids, quality engineering, design for environment, safety and reliability of machines, industrial diagnostics, predictive and monitoring maintenance, eco-sustainable design, mobile and modular robots, industrial automation. He is author/co-author of some hundred publications.

Erwin Schoitsch, born 1944 in Vienna, received his Master Degree in Technical Physics and a Bachelor degree in Computer Science (1962-1969) at the University of Technology in Vienna. He works at Austrian Research Centres - ARC for more than 35 years, focusing on software process improvement and on development and validation of safety-related real-time systems with high dependability requirements. He is/was involved in or project manager of many industrial and research projects, including the European projects ESPITI, OLOS, SPIRE, ENCRESS, ACRuDA, ECUA, ISA-EuNet, AMSD, COO-PERS, DECOS, Watch-Over, ADOSE, MOGENTES and ProSE. He is active in international working groups (EWICS TC7, ERCIM), (co-) organizer of workshops and conferences, member of international program committees and of standardization committees for functional safety (IEC 61508 and related standards, ISO WD 26262). He is head of an accredited Software Test Lab (ISO 17025). His main interest is the holistic approach to system dependability.

Donald Sofge co-leads the Natural Computation Group within the Navy Center for Applied Research in Artificial Intelligence (NCARAI) at the United States Naval Research Laboratory (NRL), and has 20 years of experience in applying computational intelligence to real-world systems. He is an acknowledged expert in several scientific disciplines including robotics, machine learning, quantum computing, artificial intelligence, and control systems. He has served as technical panel reviewer for NSF, NASA, and DARPA, and has served as an area expert for new technology evaluation for DARPA and ONR. He has served as peer reviewer for several journals in robotics and computational intelligence, as well as numerous conferences, symposia, and workshops in these and other related areas. He has over 40 peer reviewed technical publications. Educational background includes B.S. in Computer Science, MSEE, currently pursuing Ph.D. in Evolutionary Computation.

Jose Sousa, with at Master Degree in Information Systems by Minho University, Guimarães, Portugal, is a researcher and information system manager with a focus on systems for knowledge sharing and collective intelligence. He did a foundational work in information systems planning in scientific and industrial organizations. The approaches and technologies from this work are precursors to the planning of information systems using information effects in order to develop and manage information systems in web 2.0 times. At IBMC he introduced the new planning model and could develop a model that can support an organization with a great dynamic. At this point, was a pioneer in the introduction of the Web for collaboration and knowledge sharing as a need for organization information systems planning. As CIO at IBMC his current project is to implement wisdom of crowds in order to define patterns that when translated to semantic mining and ontology learning can define information ontology needs that can be used as input to the effects information systems planning model.

Malihe Tabatabaie is Ph.D. student of Computer Science at University of York, UK. She received a Bachelor degree in Software Engineering from Azad Qazvin University, Iran and the M.Sc. in Software Engineering and Ph.D. in Computer Science from the University of York. She has been active in the area of software engineering for over 6 years and recently has been a contributor to the Software Systems challenges. She did some research on organisational portals and Software Architecture for Aircraft engines. Her current research involves study of the Enterprise Information System and the challenges regarding to the software systems that have business perspectives.

Andrew Targowski was engaged in the development of social computing in totalitarian Poland (IN-FOSTRADA and Social Security # for 38 million citizens-PESEL-1972) and received political asylum in the U.S. during the crackdown on Solidarity in 1981. He has been a professor of Business Information Systems at Western Michigan University since 1980. He published 21 books on information technology, history, civilization, and political science (*Red Fascism*-1982) in English and Polish. During the 1990s he was a Director of the TeleCITY of Kalamazoo Project, one of the first digital cities in the U.S. He investigates the role of info-communication in enterprise, economy, and civilization. He is a President of the International Society for the Comparative Study of Civilizations and a former Chairman of the Advisory Council of the Information Resources Management Association (1995-2003).

Antonio Trigo, is a PhD candidate in Information Systems at Universidade de Trás-os-Montes e Alto Douro. Currently he teaches at Escola Superior de Gestão e Tecnologia de Oliveira do Hospital of the Instituto Politécnico de Coimbra. His research interests include IS management, IS strategy, IS function and organizational impacts of IT/IS solutions. António more than five years experience as a software developer having produced IT/IS solutions for such companies as Portugal Telecom, Cabo Verde Telecom, Meditel and Telesp Celular.

Hui Lien Tung is an Assistant Professor of Mathematics and Computer Science at Paine College. She has a Masters Degree in Information Science (State University of New York-Albany, 2000) and a Masters Degree in Education (National-Louis University, IL, 1990). Her research interests are in MIS, metrics of organizational information systems and performance, e-Government, Systems Analysis and Design and database. She has published several Journal articles, book chapters and peer-reviewed proceedings.

Ozden Ustun was born on 10 June 1974. He received his Master's degree and Ph.D. in Industrial Engineering in 2001 and 2007 at Eskisehir Osmangazi University in Turkey. He has worked as a research assistant at the Department of Industrial Engineering of Eskisehir Osmangazi University for ten years from 1997 to 2007. Since 02 February 2008, he has been working at the Department of Industrial

Engineering of Dumlupinar University in Turkey. He is currently an assistant professor and department chair of Industrial Engineering Department of Dumlupinar University. His studies focus on Operations Research, Multi-objective Optimization, Multi-criteria Decision Making, Nonlinear Programming, Assignment Problems, Portfolio Optimization, Facility Location, and Supply Chain Management.

Maria de los Angeles Arenas Valdes. Degree in Computer Science from the University of Veracruz in 1990. She obtained the degree of Master in Computer Science in 1999 from the Arturo Rosenblueth Foundation in Mexico City; and she is a Ph.D. candidate in Software Engineering and Artificial Intelligence, Department of Languages and Computer Science from the University of Malaga, Spain. Since 1994. she is a teacher at the School of Statistics and Informatics of the University of Veracruz, Mexico, and she is a member of the research group for Engineering and Software Technologies of the same University. Maria de los Ángeles Arenas has published various papers in conferences.

João Varajão, is currently a Professor at the Department of Engineering of the University of Trás-os-Montes e Alto Douro, where he teaches undergraduate and postgraduate courses. He supervises several Msc and PhD projects in the domain of information systems management, enterprise information systems and electronic business systems. He earned his PhD and MSc from the University of Minho, Portugal. He is the author of several books, refereed publications and communications at international conferences.

Kam Hou Vat is currently an invited lecturer in the Department of Computer and Information Science, under the Faculty of Science and Technology, at the University of Macau, Macau SAR, China. His current research interests include learner-centered design with constructivism in Software Engineering education, architected applications developments for Internet software systems, information systems for learning organization, information technology for knowledge synthesis, and collaborative technologies for electronic organizations.

Sanja Vraneš is jointly appointed as a Scientific Director of the Mihailo Pupin Institute and as a Professor of Computer Science at the University of Belgrade. From 1999 she has been engaged as a United Nations Expert for information technologies, and from 2003 as an EU Expert for intelligent content and semantics area. Her research interests include semantic web, knowledge management, intelligent agents, e-collaboration, decision support systems, multicriteria analysis algorithms, etc. In these areas she published over 150 scientific papers. She serves as a reviewer of respectable international journals, like IEEE Transaction on Computer, IEEE Intelligent Systems magazine, and also as a reviewer and evaluator of EU FP6 and FP7 projects. She has also served as a project leader and/or principal architect of more than 20 complex software projects. She is a member of IEEE, ACM and AAAI. She is also a member of Serbian Academy of Engineering Sciences and of National Scientific Council.

Richard Weston, PhD, BSc (first class honours) is founder member and Head of the MSI Research Institute, Academic Director of the UK's Centre of Excellence in Customised Assembly and Professor of Flexible Automation at Loughborough University. Richard has supervised over 60 PhD studies in areas of enterprise modelling, enterprise integration, software systems engineering, human systems modelling, methods based engineering and flexible automation. He has authored around 350 publications in refereed journals and conference proceedings and has been the Principle Investigator for over 50 UK research council grants. Previously Richard was the Pro Vice Chancellor for Research at Loughborough University; vice chair of the IFIP Working Group 5.12 on Architectures for Enterprise Integration and a Consultant Professor at Harbin Institute of Technology in China. Richard is also a member of the editorial board of five international journals.

Joseph C. Wood is the chief of a research department at an Army Medical Center. He is a physician and is board certified in Internal Medicine, Endocrine, Diabetes and Metabolism. He has a PhD in Endocrinology that was granted in 1991 from the Medical College of Georgia, and a Doctor of Medicine from the George Washington University School of Medicine in 1995. He is an academic clinician and is on the teaching staff at his institution. His research interests are experimental therapeutics in bone and soft tissue wound healing, thyroid cancer and in organizational theory, organizational performance and metrics. He has published over 8 articles and book chapters, over 38 peer-reviewed proceedings and abstracts, and he has received about $750,000 in research grants. He is a fellow in the American College of Physicians and a Fellow in the American Association of Clinical Endocrinologists.

Zdenka Ženko is Assistant Professor of Innovation Theory and System Theory at Faculty of Business and Economics, University of Maribor. Her research interest includes dialectical system theory applied in economic fields. Her research includes systemic approach to innovation management; mostly for small and medium enterprises prevalent in Slovenia and comparative studies of most developed innovative management models. Zdenka.Zenko@uni-mb.si Univerza v Mariboru, Ekonomsko poslovna fakulteta, Razlagova 14, 2000 Maribor, Slovenia.

Index

Symbols

A

B